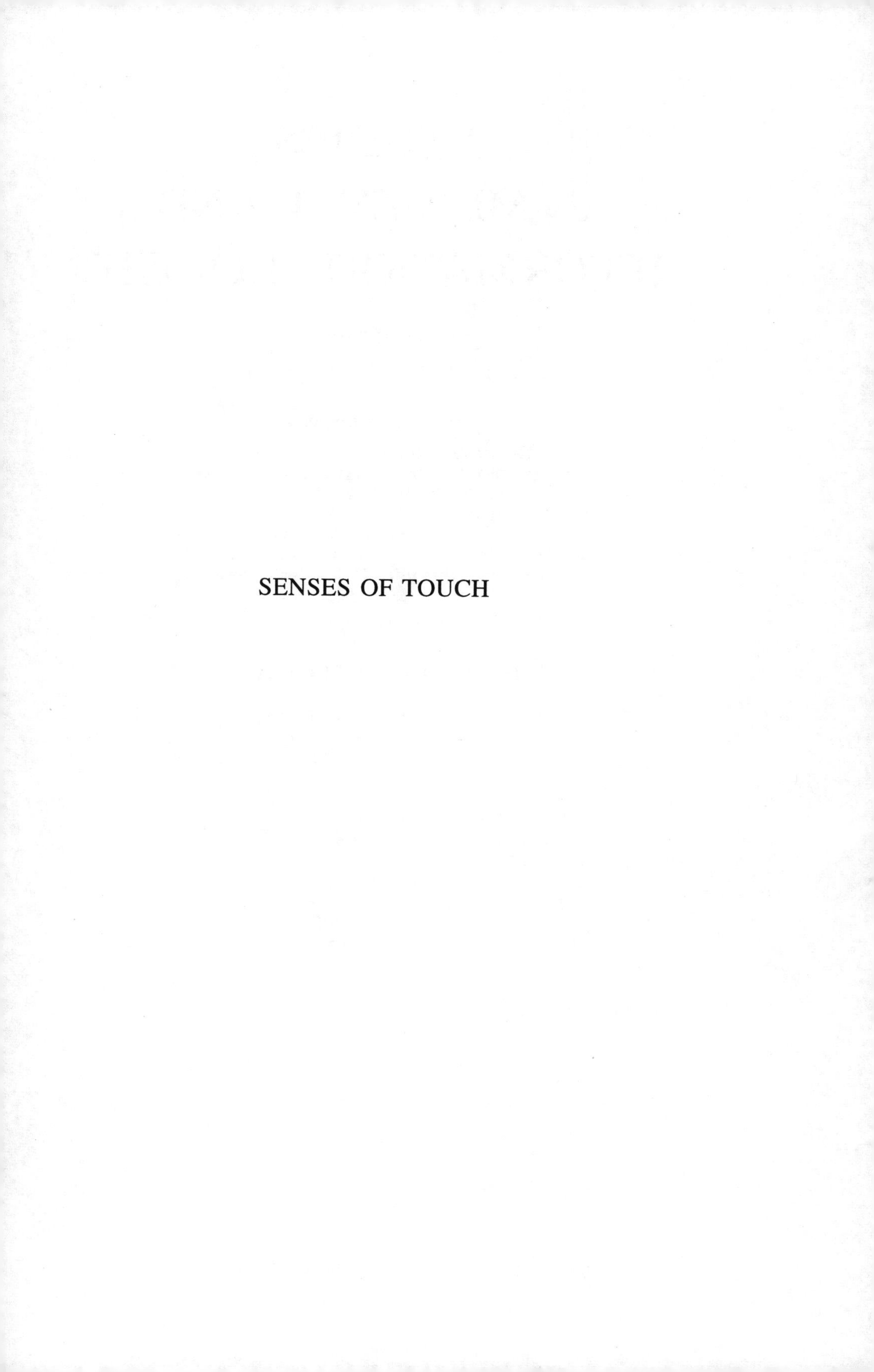

SENSES OF TOUCH

STUDIES IN MEDIEVAL AND REFORMATION THOUGHT

VOLUME LXXI

MARJORIE O'ROURKE BOYLE

SENSES OF TOUCH

SENSES OF TOUCH

HUMAN DIGNITY AND DEFORMITY FROM MICHELANGELO TO CALVIN

BY

MARJORIE O'ROURKE BOYLE

BRILL
LEIDEN · BOSTON · KÖLN
1998

This book is printed on acid-free paper.

Library of Congress Cataloging-in-Publication Data

Library of Congress Cataloging-in-Publication Data is also available.

Die Deutsche Bibliothek - CIP-Einheitsaufnahme

Boyle, Marjorie O'Rourke:
Senses of touch : human dignity and deformity, from Michelangelo to Calvin / by Marjorie O'Rourke Boyle. – Leiden ; Boston ; Köln : Brill, 1998
(Studies in medieval and reformation thought ; Vol. 71)
ISBN 90–04–11175–§

ISSN 0585-6914
ISBN 90 04 11175 1

PRINTED IN THE NETHERLANDS

To Charles Trinkaus

CONTENTS

ACKNOWLEDGMENTS

I am very grateful to Heiko A. Oberman for accepting this book for his series Studies in Medieval and Reformation Thought. I also wish to thank my valued readers of the original manuscript, William J. Bouwsma, who read the entire draft, and David Summers, who read the parts on Michelangelo.

INTRODUCTION

It was an ancient commonplace: humans surpassed other animals because they alone stood erect on two feet. Erect bipedality defined human nature as destined for contemplation of the gods by an uplifted countenance or for biological advantage especially by the liberation of the hands. Although the contemplative interpretation dominated theoretically, the biological fact prevailed actually, or else human society would have perished while everyone stood around contemplating. Handiness, as enabled by that stature, even acquired theory. *Senses of Touch* anatomizes the human hand during the sixteenth century, when physical dissection of it toward experiential knowledge commenced and when its ability was freshly discovered in the disciplines and its conduct was determined in institution, morality, and custom. The book focuses on what hands definitively did: touch, or precisely, grasp. Touch differed in traditional belief and in modern science. While touch used to be demeaned as the vilest sense, it is now researched as the primary sense.[1] Yet if the sense of touch provides still another lesson in alterity—the past as "other," its biological basis in two feet firmly on the ground coincides with the forefront of current scientific inquiry.[2]

Movement, not mind, the biological, rather than the philosophical, argument is now corroborated as the origin of humans, through hominids, by paleoanthropology.[3] That subject, the study of human fossils, has even been declared the most important in the evolutionary sciences for fulfilling the Socratic injunction to "know thyself."[4] In the modern shift from philosophy to biology not even the material brain is considered essential to human de-

---

[1] *Tactual Perception: A Sourcebook*, ed. William Schiff and Emerson Foulke (Cambridge: Cambridge University Press, 1982).

[2] Although this introduction concerns paleoanthropology, the research of modern psychology is also relevant. Consider, for example, that newborn infants, when held under the arms in an upright position with the soles of their feet on a surface, perform coordinated walking movements like mature, erect locomotion. Esther Thelen and Donna M. Fisher, "Newborn Stepping: An Explanation for a 'Disappearing' Reflex," *Developmental Psychology* 18 (1982):760-75. For the process, from this well developed neuromuscular organization, of the slow acquisition of totally erect posture and the physical structures necessary to support it, see Adolf Portmann, *A Zoologist Looks at Humankind*, trans. Judith Schaeffer (New York: Columbia University Press, 1990), pp. 82-86.

[3] For the argument that human locomotion displays a variety of patterns besides the habitual bipedal gait, see John Devine, "The Versatility of Human Locomotion," *American Anthropologist* 87 (1985):550-70. For erect status in all cultures as a basic heritage from the hominids, see Gordon W. Hewes, "World Distribution of Certain Postural Habits," *American Anthropologist* 57 (1955):231-44.

[4] Stephen Jay Gould, introduction to Delta Willis, *The Hominid Gang: Behind the Scenes in the Search for Human Origins* (New York: Viking, 1989), p. ix.

velopment. The historic feature differentiating hominids from the other primates was not a large cranial size but bipedal posture with its striding gait. Long before the development of rapid increase in brain size, the postcranial morphology of *Australopithecus afarensis*, with its relatively small brain, was an erect, striding biped.[5] The major discovery of *Australopithecus anamensis*, its possible ancestor, has a tibia indicating that hominids walked at least half a million years earlier than scientists had believed from prior evidence.[6] The calcaneus of the *afarensis* species, the largest tarsal bone that forms the prominence of the heel, shows the adaptation of bipedality of modern *Homo sapiens*. Anatomically that is defined as an inflated posterior corpus, a discrete lateral plantar process, and a specialized geometry and orientation of the posterior articular surface. Fossil specimens from Hadar in Ethiopia display features of a terrestrial bipedality that was habitual. The modifications would have inhibited the effective arboreal nature of the primates, so that significant climbing behaviors were not in the locomotor repertoire of those earliest hominids. By at least three million years ago arboreal behavior was replaced by morphological specialization to terrestrial bidpedality. Those morphological characteristics unequivocally distinguished quadrupedal pongids from bipedal hominids.[7]

The outstanding question in evolution is the pressure for selection that produced bipedality.[8] Bipedality is also essential to the understanding of

---

[5] David R. Carrier, "The Energetic Paradox of Human Running and Hominid Evolution," *Current Anthropology* 25 (1984):483.

[6] Meave G. Leakey, Craig S. Feibel, Ian McDougall, and Alan Walker, "New Four-Million-Old Hominid Species from Karapoi and Allia Bay, Kenya," *Nature* (17 August 1995):565-71. This is corroborated by the find of *Australopithecus ramidus*, for which, see Tim D. White et al., "New Discoveries of Australopithecus at Maka in Ethiopia," *Nature* 366 (1993):262.

[7] Bruce Latimer and C. Owen Lovejoy, "The Calcaneus of *Australopithecus afarensis* and Its Implications for the Evolution of Bipedality," *American Journal of Physical Anthropology* 78 (1989):369-86. See also idem, "Metatarsophalangeal Joints of *Australopithecus afarensis*," *American Journal of Physical Anthropology* 83 (1990):13-23; "Talacrural Joint in African Hominoids: Implications for *Australopithecus afarensis*," *American Journal of Physical Anthropology* 74 (1987):155-87. For the morphological change from quadruped to biped, see John Robinson, *Early Hominid Posture and Locomotion* (Chicago: University of Chicago Press, 1972), pp. 256, 258, 259. For the conservative argument that adaptation to terrestrial bipedalism was not habitual but gradual in early hominids, see William L. Jungers, "Relative Joint Size and Hominoid Locomotor Adaptations with Implications for the Evolution of Hominid Bipedalism," *Journal of Human Evolution* 17 (1988):247-65. For selection for efficiency after the transition, see Karen Steudel, "Limb Morphology, Bipedal Gait, and the Energetics of Hominid Locomotion," *American Journal of Physical Anthropology* 99 (1996):345-55. For the evolution of locomotor behavior and morphology in the vertical climbing of hominid ancestry, see Daniel L. Gebo, "Climbing, Brachiation, and Terrestrial Quadrupedalism: Historical Precursors of Hominid Bipedalism," *American Journal of Physical Anthropology* 101 (1996):55-92.

[8] A. R. E. Sinclair, Mary D. Leakey, and M. Norton-Griffiths, "Migration and Hominid Bipedalism," *Nature* 324 (1986):307-8. Against their solution of long-distance migration to scavenge, see Walter Leutenegger, "Origin of Hominid Bipedalism," *Nature* 325 (1987):305. For a sampler, see *Origine(s) de la bipédie chez les hominidé*, Colloque international de la

human culture. As the supervisor of the preservation of a unique trail of hominid footprints at Laetoli has stated, "Bipedalism led directly or indirectly to the beginning of all culture."[9] The classical topic of human definition and dignity through erect bipedality thus assumes from paleoanthropology new importance. Although bipedality was not the feature that distinguished humans from other animals, as the ancients proposed, it did distinguish hominids from other animals. The ancient argument relating erect posture to better vision has also proved correct—but in Xenophon's biological version, not in Plato's philosophical one. Creatures stood for ages before they ever philosophized. Hominids swung their forelimbs off the ground erectly for an observational advantage over other primates: to survive in an altered environment.[10] Humans in habitual continuation did not regard the heavens and wonder about the universal laws; they looked at the earth, its grasses and bushes, considering food and shelter. Human origins were not historically in contemplation, as Western culture derived from Greek philosophy has supposed. Xenophon's second assertion, relating erect bipedality to the instrumental use of the hands, is also confirmed by the fossil record. Aristotle erred in asserting that humans had hands because they were intelligent; Anaxagoras was, perhaps, more correct in stating that humans were intelligent because they had hands.

Senses of Touch explores the vitality in renaissance and reformation culture of the ancient commonplace with prehistoric reality of erect bipedality with able hands. It concerns a valuational shift from the contemplative ideal, as signified by the sense of sight, to an active reality, as signified by the sense of touch. The human body is not only literally a physical figure.

Fondation Singer Polignac, 5-8 juin, 1990, ed. Yves Coppens and Brigitte Senut (Paris: Centre national de la recherche scientifique, 1991).

9 Martha Demas, supervisor for the project of the Getty Conservation Institute, Los Angeles; cited in an article from the *Los Angeles Times*, reprinted in *The Toronto Star*, 26 November, 1995, p. F8. For physical form before cultural capacity, see G. Philip Richtmire, *The Evolution of Homo erectus: Comparative Anatomical Studies of an Extinct Human Species* (Cambridge: Cambridge University Press, 1990), pp. 397, 410. For the issue of tools, see Richard J. Klein, *The Human Career: Human Biological and Cultural Origins* (Chicago: University of Chicago Press, 1989), p. 181; Graham Richards, "Freed Hands or Enslaved Feet?" *Journal of Human Evolution* 15 (1986):143-50; Randall Susman, "Fossil Evidence for Early Hominid Tool Use," *Science* 265 (1994):1570-73, and see Leslie C. Aiello, "Thumbs Up for Our Early Ancestors," pp. 1540-41.

10 For this research, see Robinson, *Posture and Locomotion*, pp. 257-58, 260; Klein, *Human Career*, pp. 100-82, especially 180-81, 139-40, 143-44; Nina G. Jablonski and George Chaplin, "Origin of Habitual Terrestrial Bipedalism in the Ancestor of the Hominidae," *Journal of Human Evolution* 24 (1993):259-80; Kevin D. Hunt, "The Evolution of Human Bidpedality: Ecology and Functional Morphology," *Journal of Human Evolution* 26 (1994):183-202; Björn Merker, "A Note on Hunting and Hominid Origins," *American Anthropologist* 86 (1984):112-14; Mary W. Marzke, Julie M. Longhill, and Stanley A. Rasmussen, "Gluteus Maximus Muscle Function and the Origin of Hominid Bipedality," *American Journal of Physical Anthropology* 77 (9188):519-88; Carrier, "Energetic Paradox," pp. 483-89; Jeffrey A. Kurland and Stephen J. Beckerman, "Optimal Foraging and Hominid Evolution: Labor and Reciprocity," *American Anthropologist* 87 (1985):73-93.

It was appropriated historically as a rhetorical figure for human culture: for beliefs, values, customs, art, religion, government, and law. *Senses of Touch* anatomizes its hand, thrusting forth from the skeleton, as such a figure for human dignity and deformity in early modern culture.

CHAPTER ONE

ADAM'S FINGER

Adam arising is the traditional topic of human dignity portrayed by Michelangelo Buonarotti (1475-1564) on the Sistine Chapel ceiling: erect bipedality with able hands.

Yet the critical consensus has interpreted that cultural icon quite differently. "Michelangelo has represented the moment when God by the touch of a finger will endow Adam with a soul, the moment when spirit and matter will conjoin."[1] The fresco is a "heroic painting of Adam touched by the finger of God."[2] In its scene "the act of creation is performed by contact, God just touching with the tip of His finger the outstretched hand of the man."[3] Although the gesture has been acknowledged as "unusual," still, God "with his forefinger lightly touches the forefinger of Adam."[4] Or, "He extends his forefinger, about to touch that of Adam."[5] In the compositional center of the fresco are "the hands of the first man and of his Creator, all but touching each other."[6] Again, "These hands do not touch; they nearly touch."[7] Although a languid Adam lacks the strength to raise his finger to touch the Creator's, "a touch of the finger-tips will suffice."[8] Because God in his infinity and omnipotence gathers the universal forces within himself "the outstretching of a single finger of His right hand is sufficient to animate

---

1 Loren Partridge, *Michelangelo: The Sistine Chapel Ceiling, Rome* (New York: George Braziller, 1996), p. 48. For reproductions of the restored frescoes on the Sistine Chapel ceiling, see Frederick Hartt, Gianluigi Colalucci, and Fabrizio Mancinelli, *The Sistine Chapel*, 2 vols. (New York: Alfred A. Knopf with Nippon Television Network, 1991), with the Creation of Adam at 2:75, 84-95, and the hands in detail, pp. 88-89. For the restoration, see also *ichelangelo e la sistina: La technica, il restauro, il mito* (Rome: Musei Vaticani e Biblioteca apostolica vaticana with Fratelli Palombi, 1990).

2 O. B. Hardison, *Disappearing throught the Skylight: Culture and Technology in the Twentieth Century* (New York: Viking, 1989), p. 18.

3 Heinrich Wölfflin, *Classic Art: An Introduction to the Italian Renaissance* (London: Phaidon, 1968), p. 57.

4 Macdonald Critchley, *Silent Language* (London: Butterworth, 1975), p. 112.

5 Hartt, *Michelangelo*, 3 vols. (New York: Harry N. Abrams, n. d.), 3:102; idem et al., *Sistine Chapel*, 2:14.

6 Rudolf Arnheim, *The Power of the Center: A Study of Composition in the Visual Arts* (Berkeley and Los Angeles: University of California Press, 1982), p. 167.

7 Renée Weber, "A Philosophical Perspective on Touch," in *Touch: The Foundation of Experience*, eds. Kathryn E. Barnard and T. Berry Brazelton (Madison, Conn.: International Universities Press, 1990), p. 16.

8 Walter Pater, *Works of Walter Pater*, 8 vols. (London: Library, 1900-17), 1:73-97; rpt. in Charles Seymour, ed., *Michelangelo: The Sistine Chapel Ceiling* (New York: W. W. Norton, 1972), p. 164.

the titanic and still inert body of Adam." The human being "extends his left arm, supported by the left knee, to make contact with the divine finger."[9] In the mutual extension of limbs there is "the famous hand-to-hand tryst."[10]

Yet Adam's finger is not touched by the finger of God, nor on that fresco will they ever touch. There is a significant gap, the flick of a fingernail, between them. The mature divine wrist is straight, with its veins energetically taut, and the index finger is directive. The puerile human wrist is limp, with the hand drooping, so that the fingertips of God and Adam are not aligned as if to touch. Even if imaginatively they were to touch, that gesture was not creative but sportive, even adversarial. There was a renaissance adage *extremis digitis attingere*, "to touch with the fingertips." As Erasmus explained its usage, it meant to experience something slightly. The notion derived from the sport of wrestling, from the Greek word for sparring, or "fighting someone with the fingertips only without engaging the rest of the body." It was related to the adage *summis labiis*, "with the tip of the lips," for the pretence of words without action.[11] An image of superficiality, of sparring, seems inappropriate for the primordial divine-human relationship. What is happening on that ceiling?

In the consensus of interpretation the Creator infuses into Adam, finger to finger, life. "In this way the Life Force passes from God to Man."[12] The vital energy is most frequently supposed a spark of fire or of electricity.[13]

---

[9] Charles de Tolnay, *Michelangelo*, 5 vols., vol. 2: *The Sistine Ceiling* (Princeton, N.J.: Princeton University Press, 1969), p. 35.

[10] Leo Steinberg, "Who's Who in Michelangelo's Creation of Adam: A Chronology of the Picture's Self-Revelation," *Art Bulletin* 74 (1992):556. See the reproduction of the restored fresco between pp. 564-65.

[11] Erasmus, *Adagia* 1.9.94, in *Opera omnia* (Leiden), 2; *The Collected Works of Erasmus* (Toronto: University of Toronto Press, 1974-), trans. R. A. B. Mynors, 32:228. Erasmus refers to Cicero, *Pro M. Caelio* 12.18; Basil, *Epistulae*; Lucian, *Demonax* 4; Euripides, *Iphigeneia in aulis* 950-1; cited p. 367n. ad loc. The Greek is translated as "spar" in Plato, *Alcibiades* 107e in an unpublished draft by D. S. Hutchinson (Toronto: Trinity College Library, 1991). For Greek wrestling, see Michael Poliakoff, *Combat Sports in the Ancient World: Competition, Violence, and Culture* (New Haven, Conn.: Yale University Press, 1987), pp. 23-53.

[12] Critchley, *Silent Language*, p. 112.

[13] "The incipient, infecundating contact about to take place between the two index fingers has often been described as a spark or a current, a modern electrical metaphor doubtless foreign to the sixteenth century, but natural enough considering the river of life which seems about to flow into the waiting body." Hartt, *Michelangelo*, 3:102. The comparison with an electric spark dates to the turn of the nineteenth century according to Tolnay, *Sistine Ceiling*, nn. 136-37. It is still current, as in the editorial caption to the illustration in *The Sistine Chapel: Michelangelo Rediscovered* (London: Muller, Blond, and White, 1986), p. 142: "The exquisitely conceived device of isolating the moment of Creation in the convergence of two solitary fingers was an invention, one may say, anticipating that of electricity." Electricity, of course, is not an invention but a phenomenon, known experientially since antiquity, although not in scientific theory. Consider also: "Michelangelo has God stretch out a dynamic hand toward the limp and lifeless hand of Adam in order to transmit the spark of life to it. This vision of touch as the bearer of vital energy may be an early and intuitive rendering of the principle of field touch." Weber, "Philosophical Perspective," pp. 16-17. The common interpretation of the creation of Adam through the infusion of a divine spark finger to finger was repeated as re-

"The vital spark flows from the outstretched hand of God into the matter He has shaped, and in response this matter begins to live: to move physically and to feel."[14] The iconographic program of scripture is identified as profoundly informed by a Platonist conception of human existence, which Michelangelo decisively learned as a boy at the court of Lorenzo de' Medici and adhered to faithfully. That concept was the soul imprisoned in the body, remembering its divine origin and striving to attain it.[15] The hexameral stories of the Bible were thus "elevated" by the philosophical concept of deification.

The novel aspect was Michelangelo's representation of the infusion of life as a cosmic phenomenon, a spark. He metaphorically integrated with the biblical narrative the ancient belief in fire as the vital element in humans. Through the extended arms, divine and human, energies flow from heaven to earth. Portrayed is the divine origin of the human soul, ascending from its bodily imprisonment to spiritual freedom. The return to God is the return to the essence of the soul: human deification. Michelangelo's own philosophical convictions superimposed this deeper significance of spiritual ascent on the biblical scenes. The fresco was the sublime artistic expression of the philosophical and religious beliefs of humanism: earthly beauty as manifesting the divine idea, the inner renewal of the human soul as divine in nature, the possibility of its deification. The painting does not merely illustrate in image a philosophical system; it is a philosophy, "a creative synthesis in visual symbols of the transcendent idealism." Michelangelo's synthesis was more clear and coherent than those of his contemporaries in other disciplines, a summa to rival Dante's medieval *Commedia.* The fine arts in the sixteenth century composed the basic language of thought, with the Sistine Ceiling as the compendium of humanist ideals.[16] Thus, the normative interpretation.

That version of the Creation of Adam did not epitomize renaissance humanism, however, since humanism was rhetorical, not philosophical, in method.[17] Although artists appropriated rhetorical ideals for painting, those

---

cently as Joyce D. Rosa, "The Sistine Chapel Centerfold, or Why Is Eve in the Middle" (paper presented at the Sixteenth Century Studies Conference, Toronto, Canada, October 28, 1994).

14 Sydney J. Freedberg, *Painting of the High Renaissance in Rome and in Florence*, 2 vols. (Cambridge, Mass.: Harvard University Press, 1961), 1:104, and, for the sources of Michelangelo's thought as Neoplatonist, p. 97.

15 Tolnay, *Sistine Ceiling*, p. 24; Johannes Wilde, *Michelangelo: Six Lectures*, ed. John Shearman and Michael Hirst (Oxford: Clarendon, 1978), pp. 58-63; Robert Clements, *The Poetry of Michelangelo* (New York: New York University Press, 1960), pp. 325-27.

16 Tolnay, *Sistine Ceiling*, pp. 24, 36, 37, 40-41, 42-43, 44.

17 For definition, see Paul Oskar Kristeller, "The Humanist Movement," in idem, *Renaissance Thought and Its Sources*, ed. Michael Mooney (New York: Columbia University Press, 1979), pp. 21-31; Vito R. Giustiniani, "*Homo*, *humanus*, and the meaning of 'humanism,'" *Journal of the History of Ideas* 46 (1985):167-95. For criticism of a Platonist ascent for pictorial, but not philosophical, reasons, see Hartt's review of Tolnay's volume in *Art Bulletin* 32 (1950):242-44.

were principles like decorum or concepts like vividness and variety.[18] Humanism in art was not associated with a Platonist ascent of the soul. There is no historical evidence, moreover, from the Medici household of any Platonist academy in which Michelangelo could have learned its concept of deification. The gymnasium of Marsilio Ficino (1433-99), who was responsible for a renaissance revival of Platonism, was not created by Medici patronage, and no member of its family ever participated in it.[19]

That philosophy was, moreover, emphatically *anti*-tactile in its values, even metaphorically. Ficino acknowledged that touch was "the universal sense" in animals and in humans to a superior degree.[20] He denied, however, its extension beyond the body to the intellect,[21] which faculty distinguished humans from other animals by its ability to contemplate the divine.[22] As he declared, "Nature has placed no sense farther from the intelligence than touch."[23] In his commentary on Plato's *Symposium* he explained the six powers of the soul for cognition as reason and the senses, with sensation grasping the qualities of the body. Of the senses touch ranked last. It pertained to matter, not to soul, so that spiritual things even displeased it. Touch inclined to the body and perceived bodily things "through the nerves the simple qualities of the elements, such as heat, cold, and the rest." Temperatures, which considerably harmed or helped the body, "present little to the admiration or to the censure of the soul," he wrote, "and are only moderately desired by it." Contemplative love ascended from sight to mind; voluptuary love descended from sight to touch.[24] "Of all the powers of the soul which are concerned with knowing," he explained, "the highest are intellect and reason, and the lowest are taste and touch. The last two for the most part lead down to bodily nature, while the first two lead up to divine

---

18 See Carl Goldstein, "Rhetoric and Art History in the Italian Renaissance and Baroque," *Art Bulletin* 73 (1991):641-68; Brian Vickers, *In Defense of Rhetoric* (Oxford: Clarendon, 1988), pp. 340-60; David Summers, *Michelangelo and the Language of Art* (Princeton, N.J.: Princeton University Press, 1981), pp. 88-89; Moshe Barasch, *Giotto and the Language of Gesture* (Cambridge: Cambridge University Press, 1987); Rensselaer W. Lee, "*Ut pictura poesis": The Humanistic Theory of Painting* (New York: W. W. Norton, 1967); John R. Spence, "*Ut rhetorica pictura*," *Journal of the Warburg and Courtauld Institutes* 20 (1951):26-44.

19 See James Hankins, "The Myth of the Platonic Academy of Florence," *Renaissance Quarterly* 44 (1991):459-60, 461; idem, "Cosimo de' Medici and the 'Platonic Academy,'" *Journal of the Warburg and Courtauld Institutes* 53 (1990):144-62.

20 Marsilio Ficino, *Theologia platonica* 10.2, p. 60.

21 Ficino, *Commentarium in "Phaedrum"* 11.8.

22 Ficino, *Theologia platonica* 14.9, pp. 279-80.

23 Ficino, *De vita* 1.7, p. 124; *Marsilio Ficino: Three Books on Life*, trans. Carol V. Kaske and John R. Clarke, Medieval and Renaissance Texts and Studies, 57; Renaissance Texts Series, 11 (Binghamton, N.Y.: Medieval and Renaissance Texts and Studies, 1989), p. 125.

24 Ficino, *Commentarius in "Symposium" Platonis* 5.2; 6.8; *Commentary on Plato's "Symposium" on Love*, trans. Sears Jayne, 2d rev. ed. (Dallas, Tex.: Spring, 1985), pp. 84-85, 86; cited also by Louise Vinge, *The Five Senses: Studies in a Literary Tradition* (Lund: Liber Laromedel, 1975), p. 72. For the soul as independent from the influences of sensory objects, see Kristeller, *The Philosophy of Marsilio Ficino*, trans. Virginia Conant, Columbia Studies in Philosophy, 6 (New York: Columbia University Press, 1943), p. 234.

substance, which is not of the body." Consequently, a person must be considered "mad as well as miserable, who whilst thus called to the sublime through vision, plunges himself into the mire through touch. Although he could become God instead of man by contemplating the divine through human beauty, from man he returns to beast by preferring the physical shadow of form to true spiritual beauty."[25] Another Platonist, Giovanni Pico della Mirandola (1463-94), in his *Oratio* designated "the hands of the soul its irascible power." In the hands as sentient and impure resided the bodily attraction that checked the soul and hurled it down, not up, the ladder of ascent to God.[26] Hands were instruments not of deification but degradation. Hands touching is not a credible image for a Platonist program.[27]

An infusion of the divine spark—vital elemental fire—into Adam as the artistic image of Platonist transcendent idealism makes no philosophical or physical sense. The divine spark was a Stoic, not a Platonist, concept. It was the Stoics who believed that the elements were generated from fire: their very name for God was *pneuma*, the fiery breath. Stoic pneumatology comprised multiple conceptions of theodicy, psychology, epistemology, inspiration, medicine, and magic. Amorphous matter and creative fire were the two principles at the origins of existence. An immanent and material divinity was identified with the world soul, a fiery breath that penetrated the cosmos and ensured its cohesion. The human soul was a portion of that element as a microcosm participating in the universal vitality. Christians adopted the cosmology but detached the world soul from the supreme God, so that humans became not parcels but creatures of divinity. Neoplatonists were cold to the idea of a divine spark: Plotinus was decidedly negative and Augustine was categorically opposed to its materialist psychology. God was transcendent.[28] The creative infusion into Adam of a divine spark cannot climax a Platonist program for the Sistine Chapel ceiling.

---

25 Ficino, *Epistolae* 5.7; 1.42; *The Letters of Marsilio Ficino*, trans. Language Department of School of Economic Science, London, 5 vols. (London: Shepheard and Wallwyn, 1975-), 4:10; 1:85.

26 Giovanni Pico della Mirandola, *Oratio de dignitate hominis* 11; "On the Dignity of Man," trans. Elizabeth Livermore Forbes, in *The Renaissance Philosophy of Man*, ed. Ernst Cassirer, Kristeller, and John Herman Randall, Jr. (Chicago: University of Chicago Press, 1948), p. 230.

27 For the assertion of Ficino's influence, see Rudolf Edwin Kuhn, *Michelangelo: Die sixtinische Kecke: Beiträge über ihre Quellen und zu ihrer Auslegung*, Beiträge zur Kunstgeschichte, 10 (Berlin: Walter de Gruyter, 1975), pp. 84-146. For Platonism and Neoplatonism in general in Michelangelo, see Erwin Panofsky, "The Neoplatonic Movement and Michelangelo," in *Studies in Iconology: Humanistic Themes in the Art of the Renaissance* (New York: Harper and Row, 1962), pp. 171-230; Clements, *Poetry of Michelangelo*, pp. 228-37.

28 See G. Verbeke, *L'Évolution de la doctrine du "pneuma" du Stoïcisme à S. Augustin: Étude philosophique* (Louvain: Éditions de l'Institut supérieur de philosophie, 1945). For introduction to renaissance knowledge of Stoicism, see Julien Eymard d'Angers, *Recherches sur le Stoïcisme aux seizième et dix-septième siècles*, ed. L. Antoine, Studien und Materialien zur Geschichte der Philosophie, 19 (Hildesheim: Georg Olms, 1976); Michel Spanneut, *Permanence du Stoïcisme: De Zenón à Malraux* (Gembloux: J. Duculot, 1973), pp. 213-55; Léontine

In humans, moreover, that Stoic spark was not physically associated with the hand or its fingers. It was believed to arise from the blood and to reside in the heart or the brain. In all classical medicine, still dominant in renaissance theory and practice, the element of heat was believed important and immortal. But it was innate, not infused. It was not the essence of the soul but its instrument. Aristotle even denied any analogy of bodily heat with physical flame, because fire was destructive, while heat was supportive and protective.[29]

Of the four elements, "the sense of touch is connected with earth," not with fire, Aristotle declared. Aristotle decided that the peripheral organ of touch, the skin, consisted of earth as a cool element.[30] Touch as the reaction of the flesh, its sensory tissue, had to be perceived by an element contrary to heat, since heat was concentrated in the heart as vital fire.[31] In the illustration of the sense of touch for Richard de Fournival's amorous bestiary the design was hands emerging from the ground.[32] Ficino accepted the origin of the sense of touch in the cool element of earth. "Who would hesitate," he asked, "to assign touch to earth, since it comes into being through all the parts of the earthly body, is completed in the nerves, which are very earthly, and touches things which have solidity and weight, qualities which earth gives to bodies?"[33] The renaissance anatomist Alessandro Benedetti (1450?-1512) speculated that fingernails originated in the earthy part of humans and had scant heat. Moreover, "When they grow cold the humor or moisture and heat evaporate into the air and the nails take the hard form of earth, like hoof or horn. Thus they are softened by fire."[34] The notion of a spark of

---

Zanta, *La renaissance du Stoïcisme au seizième siècle*, Bibliothèque littéraire de la Renaissance, 5 (Paris: Honoré Champion, 1914).

29 Margaret Talmadge May, introduction to *Galen on the Usefulness of the Parts of the Body: Peri chreias morōn, De usu partium*, trans. eadem, 2 vols. (Ithaca, N.Y.: Cornell University Press, 1968), pp. 50-52.

30 Aristotle, *De sensu* 439a; *"De sensu" and "De memoria,"* trans. G. R. T. Ross (New York: Arno, 1973), p. 53; *De anima* 425a; cited by Vinge, *Five Senses*, p. 17. For human origins from the earth in Greek mythology and legend, see W. K. C. Guthrie, *In the Beginning: Some Greek Views on the Origins of Life and the Early State of Man* (Ithaca, N.Y.: Cornell University Press, 1957), pp. 22-25; Sue Blundell, *The Origins of Civilization in Greek and Roman Thought* (London: Croom Helm, 1986), pp. 7-8.

31 Rudolph E. Siegel, *Galen on Sense Perception: His Doctrines, Observations, and Experiements on Vision, Hearing, Smell, Taste, Touch and Pain, and Their Historical Sources* (New York: S. Karger, 1970), p. 175; May, *Galen on the Body*, p. 52.

32 Richard de Fournival, *Bestiare d'amour*, Vienna, Nationalbibliothek, MS. 2609, fol. 18v; reproduced in Carl Nordenfalk, "The Five Senses in Late Medieval and Renaissance Art," *Journal of the Warburg and Courtauld Institutes* 48 (1985):5, pl. 2a, but interpretation mine. For his sensorium, especially sight and hearing, see also Elizabeth Sears, "Sensory Perception and Its Metaphors in the Time of Richard of Fournival," in *Medicine and the Five Senses*, ed. W. F. Bynum and Roy Porter (Cambridge: Cambridge University Press, 1993), pp. 17-39.

33 Ficino, *In "Symposium"* 5.2; trans. Jayne, p. 85. For the commonplace of humans (*homines*) from the soil (*humus*), see *Theologia platonica* 10.2; *Epistolae* 1.70.

34 Alessandro Benedetti, *Historia humani corporis, sive anatomice* 1.14; trans. L. R. Lind, *Studies in Pre-Vesalian Anatomy: Biography, Translations, Documents*, Memoirs of the

fire transmitted from the divine to the human fingertip in a tactile act of creation is not a credible image.

The sense of touch was classically associated in philosophy and in medicine with temperature.[35] As modern science explains, thermal receptors in the skin regulate body temperature by behavioral escape from or avoidance of unpleasant environments or by autonomic responses such as sweating or shivering. Thermal sensibility also functions to prevent local damage to the skin. Damage from burning, unlike damage from freezing, frequently poses so immediate a threat that the aversion of harm may require a response even before pain is felt. Quick warming of the skin triggers psychological alarm and instantaneous physical withdrawal of the affected surface, often the fingers.[36]

Renaissance artists were not ignorant of the effects of heat on sensitive fingertips. Leonardo da Vinci (1452-1519) noted that touch extended "with its power as far as the finger-tips. For as soon as the finger-tips have touched the object, the senso commune is immediately made aware of whether it is hot, cold, hard or soft, pointed or smooth." The distribution of the nerves "over the tips of all the fingers" allowed such transmission of "the impression of what they touch."[37] Fire was known to be hot, as Plato's *Timaeus* explained, because of its piercing and cutting effect on the body.[38] The classical case was Livy's account of Mucius Scaevola plunging his hand into the fire, a scene replicated in renaissance art.[39] The scholastic philosopher Thomas Aquinas had stated, "Touch and taste involve physical change in the organ itself; the hand touching something hot gets hot."[40] The earliest example of the sense of touch rendered as the sense of heat was an anatomi-

---

American Philosophical Society, 104 (Philadelphia, Pa.: American Philosophical Society, 1975), p. 88.

35 See below chapter two, especially pp. 135-38.

36 Joseph C. Stevens, "Thermal Sensibility," in *The Psychology of Touch*, ed. Morton A. Heller and William Schiff (Hillsdale, N.J.: Lawrence Erlbaum, 1991), p. 62.

37 Leonardo da Vinci, *Codex atlanticus*, in *Il codice atlantico del Leonardo da Vincid della Biblioteca ambrosiana da Milano*, ed. Giovanni Piumati (Milan: Real academia dei Lincei, 1894-1904), fol. 270v, b; *MS. di Leonardo da Vinci della Reale bibliotheca di Windsor: Dell'Anatomia fogli B*, ed. T. Sabachnikoff and Piumati (Milan, 1901), fols. 1v, 2r; cited by Kenneth D. Keele, "Leonardo da Vinci's Physiology of the Senses," in *Leonardo's Legacy: An International Symposium*, ed. Charles D. O'Malley, UCLA Center for Medieval and Renaissance Studies Publications, 2 (Berkeley and Los Angeles: University of California Press, 1969), p. 53.

38 Plato, *Timaeus* 61d.

39 Livy, *Ab urbe condita* 2.13.1. For an artistic rendition, see Zanobi di Domenico, Jacopo del Sellaio, and Biagio d'Antonio, cassone and spalliera, 1472, Courtauld Institute Galleries, London; reproduced in Jill Dunkerton, Susan Foister, Dillian Gordon, and Nicholas Penny, *Giotto to Dürer: Early Renaissance Painting in the National Gallery* (New Haven, Conn.: Yale University Press with National Gallery Publications, London, 1991), p. 111, figs. 148, 149. See also Antonio Guarino, *La coerenza di Publio Mucio*. For citations, see John Calvin, *Commentarium in "De clementia" Senecae* 1.33.

40 Thomas Aquinas, *Summa theologiae* 1a.78.3; *Summa theologiae*, trans. Timothy Suttor (New York: Blackfriars with McGraw Hill, 1970), 11:131.

cal drawing of a figure putting his right hand into a fire. It was also the earliest rendition of pain, since the hand in the fire burned.[41]

The iconoclast Thomas Bilney tested that knowledge and his resolve the evening before he was to be burned at the stake for his reformist faith. As John Foxe (1516-87) related in *The Acts and Monuments*, "Thomas Bilney, putting his hand toward the flame of the candle burning before them (as he also did divers times besides), and feeling the heat thereof, 'O,' (said he) 'I feel by experience, and have known it long by philosophy, that fire, by God's ordinance, is naturally hot."[42] Then there was the ordinary adage *ignem palma*, or "fire on the hand." It was commonly used for immediate understanding, for example, if a person sensed instantly that a joke was directed against him. Usage derived, Erasmus supposed, from a game in which players "bring something burning close to other people's hands; aroused by the sudden sensation, they normally jump back, and make the bystanders laugh."[43] It was believed that if a hand were waved quickly in a flame it would not be burned because the rapid movement of the air would chill it.[44] Yet there were only two natural circumstances in which Adam would not have felt the heat and the pain of fire on his fingertip. In classical medicine perception depended on the condition of the organ, so that not every contact produced sensation. In anticipation of the modern concept of the threshold of perception, an object of the same temperature as the body was not sensed as hot. Only what was excessively hot could be felt.[45] For Adam not to feel the fire sparking from God's fingertip, his hand would have to be already at its same degree of heat. Yet if it was already as hot as the spark there would be no reason for its ignition. The other case of insensibility to heat was caused by the severance of the nerve in the hand that produced sensation. Da Vinci in a marginal drawing of fingers lettered that nerve with the comment, "This being cut, the finger no longer has sensation even though placed in fire." Yet, he observed, nature in its skill had located it carefully between the fingers, precisely so that it would not be cut.[46] Adam's hand is intact.

The fact of fire as hot was preached in the very Sistine Chapel to Michelangelo's patron, Pope Julius II, by Tommaso de Vio, Cajetan (1469-

---

41 Drawing, 15th century, London, Wellcome Institute for the History of Medicine, MS. Inc. 283; reproduced in Keele, *Anatomies of Pain* (Oxford: Blackwell Scientific Publications, 1957), pl. II, and see pp. 30-39; Nordenfalk, "Five Senses," p. 6, pl. 2c.

42 John Foxe, *The Acts and Monuments*, 4:653. For persons unwilling to burn their fingertips, see Michel de Montaigne, *Essais* 2.12, p. 567.

43 Erasmus, *Adagia* 2.10.82; trans. Mynors, 34:160.

44 Theophrastus, *De igne* 35.

45 See Siegel, *Galen on Sense Perception*, pp. 182-83.

46 Da Vinci, *Manuscripts at the Royal Library Windsor*, ed. Kenneth Clark (Cambridge, 1935), 19009v; *Corpus of the Anatomical Studies in the Collection of Her Majesty the Queen at Windsor Castle*, ed. Keele and Carlo Pedretti, 3 vols. (New York: Harcourt Brace Jovanovich, 1978-80), 143v; reproduced in Keele, "Physiology of the Senses," p. 233, fig. 10.3.

1534), in his office as procurator general of the Dominican order. Who could distinguish between fire as hot and earth as cold, he asked, if heating and cooling were foreign to sensory experience?[47] Those sensations were not foreign to Michelangelo's experience. In his poetry he typified his humor as hot, his body as combustible. God "destined me to the fire," he wrote of his flammable flesh, sulphureous heart, and tindery bones.[48] Yet all males were by definition of gender elementally hot. And it was merely conventional for passion to burn. Michelangelo's declaration, "I act like a man whose breast is on fire," was but his transcription of Francesco Petrarca's (1304-74) sonnet.[49] Michelangelo poetized about the fire necessary for smithery and for making the lime used in sculpture and architecture, about flames flickering like dynamic form. He considered the phoenix and the salamander.[50] He knew the fatality of "fire, which harms all things."[51]

That was a fate of his art: he customarily burned his preparatory drawings and cartoons.[52] His imagination was so perfect, explained his biographer, that unable to express his concepts with his hands he destroyed many sketches and designs.[53] Just before his death he burned his own drawings, except for ten cartoons. As Cosimo de' Medici, who had hoped for a contribution from his estate, angrily responded to the report, "It did not appear to us to be an action worthy of him, to have surrendered them to the fire." Yet Michelangelo had displayed his contempt for his preparations earlier, by arranging for the burning of all the cartoons in his house in Rome when he moved in 1518 to Florence. He was "wont [to give] so freely to the fire."[54] Fire and flames, which were to become important in baroque art, were not featured in Michelangelo's art. Even his fresco of the Last Judgment merely suggests the glow of hell beneath the damned bodies.[55]

Fire, as Michelangelo demonstrated, was a destructive agent. As an interlocutor in Stefano Guazzo's (1530-93) *La civil conversatione* asked, "'Among all the things in the world, which are the most harmful?'" The re-

---

47 Tommaso de Vio, Cajetan, *Oratio* 4, in *Opuscula omnia*, 186b.

48 Michelangelo, *Rime* 97; *The Poetry of Michelangelo*, trans. James M. Saslow (New Haven, Conn.: Yale University Press, 1991), p. 224.

49 Michelangelo, *Rime* A31; trans. Saslow, p. 515. See Petrarch, *Canzoniere* 236. For Petrarch's influence on his poetry in general, see Clements, *Poetry of Michelangelo*, pp. 319-24.

50 For analysis of the fiery image, see Clements, *Poetry of Michelangelo*, pp. 271-77; Saslow, introduction to *Michelangelo's Poetry*, pp. 26-27; Glauco Cambon, *Michelangelo's Poetry: Fury of Form* (Princeton, N.J.: Princeton University Press, 1985), pp. 32-33, 38-39, 108-9.

51 Michelangelo, *Rime* 122.1; trans. Saslow, p. 262.

52 Alexander Perrig, *Michelangelo's Drawings: The Science of Attribution*, trans. Michael Joyce (New Haven, Conn.: Yale University Press, 1991), p. 1.

53 Giorgio Vasari, *Vita di Michelangelo*, 1:117.

54 Perrig, *Michelangelo's Drawings*, p. 1.

55 Clements, *Poetry of Michelangelo*, p. 271.

ply was, "Fire, sea, and woman.'"[56] No artist as practiced in anatomy or observation as Michelangelo would have selected such a risible metaphor as fire for a divine gift hand to hand. When that master craftsman Prometheus stole fire from the gods, he had the sense not to use his bare hands but the pith of a giant stalk of fennel.[57] And when he fashioned humans he modeled them from clay,[58] the element of earth, not fire. Galen in his catalogue of the things humans did with their hands as pacific and sociable beings included the making of fire-tongs. Hands were instrumental, he wrote, like tongs for the smith.[59] Like the smith, even God did not handle fire in his bare hands. In a rare renaissance illustration of Adam's creation that does depict fire the Creator grasps the wrist of the man's upraised right arm with open palm and splayed fingers. In his other hand the Creator holds fire, but only intermediately on a torch. While it flames at the tip, God's hand is safely on the neutral base.[60]

So was electricity destructive to human hands. Although its definition and theory were still unscientific, the phenomenon was since antiquity very well known. The earliest bioelectric phenomenon documented was the electrical discharge of certain fish, for marine creatures with electrical organs swam the waters of the earth before any appearance of humans. The common catfish of the Nile (*Malopterurus electricus*) was the first of those electrical denizens of the deep to be drawn, quite naturalistically so on the wall of the Egyptian tomb of Ti, an architect. The depiction shows the fish being crossed by a boating pole, an accident with a terrible effect on the man: painful and paralyzing shock.[61] Ancient and medieval authors vividly described how the Mediterranean torpedo fish (*Torpedo torpedo*) also shocked its prey and how the fish could numb to insensibility the hand of a fisherman right through the line, trident, or net. The electric fish was a terror. Concerning the effects of electricity on the hand, the medical authority Galen recorded the motor and sensory loss of that human limb in contact with the discharge of the torpedo fish when harpooned. He called its effect *narkē*, or "narcotic," and he attributed it to the transfer of a toxic quality

---

56 Stefano Guazzo, *La civil conversatione* 4; cited by Thomas Crane, *Italian Social Customs of the Sixteenth Century and Their Influence on the Literature of Europe* (New Haven, Conn.: Yale University Press, 1920), p. 415.

57 Hesiod, *Theogonia* lines 562-67.

58 Blundell, *Origins of Civilization*, pp. 10-11.

59 Galen, *De usu partium* 1.2, 3.

60 *Ovide moralisée*, French, 15th century, Paris, Bibliothèque nationale, Manuscrit français 871, fol. 1; reproduced in Johannes Zahlten, *"Creatio mundi": Darstellungen der sechs Schöpfunstage und naturwissenschaftliches Weltbild im Mittelalter*, Stuttgarter Beiträge zur Geschichte und Politik, 13 (Stuttgart: Klett-Cotta, 1979), fig. 106.

61 Peter Kellaway, "The Part Played by Electric Fish in the Early History of Bioelectricity and Electrotherapy," *Bulletin of the History of Medicine* 20 (1946): 112. Bas relief from tomb of Ti, Sakkara, c. 2750; reproduced, p. 113, pl. 1.

from the fish to the fisherman.[62] He also termed the temporary insensibility *anaisthesia*. He wrote how "an unknown quantity emanating from the fish inactivated their nervous system by changing the balance of its constituent qualities." Even if the shock only partly disturbed sensation it completely abolished movement. There could result coma and stupor.[63] Galen also ascribed the cause to a frigorific quality, probably through his observation of similar effects produced on the human body by severe cold, either by contact or through a conductor. He thought the narcotic both native and unique to the fish.[64]

In the Aristotelian tradition "the torpedo narcotizes the creatures that it wants to catch, overpowering them by the shock that is resident in its body, and feeds upon them." Theophrastus knew that the fish could numb the hand of a fisherman through the line or trident. The medieval encyclopedist Vincent of Beauvais compiled that knowledge. "As Aristotle testifies, the *narkē* possess the following power: through the line and the rod the hand of the fisherman that holds it is struck by numbness and insensibility."[65] Plutarch moralized, "You know yourself the property of the torpedo or cramp fish, which not only benumbs all those that touch it, but also strikes the numbness through the very net into the hands of them that go about to take it." Even if it were captured alive on shore it affected the water being poured over it, so that the human hands were numbed and its feelings stupefied. He compared its effluviums to darts and its effects on its victim to chaining and freezing.[66]

The most accurate treatise on fish before the sixteenth century, Oppian's *Halieutica*, described the effects most comprehensively. When struck, the torpedo transmitted pain along the fisherman's line into his rod, then into his hand, so that frequently "the rod and the fishing-tackle escape from his palm. Such icy numbness straightway settles in his hand." The mere touch of the fish by a human immediately "quenches the strength of his body and his blood is frozen within him and his limbs can no longer carry him but he quietly pines away and his strength is drained by stupid torpor." The experience was nightmarish, like trying to escape in a dream from chains while one's legs buckled. "Even as in the darkling phantoms of a dream, when a man is terrified and fain to flee, his heart leaps, but, struggles as he may, a steadfast bond as it were weighs down his eager knees: even such a fetter

---

[62] Siegel, *Galen on Psychology, Psychopathology, and Function and Diseases of the Nervous System: An Analysis of his Doctrines, Observations, and Experiments* (Basel: S. Karger, 1973), p. 244, citing Galen, *De usu respirationis* 4.4; Siegel, *Galen on Sense Perception*, p. 73.

[63] Siegel, *Galen on Sense Perception*, p. 183, citing Galen, *De locis affectis* 2.2.

[64] Kellaway, "Electric Fish," pp. 123, 132, citing Galen, *De usu respirationis* 4; *De locis affectis* 2.2; 6.5; *De symptomatum causis* 1.5.

[65] Kellaway, "Electric Fish," p. 118, citing Aristotle, *Historia animalium* 630b, noting that book nine is attributable to Theophrastus, *On Biting and Venemous Animals*, as quoted by Athenaeus, *Deipnosophistae* 7.314b; Vincent of Beauvais, *Speculum naturale* 16.

[66] Plutarch, *Moralia* 978b; cited by Kellaway, "Electric Fish," p. 119.

doth the cramp-fish devise for fishes." And by craft for humans. It was Oppian who specified that the charge did not emanate from the whole body of the fish but from organs located on its sides between its head and pectoral fins. The theory was again advanced in Girolamo Cardano's (1501-76) *De rerum varietate*.[67]

Pliny popularized its amazing effect in his natural history. "Even at a distance, and that a long distance, or if it is touched with a spear or rod, to think that the strongest arms are numbed, feet as swift in racing as you like are paralysed!"[68] The electric fish was mentioned in literature as common and diverse as Cicero's *De natura deorum*, Aelian's *Historia animalium*, and Isidore of Seville's *Etymologiae*.[69] The scholastic scientist Albert the Great cited its poisonous effect if touched, even by a spear: how through emanations it numbed the human senses and drained vitality. He added an anecdote. "One of our brethren once barely grazed a torpedo with the tip of his finger, but even after six months of treatment with warm soaks and ointment he had scarcely regained the sensation in his forearm."[70]

The shocking effects of electricity were not just suffered from accidents while fishing. They were also deliberately harnessed in medicine. There was practiced in antiquity a kind of electroshock therapy for treating cases of severe headache. A live torpedo fish was placed on the patient's forehead to deliver its charge (about 50 to 60 volts for a large specimen). The effect was stupefaction,[71] not vivification. The very name of the Mediterranean

---

67 Oppian, *Halieutica* 3.149-55; 2:64-67, 81-85; *Oppian, Colluthus, Tryphiodorus*, trans. A. W. Mair (New York: G. P. Putnam's Sons, 1928), pp. 357, 287, 289. Kellaway, "Electric Fish," pp. 121-23, citing a different translation, with the organic theory at 2.63; and Girolamo Cardano, *De rerum varietate* 7.32.

68 Pliny, *Historia naturalis* 32.2.7; *Natural History*, trans. H. Rackham, W. S. Jones, and D. E. Eicholz, 10 vols. (Cambridge, Mass.: Harvard University Press, 1958-62), trans. Jones, 8:469; cited also by Kellaway, "Electric Fish," p. 120, who further notes *Historia naturalis* 9.24.42, 51; 32.9.

69 Cicero, *De natura deorum* 2.50.51; Aelian, *Historia animalium* 5.37; 9.14; 14.3; Isidore of Seville, *Etymologiae* 12.6; cited by Kellaway, "Electric Fish," p. 120.

70 Albert the Great, *De animalibus* 24.6.1; 24.58; citing Pliny, *Historia naturalis* 32.7, and Isidore of Seville, *Etymologiae* 12.6.45; *Man and the Beasts: "De animalibus" (Books 22-26)*, trans. James J. Scanlan, Medieval and Renaissance Texts and Studies, 47 (Binghamton, N.Y.: Medieval and Renaissance Texts and Studies, 1987), p. 376; cited also by Kellaway, "Electric Fish," p. 120. The torpedo fish as mentioned by Albert the Great was argued to explain the attraction between iron and a magnet by Jean Buridan, *Quaestiones octo "Physicorum" libros Aristotelis* 7.4. A precedent was Averroes, *Colliget* 5.10; cited by Kellaway, "Electric Fish," p. 123. Electricity as the cause of the stunning by the fish was only diagnosed late in the eighteenth century by Henry Cavenish, "Some Attempts to Imitate the Effects of the *Torpedo* by Electricity," Royal Society of London, *Philosophical Transactions* 66 (1776):196-225; rpt. in *The Electrical Researches of Henry Cavendish*, ed. J. C. Maxwell (Cambridge, 1879); cited by J. L. Heilbron, *Electricity in the Seventeenth and Eighteenth Centuries* (Berkeley and Los Angeles: University of California Press, 1979), p. 23.

71 Kellaway, "Electric Fish," pp. 112, 127, 129, citing Scribonius Largus, *Compositiones* 162. See also John F. Fulton, "Origins of Electroshock Therapy," *Journal of the History of Medicine* 11 (1956):229-30.

electric ray, *torpedo*, was derived from its physical effect of *torpor*.[72] The Roman physician credited with its remedy for headaches was careful to advise that the fish be removed from the patient's body as soon as numbness was felt, lest he lose all sensation. The therapy was transmitted through Dioscorides' herbal[73] and it was mentioned in Avicenna's *Canon of Medicine* as effective for arresting epileptic seizure.[74] The numbing or paralyzing charge of the fish was also recommended for curing "gout" (arthritis) and prolapsed anus. Its medical usage was current until the end of the seventeenth century.[75]

Scientists in the sixteenth century speculated on the cause of the phenomenon, whether it was frigorific or occult. Edward Wotton (1492-1555), Guillaume Rondelet (1507-66), Konrad Gesner (1516-65), Ulisse Aldrovandi (1522-1605?), Pierre Belon (1517?-64) in his great illustrated book on fishes, and even the papal physician Ippolito Salviani (1514-72) all wondered why. Gesner supposed in his *Historiae animalium* that "no one understands what power the torpedo has"; but few doubted that it had power. Thomas Erastus (1524-83) reported that fishermen in Venice denied that the electric ray possessed any great ability to numb; for himself, he was uncertain. Most scholars were certain. As Julius Caesar Scaliger (1484-1558) wrote, the "torpedo forces numbness into the hands through a line even if it is not touched—for this is no fable."[76] The fact even appeared in such an unlikely text as Laurent Joubert's (1529-83) *Traité du ris*.[77]

The phenomenon was not known only to scientists. Erasmus (?1469-1536) appropriated its venom to compare the speech of an evil tongue.[78]

---

72 Varro, *De lingua latina* 5.12; cited by Kellaway, "Electric Fish," p. 117 n. 13.

73 Scribonius Largus, *Compositiones* 11; Dioscorides, *De materia medica* 2.17; cited by Kellaway, "Electric Fish," p. 130.

74 Kellaway, "Electric Fish," p. 133, citing *Hayât-al-hayawân*, in the English translation by A. S. G. Jayakar, 2 vols. (London: Luzac, 1906-8), 1:69. See also Joshua O. Leibowitz, "Electroshock Therapy in Ibn-Sina's *Canon*," *Journal of the History of Medicine* 12 (1957):71-72.

75 Kellaway, "Electric Fish," pp. 127, 130-31. He also documents the usage of the flesh of the fish to cure lust, to ease the pain of childbirth, as a depilitory, and as an aphrodisiac, pp. 128-29. A method of boiling it, practiced since the sixth century, allowed the extraction of an oil that was a narcotic. The recipe is repeated in Jean Fernel, *Universa medicina* 6:107; cited pp. 132-33.

76 Brian P. Copenhaver, "A Tale of Two Fishes: Magical Objects in Natural History from Antiquity through the Scientific Revolution," *Journal of the History of Ideas* 52 (1991):384-85, 394, 390, citing Edward Wotton, *De differentiis animalium*, pp. 145, 149; Guillaume Rondelet, *Libri de piscibus marinis*, pp. 360-61; Konrad Gesner, *Historia animalium*, pp. 1182-94; Ulisse Aldrovandi, *De piscibus*, pp. 415-23; Ippolito Salviani, *Aquatilium animalium historiae*, fols. 142-43; Pierre Belon, *De aquatilibus libri duo cum iconibus* (Paris, 1553), pp. 90-93; Thomas Erastus, *De occultis pharamacorum potestatibus*; Julius Caesar Scaliger, *Exotericarum exercitationum. . . de subtilitate ad Hieronymum Cardanum*, fols. 290-91. Copenhaver also reviews some of the classical and medieval background, pp. 378-83, but does not cite Kellaway's precedent research.

77 Laurent Joubert, *Traité du ris* 1, prol.

78 Erasmus, *Lingua*, ed. J. H. Waszink, in *Opera omnia* (Amsterdam), 4-1-A: 87.

Michel de Montaigne (1533-92) praised it among the marvels of animals that humans could not imitate, even imagine. "As proof of this, the torpedo has the property, not only of putting to sleep the limbs that directly touch her, but of transmitting through nets and seines a sort of numbed heaviness to the hands of those who move and handle them."[79] A Jesuit missionary in the same century reported a superstitious application by the Abyssinians of the Nile catfish. As Samuel Purchas (1577?-1626) preserved the account in his *Hakluytus posthumus*, if a person held the torpedo fish without its stirring, no effect was produced. "But if it moved itself ever so little, it so torments him who holds it that his arteries, joints, sinews, and all his members feel excruciating pain with a certain numbness." As soon as the fish was dropped, immediately the pain and numbness vanished. The Abyssinians ritualized the phenomenon to exorcise demons from the human body.[80]

The effect of the torpedo fish was also a metaphorical argument in philosophy. Plato, whose doctrine of deification is wrongly said to be epitomized in Michelangelo's fresco, cited it. Menon complained to Socrates that their discussion confused him, just as the *narkē* paralyzed and numbed a person. "And if I may venture to make a jest upon you," Socrates, "you seem both in your appearance and in your power over others to be like a torpedo fish, who torpifies those who come near him and touch him, as you have now torpified me, I think. For my soul and my tongue are really torpid and I do not know how to answer you."[81] The principal Neoplatonist, Plo-tinus, also cited the fish to argue concerning sensory impressions. "The rod which is between the torpedo-fish and the hand is not affected at all in the same way as the hand; and certainly there, too, if the rod and the line were not in between, the hand would not be affected. Or even this might be disputed: for if the torpedo-fish gets into a net, the fisherman is said to receive a shock."[82] Numbness was observed to be felt more in the hands and feet than in any other bodily part,[83] and the particular effect of electricity was specified to be in the limbs. Galen wrote that the torpor the fish produced

---

[79] Montaigne, *Essais* 2.12, p. 469; *The Complete Works of Montaigne: Essays, Travel Journal, Letters,* trans. Donald M. Frame (Stanford, Calif.: Stanford University Press, 1967), pp. 344-45.

[80] Samuel Purchas, *Hakluytus posthumus, or Purchas his Pilgrimes,* 9:227; cited by Kelaway, "Electric Fish," p. 133 (modernization mine).

[81] Plato, *Meno* 80a; *Works,* trans. Benjamin Jowett, 3d ed. (New York, 1892), p. 39; cited by Kellaway, "Electric Fish," p. 118. See also for the electrostatic charge on the masts of ships, John G. Griffith, "Static Electricity in Agathon's Speech in Plato's *Symposium,*" *Classical Quarterly* 40 (1990):547-48.

[82] Plotinus, *Enneads* 4.5.1; *Plotinus,* trans. A. H. Armstrong, 6 vols. (Cambridge, Mass.: Harvard University Press, 1966-84), 4:283; also cited by Siegel, *Galen on Sense Perception,* p. 120, from Stephen McKenna's translation, which is here replaced.

[83] Aristotle, *Problemata* 6.6. The authorship was doubted by the late thirteenth century. Steven J. Williams, "Defining the Corpus aristotelicum: Scholastic Awareness of Aristotelian Spuria in the High Middle Ages," *Journal of the Warburg and Courtauld Institutes* 58 (1995):45.

was "composed of a difficulty of motion and sensation seen clearly in the whole body and especially in the limbs."[84] Finally, Ficino, whose philosophy supposedly inspired Michelangelo's fresco, also knew the tactile fact: the torpedo fish instantly numbed the hand that touched it, even distantly through a rod.[85]

Electricity, which was so very well known to numb and paralyze the human hand and even to cause stupor and coma of the entire body, is an impossible metaphor for the vivification of Adam. If in Michelangelo's fresco the Creator were infusing a spark of fire or a shock of electricity from his fingertip to Adam's, the man would instinctively, reflexively withdraw his hand from that source. He would not be so passive, so receptive as he is portrayed. The standard interpretation of his creation by the infusion of a spark is anachronistic. It has derived historically from the association of life with electricity by Luigi Galvini, an eighteenth-century scientist. The very notion of the infusion, rather than the transmission, of a spark has copied his misidentification of electricity as a chemical element and a fluid. Galvinism, a widely popular belief, inspired Mary Wollstonecroft Shelly's creation Frankenstein, who pronounced before his experiment that he would "infuse a spark of being into the lifeless thing."[86] Galvinism did not animate Michelangelo's Adam.

God is not infusing any element into Adam: not celestial fire or air, or terrestrial water or earth. No creation of a soul is depicted, although that belief was culturally implicit, cogently so from the institutional patronage and placement of the art. It crowded the ceiling of the papal chapel, on the flattened barrel-vault above the sacred rites solemnized below in the supreme Christian sanctuary. Preachers below on the floor officially lauded in epideictic rhetoric human dignity as created in the divine image and likeness (Gen. 1:26). From creation to dignity was their frequent and persistent theme but it was expressed from a considerable variety of arguments and from an impressive variety of sources. Power to command other creatures was also an argument for human dignity. So was the moral indeterminacy to be an autonomous maker. And there was excellence discerned in sharing divine causality. A philosophical, even hermetic, meditation on the skillful design of the human body adduced a knowledge of the existence of its Creator. But Adam was conceived as created with a perfection defying material categories; so that, while the nobility of the body was to be considered, more to be contemplated was the mark of the soul as participant in reason

---

84 Galen, 7:108-9; cited by Kellaway, "Electric Fish," p. 132. Sextus Empiricus, *Pyrrhonic Sketches* 14.38 also noted its numbness when applied to the extremities; cited, p. 132.

85 Ficino, *De vita* 3.16, p. 324.

86 Mary Wollstonecroft Shelley, *Frankenstein, or The Modern Prometheus*, ed. M. K. Joseph (London: Oxford University Press, 1969), p. 57 . For the science, but without reference to Michelangelo, see Frank A. J. L. James and J. V. Field, "Frankenstein and the Spark of Being," *History Today* 44 (September 1994):52.

and capable of beatitude. Papal preachers expounded in the tradition Augustine had established of the image and likeness of the Trinity formed in the tripartite faculties of the soul. The mimetic theme was determinative in the papal orators, especially those trained in scholasticism, to discern the divine vestiges in creation. Their discovery was deemed possible only by raising the eyes to heaven. People should "look up," as the preachers frequently invited their congregation precisely to do. The humanists among them exhorted the witness to open a scene of the celestial court as an exemplar of the papal court and as their final destiny. The scholastics advised attention toward contemplation of the divine nature. But the analogy of earth to heaven was their mutual presupposition.[87]

Yet, if the hearers of those sermons did tilt back their heads to look up at Michelangelo's frescoes on the ceiling, they would have seen exactly what its critics complained of: nudes. Biagio da Cesena, master of ceremonies to Pope Paul III, wanted their genitals painted over. Nudity belonged in a bathhouse, not a chapel.[88] There was nothing contemplative about bodies. Painting and philosophy—imagery and intellection—were contradictions, although some thinkers maneuvered their aesthetic alliance. Yet the depiction of human bodies, even in a chapel, was not irreverent. It was especially reverent in that chapel. The Sistine Chapel was formally dedicated to the sanctity of the human body—not the soul—through its consecration to the assumption of Mary. Although the assumption was not yet a formal dogma, it was a cherished belief that, in parallel to the resurrection of Jesus, at death Mary was taken bodily to heaven.[89]

Although Michelangelo may have believed religiously in the divine creation of a human soul, artistically he disregarded that interpretation. The artistic task was not to portray souls but bodies, although such figures were animated, his vivaciously and vigorously so. The major biographer of renaissance artists, Giorgio Vasari (1511-74), acknowledged that Michelan-

---

87 For the preaching, without reference to Michelangelo, see John W. O'Malley, *Praise and Blame in Renaissance Rome: Rhetoric, Doctrine, and Reform in the Sacred Orators of the Papal Court c. 1450-1521*, Duke Monographs in Medieval and Renaissance Studies, 3 (Durham, N.C.: Duke University Press, 1979), pp. 133-37, 130-31. For the parallel between epideictic preaching and ekphrastic art, see Hellmut Wohl, "Papal Patronage and the Language of Art," in *Umanesimo a Roma nel Quattrocent,* Atti del convegno su "Umanesimo a Roma nel quattrocento," New York, 1-4 dicembre 1981, ed. Paolo Brezzi and Maristella De Panizza Lorch (Rome: Istituto di studi romani, 1984), pp. 235-46.

88 Vasari, *Vita di Michelangelo,* 1:75 n. 4; 5:456. Pierluigi Vecchi, "Michelangelo's Last Judgment," in *Sistine Chapel*, pp. 190-94, and p. 269 nn. 27, 28; Anthony Blunt, *Artistic Theory in Italy 1450-1600* (Oxford: Clarendon, 1940), pp. 118-19; Clark, *The Nude: A Study in Ideal Form*, Bollingen Series 35-2 (New York: Pantheon, 1956), p. 376; Lee, "*Ut pictura poesis,*" p. 38. When Adam and Eve appeared on the renaissance stage, they wore suits tailored from parchment. Stella Mary Newton, *Renaissance Theatre Costume and the Sense of the Historic Past* (London: Rapp and Whiting, 1975), p. 25.

89 For background, see Martin Jugie, *La mort et l'assomption de la sainte Vierge: Étude historico-doctrinale*, Studi e testi, 114 (Vatican City: Bibliotheca apostolica vaticana, 1944).

gelo painted "the effects of the soul's passions and joys." But he declared that his artistic genius was for the body. "The intention of this singular man was never to paint anything other than the perfect and perfectly proportioned composition of the human body in its most unusual poses." Michelangelo desired to satisfy viewers with the skill in which he surpassed other artisans. He desired "to display the method of his grand style and his nudes and the extent to which he understood the problems of design, and he finally revealed the way to achieve facility in the principal aim of the art of painting—that is, the depiction of the human figure." He applied himself "to this one grace" and demonstrated profoundly "how to attain perfection." Particularly astonishing were the nudes executed on the Sistine Chapel ceiling, which Vasari argued should be discerned for "the excellence of the figures, the perfection of the foreshortenings, the truly stupendous round contours, all of which possess grace and delicacy, and the beautiful proportions." Nude bodies demonstrated "the extremes and perfection of his craft."[90]

There was not a whisper in Genesis about any creation of a soul.[91] In a scriptural tradition God did breathe into Adam's nostrils "the breath of life" (Gen. 2:7), but the interpretation of that breath as a soul was a theological inference or invention. The scriptural concept of a respiratory creation of Adam (Gen. 2:7) had been depicted artistically in medieval manuscripts as rays emanating from God to man, either mouth to mouth or mouth to ear. In variants the Creator breathed a man or a bird into Adam's mouth.[92] Respiration is not Michelangelo's depiction. Air as an element between the divine and human fingertips in his fresco has some plausibility. Unlike fire it is at least present, if only as an empty space. There was an ancient association of the fingertips with respiration but it was as a diagnostic for disease.

Symptomatic of empyema—a collection of fluid in the lungs—and of other chronic respiratory diseases, especially tuberculosis, was a morphological condition of clubbed fingers with curved nails. The condition involved a bulbous enlargement of the soft tissues of the distal phalanges, so that the

---

90 Vasari, *Vita di Michelangelo*, 1:69, 39; *The Lives of the Artists*, trans. Julia Conaway Bondanella and Peter Bondanella (Oxford: Oxford University Press, 1991), p. 461, 444. For background, see Luigi Grassi, *Il disegno italiano dal trecento al seicento*, Nuovi saggi, 18 (Rome: dell'Ateneo, n. d.).

91 For modern exegesis, see Gunnlauger A. Jonssen, *The Image of God: Genesis 1:26-28 in a Century of Old Testament Research*, trans. Lorraine Svendsen, rev. Michael S. Cheney, Coniectanea biblica, OT series, 26 (Lund: Almquist and Wicksell, 1988). For Ludwig Köhler's interpretation of the image of God as the upright posture, see pp. 107-12.

92 Mouths: Hortus deliciarum, fol. 17, 12th century, Strasbourg, Bibliothèque de la ville; reproduced in Zahlten, *Creatio mundi*, pl. 94. See also p. 396, pl. 226. Ears: Bible from Todi, Italy, 12th century, Rome, Bibliotheca apostolica vaticana, codex latinus vaticanus, 10405, fol. 4v; reproduced, pl. 51. See also pls. 36, 226, 396. Human: Peter Lombard, *Sententiae*, 1352-54, Naples; Bibliotheca apostolica vaticana, Codex vaticanus lat. 681, fol. 119v; reproduced, pl. 97. See also pls. 39, 399, 103, 400. Bird: Pantheon bible, Italian, 12th century, Rome, Bibliotheca apostolica vaticana, codex vaticanus latinus 12958, fol. 4v; reproduced, pl. 50.

fingers appeared clubbed. The nails curved and bowed over the fingertips to cover them; the beds were full and pale, without pigmentation in the cuticle.[93] The Hippocratic literature described the nails as "curved, dry and yellow-green."[94] Aretaeus, who composed the classic descriptions of respiratory disease, reported that empyema swelled the fingers of the hand. Phthisis (pulmonary tuberculosis) also affected the fingers. They became slender with thick joints, their fleshy parts so wasted that the bones remained. The fingernails were "crooked" and "bent" because they were unsupported by flesh. Among the symptoms of a pneumonia tending to fatality were "the extremities cold, the nails livid and curved."[95] Galen generally reported in his argument for the natural necessity of bones in the fingers a diseased condition of bent and distorted fingers because they were soft.[96] Albert the Great specifically recorded for medieval medicine clubbed fingers and humped fingernails as signs of pulmonary abscess. That was his primary example of the physical appearance of one part of the body as a clue to a morbid condition in another.[97]

Adam's fingernail is not diseased but healthy. Although that may be an implicit sign of normal respiration,[98] such a reference to creation by breath is recondite. The Creator is not transmitting to Adam any substance. Nor are they about to touch, nor did they ever so touch mutually in art. In the popular illustrations of the five senses in renaissance art biblical scenes became introduced into the background as moralizing exegesis. There is one such depiction of the creation of Adam, in which Peter Cool after a design by Marten de Vos (1532-1603) portrays Adam reclined in a pose copied

---

93 Robert Baran and Rodney P. R. Dawber, "Physical Signs," in *Diseases of the Nails and Their Management*, ed. idem (Oxford: Blackwell Scientific Publications, 1984), pp. 25-30; Nardo Zaias, *The Nail in Health and Disease* (New York: SP Medical and Scientific Books, 1980), pp. 213-21; Theodore J. Berry, *The Hand as a Mirror of Systemic Disease* (Philadelphia, Pa.: F. A. Davis, 1964), p. 180; Robert G. Fraser, J. A. Peter Paré, P. D. Paré, Richard S. Fraser, and George P. Genereux, *Diagnosis of Diseases of the Chest*, 4 vols., 3d ed. (Philadelphia, Pa.: W. B. Saunders, 1988), 1:403-5; Charles Coury, "Le signe du doit hippocratique," *Pagine di storia delle medicina* 12 (1968):3-12; idem, "Hippocratic Fingers and Hypertrophic Osteoarthropathy," *British Journal of Diseases of the Chest* 54 (1960):202-9.

94 Hippocrates, *Prognostica* 17, *De internis affectibus* 10, *De morbis* 50; *Hippocrates*, trans. Paul Potter, 6 vols. (Cambridge, Mass.: Harvard University Press, 1988), 5:283. See Mirko Drazen Grmek, *Diseases in the Ancient World*, trans. Mirelle Muellner and Leonard Muellner (Baltimore, Md.: Johns Hopkins University Press, 1989), pp. 185-86.

95 Aretaeus, *De causis et signis acutorum morborum* 1.9; 1.8.2.1; *The Extant Works of Aretaeus, the Cappadocian*, trans. Francis Adam (London, 1856), p. 311. See also Coury, "La pathologie pleuro-pulmonaire dans l'oeuvre d'Arétée de Cappadoce," *Presse medicale* 70 (1972):657. For the author, see Fridolf Kudlien, *Untersuchungen zu Aretaios von Kappadokien*, Mainz, Akademie der Wissenschaften und der Literatur, Abhandlungen der Geistes-und Sozialwissenschaftlichen Klasse, 11 (Wiesbaden: Franz Steiner, 1963).

96 Galen, *De usu partium* 1.12.

97 Albert the Great, *De animalibus* 22.5.10. This text is not reported in the scholarly literature on Hippocratic fingers.

98 The softness, roughness, and dryness of fingernails could aid in the diagnosis of temperament according to Avicenna, *Canon* 2.3.3.

from Michelangelo's fresco. He rests one arm on its elbow on the ground, with the other arm extended up toward a robed figure who grasps his arm traditionally to raise him. Although God touches Adam, the sense that the engraving moralizes is not touch but smell.[99] The association of human creation with the olfactory sense was owed to the biblical verse about respiration through the nostrils. "Then the Lord God formed man of dust from the ground, and breathed into his nostrils the breath of life; and man became a living being" (Gen. 2:7).

In the early Christian types of the creation formation is depicted with God's hand on Adam's shoulder; animation, with his hand on Adam's head.[100] Although God may touch Adam, the gesture is not reciprocated. The Catalan bibles illustrated in the eleventh century at the monasteries of Ripoll and Roda continued the tactile concept, as if God were a sculptor in clay, modeling from the dust of the earth (Gen. 2:7). The artisan Creator in an architectural arch, with his left hand on Adam's shoulder and his right on his chest, fashions him. Adam's own arms are at his side and his knees are crossed. Both figures are on tiptoes. In the other illustration Adam stands on a craggy pedestal but tentatively, bent sideways and looking down. God steadies him, grasping his right side behind his shoulder and encircling his arm to touch his chest, as if helping him to straighten up. In a Belgian bible of the same century the Creator places his outstretched arms on the shoulder of Adam, who emerges upright from a rock with his arms extended down.[101]

In the initial of a Canterbury bible from the mid-twelfth century God fashions Adam from clay with his right hand, his fingers splayed on the man's chest, while his left hand is curved around his head. The contemporaneous mural of an apse from a church in Osormont depicts a complex narrative. God breathes rays into Adam's face; God fashions his shoulders and back with his hands; and God sends him forth with the gesture of an uplifted hand, which Adam acknowledges with his.[102] The abbess Hildegard of Bin-

---

99 Peter Cool after Marten de Vos, Smell, engraving; reproduced in Nordenfalk, "The Five Senses in Flemish Art before 1600," in *Nederlandish Mannerism*, Papers Given at a Symposium in Nationalmuseum, Stockholm, September 21-22, 1984, ed. Görel Cavalli-Björkman, Nationalmusei Skriftserie, 4 (Stockholm: Nationalmuseum, 1985), p. 142, fig. 10c. Cf. Adriaen Collaert after Marten de Vos, p. 143, fig. 12c; p. 144, fig. 14c.

100 Helga vom Kaiser-Minn, *Der Erschaffung des Menschen auf den spätantiken Monumenten des dritte und vierte Jahrhunderts*, Jahrbuch für Antike und Christentum Ergänzungsband, 6 (Münster: Aschendorff, 1981). For the imposition of hands for the creation of Adam, see also Luc De Bruyne, "L'imposition des mains dans l'art chrétien ancien: Contribution iconologique à l'histoire du geste," *Rivista di archeologia cristiana* 20 (1943):175-82.

101 Catalan bible from Ripoll, 11th century, Rome, Bibliotheca apostolica vaticana, Cod. vat. lat. 5729, fol. 5v; reproduced in Zahlten, *Creatio mundi*, fig. 54. Catalan bible from Roda, Paris, Bibliothèque nationale, MS. lat. 6, fol. 6; reproduced in *Creatio mundi*, fig. 53. Goderannus-Bibel aus Lobbes, Belgian, 1084, Tournai, Bibliothèque du séminaire, MS. 1, fol. 6. See also the adage *manu fingere*, "to mould by hand," in Erasmus, *Adagia* 2.5.32.

102 Initial from Canterbury bible, about 1150, London, Lambeth Palace Library, MS. 3, vol. 1, fol. 1; reproduced in Mireille Mentré, *Création et apocalypse: Histoire d'un regard hu-*

gen, ever visionary, conceived for her prayer book the most tactile creation. God holds—carries—the entire body of Adam in his arms, one hand under his buttocks, the other around his upper arm.[103] In an Old Testament from the mid-thirteenth century the Creator grasps Adam's elbow, while he blesses him with his other hand. Adam's hand is uplifted, his elbow bent to receive the blessing. On a portal of the cathedral of Auxerre sculpted in the same century the Creator again fashions Adam with his hands, touching his head and his chest.[104] On a portal at the cathedral of Chartres a standing God fashions Adam's head, while the man (a mere torso) rests his hand familiarly on God's knees.[105] On the fourteenth-century reliefs on the façade of the cathedral of Orvieto, where Luca Signorelli (c.1445-1523) will paint Empedocles with his grotesques, the Creator in ancient style places his left hand on Adam's head, while his right arm touches his shoulder.[106] In a historiated German bible God blesses the sleeping Adam, touching him with his fingertips. When Adam awakes and sits up, God blesses and touches his shoulder with his hand.[107]

The human head and shoulder, then the chest, were the conventional artistic places for God to touch the male figure in the act of creation. The head and the chest were the competing locations of vitality in the medical theories of Galen and Aristotle for the brain and the heart. Touching the shoulder seems to have been a metonym for the fashioning of the entire physical frame of the upright torso; perhaps it also suggested the "shouldering" of human responsibility. In the artistic tradition God did not ever *create* Adam hand to hand or finger to finger. There are examples in which God blesses him as already created, with the traditional benediction of two fingers joined and imperiously raised. Adam is seated with outstretched hands or he is half-erect with his right arm on his knee, his left akimbo.[108] In some scenes of blessing dating from the thirteenth century the Creator also touches Adam by the arm or hand. In an English psalter the

---

main sur le divin (Paris: O. E. I. L., 1984), p. 95. Mural of church apse, Osormont, 12th century, episcopal museum, Vich; reproduced in *Création et apocalypse*, p. 107.

103 Prayerbook of Hildegard of Bingen, German, 12th century, Münich, Bayerische Staatsbibliothek, Cod. lat. 935, fol. 1v; reproduced in Zahlten, *Creatio mundi*, fig. 107.

104 Old Testament, French, 1250, New York, Pierpont Morgan Library, codex 638, fol. 1v; reproduced in Zahlten, *Creatio mundi*, fig. 20. Sockel, northwest portal, 13th century, cathedral of St. Etienne, Auxerre; reproduced, fig. 10.

105 North porch, central portal, exterior arch, cathedral of Notre-Dame, Chartres; reproduced in Mentré, *Création et apocalypse*, p. 92.

106 Attributed to Lorenzo Maitani, relief, west façade, northern pillar, 1310-30, cathedral, Orvieto; reproduced in Zahlten, *Creatio mundi*, fig. 7, and Mentré, *Création et apocalypse*, p. 93.

107 Historiated bible, German, about 1380, Stuttgart, Württ. Landesbibliothek, codex biblius 2°6, fols. 7, 8v; reproduced in Zahlten, *Creatio mundi*, figs. 174, 175.

108 See Plaque from Salerno, 11th century, Staatliche Museen, Berlin. Fresco, end of 12th century, S. Giovanni a Porta Latina, Rome. Fresco, end of 13th century, upper church of S. Francesco, Assisi. Italian bible, 12th century, Rome, Bibliotheca apostolica vaticana, Cod. vat. lat. 12958, fol. 4v. All reproduced in Zahlten, *Creatio mundi*, figs. 1, 23, 28, 50.

Creator blesses him while taking his outstretched hands in his own free hand. In a French manuscript of the Old Testament, while the Creator blesses Adam with his right hand, he grasps with the other the man's right elbow. Adam receives the blessing with his left hand upraised but bent at the elbow. In a German bible from the fourteenth century a blessing Creator touches with his fingertips the shoulder of a sleeping Adam, then with his hand the shoulder of the awakened man.[109]

Michelangelo's concept of Adam's dignity is adumbrated in a French moralized bible of the fifteenth century, although its illustration unusually depicts the Trinity in the act of creation. With the Father blessing and the Son indicating himself (and the dove of the Spirit intervening), the two divine persons each grasps a wrist of their creature to pull his body up off the ground. His buttocks tilt slightly off it, and both his knees are bent to gain the leverage to rise with divine assistance.[110] The concept of the Creator lifting Adam up, which derives from the early examples of the divine sculptor straightening his body, was not foreign to Italian renaissance art. On a chest Mariotto Albertinelli (1475-1515) painted the creation of animals and humans. While God blesses Adam with his right hand, he grasps his left hand, raising him upright. The background of quadrupeds[111] emphasizes by comparison the human dignity of an erect stature. In Michelangelo's fresco the body of Adam also rises from its supine stupor. Although the right leg rests immobile on the earth, the left leg is bent at the knee, positioning the body to arise. Adam's spine curls forward off the craggy ground. Adam raises his left arm to acknowledge the Creator's gesture toward him, just as in traditional depictions he receives his blessing.

He also extends his arm practically to facilitate his rising. As da Vinci noted, "A sitting man cannot raise himself if that part of his body which is in front of his axis [center of gravity] does not weigh more than that which is behind that axis [or centre] without using his arms."[112] As he developed the

---

109 Psalter, English, end of 13th century, London, British Library, Add. 38116, fol. 8v. Old Testament, French, about 1250, New York, Pierpont Morgan Library, Cod. 638, fol. 1v. Historical bible, German, about 1380, Stuttgart, Württ. Landesbibliothek, Cod. bib. 2°6, fols. 7 and 8 v. All reproduced in Zahlten, *Creatio mundi*, figs. 65, 121, with detail 386, 174-75.

110 See Bible moralisée, French, 1404, Paris, Bibliothèque nationale, MS. fr. 166, fol. 2v; reproduced in Zahlten, *Creatio mundi*, fig. 146, with detail 188. Since the human figure is depicted from the rear, its sex may be questionable; but it has been identified as Adam because the nude back shows the influence of classical male reliefs. Adelheid Heimann, "*Trinitas creator mundi*," *Journal of the Warburg and Courtauld Institutes* 2 (1938-39):50; reproduced, pl. 7b.

111 Mariotto Albertinelli, Creation of Animals and Humans, detail of cassone, Gambier Parry Collection, Highnam Court; reproduced in Bernard Berenson, *Italian Pictures of the Renaissance*, 2 vols. (Oxford: Phaidon, 1932), 2:1306a.

112 Da Vinci, Paris, Institut de France, MS. A, 1492, fol. 28b; reproduced in *Literary Works*, 1:264. This note belongs to the lost book on postures and movements of the human figure, according to Pedretti, *Commentary* to *The Literary Works of Leonardo da Vinci*, ed. Richter, 2 vols., National Gallery of Art, Kress Foundation Studies in the History of European Art, 5 [i. e., 6] (Berkeley and Los Angeles: University of California Press, 1977), 1:275. See

observation, "When a man is seated on the floor, the first thing he does in raising himself is to draw a leg toward him and place his hand on the ground on that side on which he wishes to arise, and he thrusts the weight of his body on that arm, and puts his knee to the ground on that side on which he wishes to arise."[113] And he sketched in a manuscript a figure to illustrate "how a man proceeds to raise himself to his feet when he is sitting on level ground."[114] It matches exactly the Adam of Michelangelo's fresco: a seated figure in profile facing left, with his left arm and left leg extended, his right arm braced on the ground and his right leg bent.

The Creator in Michelangelo's fresco does not create Adam with his extended index finger. The index finger had been compared to the activity of the Holy Spirit, so that the Father might perhaps impart spirit by it.[115] As John Calvin (1509-64) judged the metaphorical use of "finger" for the Holy Spirit, it was apt, because God worked and exercised his power through him. But scripture did not designate which finger that Spirit was.[116] Moreover, there was no iconographic tradition of the Trinity as Creator. Depiction of the other divine persons creating with the Father was rare and isolated,[117] as in the French illustration of Adam's uplifting.[118] The finger denoting the sovereignty of the Creator was not the index but the thumb. It had been designated since Hippocratic medicine "the great finger." The thumb was also called the "antihand," as the useful equivalent to an entire hand. The actions of a hand could be destroyed by severing the thumb, because the loss of the thumb rendered the fingers ineffective. The thumb was distinct in its tendons from the fingers, for its principal action was to approach or withdraw from them. The thumb was in opposition to the fingers. The index finger was next in physical position but less useful. The thumb also distinguished humans from other animals, as Galen wrote, since even the ape's thumb was "short, slender, distorted, and altogether ridiculous, just as the ape's whole body is."[119]

---

also Michael W. Kwaakelstein, *Leonardo da Vinci as a Physiognomist: Theory and Drawing Practice* (Leiden: Primavera, 1994), pp. 63-78.

113 Da Vinci, Vatican City, Bibliotheca apostolica vaticana, Codex urbinas latinus 1270, fol. 127v, in *Treatise on Painting*, vol. 2; trans. A. Philip McMahon, 1:144. This codex is a compilation by Francesco Melzi, which circulated in artistic circles in the sixteenth century but was not published until (Paris: Raphaelm Trichet du Fresne, 1651). Richter, *Literary Works*, 1:5-11.

114 Da Vinci, Windsor, Royal Library, MS. W, 1489-1516, fol. 19070a, in *Literary Works*, ed. Richter, 1:265. Da Vinci did sketch Michelangelo's David. See *The Drawings of Leonardo da Vinci in the Collection of Her Majesty the Queen at Windsor Castle*, ed. Clark and Pedretti, 2d ed., 3 vols. (London: Phaidon, 1969), fol. 12591r.

115 Esther Gordon Dotson, "An Augustinean Interpretation of Michelangelo's Sistine Ceiling," *Art Bulletin* 61 (1979):243; Hartt, *Sistine Ceiling*, 2:15.

116 Calvin, *Commentarius in harmoniam evangelicam* ad Matt. 12:28.

117 Heimann, "*Trinitas creator mundi*," pp. 42-52.

118 See above n. 110.

119 Galen, *De usu partium* 1.22, citing Hippocrates, *De officina medici* 4; 1.23, 17, 22; trans. May, 1:107.

The Christian apologist Lactantius, in praising the perfection of the hand in its palm and fingers, explicated the thumb, not the index finger, as creative. It was the thumb, he wrote concerning the divine workmanship, that played the part of God the Father. Since it was separated from the other fingers and had only two joints, rather than three, it governed and moderated the others by its power of holding and acting. The human thumb was just like the Creator governing and moderating the universe.[120] The very name for the thumb (*pollex*) derived from the verb *polleo*, "to be strong, powerful, or potent," with a classical connotation of political rule. Isidore of Seville, enumerating the perfection of the fingers, explained, "The first is named thumb because among the others it enjoys ability and power."[121] A renaissance anatomist affirmed that the thumb obtained its name from its "power equal to many needs."[122] Its power was proverbial in the adage *premere pollicem, convertere pollicem*, or "thumbs down, thumbs up," gestures signifying the essential power of life and death.[123] Montaigne devoted an essay to the power of the thumb.[124]

The second finger was called *index* and also *salutaris* or *demonstratorius* "precisely because with it we salute or signal." (The middle finger, called *impudicus*, or "shameful," was expressly not to be used for indication, because it made an obscene gesture.)[125] Gesture in Christian iconography had a history of the hand of God "speaking,"[126] and it is to this tradition that the gesture in Michelangelo's fresco belongs. The index finger of the Creator gestures to Adam as index fingers conventionally did: to point and to command. When on the façade of Orvieto's cathedral the Creator points with his right index finger to the sea, where fishes in relief are just visible under the waves, he is hardly infusing a divine soul into them.[127] He uses his index finger to indicate them and to command them alive. And, when on the Sistine Chapel ceiling he points with his right index finger to Adam, he orders him to be. Michelangelo has copied his own double deictic gesture on the same ceiling for the Creation of Light. Although the Creator's

---

120 Lactantius, *De opificio Dei* 10.82-85. For comparative ethnology of the king as distinguished by the longest nail on his thumb, see in the seventeenth century John Bulwer, *Anthropometamorphosis* 18.

121 Isidore of Seville, *Etymologiae* 11.1.66. For the thumb as short for strength, see Aristotle, *De partibus animalium* 687b.

122 Benedetti, *Historia corporis humani* 1.2; trans. Lind, p. 84.

123 Erasmus, *Adagia* 1.8.46; trans. Mynors, 32:149.

124 Montaigne, *Essais* 2:26.

125 Isidore of Seville, *Etymologiae* 11.1.66. *Medium ostendere digitum*, in Erasmus, *Adagia* 2.4.68; *Eskimalichthai* 3.3.87. For renaissance examples of this prohibition, see Benedetti, *Historia corporis humani* 1.3, ed. Lind, p. 85; Bulwer, *Chirologia*, p. 231.

126 See Martin Kirigin, *La mano divina nell'iconografia cristiana*, Studi di antichità cristiana, 31 (Vatican City: Pontificio istituto di archeologia cristiana, 1976), pp. 131-65.

127 Lorenzo Maitani, reliefs, 1310-30, west façade, cathedral, Orvieto; reproduced in Zahlten, *Creatio mundi*, fig. 7.

fingertips approach the orbs of the sun and the moon, he is not about to touch them. He commands them to be.

Hands were not only tactile but also significant. As classically "the organ of organs," hands even substituted for other bodily parts: for the eyes in the groping of the blind, for the tongue in the signs of the mute.[128] Gesture for those gifted with speech was an important part of the classical oratorical culture in renaissance revival. Not only was it necessary for the comportment of the orator, as Quintilian had best elaborated it,[129] but it also became integral to ordinary manners.[130] Even in familiar conversation the gesture of a renaissance person was to be guarded—not flapping about as if shooing flies.[131] As Erasmus instructed, gesticulating was the sign of an unstable mind.[132] Since the Hippocratic writings, odd gestures—like waving the hands in front of the face or grabbing at the air—had been observed as symptoms of disease, even portents of death.[133] Physiognomy attributed to the philosophical authority of Aristotle considered the carriage of the hand, arm, and forearm to judge a man as blustering, high-minded, effeminate, flattering, or morbid.[134] There was an ethical tradition that defined normative rules of good and bad gestures according to universal values derived from reason or revelation.[135] The principal illustrated volume on the subject, the physician John Bulwer's *Chirologia, or the Natural Language of the Hand*, was only composed in the seventeenth century; but he intended to search and scrutinize the "touches of antiquity," so that his inventory of gestures was traditional. Gesture was the lost knowledge of Adam, the idiom he had shared with other animals before his fall, and it could be restored to use by diligent observation and notation. Bulwer listed one hundred twelve actions that hands performed. Among them was "command."[136]

---

128 Marjorie O'Rourke Boyle, "Deaf Signs, Renaissance Texts," in a volume tentatively titled *Renaissance and Early Modern Studies in Honor of Nancy S. Streuver*, ed. Melinda Schlitt and Joseph Marino (Rochester, N.Y.: University of Rochester Press, forthcoming).

129 Quintilian, *Institutiones oratoriae* 11.3.63-124. See also Ursula Maier-Eichhorn, *Die Gestikulation in Quintilians Rhetorik*, Europäische Hochschulschriften, klassische Sprachen und Literaturen, 41 (Frankfurt: P. Lang, 1989); Elaine Fantham, "Quintilian on Performance: Traditional and Personal Elements in *Institutiones* 11.3," *Phoenix* 36 (1982):243-63.

130 For a survey of renaissance literature, see James W. Holme, "Italian Courtesy Books of the Sixteenth Century," *Modern Language Review* 5 (1910):145-66; and see recently Anna Bryson, "The Rhetoric of Status: Gesture, Demeanour, and the Image of the Gentleman in Sixteenth-and Seventeenth-Century England," in *Renaissance Bodies: The Human Figure in English Culture, c. 1540-1660*, ed. Lucy Gent and Nigel Llewellyn (London: Reaktion, 1990), pp. 36-53.

131 Giovanni Della Casa, *Galateo* 326.

132 Erasmus, *De civilitate*, in *Opera omnia* (LB) 1:1040.

133 Hippocrates, *Prognosis* 4.

134 Aristotle, *Physiognomia* 813a.

135 Jean-Claude Schmitt, "The Ethics of Gesture," in *Fragments for a History of the Human Body*, trans. Ian Patterson, ed. Michel Feher with Ramona Nadoff and Nadia Tazi, 3 vols. (New York: Zone, 1989), 2:129.

136 Bulwer, *Chirologia*, pp. 5-6, 18, 20, and for a list of 112-plus verbs that hands do, p. 20. For introduction to the author, see Palmer Morrel-Samuels, "John Bulwer's 1644 Treatise

There was not one single method for commanding manually. Erasmus explicated the adage *ad digitu crepitu*, or "at the snap of a finger," for a notable type. "Those who give some command in an arrogant and contemptuous manner are said to convey their meaning by the snap of a finger." He supposed the gesture typical of a master ordering his slave—a eunuch or a houseboy—to perform some menial task. It resembled Jove's nod of agreement or refusal with which mortals must hastily comply.[137] In Michelangelo's fresco God is not snapping his fingers at a subservient Adam but according him a more dignified gesture of command by the index finger. Bulwer, who thought gestures universal and innate, rather than cultural and traditional, labeled its normative gesture *indico* for "I point." Its illustration showed the index finger extended, while the thumb was tucked over the other fingers curled inward on the palm. As he explained, "The forefinger put forth, the rest contracted to a fist, is an express of command and direction, a gesture of the hand most demonstrative." That finger was called in Latin "index" from *indico* for "show"; in Greek, *deicticos*, or "demonstrator."[138]

Its direction mattered. The index finger pointed vertically signified authority, the power of the one who ordained.[139] An example current with Michelangelo's execution on the Sistine Chapel ceiling was da Vinci's portrait of John the Baptist, who points up to heaven as the source of his prophecy.[140] An index finger pointed horizontally signified a personal thought. It was a very frequent gesture of communication, characteristic of oratory (including preaching) and of instruction. When it had no imperative design, it was the prime gesture of the master in some discipline of knowledge and it was used in personifications of grammar and of wisdom.[141] An example was Matthias Grünewald's (c.1470-1528) portrayal of John the Baptist indicating the crucified Christ with the saying, "Ecce Agnus Dei"

---

on Gesture," *Semiotica* 79 (1990):341-53; James W. Cleary, "John Bulwer: Renaissance Communicationist," *Quarterly Journal of Speech* 45 (1959):391-98; H. J. Norman, "John Bulwer and his *Anthropometamorphosis*," in *Science, Medicine, and History: Essays in the Evolution of Scientific Thought and Medical Practice Written in Honour of Charles Singer*, 2 vols. (Oxford: Oxford University Press, 1935), 2:82-97.

137 Erasmus, *Adagia* 2.7.99; trans. Mynors, 34:46. See also Bulwer, *Chriologia*, pp. 216-17.

138 Bulwer, *Chirologia*, p. 124, and fig. p. 143. For deictic gestures in Greek art, see Gerhard Neumann, *Gesten und Gebärden in der griechischen Kunst* (Berlin: Walter de Gruyter, 1965), pp. 17-22; and for a survey, J. J. Tikkanen, "Zwei Gebärden mit dem Zeigenfinger," *Acta Societatis scientiarum fennicae* 43 (1913):44-98.

139 François Garnier, *Le langage de l'image au Moyen Âge: Signification et symbolique*, 2 vols. (Paris: Léopard d'or, 1982-89), 1:167-69.

140 Da Vinci, John the Baptist, c. 1509, Musée du Louvre, Paris; reproduced in *Leonardo da Vinci*, exhibition catalogue (New Haven, Conn.: Yale University Press with the South Bank Centre, 1989), p. 40, fig. 33.

141 Garnier, *Langage de l'image*, 1:170.

(Behold, the lamb of God).[142] Michelangelo knew the indicative convention perfectly. His studies for the Sistine Chapel ceiling include the Libyan sibyl and companions: a left hand with the index finger pointing and the fist properly clenched.[143] Before his fresco of the Creation of Adam, he had already painted Ham on that same ceiling boldly pointing at the nakedness of his father Noah.[144]

But the pointing forefinger communicated more than the mere indication of a person or object. The deictic gesture was also imperative and directive. As Bulwer stated, it was "an express of command and direction." It ordered. Although he specified that the accompanying thumb and fingers formed a fist, from late in the sixteenth century there had developed the theory of gesture as a natural and universal language with normative signs. The previous literature on gesture had rather differently acknowledged a variety of conventions.[145] There was renaissance artistic evidence that the indicative gesture could be conceived more loosely than Bulwer's initial illustration: by the index finger pointing but the others splayed in a curl. There was variety in the artistic execution of the gesture. An example of such a deictic gesture in the very Vatican is the angel in the upper right-hand corner of Raphael's (1483-1520) Disputa, who so indicates Christ as the Eucharist.[146] Quintilian had defined the gesture of indication as three fingers doubled under the thumb; but he mentioned that, if it were slightly dropped, it signified "affirmation." In oratory it was especially rich and impressive to extend the arm, he wrote. A becoming gesture was "fingers opening as the hand moves

---

[142] See Matthias Grünewald, Crucifixion panel, Isenheim altarpiece, Musée de Unterlinden, Colmar; reproduced in Wilhelm Frankel, *Matthias Grünewald* (Munich: C. H. Beck, 1983), p. 247, and detail p. 249.

[143] Michelangelo, Studies for the Libyan sibyl's companions and for the sibyl's right hand, Ashmolean Museum, Oxford; reproduced in Perrig, *Michelangelo's Drawings*, no. 6.

[144] Michelangelo, Nakedness of Noah, Sistine Chapel ceiling; reproduced in *Sistine Chapel*, p. 159.

[145] For the tradition and theory, see Dilwyn Knox, "Ideas on Gesture and Universal Languages, c. 1550-1650," in *New Perspectives on Renaissance Thought: Essays in the History of Science, Education, and Philosophy in Memory of Charles B. Schmitt*, ed. John Henry and Sarah Hutton (London: Duckworth and Istituto italiano per gli studi filosofici, 1990), pp. 101-36. See also Adam Kendon, "The Study of Gesture: Some Observations on Its History," *Recherches sémiotiques/Semiotic Enquiry* 2 (1982):45-62.

[146] Raphael, Disputa, Stanza della Segnatura, Vatican; reproduced in *Raffaello nell' appartamento di Giulio II e Leone X: Monumenti, musei, gallerie pontificie* (Milan: Electa, 1993), pp. 30, 254; Leopold D. Ettlinger and Helen S. Ettlinger, *Raphael* (Oxford: Phaidon, 1987), p. 85, fig. 80; John Pope-Hennessy, *Raphael: The Wrightsman Lectures* (New York: New York University Press, 1970), pp. 62-63, fig. 51; *The Complete Paintings of Raphael* (New York: Harry N. Abrams, 1966), pl. XIXb; and, for a detail of the upper right with the pointing angel, James Beck, *Raphael: The Stanza della Segnatura* (New York: George Braziller, 1993), p. 61, fig. 17. For the importance of its celestial angels, but without reference to gesture, see Christiane L. Joost-Gaugier, "Raphael's *Disputa*: Medieval Theology Seen through the Eyes of Pico della Mirandola and the Possible Inventor of the Program, Tommaso Inghirami," *Gazette des beaux arts* 139 (1997):70-71.

forward."[147] That is the very gesture of the Creator on Michelangelo's fresco: the fingers of his indicative fist opening as his hand moves forward to Adam. God's splaying fingers recall the Stoic comparative topic of the open hand of rhetoric versus the tight fist of logic. As Cicero reported Zeno's distinction, "Clenching his fist he said logic was like that; relaxing and extending his hand, he said eloquence was like the open palm."[148] The fist had its name from the meager fistful; the palm, from the extended branches of that tree.[149] The gestural attitude of Creator toward creature is more persuasive than coercive, just as renaissance art was more indebted to rhetoric than logic.

The Creator's deictic gesture toward Adam was not a novelty. It had occurred in Roman imperial statuary modeled on gods.[150] In renaissance sculpture it would be appropriated by the culminant practitioner of Florentine design, Giovanni Bologna (1529-1608), who assimilated Michelangelo's principles of interpreting the human body as dynamic.[151] Giambologna's bronze of John the Baptist has his right hand pointing to heaven with the index finger, while his other fingers are relaxed, splayed.[152] Giambologna also conceived the pagan messenger Mercury in several notable bronzes with his hand configured like those of God in Michelangelo's fresco. The index finger points conventionally straight; but the other fingers are not fused and tightly curled into a partial fist: they are separated and curved in a relaxed manner. The medium of bronze, with the tensile strength of metal and the ability to embed an iron armature in the hollow casting for support, encouraged a very different sort of sculptural composition from what marble, heavy and fragile, necessitated. A bronze statue could be centrifugal, with limbs actively projecting into space in bold, vigorous, violent, and dramatic movement, as in his Mercury. By the date when Vasari praised it, after Michelangelo's death, it was already famous as Giambologna's initial important success. It was in such demand that it was ceaselessly copied, while the sculptor reworked his versions until he inte-

---

147 Quintilian, *Institutiones oratoriae* 11.3.94, 84; *The "Institutio oratoria" of Quintilian*, trans. H. E. Butler, 4 vols. (New York: G. P. Putnam's Sons, 1933-36), 4:295, 289.

148 Cicero, *Orator* 32.113; trans. H. M. Hubbell (Cambridge, Mass.: Harvard University Press, 1939), p. 389. See also *De finibus bonorum et malorum* 2.6.7; cf. Quintilian, *Institutiones oratoriae* 2.20.7.

149 Isidore of Seville, *Etymologiae* 11.1.66.

150 See marble statue, Antoninus Pius, Thermenmuseum, Rome; reproduced in Caterina Maderna, *Iuppiter Diomedes und Merkur als Vorbilder für römische Bildnisstatuen: Untersuchungen zum römischen statuarischen Idealporträt*, Archäologie und Geschichte, 1 (Heidelberg: Archäologie und Geschichte, 1988), tafel 24, abb. 1.

151 James Holderbaum, *The Sculptor Giovanni Bologna* (New York: Garland, 1983), pp. 10, 12.

152 Giambologna, John the Baptist; reproduced in Charles Avery, *Giambologna: The Complete Sculpture* (Oxford: Phaidon Christie's, 1987), p. 199, pl. 223.

grated the human form into a superlative design.[153] Vasari himself copied it in his own Mercury: the index pointing up but the other fingers splayed with the first joint curved.[154]

In painting the variation of the deictic gesture by fingers loosely curled, rather than tightly fisted, seems original to Michelangelo's fresco. He invented it for the fresco of the Creation of Light and he repeats it for that of the Creation of Adam. Prominent artists interpreted it accurately as indicative of a divine command to humans. In an engraving by Lucas van Leyden (1491-1533) for his series of the story of Adam and Eve the scene of the prohibition copies it, as God in Eden gestures forbiddingly toward the tree of knowledge. On his right hand the index finger points out, while the others are loosely curled. God is not merely showing the primal pair the tree; he is commanding them not to touch or taste its fruit (Gen. 3:3).[155] Raphael executed for the very Sistine Chapel a cartoon for a tapestry cycle of Peter as founder of the Church that employs the same gesture. It depicts the risen Lord charging Peter to feed and tend his sheep (John 21:15-17). Jesus with an extended arm points to the kneeling disciple: his thumb is in opposition, his index finger straight, and the other fingers are curled, rather than fisted. With his other hand he gestures to a flock of sheep, ordering Peter to feed and tend them.[156] The gesture was deliberately chosen, because an earlier

---

153 Mercury, bronze, c. 1588, Kunsthistorisches Museum, Vienna; reproduced in Avery, *Giambologna*, p. 128, pl. 127, and in Holderbaum, *Giovanni Bologna*, fig. 34. Model for Mercury, bronze, c. 1563-64, Museo civico, Bologna; reproduced in *Giambologna*, p. 127, pl. 125. Mercury, bronze, 1575-79, Museo e gallerie nazionali di Capodimonte; reproduced in *Giambologna*, p. 27, pl. 19. The Medici Mercury, bronze, 1580, Museo nazionale del bargello, Florence; reproduced in *Giambologna*, p. 23, pl. 15, and *Giovanni Bologna*, figs. 108, 111-15. For his bronze statuary, see *Giambologna*, pp. 123, 137; for his Mercuries, pp. 125-30, and *Giovanni Bologna*, pp. 29-34, 116-25; and see in general, *Giambologna, 1529-1608: Sculptor to the Medici*, exhibition catalogue, ed. Avery and Anthony Radcliffe (n. p.: Arts Council of Great Britain, 1978). For the god, see *Mercure à la Renaissance*, Actes des Journées d'étude des 4-5 octobre 1984, Lille, ed. Marie-Madeleine de la Garanderie (Paris: Honoré Champion for Centre national des lettres, 1988); Joseph Porter, *Shakespeare's Mercutio: His History and Drama* (Chapel Hill: University of North Carolina Press, 1988); Barbara L. Welch, *Ronsard's Mercury: The Arcane Muse*, University Studies in Medieval and Renaissance Literature, 2 (New York: P. Lang, 1986); Douglas Brooks-Davies, *The Mercurian Monarch: Magical Politics from Spenser to Pope* (Manchester: Manchester University Press, 1983).

154 Vasari, Mercury, Palazzo Vecchio, Florence; reproduced in Sonja Brink, *Mercurius Mediceus: Studien zur panegyrischen Verwendung der Merkurgestalt im Florenz des sechzehnte Jahrhunderts*, Manuskripte zur Kunstwissenschaft in der Wernerschen Verlagsgesellschaft, 13 (Worms: Werner, 1987), pl. 3.

155 Lucas van Leyden, Prohibition from the Adam and Eve series, engraving, 1529, National Gallery, Washington, D.C.; reproduced in H. Diane Russell with Bernadine Barnes, *Eva/Ave: Woman in Renaissance and Baroque Prints*, exhibition catalogue (Washington, D.C.: National Gallery of Art with the Feminist Press at City University, New York, 1990), p. 117. See also Larry Silver and Susan Smith, "Carnal Knowledge: The Late Engravings of Lucas van Leyden," *Nederlands Kunsthistorisch Jaarboek* 29 (1978):255-56.

156 Raphael, Charge to Peter, tapestry cartoon, 1516-19, Victoria and Albert Museum, London; reproduced in Ettlinger and Ettlinger, *Raphael*, fig. 173, and see pp. 182-84; Jean-Pierre Cuzin, *Raphaël: Vie et oeuvre* (Paris: Office du livre, 1983), p. 168, fig. 174; Victoria and Albert Museum, *The Raphael Cartoons* (London: Her Majesty's Stationery Office, 1972),

stage in the design is quite different. A preparatory drawing shows Raphael's studio assistant posing for the figure of Christ with his hand pointing to heaven. That indicative style had been borrowed from da Vinci's John the Baptist and it was already used at the Vatican in Raphael's fresco of the School of Athens. In Raphael's cartoon for the final version of Jesus charging Peter the relaxed horizontal gesture is firmly a command.[157] In both van Leyden's engraving and Raphael's tapestry the gesture is not of creation or indication but of command. While those examples date to after Michelangelo's fresco, they demonstrate that major contemporary artists understood the gesture as a divine command to a human person.

There is now scientific proof from very recent experiments that the Creator's hand in Michelangelo's fresco forms the natural deictic gesture, although the experiments were performed without reference to that painting. A concern to discover the origins of language has promoted research on the development of pointing in infancy, with the earliest observation dating to only eight days old and with comprehension and intention apparent by twelve months. Pointing has been established as a uniquely human gesture; the related species of chimpanzee, gorilla, and orangutan cannot point. To test the hypothesis that the resting state of the index finger would display that topological difference, children and chimps were observed under anaesthesia. In the human subjects the index finger of the relaxed hand protruded naturally above the other fingers. The photograph in evidence replicates exactly the fingers of God's hand in Michelangelo's fresco,[158] although without the flexion of the wrist over the edge of the mattress that

---

pl. 2; Shearman, *Raphael's Cartoons in the Collection of Her Majesty the Queen and the Tapestries for the Sistine Chapel* (London: Phaidon, 1972), pl. 6, and detail p. 59, fig. III. For the placement of the tapestries, see John White and Shearman, "Raphael's Tapestries and Their Cartoons," *Art Bulletin* 40 (1958):193-221, 299-323. In the sequence the Charge to Peter hung directly to the right of the main altar and presbyterium in the first bay. See also Joyce Plesters, "Raphael's Cartoons for the Vatican Tapestries: A Brief Report on the Materials, Technique, and Condition," in *The Princeton Raphael Symposium: Science in the Service of Art History*, ed. Shearman and Marcia B. Hall, Princeton Monographs in Art and Archaeology, 47 (Princeton, N.J.: Princeton University Press, 1983), pp. 111-24.

[157] For the gesture as "a firm command," see White, introduction to *Raphael Cartoons*, p. 6. For the initial model in the Louvre, Paris, see pl. 24; Cuzin, *Raphaël*, p. 169, fig. 175; Shearman, *Raphael's Cartoons*, fig. 47. Shearman also notes "substantial revision in the pose of Christ," p. 97, and discusses gesture in the cartoons in general, pp. 129-31.

[158] Daniel J. Povinelli and D. Richard Davis, "Differences between Chimpanzees (*Pan troglodytes*) and Humans (*Homo sapiens*) in the Resting State of the Index Finger," *Journal of Comparative Psychology* 108 (1994):134-39, and p. 135, fig. 1B. For the observation of pointing at eighteen days of age, see Thomas E. Hannan and Alan Fogel, "A Case-Study Assessment of 'Pointing' during the First Three Months of Life," *Perceptual and Motor Skills* 65 (1987):187-94. For other recent study, see Laura A. Thompson and Dominic W. Massaro, "Children's Integration of Speech and Pointing Gestures in Comprehension," *Journal of Experimental Child Psychology* 57 (1994):327-54; Hannan, "An Examination of Spontaneous Pointing in 20-to 50-Month-Old Children," *Perceptual and Motor Skills* 74(1992):651-58; Josep Call and Michael Tomasello, "Production and Comprehension of Referential Pointing by Organgutans (*Pongo pygmaeus*)," *Journal of Comparative Psychology* 108 (1994):307-17.

was necessary to the experiment. (The experiment may be imitated informally by a simple flexion of the wrist, allowing the fingers to fall into position: the index will naturally protrude above the thumb and the others. The hand will replicate God's in Michelangelo's fresco.) Although the deictic gesture originated in the evolving morphology of the hand and promises some eventual understanding of the human acquisition of language, it is one that Michelangelo and other artists keen on anatomy could have discovered in their studios by experimentation on the natural position of the hand.

Michelangelo's fresco of the Creator charging Adam with the deictic gesture had been visible for several years when Raphael imitated its design for the tapestries to be displayed on important ceremonial occasions in that same Sistine Chapel. And that is precisely how Michelangelo's authorized biographer Ascanio Condivi (b. c.1520) also interpreted the divine hand extended toward Adam on the Sistine Chapel ceiling. "In the fourth [space] is *The Creation of Man*, where God is seen with arm and hand outstretched as if to impart to Adam the precepts as to what he must and must not do."[159] Portrayed was a deictic gesture, not the infusion of a soul. Michelangelo probably repeated its gesture of command for a grand altarpiece of the Raising of Lazarus. Although the painting was executed by Sebastiano del Piombo (1485-1547), Michelangelo prepared the design, as Vasari recorded. There is a series of studies for the animated figure of Lazarus, who is sitting upright, lifting his leg with bent knee as he frees a foot from the winding sheets.[160] Michelangelo probably also made the drawings for Christ.[161] The disposition of the figures recalls the design of the Creation of Adam on the Sistine Chapel ceiling.[162] The gesture of Christ toward Lazarus replicates that of the Creator toward Adam.

The charge? Exactly what Adam is portrayed as doing: arise! God commands like a renaissance activist: up and doing. Adam responds with a reciprocal gesture and with a compliant leg. Michelangelo had already painted the complementary Creation of Eve, in which God gestures with an

---

159 Ascanio Condivi, *Vita di Michelangelo* 29.5; *The Life of Michelangelo*, trans. A. S. Wohl (Baton Rouge: Louisiana State Press, 1976), p. 42.

160 Sebastiano del Piombo, Raising of Lazarus, 1519, National Gallery, London; reproduced in Hirst, *Sebastiano del Piombo* (Oxford: Clarendon, 1981), pl. 94, and detail pl. 101; Carlo Volpe, *L'opera completa di Sebastiano del Piombo* (Milan: Rizzoli, 1980), pl. XLIII, and see pp. 110-11; Ettlinger and Ettlinger, *Raphael*, p. 219, fig. 200. Michelangelo, Studies for the Raising of Lazarus, Musée Bonnat, Bayonne, pl. 95; British Museum, London, pls. 96, 97, all ireproduced n Hirst, *Sebastiano del Piombo*. For discussion of the painting, see pp. 66-75; and of Michelangelo's drawings, pp. 67, 69-70, 149-50, citing Vasari, *Vita di Michelangelo*, 5:570-1.

161 Wilde, *Italian Drawings in the Department of Prints and Drawings in the British Museum*, 7 vols., vol. 7: *Michelangelo and His Studio* (London: Trustees of the British Museum, 1953), p. 30.

162 Hirst, *Sebastiano del Piombo*, p. 70. Wilde compares the altarpiece with Michelangelo's other drawings for the Sistine Chapel, such as figures for the lunettes, *Michelangelo and His Studio*, p. 30.

uplifted, open palm for her to stand, while she complies with her legs. His biographer Condivi observed the attitude of Eve as "rising."[163] The artistic conferral of legs on humans was essential to the concept of vivification. In antiquity craftsmen had shaped statues with their feet undistinguished and together. It was the sculptor Daedalus who first separated the unformed blocks into legs, liberating limbs from torsos, and so granting them the appearance of movement. They seemed to walk; indeed, statues had to be tied down since they had become "alive."[164] For an artist like Michelangelo to express animation by giving Adam his legs, rather than his breath, was in the fundamental classical, if not scriptural, tradition.

There was since classical antiquity a vast commonplace by which human nature and dignity as bestowed by the gods or God was embodied in erect bipedality. What distinguished humans from other creatures was the ability to stand on two feet supporting a straight spine. The argument was articulated across the disciplines: in philosophy, anatomy and medicine, astronomy, theology, architecture, rhetoric, and during the Renaissance also in books of miscellany and manners. Standing on two feet with arms uplifted as essentially human in nature had alternative traditions of honor: contemplative and active, or theoretical and practical. Humans stood up to contemplate with their minds or to act with their hands, and so were distinguished from other animals. The concepts coexisted in most thinkers, with contemplation judged definitive and action useful. The preaching at the papal court favored the philosophical ideal but it also voiced the argument for the existence of the Creator from the design of the human body. There were alternative definitions of humanity. Physical teleology, rather than metaphysical idea, was the concept Michelangelo appropriated.

In considering natural history Plato had located Eros as the supreme passion for divine wisdom and immortality in the human brain at the head of its spinal marrow. The formation of the lower animals, like the differentiation of the sexes, was relegated in his *Timaeus* to an appendix, where he considered marrow as seed and Eros as intercourse. Birds, quadrupeds, and fish corresponded to his condemnation of people who failed in their proper intellectual nature. In his moralizing and teleological argument[165] animals were degraded humans,[166] perhaps in burlesque of the Pythagorean belief in

---

163 Condivi, *Vita di Michelangelo* 29.7; trans. Wohl, p. 47. For the divine gesture toward Eve as meaning "arise," see also Colalucci, *Sistine Chapel*, 2:53; Wöfflin, *Classic Art*, p. 55. For the execution of the frescoes in order from the entrance to the altar, see Tolnay, *Sistine Ceiling*, p. 22. For a break in execution between the Creation of Eve and the Creation of Adam, see Wilde, *Michelangelo and His Studio*, pp. 66, 68-71.

164 See David Freedberg, *The Power of Images: Studies in the History and Theory of Response* (Chicago: University of Chicago Press, 1989), pp. 36-37, 450 n. 29, 291.

165 G. E. R. Lloyd, *Science, Folklore, and Ideology: Studies in the Life Sciences in Ancient Greece* (Cambridge: Cambridge University Press, 1983), p. 15.

166 Francis Macdonald Cornford, *Plato's Cosmology: The "Timaeus" of Plato* (New York: Harcourt, Brace, 1937), pp. 355, 356, 357.

transmigration.[167] Birds were humans with their hair changed into feathers. The bird-brained creatures devolved from astronomers, who gazed aloft but did not establish their speculation rationally in the mathematical analysis of motion. Fish devolved from those most mindless of humans with impure souls, the criminals. In Plato's myth of the inferior species through the degradation of humans the quadrupeds were the middling creatures. They were more brutish than birds, with their harmless curiosity, for they possessed no philosophy, even in a single thought. They never considered the nature of the heavens, because, neglecting the courses of their heads, they minded the presence of the soul in their chests. Such persons were sensual and quarrelsome. Because of their passionate habits they no longer needed their heads to look up to heaven. From the distortion by disuse of the revolutions in their heads, their heads lost their perfect spherical shape. They became misshapen and elongated into snouts, then drooped to the earth by natural affinity. Front legs resting on the ground developed to prop up their heavy bodies. "Their race was made four-footed and many-footed," explained Plato, "since God set more supports under the more foolish ones, so that they might be dragged down still more to the earth." Stupider still were fish, which had no feet at all but dragged their bellies.[168] Plato derived the very etymology of *anthropos* from looking up and considering, which humans alone of all animals did.[169]

The classical alternative concerning the distinction of humans from other animals in erect bipedality was developed in Xenophon's *Memorabilia.* In the contest for wisdom Zeuxis was determined the most admirable of painters, Polyclitus of sculptors. "Which, think you," posed Xenophon, "deserve the greater admiration, the creators of phantoms without sense and motion, or the creators of living, intelligent, and active beings?" The response of his interlocutor was: "Oh, of living beings, by far, provided only they are created by design and not mere chance." The product of design was defined as "the creature that serves some useful end." The creation of human beings, as the "handiwork of a wise and loving creator," had from the beginning a useful end in mind by their endowment with the five senses. Human dignity bestowed by the gods was embodied. "In the first place, man is the only living creature that they have caused to stand upright; and the upright position gives him a wider range of vision in front

---

167 A. E. Taylor, *A Commentary on Plato's "Timaeus"* (Oxford: Clarendon, 1928), p. 640.

168 Plato, *Timaeus* 91e-92a; trans. R. G. Bury (Cambridge, Mass.: Harvard University Press, 1967), p. 253. See Taylor, *Commentary,* p. 642; Catherine Joubaud, *Le corps humain dans la philosophie platonicienne: Étude à partir du "Timée"* (Paris: J. Vrin, 1991), p. 148. For the human crowd without wisdom or virtue, their eyes bent to the earth, their heads bowed, see Plato, *Respublica* 586a. The Platonist human was defined in the sixteenth century as "a featherless biped animal." See Erasmus, *Ecclesiastes, sive de ratione concionandi,* in *Opera omnia* (Leiden), 5:923.

169 Plato, *Cratylus* 399e.

and a better view of thing above, and exposes him to less injury." That advantage of erect bipedality was biological: for survival and for protection. There was no suggestion in Xenophon that physical vision directed celestially was philosophically purposed, as in Plato's *Timaeus*, to contemplation of the universal laws of nature. "Secondly," he continued, "to grovelling creatures they have given feet that afford only the power of moving, whereas they have endowed man with hands, which are the instruments to which we chiefly owe our greater happiness." Hands beatified—and not the mind manifested in reason or speech, as in the philosophical and rhetorical traditions. Yet reflecting on the endowment of the body with a soul, Xenophon added that "the possession of hands without reason is of little worth."[170] Many concurred. Michelangelo conventionally poetized "the hand that obeys the intellect" and he affirmed that "one paints with the head and not with the hands."[171] Yet the argument for human dignity through manual labor had been established. Xenophon's assertions, relating erect bipedality to the instrumental use of the hands, would be confirmed in modern science by the fossil record of paleoanthropology. There was practical knowledge since antiquity of the function of the limbs, as in the ancient Roman curse on a person's "arms, and fingers, so that he might not aid himself. . . legs, knees, shanks, feet, ankles, heels, toes, and toe-nails, so that he may not stand on his own strength."[172] That was unspeculative.

Yet the philosophical tradition differed both from Xenophon's theory and from ordinary sense by relating erect bipedality to contemplation. Aristotle did argue that the erect stature of humans was biologically based but he compounded that science with speculation from the topic of place. Humans were the only animals that stood upright, because they possessed the largest brain (and males larger brains than females). Its size owed to the heat and blood in the region around the heart and lung. A hot substance induced growth, and a plentiful supply of blood was an indication of its presence. Aristotle asserted that "heat tends to make the body upright" as an explanation of the unique status of humans. Beyond biology, he argued from the symbolic importance of situation. "In man and man alone do the natural

---

170 Xenophon, *Memorabilia* 1.4.3, 4; 4:55; 1.4.5, 7, 11, 14; *Xenophon*, trans. E. C. Marchant, 7 vols. (Cambridge, Mass.: Harvard University Press, 1968), pp. 57, 58, 61. There was a translation commissioned by Tommaso Cardinal Parentelli, the future Pope Nicholas V, founder of the Vatican Library. The *editio princeps* was (Florence: Junta, 1516). For the literary form, see Hartmut Erbse, "Die Architektonik im Aufbau von Xenophons *Memorabilia*," *Hermes* 89 (1961):257-87; Arnaldo Momigliano, *The Development of Greek Biography: Four Lectures* (Cambridge, Mass.: Harvard University Press, 1971), pp. 52-54. See also Leo Strauss, *Xenophon's Socrates* (Ithaca, N.Y.: Cornell University Press, 1972), pp. 21-26; Olof Gignon, *Kommentar zum ersten Buch von Xenophons "Memorabilien,"* Schweizerische Beiträge zur Altertumswissenschaft, 5 (Basel: Friedrich Reinhardt, 1953), pp. 118-46.

171 Michelangelo, *Rime* 151; trans. Saslow, p. 302.

172 W. Sherwood Fox, "Cursing as a Fine Art," *Sewanee Review* 27 (1919):468.

parts appear in their natural situation: the upper part of man is placed toward the upper part of the universe." As he paraphrased that belief in his repetitive statement, "Man is the only animal that stands upright." In observing that only humans had arms and hands, rather than forelegs and forefeet, he proposed the essential philosophical argument about dignity. "Man is the only animal that stands upright, and this is because his nature and essence is divine."[173]

The business of the most divine being was "to think and to be intelligent." The task would be difficult if there were a great mass of body at the top weighing down the whole, he argued, because weight hampered intellectual motion and general sense. When the size and weight of a part became excessive, the body necessarily lurched toward the ground. The quadrupeds were for safety provided with forefeet because their souls could not sustain the bodily weight bearing them down. In comparison with humans, all other animals were like dwarfs: top-heavy. They were large at the top and small where that weight was supported and locomotion was effected. In humans the size of the trunk became proportionate through growth to the lower parts. In infancy, however, the upper portion was larger, the lower smaller. That explained why infants were unable to walk, only to crawl, and why they were initially motionless. Children were dwarfs. It was because of their inverse proportionality that animals were less intelligent than humans. So were children less intelligent than adults. The reason? "The principle of the soul is sluggish and corporeal."[174]

When the heat that elevated an organism ebbed, its body diminished into many feet. The ultimate phenomenon of the loss of heat was to lose the feet entirely and lie on the ground. It was because humans stood upright that they had no need of forelegs; instead they had arms and hands. Aristotle reported the belief of Anaxagoras that it was the possession of hands that made humans the most intelligent of living beings. Aristotle countered with the opposite belief: humans had hands because they alone were intelligent. Hands were instrumental, assigned to the animal that could use them and use them for a range of purposes.[175] The basic controversy was known through Galen in renaissance anatomy.[176] Anaxagoras had believed that nature was uniform, since all living organisms functioned similarly and all possessed mind. There was no fundamental criterion for distinguishing human from animal or from plant. Yet there was an obvious physiological dif-

[173] Aristotle, *De partibus animalium* 653a, 669b, 656a, 686a; *Parts of Animals*, trans. A. L. Peck (Cambridge, Mass.: Harvard University Press, 1968), pp. 259, 173-75, 367. Cf. *Historia animalium* 494b. See in general Lloyd, "The Development of Aristotle's Theory of the Classification of Animals," *Phronesis* 6 (1961):59-81.

[174] Aristotle, *De partibus animalium* 686a-b; trans. Peck, pp. 367, 369.

[175] Aristotle, *De partibus animalium* 687a.

[176] Berengario da Carpi, *Commentaria super "Anathomia" Mundini*, ed. Lind (summarized), *Pre-Vesalian Anatomy*, p. 160.

ference between humans and other animals: hands. Hands alone enabled people to excel even the most advanced animals in those manipulative skills and technical abilities that gave the appearance of wisdom. Aristotle preserved his thought, and so did Simplicius's commentary on his *De anima.* Plutarch cited Anaxagoras on humans as distinct from other animals by a technical skill that allowed forethought rather than chance. "Nature made the hands the most coordinated and skilful of all organs by dividing them into fingers of unequal length," he wrote. "Thus, the ancient thinker Anaxagoras was led to ascribe human wisdom and understanding to the hands." Galen, who was to compose the ultimate teleology of the hand, also cited Anaxagoras.[177] It was the belief of Anaxagoras that paleoanthropology would prove correct. His emphasis on the relation of morphology to capability—on the linkages between hands, tool-making, intelligence, and culture—remarkably anticipated a modern evolutionary biology.[178]

It was the false belief of Aristotle in erection for intellection that theoretically prevailed, however. Its dominance was forcefully demonstrated by so practical a renaissance man as Niccolò Machiavelli (1469-1527), who could exhort a confraternity to penitence by summoning the topic of the "face not turned to the earth like other animals but turned to the heavens so that he can see Him continually." And, when in the next phrase he considered the divine bestowal of hands, they were "hands to construct churches and make sacrifice in His honor."[179] That philosophical tradition of erect bipedality for contemplation was broadly articulated. Cicero argued that nature providentially lavished gifts upon people. The primary gift was an erect posture. "First, she has raised them from the ground to stand tall and upright, so that they might be able to behold the sky and so gain a knowledge of the gods." Humans were "sprung from the earth not as its inhabitants and denizens, but to be as it were the spectators of things supernal and heavenly, in the contemplation whereof no other species of animal participates."[180] People possessed nimble thought and a bodily form convenient and apt to the human mind. "For while she has bent the other creatures down toward their food, she has made man alone to look erect, and has challenged him to look up toward heaven, as being, so to speak, akin to him, and his first home."[181]

---

177 Daniel E. Gershenson and Daniel A. Greenberg, *Anaxagoras and the Birth of Physics* (New York: Blaisdell, 1964), pp. 48, 77, 113, 115, 136, citing Plutarch, *De fortuna* 3, *De fraterno amore* 2; Galen, *De usu partium* 1.3. For Simplicius's preservation of the fragments, see ed. Sider, pp. 18-32.

178 Clyde Kluckhorn, *Anthropology and the Classics* (Providence, R.I.: Brown University Press, 1961), pp. 32-33; R. J. Hankinson, "Galen and the Best of All Possible Worlds," *Classical Quarterly* 39 (1989):210.

179 Niccolò Machiavelli, "Esortazione alla penitenza," p. 210.

180 Cicero, *De natura deorum* 2.140; trans. H. Rackham (London: Heinemann, 1933), p. 257.

181 Cicero, *De legibus* 1.9.26; *De re publica, De legibus,* trans. Clinton Walker Keyes (Cambridge, Mass.: Harvard University Press, 1970), p. 326. Some of the texts of the topic are

Sallust urged humans to excel the other animals, groveling and enslaved to their bellies, by employing their minds to rule their bodies. Minds people had in common with the gods; bodies, with the brutes.[182] By implication an erect, rather than groveling, posture was associated with mind and with divinity. For Seneca virtue equalled stature, morally if not socially. A philosopher should not pretend to false grandeur by stretching himself deceitfully on tiptoes to achieve height. Station was associated with human aptitude for knowledge: if nature had provided that humans stood erect, then that was for better contemplation. To "arise," to "raise up" meant in his vocabulary "to philosophize." The upright stature was the image of pride and dignity. "Erect" described the soul of the sage. Inversely, to renounce wisdom was to live with the head bowed down.[183]

Ovid poetized mutability in verse frequently cited. After the creation in his *Metamorphoses* of fish, beast, and bird: "A living creature of finer stuff than these, more capable of lofty thought, one who could have dominion over all the rest, was lacking yet. Then man was born." Ovid declined to speculate about whether people were fashioned from the divine substance or from the new earth, as retaining some celestial element. He was certain of their distinction from other animals. "And, though all other animals are prone, and fix their gaze upon the earth, he gave to man an uplifted face and bade him stand erect and turn his eyes to heaven."[184] Silius Italicus rendered the speech of Virtue: "See you not, how the Creator raised the faces of mankind towards heaven and gave them countenances that look upwards, though he had caused all herds and flocks, all beasts and birds, to creep on their belly, inactive and unsightly? But man is born for glory, if he can appreciate heaven's gift, and in pursuit of glory he is happy."[185]

The belief that erect bipedality was intended for celestial vision and contemplation also inspired astronomical literature. Just as human eyes could perceive the sky, so human minds could penetrate it to discern the Creator divinely dwelling in them. "Why wonder that man can comprehend

---

reviewed in Michele Pellegrino, "Il 'topos' dello 'status rectus' nel contesto filosofico e biblico (A proposito di *Ad Diognetum* 10, 1-2)," in *Mullus: Festschrift Theodor Klausner*, ed. Alfred Stuiber and Alfred Hermann, Jahrbuch für Antike und Christentum, Ergänzungsband, 1 (Münster: Aschendorff, 1964), pp. 272-81; C. A. Patrides, "Renaissance Ideas on Man's Upright Form," *Journal of the History of Ideas* 19 (1958):256-58. Some others are cross-referenced in the critical editions.

182 Sallust, *Bellum Catilianae* 1.1.

183 Mireille Armisen-Marchetti, "*Sapientiae facies*": *Études sur les images de Sénèque*, Collection d'études anciennes, 58 (Paris: Belles lettres, 1989), p. 100, citing Seneca, *Epistulae* 111.3; 65.20. See also Fritz Husner, *Leib und Seele in der Sprache Senecas: Ein Beitrag zur sprachlichen Formulierung der moralischen adhortatio*, in *Philologus, Supplementband* 17, heft 3 (1924), pp. 103-9.

184 Ovid, *Metamorphoses* 1.76-78, 84-87; trans. Frank Justus Miller, rev. G. P. Goold, 2 vols. (London: William Heinemann, 1976-77), 1:7, 9.

185 Silius Italicus, *Punica* 15.84-87; trans. J. D. Duff, 2 vols. (New York: G. P. Putnam's Sons, 1934-50), 2:331.

heaven," asked Manilius in the peroration of *Astronomica*, "when heaven exists in their very beings and each one is in a smaller likeness the image of God himself?" All other animals lay prostrate on the earth, submerged in water, or hovering in the air. Sleep, food, and sex were their delights; their strength was measured by their size, their value by their limbs. Only humans, the universal rulers, were reared capable of inquiry, speech, understanding, and skills: urbanization, agriculture, husbandry, and navigation. But contemplation, not technology, was the purpose of the upright stance. "He alone stands with the citadel of his head raised high and, triumphantly directing to the stars his star-like eyes, looks ever more closely at Olympus and inquires into the nature of Jove himself; nor does he rest content with the outward appearance of the gods, but probes into heaven's depths and, in his quest of a being akin to his own, seeks himself among the stars."[186]

With the Christian assimilation of philosophy to theology erect bipedality became a sign of spiritual dignity, although contemplation was neither a scriptural term nor concept. The upright stature was an important apologetic theme. Cyprian argued it against idolatrous prostration to the gods of the earth. "God made you erect, and, although the other animals are prone and are depressed with posture bent toward earth, you have an exalted stature and a countenance raised upward toward heaven and the Lord."[187] Lactantius stated that the human form resembled the divine form, so that its origin and end must be celestial.[188] God made only humans to recline with the face upward; other animals must rest on their sides. He made the human breast "open and fully erect, because, being full of reason given from heaven, it was not befitting that it should be humble or unbecoming."[189]

Lactantius especially argued the classical topic of erect bipedality against idolatry. Other creatures with their prone bodies looked down at the earth because they lack reason and wisdom, but humans had an upright posture with uplifted countenance. Paganism was thus unworthy of them, because it worshipped the earth. "When that one and only Parent of ours fashioned man, that is, an animal, intelligent and capable of reason, He raised him up from the ground and made him stand erect for the contemplation of his Maker." Since the Greeks even called a human *anthropos*, because he looks upward, those humans who looked down renounced themselves and their

---

186 Manilius, *Astronomicon* lines 883-87, 893-95, 897-910; *Astronomica*, trans. Goold (Cambridge, Mass.: Harvard University Press, 1977), pp. 293-95. See also Firmicus Maternus, *Matheseos* 8.1.3.

187 Cyprian, *Ad Demetrianum* 16; "To Demetrian," trans. Roy J. Deferrari, in *Treatises*, Fathers of the Church, 36 (New York: Fathers of the Church, 1958), p. 181.

188 Michel Perrin, *L'homme antique et chrétien: L'anthropologie de Lactance, 250-325*, Théologie historique, 59 (Paris: Beauchesne, 1981), pp. 68-77, 86-87.

189 Lactantius, *De opificio Dei* 10; "On the Workmanship of God, or the Formation of Man," trans. William Fletcher, in *The Ante-Nicene Fathers*, ed. Alexander Roberts and James Donaldson (Buffalo, 1886), 7:292. See in general Peter A. Roots, "The *De opificio Dei*: The Workmanship of God and Lactantius," *Classical Quarterly* 37 (1987):466-86.

name. The divine will was for humans to look purposefully at heaven. While the birds and most quadrupeds could see the sky, only humans by standing erect could behold the heavens. There they were to seek religion. Although God could not be seen with the eyes in his celestial abode, he could be contemplated there with the mind. It was perverse to debase the mind to the veneration of idols of stone or bronze. "Our shape and stature signify nothing else but that the mind of man ought to look where our countenance is directed, and that his soul ought to be as upright as his body so that it may imitate that which it ought to dominate."[190]

Gregory of Nyssa considered the erect stature appropriate to the human domination of animals. That posture was a sign of "the regal dignity to command." Since among creatures humans alone were in that mode, it indicated distinctly the natural power they exercised over the bent beings.[191] Ambrose initiated his hexameral homily on the sixth day of creation by indicating every species and genus to demonstrate humans as the most divinely gifted. Their gift was not in the hand, or even in the head, but in the soul as created to the divine image. The body was not entirely negligible, however. The human form in its erectness and stature lacked the extremes of dreadful mass or puny insignificance, and so was gentle and pleasing. The body was constructed like a world, with the head as the sky in which dwelled the sun and the moon, or the eyes. "When you see a head you recognize a man," he wrote. The head was the divine director, with the human brain as the source of the nervous system and of voluntary movement, of the arteries and natural heat, and as the gathering point of the senses. In praising the head, however, Ambrose departed from the argument that only humans could regard the heavens. Other animals could also elevate their eyes, he noted, but they lacked the will to interpret their perception, while humans possessed that will. Humans fittingly had two legs, not more, as sufficient to sustain their bodily weight. Legs expressed the emotion of humility and the submission of service, with the knees flexible to appease an offended master or to induce his favors. Humans were thus unlike quadrupedal animals but like bipedal birds. They were akin to that feathered flock when they aimed aloft with their vision, flying with the sagacity of their sublime senses.[192] Minucius Felix even argued for the Christian doctrine of the resurrection of the body by praising its erect posture and uplifted countenance.[193]

---

190 Lactantius, *Divinae institutiones* 2.1; *The Divine Institutes*, trans. Mary Francis McDonald, Fathers of the Church, 49 (Washington, D.C.: Catholic University of America Press, 1964), pp. 96-97. See also *De ira Dei* 7.

191 Gregory of Nyssa, *De hominis opificio* 8.

192 Ambrose, *Hexameron* 6.1.2; 6.7.42; 6.9.54, 57, 61, 67, 74; *Hexameron, Paradise, and Cain and Abel*, trans. John J. Savage, Fathers of the Church, 42 (New York: Fathers of the Church, 1961), pp. 228, 270.

193 Minucius Felix, *Octavius* 7.11.

Augustine stated the creation of humans to the divine image and likeness as not according to the body but according to the mind, whose intellectuality was superior to the beasts. Yet he argued in *De Genesi ad litteram* that a human did have in the body "a characteristic that is a sign of this dignity in so far as he has been made to stand erect." That posture admonished humans not to seek earthly matters, like the cattle, whose pleasure was entirely earthly, so that they were inclined forward and bent downward on their bellies. The human body was "appropriate for his rational soul not because of his facial features and the structure of his limbs, but rather because of the fact that he stands erect, able to look up to heaven and gaze upon the highest regions in the corporeal world."[194] When Augustine expressly considered the question "on man made in the image and likeness of God," he again introduced it as not according to the body but according to the intellectual mind as superior to the beasts. Yet he observed the unique posture of the human body among the bodies of terrestrial animals in that it was not stretched prone on its stomach. It stood "erect in order to look at the heavens, the principle of visible things." And, although the body owed its animation to the soul, "still the human body can rightly be regarded as created more in the image and likeness of God than the other bodies of animals." That goodness was in its better adaptation for viewing the heavens.[195] In *De civitate Dei* he also mentioned the argument from bodily design. He observed that, while irrational animals had their faces toward the ground, humans were erect with their faces toward the sky. That was to admonish people to fix their thoughts on heavenly matters.[196]

Boethius in *De consolatione philosophiae* considered the varied shapes of earthly creatures. Some with stretched bodies crawled through a furrow of dust, others soared with wings in tracks through the air, some walked on the ground through woods and fields. Yet all animals looked with eyes cast down on the earth and with sluggish senses.

> Men only with more stately shape to higher objects rise,
> Who with erected bodies stand and do the earth despise.

The moral: as the upright face beheld the sky, so should the mind rise aloft.[197] Peter Lombard, whose *Sententiae* was the required text for commentary by aspirant medieval bachelors of theology, ventured to argue for a certain propriety in even the body as created in the likeness of God.

---

194 Augustine, *De Genesi ad litteram* 6.12.22; *The Literal Meaning of Genesis*, trans. John Hammond Taylor, Ancient Christian Writers, 41 (New York: Newman, 1982-), 1:193.

195 Augustine, *De diversis quaestionibus octoginta tribus* 51.3; *Eighty-Three Different Questions*, trans. David L. Mosher, Fathers of the Church, 70 (Washington, D.C.: Catholic University of America Press, 1977), pp. 86-87.

196 Augustine, *De civitate Dei* 22.

197 Boethius, *De consolatione philosophiae* 5.5; *The Theological Tractates, The Consolation of Philosophy*, trans. H. F. Stewart and E. K. Rand (New York: G. P. Putnam's Sons, 1928), p. 399.

Because the human body was erect in stature, it was congruent with its rational soul as erect to heaven.[198] Detailing the qualities of humans as civilized animals, Albert the Great mentioned only as "a final note of differentiation" that people had erect bodies. While quadrupeds were earthbound, humans had an affinity with the heavens, since their souls were in the image of the Creator and a microcosm of the universe.[199] Thomas of Cantimpré distinguished humans from apes, whose feet and placement of the leg joints were similar. Although apes could stand erect in human fashion, they accomplished that only moderately and only when trained to do so by humans. Their natural position was to face the ground. Humans alone were capable of raising their face to the heavens, so that they might perceive clearly the source of "salvation."[200] That comment advanced the argument beyond contemplation to salvation.

Thomas Aquinas thought teleologically: all nature was the divine craftsmanship, with the best possible constitution for its purpose. The purpose of the human body was to serve the rational soul and its activities, just as instruments—like a saw—served the activities of their agents. "Touch, which is the basis of the other senses, is more perfect in man than in any other animal," he argued, "and to achieve this, man had to have the most finely balanced composition of all the other animals." Humans needed the largest animal brain for the the freest and most perfect functioning of the mind and its faculties. The coldness of the brain cooled the heat of the heart, which to maintain the upright posture had to be considerable. Scholastically he enumerated four reasons why an upright stature was fitting for humans. First, their senses were not only for procuring necessities but also for attaining knowledge. Other animals delighted in sensory objects as ordered to food and sex, and so had their faces as the seat of the senses inclined toward the ground. Humans delighted in sensory objects for their beauty, and so had their faces erect. That posture was purposeful, so that the senses—especially subtle and penetrating sight—might freely survey the sensible objects all around, heavenly and earthly, to gather intelligible truth from everything. Second, for greater freedom in the acts of the interior powers, the brain in which those actions were performed was not low but lifted above other bodily parts. Third, if humans were prone on the ground, their hands would be needed as forefeet, thus rendered useless for other purposes. Fourth, people would have to grasp food with the mouth, and so would need a protruding mouth with thick, hard lips and a tough tongue as protection from external harm. Such a physique would hinder speech as the

---

198 Peter Lombard, *Sententiae* 2.16.4.2; following Bede, *In Genesin* 1:26 (*Patrologia latina*, 91:29).

199 Albert the Great, *De animalibus* 22.1.5.12; 22.2.1.13; trans. Scanlan, p. 67.

200 Thomas of Cantimpré, *De naturis rerum*; cited by H. W. Janson, *Apes and Ape Lore: In the Middle Ages and the Renaissance* (London: Warburg Institute, University of London, 1932), p. 81. For the ape in the image of humans, see pp. 73-106.

proper aspiration of reason. There was a problem of comparison with plants, he conceded, since plants, like people, were also upright. Yet plants were opposite to people, he resolved, since they had their roots, which were, as their mouths, their superior parts, underground.[201]

Gianozzo Manetti (1396-1459) in his treatise *De dignitate et excellentia hominis* repeated from Lactantius that a man was called *anthropos* from his erect stature.[202] Ficino argued that the elevation of the body to heaven like the elevation of the soul to God was uniquely human: other animals gave no sign of religion.[203] Aurelio Brandolino in the sixteenth century would also reiterate the excellence of the human body in its beauty, order, and utility.[204] A humanist miscellany would report that "infinite are the things worthy of contemplation and admiration in the composition of the human body." Pedro Mexía (1496?-1522?) in his *Silva de varia lección* singled as deserving of special merit the reason why God had created all other animals with their foreheads down gazing at the ground; trees and plants with the head and base in the earth, branches and arms on top; and humans alone capable of regarding the heavens, "the forehead high, the body straight and upright." Although it sufficed to credit the divine will, he considered the question still worthy of consideration. Mexía cited the deliberations of Lactantius, Aristotle, and Aquinas before concluding. Human posture manifested that people did not belong to this earth, he decided, but were created to imitate and to contemplate celestial truths, a destiny in which no other animal participated.[205] Montaigne was remarkable in his dissent from the anthropic principle that humans were thus privileged by nature over other animals. In his skeptical "Apologie de Raymond Sebond" he challenged the tradition: "What animals do not have their face up high and in front, and do not look straight forward like ourselves, and do not discover, in their proper posture, as much of heaven and earth as man?"[206]

Medical literature also considered the phenomenon of erect bipedality. Galen had analyzed in detail human legs as "most suitable for a reasoning, two-footed animal."[207] A late medieval collection of medical questions and answers, *Problemata varia anatomica*, began with the inquiry about why humans alone of all the animals walked with their heads erect toward the heavens. Ten reasons were cited: (1) The Creator so willed it; (2) All arti-

---

201 Thomas Aquinas, *Summa theologiae* 1.91.3; trans. Suttor, p. 27.

202 Gianozzo Manetti, *De dignitate et excellentia hominis* 1.14, citing Lactantius, *De opificio Dei* 8. For Manetti on the body, see Charles Trinkaus, *In Our Image and Likeness: Humanity and Divinity in Italian Humanist Thought*, 2 vols. (Chicago: University of Chicago Press, 1970), 1:231-34.

203 Ficino, *Theologia platonica* 14.9, p. 280.

204 Aurelio Brandolino, *De humanae vitae conditione et toleranda corporis aegritudine*, for which see Trinkaus, *In Our Image and Likeness*, 1:298-306.

205 Pedro Mexía, *Silva de varia lección* 1.16.

206 Montaigne, *Essais* 2.12, pp. 483-84; trans. Frame, p. 356.

207 Galen, *De usu partium* 3.4; trans. May, 1:161.

ficers made their best works last, so God created brutes face downward, then humans elevated to heaven; (3) Among the animals, only humans were ordained to the kingdom of heaven by contemplation; (4) Because humans were a microcosm, they ruled all animals as obedient under their feet; (5) Humans were a political and social animal, using reason; (6) It was apt to movement by analogy with heaven as a round sphere and fire as a pyramidal form; (7) The human body was light in spume and air, thus elevated; (8) It had more heat in its members, thus it rose; (9) It shared the perfect form of angels and intelligent beings; (10) It was ordained to understand, by the service of the senses, especially sight, as situated in the head.[208]

The crouching medieval skeletons of art began in the fourteenth century to be drawn standing erect. The imperfect but improving representation dated to Henri de Mondeville's anatomical lectures. Then the studies of the human skeleton by da Vinci initiated a rupture with conventional osteological illustration. Although there remains no complete drawing by him of a skeleton, he portrayed its parts in their natural forms and proportions. Those parts were figured accurately in observation and delineation, with a correction of the medieval number of the vertebrae of the spine. Da Vinci also first represented correctly the curvature of the spine, with the tilting of the sacrum that brings the weight of the trunk over the lower limbs. That renaissance artist was the first to recognize the demands, both static and dynamic, of the erect posture on the skeleton. Not even the anatomist Andreas Vesalius (1514-64) would approach him in accuracy of perception. Vesalius merely assembled bones on paper, in disregard of the conditions of an animate body. His skeletons, if they were to be animated, could neither stand nor walk.[209] Not only bones but also muscles for erectness were da Vinci's study. He compared the spinal muscles to braces for maintaining an upright posture. The braces were so designed that the upper parts of the torso were more privileged in position than the lower ones. His descriptions evidenced precise forces to guarantee the position. "Muscles support the backbone so that it does not bend when a man lowers or lifts his heavy load." That was the foundation of an anatomical analysis of movement and posture, although his description was still uncertain, with its mechanical perspective incomplete and fragmentary.[210]

The majority of the rationale or reasoning, ancient to renaissance, about the human stance was anatomically incorrect. The human development of

---

208 *Problemata varia anatomica*, p. 10.

209 J. Playfair McMurrich, *Leonardo da Vinci the Anatomist (1452-1519)*, Carnegie Institution of Washington Publications, 411 (Baltimore, Md.: Williams and Wilkins for Carnegie Institution of Washington, 1930), pp. 114, 111, 120-21; and for the leg and foot, see pp. 124-26.

210 Da Vinci, *Notebooks*, ed. Richter, 1:197; cited by Georges Vigarello, "The Upward Training of the Body from the Age of Chivalry to Courtly Civility," trans. Ughetta Lubin, in *Fragments for a History of the Human Body*, ed. Feher, 2:166.

erect bipedality did not mean a contemplative vocation or moral rectitude in the divine image. The purpose of the erect human torso is scientifically to position the hands in space for technical ability.[211] The erect posture does not in its natural stance even afford access to the heavens by vision. Humans do not naturally look up but ahead, so that, unless they have an unobstructed view of the horizon, they do not even see the sky. That fact was not unknown. When the friar Bartolomeo de las Casas (1474-1566) wanted to emphasize to his European readers the immense height of tropical trees in the Americas, he wrote that a person had to "raise his head no less than when he wants to view and contemplate the zenith of the heavens."[212] Yet, from the influence of the philosophical premise that human dignity consisted in contemplation, basic anatomy was ordinarily misrepresented. Anatomical literature acknowledged that other animals and humans differed in their form and in the position of their members: by an erect stature. Erectness was a medical commonplace. Yet at the beginning of the sixteenth century Benedetti, a Paduan physician, still explained it philosophically, not biologically, in his *Historia corporis humani, sive anatomice*. "The human body was created for the sake of the soul and stands erect among other animals, as established by divine nature and reason so that it might look upward more comfortably, whence the Greeks gave it a name." That name was *anthropos* or "man," from *anti* for "opposite, facing" and *tropos* for "turn, direction." The human head was the highest bodily part, as reflecting the universal consideration of the divine mind. It bore very little flesh on it so that it would not be bent to the ground like other animals with front legs, rather than arms and hands. Berengario da Carpi (1470-1530) in his commentary on the medieval authority Mondino da Luzzi affirmed the philosophical interpretation of the upright stature. Humans were anatomically intended to gaze at the heavens with the immensity of their intellects. Niccolò Massa (1485-1569), who had degrees in both philosophy and medicine, simply cited Ovid's verse. "He gave a sublime face to man and ordered him to look at the sky and to lift an upright countenance to the stars."[213]

---

211 See Emmanuel B. Kaplan and Morton Spinner, "The Hand as an Organ," in *Kaplan's Functional and Surgical Anatomy of the Hand*, ed. Spinner, 3d ed. (Philadelphia, Pa.: J. B. Lippincott, 1984), p. 3.

212 Bartolome de Las Casas, *Apologética historia sumaria* 21.

213 Alessandro Achellini (1463-1512), *Annotationes anatomicae*, ed. Lind, *Pre-Vesalian Anatomy*, p. 42; Benedetti, *Historia corporis humani* 2, ed. Lind, p. 83 and n. 9; Berengario da Carpi, *Commentaria*, ed. Lind (summarized), p. 160; Niccolò Massa, *Liber introductorius anatomiae*, ed. Lind, p. 176. Cf. Ovid, *Metamorphoses* 1.85-86. Also cited by Berengario da Carpi, *Commentaria* 24, ed. Lind (summarized), p. 176 n. 7. For his method, see R. K. French, "Berengario da Carpi and the Use of Commentary in Medical Teaching," in *The Medical Renaissance of the Sixteenth Century*, ed. A. Wear, French, and I. Lonie (Cambridge: Cambridge University Press, 1985), pp. 42-74. For the accommodation of philosophy in medicine, see Charles B. Schmitt, "Aristotle Among the Physicians," in *Medical Renaissance*, pp. 1-15.

An erect posture as the sign of human nature became, by deduction from its contemplative purpose, the index of moral character. In the extensive catalogue of evils befalling a lover of pleasure Philo characterized him as failing in the dignity of rectitude as erectness: "unstable," "wavering," "pliable," "dawdling," "vagrant," "tripping," in sum, "beast-like." That distinction of vice from virtue occurred in his commentary on Cain and Abel,[214] where he decisively transformed the rival personalities of the biblical brothers into rival principles of all humanity.[215] Like the serpentine tempter slithering on his belly, the lover of pleasure was "so weighted and dragged downwards that it is with difficulty that he lifts up his head, thrown down and tripped up by intemperance."[216]

Since the physiognomy attributed to Aristotle, only a right posture signified right living. The characteristic of a brave man was "an erect carriage of body," while that of a coward was "a body of sedentary habit, not energetic." A coward's extremities were "weak," with "small legs and long thin hands," so that the movement of his figure was "constrained." Typically, "he is not eager but supine and nervous." A shameless man was similarly "bowed." Although quick in movement, "his figure is not erect but inclines to stoop forward." The man of low spirits was "stooping in figure and feeble in his movements." A morbid character was "knock-kneed" with two gaits, either wiggling or stiff in the hips. A small-minded man was "small limbed." An abusive man leaned forward. Concerning the passionate temperament, in contrast, "the body is erect." As for a gentle man, "his figure is upright." In sum: "Those who have well-made, large feet, well-jointed and sinewy, are strong in character; witness the male sex. Those who have small, narrow, poorly-jointed feet, are rather attractive to look at than strong, being weak in character; witness the female sex." The rule for the feet applied strictly to the legs: strong limbs, strong morals, strong males. What the feet and the legs supported—the back—also complied with uprightness as rectitude. "Those whose back is very large and strong are of strong character; witness the male. Those which have a narrow, weak back are feeble; witness the female." In either sex, however, the back was to be straight. A back bent well forward, with the shoulders pressed into the chest, meant an "evil disposition." A back curved backwards belonged to "vain and senseless persons." Although the eyes were classically the clear-

---

214 Philo, *De sacrificiis Abelis et Caini* 32; *On the Sacrifices of Abel and Cain*, trans. F. H. Colson and G. H. Whitaker, in *Philo*, 12 vols. (Cambridge, Mass.: Harvard University Press, 1961), 2:117, 119.

215 Ricardo J. Quinones, *The Changes of Cain: Violence and the Lost Brother in Cain and Abel Literature* (Princeton, N.J.: Princeton University Press, 1991), pp. 23-24.

216 Philo, *De opificio mundi* 56.157; trans. Colson and Whitaker, 1:125.

est windows of the soul,[217] the legs and feet were also displays of character.[218]

Aristotle had noticed the basic biology of feet. Among all the animals, humans had the largest for their size and reasonably so. Humans were the only animals to stand upright, and since the two feet had to bear the entire weight of the body, it was necessary that they be long and broad. "The business of the feet is to get a firm and reliable footing,"[219] he stated. It was an opinion repeated in renaissance anatomy.[220] Yet most thinkers were more concerned about the morality, rather than the biology, of feet: a theoretical, rather than practical, reason for standing.

From birth a human being was to be straight. A newborn, fresh from his initial bath, was grasped by the ankles and hung upside down: to separate the vertebrae, give the spine the right curves, and untangle the sinews. His body was anointed with olive oil, stretched out, and rubbed down, with the nurse bending it to make the sinews of the joints supple and mobile.[221] Because of the cultural belief in a tight relation between body and soul—erectness as rectitude, posture was formed from infancy by manipulation. The body of a baby was considered excessively hot and liquid in its humors, with its bones in danger of being unaligned or dislodged. Its very weakness subjected it to correction. The body was manipulated to straighten it, as a precaution against deformation or displacement of the vertebrae, and to guarantee a postural control that would be elegant. The aims were physical strength and moral decorum. As a body grew it solidified, affected by pressures that could impress malformed positions. The period just after birth was thus the time for molding the bones into proper form, when they were soft and tender and would comply with compressing, bending, and shaping. A delay in the process risked the hardening of the bones from internal heat and external air. In analogy with the sculptor molding a figure in malleable clay the surgeon or nurse shaped the infant by repositioning the vertebrae of the spine. Soranus, who wrote the definitive text on gynecology, specified "a full hand massage, while the torso is kept in traction" to avoid curvature of the spine. He detailed the application of the index and middle fingers above the buttocks to "dig a graceful depression." The initial molding after birth was continued through infancy by swaddling cloths, which replaced the hands in supplying erectness. By applying pressure to impose shape, the cloths were thought to be endowed with a corrective power to which the infant's body submitted. They were specified as clean, soft woolen strips of three- or four-fingers width. The bands were considered like the stakes that

217 Plato, *Phaedrus* 255c.

218 Aristotle, *Physiognomica* 807a-b, 808a, 809a, 810a-b, 814a; *Minor Works*, trans. W. S. Hett (Cambridge, Mass.: Harvard University Press, 1936), pp. 99, 101, 103, 105, 115, 117, 119.

219 Aristotle, *De partibus animalium* 690a; trans. Peck, p. 391.

220 Benedetti, *Historia corporis humani* 1.2.

221 Soranus, *Gynaecia* 2.16.32.

supported a sapling, since the spinal column was analogous to a stem that was a bendable green twig. The rules for their application and removal were elaborate. They had to be applied correctly, since defective cloths could cause the very deformity they were supposed to prevent.[222]

In the practice of swaddling the midwife began the process of ensuring a right spine by swaddling the hand: taking the end of the bandage and winding it around the extended fingers, then over the middle of the hand; then, compressing the wrist slightly, wrapping it to the forearm and upper arm, loose to the arm pit. The swaddling of the hand was especially to prevent its becoming twisted by excessive movement. When the infant was finally bound circularly from thorax to feet, the hands were placed inside the wrapping to accustom them to extension. The confinement of the joints was believed to thicken the sinews.[223] There were complaints about the practice since Roman medicine, however. Swaddling was blamed for indoor confinement, inadequate diet, and lack of exposure to sunlight causing rickets. If the cloths were not changed often enough they would emit the foul odor of excrement.[224] Even their advocate Soranus allowed for some difficulty. If the swaddled infant became chafed by the friction of the bandages, they should be abandoned for a simple little shirt until the sores were healed.[225] Yet swaddling was normative from ancient to renaissance societies,[226] although the practice could be simplified. Late medieval illustrations show the infant only bundled in a blanket that is crisscrossed with a single band, from behind the shoulders to a tie at the ankles.[227]

Swaddling had not only medical but also scriptural authority. "And she gave birth to her first-born son and wrapped him in swaddling cloths" (Luke 2:7). God incarnate conformed to the custom of erect posture. A female saint had a vision of the infant Jesus customarily swaddled.[228] A devout woman, wrapped in the imaginative meditations of late medieval piety,

---

222 Vigarello, "Upward Training of the Body," pp. 168-73. See Soranus, *Gynaecia* 2.9.14-15; 2.19.42. For swaddling, see also Lloyd, *Science, Folklore, and Ideology*, pp. 172, 175-76.

223 Soranus, *Gynaecia* 2.9.15.

224 Peter Garnsey, "Child Rearing in Ancient Italy," in *The Family in Italy from Antiquity to the Present*, ed. David I. Kertzer and Richard P. Saller (New Haven, Conn.: Yale University Press, 1991), p. 57; Keith R. Bradley, "Wet-Nursing at Rome: A Study in Social Relations," in *The Family in Ancient Rome: New Perspectives*, ed. Beryl Rawson (London: Croom Helm, 1986), pp. 215, 219; Shulamith Shahar, *Childhood in the Middle Ages* (London: Routlege, 1990), pp. 84-86.

225 Soranus, *Gynaecia* 2.19.42.

226 See Luke Demaitre, "The Idea of Childhood and Child Care in Medical Writings of the Middle Ages," *Journal of Psychohistory* 4 (1976-77):471-73. For illustrations of swaddling, see Suzanne Dixon, *The Roman Mother* (London: Croom Helm, 1987), pl. 9; Ilene H. Forsyth, "Children in Early Medieval Art: Ninth through Twelfth Centuries," *Journal of Psychohistory* 4 (1976-77):36-39.

227 Danièle Alexandre-Bidon and Monique Classon, *L'Enfant à l'ombre des cathedrales* (Lyon: Presses universitaires de Lyon, 1985), pp. 94-102.

228 See *Acta sanctorum*, March 2; cited by Shahar, *Childhood*, p. 86.

wanted to swaddle him herself. Margery Kempe (b. c.1373), who as the wife of a burgess would not have swaddled her own large brood, begged in her imagination for Jesus' cloths. She watched Mary swaddle him with a white kerchief, then imitated the process, assuring the divine infant that she would not bind him too tightly,[229] which could dislocate his hips.[230]

The infant was also not to be laid down on any surface too hard or too soft that might flatten or distort the head, neck, and backbone. The correct bedding was a pillow filled with flock or hay, with the mattress hollowed out like a channel.[231] An infant attempting to sit or to stand was to be helped in its motions. As Soranus's gynecology explained, "For if it is eager to sit up too early and for too long a period it usually becomes hunchbacked (the spine bending because the little body has as yet no strength). If, moreover, it is too prone to stand up and desirous of walking, the legs may become distorted in the region of the thighs." When an infant first sat up, its body should be supported by a cloth wrap and propped up at its sides. Once it progressed to crawling and to standing a little, it should be placed against a wall.[232] Erect bipedality was assumed to be innate and natural to humans. Galen and his successors cautioned eager parents not to force an infant to walk "before the desire comes to him naturally." A common practice toward baby's first steps was to position him for support near a round bench or log and for security in front of his nurse. The toddler could see the nurse over the object and walk confidently toward her with encouragement. It should not be led into walking by the arm, because a jerk might dislocate the limb. After the initial toddling a walker (*cariolo*), a chair with wheels on its legs, could be employed. The next step toward stepping was to place the child near a wall, but at a distance from it, and to throw an object there—a box, purse, or apple—to entice him to walk to it. By that method his distance and confidence would be increased. As the toddler approached his second birthday, he should be allowed to exercise with other children by climbing, running, and throwing.[233]

Once walking was habitual, there were rules governing its comportment. Erasmus in his behavioral manual for children prescribed renaissance civility. A drooping neck and hunched shoulders spoke laziness; yet tossing the head back, haughtiness. "It should be held gently erect," he instructed, inclined to neither side except as conversation required. Hunching through

---

229 *The Book of Margery Kempe* 1.6, 85.

230 Shahar, *Childhood*, p. 88.

231 Soranus, *Gynaecia* 2.10.16. For cradles, see Shahar, *Childhood*, pp. 89-90.

232 Soranus, *Gynaecia* 2.20.43; *Gynecology*, trans. Owsei Tempkin, with Nicholson J. Eastman, Ludwig Edelstein, and Alan F. Guttmacher, Publications of the Institute of the History of Medicine, Texts and Documents, 3 (Baltimore, Md.: Johns Hopkins University Press, 1956), p. 115.

233 Demaitre, "Childhood and Child Care," p. 475; Shahar, *Childhood*, p. 92. The cited advice against forced walking is Arnoul de Villeneuve, *De regimine sanitatis*, in his *Opera* (Lyon, 1509), 63v; *Opera omnia* (Basel, 1585), col. 667.

laziness resulted in humpback; inclination to the side, in fixation. "The shoulders should be held evenly balanced," not raised or lowered like sails. "If neglected in boyhood, bodily habits of this sort become ingrained and deform the natural posture of the body." In general "young bodies resemble young shoots, which come to maturity and acquire the fixed characteristics of whatever you determine for them with a pole or trellis." The guide to decency was conformity with nature and with reason, not the taste of fools. The human stance was morally determined. In standing still the feet were to be placed together or only slightly apart—not wide apart or crossed like a braggart. Erasmus deplored the Italian custom of standing with respect for others "like storks," with one foot pressed against the other. In walking the gait was to be neither effeminate mincing nor headlong raging nor silly half halting.[234]

Since external appearance reflected moral character, renaissance guides to courtesy emphasized walking with a dignity that was "straight."[235] Giovanni della Casa (1503-56) taught in his manual *Galateo* that the correct stance was erect—not leaning against or over another person. In their gait men should neither run in the streets nor pace slowly like brides. They should not lift their legs prancingly, or stamp their feet on the ground, or bend at every step to pull up their stockings, or wiggle their behinds excessively, or strut like peacocks.[236] The polite ideal defined by Baldassare Castiglione's (1478-1529) *Il libro del cortegiano* was a moderate build with "finely proportioned members." Legs should be fair to behold and able at physical exercise; specifically, legs should not be languid in their gait, as if they threatened to fall off.[237] As Montaigne summarized, "The other kinds of beauty are for women; the beauty of stature is the only beauty of men."[238]

Attention to erect posture as the expression of human dignity through contemplation and character did not eclipse consideration of the alternate theory, however. Xenophon had stated that people stood for the advantage and protection of better physical vision and for the usage of able hands.

---

234 Erasmus, *De civilitate* 1, in *Opera omnia* (Leiden), 1:1035-36; *On Good Manners for Boys*, trans. Brian McGregor, in *Collected Works of Erasmus*, 25:277, 278. For classical background on gait and standing, see Jan Bremmer, "Walking, Standing, and Sitting in Ancient Greek Culture," in *A Cultural History of Gesture: From Antiquity to the Present*, ed. idem and Herman Roodenberg (Cambridge: Polity, 1991), pp. 16-23, 23-35. Quintilian, the ancient authority on gesture, wrote that an upright head was natural, thus graceful. *Institutiones oratoriae* 11.3.69.

235 Vigarello, "Upward Training of the Body," p. 150.

236 Della Casa, *Galateo* 59, 300-1. For recent study of that author on manners in general, see Mariella Mazzeschi Porretti, *Il monsignore: Vita e opere di Giovanni della Casa* (Rome: Ellemme, 1990), pp. 179-205; Klaus Ley, *Die "Scienza civile" des Giovanni della Casa: Literatur als Gesellschaftskunst in der Gegenreformation* (Heidelberg: Carl Winter Universitätsverlag, 1984), pp. 123-80.

237 Castiglione, *Cortegiano* 1.20, 19, 17; cf. 2.8; *The Book of the Courtier*, trans. George Bull (Harmondsworth, Middlesex: Penguin, 1967), p. 61.

238 Montaigne, *Essais* 2:17, p. 641; trans. Frame, p. 486.

Anaxagoras had declared that humans were intelligent because they had hands, not vice versa. In comparison with the penetrating focus of intellectuals and scientists on the mind, the hands could be ignored, disparaged, slighted: hidden behind the back. Yet they could be duly admired. Aristotle praised hands in defense against their invidious comparison with the claws of animals.[239] Cicero exclaimed, "Then what clever servants for a great variety of arts are the hands which nature has bestowed on man! The flexibility of the joints enables the fingers to close and open with equal ease, and to perform every motion without difficulty." By manipulating the fingers, humans could paint, model, carve, and play musical instruments. Beyond artistic recreation, there was the basic utility of hands for agriculture, building, weaving and stitching cloth, and forging in bronze and iron. "We realize that it was by applying the hand of the artificer to the discoveries of thought and observations of the senses that all our conveniences were attained." Hands were active for food, shelter, clothing; for husbandry, mining, forestry, fire, navigation, fishery, and agriculture. "In fine," he wrote, "by means of our hands we essay to create as it were a second world within the world of nature."[240]

Among the Christian apologists for the creation, Lactantius considered the rational and the manual as part of the same divine plan. Like the upright stature, hands were among the characteristics distinguishing humans from animals that needed tremendous bodily force. The freedom of their various movements was wisely designed by the Creator to give them the greatest mobility compatible with human dignity. The palm was the perfect concave form for holding objects; the fingers with their flexible phalanges and protective nails were of a perfect number, order, and gradation. The apologist marveled at the hands as "the ministers of reason and wisdom."[241] Augustine acknowledged the mobility of the hands as appropriate and adapted for writing and for arts and crafts. "Is this not sufficient indication that a body of this kind was designed as an adjunct to the soul?" he asked, if only tersely.[242] Medieval etymology derived "hand" (*manus*) from its "service" (*munus*).[243] A renaissance anatomical notice, inserted between directions for dissection—stripping the hand and examining its tendons—also praised its creation. "What is most beautiful to see, not without giving the highest praise to the most blessed Lord, is the composition of the hand itself or of

239 Aristotle, *De partibus animalium* 687b.

240 Cicero, *De natura deorum* 2.60.150-52; trans. Rackham (Cambridge, Mass.: Harvard University Press, 1972), pp. 267, 269, 271.

241 Lactantius, *De opificio Dei* 3.17, 20; 5.11-13; 10.21-25, 22; trans. Fletcher, p. 291. See also Perrin, *Homme antique et chrétien*, pp. 79-85.

242 Augustine, *De civitate Dei* 22; *The City of God*, trans. Henry Bettenson (Harmondsworth, Middlesex: Penguin, 1972), p. 1073.

243 Isidore of Seville, *Etymologiae* 11.1.66.

the instruments which move the hand."[244] Such praise occurred in consideration of the entire design of the human body, however, with praise for each and every part. The uniqueness of the human hand was noticed but it was not scientifically explained or coordinated with the philosophical belief in erect bipedality for the purpose of contemplation. *Problemata varia anatomica* asked why people alone had hands but it did not answer the question, except to state that humans had many operations not shared by brutes. In the phrase of Aristotle frequently repeated, the hand was "the organ of organs." Yet its ten reasons advanced for the erect stature of humans included no function for hands.

In the classical tradition civilization was monumental and remarkable, whether from divine benevolence, human ingenuity, or neutral chance. Yet authors might appeal in the same narrative to unrelated, or even contradictory, tendencies. Arguments for the biological and physiological advantages of humans over other animals could appear in both naturalistic and teleological contexts. An example of a mixed version was preserved in the account of the origins of building by Vitruvius,[245] whose singular *De architectura* was so influential for the renaissance theory of proportion.[246] People were born like animals in the forests and caves and woods, he wrote, and they foraged in the fields. Once upon a time, trees in thick profusion tossed by the winds of a storm rubbed branches together and kindled fire. Terrified by the conflagration, people fled. But in reflecting on the advantage of heat, they added fuel to maintain it and by signs—breaths, words, then conversation—they indicated its advantages. Sociability originated in the discovery of fire. "Many came together into one place, having from nature this boon beyond other animals, that they should walk, not with head down, but upright, and should look upon the magnificence of the world and of the stars. They also easily handled with their hands and fingers whatever they wished." After meeting they began to make shelters from leaves or from mud and wattles, like the nests of swallows, and to dig caves. By observation of the houses of others, people made improvements, and so produced

---

244 Massa, *Liber introductorius anatomiae* 42; trans. Lind, *Pre-Vesalian Anatomy*, p. 246.

245 Thomas Cole, *Democritus and the Sources of Greek Anthropology*, American Philological Association Monograph Series, 25, rev. ed. (Atlanta, Ga.: Scholars, 1990), pp. 2, 3, and nn. 7, 8.

246 Frank Zollner, *Vitruvius Proportionsfigur: quellenkritische Studien zur Kunstliteratur im fünfzehnte und sechzehnte Jahrhundert*, Manuskripte zur Kunstwissenschaft in der Wernerschen Verlagsgesellschaft, 14 (Worms: Wernersche Verlagsgeslleschaft, 1987); Louis Callebat, "La tradition vitruvienne au Moyen Âge et à la Renaissance: Éléments d'interprétation," *International Journal of the Classical Tradition* 1 (1994):3-14; Bruno Reudenbach, "*In mensuram humani corporis*: Zur Herkunft der Auslegung und Illustration von Vitruv III 1 im fünfzehnte und sechzehnte Jahrhundert," in *Texte und Bild: Aspekte der Zusammenwerkens zweier Künstler der frühen Neuzeit*, ed. Christel Meier and Uwe Ruberg (Wiesbaden: Reichert, 1980), pp. 651-88.

better huts.[247] Vitruvius then compounded the biological idea of cooperation between the human upright status and its qualities with an alien teleological commonplace: erect posture enabled the observation of the world and the heavens. Conscious sight of the starry skies stirred people to a destiny higher than that of the creatures creeping and crawling about them.[248] Erect posture as a natural gift for observation of both earth and heaven was associated with "magnificence," although not explicitly with contemplation. The use of hands and fingers immediately followed for easy management of materials for housing.

The traditions, contemplative and active, comfortably coexisted in the mind of a renaissance anatomist. Benedetti argued that erect posture reflected the universal consideration of the divine mind, since the head occupied the highest position in the body. Yet he also praised the utility of the hands. "Arms and hands were provided for man as the most foresighted of all animals so that he might use them suitably for many crafts." He admired the design of the arms and legs, "bent in wondrous fashion, the legs inward, the arms outward, the latter for handcrafts and the former for walking." He acknowledged that the legs "preserve the entire body erect" and he supposed that was why they were proportionately the largest human member. Yet although he knew that it was the legs that made the body upright, he thought that it was the head that provided the rationale, in being positioned highest.[249] Situation, as the criterion of Aristotle, ruled.

Yet *Homo* stood for ages before he ever contemplated. And although renaissance scientists had no record of hominid fossils, they were not ignorant of an evolutionary, rather than creational, model. There was an alternative to the religious belief that the primordial humans were created pristine, like Adam freshly appearing from Michelangelo's brush on the wet plaster of the Sistine Chapel ceiling. Empedocles had initially hinted at Charles Darwin's theory of the natural selection of the species,[250] although the modern concept was a revolutionary, not cumulative, knowledge.[251] Empedocles thought that the environment was constantly changed with intermingling elements. The earliest generation of animals and plants consisted of separate limbs; then limbs joined into monsters; then whole forms; finally life through sexual reproduction. He wrote of bodily parts existing separately, scattered

247 Vitruvius, *De architectura* 2.1-2; *On Architecture*, trans. Frank Granger, 2 vols. (Cambridge, Mass.: Harvard University Press, 1931), 1:79.

248 Cole, *Democritus and Greek Anthropology*, p. 42.

249 See Benedetti, *Historia corporis humani* 1.3; trans. Lind, *Pre-Vesalian Anatomy*, p. 84.

250 Blundell, *Origins of Civilization*, pp. 73-99; Guthrie, *In the Beginning*, p. 45 on Empedocles, and see also pp. 32-33, 35-39; Kluckhorn, *Anthropology and the Classics*, p. 32 on Empedocles, and see also pp. 31-33.

251 Peter J. Bowler, *Evolution: The History of an Idea* (Berkeley and Los Angeles: University of California Press, 1984), p. 19. For the differences between Empedocles' perspective and modern theory, see Blundell, *Origins of Civilization*, pp. 86-89.

in space: "limbs wandered alone." On earth "many foreheads without necks sprang forth, and arms wandered unattached, bereft of shoulders, and eyes strayed about alone, needing brows." The parts then combined at random to form monstrosities. Either anatomical parts like limbs were doubled, or human parts were mixed with bestial parts to form a creature half-human and half-oxen. Only combinations that were appropriate and functional survived. The gradualism of animate development was emphasized. Humans and other animals were subject to biological change; they did not issue whole from the hand of a god.[252]

A renaissance artist, Signorelli, dared to portray Empedocles in a church, in a roundel in Orvieto's cathedral. In the vogue for the grotesque ornamental art that combined human, animal, and vegetable forms,[253] Empedocles gazes wondrously with an upraised hand at the imaginative prodigies surrounding him. Grotesque men point with their index fingers to a box with the signature "L. S." of the artist.[254] Empedocles' turban, a frequent attribute for the renaissance artist, including Michelangelo,[255] suggests

---

252 Empedocles, frag. 57-62, citing 58, 57; *Ancilla to the Presocratic Philosophers: A Complete Translation of the Fragments in Diels, Fragmente der Vorsokratiker*, trans. Kathleen Freeman (Oxford: Basil Blackwell, 1948), p. 58. See Blundell, *Origins of Civilization*, pp. 84, 35-45.

253 For the origins of grotesque art in the excavation of Nero's golden palace, see Nicole Dacos, *La découverte de la "domus aurea" et la formation des grotesques à la Renaissance*, Studies of the Warburg Institute, 31 (London: Warburg Institute, University of London, 1969), pp. 3, 9-13, 93-95. Michelangelo, tomb of Julius II, St. Peter-in-Chains, Rome, fig. 151. For Signorelli's visit to that site, see Leopold Ettlinger, *The Sistine Chapel before Michelangelo: Religious Imagery and Papal Primacy* (Oxford: Clarendon, 1965), pp. 120-23. For its influence, see Rose Marie San Juan, "The Function of Antique Ornament in Luca Signorelli's Fresco Decoration for the Chapel of San Brizio," *RACAR: Revue d'art canadienne/Canadian Art Review* 12 (1985):235-36, 238. For the historical circumstances of the composition of the frescoes, see Jonathan B. Riess, "Luca Signorelli's Frescoes in the Chapel of San Brizio as Reflections of Their Time and Place," in *Renaissance Studies in Honor of Craig Hugh Smyth*, ed. Andrew Morragh, Fiorelli Superbi Gioffredi, Piero Morselli, and Eve Borsook, 2 vols. (Florence: Villa I Tatti, 1985), 2:383-84. See also idem, "La genesi degli affreschi del Signorelli per la cappella nova," in *Il duomo di Orvieto*, ed. Lucio Riccetti (Rome: Laterza, 1988), pp. 247-71; *The Renaissance Antichrist: Luca Signorelli's Orvieto Frescoes* (Princeton, N.J.: Princeton University Press, 1995). See also in general, Geoffrey Galt Harpham, *On the Grotesque: Strategies of Contradiction in Art and Literature* (Princeton, N.J.: Princeton University Press, 1982), pp. 3-47; Frances K. Barasch, *The Grotesque: A Study in Meanings* (The Hague: Mouton, 1977), pp. 17-25; Wolfgang Kayser, *The Grotesque in Art and Literature*, trans. Ulrich Weisstein (New York: McGraw Hill, 1966), pp. 19-22.

254 For the attribution of Empedocles, see Ludovico Luzi, *Il duomo di Orvieto* (Florence, 1866); reproduced in Enzo Carli, *Luca Signorelli, gli affreschi nel duomo di Orvieto* (Bergamo: Istituto italiano d'art grafiche, 1946), pls. 54, 57; Dacos, *"Domus aurea" et grotesques*, p. 73, and fig. 109; Mario Salmi, *Luca Signorelli* (Novara: Istituto geografico de Agostini, 1953), fig. 56; Luitpold Dussler, ed., *Signorelli: Des Meisters Gemälde* (Stuttgart: Deutsche Verlags, 1927), p. 109; Harpham, *On the Grotesque*, p. 39, fig. 22.

255 See John F. Paoletti, "Michelangelo's Masks," *Art Bulletin* 74 (1992):432 n. 21. Jan van Eyck's painting called the Man in the Red Turban wears, instead, a dangling scarf wound and tied around a hat. Margaret Scott, *Late Gothic Europe, 1400-1500*, History of Dress, 1 (London: Mills and Boon, 1980), p. 11; Jacqueline Herald, *Renaissance Dress in Italy, 1400-1500*, History of Dress, 2 (New Jersey: Humanities, 1981), p. 55; Lorne Campbell, *Renaissance*

that Signorelli the artist invents from the disparate forms that philosopher had envisioned. The surgeon Ambroise Paré (1510-90) also cited Empedocles as an authority in his book of marvels and monsters.[256] Debate was lively on the status of monsters, whose existence was reported in the accounts of crusaders, the journals of diplomatic missionaries to Asia, the maritime explorers, and even the armchair travelers.[257] Did the mixed creatures descend in some confusion from Adam, perfect as on the Sistine Chapel ceiling, or from Ham, depicted there as pointing maliciously at Noah's nakedness? The influential decision for the Adamic status and human lineage of the monstrous peoples was rendered by Augustine. "Whoever is born anywhere as a human being, that is, as a rational mortal creature, however strange he many appear to our senses in bodily form or colour or motion or utterance, or in any faculty, part or quality of his nature whatsoever, let no true believer have any doubt that such an individual is descended from the one man who was first created." Rationality, not corporeality, distinguished humans from other animals.[258]

Yet bodily integrity, and not only mental capacity, remained at issue for the definition of human nature. The legs supporting an erect torso, which so distinguished humans from other animals, and the hands those legs enabled were examined for correctness. A strange corporeality horrified yet fascinated people. In antiquity monsters were omens of misfortune, eruptions of cosmic disorder that portended civic danger. Anomalous infants were immediately killed by their fathers. Human form was necessary for human status, social and legal. In the medieval version of the Roman law compiled under Justinian, while outright monsters were excluded from humanity, children born with an abnormal number of limbs were included, as humanly formed. A body with extra members, providing the members were human, was considered human. The ponderous medieval commentary on the Roman digest established the legal status of formal humanity as the basis for human dignity. While lawyers defined the human by the visible, canonists were preoccupied with the invisible. What if the extra members were heads? Did two heads mean two souls? Canonists

---

Portraits: European Portrait-Painting in the Fourteenth, Fifteenth, and Sixteenth Centuries (New Haven, Conn.: Yale University Press, 1990), p. 12, fig. 22.

256 Ambroise Paré, *De monstres* praef., 5, 9, 10.

257 Annemarie De Waal Malefijt, *Images of Man: A History of Anthropological Thought* (New York: Knopf, 1974), pp. 36-37, 47; J. S. Slotkin, ed., *Readings in Early Anthropology* (Chicago: Aldine, 1965), pp. xi-xii.

258 Augustine, *De civitate Dei* 16.8. See John Block Friedman, *The Monstrous Races in Medieval Art and Thought* (Cambridge, Mass.: Harvard University Press, 1981), pp. 90-91; Rudolf Wittkower, "Marvels of the East: A Study in the History of Monsters," *Journal of the Warburg and Courtauld Institutes* 5 (1942):167-68. For sixteenth-century views on origins, see Gordon R. Willey and Jeremy A. Sabloff, *A History of American Archaeology* (San Francisco, Calif.: W. H. Freedman, 1980), pp. 12-19; Ignacio Bernal, *A History of Mexican Archaeology: The Vanished Civilizations of Middle America* (London: Thames and Hudson, 1980), pp. 21-28; De Waal Malefijt, *Images of Man*, pp. 36-37, 42-44.

debated the validity of baptism in that case—once, twice, or conditionally? When theologians deliberated the fine distinctions about monsters, whose human identity was in question for their evangelization and salvation, they tended to focus on the head as determinative. The dogheads were argued to be beasts, rather than humans, because, while people had rounded heads to observe the heavens, those had oblong heads to look at the earth.[259]

Among the monstrous features in question were legs and feet. As the base for the erect human stature they figured in the determination of human status. There were legendary creatures with feet like leather thongs who crawled on all fours prone as animals; there were some with feet turned backwards, and some with red feet. Others had an odd number of toes—eight (perhaps from a mutated gene through inbreeding). Frequent were the sciopods with one gigantic leg on which they sped. Or its foot shaded their heads from the sun like an umbrella, while they reclined on their backs, a posture perhaps derived from travelers' observations of Hindus in yoga positions. Sciopods were among the most commonly depicted of the odd creatures, a striking subject in the margins of medieval manuscripts and in sculptural programs. They were conservatively reported in the sixteenth century in Cornilius Gemma's *De naturae divinis characterismis* as symbols of the degeneration through Adam's fall of the original human union with God. While the sciopods were often located opposite Europe in the sunny climate of Africa, or in the Antipodes,[260] the global region opposite to Europe, more troublesome were the peoples named for that region. The antipodeans were imagined as heathens living on the globe upside down, foot to foot with Christians. The notion was so disturbing that theologians declared it heretical, while geographers collaborated by defining the equator as a fiery barrier that Adam's descendents could never have crossed.[261]

---

[259] Friedman, *Monstrous Races*, pp. 179-83, 188, 60. For two-headed births, see Eugen Holländer, *Wunder, Wundergeburt, und Wundergestalt: In Einblattdrucken des fünfzehnten bis achtzehnten Jahrhunderts*, Beiträge aus dem Grenzgebiet zwischen Medizingeschichte und Kunst-Kultur-Literatur, 4 (Stuttgart: Ferdinand Enke, 1921), pp. 61-83. For a particular example, consider the political implications of the Siamese twins born at Worms, pp. 336-46; Claude Kappler, "L'interprétation politique du monstre chez Sébastien Brant," in *Monstres et prodiges au temps de la Renaissance*, ed. T. T. Jones-Davies, Université de Paris-Sorbonne, Institut de recherches sur les civilisations de l'Occident moderne, 5 (Paris: Jean Touzot, 1980), pp. 100-9. For an example of artistic interest, see E. H. Gombrich, "The Grotesque Heads," in idem, *The Heritage of Apelles: Studies in the Art of the Renaissance* (London: Phaidon, 1976), pp. 57-76.

[260] Friedman, *Monstrous Races*, pp. 9, 11, 16, 18, 24, 23, 25, 48-49, 135, 136-39, 198, citing Cornilius Gemma, *De naturae divinis characterismis* 1.6; Hodgen, *Early Anthropology*, pp. 38, 66, 53, 57; Wittkower, "Marvels of the East," pp. 160, 162, 182. For Gemma, see Jean Céard, "Tératologie et tératomancie au seizième siècle," in Centre de recherches sur la Renaissance, *Monstres et prodiges*, p. 9. For the sciopods as depicted in central south Africa on the earliest known globe, Martin Behaim's (1459-1507) *Erdapfel*, see Wittkower, "Marvels of the East," pp. 194-95.

[261] Hodgen, *Early Anthropology*, pp. 52, 56; Friedman, *Monstrous Races*, pp. 11, 47-48; William D. McCready, "Isidore, the Antipodeans, and the Shape of the Earth," *Isis* 87 (1996):108-27.

Although Montaigne noted that the Antipodes only used to be heresy,[262] toward the end of the century José de Acosta in his *Historia natural y moral de las Indias* was still repeating the patristic apologetic against them.[263]

Monsters were a complex renaissance subject of anxiety and curiosity, superstition and knowledge.[264] They were popularized in pamphlets for prognostication, satire, and propaganda, both political and religious, but especially they were just exploited for business from a human fascination with the horrible. The fictive tradition oddly merged with personal observation. There developed the systematic study of monstrosities as a branch of natural science: teratology. An increasing literature compiled material since classical sources, arranged it methodically, and interpreted it with new anatomical and biological information. Scientists became assiduous for the pathological causes of monstrosities. Some grouped deformities in a formal system and with encylopedic spirit according to the part of the body in which the abnormality occurred. A progressive attempt was to classify by the biological cause of the monstrosity, from the Aristotelian conviction that the effect was not random but teleological. A pioneer teratologist was Paré,[265] who rose from a surgical practice on the battlefield to become personal physician to four French kings. He was ridiculed for inserting monsters into his medical literature. Physicians accused him of debasing himself to a quadruped, "going on all fours." Yet he asserted that "there are divine things, hidden, and to be wondered at, in monsters—principally in those that occur completely against nature; for in those, philosophical principles are at want, so that one cannot give any definite opinion in their case." He believed that marvels issued from the wrathful will of God to warn of misfortune from some great disorder, as when Pope Julius II caused such calamities in Italy, then fought against Louis XII in a bloody battle near Ravenna. Shortly afterwards a hermaphrodite monster was born there with a horn on its head, two wings, a single foot like a bird of prey, and an eye in its knee. Paré did not know it as an example of symmelus with monopodia, a fetal monster with fused legs. He did cite from ancient theory both Hippocrates and Empedocles for the attribution of monstrous and deformed births to a superabundance, lack, or corruption of seed, or to the indisposition of the womb.[266]

---

262 Montaigne, *Essais* 2.12, p. 572.

263 José de Acosta, *Historia natural y moral de las Indias*, p. 27, citing Lactantius, *Divinae institutiones* 3.24; cited by Anthony Pagden, *The Fall of Natural Man: The American Indian and the Origins of Comparative Ethnology* (Cambridge: Cambridge University Press, 1982), p. 155.

264 Centre de recherches sur la Renaissance, *Monstres et prodiges au temps de la Renaissance*; Gilbert Lascault, *Le monstre dans l'art Occidental: Un problème esthétique* (Paris: Klincksieck, 1973); Wittkower, "Marvels of the East," pp. 190-94.

265 Wittkower, "Marvels of the East," pp. 193, 195, 188-90.

266 Janis L. Pallister, introduction to her translation of Paré, *On Monsters and Marvels* (Chicago: University of Chicago Press, 1982), p. xxv. See Paré, *De monstres* 20, 3; trans., p.

Paré was interested not only in the misconception of monsters but also in their lives and livelihood—if they survived infancy. He related a case of the ingenious use of feet for lack of hands. "Some while ago one could see in Paris a man without any arms, forty years old, or thereabouts, strong and robust, who performed almost all the actions that another might do with his hands." With his stump of a shoulder and his head he could strike a hatchet against a piece of wood as decisively as another man did with his arms. He could snap a carter's whip and perform several other actions. "With his feet he ate, drank, and played cards and dice, which is shown to you in this picture." Alas, he became a robber and a thief—worse a murderer, for which crimes he was executed: hanged then fastened to a wheel.[267]

The man's adroitness would have been of keen interest to that surgeon, for it was Paré who invented the artificial hand. In his *Dix livres de la chirurgie* he considered the "means of accommodating artificial hands, arms, and legs in the place of the extirpated members." His surgical fame was for the substitution of litigation for cauterization in amputations. Although it was "very inhuman" to amputate a limb, he considered, the life of the whole body was more important than the loss of a part. "This remedy is miserable and worthy of compassion, to the patient as well as to the surgeon, but it is the only and last refuge, which one must still prefer to death, which will follow if one seeks other means than section of the mortified part." He was the first to describe the phenomenon of the phantom limb, how amputees complained strongly of extreme pain where the arm had once been. That loss of feeling must be explored with good judgment, he instructed, because many surgeons were deceived by the avowal of patients that they had feeling when pricked, pressed, or otherwise touched. It was like an ordinary person saying that he felt a shirt being pulled off his body, although the garment was insensitive and only contiguous to the flesh. Paré pronounced it a "false feeling," although he conceded that it was "a thing worthy of wonder, and almost incredible to people who have not experienced this." He cautioned surgeons not to falter because of it in their duty of a perfect cure. He had witnessed mortified members cut two or three times because the surgeon stopped at a false and uncertain feeling. Concerning the treatment of the amputated member, he recommended cold astringent and he also supplied prescriptions for powdered remedies. He repeated that it was true that long after amputation patients thought they still had the missing member in its entirety. "This happens to them, as it seems to me, because the nerves withdraw toward their origin and in withdrawing make great pain, almost similar

---

73, with diagnosis at p. 177. For illustrations of the famous Ravenna monster, see p. 7, fig. 2 of the translation, and also Céard's edition, pp. 154-55. Paré, *De monstres* 4, 8. For Empedocles, see *De monstres*, praef., 5, 9, 10. For a biography, see Paule Dumaître, *Ambroise Paré, chirurgien de quatre rois de France* (Paris: Librairie académique Perrin; Fondation Singer-Polignac, 1986).

[267] Paré, *De monstres* 8; trans. Pallister, p. 36, and fig. 25, p. 37.

to the retractions which are are made in spasms." The edition of 1579 inserted an explanation from Galen's *De motu musculorum* that "contraction is the true and proper action of the nerve and muscle, and as for extension, it is not so much action as movement." Paré's remedy was to rub the neck of the amputation and the whole affected part with liniment. Another remedy was of his own invention: the artificial limb. Nature was imitable. In his illustrated description of the iron hand that he devised gears serving each finger were assembled at the back of the hand. The gears turned on an iron rod that passed through their middle. Catches secured the fingers, and devices—more catches, buttons, and springs—opened and closed the fingers and hand. But Paré did not dismiss the reality of the felt pain in missing limbs.[268]

Although as a surgeon he simulated nature with artifice in creating an iron hand and arm, he was frank in exposing those who faked deformity to exploit others. He told in *De monstres* of a scoundrel who had severed a stinking and infected arm from a hanged man and fastened it to his own vest, propped up on a small fork against his side. The man hid his natural arm behind his back in his cloak so that people would mistake the hanged man's arm for his. The faker shouted at the church door for alms, which people gave, supposing the rotted limb his. Since the beggar wiggled the offending arm about, in time it came loose and fell to the ground. He was caught in the act of picking it up with his two good hands. As punishment he was imprisoned, flogged with the corrupt limb hung about his neck, and banished. Paré also reported on "even some who have kidnapped little children and have broken their arms and legs" just to collect pennies as beggars.[269] Such deformed persons were exhibitionists for money. Montaigne reported at his door a manikin "born without arms, who has so well adapted his feet for the service his hands owed him that in truth they have half for-

---

[268] Paré, *Chrirurgie* 7.19, 10, 18; *Ten Books of Surgery with the Magazine of the Instruments Necessary for It*, trans. Robert White Linker and Nathan Womack (Athens: University of Georgia Press, 1969), pp. 143, 134, 142. Galen discussed loss of sensibility and the desire to move a limb in *De Hippocratis et Platonis placitus* 4. The text (ed. Kuhn, 5:611-14) is translated by Siegel, *Galen on the Nervous System*, p. 87. The term "phantom limb" was coined by the neurologist S. Weir Mitchell (1829-1914), who published the phenomenon anonymously as "The Case of George Deadlow," *Atlantic Monthly* (July 1866; rpt. in *The Autobiography of a Quack and Other Stories* [New York: Century, 1905], pp. 81-109), and later in idem, *Injuries of Nerves and Their Consequences*, 1872 (rpt. New York: Dover, 1965), where he cites Paré as precedent, p. 342. Paré is also acknowledged in G. D. Shukla, S. C. Sahu, R. P. Tripathi, and D. K. Gupta, "Phantom Limb: A Phenomenological Study," *British Journal of Psychiatry* 141 (1982):56; Debra Journet, "Phantom Limbs and 'Body-ego': S. Weir Mitchell's George Deadlow," *Mosaic* 23 (1990):89. For a review of the recent scientific literature, see Margaret S. Bowser, "Giving Up the Ghost: A Review of Phantom Limb Phenomena," *Journal of Rehabilitation* 57 (1991):55-62; and for some popular introduction to the research, James Shreeve, "Touching the Phantom," *Discover* 14 (June 1993):34-42; Ronald Melzack, "Phantom Limbs," *Scientific American* 266 (April 1992):120-26.

[269] Paré, *De monstres* 21.23; trans. Pallister, p. 78. For the beggar's trick of feigning a broken or lame leg, see also Erasmus, *Lingua*, p. 83.

gotten their natural function. Moreover he calls them his hands; he carves, he loads a pistol and fires it, he threads his needle, he sews, he writes, he doffs his hat, he combs his hair, he plays cards and dice, and moves them with as much dexterity as any other could do. The money I gave him—for he gains his living by exhibiting himself—he carried off in his foot as we do in our hand."[270]

There were not only monsters without hands: there were also those with too many. Creatures with "innumerable hands" had been observed since the fragmentary speculations of Empedocles,[271] and Isidore of Seville transmitted their classical sources to medieval lore. Their first original mention was by the traveler Marco Polo, who reported that the idols of the island of Zipangri (Japan) had many hands—four, twenty, a hundred—and that the ones with the most hands were esteemed as the truest. Thomas of Cantimpré in his examination of the nature of things insisted on a Hindu provenance for the concept, which he mitigated by moralization. A person with six hands symbolized multiple gifts redeeming faults, from the play on words "pardon—par don." In Giovanni Boccaccio's (1313-75) *Decameron* fortune as a hideous monster appeared as an idol of Zipangri with a hundred arms and hands to give or take worldly goods from people, or to debase or exalt them. One illustration of the manuscript has ten hands, while others show six. The same prodigy was reproduced in a presentation manuscript of Petrarch's *De remediis utriusque fortunae*, with ten arms distributing to the world felicitous and infelicitous gifts.[272]

Paré recorded with illustrations such medically superfluous limbs, four arms or legs, or six digits on the hands or feet. That formation of the sixth finger, he repeated from Aristotle, resulted from an excess of matter during conception.[273] The perfection of measurement, the number ten, had been derived classically from the ten fingers of the human hand,[274] so that an excess or want of fingers deviated from the universal order. In scripture the man with the six fingers was a giant, an enemy to be slain (2 Sam. 21:20). An extra digit was topical. Cajetan preached about it to the pope in the Sistine Chapel, in a sermon on the union of the divine Word with human nature as

---

270 Montaige, *Essais* 1:23; trans. Frame, p. 79. He also reports seeing as a child one "who handled a two-handed sword and a halberd in the crook of his neck for lack of hands, threw them in the air and caught them again, hurled a dagger, and cracked a whip as well as any wagoner in France."

271 Empedocles frag. 60.

272 Jurgis Baltrušaitis, *Le Moyen Âge fantastique: Antiquités et exotismes dans l'art gothique*, Collection Henri Focillon, 3 (Paris: Armand Colin, 1955), pp. 197-200. For the Indian gods, see Partha Mitter, *Much Maligned Monsters: History of European Reactions to Indian Art* (Oxford: Clarendon, 1977), pp. 8-9.

273 Paré, *De monstres* praef.; 4, and fig. 14; 8; and 5, citing Aristotle, *De generatione animalium* 4.4. For the monster with four legs and four arms, see also Wittkower, "Marvels of the East," p. 187; for eight toes or fingers, p. 162.

274 Bernard Schultz, *Art and Anatomy in Renaissance Italy*, Studies in the Fine Arts, Art Theory, 12 (Ann Arbor, Mich.: UMI Research, 1985), p. 41.

the incarnation. The human nature of Christ he likened to the instrument of the Word by analogy with the hands and the tools a craftsman used in productive work. Bodily parts were defined as integral organs because they were properly accommodated to offices and duties. Cajetan distinguished conjoined instruments, which were not integral to human nature. His example was the sixth finger.[275] Christ did not have one, but someone who was mightily to disturb the papacy allegedly did: Anne Boleyn. In the principal Catholic polemic against the English Reformation, *De origine ac progressu schismatis Anglicani*, Nicholas Sander (1530?-81) gave her a sixth finger on the right hand. Although he probably never saw her, his scurrilous detail of deformity portrayed her by an ugly physique as villainous in character. George Wyatt (1554-1624), grandson of the poet who was her lover, reduced the sixth finger to an extra fingernail: "upon the sides of her nail upon one of her fingers, some little show of a nail." He argued that the divine craftsman had left it "as an occasion of greater grace to her hand." It was usually hidden, he observed, by the adjacent fingertip, so that the "blemish" was less noticeable. Wyatt invented a card game between Boleyn and Catherine of Aragon in which the mitigated deformity became evident. His ploy was unlikely, since Henry VIII had already rejected Madame Renée as his mistress just for a discolored spot on her fingernail, considered a bad omen.[276]

The issue of bodily rectitude and integrity became momentous when people accustomed to gawking at the monstrous and the maimed in European streets encountered them through the voyages of discovery in alien cultural contexts.[277] The comparative perspective, an interest in human differences, originated in renaissance archaeology.[278] Classical and medieval thought had included no systematic study of antiquity. Antiquities were valued for their rare material or excellent craft, not for their old age. Ruins were precious and useful not as sources of historical information associated with personages or events but as potential quarries for churches

---

275 Tommaso da Vio, *Oratio* 2, in *Opuscula omnia*, 184a-b. See also Jared Wicks, "Thomism between Renaissance and Reformation," *Archiv für Reformationsgeschichte* 68 (1977):15, 16.

276 Nicholas Sander, *De origine ac progressu schismatis Anglicani* 24-25; George Wyatt, "The Life of Queen Anne Boleigne," pp. 424-28. See Retha M. Warnicke, *The Rise and Fall of Anne Boleyn: Family Politics at the Court of Henry VIII* (Cambridge: Cambridge University Press, 1989), pp. 3, 58, and Appendix A, "The Legacy of Nicholas Sander," pp. 243-47; eadem, "The Physical Deformities of Anne Boleyn and Richard III: Myth and Reality," *Parergon* 4 (1986):139, 141-43.

277 For background, see Mary B. Campbell, *The Witness and the Other World: Exotic European Travel Writing, 400-1600* (Ithaca, N.Y.: Cornell University Press, 1988); Boies Penrose, *Travel and Discovery in the Renaissance, 1420-1620* (Cambridge, Mass.: Harvard University Press, 1955).

278 John Howland Rowe, "The Renaissance Foundations of Anthropology," *American Anthropologist* 67 (1965):1; rpt. in *Readings in the History of Anthropology*, ed. Regna Darnell (New York: Harper and Row, 1974), pp. 61-77.

or fortresses. A sarcophagus became a tomb, an idol a statue. Renaissance builders also destroyed classical ruins, more so than in any other age,[279] but not before renaissance humanists had learned some cultural distinctions between the past and the present from them. From classical monuments—objects as documents—they extrapolated contrasts with current languages, institutions, and customs.[280] Although Herodotus is credited as the father of anthropology,[281] there was no comparative tradition in classical or medieval learning, only a small number of individual authors interested in cultural differences. Herodotus was libeled as a liar until Henri Estienne (1531-98) protested. His only enduring influence before renaissance thought, when Lorenzo Valla (1407-57) translated him, was through a pedagogic topic in rhetoric and ethics. That debated whether there was an absolute standard of honor and shame, considering national variations in customs, especially Herodotus's sensational example of eating dead parents. Megasthenes wrote on the Indians, Tacitus on the Germans, and there were scattered comparative references in geography and natural history, although Pliny lacked any anthropological perspective. In medieval accounts, even in Roger Bacon's *Opus maius*, divergent customs were ascribed to astrological influences, so that the method of study was not comparative behavior but, rather, the latitude or longitude of a region. Ethnographical sources before the Renaissance were not numerous and the best ones were neglected or disbelieved. From Petrarch ruminating on the Roman ruins, to the explorations and excavations of others, antiquity became recognized as remote from renaissance culture, however accessible through its inscriptions. In response to the question of the clergy about his business—studying monuments, copying inscriptions, and recording sculpture and architecture, from Italy to Egypt—Ciriaco de' Pizzicoli (1391-c.1452) replied that he was "restoring the dead to life."[282]

---

279 Roberto Weiss, *The Renaissance Discovery of Classical Antiquity* (Oxford: Basil Blackwell, 1969), pp. 2, 203-4, 205.

280 Rowe, "Renaissance Foundations of Anthropology," p. 1.

281 Kluckhorn, *Anthropology and the Classics*, p. 5, cf. p. 27.

282 Rowe, "Renaissance Foundations of Anthropology," pp. 1, 4-12, 14, citing Pizzicolli, *Itinerarium*, p. 55. For Pizzicolli, see Weiss, *Renaissance Discovery of Classical Antiquity*, pp. 137-42; Richard Stoneman, *Land of Lost Gods: The Search for Classical Greece* (London: Hutchinson, 1987), pp. 22-36. For the renaissance background of modern cultural anthropology, see also Kluckhorn, *Anthropology and the Classics*, p. 23; De Waal Malefijt, *Images of Man*, pp. 46-58. For ruins, see also Vincenzo de Caprio, "*Sub tanta diruta mole*: Il fascino delle rovine di Roma nel quattro e cinquecento," in *Poesia e poetica delle rovine di Roma: Momenti e problemi*, ed. idem, Quaderni di studi romani, 47 (Rome: Istituto di studi romani, 1987), pp. 21-52; Angelo Mazzoco, "Linee di sviluppo dell'antiquaria del rinascimento,' *Rovine di Roma*, pp. 53-71; Paul Zucker, *Fascination of Decay: Ruins: Relic—Symbol—Ornament* (Ridgewood, N.J.: Gregg, 1968), pp. 11-43; *Zwischen Phantasie und Wirklichkeit: Römische Ruinen in Zeichnungen des sechzehnte bis neunzehnte Jahrhunderts* (Mainz: Phillip von Zahern, 1988). For antiquarianism, see also Eric Cochrane, *Historians and Historiography in the Italian Renaissance* (Chicago: University of Chicago Press, 1981), pp. 423-44.

Renaissance voyagers on discovery confronted a more immediate cultural challenge than ancient monuments: strange people alive. Travel and discovery fostered the development of anthropology, a discipline derived from the humanities and the natural sciences. The antecedents of modern field manuals date to the sixteenth century, although neither anthropology nor ethnology was yet a scholarly discipline. Questions were designed to recover cultural, social, and psychological data on colonial possessions for governmental agencies. Or inquiries occurred in the guides, pamphlets, and books of travelers.[283] When Christopher Columbus (1446-1506) wrote in his journal about his first day ashore on a Caribbean isle, he had not discovered prehistoric human hands painted on caves but living natives whose palpitating bodies were painted black, or white and red.[284] And, when Alonso de Molino compiled a dictionary for Castilian-Nahuatl, he could find no equivalent for *hombre*, "human being," only for social groups and particular types, such as "man with big feet," and "man with six fingers on his hands," or "man with six toes on his feet."[285] Although physical anthropology was delayed as a subject, since classical antiquity offered little precedent for such comparison,[286] renaissance thinkers did have a moral compulsion for considering the bodies of others.

Aristotle, whose *Politica* justified for theologians the practice of slavery, had stated that bodies were distinguished by nature as free or slave: as upright for politics or as strong for labor.[287] Humans were hierarchically ordered: soul over body, intellect over emotion, male over female. The same natural principle applied to slaves, who resembled body because they apprehended, but did not possess, reason—they were like base animals. "The intention of nature therefore," he wrote, "is to make the bodies also of freemen and of slaves different—the latter strong for necessary service, the former erect and unserviceable for such occupations, but serviceable for a life of citizenship."[288] It was typical since classical antiquity that the heads of slaves were never straight but, rather, crooked at the neck.[289] The moral contest for the right to exploit or enslave the natives of the Americas necessarily argued about their mortal bodies, not only their immortal souls. In the fashion of applying the ancient legends about the odd creatures to the

283 See Don D. Fowler, "Notes on Inquiries in Anthropology," in *Toward a Science of Man: Essays in the History of Anthropology*, ed. Timothy H. H. Thoreşen (The Hague: Mouton, 1973), pp. 16-17.

284 Christopher Columbus, *The Voyages of Christopher Columbus*, p. 149; cited by Hodgen, *Early Anthropology*, p. 17.

285 Alonso de Molina, *Vocabulario en lengua castellana y mexicana*, fol. 90v; cited by Pagden, *Fall of Natural Man*, p. 17.

286 Rowe, "Renaissance Foundations of Anthropology," p. 1.

287 Pagden, *Fall of Natural Man*, p. 45, citing Aristotle, *Politica* 1254b.

288 Aristotle, *Politica* 1254b; trans. Rackham (New York: G. P. Putnam's Sons, 1932), p. 23.

289 Bremmer, "Walking, Standing, and Sitting," p. 23.

new situations Las Casas asserted that the true barbarian was very rare, as rare as a man born lame or those creatures with "the soles of their feet upwards," the sciopods. The theologian Francisco de Vitoria (1486?-1546) argued that a cripple was an aberration of nature, because his gait was contrary to the natural way of walking, just as a simpleton was contrary to the natural mode of reasoning. But the Amerindians did have a certain use of reason, he countered, manifested in their cities, marriage, rulers, laws, industry, commerce, and even religion. God could create a limbless person, but such a creature was still human if he possessed a rational mind. The Amerindians were like the limbless.[290]

A more serious objection to their humanity arose with reports of something they did with human limbs: eat them. Even the Scythians were not cannibals, although they were careless with the limbs of their victims, once they had sacrificed them by slitting their throats over a vessel. As Herodotus reported, "They cut off the slain men's right arms and hands and throw these into the air. . . . The arm lies where it has fallen, and the body apart from it."[291] Pietro Martire d'Anghiera (1455-1526) related in *De orbe novo* at the beginning of the sixteenth century how the foreign "cannibals" ate raw the arms and legs and intestines of their enemies, then salted the rest of the body for later consumption like ham hocks.[292] Relations of a Jesuit missionary among the Tupinambá in Brazil mentioned seeing severed human hands being prepared for eating, smoked on a moquem or cooked in an earthenware pot. Another lurid account told how those cannibals "eat their victims down to the last fingernail."[293]

---

290 Pagden, *Fall of Natural Man*, pp. 133, 68, 95, citing Las Casas, *Argumentum*, fol. 17v; Francisco de Vitoria, *Relectio de Indis*, p. 29; *Comentarios a la Secunda secundae de Santo Tomás*, 3:11.

291 Herodotus, *Historiae* 4.62; *Herodotus*, trans. A. D. Godley, 4 vols. (London: Heinemann, 1921-25), 2:261.

292 Pietro Martire d'Anghiera, *De orbe novo decades octo* 1.1; cited from English translation by Hodgen, *Early Anthropology*, p. 30.

293 Juan de Aspilcueta Navarro, in *Cartas dos primeiros jesuitas do Brasil*, 1:282, 182, 183; cited by Donald W. Forsyth, "The Beginnings of Brazilian Anthropology: Jesuits and Tupinambá Cannibalism," *Journal of Anthropological Research* 39 (1983):163. José de Anchieta, *Cartas dos primeiros jesuitas do Brasil*, 2:113; cited by Forsyth, "Brazilian Anthropology," p. 155; Pagden, *Fall of Natural Man*, p. 83. For illustrations of the Tupinambá slaughtering, boiling, and eating the prisoner, with various legs and hands visible, see Bernadette Bucher, *Icon and Conquest: A Structural Analysis of the Illustrations of de Bry's "Great Voyages,"* trans. Basia Miller Gulati (Chicago: University of Chicago Press, 1981), pls. 1-5; *Discovering the New World: Based on the Works of Theodore de Bry*, ed. Michael Alexander (London: London, 1976), pp. 113-14, 121. For Montaigne on the reports of cannibalism in *Essais* 1.31, see Claude Rawson, "'Indians' and Irish: Montaigne, Swift, and the Cannibal Question," *Modern Language Quarterly* 53 (1992):299-363; David Quint, "A Reconsideration of Montaigne's 'Des cannibales,'" *Modern Language Quarterly* 51 (1990):459-89; François Rigolot, "Montaigne: European Reader of America," trans. Sophie Hawkes, *Diogenes* 164 (1993):1-12. For comparative ethnology on arms, hands, and nails, see in the seventeenth century Bulwer, *Anthropometamorphosis* 18.

Fingernails were not supposed to be eaten—not with corpses attached. The habit of biting one's own fingernails was an emotional sign of anger or concentration, jealousy or desire, embarrassment or sorrow.[294] It was a disturbance classically ascribed to a vice: wrath.[295] Polite renaissance society even disdained to use hands *for* eating, although the fork was still a rare item of tableware. In its earliest description, in a fifteenth-century inventory, there was "a small crystal fork for green ginger, mounted in gold." From such limited use for candied fruits or preserves larger forks were developed for taking meat from a common dish and placing it on an individual trencher or for steadying the joint during carving. The arrival of forks for eating and serving was earliest in Italy, where they were two-pronged and hafted of silver—engraved, embossed, inlaid, even with the familial coat of arms. Their use was not general in Europe before the end of the sixteenth century, when it was perhaps occasioned by the fashion for enormous ruffs. Forks were items of luxury, with the silversmith, jeweler, ivory-carver, steelworker, potter, or glassman involved in crafting the handles. In the eighteenth century the fork was still a newfangled item, since it was argued that the hand could be as clean as a fork.[296]

Rules were articulated in manuals on courtesy for the necessary use of the clean hand at the common board. A diner was not to thrust greedily into a platter just upon sitting down—wolves did that. Such animalistic feeding offended deference to superiors or elders; besides, it was dangerous: one might burn one's hand on hot food. Nor was it nice to poke about the platter searching for a choice morsel.[297] A knife or fork should transfer the food to the fingers—three fingers precisely—or to a plate. To grasp bread in the palm and break it with the fingertips was the affected practice of courtiers. It should be cut properly with a knife. To pick clean an eggshell one was not to use the fingernails and thumb but a small knife. To take salt the fingers should not be thrust into the cellar; again a small knife, or a plate, was to be used.[298] The thumb had its particular rules. In serving a plate it was to be kept on the rim of the dish—the better to set it down in place on the board. In offering a cup the thumb was never boorishly to touch the upper

---

294 Betty J. Baüml and Franz H. Baüml, *A Dictionary of Gestures* (Metuchen, N.J.: Scarecrow, 1975), p. 110; Carl Sittl, *Die Gebärden der Griechen und Römer* (Leipzig, 1890), pp. 17-18.

295 Horace, *Epodes* 5.48; Persius, *Saturae* 5.162.

296 *Knives and Forks in the Netherlands, 1500-1800* (The Hague: Gemeentmuseum, 1972), introduction n. p.; C. T. P. Bailey, *Knives and Forks* (London: Medici Society, 1927), pp. 5, 9, 10. There was but one fork in the inventory of a bishop of Utrecht. Pieter Spierenburg, *Elites and Etiquette: Mentality and Social Structure in the Early Modern Northern Netherlands*, Centrum voor Maatschappijgeschiedenis, 9 (Rotterdam: Erasmus Universiteit, 1981), p. 8.

297 Bonvesin da Riva, *Da quinquaginta curialitabus ad mensam* 21.85-88; Erasmus, *De civilitate* 1039; and for the adaptation, see Spierenburg, *Elites and Etiquette*, p. 6.

298 Erasmus, *De civilitate* 1039, 1038, 1040.

edge of its bowl; a cup should be held beneath and presented with one hand.[299] Food was not to be offered or drink poured with the left hand.[300] One manual stated that food should be eaten ambidextrously. If the dish was on the left side, it was to be eaten with the right hand; and vice versa.[301]

Other uses of the hand at table involved sociability, rather than eating. From the earliest Italian treatise on etiquette for meals, Bonvesin da Riva's medieval verse *De quinquaginta curialitabus ad mensam*, to the cosmopolitan renaissance prose of Erasmus's *De civilitate*,[302] there developed rules of manual comportment toward others and toward oneself. "When sitting down," Erasmus wrote, "have both hands on the table, not clasped together nor on the plate. It is bad manners to have one or both hands on one's lap as some do."[303] Servants were also regulated in deportment. In Della Casa's *Galateo* they were not to tuck their meticulously clean hands in shirts or behind backs but to maintain them "in sight and above suspicion."[304] There seems to have been fear or suspicion of concealed hands in company. Knives, with a short broad blade tapering to a sharp point, were in the fifteenth to sixteenth century an item newly brought to table. Ordinary citizens carried on their girdle a knife of multiple purposes; only princes and nobles of rank owned special knives for cutting food. Whether precious or simple in material, they were in Erasmus's native Netherlands crafted with great care and with individual character. The knife was a personal possession carried about, with a lingering medieval fear of poisoning. Until the middle of the sixteenth century, cutlers were bound to fill the hollows of the stamped mark on the blade (the signature) with brass, lest someone else fill it with poison.[305] Erasmus instructed against playing with the dinner knife. As for twisting one's arms behind the back, that was the mark of an idler and

---

299 Bonvesin da Riva, *Ad mensam* 42.169-72; 43.173-76.

300 Erasmus, *De civilitate* 1041.

301 "Dit is hoversheit: Uit een handschrift van het klooster Bursveld (in Westfalen)," cited by Spierenburg, *Elites and Etiquette*, p. 5.

302 For Bonvesin da Riva, a Milanese friar of the late 13th century, see Crane, *Italian Social Customs*, pp. 351-52. For Erasmus's treatise, see Franz Bierlaire, "Erasmus at School: The *De civilitate morum puerilium libellus*," in *Essays on the Works of Erasmus*, ed. Richard L. DeMolen (New Haven, Conn.: Yale University Press, 1978), pp. 239-51; Norbert Elias, *The Civilizing Process*, trans. Edmund Jephcott (New York: Urizen, 1978), 1:53-58, 70-79; Roger Chartier, "From Text to Manners, A Concept and Its Books: *Civilité* between Aristocratic Distinction and Popular Appropriation," in idem, *The Cultural Uses of Print*, trans. Lydia G. Cochrane (Princeton, N.J.: Princeton University Press, 1987), pp. 71-109; Bierlaire, "Erasme, la table, et les manières de table," in *Pratiques et discours alimentaires à la Renaissance*, Actes du colloque de Tours de mars 1979, Centre d'études supérieures de la Renaissance, ed. Jean-Claude Margolin and Robert Sauzet (Paris: Maisonneuve et Larose, 1982), pp. 147-60. For some adaptations of Erasmus's manual, see Spierenburg, *Elites and Etiquette*, pp. 5-6, 8.

303 Erasmus, *De civilitate* 1038.

304 Della Casa, *Galateo* 42; trans. Konrad Eisenbichler and Kenneth R. Bartlett, Centre for Reformation and Renaissance Studies Translation Series, 2 (Toronto: Centre for Reformation and Renaissance Studies, 1986), p. 9, with my change.

305 See *Knives and Forkss*, introduction, n. p.; Bailey, *Knives and Forks*, p. 1, and for carving as part of table service, pp. 2-3.

thief. Nor was a diner even to gesticulate with his hands, the sign of an unstable mind.[306] A polite person did not lean forward on the table as a prop or stretch his arms along its surface.[307] He did not pet the household cats and dogs, so familiar at table—even on the table—in depictions of banquets. As the friar da Riva versified:

> Stroke not with hands,
> As long as you at at the board, cat or dog.
> A courteous man is not warranted in stroking brutes
> With the hands with which he touches the dishes.[308]

He did not elbow the person seated beside him or fidget in his own seat either but maintained his body, as Erasmus wrote, "upright and evenly balanced."[309]

A polite diner not only kept his hands to himself but he also kept his hands off himself. Della Casa blamed as unmannerly first of all "dirty, foul, or repulsive things, which were not to be done in public, or even mentioned or recalled." There was "an indecent habit, practised by some people who, in full view of others, place their hands on whatever part of their body it pleases them."[310] His allusion was likely to the resting of the hand on the groin, which gesture some thought elegant or military but Erasmus agreed was loathsome.[311] A gentleman also did not jab his fingers into his ears to clear wax. As da Riva admonished,

> The man who is eating must not be cleaning,
> By scraping with his fingers at any foul part.[312]

He did not poke his fingers into his nostrils to clear mucus either but, rather, used a handkerchief.[313] Nor did he scratch himself.[314] A courteous diner especially did not scratch his head (for lice); but, as one author qualified that

---

306 Erasmus, *De civilitate* 1040, 1035, 1040.

307 Bonvesin da Riva, *Ad mensam* 6.26-28; Erasmus, *De civilitate* 1040.

308 Bonvesin da Riva, *Ad mensam* 33.133-36; *Italian Courtesy Books: Fra Bonvicino da Riva's "Fifty Courtesies for the Table" (Italian and English) with Other Translations and Elucidations*, trans. William Michael Rossetti, Early English Text Society, e.s., 8 (London, 1869), p. 27 (modernization mine). For dogs on the table, see Limbourg brothers, January from the calendar of the Très riches heures du Duc de Berry, before 1416, fol. 1v, Chantilly, Musée Condé; reproduced in Millard Meiss, *French Painting in the Time of Jean de Berry: The Late Fourteenth Century and the Patronage of the Duke*, 2 vols., National Gallery of Art Kress Foun-dation Studies in the History of European Art, 2 (London: Phaidon, 1967), 2:pl.489.

309 Erasmus, *De civilitate* 1038; trans. McGregor, p. 281.

310 Della Casa, *Galateo* 12, 13; trans. Eisenbichler and Bartlett, p. 5.

311 Erasmus, *De civilitate* 1035.

312 Bonvesin da Riva, *Ad mensam* 32.128-32; trans. Rossetti, p. 27 (modernization mine).

313 Bonvesin da Riva, *Ad mensam* 31.125-28; Erasmus, *De civilitate* 1033-34. See also *cubito emungere*, in Erasmus, *Adagia* 2.4.8.

314 Della Casa, *Galateo* 293, 42.

prohibition, only "if someone can see it."[315] Erasmus explained in his *Adagia* that scratching the head was the sign of effeminate men.[316] Most important, perhaps, a polite diner did not put his hands or fingers into his own mouth, unless conveying food to it. Da Riva wrote:

> As long as you are eating with men of breeding,
> Put not your fingers into your mouth to pick your teeth.
> He who sticks his fingers into his mouth, before he has done eating
> Eats not, with my good will, on the platter with me.[317]

Erasmus developed the courtesy. "Food particles should be removed from the teeth, not with a knife or with the nails, in the manner of dogs or cats, and not with a napkin, but with a toothpick of mastic wood, or with a feather, or with small bones taken from the drumsticks of cocks or hens."[318] Della Casa also advised against rubbing the teeth with the fingers.[319]

Just as the fingers were not to clean the mouth, so the mouth was not to clean the fingers. In verse:

> You must not lick your fingers.
> He who thrusts them into his mouth cleans them nastily.
> The man who thrusts into his mouth his besmeared fingers,
> His fingers are none the cleaner, but rather the nastier.[320]

Erasmus concurred. "It is equally impolite to lick greasy fingers or to wipe them on one's tunic: you should wipe them with a napkin or cloth."[321] An adaptation toward the end of the century, *Regel der Duytsche schoolmeesters*, specified that said cloth was not to be the tablecloth.[322] Della Casa was more finicky. He complained about people who at table soiled their hands to their elbows but he offered slight remedy, for even the napkin was to be neat. "A well-mannered man must therefore take heed not to smear his fingers so much that his napkin is left soiled, for its is a disgusting thing to see." Fingers were not to be wiped clean in the bread either.[323]

---

315 "De bouc van Seden," in *Denkmäler altniederländischer Sprache und Literatur*, ed. Eduard Kausler, 3 vols. (Tübingen, 1840-66), 2:582-83; cited by Spierenburg, *Elites and Etiquette*, p. 5.

316 Erasmus, *De civilitate* 1040; *Unico digitulo scalpit caput, Summo digito caput scalpere*, *Adagia* 1.8.34, 35. Against scratching the head, picking the ears, stroking the face, or rubbing the back of the head, see also *De civilitate* 1041.

317 Bonvesin da Riva, *Ad mensam* 34.137-40; trans. Rossetti, p. 27 (modernization mine).

318 Erasmus, *De civilitate* 1034, 1040; trans. McGregor, p. 276.

319 Della Casa, *Galateo* 306.

320 Bonvesin da Riva, *Ad mensam* 35.141-44; trans. Rossetti, p. 27 (modernization mine).

321 Erasmus, *De civilitate* 1038; trans. McGregor, p. 283.

322 D. Adriaenz. Valcoogh, *Regel der Duytsche schoolmeesters*, p. 52; cited by Spierenburg, *Elites and Etiquette*, p. 8. He also added to the list of not picking the nose or teeth, nor scratching the head, not catching fleas.

323 Della Casa, *Galateo* 40-41; trans. Eisenbichler and Bartlett, p. 9.

A final rule was to wash the hands, drink a choice wine, then after the meal to wash the hands a bit more to clean the grease.[324]

During the development of manual manners for dining the matter of the cannibals discovered eating hands was blamed on a global theory of the sense of touch. Cultural diversity was never associated with racial distinctions, for racialism was virtually non-existent. Even the issue of pigmentation was whitewashed by the confidence that variation in complexion was due to the difference of exposure to the sun of skins that had all been originally white. Blacks and Orientals were thus included in Adam's family with human dignity. Even the inimical Arabs and Jews were not discriminated against by Christians on the basis of race, as Semites, but of religion. Peoples were differentiated as "nations"; the term "race" had a zoological connotation. Humans were believed monogenetic in origin and homogeneous in descent, thus not subject to zoological divisions or terms.[325] Cultural diversity was traced, rather, to the influence of physical environment—geographical location, climate, and terrain—as determinative of actions, psychology, and sometimes physique. The classical argument revolved around the Scythians, who lived in cold climates and therefore had hot humors, which made them cruel and stupid.[326] Like diverse peoples, the monstrous creatures were determined so by the sense of touch, not in its organic definition as hands but through what hands essentially felt: temperature.

Medieval maps visually displayed a cosmology and a theology in their disposition of the zones and continents. Such maps were not only scientific but also catechismal, appearing in stained-glass windows and on floor mosaics of churches, and in bibles, psalters, and other religious books. In the type that developed to illustrate Macrobius's commentary on Cicero's *Somnium Scipionis* the sphere was divided into excessively hot and cold regions—polar and equatorial—with temperate zones mediate. Only the temperate belts were regarded inhabitable by humans. As did the ancients, medieval people thought typologically, not racially, about one another. The concept—as old as the Hippocratic literature on airs, waters, and places—was expressed by Isidore of Seville in his encyclopedia, where climate determined the basic physical characteristics of appearance, skin color, and stature, as well as the emotional dispositions. The uncommon appearance and habits of the odd creatures were explained by locating them at the global extremities. The sciopods, whom Pliny had reported as living in In-

---

324 Bonvesin da Riva, *Ad mensam* 50.201-4.

325 Hodgen, *Early Anthropology*, pp. 213-14. See also Frank M. Snowden, Jr., *Before Color Prejudice: The Ancient View of Blacks* (Cambridge, Mass.: Harvard University Press, 1983); Y. A. Dauge, *La barbare: Recherches sur la conception romaine de la barbarie et de la civilisation*, Collection Latomus, 176 (Brussels: Latomus, 1981), pp. 468-71. For Hodgen's history of anthropology, see James A. Boon, "Comparative De-enlightenment: Paradox and Limits in the History of Ethnology," *Daedalus* 109 (1980):73-91.

326 Pagden, *Fall of Natural Man*, pp. 137-38.

dia, were transferred as that country became more familiar, less exotic, to the hot Antipodes at the southern edge of the world. Extreme creatures were located in extreme places. They were distanced from the center defined as Jerusalem, and in one map they even appear at Christ's left hand.[327]

In thought about the environment physical appearance and moral disposition were dependent on place. Zonal maps, which separated distinct climates by definite bodies of water, explained the distinct features of various peoples and creatures. Place influenced the inhabitants of a region astrally, for there was a dominant planet for each climate, and environmentally through the prevalent medical theory of the balance or imbalance of humors. A temperate zone assured normal growth through a balance of physiological humors. A climate of nothing extreme, nothing wild promoted physical health and moral and social well-being. A moderate climate was advantageous, while an extreme one disturbed mind and soul. In the middle climate was a healthful mixture of hot and cold elements that produced people of medium stature, even complexion, gentle customs, clear senses, and good government. Albert the Great wrote in *De natura locorum* that mediate climates produced strong people, who were handsome and brave, with long life, good customs, and social justice. They were "noble of stature." European peoples vied to be the middle people of superior climate, thus superior morality.[328]

The superiority of a culture had, ever since the topic of the Greeks versus the barbarians, legitimated its oppression of others.[329] So a nation like the Scythians was revived rhetorically for comparison with the ferocity of the Mexicans. The topic of temperature was advanced as proof that they were naturally slaves.[330] A savage climate bred savage people, since hot and cold temperatures produced crudity and violence.[331] Apologists for the humanity of the natives of the Americas, arguing against their exploitation as enslaved beasts of burden, were thus careful to praise their fortunate environment. Description of the newly discovered continents was not superficially a matter of geographical documentation but of moral argumentation with political consequence. Through temperature the sense of touch determined character and behavior.

---

327 Friedman, *Monstrous Races*, pp. 38-43. Hippocrates, *De aere, locis, et aquis*, which he claims was generally not known in the West before the ninth century, p. 219 n. 18; but for its translation into Latin in the late fifth to early sixth century, see Pearl Kibre, "Hippocrates latinus," *Traditio* 31(1975):123-24. Macrobius, *Commentarium in "Somnium Scipionis"* 5.

328 Friedman, *Monstrous Races*, pp. 50-54.

329 Edith Hall, *Inventing the Barbarian: Greek Self-Definition through Tragedy* (Oxford: Clarendon, 1989).

330 Pagden, *Fall of Natural Man*, p. 117, cf. p. 152. For Herodotus in the sixteenth century, see François Hartog, *The Mirror of Herodotus: The Representation of the Other in the Writing of History*, trans. Janet Lloyd, New Historicism, 5 (Berkeley and Los Angeles: University of California Press, 1988), pp. 306-9.

331 Hartog, *Mirror of Herodotus*, p. 52, citing Pliny, *Historia naturalis* 2.80.

In his only comment on his work on the Sistine Chapel ceiling Michelangelo characterized himself as uncivilized. His caudate sonnet complained:

> In front of me my hide is stretching out
> and, to wrinkle up behind, it forms a knot,
> and I am bent like a Syrian bow.[332]

Michelangelo also applied the comparison with the Syrian bow in another sonnet for the curve of the eyebrows in a burlesque praise of some woman's beauty.[333] But his personal comparison was more than comedic: barbaric. The archers of antiquity were never Greeks or Romans, always foreigners, defined as uncivilized. The best marksmen were the Scythians,[334] not the Syrians, so that Michelangelo implied a poor comparison. Not only were the Scythians handsomely depicted with bow and quiver on Attic vases,[335] but also they were themselves artists and craftsmen of distinguished technical skill.[336] Bows were the almost exclusive weapon in ancient Syria, a usage from Africa where shafted projectiles were preferred.[337] No bows dating from antiquity have been discovered in Syria, however, and their depiction on native monuments is very rare. There are a fair number of Egyptian paintings and reliefs commemorating Syrian events, however, and on those monuments Syrian hunters or archers carry two types: a long composite bow of the Hurrian type and a simple bow similar to the Egyptian doubly convex one. On a Roman monument, on the emperor Trajan's column in his

---

332 Michelangelo, *Rime* 5; trans. Saslow, p. 70. He also used bow in general as symbolic of love and of force. Clements, *Poetry of Michelangelo*, p. 277.

333 Michelangelo, *Rime* 20. For Francesco Berni's influence on this image, see Clements, *Poetry of Michelangelo*, pp. 92, 259.

334 For Scythian archers, see A. Plassart, "Les archers d'Athènes," *Revue des études grecques* 26 (1913):151-213; Timothy Long, *Barbarians in Greek Comedy* (Carbondale: Southern Illinois University Press, 1986), pp. 105-7; Hall, "The Archer Scene in Aristophanes' *Thesmophoriazusae*," *Philologus* 133 (1989):38-54. For the Scythians, see Renate Rolle, *The World of the Scythians*, trans. Gayna Walls (Berkeley and Los Angeles: University of California Press, 1989); for their social status, Oscar Jacob, *Les esclaves publics à Athènes*, Bibliothèque de la faculté de philosophie et lettres de l'Université de Liége, 35 (Paris: H. Vaillant-Carmane, 1928), pp. 53-78. For the Hellene-barbarian antithesis, see Hall, *Inventing the Barbarian*, especially on Scythian archers, pp. 138-39; Long, *Barbarians in Greek Comedy*, pp. 129-56; Steven W. Hirsch, *The Friendship of the Barbarians: Xenophon and the Persian Empire* (Hanover, N.H.: University Press of New England for Tufts University, 1985); Anastasios G. Nikolaides, "*Hellenikos-barbarikos*: Plutarch on Greek and Barbarian Characteristics," *Wiener Studien* 20 (1986):229-44; Reimar Müller, "Hellenen und 'Barbaren' in der griechischen Philosophie," in *Menschenbild und Humanismus der Antike: Studien zur Geschichte der Literatur und Philosophie* (Frankfurt: Röderberg, 1981), pp. 111-34.

335 M. F. Vos, *Scythian Archers in Archaic Attic Vase-Painting*, Archaeologica traiectina, 6 (Groningen: J. B. Wolters, 1963). See also Harvey Allen Shapiro, "Amazons, Thracians, and Scythians," *Greek, Roman and Byzantine Studies* 24 (1983):110-12.

336 See M. I. Artamanov, *Treasures from Scythian Tombs in the Hermitage Museum, Leningrad* (London: Thames and Hudson, 1969).

337 Manfred Korfmann, "The Sling as a Weapon," *Scientific American*, 229 (October 1973):42.

forum, there is among the reliefs a member of the Syrian auxiliary. He holds a short, composite segment bow with its horns bent forward. All of the bows depicted there appear quite small, with the Syrian and the Scythian bows about the same size. But they are distinguished in design: the Syrian bow is in an unbroken curve, while the Scythian examples have a sunken grip.[338]

Trajan's column was a subject of renaissance interest at the papal court and of intent copying and imitation among painters and sculptors.[339] Michelangelo could readily have known the example. By his comparison of himself as a working artist to a Syrian bow he disparaged his skill, for Syrian archers were of no distinction. "David with his sling, and I with my bow," wrote Michelangelo on a sheet of sketches of his Davidic sculpture.[340] The two weapons were parallel and equal in war since the eighth millennium B.C., and ancient art depicted slingers and archers in tandem.[341] Da Vinci had contributed to theoretical mechanics on the crossbow.[342] Michelangelo's comparison was practical and artistic: with the sculptor's manual drill (*archetto*), a metal drill twirled by a taut string as the handle of the bow was moved back and forth.[343] In his poem about his work on the Sistine Chapel ceiling the bow is not a drill or other tool, however, but his very body—strung out and stretched out to its limits of endurance. Art is embodied as tense physical labor.

Although his body could be stretched as a bowed instrument for art, its proper stature by tradition was erect. The popular notion that Michelangelo

---

338 Gad Rausig, *The Bow: Some Notes on its Origin and Development* (Lund: Berlingska Boktryckeriet, 1967), pp. 90-91, 100-1, citing Conrad Cichorius, *Die Reliefs der Traianssäule*, 2 vols. (Berlin: Walter de Gruyter, 1927), but in this edition, 1:111-21. For the auxiliaries, see Lino Rossi, *Trajan's Column and the Dacian Wars*, trans. J. M. C. Toynbee (London: Thames and Hudson, 1971), pp. 102-3; in general, Anne-Marie Leander Touati, *The Great Trajanic Frieze: The Study of a Monument and of the Mechanisms of Message Transmission in Roman Art*, Skrifter Utgivra av Svenska Institutet i Rom, 4, 45 (Stockholm: Paul Aströms, 1987). For a relief comparing Syrian and Scythian bows, see *La colonna traiana*, ed. Salvatore Settis (Turin: Giulio Einaudi, 1988), pl. 30 (XXIV, 59-61). Unavailable to me was James E. Parker, *The Forum of Trajan at Rome*, 3 vols. (Berkeley and Los Angeles: University of California Press, 1997).

339 Giovanni Agosti and Vincenzo Farinella, "Nuove richerche sulla colonna traiana nel Rinascimento," in *La colonna traiana*, ed. Settis, pp. 549-89. For a particular, see Giangiacomo Martines, "La colonna Traiana e chiaroscuro della sala di Costantino in Vaticano: Note sul monocromo," *Bollettino d'arte* 71 (1986):31-36.

340 Michelangelo, *Rime* A3; trans. Saslow, p. 504. For the polarity of the sling and bow, see Korfmann, "Sling as a Weapon," p. 42. Slingers are depicted on Trajan's column, although the weapon is held down, whereas in ancient orthographs it is raised over the head. See idem, "Die Waffe Davids: Ein Beitrag zur Geschichte der Fernwaffen und zu den Anfägen organisierten Kriegerischen Verhaltens," *Saeculum* 37 (1986):129.

341 Korfmann, "Sling as a Weapon," pp. 35, 42.

342 Vernard Foley and Werner Soedel, "Leonardo's Contributions to Theoretical Mechanics," *Scientific American* 255 (September 1986):108-13, with reference to the crossbow in Codex Madrid I.

343 Seymour, *Michelangelo's "David": A Search for Identity* (Pittsburgh, Pa.: University of Pittsburgh Press, 1967), pp. 7-8, and see figs. 3 and 4.

executed the ceiling fresco flat on his back on a scaffold is mistaken. In the left corner of his study for God in the Creation of Adam there is a sketch of another figure on an arched structure with steps ending at a platform. He positions his left foot on the bottom step, his right with bent knee on the third step. In his left hand he holds an object, possibly a pot of paint, while he extends his right as if he were painting the surface of a lunette. Another figure is sketched reclining on the only spot in the project that would have required Michelangelo to paint lying down—on the upper deck of the scaffolding—to execute the mask above each of the ancestral name tablets.[344] A diagrammatic sketch, it was probably done impromptu to demonstrate to the foreman the consequences of constructing the platform and steps of the scaffolding too close to the vault. The central platform, the place of maximum activity, had to accommodate Michelangelo's height at full stretch with brush in hand. Any less room would have inconvenienced the artist and the mason. The crouching figure in the sketch demonstrates the hypothetical situation of boarding placed too close to the ceiling. Michelangelo logically painted the ceiling standing up and at the optimal distance from the surface for the application. The renaissance remark that he painted it *resupinus* did not mean "lying down" but "bent backwards." As Vasari wrote, "These frescoes were done with the greatest discomfort, for he had to stand there working with his head tilted backwards."[345]

In the very sketch appended to the sonnet comparing his body as artist to a Syrian bow Michelangelo drew himself upright on the scaffold, his arm stretched upwards in the act of painting. He thus fulfilled his portrayal of Adam created erectile and stirring. Michelangelo's composition of the Creation of Adam is not ideally contemplative but really active. Although Adam gazes into the face of God, God does not reciprocate his gaze. The omission is significant. Only in primates and humans is gazing an affiliating, rather than aggressive, signal. Mutual gazing appears early in human infancy and may be the origin of intersubjectivity.[346] It was in renaissance art an amatory motif.[347] It is in Michelangelo's fresco of the Creation of Eve that Creator and creature see eye-to-eye.[348] In the scene of the Creation of

[344] Hartt, "The Evidence for the Scaffolding of the Sistine Ceiling," *Art History* 3 (1982): 280. Drawing of Michelangelo on scaffolding, Uffizi, Florence, 18722Fr; reproduced, pl. 6; Clements, *Poetry of Michelangelo*, pl. 2.

[345] Mancinelli, "Michelangelo at Work," in *Sistine Chapel: Michelangelo Rediscovered*, pp. 222, 232, 234, citing Paolo Giovio on *resupinus*, in *Scritti d'arte del cinquecento*, ed. Paola Barocchi, 3 vols., Letteratura italiana, storia e testi, 32 (Milan: R. Ricciardi, 1971-73), 1:10; Vasari, *Vita di Michelangelo*, 1:38, trans. Bondanella and Bondanella, p. 443.

[346] Michael Argyle and Mark Cook, *Gaze and Mutual Gaze* (Cambridge: Cambridge University Press, 1976), pp. 4, 33.

[347] Robert Baldwin, "'Gates Pure and Shining and Serene': Mutual Gazing as an Amatory Motif in Western Literature and Art," *Renaissance and Reformation* 10 (1986):23-48.

[348] Also noted by Hartt, *Sistine Chapel*, 2:12.

Adam, God looks intently, rather, at the man's hand extended toward him. Not the human eye, but the human hand, is the focus of divine attention.

What is a hand but a divine design? and what is a hand for but to design divinely? The concept was important from the teleology of Galen. Hands had not been without praise. Ambrose in his hexameral homilies recognized their utility and even their sanctity. Hands, with the strong muscles of the forearm, were able for action and adaptable for holding objects in their long fingers. Humans thus acquired an aptitude for work, for elegance in writing, for serving the mouth with food, for eminence in great deeds, for the ritual dispensation of divine mysteries through the mediation of prayer and participation in the sacraments.[349] Aquinas had devoted half of his reasoning on hands to their importance as tools, especially for liberating the mouth for speech. His mentor Albert the Great had argued that humans, pygmies, and apes all shared the hand in common but that only humans had developed it into an intellectual tool. Apes and pygmies used it for locomotion and for eating; humans, for works of art.[350] Yet that was the crux of the problem: precisely because people used their hands for works of art philosophers disparaged that organ. There perdured an ancient antithesis between philosophy and art, the works of the mind and those of the hand. In Seneca's argument technical inventions, tools, were not obtained by wisdom but by ingenuity. Manual skills, such as weaving, farming, shipbuilding, were devised by reason—but not by right reason.[351] The work of the hands was undignified.

It was the physician Galen who, among the ancients, most exalted a purpose in the structure of the human body that conferred dignity on hands and their labor. Although as a naturalist Galen opposed the theory of the individual creation of a soul infused into each body,[352] he did in *De usu partium* argue cogently from anatomical design. His teleology well surpassed the tendencies of Plato and Aristotle, for it affirmed against mechanism the strict and literal truth that nature never acted in vain.[353] Galen's teleology dominated medicine almost to the end of the seventeenth century, with a persistence that distinguished it as an outstanding phenomenon in intellectual history.[354] Galen termed *De usu partium* "a sacred discourse" and "a

---

349 Ambrose, *Hexameron* 6.9.69.

350 For Aquinas, see above, pp. 40-41. Albert the Great, *Historia animalium* 21.1-2; cited by Janson, *Apes and Ape Lore*, p. 88.

351 Seneca, *Epistulae morales* 90.11, 24.

352 Siegel, *Galen on the Nervous System*, p. 117. For his opposition to the immortality of the soul, because diseases dominated it, see Temkin, *Hippocrates in a World of Pagans and Christians* (Baltimore, Md.: Johns Hopkins University Press, 1991), p. 204.

353 R. J. Hankinson, "Galen and the Best of All Possible Worlds," *Classical Quarterly* 39 (1989):206-27; John D. Barrow, *The Anthropic Cosmological Principle* (Oxford: Oxford University Press, 1986), p. 44.

354 Carlo M. Cipolla, *Public Health and the Medical Profession in the Renaissance* (Cambridge: Cambridge University Press, 1976), p. 5. Although the text was unpublished until

true hymn of praise to our Creator." It treated the suitability of each bodily part for its action, the particular characteristics of its structure, the reason or advantage for its utility. He concluded that, as a whole and in its parts, the human body was perfectly fashioned for its functions.[355]

Galen commenced on its divine design with an exposition of the hand, "because that is most characteristic of mankind." As he explicated, "Man is the only one of all the animals to have been provided with hands, instruments suitable for an intelligent animal; likewise, of animals that go afoot he alone was made biped and erect, for the reason that he had hands." Animal limbs were for locomotion. In humans the forelimbs became hands, for, since with their skills they were to tame other animals for riding, they had no need of four legs. Better than usage for speed, hands were instruments of the arts. Humans were not constructed like marvelous centaurs, with four legs and two hands, since nature could never mix such disparate parts. "For it was not merely their shapes and colors that she would have had to combine, as sculptors and painters do; she would also have been obliged to blend their very substances, which are absolute and will not mingle." A centaur could not build a ship or scramble up its mast to the yardarm or build a house and scale ladders to the top of its walls. It could not be a farmer, blacksmith, cobbler, weaver, or mender. For animals to be bipeds like humans would be as useless as if they had hands, for they were not meant to practice any art. "What advantage, indeed, would they gain from standing erect on two feet if they had no hands?" They would gain nothing, Galen asserted, but would lose the advantages normally theirs: ease in feeding, protection for vital parts, and swiftness in movement. Yet animals had the advantage in swiftness only on level plains, for human legs were better for leaping obstacles, climbing rocks, and traversing difficult terrain. "Man is the only one of all the animals to stand erect," he affirmed. All of the ac-

---

1528, it was well known from Niccolò da Reggio's 1317 translation. Richard J. Durling, "A Chronological Census of Renaissance Editions and Translations of Galen," *Journal of the Warburg and Courtauld Institutes* 24 (1961):233. For his reputation, see Temkin, *Galenism: Rise and Decline of a Medical Philosophy* (Ithaca, N.Y.: Cornell University Press, 1973). See also Andrew Wear, "Galen in the Renaissance," in *Galen: Problems and Prospects*, A Selection of Papers Submitted at the 1979 Cambridge Conference, ed. Vivian Nutton (London: Wellcome Institute for the History of Medicine, 1981), pp. 229-62; Durling, "Chronological Census," pp. 230-305; Nancy G. Siraisi, "Vesalius and the Reading of Galen's Teleology," *Renaissance Quarterly* 50 (1997):1-37; and for individual works, Stefania Fortuna, "Galen's *De constitutione artis medicae* in the Renaissance," *Classical Quarterly* 43 (1993):302-19; Jerome J. Bylebel, "Teaching *Methodus medendi* in the Renaissance," in *Galen's Method of Healing*, Proceedings of the 1982 Galen Symposium, ed. Fridolf Kudlien and Durling, Studies in Ancient Medicine, 1 (Leiden: E. J. Brill, 1991); Nutton, "*De placitis Hippocratis et Platonis* in the Renaissance," in *Le opere psicologiche di Galen,* Atti del terzo colloquio galenico internazionale Pavia, 10-12 settembre 1986, ed. Paola Manuli and Mario Vegetti, Elenchos, 13 (Pavia: Bibliopolis for Centro di studio del pensiero antico del Consiglio nazionale delle richerche, 1986), pp. 281-309.

355 Galen, *De usu partium* 3.10; trans. May, 1:189, and introduction to *Galen on the Body*, pp. 9-11.

tions the hands performed in exercising the arts required bipedality, for "nobody does anything lying supine or prone." Thus nature justly denied the other animals a structure enabling them to stand erect, since they were not intended to make use of hands.[356]

Erect bipedality was in his anatomy for handiness, not for contemplation. Galen repudiated the philosophical tradition about posture by spurning a fragment by Empedocles. "To think that man has an erect posture for the sake of looking readily up to heaven and being able to say, 'I reflect light from my undaunted countenance,' is to be expected of men who have never seen the fish called *uranoscopus* (heaven-gazer), which looks perpetually up to heaven whether it wants to or not, whereas man would never see the heavens if he did not bend his neck back." The ability to bend the neck back people shared with asses and with cranes. Galen did concede that people were grossly careless if they failed to heed Plato's interpretation, which he paraphrased as "'looking up does not mean lying on one's back and yawning, but in my opinion means using one's reason to meditate on the nature of things.'" But, in Galen's judgment, few before himself, in meditating on the nature of things, had correctly understood the utility of the bodily parts, especially the hands.[357]

Although he scorned the contemplative rationale of human anatomy, Galen did not deny human rationality. "Only man has a hand actually perfected and the reasoning power to use it as well, a power than which there is nothing more godlike in mortal animals." The usefulness of bodily parts was related to the soul, of which the body was the instrument. "Now to man—for he is an intelligent animal and, alone of all creatures on earth, godlike—nature gave hands as a defensive weapon and for pacific skill." As a pacific and sociable animal, "with his hands he writes laws for himself, raises altars and statues to the gods, builds ships, makes flutes, lyres, knives, fire-tongs, and all the other instruments of the arts," and in his literature he comments on theories. Since "man is the most intelligent of the animals and so, also, hands are the instruments most suitable for an intelligent animal." Galen agreed with Aristotle against Anaxagoras that people had hands because they were intelligent, not vice versa. Humans were instructed in the arts by their reason, not by their hands; yet their hands were instrumental, like the lyre for the musician or the tongs for the smith. Reason depended upon manual instruments for accomplishing its natural disposition. Hands were, as Aristotle wrote, "an instrument for instruments."[358]

The work of the hands was common knowledge: they were made for grasping. Yet not everyone knew how the parts of the hand cooperated in

---

[356] Galen, *De usu partium* 2.1; 3.1, 2; trans. May, 1:113, 154, 157, 160.

[357] Galen, *De usu partium* 3.2, citing Empedocles, 1:330; Plato, *Respublica* 7.529; trans. May, pp. 160-61.

[358] Galen, *De usu partium* 14.6; 1.2, 3, 4; trans. May, 2:630; 1:68, 69, 71.

that work, Galen criticized. He thus investigated every part of the human hand to the minutest detail. He discoursed on fingers as bone and as flesh. He explained the fingers and their "marvelous workmanship" in number, size, shape, and organization, "constructed so advantageously for the action of the hand as a whole that no better construction could possibly be imagined." Then he examined the movement of the fingers, the usefulness of each, and the tendons in control.[359] In his discussion of the hand as prehensile he treated the focus of Michelangelo's fresco of the Creation of Adam: the fingertip and the fingernail.

Human fingertips were soft and round and, rather than being just bone, they ended in nails. They were neither too hard nor too soft, because the objects to be grasped varied in consistency. By mutual arrangement the flesh in the extremities seized soft objects, while the nails on the outside, as a base for the flesh, aided in picking up hard objects. The flesh of the fingertip compensated for the slipperiness of the nails, and the nails supported the easily damaged flesh. Nails that were out of proportion, excessively long, could not pick up a thorn or a hair because they would strike against the object. Those that were shorter than the tips deprived the flesh of support and rendered them incapable. "Only nails that come even with the ends of the fingers will best provide the service for the sake of which they were made." Galen quoted Hippocrates on the norm of "the nails neither to project beyond, nor to fall short of, the fingertips." A duly proportioned size was most useful. Fingernails served multiple uses other than picking up tiny objects. They were for scraping, scratching, skinning, and tearing apart. They were needed in almost all circumstances of life and in all the arts, especially in those requiring precise manual skill. But it was as a prehensile instrument for seizing small, hard objects that the hand most needed the fingernails.[360]

Galen asked why Plato, although a follower of Hippocrates, slighted fingernails. And why Aristotle, so clever at explaining nature's workmanship, overlooked most of their utility. "Plato says," he repeated, "that like certain bad workmen the gods who fashioned man made nails grow on his finger tips, as if they were practicing in advance the formation of the claws that would be necessary in other animals." As for Aristotle, he had remarked that fingernails were formed for protection, without specifying whether from temperature or from injury. Galen denied the theory. It was precisely from the difference of opinion among ancient physicians and philosophers about fingernails—whether skillless or skillful—that he sought to discover a standard of judgment and to devise a single universal method for further

---

359 Galen, *De usu partium* 1.5, 8, 12-14; 2.1; trans. May, 1:113.

360 Galen, *De usu partium* 1.6, citing Hippocrates, *De officina medici* 4; trans. May, p. 74. For ancients on the formation of fingernails, see Charles Daremberg, trans., Galen, *Oeuvres anatomiques, physiologiques, et médicales*, 2 vols. (Paris, 1854-56), 1:122-24 n. 1.

discovering the utility of each part of the body and its attributes. The ancient writings were incomplete and incorrect, he thought, as in the prime case of fingernails. "The best philosophers are plainly ignorant of their usefulness."[361]

The fingernails, he explained, were for bettering the action of the hands, which could grasp—but not small, hard objects. Why were they made just so hard and rounded? he posed. If they were harder, he answered, they could not bend, even a little, and they would be easily broken, like all brittle substances. So they were made moderately hard to pick up objects and to be protected from breakage. They were made softer than bone so that they could yield to violently falling objects and blunt the force of the blow. All exposed parts of animals were made from a substance resistant to bruising or breakage: thus hoofs, spurs, and horns, which yielded to impact. Fingernails were formed softer and more delicate than the claws of wild beasts, as appropriate to a civilized and social animal and as adapted to grasping objects accurately. They were rounded on all sides for safety, since a circular shape was adapted for resistance, without an exposed angle to be broken off. But, since their ends were worn down by scraping and other use, fingernails were the only bodily parts capable of growth even when the whole body had stopped growing. They grew in length, like hair, with the new nails increasing from below and pushing forward the old ones. "Thus," concluded Galen's teleology, "everything about the fingernails shows the utmost foresight on the part of Nature."[362]

The science of fingernails continued. Avicenna's *Canon*, which perpetuated Galen's thought in medieval medicine, noted that they were made of a soft bone to protect underlying structure from damage. They grew continuously to replace loss by friction. Nails served three purposes in humans: to support the fingers in grasping objects firmly, to assist them in picking up the minutest objects, and to scratch. In animals they were used as weapons or instruments for tearing thin and delicate coverings.[363] Renaissance anatomists also studied fingernails both objectively and teleologically. Benedetti thought they arose from the bone and hardened but clung with their roots to the flesh, not the bone. The nails of the hand grew more than those of the foot because their higher position in the body meant an increase.[364] Jacopo Berengario da Carpi (d. 1550) repeated the ancient belief that fingernails continued to grow even on a corpse. He supposed it was because they were generated like hair from superfluities. He repeated their

---

361 Galen, *De usu partium* 1.8, citing Plato, *Timaeus* 76; Aristotle, *De partibus animalium* 687b; trans. May, pp. 74, 77.

362 Galen, *De usu partium* 1.11; trans. May, p. 82.

363 Avicenna, *Canon*, 1.5.24. For the fortune of the text, see Siraisi, "The Changing Fortunes of a Traditional Text: Goals and Strategies in Sixteenth-Century Latin Editions of the *Canon* of Avicenna," in *Medical Renaissance*, ed. Wear et al., pp. 16-41.

364 Benedetti, *Historia corporis humani* 5.28; 1.14.

utility. "At the end of the fingerbones are the nails, which are for the comeliness of the hand, the protection of the fingertips, and for picking up minute objects."[365] Paré, writing on the hand as "the organ of organs and instrument of human instruments," typically recounted the utility of fingernails: "to scratch, to scrape, to flay, to tear something, or to fasten and unfasten, to take and to hold, and to catch and kill vermin."[366]

Galen complained that those who claimed that nature had no skill praised sculptors for matching the right and left sides of a figure precisely. Yet nature not only made those parts equal but also provided them with actions and with usefulness innate from birth. Galen asked whether it was right to praise Polyclitus for the symmetry of his statue the "canon," while depriving nature of praise and artistry, since it exhibited symmetry not only externally, as did sculptors, but also internally. Polyclitus was the imitator of nature to the best of his ability. "But he could imitate her only in the external features, where he had seen the skill involved, and he began with those that are the most obvious, such as the hand, an instrument most characteristic of man, for it has five fingers with flat nails at their ends, three joints in each finger, and movements. . . everything displaying the utmost skill." Natural symmetry was indicative of a marvelous skill, which sculptors, who employed many tools in the making of their statues, achieved only with difficulty. The human arm was prehensile, the leg locomotive. Nature had used the very best proportion in establishing the size of the arm: neither too long, so that it was slow, nor too short for grasping objects. While the mere sight of the arm before dissection was sufficient for wonder, its interior parts were exceedingly marvelous. They corresponded proportionately between the upper arm and forearm, the arm and hand, and the different parts of the hand—all displaying the Creator's skill. The proper proportions of the fingers alone sufficiently demonstrated its skill. No one ever had them too large or too small, Galen observed. Occasionally, he conceded, in ten thousand times ten thousand chances, there was the rare human born with six fingers. Yet, if Polyclitus made one such small error in a thousand statues, he would not be blamed.[367]

But Galen had made mistakes, as renaissance anatomists would discover, because he had failed to dissect human hands. Italian culture was keen on anatomy, since dissection had originated in Bologna around the figure of Mondino da Luzzi,[368] who discoursed from experience on the arm and the

---

365 Jacopo Berengario da Carpi, *Isagogae breves*, p. 172. For the ancient belief, see Tertullian, *De anima* 51.2 after Democritus; cited by David Satran, "Fingernails and Hair: Anatomy and Exegesis in Tertullian," *Journal of Theological Studies* 40 (1989):119.

366 Paré, *Chirurgie* 4.20.

367 Galen, *De usu partium* 17.1.1; trans. May, 2:727.

368 See Giovanna Ferrari, "Public Anatomy Lessons and the Carnival: The Anatomy Theatre of Bologna," trans. Chris Woodall, *Past and Present* 117 (1987):53. See also Katharine

hand.[369] By the end of the sixteenth century, through the influence of Vesalius, there was a permanent theater for dissection erected by its university. Although anatomy was still scorned as a mechanical art, the social position of its practitioner improved. Anatomical books became increasingly available, for sale in the Florentine apothecary shops, where painters purchased their colors.[370] There was common membership of physicians and painters in the guild *Medici e Speziali*.[371] More learned illustrations were designed to be useful also to artists. Collaboration developed between the anatomist and the designer or painter, many of whom especially studied the subject. Other artists actually practiced human anatomy to discover muscular proportion and form.[372]

Aristotle had compared the practice of sculptors with the method of nature: to work from a hard and solid core of bone or clay, then mold the figure around it.[373] A similar rationale was articulated by Leon Battista Alberti (1404-72) in the initial renaissance primer on painting, *Della pittura*, where he defined academic composition. "In painting the nude begin with the bones, then add the muscles and then cover the body with flesh in such a way as to leave the position of the muscles visible." To the objections that artists should not represent the invisible, he countered that the procedure was "analogous to drawing a nude and then covering it with draperies."[374] To that purpose the method of Galen's *De usu partium* proved serviceable to artists. During the period when Michelangelo was painting the frescoes on the Sistine Chapel ceiling, da Vinci was drawing on myology, precisely from Galen's text.[375] Da Vinci made an artistic study of arms and hands[376] but also a scientific rendition of the upper extremity, in which he displayed hands.[377] His note accompanying drawings of dissections of the hand in

---

Park, "The Criminal and the Saintly Body: Autopsy and Dissection in Renaissance Italy," *Renaissance Quarterly* 47 (1994):1-33.

369 Mondino da Luzzi, *Anathomia*, pp. 48-49.

370 Ferrari, "Anatomy and Carnival," pp. 72, 55-56.

371 Schultz, *Art and Anatomy*, p. 60.

372 Ferrari, "Anatomy and Carnival," pp. 55-56. See also Roberto Paolo, "Il corpo: Progetto e rappresentazione," in *Immagini anatomiche e naturalistiche nei disegni degli Uffici, seccoli sedicesimo e diassetticesimo*, ed. idem and Lucia Tongiorgi Tomasi, Gabinetto desegni e stampe degli Uffizi, 60 (Florence: L. S. Olschki, 1984), pp. 9-30; Charles Singer, "The Confluence of Humanism, Anatomy, and Art," in *Fritz Saxl, 1890-1948: A Volume of Memorial Essays from his Friends in England*, ed. D. J. Gordon (London: T. Nelson, 1957), pp. 261-69.

373 Aristotle, *De partibus animalium* 654; cited by Schultz, *Art and Anatomy*, p. 31.

374 Clark, *Nude*, p. 351.

375 See Charles D. O'Malley and J. B. de C. M. Saunders, *Leonardo da Vinci on the Human Body* (New York: Henry Schuman, 1952), pp. 27-28; Schultz, *Art and Anatomy*, p. 57.

376 Leonardo da Vinci, Study of arms and hands, c. 1471, Windsor Leoni volume; reproduced in *Leonardo da Vinci*, Yale exhibition catalogue, p. 51 n. 4.

377 Da Vinci, Drawings of hands; reproduced in O'Malley and Saunders, *Da Vinci on the Human Body*, figs. 56, 57. For the mechanism of pronation and supination in the arms and hands, see McMurrich, *Da Vinci the Anatomist*, p. 123.

layers emphasized the importance of mechanics for understanding human forces.[378] It was he who discovered, concerning the movements of the forearm, the functions of the biceps and of the brachioradialis muscles and it was he who demonstrated them with accurate drawings. His achievement was rediscovered only two hundred years later.[379] Da Vinci was also the first to illustrate accurately the bones of the hand. Observing twenty-seven sesamoid bones, he described the mechanical principles of their function.[380]

Michelangelo was eagerly among the artists who anatomized. As Vasari testified, "In order to become completely perfect in this art, he did anatomical studies on countless occasions, dissecting human beings in order to observe the principles and the ligatures of the bones, muscles, nerves, veins, and their various movements, as well as all of the positions of the human figure."[381] Not only did Michelangelo practice dissection; he also intended to write a treatise on the subject.[382] Early in his career, after leaving the Medici household upon the death his patron, Michelangelo was performing dissections in the convent of Santo Spirito in Florence. The prior provided him a room there and supplied him, by permission of a papal brief, with corpses. "Nothing could have given him greater pleasure," wrote Condivi, his biographer. In exchange for the cadavers Michelangelo carved a wooden crucifix just under life-size for display above the main altar of the church. The artist applied himself to dissection there, while he had the opportunity, and likely continued the practice in Bologna. The results of his anatomy were an accurate myological presentation in his sculptures of Proclus, Bacchus, and the initial Pietà. The musculature of the thigh of his Proclus is more correctly conceived and differentiated than in his earlier work, as is also the treatment of the hands. The pronounced extensor tendons in the left hand clutching the cloak reinforce the facial tension. In his Pietà the right forearm of Christ correctly depicts the accessory cephalic vein running over the wrist and ramifying the interosseous veins. The musculature of his wrist bones is naturalistic—not the expressive distortion of northern prototypes. As Vasari exclaimed, "It is absolutely astonishing that the hand of an artist could have properly executed something so sublime and admirable in a brief time, and clearly it is a miracle that a stone, formless in

---

378 Keele, *Leonardo da Vinci's Elements of the Science of Man*, pp. 276-80; and see *Corpus of the Anatomical Studies*, ed. Keele and Pedretti, 143r, p. 279, fig. 13.10.

379 J. G. Bearn, "Leonardo da Vinci and the Movements of the Forearm," *Medical and Biological Illustration* 13 (1963):250-54.

380 Elmer Belt, *Leonardo the Anatomist*, Longan Clendening Lectures on the History and Philosophy of Medicine, 4 (Lawrence: University of Kansas Press, 1955), p. 15. For Vesalius on the bones of the hand, see Saunders and Charles D. O'Malley, *The Illustrations from the Works of Andreas Vesalius of Brussels* (Cleveland: World, 1950), p. 74, and p. 75, pl. 16.

381 Vasari, *Vita di Michelangelo*, 5:108; trans. Bondanella and Bondanella, p. 471.

382 See Summers, *Michelangelo and the Language of Art*, pp. 20-21, 397-405, 426-28.

the beginning, could ever have been brought to the state of perfection which Nature habitually struggles to create in the flesh."[383]

Another amazing hand before the gesture in his fresco of the Creation of Adam was on his sculpture of David in the antique colossal mode. An enormous right hand with a prominent thumb hangs at David's thigh.[384] The study sketches an arm thrust erect from a supine shoulder, with the index finger prominent. Among Michelangelo's anatomical drawings was even one that appears to be a sketch from memory of his own writing hand.[385] His knowledge of anatomical forms was from such ancient models, from observation of live models, and from dissection of dead ones. Although Michelangelo rarely altered anatomy, in the right hand of David he extended a muscle, despite his knowledge of its natural boundary. He deliberately altered it to make the hand appear more massive on a part whose mass was otherwise due to its proportion to the whole figure. In another aspect that hand was remarkably scientific. The forms of deep muscles and deep tissues, which only the practice of anatomy could disclose, were only slightly represented in Michelangelo's art. Yet one of the only two structures invisible to the naked eye was in that right hand of David: in the posterior distal margin of the radius, visible through the tendons and extensor retinaculum. Despite the muscular invention, his anatomical depictions were extremely accurate. His knowledge of surface contours was mostly from observation of live models. Michelangelo applied his anatomical practice to understand and to delineate the difficult contours, such as shoulder blades. He also retrieved from its imaginative storage a vast and distinctive collection of forms remembered from dissections. He drew from memory for a study of the Last Judgment a figure of a leg that was an extremely rare form in life, one only obvious from dissection.[386]

Before the execution of the frescoes on the ceiling of the Sistine Chapel, Michelangelo had already done a highly polished study of a left leg with ac-

---

383 Schultz, *Art and Anatomy*, pp. 3, 67-68, 78-79, 81, citing Condivi, *Vita di Michelangelo* 10.8; trans. Wohl, p. 17; Vasari 7:151, trans. Bondanella and Bondanella, p. 425. For the attributed crucifixes, see figs. 58, 59; and also Proclus, p. 79, fig. 60. The interossei of the hand were first described by Galen. May, introduction, *Galen on the Body*, p. 42.

384 Seymour, *Michelangelo's "David,"* p. 48. See also Hartt, *David by the Hand of Michelangelo: The Original Model Discovered* (New York: Abbeville, 1987), although the model lacks the arms. For description, see Vasari, *Vita di Michelangelo*, 1:18-21. For the phenomenon, see Creighton Gilbert, "A New Sight in 1500: The Colossal," in *"All the World's a Stage. . .": Art and Pageantry in the Renaissance and Baroque*, ed. Barbara Wisch and Susan Scott Munsbower, 2 vols., Papers in Art History from the Pennsylvania State University, 6 (University Park, Pa.: Pennsylvania State University, Department of Art History, 1990), 2:396-415.

385 Michelangelo, arm study, David sketch, Louvre, Paris; reproduced in Perrig, *Drawings of Michelangelo*, fig. 5; and for his own hand sketched, p. 69.

386 James Elkins, "Michelangelo and the Human Form: His Knowledge and Use of Anatomy," *Art History* 7 (1984):176-82. Michelangelo, Studies for an angel and for the damned in the Last Judgment, London, British Museum, H 379; reproduced, pl. 21.

curate surface modeling of the myological and skeletal construction. He had obeyed Alberti's recommendation that an artist should assiduously observe the human bones as occupying "a central determined position." It was from the skeleton that the artist worked outward, covering the bones in muscle and skin. Anatomical structure in Florentine drawing began specifically with the tibia. The only extant drawing, perhaps, for his projected illustration of Realdo Columbo's (1515?-59) text on anatomy was a skeletal and myological structure of the legs.[387] When Michelangelo on his own legs climbed the scaffolding to the Sistine Chapel ceiling, he had more in his mind than philosophical speculation about the immortality of the soul. He had practical experience in a holy anatomy, supported by a classical and Christian tradition of human dignity through erect posture. Michelangelo knew more than the position of bones: he knew the function and purpose of legs. They had a divinely conferred dignity.

Da Vinci criticized him as an "anatomical painter," for "a too strong indication of bones, sinews, and muscles" that rendered humans wooden. His thought, committed to private manuscript, probably in response to the Sistine Chapel ceiling, became public criticism by the middle of the century. Conspicuous torso muscles, as in the frescoed body of Christ in the Last Judgment or in his sculpted body in the Resurrection, seemed to some an exaggerated, even extreme, physical delineation.[388] But as an inquisitor more astutely perceived the design, "Do you not know that in these figures by Michelangelo there is nothing that is not spiritual?"[389]

In classical argument the intelligence pervading the universe was evidence of "a wise Creator." Galen commended his argument from the design of the human body to the significant detail of the fingernail. It was "the source of a perfect theology, which is a thing far greater and far nobler than all of medicine." He termed his conclusion an "epode," because the lyric poets chanted such a theme before the altars, "singing hymns of praise to the gods." The proofs of the mysteries were feeble in comparison with the proofs of nature, which were manifest in all animals. Nature's skill was not evident in humans alone but in any creature one cared to dissect—the smaller the animal, the greater the wonder, "just as when craftsmen carve something on small objects."[390] Galen predicted that his argument from design would be useful not only for physicians but also for philosophers and theologians, indeed, for all religious persons.

---

387 See Schultz, *Art and Anatomy*, pp. 33, 38. Michelangelo, Studies for a left leg, c. 1504; reproduced, p. 33, fig. 31; James Byam-Shaw, *Old Master Drawings from Christ Church Oxford* (Washington, D.C.: International Exhibitions Foundation, 1972), pp. 37-38. See Schultz, *Art and Anatomy*, p. 104, and fig. 80.

388 Schultz, *Art and Anatomy*, pp. 92, 68; Clark, *Leonardo da Vinci*, p. 121, citing Da Vinci, MS. E, folio 19v.

389 Clark, *Leonardo da Vinci*, pp. 26-27.

390 Galen, *De usu partium* 17.1.3; trans. May, 2:731.

And in renaissance thought and practice his text was used. Alberti had already cited it in composing the initial renaissance primer on painting,[391] and it was a principal influence on da Vinci's late anatomical drawings.[392] Michelangelo's personal physician, Columbo, in his *De re anatomica*, which the artist would be commissioned to illustrate, will cite it immediately after Aristotle's dictum on the hand as the supreme organ. Colombo introduced his own commentary on the "wondrous structure" of its muscles in movement—"a kind of miracle"—by acknowledging that Galen had noticed and considered it. "This the best and supreme God has granted to a human being so that by this power he might exercise all the arts and be protected from external injuries, concerning which Galen that most eloquent man in such a long course first in *De usu partium* had spoken."[393] Vasari in his anatomy also acknowledged Galen's teleology.[394] Michelangelo as an artist who anatomized stole inspiration for his Creation of Adam from that classical teleological tradition.

The concept would not have been misplaced on that ceiling. When Cajetan preached initially to Julius II in the Sistine Chapel, his theme was alternatively the immortality of the soul, rather than a dignity manifested in the body. Yet even Cajetan's argument progressed from the mental experience of humans, such as the discernment of intelligence and the desire for immortality, to their bodily experience. His text for that first Sunday of Advent was: "Look up and lift up your heads" (Luke 21:28). External nature he pleaded as a witness to a godlike soul, which originated from chaos in an order with a hierarchical plan and concomitant perfection. In natural ascent species followed species without intervals, so that the contiguous ones were difficult to distinguish. But the steady ascent, slow and gradual, from bodies, to plants, to animals, to humans was not maintained. "Nature is suddenly drawn aloft and raised to another and far distant level." Humans were separated from the neighboring species by a distance greater than that between the highest and lowest animals. Animals originated within matter; humans, without. They differed also in conditions. Animals possessed from nature their basic equipment at birth: for clothing they had bark, shells, hides, quills, shag, bristles, hair, feathers, wings, scales, fleeces; for defense they had horns, nails, teeth, jaws, beaks, stings, bites, hooves, and poison. Then gapped a crucial difference: "To take the place of all these and host of various other marvellous things, man has been

---

391 Leon Battista Alberti, *De pictura* 3.57.

392 Schultz, *Art and Anatomy*, pp. 57, 96, cf. 64; Martin Kemp, "Dissection and Divinity in Leonardo's Late Anatomies," *Journal of the Warburg and Courtauld Institutes* 35 (1972):200-25.

393 Realdo Columbo, *De re anatomica* 5.33. For their relationship, see Schultz, *Art and Anatomy*, pp. 100-8; Summers, *Michelangelo and the Language of Art*, p. 398; Steinberg, "Michelangelo and the Doctors," *Bulletin of the History of Medicine* 56 (1982):543-53.

394 Siraisi, "Vesalius and Galen."

given only his versatile and skilful hands." Cajetan's explanation for the divide between other animals and humans, the sudden leap from the gradual ascent, from analogy to difference, was not ultimately hands with Anaxagoras, but soul with Aristotle. It was the soul as "vivifying a body of clay" in the pinnacle of a human being that transposed nature.[395] Yet he discerned a bodily manifestation of that spiritual and intellectual principle and it was actively in hands. As Cajetan preached, hands had replaced in humans the various instruments of other animals.

Body and soul were continuous, not dichotomous. In classical medicine hands acted in accordance with the discernment of the brain.[396] Artists understood that. As da Vinci observed, "Whatever exists in the universe, in essence, in appearance, in the imagination, the painter has first in his mind and then in his hands."[397] Michelangelo himself wrote, "You can't work on one thing with your hands and on another with your brain." Also, "One paints with the brain and not with the hands."[398] His biographer Vasari confirmed his "miraculous and magnificent works created through his hands and his genius."[399] Since Cajetan's sermon was preached in the Sistine Chapel in 1503, his injunction to "look up and lift up your heads" could not have included a congregational vision of Michelangelo's fresco. The concept of the Creator charging Adam to erect bipedality with able hands was, nevertheless, a traditional understanding of human nature and dignity as distinct among creatures. Standing had been since classical antiquity the position of the hero in glory.[400] Most renaissance portraits that were full-length showed the subject standing, rather than sitting or reclining.[401] Da Vinci advised for the better comparison of a human with a brute showing him on tiptoe.[402] That was the position of superiority, as Quintilian faulted orators who "rise on tiptoe, whenever they say anything of which they are especially proud."[403]

In renaissance art the hand—whether in motion or at rest, depicted with prominent gesture or anatomical skill—became a metonym for the human

---

395 Tommaso da Vio, "Oratio" 4, in idem, *Opuscula*, 186b-1881, especially 187b; "On the Immortality of Minds," trans. James K. Sheridan, in *Renaissance Philosophy*, ed. Leonard A. Kennedy (The Hague: Mouton, 1973), pp. 52, 53. For the dating of the sermon, see the intoduction to the translation, p. 43; Wicks, "Thomism between Renaissance and Reformation," p. 16.

396 Hippocrates, *De morbo sacro* 19; Galen, *De usu respirationis*, p. 13.

397 Da Vinci, *Literary Works*, ed. Richler, 1:54; *Leonardo on Painting*, ed. Kemp (New Haven, Conn.: Yale University Press, 1989), p. 32.

398 Michelangelo, *Lettere*, ed. Milanesi, p. 450, 489; cited by Clements, *Poetry of Michelangelo*, p. 26.

399 Vasari, *Vita di Michelangelo*, 1:5; trans. Bondanella and Bondanella, p. 415.

400 Bremmer, "Walking, Standing, and Sitting," p. 24.

401 See Campbell, *Renaissance Portraits*, p. 56.

402 Da Vinci, *Notebooks*, ed. MacCurdy, 1:201; cited by Slotkin, *Readings in Early Anthropology*, p. 6.

403 Quintilian, *Institutiones oratoriae* 11.3.120; trans. Butler, 4:307.

body.[404] Da Vinci's portrait of the lady with the ferret shows a greatly enlarged right hand stroking the pet.[405] Parmigianino's self-portrait displays his own artistic hand exaggerated in a convex mirror as a sign of his skill through its instrumentality.[406] In Michelangelo's fresco of the Creation of Adam all of the principles of artistic design converge in its center:[407] on the line and movement of two arms, hands, fingers. Vasari's evaluative description commenced with the form and movement of God and with the posture of his arm toward the angels, then it described his divine gesture toward the man. "With the other he stretches out his right hand to Adam, a figure whose beauty, pose, and contours are of such a quality that he seems newly created by his Supreme and First Creator rather than by the brush and design of a mere mortal." Vasari recognized that divinity as Michelangelo's genius and he praised him as the master of artistic design. The Creator had determined in Michelangelo a marvelous project: "a spirit who, working alone, was able to demonstrate in every art and every profession the meaning of perfection in the art of design." God purposed the creature Michelangelo as the supreme human exemplar, so that he might be acclaimed "divine rather than mortal." Of Michelangelo's mimetic development Vasari wrote, "All the knowledge and ability of true grace was, in his nature, enhanced by study and practice, for it Michelangelo it produced more sublime works every day." Even a cartoon aroused wonder for its sublimity. The cartoon was taken to the papal sala, copied by many artists, then divided and scattered in remnants "divine rather than human." His statue of Moses possessed a face of such beauty that the viewer was prompted to demand its veiling—"so resplendent and radiant does it appear to onlookers." Michelangelo had in marble "perfectly expressed the divinity that God has endowed upon his most holy face" so that the sculpture was "not human but divine." The Jews flocked like starlings to adore it, the highest compliment, since by the Mosaic law they did not worship graven images. Divinity was manifested in design. From his very apprenticeship Michelangelo was acknowledged as much given to design, and soon he flayed bodies to acquire a more accurate knowledge of design. His Last Judgment in the Sistine Chapel would be summed as "all that the art of design was capable of

---

[404] Mirollo, *Mannerism and Renaissance Poetry: Concept, Mode, Inner Design* (New Haven, Conn.: Yale University Press, 1984), p. 140.

[405] Campbell, *Renaissance Portraits*, p. 59. Leonardo da Vinci, Lady with a ferret, 1485-90, Muzeum Narodowe, Cracow; reproduced, pl. 67.

[406] Mirollo, *Mannerism and Renaissance Poetry*, p. 141. Parmigianino, Self-portrait with hand, Kunsthistorisches Museum, Vienna; reproduced in Paola Rossi, *L'opera completa del Parmigianino* (Milan: Rizzoli, 1980), pl. XXV; Armando Ottaviano Quintavalle, *Il Parmigianino* (Milan: Istituto editoriale italiano, 1948), pl. 25.

[407] Arnheim, *Power of the Center*, pp. 167, 169.

achieving." Michelangelo's epitaph admired his genius and acknowledged the benefits of the "divine works" erected "from his own hands."[408]

But in what did the design of the Creation of Adam consist? No Platonist infusion of a soul finger to finger is depicted on that fresco but, rather, a horizontal man tending toward verticality. Adam is divinely charged to stabilize his feet on the clay from which he was formed and to stand erect in dignity and responsibility as thinker and maker. The classical argument from design perfectly complemented the genius of that renaissance artist, so celebrated as the supreme master of design. Michelangelo concentrates the divine focus on a human detail as indicative of a providential design: the fingernail. God and Adam are not about to touch fingertip to fingertip. God charges with his straight fingertip Adam's bent fingernail. The fingernail was traditionally a measurement. There was the adage *ad unguem*, or "to the fingernail." It meant "by rule," from the practice of stone-cutters and carpenters who tested work for evenness with a measuring line. As Erasmus explained, "The metaphor is taken from workers in marble"—like Michelangelo—"who draw the nail over the surface to test the joins in the stone." A person "finished to the finger-nail" was very polished; so was a poem "smoothed to the nail." An alley of trees was planted "square to the nail"; a calendar year was "refined as it is to the nail." In some contexts "to the finger-nail" meant an object "exact and precisely finished," like Adam as God's creation. There was a related adage *notari ungui et similia*, or "to be marked with the finger-nail," from the custom of noting anything unsatisfactory in workmanship. The marking with the fingernail served the same function as the sponge, the file, and the chisel as instruments of emendation.[409]

There was yet another adage interpretative of Adam not touching God by the space of a fingernail: *latum unguem*, or "a nail's breadth." Erasmus reported as a common saying in Cicero to swerve by the breadth of a finger or its nail as meaning "'by the least distance.'" The metaphor was used "to convey perfect imitation as full agreement," from which rule or honor or conscience a person should not swerve or stray "a finger's breadth" or "by a nail's breadth." The metaphor partly derived from those who measured a plank or a piece of stone by fingers' breadth, for perfect measurement, rather than by cubits. "A fingerbreadth is the smallest possible measurement," Erasmus explained. The metaphor was also partly derived from surveyors

---

[408] Vasari, *Vita di Michelangelo*, 1:43, 3, 4, 8, 27, 30-31, 6, 13, 70, 160; trans. Bondanella and Bondanella, pp. 445, 414, 418, 431, 434, 458. For the renaissance artist as another god, see Giancarlo Maiorino, *Adam, "New Born and Perfect": The Renaissance Promise of Eternity* (Bloomington: Indiana University Press, 1987), pp. 112, 113. For Michelangelo as "the greatest exponent of *disegno*," see James Beck, "The Sistine Ceiling Restorations: Second Thoughts," *Arts Magazine* 61 (1986):60-61.

[409] Erasmus, *Adagia* 1.5.91; 1.5.58; trans. Phillips, 31:463, 435-37.

of land, who measured by stadia, paces, or feet.[410] The principal unit of length was the arm (*braccio*), in Florence 58 cm, while shorter references were to span, palm, finger (*spanna*, *palmo*, *dito*).[411]

There was since the classical belief in measurable proportion an analogy between anatomy and art. The parts of the human body provided the measurements for architecture, sculpture, and painting. The concept was known as the canon of Polyclitus, and it survived in three medical texts by Galen and in Pliny's natural history. Its statement in Vitruvius's *De architectura* decisively influenced renaissance art. As he explained, "It was from the members of the human body that they derived the fundamental ideas of measures which are obviously necessary in all works, as the finger, palm, foot and cubit." With arms and legs extended the human body was a model of proportion because it fitted into the square and the circle, which were perfect geometrical forms.[412] Not only art but also life obeyed the rule. Della Casa compared his book on manners *Galateo* to that artistic canon because he dealt with humanity in its proper measures.[413]

That fingernail of Adam's was also the tiniest tool of the human hand, grasper of things. There was a new opinion among renaissance scientists about tools: their recognition as artifacts that were ancient and primitive. That recognition was an initiative toward the eventual discovery of humans themselves as old creatures and old creators. Stone artifacts had been lumped with other shaped objects of mineral accidentally found in or on the ground, which were called fossils. The tools were commonly called *ceraunia*, or "thunderstones," from the superstition that they fell like meteorites from the sky during storms.[414] Thunderstones had been tentatively ques-

---

410 Erasmus, *Adagia* 4.5, citing Cicero, *Academica* 2.18.58, cf. 2.36.116; *Ad Atticum* 7.3.11; *Ad familiares* 7.25.2.; trans. Phillips, 31:390-91. Reference to Jerome, *Epistolae* 120.10.3 was added in the 1515 edition. For the adage, see also Montaigne, *Essais* 3.10, p. 1007.

411 "A Note on Systems of Measurement and Coinage," in Dunkerton et al., *Giotto to Dürer*, p. 390; Herald, *Renaissance Dress*, p. 12. For *bracchia* as a unit of measurement in Italian renaissance architecture, see Spiro Kostoff, *A History of Architecture: Settings and Rituals* (Oxford: Oxford University Press, 1985), p. 405; and for the derivation of Greek measurement from the human body, p. 126. For Michelangelo's poems that pun on the name Bracchi, see Clements, *Poetry of Michelangelo*, pp. 134-53.

412 Rudolf Wittkower, *Architectural Principles in the Age of Humanism*, 3d rev. ed. (London: Academy, 1973), p. 15; Clark, *Nude*, p. 15; Schultz, *Art and Anatomy*, pp. 40, 41, citing Vitruvius, *De architectura* 3. For the body as a model for architecture, see also Joseph Rykwert, *The Dancing Column: On Order or Architecture* (Cambridge, Mass.: MIT Press, 1996); G. L. Hersey, *Pythagorean Palaces: Magic and Architecture in the Italian Renaissance* (Ithaca, N.Y.: Cornell University Press, 1976), pp. 88-127.

413 Della Casa, *Galateo* 262-64, 265.

414 Donald K. Grayson, *The Establishment of Human Antiquity* (New York: Academic Press, 1983), pp. 5-8; A. Irving Hallowell, "The History of Anthropology as an Anthropological Problem," in *Readings in the History of Anthropology*, ed. Darnell, p. 310. The spontaneous generation of pots from the earthen womb was also challenged by excavations of burial urns. Karel Sklenár, *Archaeology in Central Europe: The First 500 Years* (Leicester: Leicester Univeristy Press, 1983), pp. 16-19, 34, 37-38; Andrzej Abramowicz, "*Sponte nascitur*

tioned but they were decisively challenged by Michele Mercati (1541-93), a physician and philosopher who supervised the papal botanical gardens and collected fossils and metals for a lithological museum there. In *Metallotheca vaticana* he declared the points of arrows and spears to be the artifacts of primitive peoples, ignorant of metallurgy, who had chipped them out of flint for use as weapons.[415] Gesner retained the ancient term of thunderstones, but skeptically so, describing with illustrations the varying color, weight, proportions, and shapes of the items: how some were like hammers or wedges, others discoid or claviform.[416] The very classification of *ceraunia* disappeared with Aldrovandi's *Musaeum metallicum*, which considered them as familiar human tools. Aldrovandi, who was an intimate of Michelangelo's inner circle[417] and had a personal museum of stone tools and flint arrowheads, distinguished between the natural and the manufactured and he described the uses of weapons and utensils.[418] Exploration of the Americas provided comparative sources when the natives were judged representatives of earlier cultural development. A notice from Columbus's second voyage observed that the Caribbean natives did not work with iron or steel, which they lacked, but with "sharply pointed stones filled with a wooden handle."[419] When Mercati declared *cerauniae* manufactured items, he

---

ollae. . ." in *Towards a History of Archaeolog*, Being the Papers Read at the First Conference on the History of Archaeology in Aarbus, 29 August- 2 September 1978, ed. Glyn Daniel (London: Thames and Hudson, 1981), pp. 146-47.

415 Michele Mercati, "De ceraunia cuneata," pp. 73-77, and see p. 75, fig. 10. See also Bruce G. Trigger, *A History of Archaeological Thought* (Cambridge: Cambridge University Press, 1989), pp. 47, 51-53; Graeme Barker and Richard Hodges, "Archaeology in Italy, 1980: New Directions and Mis-Directions," in *Archaeology and Italian Society: Prehistoric, Roman, and Medieval Studies*, BAR International Series, 102, ed. idem (Oxford: BAR, 1981), pp. 1, 33-34; Jaroslav Malina and Zdenek Vasícek, *Archaeology Yesterday and Today: The Development of Archaeology in the Sciences and Humanities*, trans. and ed. Marek Zvelebil (Cambridge: Cambridge University Press, 1990), p. 21; Slotkin, ed., *Readings in Early Anthropology*, p. x.

416 Judith Rodden, "The Development of the Three Age System: Archaeology's First Paradigm," in *Towards a History of Archaeology*, ed. Daniel, p. 54.

417 Phyllis Pray Bober, "Ligorio and Aldrovandi," in *Pirro Ligorio: Artist and Antiquarian*, ed. Robert W. Gaston, Villa I Tatti Studies, 10 (Milan: Silvana, 1988), p. 289.

418 Hodgen, *Early Anthropology*, pp. 122, 123.

419 Rodden, "Three Age System," pp. 59-60, citing *Journals and Other Documents on the Life and Voyages of Christopher Columbus*, ed. Morison, p. 235; Hallowell, "Anthropology as an Anthropological Problem," p. 310; Daniel, "Stone, Bronze, and Iron," in *To Illustrate the Monuments: Essays on Archaeology Presented to Stuart Piggott*, ed. J. V. S. Megaw (London: Thames and Hudson, 1976), p. 36. For Aldrovandi's artifacts from the Americas, see Rodden, "Ideas about a Stone Knife," *Antiquity* 59 (1985):219-20; Detlef Heikamp, "American Objects in Italian Collections of the Renaissance and Baroque: A Survey," in *First Images of America: The Impact of the New World on the Old*, ed. Fredi Chiappelli with Michael J. B. Allen and Robert L. Benson, 2 vols. (Berkeley and Los Angeles: University of California Press, 1976), 1:459, fig. 35, and p. 460, fig. 36.

argued not only from scriptural and classical texts but also from Amerindian specimens accumulating in the Vatican as gifts from explorers.[420]

Preaching at the papal court reasoned from human participation in the divine nature toward a dignity to be realized in action.[421] Activity was a renaissance virtue. As the activist Alberti argued, idleness was the pernicious source of all vice. "Whatever is endowed with life is also able by nature to move and feel." A creature who failed to use the features, the senses, that distinguished life was not alive. Animals—fish, quadrupeds, and birds—were busy at utility, building and foraging. "It seems to me that man, too, is not born to stagnate at rest, but to be up and doing." The divinely endowed powers by which humans surpassed other animals in strength, speed, and ferocity were to be used generously. Alberti objected to the classical notion that God's supreme happiness consisted in "doing nothing," so that he permitted to people a "simply aimless being." More plausible was the opinion of Anaxagoras, he thought, that humans were created to contemplate the celestial works. "This is a most plausible idea, especially when we observe that there is no animal but is bent and bowed with its head close to pasture and to earth. Man alone stands erect with brow and countenance raised up, as though made by nature herself to gaze upon and know the paths and bodies of the heavens."[422] Alberti's argument for civic responsibility established on familial bonds betrayed a confusion with the classical norm of contemplation. Erect bipedality to consider the stars was not the idea of Anaxagoras but of Aristotle and of a massive philosophical tradition. Perhaps Alberti recommended a consideration of the revolution of the heavens not for abstract intellection of the deity, however, but as a practical mathematical model for human creativity in imitation of the divine creation. In his plea for activity against leisure—the classical condition for thought and art—people were to be "up and doing." Motion and sensation, the values that established animation, were renaissance vocations against the classical culture of leisure, which was founded on rest and intellection.

In art it was Michelangelo who most aroused the human imagination to the sense of touch. "Tactile values" occurred when representations of solid objects communicated to stir the mind to feel, to weigh, to measure them and their potential and to perform the essential function of the human hand: to grasp. The artist perceived the occupation of the body in space: its shape, dimension, contour, spot and shadow, color—the whole as a unique pattern of objects enhancing life. He communicated those through tactile values, then movement. Touch and motion were the distinctive artistic

---

420 Trigger, *History of Archaeological Thought*, p. 53; Daniel, "Stone, Bronze, and Iron," p. 37.

421 O'Malley, *Praise and Blame*, pp. 109-10.

422 Alberti, *Il libro della famiglia* 2; *The Family in Renaissance Florence*, trans. Renée Neu Watkins (Columbia: University of South Carolina Press, 1969), p. 133.

qualities in figure painting, for through those sensual values art heightened life. Since the excellence of Greek art, Michelangelo alone achieved works of form whose tactile values so increased the human sense of capacity, whose movements were so communicative and inspirational. No other artist employed those values as did he on the subject that so eminently manifested them: the nude.[423]

Adam on the fresco is not merely to pick up things with his hand, the tool. He is to do what his endowment with hands largely implies: to pick up himself. He is divinely charged to stabilize his feet on the clay from which he was formed and to stand erect in dignity and responsibility. His vocation is to be a maker. He is to be an artist, like Michelangelo, in imitation of the divine Creator.[424] The artistic brush only extended the instrumentality of the finger.[425] The particular instrumentality of the human hand, down to its parts of finger, phalanges, and fingernail, is painted in the focal detail of Adam's sweeping gesture raised to acknowledge and accept the divine command. The Creator charges Adam, and Adam complies. He does so almost divinely by the significant breadth of a fingernail.

---

[423] Berenson, *The Florentine Painters of the Renaissance*, 3d ed. rev. (New York: G. P. Putnam's Sons, 1909), pp. 85, 88, 89; idem, *Aesthetics and History* (London: Constable, 1948), pp. 60-61. For tactile values, see also Clark, *Nude*, p. 200.

[424] For art as the imitation of God, see Clements, *Poetry of Michelangelo*, pp. 62-64.

[425] Some renaissance artists, like da Vinci, even continued to paint with their fingers, or toes, in the prehistoric tradition. Thomas Brachert, "A Distinctive Aspect of the Painting Technique of 'Ginevra de' Benci' and of Leonardo's Early Works," trans. C. P. Casparis, in National Gallery of Art, *Report and Studies in the History of Art, 1969* (Washington, D.C.: National Gallery of Art, 1970), pp. 84-104; "Radiographische Untersuchungen am Verkündignungs von Monte Oliveto," *Maltechnik/Restauro* 80 (1974):180; "Die beiden Felsgrottenmadonnen von Leonardo da Vinci," *Maltechnik/Restauro* 83 (1977):11. Cornelis Ketzel painted portraits with his fingers, or even toes, but was considered eccentric for it. Campbell, *Renaissance Portraits*, p. 152. For the use of brushes in the period, see Dunkerton et al., *Giotto to Dürer*, p. 141.

CHAPTER TWO

EVE'S PALM

God is not about to touch her. He stands apart, while Eve emerges whole from behind Adam's side, her right leg bent at the knee but her left leg braced. She is about to stand erect, a human by the classical topic of dignity in posture. The Creator himself summons her to achieve that stance, for he extends his right arm, palm open and up, to gesture: arise![1] Only in the Creation of Eve does God himself stand erect on the earth; in all of Michelangelo's other creational scenes he flies and floats ethereally in the sky.[2] The Creation of Eve is a vertical design.

Erect bipedality was not an ordinary renaissance argument for the dignity of woman, which contentious question depended on her soul or her semen,[3]

---

1 Michelangelo, fresco, Creation of Eve, Sistine Chapel, Vatican. For reproductions of the restored fresco, see Frederick Hartt, Gianluigi Colalucci, and Fabrizio Mancinelli, *The Sistine Chapel*, 2 vols. (New York: Alfred A. Knopf with Nippon Television Corporation, 1992), 2:53-61, with her hands at p. 60. For its restoration, see Mancinelli, "La technique de Michel-Ange et les problèmes de la Chapelle Sixtine: La Création d'Eve et le Péché originel," *Revue de l'art* 81 (1988):9-19. The gesture is still observable in modern Catholic ritual, in papal and episcopal audiences and processions and in parochial liturgy, where the prelate indicates to the congregation that it should stand. Michelangelo's biographers Vasari and Condivi both erroneously interpreted the gesture as a benediction, as noted by Charles de Tolnay, *Michelangelo*, vol. 2: *The Sistine Ceiling*, 5 vols., 2d ed. rev. (Princeton, N.J.: Princeton University Press, 1969), p. 134. But there is no evidence for Tolnay's interpretation that "the gesture of his right hand is like a magician's gesture of conjuration," p. 33; or for the "magic power of God's gesture," by Sydney J. Freedberg, *Painting of the High Renaissance in Rome and Florence*, 2 vols. (Cambridge, Mass.: Harvard University Press, 1961), 1:102.

2 Hartt, "The Evidence for the Scaffolding of the Sistine Ceiling," *Art History* 3 (1982):282; Heinrich Wölfflin, *Classic Art: An Introduction to the Italian Renaissance*, trans. Peter and Linda Murray (London: Phaidon, 1968), p. 57.

3 For introduction to the arguments, see Constance Jordan, *Renaissance Feminism* (Ithaca, N.Y.: Cornell University Press, 1992); Pamela Joseph Benson, *The Invention of the Renaissance Woman: The Challenge of Female Independence in the Literature and Thought of Italy and England* (University Park: Pennsylvania State University Press, 1992); Ian Maclean, *The Renaissance Notion of Woman: A Study in the Fortunes of Scholasticism and Medical Science in European Intellectual Life* (Cambridge: Cambridge University Press, 1980). For the medieval typology, see John Cadden, *Meanings of Sex Difference in the Middle Ages: Medicine, Science, and Culture* (Cambridge: Cambridge University Press, 1993), pp. 167-227. For the quarrel about women, see also Linda Woodbridge, *Women and the English Renaissance: Literature and the Nature of Womankind, 1540-1620* (Urbana: University of Illinois Press, 1984); Richard Harvey, "Early English Feminism and the Creation Myth," *Historian* 54 (1991):35-48; Joan Kelly, "Early Feminist Theory and the *Querelle des femmes*, 1400-1789," in eadem, *Women, History, and Theory: The Essays of Joan Kelly* (Chicago: University of Chicago Press, 1984), pp. 65-109; Ruth Kelso, *Doctrine for the Lady of the Renaissance*, 2d ed. (Urbana: University of Illinois Press, 1978), pp. 5-23; Francis Lee Utley, *The Crooked Rib: An Analytical Index to the Argument about Women in English and*

rather than her stature. In the next century the humanist Anna Maria van Schurman (1607-78) would assert that "God has created woman also with a sublime and erected countenance." That physique fitted her conformably for divine contemplation. "To what purpose would he have given us erect stature," she inquired, "unless to direct our eyes and minds toward contemplation of him? Certainly we would be tree trunks, not human beings."[4] Renaissance "feminists" asserted their humanity by assumption of the male norm, which was philosophically determined as rational, ultimately intellectual. As Cassandra Fedele (1465?-1558) conceded, "Even an ignorant man—not only a philosopher—sees and admits that man is rightly distinguished from a beast above all by reason."[5] Women thus strove to establish themselves as reasonable creatures, even sublimely contemplative, and they did so exceptionally through humanist study, discourse, and literature.[6] In

---

Scot Literature to the End of the Year 1568 (New York: Octogon, 1970); Conor Fahy, "Three Early Renaissance Treatises on Women," *Italian Studies* 11 (1956):30-55. Recent studies of women in the sixteenth century include Margaret L. King, *Women of the Renaissance* (Chicago: University of Chicago Press, 1991); *Refiguring Woman: Perspectives on Gender and the Italian Renaissance*, ed. Marilyn Migiel and Juliana Schiesari (Ithaca, N.Y.: Cornell University Press, 1991); *Women in Reformation and Counter-Reformation Europe: Public and Private Worlds*, ed. Sherrin Marshall (Bloomington: Indiana University Press, 1989); *Seeking the Woman in Late Medieval and Renaissance Writings*, ed. Sheila Fisher and Janet Hadley (Knoxville: University of Tennessee Press, 1989); *Women Writers of the Renaissance and Reformation*, ed. Katharina M. Wilson (Athens: University of Georgia Press, 1987); Romeo de Maio, *Donna e rinascimento*, Cultura, 61 (Milan: Saggiatore, 1987); *Ambiguous Realities: Women in the Middle Ages and Renaissance*, ed. Carole Levin and Jeanie Watson (Detroit, Mich.: Wayne State University Press, 1987), pp. 133-251; Elaine V. Beilin, *Redeeming Eve: Women Writers of the English Renaissance* (Princeton, N.J.: Princeton University Press, 1987); *Rewriting the Renaissance: The Discourses of Sexual Difference in Early Modern Europe*, ed. Margaret W. Ferguson, Maureen Quilligan, and Nancy J. Vickers (Chicago: University of Chicago Press, 1986); *Women in the Middle Ages and the Renaissance: Literary and Historical Perspectives*, ed. Mary Beth Rose (Syracuse, N.Y.: Syracuse University Press, 1986); *Silent But For the Word: Tudor Women as Patrons, Translators, and Writers of Religious Works*, ed. Margaret Patterson Hannay (Kent, Ohio: Kent State University Press, 1985).

[4] Anna Maria van Schurman, *Amica dissertatio de capacitate ingenii muliebris ad scientias*; cited in its English translation, *The Learned Maid, or Whether a Maid May Be a Scholar?* p. 8, by Simon Schama, *The Embarrassment of Riches: An Interpretation of Dutch Culture in the Golden Age* (New York: Alfred A. Knopf, 1987), p. 412. Van Schurman, *Amica dissertatio de capacitate ingenii muliebris ad scientias*, in *Opuscula hebraea, graeca, latina, gallica, prosaica et metrica*, pp. 71-72; cited by Joyce Irwin, "Anna Maria van Schurman: From Feminism to Pietism," *Church History* 46 (1977):52, with my change. For her art, see Katlijne van der Stighelen, *Anna Maria van Schurman, of 'Hoe hooge dat een maeght kan in de konsten Stijgen,'* Symbolae, B4 (Louvain: University Press, 1987).

[5] Cassandra Fedele, *Epistolae et orationes*, pp. 201-7; *Her Immaculate Hand: Selected Works By and About the Women Humanists of Quattrocento Italy*, trans. King and Albert Rabil, Jr., Medieval and Renaissance Texts and Studies, 20 (Binghamton, N.Y.: Medieval and Renaissance Texts and Studies, 1983), p. 75.

[6] For female education, see King, *Women of the Renaissance*, pp. 167-72; for literacy, pp. 172-88; for learned women, pp. 194-218. See also Paul Oskar Kristeller, "Learned Women of Early Modern Italy: Humanists and University Scholars," in *Beyond Their Sex: Learned Women of the European Past*, ed. Patricia H. Lablame (New York: New York University Press, 1980), pp. 91-116; Kelso, *Doctrine for the Lady*, pp. 58-77. Women were traditionally believed to suffer from a "defect of contemplation" that rendered them suitable for

accepting a classical dualism of mind and body, however, they separated themselves from physiological functions that defined them sexually: conception, gestation, and parturition. They endeavored to escape the constraints of their bodies. As the studious, but necessarily chaste, Isotta Nogarola (1420?-66) urged Costanza Varano, "Nothing could be more expedient and fruitful for women than to forget the needs of the body and to reach out strenuously for those goods which fortune cannot destroy."[7] The aspirant female grasp was for spirit, not flesh.

The equality of the sexes in flesh, differing only in the function of the generative organs, was argued by Henrich Cornelius Agrippa von Nettesheim (c.1486-1535) in a declamation on the excellence of woman. He did not fail in his catalogue of female beauty to include the "straight and erect back."[8] Yet there appeared a specific argument for the dignity of woman by erect bipedality, although it conformed to philosophical speculation, rather than biological reality. Agnolo Firenzuola (1493-c.1545) in his dialogue *Delle bellezze delle donne* considered "the shape of the entire person, which almighty God, who created us to His own end and so that we should contemplate His heavenly order, turned and lifted up toward the heavens." As he explained conventionally, other animals, created to benefit humanity or to adorn the universe, were physically turned toward the ground, gazing at it with lowered eyes and crawling on it with forelegs. "To humanity, however, He granted an upright carriage, the ability to turn his eyes to the sky and keep them forever fixed upon the virtues of those higher beauties" with which he would be rewarded in celestial rest after his terrestrial labors. Although Firenzuola elaborated on the perfect proportionality of humans, illustrated after Vitruvius with male figures in the circle and the square, he did so in the context of a statement of the equality of the sexes. As he explicated, "And what we say about men, we always understand to be the same for women, be it in this or in any other measurement."[9] In discussing the composition of female beauty in its individual parts, he began with the carriage. He defined its ideal as majestic, the character of a woman who was "tall, well-shaped, carries herself well, sits with grandeur." Since that quality derived from the authority of the throne, "majesty is nothing else but

---

devotional, rather than intellectual, activities. See, for example, Thomas Aquinas, *Summa theologiae* 2a2ae.82.3

[7] Isotta Nogarola, *Opera* 2:3-6; trans. King and Rabil, *Her Immaculate Hand*, p. 56. For the author, see Lisa Jardine, "Isotta Nogarola: Women Humanists—Education for What?" *History of Education* 12 (1983):231-44; King, "The Religious Retreat of Isotta Nogarola," *Signs* 3 (1978):807-22.

[8] Henrich Cornelius Agrippa von Nettesheim, *De nobilitate et praecellentia foeminei sexus*, pp. 49, 56. For the work, see Barbara Newman, "Renaissance Feminism and Esoteric Theology: The Case of Cornelius Agrippa," *Viator* 24 (1995):337-56.

[9] Agnolo Firenzuola, *Delle bellezze delle donne* 1; *On the Beauty of Women*, trans. Konrad Eisenbichler and Jacqueline Murray (Philadelphia: University of Pennsylvania Press, 1992), pp. 21, 23.

the movement and carriage of a lady who moves with a certain royal pomp, of a woman, I say, who is somewhat tall and robust." So he instructed, "The body of a gentlewoman must move with gravity and in a certain genteel way so as to carry her uprightly, yet not stiffly, giving her that majesty."[10] That personal quality differed from the sexual norm more typically articulated by Leon Battista Alberti (1404-72), who also thought female beauty was manifested in bodily grace. It consisted, however, only in a physique and constitution "well made for bearing children." He specified that the desirable wife was "fairly big" with "limbs of ample length."[11]

Women as embodied were instructed in good posture. Christine de Pisan (c.1364-c.1431), the first female author who was professional, noted in her *Livre de trois vertus* that a noble woman should be of "courteous bearing" and "in her stature stately."[12] A girl was taught to stand still, feet together, without unnecessary and affected movement of parts.[13] Even she who necessarily moved, a female dancer, was instructed on the bearing of her head. "She should carry it upright, aligned with the body, as nature itself—as it were—teaches us."[14] The erect female carriage even acquired religious decorum. *Le ménagier de Paris*, a late medieval manual from husband to wife, specified that en route to church a woman should bear her head straight, glancing neither to the left nor the right; while in church she should hold her head upright.[15] The book by Geoffroy de La Tour-Landry, composed for the edification of his daughters, indicated that a woman at prayer or at liturgy should not twist or turn her body. She should not imitate the crane or the tortoise but, rather, be like a wolfhound: with a straight head.[16] Even counsel toward adultery advised that a woman should look forward, neither gazing at the stars nor at her feet. In her bearing she should

---

10 Firenzuola, *Delle bellezza delle donne* 1, 2; trans. Eisenbichler and Murray, pp. 41, 49. For his exposition of ideal female beauty, see also Elizabeth Cropper, "On Beautiful Women, Parmigiano, *Petrarchismo*, and the Vernacular Style," *Art Bulletin* 58 (1976):374-75; in general, Murray, "Agnolo Firenzuola on Female Sexuality and Women's Equality," *Sixteenth Century Journal* 22 (1991):199-213.

11 Leon Battista Alberti, *Il libro della famiglia* 2; *The Family in Renaissance Florence*, trans. Renée Neu Watkins (Columbia: University of South Carolina Press, 1969), p. 116.

12 Christine de Pisan, *Livre de trois vertus* 1.18, 27; *A Medieval Woman's Mirror of Honor: The Treasury of the City of Ladies*, trans. Charity Cannon Willard (New York: Persea, 1989), pp. 113, 140. For a survey of the text, see Diane Bornstein, *The Lady in the Tower: Medieval Courtesy Literature for Women* (Hamden, Conn.: Archon, 1983), pp. 67-71. For Pisan as a feminist, see Beatrice Gottlieb, "The Problem of Feminism in the Fifteenth Century," in *Women of the Medieval World: Essays in Honor of John H. Mundy*, ed. Julius Kirshner and Suzanne F. Wemple (Oxford: Basil Blackwell, 1985), pp. 337-62.

13 Kelso, *Doctrine for the Lady*, pp. 50, 106.

14 Guglielmo Ebreo da Pesaro, *De practica seu arte tripudii* 1; *On the Practice or Art of Dancing*, trans. Barbara Sparti (Oxford: Clarendon, 1993), p. 109.

15 *Ménagier de Paris* 1.2. For a survey of the text, see Bornstein, *Lady in the Tower*, pp. 53-59.

16 Geoffrey de La Tour-Landry, *Le livre du Chevalier de La Tour Landry pour l'enseignement de ses filles* 11.

not thrust forward, or run quickly, or amble slowly, or walk like a statue, or strut like a peacock.[17]

Baldassare Castiglione's (1478-1529) *Il libro del cortegiano* specified that female bearing was very distinct from male bearing, "for just as he must show a certain solid and sturdy manliness, so it is seemly for a woman to have a soft and delicate tenderness, with an air of womanly sweetness in her every movement." Her every action was to be "naturally graceful." She was to avoid "robust and strenuous manly exercises," and even in dancing to shun "movements that are too energetic or violent."[18] In Philo's personification of vice and virtue as female the posture of vice was unnatural. "Her neck is held high; she assumes a stature which Nature has not given her." Neither was her footing sure. "Her gait has the looseness which her extravagant wantonness and luxury has bred." Virtue had a contrasting posture and gait. "Her carriage was unaffected, her movements quiet," while she walked with "a firm tread."[19]

The renaissance expectation of moral rectitude required the imitation of physical erectness. There was even a poetic topic, derived from Petrarchan sonnets, of the beautiful foot of the lady as generative, animating nature as she stepped.[20] For females the requirement of erectness extended beyond the molding and swaddling of both sexes in infancy. There was a conviction of the body as a microcosm, evoking by its measures and relationships the cosmic order in its universal geometry. From that belief, clothing assumed a formal importance on the frame of the body that surpassed medieval emphasis on neatness and modesty.[21] For ease of getting into clothes and the assurance of keeping them on, there developed fastenings: buttons, hooks and eyes, and especially laces. Those devices soon exceeded function with aesthetics. Fastenings became important in renaissance dress for ensuring a

---

17 Alessandro Piccolomini, *Dialogo de la bella creanza de le donne*, p. 30. For women in this text, see Marie-Françoise Piéjus, "'Venus bifrons': Le double idéal féminin dans *La Raffaela* d'Alessandro Piccolomini," in *Images de la femme dans la littérature italienne de la Renaissance: Préjugés, misogynes, et aspirations nouvelles*, ed. André Rochon, Recherches sur la Renaissance italienne, 8 (Paris: Université de la Sorbonne nouvelle, 1980), pp. 81-156.

18 Baldassare Castiglione, *Cortegiano* 3.4, 8; *The Book of the Courtier*, trans. George Bull (Harmondsworth, Middlesex: Penguin, 1976), p. 206.

19 Philo, *De sacrificiis Abelis et Caini* 26; *On the Sacrifices of Abel and Cain*, trans. F. H. Colson and G. H. Whitaker, in *Philo*, 12 vols. (Cambridge, Mass.: Harvard University Press, 1961), 2:113, 111.

20 See James V. Mirollo, "'Where'er you walk': My Lady's Beautiful Foot and Generative Footsteps: The Literary Context of Parmigianino's Madonna del bel piede," in *Reconsidering the Renaissance*, Papers from the Twenty-First Annual Conference, ed. Mario A. De Cesare, Medieval and Renaissance Texts and Studies, 93 (Binghamton, N.Y.: Medieval and Renaissance Texts and Studies, 1992), pp. 177-89; James Villas, "The Petrarchan Topos *bel piede*: Generative Footsteps," *Romance Notes* 11 (1969):167-73.

21 Georges Vigarello, "The Upward Training of the Body from the Age of Chivalry to Courtly Civility," trans. Ughetta Lubin, in *Fragments for a History of the Human Body*, ed. Michel Feher with Ramona Naddaff and Nadia Tazi, 3 vols. (New York: Zone, 1989), 2:154-55.

good fit toward a good appearance. Clothing for both sexes was commonly fastened in the center front, from neck to waist or below, with a lengthy cord. It was secured with a knot at one end, then threaded with a metal-tipped lacing horizontally or diagonally through eyelets on either side of the opening.[22] With the progress of fashion, fit became tightness and tightness stiffness. The outstanding feature of female dress in the sixteenth century was its rigidity. The look was achieved partly by an increase in lacing tightly, partly by the introduction of artificial stiffening. Although artificial stiffening did not appear before that century, there developed a variety of methods to achieve a firm and straight torso. Usual were the buckram—a front attached to the bodice that flattened the stomach—and beneath the bodice a separate laced corset.[23]

By the middle of the sixteenth century there appeared in vogue for women rigid corsets with stays of whalebone to replace the tightly fitting bodices fashioned only of cloth. The more rigid bone molded the bust and the back into a set shape. As Henri Estienne (1531-98) remarked, "The ladies call a whalebone (or something else in the absence of the latter) their stay, which they put under their breast, right in the middle, in order to keep straighter." The custom, he noted, originated with the Italians. In the fashion for postural rectitude and rigidity, the garment imposed a shape on the body: laced and braced.[24] Garments, believed natural and honest by tradition, were blamed for a novelty that not merely decorated but distorted the female frame. As the translator of the *Shyp of Folys of the World* accused, "They deform that figure that God himself has made." Another censor complained that women were purchasing wire waists, as if their fleshy ones were insufficient. Stays were condemned as a deformation, as yet another moralist urged women to reflect on the divine indwelling in their bodies. Moralists, implicitly acknowledging female maturity as ideal, complained that fashion reduced women to "babyishness," since in their layers they could not walk but had to be conveyed in coaches. Not only did stays deform the wearer's body but they also imperiled the procreation of new bodies. As intimate to the body, women often awarded their stays to men as amatory tokens. There were ribald comments on their shape, which was somewhat phallic and, when in position, pointed down to the genitals. There were even suggestions that the constriction of stays caused miscarriages and that dissolute women wore them precisely to abort. "The baudy busk keeps down flat the bed wherein the babe should breed."[25] Yet stays for rigidity

---

22 Elizabeth Birbari, *Dress in Italian Painting: 1460-1500* (London: John Murray, 1975), pp. 74-79.

23 Aileen Ribeiro, *Dress and Morality* (London: B. T. Batsford, 1986), p. 70.

24 Vigarello, "Upward Training of the Body," pp. 154-55, citing Henri Estienne, *Dialogue du nouveau langage français, italianisé*, 1:210.

25 Ribeiro, *Dress and Morality*, pp. 59, 70-73 (translations modernized).

affected not only fronts but also backs, spines as well as stomachs, and so became integral to erect posture for women.

Such corsets with whalebones for adult wear no longer served the same straightening function as swaddling cloths for baby use. They were a matter of etiquette, not morphology. Corsets related to the temporary outline of the body, not its permanent distortion, to the definition of a silhouette, rather than the modification of a defect. Straightening by corset was merely illusory. Yet the constraints of swaddling cloths continued even for girls in a system of tightening dress. Girlish bodies were subjected to correctives that would guarantee a waist in a practice of perfection through bandages. Ambroise Paré (1510-90) lamented those who had become "hunched and deformed by having their bodies too tightly bound." For real deformity a corset was simply a disguise. Paré described with illustrations a metal cage for girls who were hunchbacked and deformed. It was an iron corset, perforated so that it was not too heavy, padded so that it was not too hurtful, and changed to accommodate growth. The mechanical pressure of iron on vertebrae already formed evidenced a renaissance faith in technology for change. Whalebone stays were for aesthetics, the creation of tailors for fashion; metal fastenings were for therapeutics, the instrument of surgeons for pathology. Yet both types of corsets displayed a sensibility toward an erect posture for women that was new.[26]

Michelangelo portrays Eve bodily, as a painter must, conferring her human status by an erectile posture. Nude as pristine, she straightens herself. There is nothing of the Eve at creation on Lorenzo Ghiberti's (1378-1455) doors of paradise, where she is borne aloft by angels who must straighten and stretch her arm toward the divine shoulder.[27] No swaddling cloth or stiffened corset is in evidence. Nor does she require that caprice of medieval fashion for women, the walking stick of valuable wood with an ornamental top, although the accessory was just passing out of vogue.[28] Eve is perfect from God's own hand: alert and arising. She steps out of Adam's side, in the medieval artistic convention for her scriptural making from his rib (Gen. 2:21-22). In the Roda bible, on the same folio that perches Adam divinely steadied on a craggy pedestal, God is depicted as holding that formative rib in his hand. He blesses a supine Adam, while Eve emerging erect from his side replicates the divine benediction of man.[29]

---

[26] Vigarello, "Upward Training of the Body," pp. 174-75, citing Ambroise Paré, *Chirurgie* 17.8.

[27] Lorenzo Ghiberti, Door of paradise, 1425-27, baptistry, Florence; reproduced in Richard Krautheimer, *Ghiberti's Bronze Doors* (Princeton, N.J.: Princeton University Press, 1971), pl. 75.

[28] For the walking stick, see Katherine Morris Lester and Bess Viola Oerke, *Accessories of Dress* (Peoria, Ill.: Chas. A. Bennett, 1954), pp. 391-92.

[29] Bible, Roda, 11th century, Paris, Bibliothèque national, MS. latin 6, fol. 6; reproduced in Johannes Zahlten, *Creatio mundi: Darstellungen der sechs Schöpfunstage und naturwis-*

Exactly how many ribs Adam had left after Eve became a test of orthodoxy. William of Conches had argued in medieval philosophy that woman's body was molded from the clay beside Adam, not literally taken from a rib in his side.[30] Bartolomeo Goggio (b.c.1430) declared in renaissance praise that she was indeed fashioned from his rib but miraculously so, since a rib naturally would have produced a rib and not a woman. Eve was a nobler creature than Adam because she was made from man, while he was molded from mud like a frog.[31] The rib was a bone of contention. *Malleus maleficarum* declared that witchcraft necessarily attracted women because they were more carnal than men, as proved by their crooked matter. "There was a defect in the formation of the first woman, since she was formed from a bent rib, that is, a rib of the breast, which is bent as it were in a contrary direction to a man. And since through this defect she is an imperfect animal, she always deceives."[32] A treatise on marriage argued contrarily that the formation of woman from the rib, rather than the hand, of man proved that she was not subservient to him. Because she was taken from his side, she should be sheltered beneath his protection.[33]

When Andreas Vesalius (1514-64) published *De humani corporis*, his science did not corroborate the doctrine extrapolated from the biblical etiology that man had one less rib than woman on one side. That popular opinion he criticized as "simply ridiculous." Even if Adam were so created, he argued, it did not follow that all men lacked a rib. The illustrations to his text show evenly matched ribs on all of the skeletons.[34] Those were invariably male. Although renaissance anatomists drew human skeletons from observation and dissection, they were all male, with the first illustration of a female skeleton dating only to the eighteenth century. Vesalius did not distinguish human bones sexually. Although he drew a male nude and a female nude with differences in lines and curves, he disbelieved that such differences involved the skeleton. His model was a single human skeleton from

---

senschaftliches Weltbild im Mittelalter, Geschichte und Politik, 13 (Stuttgart: Klett-Cotta, 1979), abb. 53, and detail 389.

[30] William of Conches, *Philosophia mundi*, British Museum Royal 9.A.XIV, fol. 261rb; cited by Peter Dronke, *"Fabula": Explorations into the Uses of Myth in Medieval Platonism*, Mittellateinische Studien und Texte, 9 (Leiden: E. J. Brill, 1974), p. 19, who reports the text as garbled in *Patrologia latina*, 90:1138; 172:56; J. S. Slotkin, *Readings in Early Anthropology* (Chicago: Aldine, 1965), p. 6.

[31] Bartolommeo Goggio, *De laudibus mulierum* 1.6; cited by Werner L. Gundersheimer, "Bartolommeo Goggio: A Feminist in Renaissance Florence," *Renaissance Quarterly* 33 (1980):188.

[32] Jacob Sprenger and Heinrich Institoris, *Malleus maleficarum* 1.6; trans. Montague Summers (London: John Rodker, 1928), p. 44.

[33] Vicente Mexía, *Saludable instrucción del estado del matrimonio*, pp. 34r-35r; cited by Mary Elizabeth Perry, *Gender and Disorder in Early Modern Seville* (Princeton, N.J.: Princeton University Press, 1990), p. 60.

[34] Andreas Vesalius, *De humani corporis* 1.19; reproduced in J. B. de C. M. Saunders and Charles D. O'Malley, *The Illustrations from the Works of Andreas Vesalius of Brussels* (Cleveland: World, 1950), p. 69, pl. 13; pp. 85, 87, 89, pls. 21-23.

which were derived male and female versions. And although textual notes reveal that his exemplar was drawn from a young male, he did not masculinize it. Sexual differences were limited to the curvaceous outline of the body and the organs of reproduction only. That depiction was not from anatomical ignorance. Women had been dissected since the fourteenth century, and on the very frontispiece of his text it is a woman who is under the knife.[35] Later in the century John Banister (1540-1610) stated in *The Historie of Man* that the notion that woman had more ribs than man was impudent. Worse, it was "extreme madness and folly," since such more and less parts happened only by the excess or lack of the matter of generation, just as there occurred "more or less than five fingers on one hand."[36] Just as the male torso equaled the female in the number of ribs, so did the female skeleton match the male in erect bipedality. The implication of renaissance anatomy was her dignity as created his equal.

The female torso in late medieval art had been elongated, with a wider pelvis than in Hellenistic art. The chest was narrower, the waist higher, and the emphasis was on the generative belly. A fundamental difference in bodily attitudes was displayed in the alteration from the ancient curve of the hip to the medieval curve of the stomach. The curve of the hip had been created by a vertical thrust, with bone and muscle beneath it, supporting the bodily weight. It provided an energetic, controlled image. The curve of the stomach denoted gravity and relaxation, with its heavy lack of structure, suggesting biology, rather than will.[37] Not only was the nude female figure prominent in the middle but also her dressed figure featured a high girdlestead with garments tight and flattened across the breasts while expansive below.[38] Even virgins appeared perpetually pregnant. Michelangelo does not focus on that medieval anatomical zone. Eve's belly is shown, but his emphasis is on her massive buttock and thigh and on a leg heavy in the calf. While Adam's sexual organs are at his creation visible on the fresco to all, hers are visible only to God. In its lateral view her genitals are hidden by her emerging leg, and even her breasts are mostly covered by her upper arms. Eve's vertical direction at creation is reminiscent of classical will toward achievement. Michelangelo's portrayal is of the erectile female form: upright head, thrusting spine, enabled limbs.

An inspiration for his postural design for Eve's upper limbs was Jacopo della Quercia's (1372?-1436) relief, although there God grasped Eve's left

---

35 Londa Schiebinger, "Skeletons in the Closet: The First Illustrations of the Female Skeleton in Eighteenth-Century Anatomy," *Representations* 14 (1986):42-49; eadem, *The Mind Has No Sex?: Women in the Origins of Modern Science* (Cambridge, Mass.: Harvard University Press, 1989), pp. 181-84.

36 John Banister, *The Historie of Man* 1, fol. 23.

37 Kenneth Clark, *The Nude: A Study in Ideal Form*, Bollingen Series 35-2 (New York: Pantheon, 1956), pp. 317-18.

38 Anne Hollander, *Seeing Through Clothes* (New York: Viking, 1978), pp. 97-100.

arm with his left hand, as he blessed her with his right.[39] It was traditional for the Creator so to touch woman. Just as he was portrayed with his hands upon the head or shoulders of Adam, to fashion or to right him, so was he tactile with Eve. On an ivory plaque of the eleventh century from Salerno he touches her shoulders, while her hands slacken at her side. On a relief on the cathedral of Auxerre, where he feels Adam on the head and chest, he touches Eve's outstretched hands as she emerges tiny from man. A mosaic in San Marco, Venice, of Eve fully erect—plainly on her own two feet—depicts God placing his right hand on her shoulder and holding her by the right wrist. A fourteenth-century fresco in the collegiate church in San Gimignano shows Eve emerging diagonally from a slit in the side of supine Adam, her arms extended with joined hands, just as in Michelangelo's fresco. The Creator blesses her with his right hand, while with his left he grasps her wrists.[40]

In manuscript illustrations from the eleventh and twelfth centuries the Creator grasps by both his hands the upper arms of Eve emergent or he takes her by the crook of her elbow. In an English psalter of the thirteenth century he touches her shoulders, while she crosses her hands on her breasts. In a French moralized bible from the same century he embraces her shoulder and grabs her by the crook of her elbow out of Adam's body. In another version he grasps her wrists together, while he curves his other hand over the top of her head. In Italian bibles from the fourteenth century he grasps her outstretched arms or he takes her by the wrist Or he blesses her with one hand, while with the other he takes her hands, wrist, or elbow; or he touches her shoulder. Her gestures include hands at her side and receiving the blessing with her free hand.[41] In an illustration for Martin Luther's

---

[39] Tolnay, *Sistine Ceiling*, p. 34. Jacopo della Quercia, relief, Creation of Eve, San Petronio, Bologna; reproduced, fig. 307. See also James Beck, *Jacopo della Quercia*, 2 vols. (New York: Columbia University Press, 1991), reproduced, 2:pl. 102, and see 1:168-77; Hartt, *Michelangelo*, 3 vols. (New York: Harry N. Abrams, n. d.), 3:15, fig. 7.

[40] Ivory plaque, 11th century, Salerno, Staatliche Museen, Berlin; reproduced in Zahlten, *Creatio mundi*, fig. 1. Relief, 13th century, cathedral of St. Etienne, Auxerre; reproduced, fig. 10. Mosaic, 13th century, vestibule ceiling, San Marco, Venice; reproduced, fig. 39. Fresco, Bartolo di Fredi, 1367, collegiate church, San Gimignano; reproduced, fig. 30.

[41] Historical bible from Guiart des Moulins, French, 14th century, Montpellier, Bibliothèque de la faculté de médecine, MS. H 49, fol. 9; reproduced in Mireille Mentré, *Création et apocalypse: Histoire d'un regard humain sur le divin* (Paris: O. E. I. L., 1984), p. 115. Historical bible, French, 1380, Paris, Bibliothèque nationale, MS. fr. 20090, fol. 3; reproduced in Zahlten, *Creatio mundi*, fig. 132. Queen Mary psalter, English, 14th century, London, British Library, Royal 2.B.VII, fol. 3; reproduced, fig. 169. Bedford missal, French, 1423-30, London, British Library, Add. 18850, fol. 14; reproduced, fig. 134. Stained glass window, about 1370, choir, cathedral, Erfurt; reproduced, fig. 44. Relief, Lorenzo Maitani, cathedral, Orvieto, 1310-30; reproduced, fig. 8, and better in *La cattedrale di Orvieto: Santa Maria Assunta in cielo*, ed. Giusi Testa (Umbria: Istituto poligrafico e zecca dello stato, 1990), p. 67. For the derivation of this Creation of Eve from a Nereid sarcophagus, see Clark, *Nude*, pp. 286, 316, and p. 287, fig. 227. Historical bible, French, c. 1380, Stuttgart, Württ. Landesbibliothek, Cod. bib. 2°6, fol. 9; reproduced in Zahlten, *Creatio mundi*, fig. 176.

(1483-1546) translation of the Bible God places his hands traditonally on Eve's shoulders, while in a chronicle he takes her wrist and blesses her. Later versions replace the anthropomorphic deity with symbolic light and fire. In Jost Amman's (1539-91) invention Adam sprawls on his stomach while Eve lifts her knee limply from his back as she leans back awkwardly. A flaming and smoking shaft of light penetrates her breastplate.[42]

The tactile tradition of the divine hand on the female body continued well into renaissance art. In Parmigianino's (1503-40) drawing an aerial Creator grasps Eve on both of her uplifted elbows as she steps out of Adam's side.[43] The tradition achieved a remarkable expression in an engraving by Lucas van Leyden (1494-1533). While Adam reclines, Eve stands—one leg out of his body, one leg in a slit in his side up to her calf. Her arm is outstretched toward Adam's head, reminiscent of her medieval blessing of him. But it is the Creator's posture that is exceptional, for he stoops crouching and kneeling, leaning awkwardly to grasp woman from man. With one arm behind Eve on her buttocks, with his other splayed hand he reaches across her breasts toward her side.[44] God wears a splendid turban, perhaps as a patriarch or potentate, but more wonderfully as the person whose attribute in renaissance portraiture it was: an artist. In a version of the blessing of Eve by Marten de Vos (1532-1603) the Creator even touches her index and middle fingertips with his, while she gestures to Adam with her other hand.[45]

In other examples the Creator does not touch Eve but simply blesses her with his hand. Responsively she assumes the traditional gesture (*orans*) for prayer: arms extended and uplifted with palms displayed.[46] When manual

---

42 Bible by Nikolaus Wolrab, 1541, Leipzig; reproduced in Philipp Schmidt, *Die Illustration der Lutherbibel, 1522-1700* (Basel: Friedrich Reinhardt, 1962), p. 220, fig. 154. Hartmann Schedel, *Weltchronik* (Nürnberg: Anton Koberger, 1493); reproduced, p. 58, fig. 17. Jost Amman, Creation of Eve, 1571; reproduced, p. 272, fig. 104. Cf. his bible of Feyeraband, 1583, Frankfurt, p. 266, fig. 189; and the version by Ehlich Pflicht, p. 298, fig. 217.

43 Parmigianino, Creation of Eve, drawing, British Museum, London; reproduced in Freedberg, *Parmigianino: His Works in Painting* (Cambridge, Mass.: Harvard University Press, 1950), fig. 41.

44 Lucas van Leyden, Creation of Eve, engraving, 1529, Staatliche Museen Preussischer Kulturbesitz Kupferstichkabinett, Berlin. Reproduced in Ellen S. Jacobowitz and Stephanie Loeb Stepanek, *The Prints of Lucas van Leyden and His Contemporaries* (Princeton, N.J.: National Gallery of Art, Washington, D.C., with Princeton University Press, 1992), p. 235; Max J. Friedländer, *Lucas van Leyden*, ed. F. Winkler (Berlin: Walter de Gruyter, 1963), pl. 28. God, wearing a crown and kneeling down on the ground with Eve among the animals, imposses his left hand on her head while with the right he blesses her. Title page, German bible, 1536, Fraschauer, Zürich; reproduced in James Strachan, *Early Bible Illustrations* (Cambridge: Cambridge University Press, 1957), fig. 84.

45 Marten de Vos, Creation of Eve; reproduced in Armin Zweite, *Marten de Vos als Maler: Ein Beitrag zur Geschichte der Antwerpener Malerei in der zweite Hälfte des sechzehnte Jahrhunderts* (Berlin: Gebr. Mann, 1980), fig. 16, and see pp. 269-70.

46 Missal from Hildesheim, German, 12th century, Brabecke, Sgl. Fürstenberg, fol. 10v; reproduced in Zahlten, *Creatio mundi*, fig. 56. Flavius Josephus, *Historia*, French, 12th century, Paris, Bibliothèque nationale, MS. lat. 5047, fol. 2; reproduced, fig. 71. Bible from Sou-

gestures were codified and illustrated in John Bulwer's (fl. 1654) *Chirologia*, this extension toward heaven was explained as "the habit of devotion, in a natural and universal form of prayer." It was practiced from adversity and anguish or to give thanks and praise. Expressing fervent affections, the extension of the hands was compared to wings spread to assist the ascension of the heart. Even atheists and hypocrites resorted to it in desperation during extreme danger, he reported, although, since they lacked belief, they practiced it like groveling apes. The gesture of joining hands was among the current customs of praying in church; others were a moderate uplifting of the the hands and the cupping of them by ten fingers in the form of the letter *X*. The practice at the *oremus* (let us pray) of the Mass was for the celebrant to extend, then join, his hands, both gathering and uniting the people. The liturgy was difficult manually, Bulwer thought: not for the hands of just anyone—the priest had to be well trained in gesture.[47] Eve's medieval responses to the divine blessing also range from arms outstretched to bent at the elbow but with the palms of her hands joined in the novel style.[48]

That was the gesture Michelangelo adopted for Eve: arms extended with joined hands. Although it was by the sixteenth century a common pose for the faithful, as in portraits of donors before saints,[49] it was introduced in art through papal portraiture. The thirteenth-century portrait of Pope Gregory IX in a mosaic on the restored façade of old St. Peter's in Rome supplanted the ancient prayerful type of parted and uplifted arms. The pope is

vigny, French, 12th century, Moulins, Bibliothèque municipale, MS. 1, fol. 4v; reproduced, fig. 113. Right hand only: Hexameron, from Weissenau, German, 12th century, Amiens, Bibliothèque de la ville, MS. L'Escalopier 30, fol. 10v; reproduced, fig. 112. Bible, French, 13th century, Bibliothèque de l'Arsenal, Cod. 5211, fol. 3v; reproduced, fig. 122. Bible from Maerlant-Reim, Netherlands, 1332, Hague, Rijks Museum, MS. 10 B 21, Fol. 1v (MS. 186); reproduced, fig. 127. For the open, uplifted hand, see Heinz Demisch, *Erhobene Hände: Geschichte einer Gebärde in der bildenden Kunst* (Stuttgart: Urachhaus, 1984); for upraised arms, see also Arturo Schwarz, "La dimensione verticale dell'andragino immortale," in *The Intellectual Expressions of Prehistoric Man, Art, and Religion*, Acts of the Valcamonica Symposium '79, ed. Antonio Beltrán (Brescia: Edizioni del Centro, Centro comuno di studi prehistorica, 1983), pp 79-95.

47 John Bulwer, *Chirologia*, pp. 23-28, 31.

48 Outstretched: Altar design on ivory table, 12th century, cathedral museum, Salerno; reproduced in Zahlten, *Creatio mundi*, fig. 6. Processional cross, detail, end of 13th century, treasury room, St. John Lateran, Rome; reproduced, fig. 21. Bent: Flavius Josephus, *Antiquitates judaicae*, English, 12th cenutry, Paris, Bibliothèque nationale, MS. lat. 16730, fol. 3; reproduced, fig. 85. Fresco, about 1200, S. Paolo inter vineas, Spoleto; reproduced, fig. 25. Mosaic, 13th century, cuppola, bapistry of S. Giovanni, Florence; reproduced, fig. 38 (fingers splayed). Universal history, French, 1300, Paris, Bibliothèque nationale, MS. fr. 20125, fol. 3; reproduced, fig. 125. Benedictine bible, German, 1446, Münich, Bayerische Staatsbibliothek, Cod. lat. 4501a, fol. 4; reproduced, fig. 92. Bible of Federigo da Montefeltre at Urbino, Italian, 1476-78, Rome, Bibliotheca apostolica vaticana, Cod. urb. lat. 1, fol. 7; reproduced, fig. 95. Variant with hands not joined: Bible, Italian, 12th century, Perugia, Bibliotheca augustana, MS. L. 59, fol. 2v; reproduced, fig. 166.

49 For the feudal gesture of commendation in paintings of saints and their venerators, see Corine Schleif, "Hands That Appoint, Anoint, and Ally: Late Medieval Donor Strategies for Appropriating Approbation through Painting," *Art History* 16 (1993):3-7.

represented before an enthroned Christ as small, although not miniature, kneeling with his upper body erect and his hands joined before his breast. As in Michelangelo's Creation of Eve, the hands are extended out, not held close to the body. The figure of the kneeling pope who prayed with hands joined became by the end of that century a Roman iconographic scheme for the papacy. The gesture derived immediately from commendation, as feudal forms became adopted ecclesiastically, especially in the liturgy. Commendation in feudal homage involved the vassal's placement of his joined hands in the hands of the lord as a sign of his surrender to dependency and also of his trust and fidelity.[50]

There was a a similar religious gesture. When Margery Kempe's (b. c.1373) husband agreed to a common vow of chastity, he appealed to the local bishop in whose hands he placed his own in agreement.[51] The Roman pontifical stipulated that the bishop during his consecration keep his hands joined while the pope bestowed the crozier as the sign of office. The same gesture was required of the priest during his ordination, in receiving the paten and chalice. Joined hands was a female practice in the rite for the consecration of virgins. The gesture of joining hands would be formally incorporated into the liturgical reforms of the Council of Trent, as published in the Roman missal. An instance was the joining of hands for the elevation of the host, a Franciscan practice dating to medieval usage in the papal chapel in the Lateran palace. The increasing popularity of the gesture developed from Eucharistic devotion to the elevated host, popularly supposed the principal reason for attending Mass. The gesture of joined hands was, however, usually associated, even for the pope, with the posture of kneeling,[52] so that Eve's usage, as she rises to an erect stance, is bold. But, then, the Creator himself motions her to stand.

Those gestures of feudal commendation and investiture, as adopted for ecclesiastical ritual, had precedents in Roman juridical symbolism. Joined hands derived further still from the practical attitude of prisoners who had surrendered and so held their hands together before being tied.[53] As Erasmus (1469?-1536) explained the adage *dare manus*, "to put one's hands up," it was to confess oneself beaten, "for those who surrender to the man who

---

50 See Gerhart Ladner, "The Gestures of Prayer in Papal Iconography of the Thirteenth and Early Fourteenth Century," in *"Didascaliae": Studies in Honor of Anselm M. Albareda*, ed. Sesto Prete (New York: Bernard M. Rosenthal, 1961), pp. 251-52, 255, 258-59, 261; Moshe Barasch, *Giotto and the Language of Gesture* (Cambridge: Cambridge University Press, 1987), pp. 59-64. Ciaconius, Gregory IX, façade, Old St. Peter's, Rome, reproduced in *"Didascaliae,"* p. 251, fig. 5. For the ceremony and gesture of homage, see also Marc Bloch, *Feudal Society*, trans. L. A. Manyon, vol. 1: *The Growth of Ties of Dependence* (Chicago: University of Chicago Press, 1964), pp. 130, 145-46, 151, 162.

51 *The Book of Margery Kempe* 1.15.

52 Ladner, "Gestures of Prayer," pp. 262, 264, 265, 268.

53 Ladner, "Gestures of Prayer," pp. 262-63, 258 n. 33. See also Jean-Claude Schmitt, *La raison des gestes dans l'Occident médiévale* (Paris: Gallimard, 1990), pp. 295-97.

has defeated them to avoid being killed voluntarily hold out their hands to be shackled."[54] Although the gesture in modern practice is devotional, its historical usage was political and legal, from the original meaning of religion from *religo* for "I bind." The gesture for prayer, *oro* ("I pray") as uplifted hands, was still distinguished into the seventeenth century from joined hands for *libertatem resigno* ("I resign my liberty"). As Bulwer defined, "To hold forth the hands together is their natural expression who yield, submit, and resign up themselves with supplication into the power of another." The ancient term was "to surrender the hand" (*manum dare*), just as Ovid yielded to Cupid in triumphal procession.[55] Michelangelo could have known the gesture even from that single reference, for he had a personally inscribed copy of Ovid's *Amores* in his library.[56]

But there were more serious examples from Roman political history, as Bulwer detailed them. In Dio Cassius's text Veringetorix "falling on his knees before Caesar and holding forth his hands exhibited the gesture of a suppliant." So did Diridates, king of Armenia, perform the same gesture of obedience and submission to Nero. The legates of Decebalus acted similarly like captives before the Senate—to the triumph of Trajan over the Dacians. Plutarch related how the the Romans in the galley, carrying the golden cup fashioned from the jewels of matrons, "held up their hands and entreated, making no resistance." In another example Tigranes, king of Armenia, was waited upon by four kings who held their hands together while he held audience in his chair of state. The gesture, as Bulwer expounded it, was "the most manifest confession and token of bondage," demonstrating that "they resigned all their liberty and offered their bodies unto their lord and master, more ready to suffer than anything to do."[57]

Since the concept of prayer can include submission to the divine sovereignty and will, the modern adoption of joined hands as its comprehensive gesture is intelligible. Yet Eve's gesture on Michelangelo's fresco is in its historical situation not devotional but submissive. It is a variant on medieval depictions of Eve at creation as divinely grasped on her wrist. The gesture of grasping by the wrist denoted the subjugation or dependency of weaker persons to or upon stronger authorities.[58] It affirmed power, spiri-

---

[54] Erasmus, *Adagia* 1.9.79, in *Opera omnia* (Leiden) 2; *The Adages of Erasmus*, trans. R. A. B. Mynors, *The Collected Works of Erasmus* (Toronto: University of Toronto Press, 1989), 32:223.

[55] Bulwer, *Chirologia*, p. 41, citing Ovid, *Amores* 1.2.33.

[56] E. Grisebach, "Ein Buch aus Michelangelos Bibliothek," *Zeitschrift für Bücherfreunde* 1 (1897-98); cited by Robert J. Clements, *The Poetry of Michelangelo* (New York: New York University Press, 1965), p. 8.

[57] Bulwer, *Chrirologia*, pp. 41-42, citing Cassius Dio, *Historia romana* 40.41.1-2; 62.2.4; 68.10.1; Plutarch, Camillus in *Vitae parallelae* 42.3-4; and the final reference unlocated by the editor.

[58] See Schleif, "Hands That Appoint, Anoint, and Ally," p. 18.

tual and physical—by possession, protection, or constraint.[59] The gesture was frequent since early Christian art in scenes of the harrowing of hell, in which the resurrected Jesus grasps Adam or Eve by the wrist to pull them from the bowels of the earth as a sign of his saving power.[60] Other scriptural scenes of life over death illustrated by the gesture included the raising of the daughter of Jairus and the rescue of Peter on the sea. The gesture may have been introduced to medieval art from late antique ceremonies at court, in which a superior as a sign of his magnanimity grasped a kneeling subject by the wrist and assisted him to his feet. The motif became common in allegorical scenes, such as the devil grasping by the wrist a vice, or death, or the pope. The gesture also applied in a legal context, such as a creditor seizing a debtor by the wrist. A grasp on the wrist also denoted crimes of sexual violence.[61] Other examples of force in the use of the grasp were religious depictions of a devil and and angel struggling over a soul, of the guards arresting Samson, and of the massacre of the innocents. Yet the crucial artistic motif for rape, the very emblem of sexual assault, was the hold of the male rapist on the wrist of his female victim. Her constraint in rape contrasted with traditional portrayals of marriage, in which the wife gave her body freely to her husband in the couple's joining of their right hands in consent. Although the notion of a religious authority as a rapist was not unthinkable, since the majority of the accused in documented medieval cases of rape were clergy,[62] in a creational context God is not about to violate Eve.

The iconography, in which the Creator grasps his creature as she emerges from the side of another human, is reminiscent of illustrations of the Caesarean delivery for childbirth. The medically preferred incision was lateral, not median, and on the left side as Guy de Chauliac (d.1368), the papal surgeon, first precisely instructed. Delivery was a process of the midwife pulling the infant out of the mother's side, for which exercise long slim fingers and short nails were recommended.[63] Although scripture never men-

---

59 François Garnier, *Le langage de l'image au Moyen Âge: Signification et symbolique*, 2 vols. (Paris: Léopard d'or, 1982-89), 1:199, 202-5; Barasch, *Giotto and the Language of Gesture*, pp. 133-34.

60 Walter Loeschke, "Der Griff ans Handgelenk: Skizze einer Motivgeschichtlichen Untersuchung," in *Feschrist für Peter Metz*, ed. Ursula Schlegel and Claus Zoege von Manteuffel (Berlin: Walter de Gruyter, 1965), pp. 46-73; Barasch, *Giotto and the Language of Gesture*, pp. 137-38; and for classical background, Gerhard Neumann, *Gesten und Gebärden in der griechischen Kunst* (Berlin: Walter de Gruyter, 1965), pp. 59-66. See also Gertrud Schiller, *Ikonographie der christlichen Kunst*, 2d ed., 3 vols. (Gütersloh: Gerd Mohn, 1969), 3:348-77. Among the renaissance examples the most suggestive adoption is by Agnolo Bronzino, in which Christ grasps the wrists of Adam, whose hands are joined, while a woman below in imitation assists another person. Bronzino, Harrowing of hell, 1552, S. Croce, Florence; reproduced, p. 377, fig. 172.

61 Schleif, "Hands that Appoint, Anoint, and Ally," pp. 18-19.

62 See Diane Wolfthal, "'A Hue and a Cry': Medieval Rape Imagery and Its Transformation," *Art Bulletin* 75 (1993):40-43, 51, without reference to Eve.

63 See Renate Blumenfeld-Kosinski, *Not of Woman Born: Representations of Caesarean Birth in Medieval and Renaissance Culture* (Ithaca, N.Y.: Cornell University Press, 1990), pp.

tions or implies any birth by Caesarean section,[64] in the iconographic creation of Eve a slit in Adam's left side can be visible. In the fresco from San Gimignano it appears with surgical precision. Eve is even in other examples born tiny, as an infant.[65] Her consistent presentation at creation or by Caesarean is headfirst, medically regarded as the correct position,[66] from the classical and renaissance preference for the head, rather than the feet (as in breech birth), as the noblest human part.[67] As the medieval physician Henri de Mondeville affirmed, "God himself practiced as surgeon when He made the first man out of clay and from his ribs made Eve." The initial iconography of dissection in a printed book depicts a man standing upright with his abdomen slit. Behind him is a walled garden of Eden in which God is pulling Eve from the side of Adam, with her one foot still in his slit.[68] In such depictions the Creator plays the role of midwife, in delivering Eve bodily by hand in a pulling motion. His touch is vital, not violent.

Jacopo Carruci da Pontormo's (1494-1557) study of the creation of Eve[69] emphasizes her human dignity from the sense of touch, which erect posture

---

23, 35, 36, 37, 39, 40, 41, 45 for lateral incision, and see figs. 4-6, 8-10, 13, 17, 19-20. For the midwife's hands, dating to Soranus's gynecology, see pp. 34, 101; and for pulling out, pp. 21, 63.

64 Jeffrey Boss, "The Antiquity of Caesarean Section with Maternal Survival: The Jewish Tradition," *Medical History* 5 (1961):128.

65 For the surgical slit, see Bartolo di Fredi, fresco, 1367, collegiate church, San Gimignano; reproduced in Zahlten, *Creatio mundi*, fig. 30, cf. figs. 71, 134. For Eve as miniature, see figs. 10, 18, 41, 44, 92; and Fritz Weindler, "Der Kaiserschnitt nach den ältesten Überlieferungen unter Zugrundlegen von 18 Geburstdarstellungen," *Janus: Archives internationales pour l'histoire de la médecine et la géographie médicale* 20 (1915):figs. 7, 8. The creation of Eve as the artistic scheme for the Caesarean birth was published in pp. 1-40. Blumenfeld-Kosinksi suggests that only one of her illustrations of Caesarean sections corresponds somewhat to Eve's creation. *Not of Woman Born*, p. 73, and fig. 9, Jean Bondel, *Les faits des romains*, c. 1375, fol. 199r. Although her survey of illustrated Caesarean sections is comprehensive, her comparative sample for Eve's birth is merely the two examples from the thirteenth century proposed by Weindler. Nor has the possibility been considered that the influence is the reverse: that the practice of the Caesarean section influenced the iconography of Eve's birth.

66 See Mireille Laget, *Naissances: L'accouchement avant l'âge de la clinique* (Paris: Seuil, 1982), pp. 240-41; Blumenfeld-Kosinski, *Not of Woman Born*, pp. 33, 34.

67 See Marsilio Ficino, *Epistolae* 5.27; 6.42.

68 Henri de Mondeville, *Chirurgia*, p. 202; cited by Marie-Christine Pouchelle, *The Body and Surgery in the Middle Ages*, trans. Rosemary Morris (London: Polity, 1990), p. 43. Miniature, Bartholomaeus Anglicus, *De proprietate rerum* (Harlem: J. Bellaert, 1485); reproduced in André Hahn and Paule Dumaître, ed. Janine Samion-Contet, *Histoire de la médicine et du livre médical à la lumière des collections de la bibliothèque de la faculté de médicine de Paris* (Paris: Olivier Perrin, 1962), p. 59; cited by Pouchelle, *Body and Surgery*, p. 85. For a renaissance midwife on presentations at birth, see Louise Boursier (1563-1636), *Observations diverses, sur la sterilité, perte de fruict, foecondité, accouchements, et maladies des femmes, et enfants nouveaux naiz.*

69 Pontormo, Study for a creation of Eve, c. 1519-20, Uffizi, Florence; reproduced in Janet Cox Rearick, *The Drawings of Pontormo*, 2 vols. (Cambridge, Mass.: Harvard University Press, 1964), 2:fig. 114, and see 1:166-67. Cf. Pontormo, Compositional study for Christ in glory and the creation of Eve, Uffizi, Florence; reproduced in *Pontormo: Drawings*, ed.

conferred on the able hand. He portrays God bending down to her, his free hand posing his thumb and fingers in opposition. That opposition was a classical distinction of humans from other animals, especially apes. The Creator's digital opposition is also reminiscent of medieval and renaissance illustrations of the compass in hand with which the demiurge measures creation.[70] In a late fifteenth-century bible of Federigo da Montefeltre from Urbino the Creator, seated with the globe between his spread legs, extends both arms widely, palms open and down and thumbs in opposition, to gesture expansively at his work. In a late fourteenth-century manuscript he holds a book and compass while measuring the earth. In its adjacent illustration he holds the book in one hand but, rather than the compass, Eve's hand. She acknowledges his blessing with her free hand.[71] In Pontormo's interpretation God with his free hand grasps Eve by both her wrists, as she emerges from behind Adam's flank. The Creator lends her a hand for emergence and erection, yet his hand on her wrist essentially signifies his power over her. His gesture means not only the power of divine over human but also of male over female. In the medical and philosophical convention the male was active and creative, the female passive and created. As Alessandra Macinghi Strozzi (1407-71) stated the reality in a chiding letter to her son on how to handle a wife, "A man, when he really is a man, makes a woman a woman."[72]

Women had been depicted artistically since prehistory, although then they were always engraved—only men were painted.[73] In the earliest periods of art females were more numerous than males, but in archaic or archaistic

Salvatore S. Nigro (New York: Harry N. Abrams, 1992), pl. 68; Cox-Rearick, *Drawings of Pontormo*, 2:fig. 345, and see 1:331-34.

70 See Bible moralisée, 13th c., Vienna, cod. 1179, fol. 1v; reproduced in Zahlten, *Creatio mundi*, fig. 269. Bible moralisee, 13th c., Vienna, cod. 2554, fol. 1v; reproduced, fig. 270. Psalter, English, 13th c., Paris, Bibliothèque national, MS. lat. 8846, fol. 1; reproduced, fig. 283. Universal history, c. 1285, London, British Library, Add. 15268, fol. 1; reproduced, fig. 284. Composite manuscript, 13th c., Eton College Library, Eton, MS. 177, fol. 1v; reproduced, fig. 286. Holkham bible, English, 1326-31, British Library, Add. 47682, fol. 2; reproduced, fig. 290. Augustine, *De civitate Dei*, French, 1376, Paris, Bibliothèque national, MS. fr. 22913, fol. 2v; reproduced, fig. 180. Historical bible, c. 1380, Stuttgart, Württ. Landesbibliothek, Cod. Bibl. 2°6; reproduced, fig. 287. Orosius, French, 14th c., Munich; reproduced, fig. 288. Window, middle 15th c., Great Malvern Priory church, Worcestershire; reproduced, fig. 289. For the compass in medieval and renaissance scenes of creation, see also Anthony Blunt, "Blake's 'Ancient of Days': The Symbolism of the Compasses," *Journal of the Warburg and Coutauld Institutes* 2 (1938):53-55.

71 Bible of Federigo da Montefeltre at Urbino, Italian, 1476-78, Rome, Bibliotheca apostolica vaticana, Cod. Urb. Lat. 1, fol. 7; reproduced in Zahlten, *Creatio mundi*, fig. 332, detail of 95. Augustine, *De civitate Dei*, French, 1376, Paris, Bibliothèque nationale, MS. fr. 22913, fol. 2v; reproduced, fig. 180.

72 Alessandra Macinghi Strozzi, *Lettere* 33; cited by Lauro Martines, "A Way of Looking at Women in Renaissance Florence," *Journal of Medieval and Renaissance Studies* 4 (1974):22.

73 Patricia C. Rice and Ann L. Paterson, "Anthropomorphs in Cave Art: An Empirical Assessment," *American Anthropologist* 90 (1988):671-72.

groups they were only represented as the vulva. They tended to be central in the composition, with males peripheral,[74] yet passive, with males active.[75] Michelangelo's composition reverses that tradition: his Eve is central and active, with Adam peripheral and passive. While she is awake and arising, he is asleep on his buttocks slumped against a bare tree trunk. Yet not all renaissance observers of that fresco would have interpreted Eve's stance so affirmatively. Tomasso da Vio, Cajetan (1469-1534), who preached officially below that ceiling, explained in his commentary on Genesis that the sleep of Adam was a metaphor for the defect in male power from which woman was produced. "For a sleeping man is only half a man; similarly, the principle creating woman is only semi-virile. It is for this reason that woman is called an imperfect version of the male by the philosophers."[76] Thus was the debility of Adam transferred to her. In her gesture of joined hands on that fresco Eve remains traditionally submissive.

Eve's submission is not to man, however, but to God. It is the Creator to whom she relates posturally and gesturally, ignoring Adam who slumbers unconscious of her presence. The conviction of female submission to God, rather than to man, would be articulated by Erasmus in his colloquy "Puerpera," on the new mother. The protagonist asserted that males were only believed better than females on the authority of males. When her interlocutor conceded that all humans were incorporated into Christ by faith, she wondered why all members did not share equally, then, in that one head of the Church, his body. When God created human beings he expressed his image in mental, not bodily, gifts—and in those women were obviously superior, she stated. Fabulla pressed a clever argument that subverted the scriptural order: "For Adam was formed first, then Eve" (1 Tim. 2:13).

> Eutrapelus. Well, but the male was created first.
> Fabulla. Adam was created before Christ. And artists usually surpass themselves in their later works.[77]

---

74 André Leroi-Gourhan, *Treasures of Prehistoric Art*, trans. Norbert Gutterman (New York: Harry N. Abrams, 1964), p. 113. See also Henri Delporte, *L'image de la femme dans l'art préhistorique* (Paris: Picard, 1979). For recent interpretation of the "Venus" figurines, see Marcia-Anne Dobres, "Re-Considering Venus Figurines: A Feminist Inspired Re-Analysis," in *Ancient Images, Ancient Thought: The Archaeology of Ideology*. Proceedings of the Twenty-Third Conference of the Archaeological Association of the University of Calgary, ed. A. Sean Goldsmith, Sandra Garvie, David Selin, and Jeanette Smith (Calgary, Alta.: University of Calgary Archaeological Association, 1992), pp. 245-62; Paul G. Bahn and Jean Vertut, *Images of the Ice Age* (New York: Facts on File, 1988), pp. 138, 164-65; Marija Gimbutas, "Vulvas, Breasts, and Buttocks of the Goddess Creatress: Commentary on the Origins of Art," in *The Shape of the Past: Essays in Honor of Franklin D. Murphy*, ed. G. Buccellati and C. Speroni (Los Angeles, Calif.: Institute of Archaeology, 1981), pp. 15-42.

75 Rice and Paterson, "Anthropomorphs in Cave Art," pp. 671-72.

76 See Tommaso de Vio, Cajetan, *Commentarii in quinque mosaicos libros* ad loc. Gen. 2:21, p. 25; cited by Maclean, *Renaissance Notion of Woman*, p. 12.

77 Erasmus, "Puerpura," in *Colloquia*, in *Opera omnia* (Amsterdam), 1-3:455-57; *Collected Works of Erasmus*, trans. Craig R. Thompson, 2 vols. (Toronto: University of Toronto

Eve's manual submission to her Creator in Michelangelo's fresco is not particularly female but universally human. His artistic exception was the resurrected Christ, whom he sketched emerging from the tomb, like Eve from Adam, but with his arms thrown up in liberation.[78] Eve's gesture of joined hands imitates the servility of even the pope at the altar before God. Only, while he on the floor below her must kneel, she in her pristine creation on the ceiling above may by divine invitation stand.

Ambrose in his exegesis of the creation had so discoursed on the liturgical dignity of human hands. "Great are the deeds for which the hand is eminent. The hand is placed on the holy altars as conciliator of divine grace. Through it we offer as well as partake in the celestial sacraments. It is the hand which performs and at the same time dispenses the divine mysteries."[79] The priesthood of the laity was a scriptural teaching of Peter (1 Peter 2:9), prototype of the papacy. It would be preached also in the Protestant Church,[80] although women would remain excluded from clerical ordination. No Catholic woman dared even touch the Eucharist, much less elevate it solemnly before the congregation with joined hands.[81] She was only to imitate the priestly gesture privately at her place. As Robert de Blois taught in his medieval manual on female courtesy, *Le chastoiement de dames*, "At the elevation of the body of Christ, you also should raise joined hands." But she was simultaneously "to bow the head and neck."[82] God incarnate, believed really present to the faithful in the Eucharist, implied submission, rather than dignity, for women in their liturgical gestures of joined hands and bent heads. There was in the church nave and at its communion railing no erect posture with able hands.

Erasmus in his colloquy questioned the inequality of women as members of the one body of Christ, but his character Fabulla was what her name meant: fond of talk. Yet males were not allowed to touch that sacrament

---

Press, 1997), 39:593. For authors who perpetuated Erasmus's argument against priority as superiority, but without acknowledging him as a source, see Kelso, *Doctrine for the Lady*, p. 15. The rule of males over females as the arrogation of male authority was also argued in Castiglione, *Cortegiano* 3.16. See also Dain Trafton, "Politics and the Praise of Women: Political Doctrine in the *Courtier's* Third Book," in *Castiglione: The Ideal and the Real in Renaissance Culture*, ed. Robert W. Hanning and David Rosand (New Haven, Conn.: Yale University Press, 1983), pp. 29-44; José Guidi, "De l'amour courtois à l'amour sacré: La condition de la femme dans l'oeuvre de B. Castiglione," in *Images de la femme*, ed. Rochon, pp. 9-80.

78 See Michelangelo, Resurrection; reproduced in Clark, *Nude*, p. 306, fig. 244. The comparison is mine.

79 Ambrose, *Hexameron* 6.9.69; *Hexameron, Paradise, and Cain and Abel*, trans. John J. Savage, Fathers of the Church, 42 (New York: Fathers of the Church, 1961), p. 278.

80 John Calvin, *Institutio religionis christiani* 4.19.25. For a survey, see G. D. Henderson, "Priesthood of Believers," *Scottish Journal of Theology* 7 (1954):5-15.

81 For the traditional arguments against women's ordination, see Francine Cardman, "The Medieval Question of Women and Orders," *The Thomist* 42 (1978):582-99.

82 Robert de Blois, *Le chastoiement des dames* lines 417-19. For this work, see Bornstein, *Lady in the Tower*, pp. 59-61; for female courtesy in general, see Angela Giallongo, *Il galateo e le donne nel medioevo* (Rimini: Maggioli, 1987).

either, unless they were so ordained.[83] Although the scriptural command of Jesus to his disciples was "Take," "Take this," or "Take, eat" (Mark 14:22; Luke 22:17; Matt. 26:26), in a liturgical reversal of gesture as language the tongue became substituted for the hand. On a fresco in the cathedral of Orvieto, whose foundation recorded a miraculous Mass,[84] persons kneel in the sanctuary before the altar, receiving on their extended tongues the host distributed by a priest from a paten.[85] The practice is documented to the sixth century at the synod of Auxerre, when the Frankish bishops ruled that women, because of their impurity, could not touch any consecrated object. "It is not lawful for a woman to receive the Eucharist with her bare hand."[86] There developed a custom of communicants having a cloth draped over their hands,[87] lest the host drop accidentally onto their bare skin. Its authority was dated to a dubious sermon of Augustine, which prescribed that all males before communicating should wash their hands, while all females should employ a neat linen cloth.[88]

In theological argument tasting the Eucharist compensated by ritual reversion for the original sin of Adam and Eve in tasting the forbidden fruit.[89] The friar Marco Cardinal Vigerio, who has been designated Michelangelo's probable advisor for the theological program of the Sistine Chapel ceiling, opposed the fruit of the tree of knowledge in Eden with the fruit of the tree of life as the Eucharist.[90] Yet the sense of touch, not taste, is what Michelangelo distinctly painted on that ceiling. Theologians did not reason that before the pair ate the fruit they necessarily had to touch it, since Eve took it, then handed it to Adam. "She *took* of its fruit and ate; and she also gave some to her husband, and he ate" (Gen. 3:6). In scripture both senses of taste and touch were explicated in the divine command. "But God said, 'You shall not eat of the fruit of the tree which is in the midst of the garden, neither shall you *touch* it, lest you die (v. 3).'" Yet it was not argued theologically that touching the Eucharist compensated for the sin of

83 See Miri Rubin, *Corpus Christi: The Eucharist in Late Medieval Culture* (Cambridge: Cambridge University Press, 1990), p. 255.

84 See Andrea Lazzarini, *Il miracolo di Bolsena, testimonianze e documenti dei secoli tredicesimo e quattrodicesimo*, Temi e testi, 1 (Rome: Edizioni di storia e letteratura, 1952).

85 Ugolino di Prete Ilario, 14th century, chapel of the corporal, cathedral, Orvieto; reproduced in *Il duomo di Orvieto*, ed. Lucio Riccetti (Rome: Laterza, 1988), pl. VII.

86 *Synodis dioecesana autisioderensis* 36; cited by Suzanne Wemple, *Women in Frankish Society: Marriage and the Cloister, 500 to 900* (Philadelphia: University of Pennsylvania Press, 1981), p. 141; Barasch, *Giotto and the Language of Gesture*, p. 103.

87 See Rubin, *Corpus Christi*, pp. 41, 43.

88 Augustine, *Sermones supposititos* 229.5, in *Patrologia latina*, 39:2168; cited by Barasch, *Giotto and the Language of Gesture*, p. 103. The rationale was that, as men washed their hands with water, so almsgiving cleansed their souls, while women employed a linen cloth, thus presenting a chaste body and clean heart.

89 Rubin, *Corpus Christi*, p. 27.

90 Hartt, *Michelangelo*, 3 vols. (New York: Harry N. Abrams, n.d.), 1:31, 96; idem et al., *Sistine Chapel* 1:14, 243.

touching the fruit, because original sin was in literature consistently interpreted as tasting, not touching. The knight of La Tour-Landry, in enumerating the follies of Eve to his daughters, meditated on her fifth fault, which was to touch the fruit. It would have been better, he taught them, "if she had none hands," because she introduced to humanity the vice of lust. Yet her crucial sixth folly was to eat the fruit, "when the serpent made her to break the commandment of God in Paradise, when she bit upon the apple." Taste, not touch, was the decisive act. "And for that deed," he taught, "we were delivered all to the pain of death and of hell, and estranged from great joy and bliss."[91] Cardinal Vigerio explicated that Adam "fell while eating."[92]

Although the theological favoring of taste prevailed in textual interpretation, art consistently depicted the primordial fault as touching, rather than tasting, the fruit. The serpent, who offers the fruit by its mouth in early reproductions on sarcophagi, even acquires after the twelfth century a human hand.[93] It typically passes the fruit to Eve's hand, or she reaches above her head to pluck it, then places it in Adam's hand,[94] as in Albrecht Dürer's (1471-1528) ideal engraving.[95] In Michelangelo's fresco on the Sistine Chapel ceiling the sinning sense is touch, not taste. Artists interpreted the fall better than exegetes did. Touch was the better depiction of human will than taste, since the grasp of an object by the hand is particular to people. All animate creatures can taste and also touch; only humans can grasp.

Aristotle favorably compared the human hand to the animal claw "because it can seize and hold." The shape of the hand was naturally contrived to suit that purpose: not of one piece but several to allow a convergence, with joints well-constructed for grasping things. "The business of the hands is to take hold and to keep hold of things,"[96] he stated. As Galen argued, "One and indeed the chief characteristic of a prehensile instrument constructed in the best manner is the ability to grasp readily anything of whatever size or shape man would want to move." The hand was divided into many members to grasp larger masses or to fasten on the smallest ob-

---

91 *Livre du Chevalier de La Tour-Landry* 39-46, 109; *The Book of the Knight of La Tour-Landry*, trans. G. S. Taylor (London: John Hamilton, 1930), pp. 81, 214-15, 82 (italics mine).

92 Hartt, *Michelangelo*, 3:96.

93 J. B. Trapp, "The Iconography of the Fall," in *Approaches to "Paradise Lost": The York Tercentennary Lectures*, ed. C. A. Patrides (London: Edward Arnold, 1968), p. 228, with 28 plates.

94 Roland Mushat Frye, *Milton's Imagery and the Visual Arts: Iconographic Tradition in the Epic Poems* (Princeton, N.J.: Princeton University Press, 1978), pp. 246-47, and see pls. 152, 155-74, 185-86, 190.

95 Albrecht Dürer, Adam and Eve, engraving, 1504; reproduced in H. Diane Russell with Bernadine Barnes, *Eva/Ave: Woman in Renaissance and Baroque Prints* (Washington, D.C.: National Gallery of Art with the Feminist Press at the City University of New York, 1990), pp. 116-17.

96 Aristotle, *De partibus animalium* 687b, 690a; *Parts of Animals*, trans. A. L. Peck (Cambridge, Mass.: Harvard University Press, 1968), pp. 373, 391.

jects. Handling ranged from two fingertips to two hands. For larger items the hand was extended with its fingers spread; for smaller ones, the tips or two fingers or the thumb and forefingers could be used. The hand was excellently constituted for a firm grasp. It was divided for different shapes, whether curving around a sphere from all sides or firmly surrounding objects with straight or concave sides. Two hands could cooperatively grasp a large mass like a log or a rock on opposite sides, as if it were one great hand. For that reason hands faced one another, as made for each other and as equal: to share some action. Manual activity depended on the formation of different fingers, with the thumb in opposition, rather than all five digits in a straight row. Galen cited the medical knowledge since the Hippocratic writings of the utility of the opposition of the thumb to the fingers. The opposition functioned so that the fingers could spread apart to the maximum extent, often a most advantageous position. It proved that the human body was constructed in the best possible design, since "all the parts contribute services sufficient for the actions of the instruments as a whole." The work of the hand was grasping, and the the fingers cooperated in that effect by their wide spacing in between and by the opposition of the thumb. There was correlation of structure and action. "This is your standard, measure, and criterion of proper form and true beauty, since true beauty is nothing but excellence of construction, and in obedience to Hippocrates you will judge that excellence from actions."[97] The agreement of utility and beauty was specified by Firenzuola's renaissance manual in praising "the arms, with the bend of the elbow, and with the admirable and necessary use of the hands, the most eminent ministers of the sense of touch." As he continued, "With their concave palm and the flexibility of their fingers, they are capable of picking up and holding whatever they like." Ultimately, he wrote, "It is difficult to decide which is greater, their usefulness or their beauty."[98]

The typification in Michelangelo's art of original sin as grasping, rather than eating, the forbidden fruit specified a human action. Galen's anatomical knowledge of the hand was inaccurate in its description of the muscles extensor proprius and flexor digitorum profundus, because he had dissected not anthropoids but only species of small, tailless apes.[99] Yet he did distinguish humans from simians concerning the hand. The ape he declared a ridiculous imitation of people in its limbs, since the arms and legs were very different. The ape as "an animal with a ridiculous soul, has its whole body for this reason ridiculously arranged." It was "like a defective biped (for it

---

97 Galen, *De usu partium* 1.5, 9, citing Hippocrates, *De officina medica* 4; *Galen on the Usefulness of Parts of the Body: Peri chreias moriōn, De usu partium*, trans. Margaret Talmadge May, 2 vols. (Ithaca, N.Y.: Cornell University Press, 1968), 1:72, 79. For uneven fingers for grasping, cf. 1.24; for bones for grasping, 1.13 and 17.

98 Firenzuola, *Delle bellezze delle donne* 1; trans. Eisenbichler and Murray, p. 31.

99 May, introduction, *Galen on the Parts of the Body*, pp. 40, 41. Galen, *De usu partium* 13.11; 1.22; trans. May, 1:108; 2:611.

cannot stand quite erect) and a quadruped that is crippled and slow." The body of an ape caricatured the body of a human. A human, because he possessed "a reasoning soul and is the only godlike animal of those on earth, his body is very well constructed for the faculty of his soul." Galen reiterated the uniquely erect posture of a human, who "alone makes proper use of his hands." An ape mimicked human actions but performed laughably and failed, except to amuse children. This was so true of the hands that "if an artist or a sculptor intended to produce a caricature of the human hand, the result would be exactly like what we see in the ape." There was no advantage in possessing four well-formed fingers if the thumb was poorly arranged. "Surely, this is its condition in the ape, where it is only separated slightly from the forefinger, and is utterly ridiculous besides."[100]

In Michelangelo's fresco of the Temptation and Fall the humans are touching, not tasting. Eve is seated in counterposition in a languid pose. She reaches back with her left hand, arm fully extended up, to take the fruit from the hand of a serpentine woman twined about the tree. In Galen's teleology it was by virtue of the palm that the hand was a prehensile instrument. Although the entire hand cooperated in grasping and had suitably tight skin for the firm and accurate grasp of small objects, the skin of the palm was "more sensitive than that of any other part, for it was not necessary that there should be one instrument for prehension and another for touch." As he considered, "On the contrary, it was better that as we grasp an object we should at the same time determine its nature" according to the contrary tactile qualities.[101]

In Michelangelo's fresco of the Temptation and Fall, the palms of Eve, which had at creation been submissively joined and extended toward the Creator, open to grasp the fruit forbidden by him. Adam stands actively erect. With his left arm he grabs a limb of the tree; with his right he stretches to pick a fruit for himself: its index finger is bent. His arm grasping up parallels the serpent's arm extending down.[102] The logical and symbolic consequence of scripture, as depicted on Michelangelo's fresco, would have been to extend to the congregation below in the nave the reception of the sacramental food in their hands. But the Eucharist was customarily reserved in a tabernacle, under lock and key as the tactile privilege of the clergy.[103] The laity had to be satisfied with the application to the Eucharist

---

[100] Galen, *De usu partium* 13.11; 1.22; trans. May, 2:611, 1:107-8.

[101] Galen, *De usu partium* 2.6; trans. May, 1:125. For the metacapus, see also Markwart Michler, "Die Mittelhand bei Galen und Versal," *Sudhoffs Archiv für Geschichte der Medizin und der Naturwissenschaften* 48 (1964):200-15.

[102] Michelangelo, Temptation and Fall of Adam and Eve, fresco, Sistine Chapel, Vatican; reproduced in Hartt et al., *Sistine Chapel*, 1:209-28, and for the bent right index finger, p. 243.

[103] See Hans Caspary, *Das Sakramentstabernakel in Italien bis zum Konzil von Trient: Gestalt, Ikonographie und Symbolik, kultische Funktion* (Munich: Uni-Druck, 1965).

of senses judged nobler than touch: taste and especially sight. Those sick persons who were unable to swallow the host gazed upon it in a "communion of the eyes." That was but a case of the general visual enhancement of the sacrament, through its elevation at the consecration and through its exposition in a monstrance on the altar and in processional.[104]

The avoidance of touch could be extended imaginatively, although not practically, even to priests. In art even the clergy are depicted as receiving communion like the laity, not only kneeling, rather than standing, but also on the tongue, rather than in the hand. Luca Signorelli (c.1445-1523) portrays the disciples at the Last Supper as if they attend the institution of the Eucharist. Jesus stands in the midst of the twelve, who are in various stances, poses, and gestures, holding the paten in one hand and the host in liturgical correctness between the thumb and forefinger of his other. He gives the host to a kneeling disciple, who receives it from his hand, not correspondingly in his own hand, for the fingertips are loosely joined, but in his mouth.[105]

Sandro Botticelli's (1444?-1510) painting of the last communion of Saint Jerome dramatizes a tonsured priest holding the host in his right hand, the paten in his left, while the kneeling saint with folded hands opens his mouth.[106] In his painting of Mary Magdalen's viaticum for a Florentine convent of repentant prostitutes and courtesans she kneels as bishop Maximin extends her the host. By analogy with Jerome, she is about to receive it on her tongue, since her hands are folded.[107] The viaticum of the saints became a popular theme in sixteenth-century art, with even the Virgin depicted holding a cloth lest the host drop on her hands. In such a scene for the hospital of St-Jacques in Aix-en-Provence angels courteously hold the

---

104 See Charles Zika, "Hosts, Processions, and Pilgrimages: Controlling the Sacred in Fifteenth-Century Germany," *Past and Present* 118 (1988): 33. For the elevation of the host and chalice, see Peter Browe, *Die Verehrung der Eucharistie im Mittelalter* (Rome: Herder, 1967), pp. 26-48; Hans Bernhard Meyer, "Die Elevation im deutschen Mittelalter und bei Luther," *Zeitschrift für katholische Theologie* 85 (1963):162-217; V. L. Kennedy, "The Moment of Consecration and the Elevation of the Host," *Mediaeval Studies* 6 (1944):121-50.

105 Luca Signorelli, Communion of the disciples, 1512, diocesan museum, Cortona; reproduced in Mario Salmi, *Luca Signorelli* (Novara: Istituto grafico de agostini, 1953), fig. 74, and detail of table XII.

106 Sandro Botticelli, Last communion of Saint Jerome, Metropolitan Museum of Art, New York; reproduced in Ronald Lightbown, *Sandro Botticelli*, 2 vols. (London: Paul Elek, 1978), 1:pl. 45, and see pp. 120-21; 2:86-87; Nicoletta Pons, *Botticelli: Catalogo completo* (Milan: Rizzoli, 1989), p. 86 n. 118; Herbert Percy Horne, *Botticelli, Painter of Florence* (Princeton, N.J.: Princeton University Press, 1980), p. 175, and see pp. 174-77; idem, "Botticelli's Last Communion of S. Jerome," *Burlington Magazine* 28 (1915):44; Bernard Berenson, *Italian Pictures of the Renaissance*, 2 vols. (Oxford: Phaidon, 1932), 2:1087. For the origins of the sacramental practice, see Gregory Grabka, "Christian Viaticum: A Study of its Cultural Background," *Traditio* 9 (1953):1-43.

107 Botticelli, Last communion and death of Mary Magdalen, predella for the Pala delle convertite of Florence, Museum of Art, Philadelphia; reproduced in Lightbown, *Sandro Botticelli*, 1:pl. 35; 2:77-78, B66; Pons, *Botticelli*, p. 84, fig. 112D.

napkin for her.[108] Since communion was a condition for entrance to the hospital and for its dole of bread and medicine,[109] the Virgin's devotion was exemplary for its patients.

Yet the concept was odd: in numerous paintings she holds in her bare hands the naked body of Jesus, as child or as corpse, which the Eucharist really represented. In Fra Angelico's (1387-1455) painting of the last supper the Virgin kneels with joined hands to receive communion on the tongue from her very Son.[110] The notion that even she could not touch the host, moreover, that she required draped hands as a precaution against accidental touching, epitomized the extreme of a sacral, transcendent Eucharist. Catholic devotion may have been compelled to such hyperbole in reaction to reformed teachings, which substituted a spiritualized interpretation for the scholastic doctrine of transubstantiation. The Catholic culture of the Eucharist deprecated the sense of touch, in reversal of the scriptural command, "Take."

Not only were the immaculate Virgin's hands distanced from their proper tactile function. The sinful Magdalen's hands were notoriously rebuffed, as in another scene from Botticelli's predella portraying her reception of the viaticum with hands joined. The *Noli me tangere* was so called from the Vulgate translation of *mē mou haptou*, the command of her risen Lord: "'Do not touch me'" (John 20:17). In Botticelli's version Magdalen is portrayed kneeling in a walled garden, about to touch Jesus with her raised left hand. He has his back to her, while in counterposition he turns his face to her. He gestures close to her outstretched right hand, while toting a hoe over his shoulder.[111] Their poignant encounter captivated renaissance artists from Duccio (d.1319) to Titian (c.1488-1576).[112] In all depictions—save a

---

108 Émile Mâle, *L'art religieux de la fin du quatorzième siècle du dix-septième siècle et du dix-huitième siècle: Étude sur l'iconographie après la Concile de Trent*, 2d ed. rev. (Paris: Armand Colin, 1951), p. 77. J. B. Speranza, Virgin communicating from the hand of St. John, S. Lucia in Selci, Rome; reproduced, p. 81, fig. 45.

109 Cissie C. Fairchilds, *Poverty and Charity in Aix-en-Provence, 1640-1789*, Johns Hopkins University Studies in Historical and Political Science, 91-1 (Baltimore, Md.: Johns Hopkins University Press, 1976), p. 46. Athough Mâle does not offer an artist or date for the painting, the hospital was founded by a bourgeois merchant in 1532, according to Fairchilds, pp. 21-22.

110 Fra Angelico, Last supper; reproduced in Umberto Baldini, *Fra Angelico* (Florence: D'Arte il Fiorentino, 1986), p. 219, and see p. 218.

111 Botticelli, Noli me tangere, Museum of Art, Philadelphia; reproduced in Lightbown, *Sandro Botticelli*, 1:pl. 35; 2:77-78, B65; Pons, *Botticelli*, p. 84, fig. 112C; Berenson, *Italian Pictures*, 2:pl. 1076. For the altarpiece, which includes scenes of her conversion and of her anointing of Christ's feet, see Lightbown, *Sandro Botticelli*, 1:109-11.

112 Duccio, di Buoninsega, Noli me tangere, Museo dell'opera della metropolitana, Siena; reproduced in Florens Duechler, *Duccio* (Milan: Electa, 1984), pp. 110-11, pls. 131-32; Giovanna Ragionieri, *Duccio, catalogo completo dei dipinti*, Gigli dell'arte, 4 (Florence: Cantini, 1989), p. 87 n. 26; James H. Stubblebine, *Duccio di Buoninsega and His School*, 2 vols. (Princeton, N.J.: Princeton University Press, 1979), 2:pl. 113, and see 1:61; John White, *Duccio: Tuscan Art and the Medieval Workshop* (London: Thames and Hudson, 1979), pl. 50. Anonymous, façade, cathedral, Orvieto; reproduced in White, "The Reliefs on the Façade of

significant one—Jesus stands erect on two feet, while Magdalen crouches or kneels, or even sits. In one renaissance painting only does she match his stature by standing. It was executed by Pontormo, but from a cartoon by Michelangelo, who recommended that artist for the commission. Pontormo

---

the Duomo at Orvieto," *Journal of the Warburg and Courtauld Institutes* 22 (1959):pl. 29c. Giotto, fresco, c. 1305-6, Capella degli Scrovegni, Padua; reproduced in Giovanni Previtali, *La cappella degli Scrovegni* (Milan: Fratelli Fabri, 1969), p. 57; Berenson, *Italian Pictures*, 1:frontispiece. For analysis, see also Barasch, *Giotto and the Language of Gesture*, pp. 169-70, 176-82. Fra Angelico, (cell 1) San Marco, Florence; reproduced in William Hood, *Fra Angelico at San Marco* (New Haven, Conn.: Yale University Press, 1993), p. 213, pl. 211; Baldini, *Fra Angelio*, p. 199, and see p. 198; Giovanni Falloni, *Vita e opere di fra Giovanni Angelico* (Florence: Sansoni, 1984), pl. XL; Germain Bazin, *Fra Angelico*, trans. Marc Lagé (London: Hyperion, n.d.), p. 141; Cesare Fasola, *The Convent of San Marco in Florence and the Paintings of Fra Angelico: Handbook and Itinerary* (Florence: Azienda libreria editoriale fiorentina, 1957), II corriodoi-I cella; Maria Luisa Gengaro, *Il Fra Angelico a San Marco* (Bergamo: Istituto italiano d'arti grafiche, 1944), pl. 31; and for a detail of their hands, Georges Did-Huberman, *Fra Angelico: Dissemblance et figuration* (Paris: Flammarion with Centre national des lettres, 1990); John Pope-Hennessy, *Fra Angelico* (Ithaca, N.Y.: Cornell University Press, 1974), pl. 77, and detail of Christ, pl. 78, and see p. 206. Style of Orcagna, c. 1343-68; reproduced in Martin Davies, *Earlier Italian Schools*, National Gallery Catalogues, 2 vols. (London: The Trustees, 1953), 2:pl. 3894, and see p. 327. Fra Bartolommeo (1475-1517), Louvre, Paris; Uffizi, Florence; reproduced in Hans von der Gabelentz, *Fra Bartolommeo und die Florentiner Reniassance*, 2 vols. (Leipzig: Karl W. Hiersemann, 1922), 1:fig. 5, and see pp. 141-43, 2:pl. 20. Andrea del Sarto (1486-1530), Museo del cenacolo di san Salvi, Florence; reproduced in *Andrea del Sarto, 1486-1530, dipinti e disegni a Firenze*: Firenze, Palazzo Pitti, 8 novembre 1986-1 marzo 1987, ed. Centro mastre di Firenze (Milan: D'Angeli-Haeusler, 1986), p. 93, and for the restoration, see pp. 91-93; Raffaele Monti, *Andrea del Sarto*, 2d ed., Studi e documenti di storia dell'arte, 8 (Milan: Communità, 1981), pl. 30; John Shearman, *Andrea del Sarto*, 2 vols. (Oxford: Clarendon, 1965), 1:pl. 18a, and see pp. 203-4; Freedberg, *Andrea del Sarto*, 2 vols. (Cambridge, Mass.: Belknap Press, Harvard University Press, 1963), 1:fig. 21; 2:20-21. Correggio, Noli me tangere, c. 1520, Prado, Madrid; reproduced in Giuliano Ercoli, *Arte e fortuna del Correggio* (Modena: Articoli, 1982), pl. XXXVI, and detail XXXVII; Stefano Bottari, *Correggio*, Collana d'arte, 1 (n. p.: G. Barbèra, n. d.), pl. XIII; Cecil Gould, *The Paintings of Correggio* (London: Faber and Faber, 1976), pl. 98, and see pp. 224-26; Corrado Ricci, *Antonio Allegri da Correggio: His Life, His Friends, and His Time*, trans. Florence Simmonds (London, 1896), pp. 234-35. Vincenzo Civerchio, fresco, c. 1520, chiesa del Carmine, Brescia; reproduced in Antonio Morassi, *Brescia*, Catologo delle cose d'arte e di antichità d'Italia, 11 (Rome: Libreria dello stato, 1939), p. 114. Franciabigio, c. 1523-24, Museo Horne, Florence; reproduced in Susan Regan McKillop, *Franciabigio*, California Studies in the History of Art, 16 (Berkeley and Los Angeles: University of California Press, 1974), pp. 172-73; Berenson, *Italian Pictures*, 2:pl. 1359. And see Elizabeth Pilliod, "Le *Noli Me Tangere* de Bronzino (1503-1572) et la décoration de la chapelle Cavalcanti de l'Eglise santo Spirito à Florence," *Revue du Louvre et des musées de France* 41 (December 1991):50-61. For some northern examples see: Albrecht Altdorfer, 1516-18, Alte Pinakothek, Munich; reproduced in Franz Winzinger, *Albrecht Altdorfer: Tafelbilder, Miniaturen, Handbilder, Bildhauerbeilen, Wekstatt, und Umkreis* (Munich: Hirmer, 1975), pl. 25, and see p. 82. Martin Schongauer, c. 1480-90, National Gallery of Art, Washington, D.C.; reproduced in Russell with Barnes, *Eva/Ave*, p. 104. Lucas van Leyden, engraving, 1520; reproduced in Craig R. Harbison, "Lucas van Leyden, the Magdalen, and the Problem of Secularization in Early Sixteenth-Century Northern Art," *Oud Holland* 98 (1984):122, fig. 5. Hans Baldung Grien, Darmstadt; reproduced in Georg Bussman, *Manierismus im Spätwerk Hans Baldung Griens: Die Gemälde der zweiten Strassburger Zeit* (Heidelberg: Carl Winter-Universität, 1966), pl. XXXII, fig. 73. For medieval examples, see Schiller, *Ikonographie der christlichen Kunst*, 3:495-98; Barasch, *Giotto and the Language of Gesture*, pp. 170-75.

may even have painted it directly under Michelangelo's supervision. His effort was so successful that he was commissioned to do a replica, and Battista Franco also copied Michelangelo's cartoon for a painting on a larger scale. Yet, even from the cartoon, Magdalen is so unmistakably Michelangelo's creation that she could have stepped out of his Sistine Chapel frescoes,[113] like Eve from Adam's side. It was the official preacher for that chapel, Cajetan, who so unusually thought that Magdalen stood in the garden scene.[114] Although in Michelangelo's artistic conception she uniquely stands, her arms do not conform to Cajetan's exegesis of her reaching toward the face or neck of Jesus. They are widely out-flung, more dramatically expansive than in any other representation, with one arm even disappearing behind his back. Giorgio Vasari (1511-74) called the design a rarity.[115]

Jesus' figure in such scenes tends to be in counterposition.[116] Magdalen's posture of subordination to him is not scriptural, although it was likely borrowed from a synoptic gospel in which she and another Mary worshipfully take hold of the feet of their risen Lord (Matt. 28:9). Not only were the different gospel accounts of the resurrection frequently confused but also the papal authority of Gregory the Great had conflated the distinct pericopes about the different Marys into a singular personage named Magdalen. The renaissance editor and exegete Jacques Lefèvre d'Étaples (d. 1536) challenged her cult by asserting that there was no textual evidence for such identification of the Marys. Among his arguments for distinguishing the women was the contradiction at the tomb between Mary embracing Jesus' feet (Matt. 28:9) and Mary being forbidden to touch him (John 20:17). But Lefèvre's humanist reform was both resisted and censured as an innovation that would obliterate Magdalen's pastoral utility as a mirror of penitence. It was even feared to undermine the universal liturgy and the very concept of tradition.[117] The cult of a repentant prostitute was too appealing

---

113 For the attribution, see William E. Wallace, "Il 'Noli me Tangere' di Michelangelo: tra sacro e profano," *Arte cristiana* 76 (1988):443-50, with reproductions of Pontormo, Noli me tangere, private collection, Milan; Pontormo, Noli me tangere, Casa Buonarroti, Florence, pp. 444-45, figs. 1-2; and Battista Franco, Noli me tangere, Casa Buonarroti, Florence, p. 447, fig. 3. See also Giorgio Vasari, *Vita di Michelangelo*, 4:1936-39. Wallace relates Magdalen to the sibyls of the Sistine Chapel ceiling, p. 446, and also discusses the originality of her gesture and that of Christ, p. 448. Consider also Vergil, *Aeneid* 6.48-49 on the Cumaean sibyl, who conducted Aeneas to the underworld.

114 Tommaso de Vio, *In quatuor evangelia*, p. 495.

115 Vasari, *Vita di Michelangelo*, 1:122.

116 For this figuration, see David Summers, "*Maniera* and Movement: The *figura serpentinata*," *Art Quarterly* 35 (1972):269-301; idem, "*Contrapposto*: Style and Meaning in Renaissance Art," *Art Bulletin* 59 (1977):336-61.

117 Gregory the Great, *Homilia* 25; Lefèvre d'Étaples, *De Maria Magdalena* and subsequent treatises. For the controversy, see Anselm Hufstader, "Lefèvre d'Étaples and the Magdalen," *Studies in the Renaissance* 16 (1969):31-60, with citation at p. 54.

in the devotional fashion for sensationalism and in the cultural relish for antithesis.

The tactile, concupiscent hands of Magdalen and the wounded, redemptive hands of Jesus provided a fascinating contrast, as in Martin Schongauer's (c.1430-91) engraving where their hands overlap on the vertical axis but are separated.[118] Renaissance versions of the scene are sympathetic, rather than severe. Gesturally they are quite similar. Magdalen extends her arms or arm toward Jesus, while with a hand he gestures defensively against her attempt to touch him. In his other hand he holds a gardening tool or, in a minor variant, a standard with a banner of victory over death.[119] The hoe or spade in the one hand is not less significant than his gesture of dismissal with the other. It renders realistic Magdalen's mistaking of him for the gardener (John 20:15). It also alludes theologically to Jesus as the second Adam, since the hoe or spade became Adam's attribute after the fall, from the curse of tilling the soil (Gen. 3:17-19). Adam at the gates of paradise on Ghiberti's bronze doors for the Florentine baptistry[120] holds a hoe such as Jesus carries in *Noli me tangere* scenes. By her association in a garden with that second Adam, Magdalen becomes the second Eve.[121] The gospel of John is the only version to locate the tomb (and the cross) of Jesus in a garden, in allusion to the paradise from which Adam was expelled. Just as the first man had been created from the dust regally to tend the garden, so was the second man raised from the dust to assume the abandoned and ruined task.[122] When Jesus forbade Magdalen to touch him, perhaps he replicated the divine command against touching in Eden the fruit of the tree of life. Her obedience, as the prime witness to the resurrection, would then symbolically reverse Eve's primordial disobedience as the woman who introduced death to creation.

Commentators, ancient to renaissance, labored to explain *Noli me tangere*. For that is how they rendered the verse, although current exegesis ex-

---

118 Martin Schongauer, Noli me tangere, engraving, c. 1480-90, National Gallery, Washington, D.C.; reproduced in Russell with Barnes, *Eva/Ave*, p. 104.

119 Hoe: Fra Angelico, Painting in style of Orcagna, Fra Bartolommeo, Signorelli, Franciabigio, Corregio. Spade: The earliest example, perhaps, is in a gospel book, c. 1230-39 for St. Chapelle, Paris, Bibliothèque national, MS. lat. 8892, fol. 12. Aina Trotzig, "Kristus som örtgårdmästare—den nye Adam," *Iconographisk Post* (1982): fig. 8; cited by Clifford Davidson, "The Middle English Saint Play and Its Iconography," in *The Saint Play in Medieval Europe*, ed. idem, Early Drama, Art, and Music Monograph Series, 8 (Kalamazoo: Medieval Institute Publications, Western Michigan University Press, 1986), p. 89 and n. 309. See also Steven May, "A Medieval Stage Property: The Spade," *Medieval English Theatre* 4 (1982):77-83. For spades, see also the works by Lucas van Leyden, Bronzino, Correggio, Fontana. For the standard with banner or cross, see the works by Duccio, Giotto, Andrea del Sarto, Altdorfer, Schongauer.

120 See Lorenzo Ghiberti, Adam, Gates of paradise, baptistry doors, Florence; reproduced in Krautheimer, *Ghiberti's Bronze Doors*, pl. 129.

121 Gregory the Great, *Homilia* 25.

122 Nicholas Wyatt, "'Supposing Him to Be the Gardener' (John 20, 15): A Study of the Paradise Motif in John," *Zeitschrift für die neutestamentliche Wissenschaft* 81 (1990):21-38.

ploits the present tense of the imperative, which literally means "Stop touching me." The modern translation, "Do not cling to me," implies a divine prohibition not against touching but against dalliance and detention in touch. The present imperative can mean, however, that Magdalen is attempting to touch Jesus and should desist,[123] just as the scene is portrayed in medieval and renaissance art. Augustine assumed that Jesus the gardener was sowing in Magdalen's heart, as in his personal plot, a grain of mustard seed for faith. Yet Augustine was baffled by his prohibition against her touch before the ascension. What sense did it make? he posed in a homily. If Jesus were not touched on earth, how would he be touched in heaven? Before his ascension he certainly offered his body to be touched by his disciples, notably Thomas the doubter. The opinion that he was willing to be touched by his disciples before his ascension, but not by the women until after it, Augustine dismissed as absurd. The gospel plainly stated that the women, including Magdalen, did touch him when they grasped his feet (Matt. 28:9). A spiritual meaning had to be latent, he proposed. The woman Magdalen might be a figure of the Church of the gentiles, who did not believe before the ascension. Or in the explanation Augustine favored Jesus desired persons to believe in him—to touch him spiritually—as a union with the Father. People did not rightly "touch," or believe, him unless they perceived interiorly that he was ascended, as equal to the Father in divinity. The belief of Magdalen rested in Jesus, without transcending him to the Father. She believed only carnally, since she wept for him as for a human being. The prohibition against touching Jesus until after his ascension meant: "There you shall touch me, when you believe me to be God, not unequal to the Father."[124]

---

123 Modern translations argue that the aorist means to "touch," while the present means to "hold, grasp, cling." The text has also been emended to *me ptoou* for "Don't fear" and to *mou haptou*, eliminating the negative, for "Touch me." For a survey, see Raymond Brown, *The Gospel according to John*, Anchor Bible, 29, 2 vols. (New York: Doubleday, 1964), 2:992-93. For the argument that the explanatory *gar* should be placed grammatically with the following sentence, see Michael McGehee, "A Less Theological Reading of John 20:17," *Journal of Biblical Literature* 105 (1986):299-302. For the prohibition against touch as regarding purity and danger, see Mary Rose D'Angelo, "A Critical Note: John 20:17 and Apocalypse of Moses 31," *Journal of Theological Studies* 41 (1990):529-36. Other recent interpretations repeat the spiritualized tradition. Pheme Perkins, "'I Have Seen the Lord': Women Witnesses to the Resurrection," *Interpretation* 46 (1992):31-41; Gerald O'Collins and Daniel Kendall, "Mary Magdalen as a Major Witness to Jesus' Resurrection," *Theological Studies* 48 (1987):631-46; Frank J. Matera, "John 20:1-18," *Interpretation* 43 (1989):402-6; Ignace de La Potterie, "Genèse de la foi pascale d'après John 20," *New Testament Studies* 30 (1984):26-49; François Bovon, "Le privilège pascale de Marie-Madeleine," pp. 50-62; Frans Neiryack, "John and the Synoptics: The Empty Tomb Stories," pp. 161-87; Edward Lynn Bode, *The First Easter Morning: The Gospel Accounts of the Women's Visit to the Tomb of Jesus*, Analecta biblica, 45 (Rome: Pontifical Institute Press, 1970), pp. 72-75.

124 Augustine, *In evangelium Iohannis tractatus* 121.3.

Gregory the Great, who was responsible for the conflation of the Marys[125] and for the influential identification of Magdalen with the erotic spouse seeking her beloved (Song 3:2), concurred. The risen Jesus did not hinder Magdalen from a refusal of female touch, since she and another woman had already clasped his feet (Matt. 28:9). His reason for the prohibition was that he had not yet ascended to the Father, with whom he was eternally equal in substance.[126] A sermon attributed to Odo of Cluny agreed that she wished to hold his feet in adoration but was forbidden contact, because she did not perceive him with the perfect mind of faith, since she sought him living among the dead.[127] Augustine's interpretation was also copied in her principal medieval legend, down to the detail of the mustard seed planted in her soul. "Do not touch me with a fleshly embrace," Jesus commanded Magdalen, since she sought him among the dead, rather than the living. "Touch me with the embrace of your heart, believing firmly in my resurrection. I have not yet ascended to the Father in your heart, for though I have risen, you do not believe that I am equal to God the Father." Magdalen doubted no longer but believed. Although touch was denied her, from the sensual perceptions of hearing his voice and seeing his face, she developed faith. The hagiography lauded her as "first servant and special friend," "evangelist of his resurrection. . . apostle of his ascension." Her privilege of witnessing Jesus' prime and profoundest apparition distinguished her, after his mother, as the most divinely loved and cherished of all women.[128]

Yet an overtly misogynist interpretation of touching was proposed among patristic authors by John Chrysostom, who contrasted Magdalen's tender, sympathetic weeping as womanish with Peter's lack of emotional display as manly. She was, he preached, "by nature very easily discouraged, and she did not yet understand clearly the doctrine of the Resurrection as the others did." Although the male disciples had immediately seen and believed on the evidence of the discarded linens in the empty tomb, "since the woman was not sufficiently spiritual-minded to grasp the fact of the Resurrection from the grave cloths," angels were provided for her consolation. As warm and tender, she had to be led gradually to understand the sublime doctrine she had not yet accepted. Jesus' words to her thus aroused her "curiosity," since it was "not desirable to lead so lowly a person as this woman suddenly to lofty considerations." Magdalen was paralleled to the Jews in her carnal unbelief. It was "evident" from the command "Do not

[125] Victor Saxer, *La culte de Marie Madeleine en Occident: Des origines à la fin du Moyen Âge*, Cahiers d'archéologie et d'histoire, 3 (Paris: Clavreuil, 1959), p. 3.

[126] Gregory the Great, *Homilia in evangelia* 25.2, 5-6.

[127] Odo of Cluny, "Sermo de Maria Magdalena," in *Patrologia latina*, 133:720.

[128] *Vita beatae Mariae Magdalenae* 26, 27; *The Life of Saint Mary Magdalen and of Her Sister Saint Martha: A Medieval Biography*, trans. David Mycoff, Cistercian Studies, 108 (Kalamazoo, Mich.: Cistercian Publications, 1989), pp. 72, 73; Jacobus da Voragine, *Legenda aurea* 96.

touch me," thought John Chrysostom, that she had indeed touched him and fallen at his feet. Why then did Jesus so speak? "It seems to me that she wished to enjoy His presence still, in the same way as before, and because of her joy at seeing Him, had no realization of His greatness, even though he had become much more excellent in bodily appearance." It was to induce her to abandon the notion and to to refrain from addressing him familiarly that he "elevated her thoughts so that she would treat Him with a more reverential attitude." His speech to her was indirect, because a statement that her accustomed touching was no longer appropriate in a changed situation would have been harsh and boastful.[129]

The substance, if not the tenor, of his interpretation perdured. One sixteenth-century preacher in France, which hosted her cult, defined Magdalen as being of the weak sex and scant virtue. She desired to hold Jesus "because of her imbecillity."[130] Erasmus in his paraphrase of the gospel expressed the traditional low estimation of the sense of touch. He imagined that Magdalen tried to kiss Jesus' feet but did not succeed. Jesus prevented her from touching his body because she did not consider his magnitude, although she loved him truly and ardently. Magdalen saw him resurrected but supposed that he would resume his usual relations with his disciples. She did not realize that he possessed a body now immortal, which demanded a more reverential treatment. It was a body he would never display to the wicked or allow to be touched by just anyone, so that he might gradually remove people from love of the body. "'Do not touch me,' he said; 'it is the same body that hung on the cross, but now adorned with the glory of immortality. But your feelings still smack of the flesh, because I have not yet ascended to my Father; when I do, I shall send you all the Spirit as comforter who will make you perfect and worthy of My spiritual fellowship. For now, Mary, let your longing be satisfied to have looked at me and heard me speaking.'" Her commission to announce the resurrection to the disciples involved their renunciation of earthly feelings and their direction to heavenly truths, since the enjoyment of his physical presence would be brief.[131]

Cajetan, the papal orator, agreed that the prohibition was not against touch but against her familiar and customary touch. Although Jesus had not yet ascended to the Father but was still with her on earth, she did not have

---

[129] John Chrysostom, *Homilia* 86; *Commentary on Saint John the Apostle and Evangelist: Homilies 1-88*, trans. Thomas Aquinas Goggan, 2 vols., Fathers of the Church, 33, 41 (New York: Fathers of the Church, 1957-60), 2:446, 447, 448, 449.

[130] François Le Picart, *Les sermons et instructions chrestiennes, pour tous les ious de caresme, and feries de Pasques*, fol. 171; cited by Larissa Taylor, *Soldiers of Christ: Preaching in Late Medieval and Reformation France* (New York: Oxford, 1992), p. 175. For French preaching on Magdalen, see also Jacques Roussiaud, *Medieval Prostitution*, trans. Lydia G. Cochrane (Oxford: Basil Blackwell, 1988), pp. 140-44 and n. 26.

[131] Erasmus, *Paraphrasis in evangeliam Ioannis*, in *Opera omnia* (Leiden), 7, ad loc.; *Paraphrase on John*, trans. Jane E. Phillips, in *Collected Works of Erasmus* (Toronto: University of Toronto Press, 1991), 46:218.

the faculty to touch him as she used to, for he was no longer passible. By the prohibition the evangelist insinuated that Magdalen, in an impulse of love and joy, had rushed to embrace Jesus. Cajetan further inferred that, since the prohibition was not against clasping his feet (Matt. 28:8), Magdalen must have been standing, not kneeling. She was stretching her arms toward his face or his neck.[132] Her principal medieval legend poised her to throw herself on the shoulders of the gardener, although when she recognized him as Jesus she approached only to humble herself at his feet.[133]

Magdalen's relationship with Jesus was characterized as amorous, even erotic. The *Noli me tangere* scene could be accompanied by an image of their encounter as bride and bridegroom (Song 3:4).[134] The precise touch she desired was usually speculated to be a kiss. In one mystery play, although she dared not kiss his head, she desired to kiss his feet.[135] The Digby play of "Mary Magdalen" dramatized her attempt as an anointment and a kiss.[136] The popular meditations on the life of Christ specified that she ran toward Jesus' feet to kiss them, when his command interrupted her by elevating her mind from earth to heaven. Yet the pair lingered together lovingly. "Although it seemed at first that the Lord held back from her," romanced the author, "I can hardly believe that she did not touch him familiarly before He departed, kissing His feet and His hands." Jesus visited Magdalen (with his mother's permission) for her pleasure, not for her distress.[137]

There was even in that artistic garden a reverse encounter in which *he* touched *her*. Its visualization by van Leyden[138] depicts Jesus tapping Magdalen's forehead lightly with an index and middle finger. The legend was propagated by *Aurea rosa*, which related her apparition to Charles II of Anjou to reveal that the risen Lord had left his mark on her forehead. The church of St.-Maximin near her cave of Sainte-Baume preserved her reliquary skull, supposed miraculously marked with the imprint of Jesus' fingers.[139] That medieval reliquary had a removable golden face to expose her skull through a crystal mask. There were renaissance illuminations of it by Gode-

---

[132] Tommaso de Vio, *In quatuor evangelia*, p. 495.

[133] *Vita beatae Mariae Magdalenae* 26.

[134] *Biblia pauperum*, pl. 31; cited by Mary Pardo, "The Subject of Savoldo's Magdalen," *Art Bulletin* 71 (1989):75.

[135] *The Cornish Mystery-Play of the Three Maries*, p. 126.

[136] "Mary Magdalen," in *Late Medieval Religious Plays* lines 1070-73. For the play, see Darryll Grantley, "The Source of the Digby Mary Magdalen," *Notes and Queries* 31 (1984):457-59.

[137] Pseudo-Bonaventure, *Meditationes vitae Christi* 88; *Meditations on the Life of Christ: An Illustrated Manuscript of the Fourteenth Century*, ed. Isa Ragusa and Rosalie B. Green (Princeton, N.J.: Princeton University Press, 1961), p. 363.

[138] See Harbison, "Lucas van Leyden, Magdalen, and Secularization," p. 117. Van Leyden, Christ appearing to Magdalen, engraving, 1519; reproduced, p. 120, fig. 3.

[139] Mâle, *Art religieux*, pp. 294-95. For the relics at St.-Maximin, see also Saxer, *Culte de Marie Madeleine*, pp. 230-47.

froy le Batave in *Vie de la Magdalene* by Francis Du Moulin, who had been commissioned by the mother of Francis I to write a souvenir of his royal pilgrimage to the site. Females were not allowed into Magdalen's crypt, although she and the other women had been first to enter Jesus' tomb. So the relics had to be brought up for veneration: hair, arm, head. In the miniature of the king kneeling before the reliquary her skull wears a crown and long curling locks—Magdalen's penitential attribute, since she had wiped Jesus' feet with her hair. Its left temple has an angled rectangular patch of skin, the spot of the marvelous fingerprints. The author remarked that the friars displaying the item called it *Noli me tangere* (touch me not) but that he called it *Noli me credere* (believe me not). The evangelists who wrote that Magdalen touched the feet of Jesus never added that he touched her forehead, he stated. Du Moulin's book incited the upset of her cult, for he had sought advice from Lefèvre, who had dedicated to the king his own contentious *De Maria Magdalena*.[140] Lefèvre declared himself indifferent to the relic, investing his faith rather in the narratives celebrated by the Church that elevated the mind to the celestial exemplars of things bodily visible.[141] John Calvin (1509-1564) in his inventory of relics dismissed it. The supposed imprints of Christ's fingers were only "a bit of wax."[142]

Yet Magdalen's hands were valued by the faithful, for they had once embraced and anointed Jesus' feet. The first sanctuary dedicated to her was in the tenth century at the cathedral of Exeter, which claimed to have a finger of hers. In the sixteenth century her fingers were still desirable. The abbey of Sainte-Pons outside the walls at Nice acquired another one as a relic.[143] Hands figured in the catalogue of feminine beauty. Roman erotic poets had decided that nature best created feminine hands that were slim, with long slender fingers.[144] As the medieval rhetorician Geoffrey of Vinsauf dictated the topic of *effictio*, the amplification of female beauty, "So let the radiant description descend from the top of her head to her toe, and the whole be polished to perfection." Literally he wrote "toenail." When that author came to the upper limbs, he prescribed: "Let her arms be a joy to behold,

---

140 Myra Dickman Orth, "The Magdalen Shrine of la Saint-Baume in 1516: A Series of Miniatures by Godefroy le batave (B. N. MS. fr. 24.955)," *Gazette de beaux arts* 98 (1981):209, citing De Moulin, *Vie de la Magdalene*, fol. 71v. Godefroy le Batave, reliquary skull of the Magdalen, Paris, Bibliothèque nationale, MS. fr. 24.955, fol. 72; reproduced, p. 207, fig. 12.

141 Lefèvre d'Étaples, *De Maria Magdalena, triduo Christi, et ex tribus una Maria disceptatio. . . secunda emissio*, fol. 36v; cited by Hufstader, "Lefèvre d'Étaples and the Magdalen," p. 59.

142 Calvin, *Traité des reliques*, p. 86, and see also p. 54.

143 See Saxer, *Culte de Marie Madeleine*, pp. 54, 282.

144 M. B. Ogle, "The Classical Origin and Tradition of Literary Conceits," *American Journal of Philology* 34 (1913):125-26. See also D. S. Brewer, "The Ideal of Feminine Beauty in Medieval Literature, especially 'Harley Lyrics,' Chaucer, and Some Elizabethans," *Modern Language Review* 50 (1955):263; Margaret Scott, *Late Gothic Europe, 1400-1500*, History of Dress, 1 (London: Mills and Boon, 1980), pp. 204-7.

charming in their grace and their length. Let soft and slim loveliness, a form shapely and white, a line long and straight flow into her slender fingers. Let her beautiful hands take pride in those fingers."[145] Agrippa von Nettesheim in his declamation on female excellence praised "extensive arms, smooth hands, fingers lengthened with pleasing joints."[146] Renaissance artists, in portraying sacral and secular beauties, conferred that ideal on women. From Madonna to whore they were a manual type: long slender hands and fingers.[147] Hands were also to be "smooth," with no flabby skin hanging.[148] They should be as soft as fine silk or downy cotton. Even a finger should comply with the aesthetic norm. "We call such a finger beautiful," wrote Firenzuola, "not because of the universal beauty philosophers demand, but because of its appropriate and particular beauty." That derived from proportion and purpose.[149]

It was Firenzuola who most considered the beauty of the hands in his description of the perfect woman, part by part, like Zeuxis's ancient painting from composite bodies. The arms of a woman were to be in color white and of well-proportioned length, "fleshy and muscular, but with a certain softness," like Athena, rather than Hercules. Their natural substance should make for a firmness, testable by pressing the flesh for white and pink tones. The hands were to be large, slightly full, and white, especially on the backs. The palms were to be slightly hollow and shaded in rose. Their markings should be clear and distinct, well delineated without tangling or crossing of lines; their mounds also distinct but not exaggerated. The hollow between the index finger and the thumb was to be well defined, without wrinkles, and vivid in color. Finally in praise of fingers: "Fingers are beautiful when they are long, straight, delicate, and slightly tapering toward the end, but so little as to be scarcely perceptible."[150] Agostino Nifo (c.1473-1545?), writing on the beautiful Jeanne d'Aragon, described her hand as a little plump, snowy on the exterior, ivory on the interior, the fingers fleshy and rounded, with fine curved nails of a soft coloration.[151]

---

145 Geoffrey of Vinsauf, *Poetria nova* lines 597-99, 587-90; *"Poetria nova" of Geoffrey of Vinsauf*, trans. Margaret F. Nims (Toronto: Pontifical Institute of Mediaeval Studies, 1967), p. 37. See also Ernest Gallo, *The "Poetria nova" and Its Sources in Early Rhetorical Doctrine* (The Hague: Mouton, 1971), pp. 182-87.

146 Agrippa von Nettesheim, *De nobilitate*, p. 56.

147 For the modern version of renaissance chironomy, diagnosing such hands as lacking in vitality and strength, as the property of introverted, shallow personalities, see Charlotte Wolff, *The Human Hand* (London: Methuen, 1942), pp. 65, 70; eadem, *The Hand in Psychological Diagnosis* (London: Methuen, 1951), pp. 66-67.

148 Matthew of Vendôme, *Ars versificatoria* line 57; *Cour d'amour* lines 675-76.

149 Firenzuola, *Delle bellezze delle donne* 2, 1; trans. Eisenbichler and Murray, p. 13.

150 Firenzuola, *Delle bellezze delle donne* 2; trans. Eisenbichler and Murray, p. 67. Cited also by Mirollo, *Mannerism and Renaissance Poetry: Concept, Mode, Inner Design* (New Haven, Conn.: Yale University Press, 1984), pp. 138-39, and see his summary of Federico da Udine, *Il libro della bella donna* 2, p. 139.

151 Agostino Nifo, *De pulchro* 5.

Hands were ideally white; nails desirably rosy.[152] To blanch the skin, hands were washed in the juice of nettles.[153] Hands whose whiteness and sweetness were owed to honey and to almond oil were also praised.[154] Alessandro Piccolomini's (1508-78) amorous art, *Dialogo de la bella creanza de le donne*, observed that "beauty of hands is much esteemed in a young woman." Although the common hand care was a tepid solution of lemon juice and candy sugar, the bawd Raffaela recommended a paste of finely sieved mustard, honey, and bitter almonds smoothed on the hands at night, then chamois gloves pulled on tightly for sleeping. In the morning the lady was to rinse her hands with rainwater and a little oil of benjamin.[155] Women strove to obtain purity of complexion.[156] The lady at toilet, posed with a mirror in scrutiny or admiration of her skin, was an epideictic theme of renaissance art.[157] Not a single vein was to protrude,[158] not a wrinkle to surface. Worse was the eruption of blotches (strawberry marks) or freckles, pimples, and sores, for the removal of which there were daunting recipes.[159] Renaissance women concocted numerous and various recipes such as facial masks to refresh the skin, cleanse impurities, and slough off dead cells. There were treatments with grains, oils, and creams and with a range of waters distilled from minerals, vegetables, and birds. Such resorts were criticized, echoing classical protestations, as manifestations of the capital vices of lust and pride. In exempla and in sermons moralists excoriated plaster to hide wrinkles and makeup to whiten the skin. By the Stoic topic of nature versus artifice, the use of cosmetics was a refusal of the divine art as imperfect and a disfigurement of the divine creation. Among all creatures only humans were created in the divine image and likeness, so that any falsification of even the body was quasi idolatrous. The coquette was a deviant

---

152 Ogle, "Literary Conceits," p. 126; idem, "White Hand"; Lester and Oerke, *Accessories of Dress*, p. 142. For the blond ideal, see Marie-Claude Phan, "Pratiques cosmétiques et idéal feminin dans l'Italie des quinzième et seizième siècles," in *Soins de beauté: Moyen Âge, début des temps modernes*, Actes du troisième colloque international Grasse (26-28 avril 1985), ed. Denis Menjot (Nice: Université de Nice, 1987), pp. 114-15. For some texts, see Christine de Pisan, *Livre de trois vertus* 2.11; Firenzuola, *Delle bellezze delle donne* 2.

153 Herald, *Renaissance Dress*, p. 162.

154 *Amiria*; cited by Phan, "Pratiques cosmétiques," p. 112. The attribution of *Amiria* to Leon Battista Alberti is not accepted by Cecil Grayson in his critical edition of *Opere volgare*, 3:431-32.

155 Piccolomini, *Dialogo de la bella creanza de le donne*, p. 26.

156 Phan, "Pratiques cosmétiques," p. 116.

157 See Elise Goodman-Soellner, "Poetic Interpretations of the 'Lady at her Toilette' Theme in Sixteenth-Century Painting," *Sixteenth Century Journal* 14 (1983):426-42.

158 Ghislaine Pillivuyt, *Histoire du parfum: De l'Egypte au dix-neuvième siècle* (Paris: Denoël, 1988), p. 132, citing Jean Liébault, *Trois livres de l'embellissement et ornement du corps humain*, which was compiled largely from Giovanni Marinelli, *Gli ornamenti delle donne, tratti dalle scritture d'una reina graeca* (Venice, 1562).

159 For examples, see *L'ornement des dames (Ornatus mulierum): Texte Anglo-normand du troisième siècle* 35-38, 46, 48, 49-51, 52, 53, 61; Piccolomini, *Dialogo de la bella creanza de le donne*, pp. 22-25.

from humanity, a hybrid in the service of the devil. Her sacrifices for beauty mimicked religious martyrdom. In contrast, a natural beauty of divine origin was praised as a sign of moral character, especially in females of chastity.[160]

The argument against cosmetics because a woman's face, or other bodily part, was created in the divine image derived from Christian appropriation of the classical topic of human dignity through erect posture. The argument surfaced in the cosmetic topic. While it blamed women for their practices, it affirmed the essential dignity of their bodies. The apologist Tertullian complained of cosmetic women, who, dissatisfied with the creative skill of God, censured it by adding to his work from a rival artist, the devil. "Whatever is born, that is the work of God." Any addition to that divine handiwork was the invention of the devil.[161] The argument developed from the female body as divine art to the female body as divine image. Ambrose maintained that the flesh was not to the divine image, not even in the sense of sight. Yet he imagined humans as truthful and graceful paintings by God. "I speak, also, of women," he affirmed. When women applied white and rouge cosmetics they erased the divine painting. They obliterated the art of the Creator, who became displeased at their ugly and deceitful artifice. "Tell me," asked Ambrose, "if you were to invite an artist of inferior ability to work over a painting of another of superior talent, would not the later be grieved to see his own work falsified?" So he urged, "Do not displace the artistic creation of God by one of meretricious worth," making a Christian a harlot. To adulterate the work of God was a grave offense. "It is a serious charge to suppose that a human is to be preferred to God as an artist!" God would accuse the cosmetic woman that he did not recognize his colors, or image, or even countenance. He would reject her as his work of art.[162] The knight of La Tour-Landry advised his daughters not to use cosmetics, because their visage was "made after God's image."[163]

The opposition to cosmetics was severe in Spanish manuals, where their application, even by a married woman on her husband's order, was considered a damnable mortal sin. A confessor was to impose his hand against any

160 Marie-Anne Polo de Beaulieu, "La condemnation des soins de beauté par les prédicateurs du Moyen-Âge (troisième-quatorzième siècles)," in *Soins de beauté*, ed. Menjot, pp. 297-309. For Christian condemnation of cosmetics, see also Marcia Colish, "Cosmetic Theology: The Transformation of a Stoic Theme," *Assays: Critical Approaches to Medieval and Renaissance Texts* 1 (1981):3-14; Wykes-Joyce, *Cosmetics and Adornment*, pp. 32-33. For the human body as probably the most ancient surface for paint, with personal adornment dating to the paleolithic age, see Justine M. Cordwell, "The Very Human Arts of Transformation," in *The Fabrics of Culture: The Anthropology of Clothing and Adornment*, ed. idem and Ronald A. Schwartz (The Hague: Mouton, 1979), pp. 47-75.

161 Tertullian, *De cultu feminarum* 5.2-4; "The Apparel of Women," trans. Edwin A. Quain, in *Disciplinary, Moral, and Ascetical Works*, Fathers of the Church, 40 (New York: Fathers of the Church, 1959), p. 136.

162 Ambrose, *Hexameron* 6.8.44-45, 47; trans. Savage, p. 260. For the soul as painted by a divine artist, see also 6.7.42-43.

163 *Livre du Chevalier de La Tour Landry* 51; trans. Taylor, p. 99.

female who raised hers with rouge rather than virtue. The rationale was the acceptance of what God had done and how he had done it as his absolute will. The fatalism not only meant the socioeconomic condition into which a female was born but it also extended to her very physical appearance. If a woman altered her countenance or figure, moralists feared that, perhaps, God might not recognize her at the last judgment as being in his image.[164] Implicit, even explicit, in that argument was the belief that her body was created as his handiwork in his divine image. Luis de León (1528-91), editor of Teresa of Avila's *El castillo interior*, railed for folios in his *La perfecta casada* against the use of cosmetics. Yet he did so from the premise that a woman was a divine work of art in her very body. From fear of God and from charity toward women, he felt compelled to warn them that "in no manner whatever is it fitting or licit for them to adulterate the work of God and His workmanship by adding either red paint, or stibium, or rouge, or any other admixture which may change or corrupt their natural features." The reason? "God has said, 'Let us make man in our image, after our likeness,' and does any woman make so bold as to alter the semblance of what God has made into something different? Such as these lay hands on God Himself when they try to make over, and change the appearance of what He has formed." As he affirmed, "Every living thing is God's handiwork," while what deviated from its nature was diabolical. Luis de León applied the analogy of a master painter justly indignant at a touch-up by an inferior artist. Women who boldly colored their skin would not go unpunished for such perversion and insanity toward the divine artificer. Even if they did not become unchaste through the seduction of their paints, because of their corruption and violation of the divine workmanship in themselves they were guilty of a worse adultery. Female bedizening contradicted God's work and betrayed truth. At judgment day the Creator might fail to recognize them, pronouncing with authority and severity: "'This is not my handiwork, nor is it in our image: you have muddied your skin with counterfeit makeup, changed your hair into an unnatural colour, waged war upon your own countenance, and wrecked it. You have corrupted your face with lies. This is not your true aspect: you cannot behold God.'"[165]

The polemic was patristic in authority, as old as Cyprian's *De habitu virginium*, and it contradicted the prevalent theology of women as not created in the divine image. Scholastic doctrine stated that males only were created in the divine image, while females were merely the reflection of that

---

164 José Sanchez Herrero, "Los cuidados de la belleza corporal femenina en los confesionales y tratados de la doctrina cristiana de los siglos décimotercio al décimosexto," in *Soins de beauté*, ed. Menjot, pp. 280-81, 286-87.

165 Luis de León, *Perfecta casada* 11, citing Cyprian, *De habitu virginium* 15-16; *The Perfect Wife*, trans. Alice Philena Hubbard (Denton: College Press, Texas State College for Women, 1943), pp. 57, 58-59.

imaged image.[166] The cosmetic topic was not only applied to women, moreover. Giovanni Della Casa (1503-56) also censured renaissance men for applying so much make-up to their hands that their appearance was unseemly even for a harlot.[167] Yet a female humanist did not necessarily capitalize on the moralizing against cosmetics to argue for her own dignity. Laura Cereta (1469-99) in an epistolary exercise typically blamed cosmetic women who "strive by means of exquisite artistry to seem more beautiful than the Author of their beauty decreed." Then, rather than praise natural female beauty as created in the divine image, Cereta reverted to the opposite argument against cosmetics: bodily corruption. "Mindful of the ashes from which we come, we should renounce sins born from desires."[168] Yet at the turn of the century Lucrezia Marinella (1571-1653) could argue in *La nobiltà e l'eccellenze delle donne* that beauty was a gift from God's hand, so that women had the right to care for and enhance it.[169]

With or without cosmetics, hands and fingernails were expected to be neat. The character of Magdalen, dramatically performed as a courtesan, inquired in a passion play at the beginning of the sixteenth century about the physical appearance of Jesus, part by bodily part. "His hands?" she asked. Magdalen was assured that they were "fine, long, and clean."[170] As in the practice of swaddling, even God incarnate was expected to conform to custom. An important part of medieval and renaissance grooming was the manicure. The duly proportioned size of the fingernails was a teaching of Hippocratic medicine: "the nails neither to project beyond, nor to fall short of, the fingertips." Galen had instructed practically that nails were to be neither long nor short. If they were too long, they would be useless as a tool for picking up tiny objects, since they would strike against them. If they were too short, they would deprive the flesh of support against damage and also

---

166 Thomas Aquinas, *Summa theologiae* 1a.93.4.

167 Della Casa, *Galateo* 293.

168 Laura Cereta, *Epistolae*, pp. 66-70; *Her Immaculate Hand*, trans. King and Rabil, pp. 79, 80. For the author, see Rabil, *Laura Cereta: Quattrocento Humanist*, Medieval and Renaissance Texts and Studies, 3 (Binghamton, N.Y.: Center for Medieval and Early Renaissance Studies, 1981).

169 Lucrezia Marinella, *La nobiltà e l'eccellenze delle donne*, pp. 153-54. For the author, see Patricia H. Labalme, "Venetian Women on Women: Three Early Modern Feminists," *Archivio veneto* 117 (1981):92-98; and for her social context, Virginia Cox, "The Single Self: Feminist Thought and the Marriage Market in Early Modern Venice," *Renaissance Quarterly* 48 (1995):513-81. For continuity of the cosmetic topic, see Frances E. Dolan, "Taking the Pencil Out of God's Hand: Art, Nature, and the Face-Painting Debate in Early Modern England," *Publications of the Modern Language Association* 108 (1993):224-40; Annette Drew-Bear, *Painted Faces on the Renaissance Stage* (Lewisburg, Pa.: Bucknell University Press, 1994).

170 Jean Michel, *Le mystère de la passion*, pp. 213-14; cited by Marjorie M. Malvern, *Venus in Sackcloth: The Magdalen's Origins and Metamorphoses* (Carbondale: Southern Illinois University Press, 1975), p. 111 (italics mine). See also Graham A. Runnalls, "La circulation des textes des mystères à la fin du Moyen Âge: Les éditions de la *Passion* de Jean Michel," *Bibliothèque de humanisme et Renaissance* 58 (1996):7-33.

render the fingertips incapable as tools. "Only nails that come even with the ends of the fingers will best provide the service for the sake of which they were made."[171] Nothing was indicated about their cleanliness, although the Greeks proverbially disdained dirty fingernails.[172] The Romans also cared about the appearance of their nails. There were recipes for the cure of hangnails, such as the ash of a dog's head. For smoothing roughness on nails a mixture of locusts fried with suet of goat or more pleasantly of mistletoe and purslane was recommended.[173]

In medieval medicine the papal physician Chauliac devised remedies for gibbosity and curvature of the nails and for those that were crazed or blotched.[174] But the versified *La clef d'amours* passed beyond health to honor. It advised a lady to trim her nails often and care for them as the most important part of her body after the face, for hands conferred fame.[175] *Chastoiement des dames* instructed medieval women frankly on manicure:

> You ought to keep your hands very clean,
> And often cut the fingernails,
> Not letting them grow beyond the flesh,
> So that filth cannot accumulate there.[176]

The renaissance treatise *Amiria* admired nails that were "clean, short, and cut slightly rounded."[177] Although inventories did not list any item for manicure, there was a literary reference to small scissors called in French *forcettes*.[178]

Firenzuola was most detailed about manicure. "Fingernails should be clear and like balas rubies tied with flesh-pink roses and pomegranate leaves; not long, not round, not completely square, but with a fine shape and a very slight curve; bare, clean, well kept, so that that little white crescent at their base is always visible." He departed, however, from the standard of cutting them so short that no white showed. "At top the nail should extend past the flesh of the finger the thickness of a small knife, without the least

---

171 Galen, *De usu partium* 1.6, citing Hippocrates, *De officina medici* 4; trans. May, 1:74. Long nails appeared as a sign of gentility in the seventeenth century because they hindered manual labor. See the comparative ethnology of Bulwer, *Anthropometamorphosis* 18; Michel de Montaigne, *Essais* 1.23, 26.

172 See Erasmus, *Adagia* 4.1.82.

173 Pliny, *Naturalis historia* 30.37.111.

174 Chauliac, *Chirurgia magna* 6.2; cited by Jacques Rovinski, "Cosmétologie de Guy de Chauliac," in *Soins de beauté*, ed. Menjot, p. 172.

175 *Clef d'amours* lines 2349-64.

176 Robert de Blois, *Chastoiement des dames* lines 463-66. The hands were also to be white, line 198.

177 *Amiria*, cited without documentation by Phan, "Pratiques cosmétiques et idéal feminin," p. 112.

178 Danièle Alexandre Bidon and Françoise Piponnier, "Gestes et objets de la toilette aux quatrième et cinquième siècles," in *Soins de beauté*, ed. Menjot, p. 218, citing Aldobrandino of Siena without documentation.

suspicion of a black rim at the tip."[179] The more common courtesy of not allowing the fingernails to exceed the fingertips was obeyed by medieval and renaissance artists. They depicted them cut very short, with no white visible. Even the Creator obeyed the nicety. When in Michelangelo's frescoes he charges Adam and elevates Eve to human dignity by erect posture with able hands, his own hands are divinely clean with their nails cut short.

Long fingernails were considered not only diabolical but also avian, barbaric, and even quite mad. Nebuchadnezzar, who was a medieval model of insanity, had nails long like claws (Dan. 4:33); his bestial appearance was interpreted as a projection of moral deformity.[180] A medieval saint (male) complained to an abbess about the finery of her nuns, from their satin underwear to the detail of fingernails "sharpened like the talons of hawks or owls seeking their prey."[181] When Ignatius Loyola (1491-1556), upon his conversion, adopted his ascetical regimen, he let his nails grow long. Then, with a moderation issuing from some pastoral practice, he thought that practice "extreme" and so cut them. And he exemplified his reform in religious *Constitutiones*: the Jesuits were required to maintain a good personal appearance, the better to edify others.[182] Lack of manicure was not socially nice. Tullia d'Aragona (1508-56), a notable poet and courtesan, was blamed for sullying her reputation and her beauty by sexual intercourse with a slovenly foreigner. He cut her body with his unkempt toenails and tore at the delicate flesh of her breast with his ungroomed fingernails.[183]

There was more variety in the description of ugliness than of beauty, because the comparison was less fixed, so that a poet was freer to invent.[184] When a renaissance author descended to the dregs of filthy fingernails, they were loaded with gore, not dirt, and they belonged to a woman. She was the apothecary's wife in Tifi Odasi's "Macaronea," who prepared and served dinner to her husband with her fingernails "full of lots of blood." Since that was her menstrual blood,[185] the female touch as impure was obscenely articu-

---

179 Firenzuola, *Delle bellezze delle donne* 2; trans. Eisenbichler and Murray, p. 67.

180 See Penelope B. R. Doob, *Nebuchadnezzar's Children: Conventions of Madness in Middle English Literature* (New Haven, Conn.: Yale University Press, 1976), pp. 55-94, especially p. 70, citing Richard of St. Victor, *De eruditione hominis interioris* 19.

181 Aldhelm, *De virginitate* 58; cited by Ribeiro, *Dress and Morality*, p. 33.

182 Luis Gonçalves da Câmara, *Acta patris Ignatii* 3.29; Society of Jesus, *Constitutiones* 1.2.10. See Marjorie O'Rourke Boyle, *Loyola's Acts: The Rhetoric of the Self*, New Historicism, 36 (Berkeley and Los Angeles: University of California Press, 1997), pp. 70-73.

183 Giovanbattista Giraldi Cintio, *Gli Hecatommithi* 1.intro.3; cited by Lynne Lawner, *Lives of the Courtesans: Portraits of the Renaissance* (New York: Rizzoli, 1987), p. 73. For that author on women, see also Diana Handley, "'Amore' and 'maestà': Giambattista Giraldi's Tragic Heroines," *Modern Language Review* 80 (1985):330-39.

184 Jan Zialkowski, "Avatars of Ugliness in Medieval Literature," *Modern Language Review* 79 (1984):1-20.

185 Tifi Odasi, "Macaronea" lines 547-58; cited by Barbara Spackman, "*Inter musam et ursam moritur*: Folengo and the Gaping 'Other Mouth,'" in *Refiguring Woman*, ed. Migiel and Schiesari, p. 21.

lated. Even butchers, of humble occupation and low society, knew better than that woman. Those preparers of salted and pickled meats, when their hands were soaked with brine, would not clear their noses with their fingernails but wipe them on their forearm, as the adage *cubito emungere* joked.[186]

Beyond a change in emphasis from utility to cleanliness, manicure developed from a public to a private matter. In Roman society manicure had been the task of the barber or the hairdresser, who trimmed and polished the nails and removed any callouses from the palms and joints of the hand.[187] The practice occasioned the adage *ad vivum resecare*, "to cut to the quick," for, as Erasmus explained, those professionals were "tiresome with their efforts to be needlessly precise."[188] The renaissance manicure was no longer a public but a private act, however. Cutting the fingernails was considered rude at table but even in any company. "You shall do it when you are alone," stated one manual.[189] Della Casa's *Galateo* detailed among the offenses against guests, such as fidgeting and pacing, the inappropriate manicure. "Someone who pulls out his nail clippers and devotes himself to his manicure acts even worse, appearing to hold the company in no esteem at all and so tries to find some other amusement for himself in order to pass the time."[190] Erasmus's *De civilitate* instructed on table manners with humanist refinement. "Never sit down without having washed and without first trimming your nails lest any dirt stick to them and you are called *r hupokondulos* 'dirty-knuckled.'"[191] By the end of the sixteenth century an adaptation of his manual dictated privacy for such grooming. "You shall not have long nails; you shall cut them in secrecy."[192] A seventeenth-century genre painting by Jacob Ochtervelt (1634-82) will display a young woman trimming her fingernails in the privacy of her boudoir.[193]

---

186 See Erasmus, *Adagia* 2.4.8.

187 Plautus, *Aulularia* 2.4.33; cited by Arnold J. Cooley, *The Toilet in Ancient and Modern Times: With a Review of the Different Theories of Beauty and Copious Allied Information Social, Hygienic, and Moral* (New York: Burt Franklin, 1866; rpt. 1970), p. 37.

188 Erasmus, *Adagia* 2.4.13; trans. Mynors, 33:196.

189 "Dit is hoversheit: Uit een handschrift van het klooster Bursveld (in Westfalen)"; cited by Pieter Spierenburg, *Elites and Etiquette: Mentality and Social Structure in the Early Modern Northern Netherlands,* Centrum voor Maatschappijgeschiedenis, 9 (Rotterdam: Erasmus Universiteit, 1981), p. 5.

190 Della Casa, *Galateo* 54-55; trans. Eisenbichler and Bartlett, p. 11.

191 Erasmus, *De civilitate*, in *Opera omnia* (Leiden), 1:1038, citing Julius Pollux *Onomasticon* 6.4; *On Good Manners for Boys*, trans. Brian McGregor, in *Collected Works of Erasmus*, 25:280-81. Cf. *Adagia* 4.1.82.

192 D. Adriaenz. Valcoogh, *Regel der Duytsche schoolmeesters*, p. 14; cited by Spierenburg, *Elites and Etiquette*, p. 6.

193 Jacob Ochtervelt, Young woman trimming her fingernails; reproduced in Susan Donahue Kuretsky, *The Paintings of Jacob Ochtervelt, 1634-1682: With Catalogue Raisonée* (Montclair, N.J.: Allanheld and Schram, 1979), p. 164, fig. 88, and see p. 85; Neil MacLaren, rev. Christopher Brown, *The Dutch School 1600-1900*, 2d ed., 2 vols. (London: National Gallery, 1991), 2:pl. 251, and see 1:293.

The ordinary care of hands by both sexes was to wash them in water—and not just to spit on them.[194] Hands were the singular part of the body consistently cleaned from ancient to renaissance cultures. Washing the hands had been a practice common to all peoples of the ancient Near East, the custom upon rising and before (also usually after) meals. The Greeks had used perfumed warm water and a common towel.[195] The washing of hands survived as a medieval practice. The usual occasions for washing were upon rising[196] and at meals. *Disciplina clericalis*, with perhaps the earliest medieval code of table manners, indicated washing the hands before and after meals as hygienic, with reference to the contraction of ocular disease from contamination with food.[197] Cistercian monasteries, renowned for their plumbing, despite other austerities, had piped water for washing hands before meals.[198] In the great houses of France in the fifteenth century the washing of hands before sitting to table or leaving it was announced by a hunting-horn. Ewers of precious and delicately wrought metals, filled with scented rosewater, were borne in silver basins by pages or squires who handed them to the ladies.[199]

The earliest Italian book on etiquette at table pronounced as its second rule (after feeding the poor):

> If you offer water for the hands,
> Offer it neatly: see that you are not rude.
> Offer enough water, not too much, when it is summer;
> In winter, for the cold, in small quantity.[200]

Galateo banished the washing of hands to the privacy of the bedroom, with the exception of the practice at table. "For then it should be done in full sight of others, even if you do not need to wash them at all, so that whoever dips in the same bowl as yours will be certain of your cleanliness."[201] The first Italian book on manners for women, Francesco da Barberino's medieval

---

194 Della Casa, *Galateo* 328.

195 Michal Dayagi-Mendels, *Perfumes and Cosmetics in the Ancient World* (Jerusalem: Israel Museum, 1989), p. 14.

196 Bidon and Piponnier, "Gestes et objets de la toilette," pp. 214-15.

197 *Disciplina clericalis* 26.

198 Christopher Brooke, "St. Bernard, the Patrons, and Monastic Planning," in *Cistercian Art and Architecture in the British Isles*, ed. Christopher Norton and David Park (Cambridge: Cambridge University Press, 1986), p. 15.

199 Paul Lacroix, *France in the Middle Ages: Customs, Classes, and Conditions* (New York: Ungar, 1963), pp. 174-76.

200 Bonvesin da Riva, *De quinquaginta curialitabus ad mensam* 2.9-12; *Italian Courtesy Books: Fra Bonvicino da Riva's "Fifty Courtesies for the Table" (Italian and English) with Other Translations and Elucidations*, trans. William Michael Rossetti, Early English Text Society, extra series, 8 (London, 1869), p. 17 (modernized).

201 Della Casa, *Galateo* 319; trans. Eisenbichler and Bartlett, p. 60. For the medieval practice as decency, not hygiene, see Vigarello, *Concepts of Cleanliness: Changing Attitudes in France Since the Middle Ages*, trans. Jean Birrell (Cambridge: Cambridge University Press, 1988), pp. 17, 45-48, 226, 227.

Reggimento e costume di donna, also intimated that the rite was more for courtesy than for cleanliness: sheer display. He counseled women to wash their hands privately before meals, so as not to silt the communal basin.[202] Female hands did get dirty, even virginal ones, as Lea Ráskai's sixteenth-century hagiography of blessed Margaret testified. When that daughter of the Hungarian king desired to debase herself to the worst drudgery in a convent, she emptied the water made filthy by the hand washing of the nuns in the refectory, then for added mortification let another nun splash her with it.[203]

The most frequently mentioned medieval item for cleanliness was the basin, the bucket, or the ewer, for washing hands and other limited ablutions. Those were utilitarian objects for domestic use, of brass or tin, circular in form, and undecorated. Barbers also used basins. And there were supplies of linen for drying hands.[204] The adage *illotibus manibus*, "with unwashed hands," meant simply to be unprepared.[205] Erasmus fastidiously instructed that hands were to be washed upon rising and before eating. He added a note of sociability. When you wipe your hands, he wrote, wipe away trouble, for it was bad manners to be sad at table.[206]

There was a cultural belief, preserved in cliches and epigrams of late antiquity, that baths had the ability to relieve pain and worry. Augustine's response to his mother's death had been resort to the baths.[207] A remnant of the belief was implied in Erasmus's advice to wash the hands in a basin before meals to banish care. Thermal sensibility was a relaxant and purifier that promoted optimism. It was precisely because bathing relaxed the body that Christian moralists believed it conduced to lust. Hands were not always to be washed reassuringly in public—certainly not after relieving one-

202 Francesco da Barberino, *Reggimento e costume di donna* 5.6.59-60. For this work, see Charles Franco, *Arte e poesia nel "Reggimento e costume di donna" di Francesco da Barberino* (Ravenna: Longo, 1982); Bornstein, *Lady in the Tower*, pp. 61-62; Ramiro Ortiz, *Francesco da Barberino e la letteratura didattica neolatina* (Rome: Angelo Signorelli, 1948), pp. 85-146; Thomas Crane, *Italian Social Customs of the Sixteenth Century and Their Influence on the Literature of Europe* (New Haven, Conn.: Yale University Press, 1920), pp. 353-61; G. B. Festa, *Un galateo femminile italiano del trecento (Il "Reggimento e costumi di donna" di Francesco da Barberini)* (Bari: Gius. Laterza e Figli, 1910). Raffaela instructed Margherita not to clean herself publicly about the house. Piccolomini, *Dialogo de la bella creanza de le donne*, p. 32.

203 Lea Ráskai, *Boldog Margit legendája*; cited by Wemple, introduction to "The Legend of Blessed Margaret," in *Women Writers of the Renaissance and Reformation*, ed. Wilson, p. 437. See also Gábor Klaniczay, "Legends as Life-Strategies for Aspirant Saints in the Later Middle Ages," in idem, *The Uses of Supernatural Power: The Transformation of Popular Religion in Medieval and Early-Modern Europe*, trans. Susan Singerman, ed. Karen Margolis (London: Polity, 1990), pp. 95-110.

204 Bidon and Piponnier, "Gestes et objets de la toilette," pp. 212, 214-15, 216-17.

205 Erasmus, *Adagia* 1.9.55.

206 Erasmus, *De civilitate* 1038.

207 Augustine, *Confessiones* 9.12.32. See also Fikret Yegül, *Baths and Bathing in Classical Antiquity* (Cambridge, Mass.: MIT Press for the Architectural History Foundation, 1992), p. 5.

self, since that recalled to the imagination of the company a disgusting act.[208] Bathing the entire body was a different matter in a Christian, rather than classical, culture, although it had been practiced religiously in ancient societies for ritual purity.[209] Herodotus typified barbarism by those Scythians who "howl in joy for the vapour-bath. This serves them instead of bathing, for scarce ever do they wash their bodies with water." He described how they produced the steam by throwing hemp into a pit with red-hot stones in the center of rugs propped on three poles leaning to a point (a sort of tepee). The women ground fragrant woods mixed with water and anointed the bodies with a paste, removing it the next day to clean and shiny skins.[210] Not so for the civilized. The Romans prized water running freely from their aqueducts into the public baths built by their civil engineering. Their moralists, especially the Stoics, opposed bathing, however;[211] and the most horrifying fate of a bather was a classical invention. Scylla in Ovid's *Metamorphoses* waded waist-deep into the water to bathe, only to see her loins and legs suddenly disfigured into barking creatures. She tried to drive them off, then fled in panic, only to drag them with her. "And, feeling for her thighs, her legs, her feet, she finds in place of these only gaping dogs'-heads, such as a Cerebus might have. She stands on ravening dogs, and her docked loins and her belly are enclosed in a circle of beastly forms."[212] Bathing was feared to destroy the dignity of erect bipedality, reducing human legs to animal all fours.

Christian moralists also blamed bathing on and for vice,[213] although they never equalled with their rhetoric the classical metamorphosis of Scylla. Pisan advised women that bathing was unnecessary. "Bathing establishments, public baths, and other such gatherings which women too often frequent are needless convivialities and superfluous expenditures which lead to no good."[214] Yet there remained tubs for bathing[215] in medieval public establishments. Literature catalogued baths as purifying, therapeutic, and hygienic; but commonly as recreational, for pastime.[216] Bathing was for pleasure: play, and not cleanliness, was the real purpose.[217] When a virginal saint indulged her imagination in bathing the infant Jesus in her soul, the

---

208 Della Casa, *Galateo*, 14.

209 See Dayagi-Mendels, *Perfumes and Cosmetics*, p. 14.

210 Herodotus, *Historiae* 4.77; *Herodotus*, trans. A. D. Godley, 4 vols. (London: Heinemann, 1921-25), 2:275.

211 Yegul, *Baths and Bathing*, pp. 40-43.

212 Ovid, *Metamorphoses* 14.59-69; trans. Frank Justus Miller, 2 vols. (Cambridge, Mass.: Harvard University Press, 1976), 2:305.

213 For Christian criticism, see Roy Bown Ward, "Women in Roman Baths," *Harvard Theological Review* 85 (1992):142-46; Yegul, *Baths and Bathing*, pp. 314-20.

214 Pisan, *Livre de trois vertus* 3.2; trans. Willard, p. 193.

215 Bidon and Piponnier, "Gestes et objets de la toilette," pp. 215-16.

216 Jean Larmat, "Les bains dans la littérature française du Moyen Âge," in *Soins de beauté*, ed. Menjot, pp. 195-210.

217 Vigarello, *Concepts of Cleanliness*, pp. 27-28, 226-27.

object was not to cleanse his body. In the imaginative event she placed him in a tub of tepid water and tended him "with both hands" as he swished about, splashing her all wet before she could even wash him. Towelling him dry she played intimately with him.[218] Her hands in the water and inside the towel indulged the sense of touch, a sensuality toward the divine body that her chastity forbade but his infancy allowed. Bathing was luxuriously tactile.

Among the Romans, who perfected the pleasure, mixed bathing had been common practice for all classes and both sexes. Literature betrayed amatory encounters.[219] Medieval art depicted baths as places of amorous, even lascivious, encounter, with both sexes indiscriminately displayed naked in tubs. Literally baths were steamy places and they acquired that connotation morally.[220] Nude female bathing as pleasurable became a topic of renaissance art.[221] When opponents of Luther wished to discredit his reform, they alleged that his mother had conceived him by intercourse with the devil in a public bathhouse.[222] When critics gasped at Michelangelo's nudes frescoed in the Sistine Chapel, they were contemned as belonging in a sumptuous bathtub.[223] Beyond promiscuity, a threat loomed from proximity. As sixteenth-century physicians discerned the causes of the plague, the heat and steam of the bath were believed to open the pores of the skin to infection by its pestiferous vapors. Not only the element of air but even water seeping into the body was avoided as deadly, except for its controlled therapeutic use at spas.[224] Yet there was a famous steam bath already installed in the Vatican apartments. Bernardo Cardinal, da Bibbiena, Dovizi (1470-1520) commissioned its erotic frescoes of scenes from the *Metamorphoses*, after sketches by Raphael (1483-1520), above his loggie.[225] The inclusion of

---

218 *Acta sanctorum*, 2 April, p. 177; cited by David Herlihy, *Medieval Households* (Cambridge, Mass.: Harvard University Press, 1985), p. 127.

219 Ward, "Women in Roman Baths," pp. 137, 134-36.

220 Roussiaud, *Medieval Prostitution*, pp. 5-7, 186-93; Vigarello, *Concepts of Cleanliness*, pp. 28-31, 226-27.

221 For numerous illustrations, see Raimond Van Marle, *Iconographie de l'art profane au Moyen Âge et à la Renaissance*, 2 vols. (The Hague: Martinus Nijhoff, 1931-32), 1:497-515.

222 See Heiko A. Oberman, *Luther: Man Between God and the Devil*, trans. Eileen Walliser-Schwarzbart (New Haven, Conn.: Yale University Press, 1989), p. 88.

223 E. g., Pietro Aretino, in "Dokumente und Forschungen zu Michelangelo," ed. Ernst Steinmann and Heinrich Pogatscher, p. 492. See also Pierluigi de Vecchi, "Michelangelo's Last Judgment," in *The Sistine Chapel: Michelangelo Rediscovered* (London: Muller, Blond, and White, 1986), pp. 190-94. For courtesans and prostitutes as the frequenters of the baths of renaissance Rome, see Lawner, *Lives of the Courtesans*, pp. 8-9.

224 Vigarello, *Concepts of Cleanliness*, pp. 9-11. See also D. S. Chambers, "Spas in the Italian Renaissance," in *Reconsidering the Renaissance*, ed. Di Cesare, pp. 3-27.

225 Luitpold Dussler, *Raphael: A Critical Catalogue of His Pictures, Wall-Paintings, and Tapestries*, trans. Sebastian Cruft (London: Phaidon, 1971), pp. 92-93; Innis H. Shoemaker and Elizabeth Brown, *The Engravings of Marcantonio Raimondi* (Lawrence, Kan.: Spencer Museum of Art, 1981), pp. 184-89; Russell with Barnes, *Eva/Ave*, p. 136. The project was executed by Raphael's pupils Giovanni Francesco Penni and Giulio Romano, perhaps after his cursory sketches, although they did the preparatory drawings. See also "La Stuffeta," Vati-

baths in renaissance episcopal and imperial palaces continued early Christian practice, which had discouraged bathing by the ordinary laity and clergy, while reserving it as a symbol of status for nobles and prelates.[226] The ultimate rejection of the ascetical contempt of such steamy leisure was the hanging of Leonardo da Vinci's portrait of John the Baptist, gesturing toward heaven, in the baths at Fontainebleau.[227]

Bathing involved changes in the temperature of the skin, and so was essentially tactile. In the Roman establishments there had been an orderly movement through a formal series of rooms: from the tepedarium to the caldarium—from warm to hot—climaxing in the frigidarium with a cold plunge.[228] Because bathing could alter temperature through the contact of regulated water with the skin, it had moral potential for good or ill. Just as the various global zones of hot, cold, and temperate climates governed the morality of nations, so the fluxing temperatures of human bodies determined the character of individuals. Temperature, not sexuality, was the primary classical association of the sense of touch. The conviction survived intact in medicine, if not in morality. Medical diagnosis was tactile and it included temperature and other qualities of touch as determinant of character.

As was the common practice in classical Greek medicine, Galen used in diagnosis what he proclaimed his "exceedingly sensitive touch": taking the pulse, taking the temperature, and palpating the body, especially the abdomen in gynecology. For the detection of temperature, notably in the crisis of fever, a major diagnostic since the Hippocratic writings had been the use of the hand—more the palm than the fingers. Galen praised the divinely wise design of "the palm of the human hand to respond to the smallest of stimuli and to be able to notice the smallest changes. Of all the body the palm is the best-tempered, and hence can be used as a measuring rod whereby to judge temperature. With such a natural and god-ordained instrument, the well-trained physician can easily judge degrees of heat or cold all over the body and diagnose accordingly."[229] Avicenna in his *Canon of Medicine* explained its application. "The temperament of a person is diag-

---

can Palace, Rome; reproduced in Leopold D. Ettlinger and Helen S. Ettlinger, *Raphael* (Oxford: Phaidon, 1987), p. 203, fig. 188.

226 Yegül, *Baths and Bathing*, p. 319; and for private baths for a privileged minority, Vigarello, *Concepts of Cleanliness*, pp. 23-24, 34-36.

227 See Henri Zerner, "La dame au bain," in *Le corps à la Renaissance*, Actes du trentième colloque de Tours 1987, ed. Jean Céard, Marie Madeleine Fontaine, Jean-Claude Margolin (Paris: Amateurs du livres, 1990), pp. 109, 110, with reference to Cardinal Bibiena's *stuffeta*.

228 Yegul, *Baths and Bathing*, pp. 5, 352-55, 314-20, 38, for temperature citing Vitruvius, *De architectura* 5.10.1-2, 5; Pliny, *Epistolae* 5.6.26; Seneca, *Epistulae* 86.11; Celsus, *De medicina* 1.3, 4; Galen, *De methodo medendi* 11.10.

229 Vivian Nutton, "Galen at the Bedside: The Methods of a Medical Detective," in *Medicine and the Five Senses*, ed. W. F. Bynum and Roy Porter (Cambridge: Cambridge University Press, 1993), pp. 11-13, citing Galen, *De praenotatione ad posthumum* 12 on his personal sensitivity and *De usu partium* 2.6 on taking the temperature.

nosed by comparing the feel of his body with that of a normal person under equitable climatic and atmospheric conditions." If they were the same in both cases, the client's temperament was balanced, though its temperature might be relatively hot or cold. If a person of balanced temperament found the feel of another's body hot or cold, hard or soft, smooth or rough, then it was abnormal, providing there had been no alteration of the skin, such as from bathing.[230] The *Problemata* attributed to Aristotle also considered the effects of temperature and touch. "Why do we shudder more readily when someone else touches us anywhere than when we touch ourselves?" it asked. Was it because the touch of another had more power to provoke sensation? Or because its suddenness, catching a person unexpectedly, caused fright and initiated a process of cooling? "Why is it that, although summer is hot and winter cold, bodies are colder to the touch in summer than in winter?" And, "Why do the hairs bristle on the skin?" Certainly that was because of their contraction from the cold, it concluded.[231]

It was from the association of temperature with touch that touching acquired a sexual connotation. The basic medical distinction of temperatures in the human body—not superficially on the skin but internally in the humors and the organs—was sexual. Touch was concerned with temperature, and temperature determined sexual difference; therefore, touch involved sexuality. Medicine, ancient to renaissance, distinguished the sexes[232] by bodily temperature: males were hot, females cold. The theory was not scientific but speculative, for there existed not a thermometer, not even a thermoscope, for verification of the principle.[233] Hippocratic medicine had emphasized the influence of temperature not only on nationalities but also on the sexes. Just as nationalities varied in stature and shape because of the seasons, so did generation differ in the coagulation of the seed. Its activity altered in summer or winter, in rain or drought. The Scythian males may have been the absolute archers but, as influenced by the excessive cold and damp of their climate, they developed effeminate personalities. Moist constitutions and chill abdomens so checked their desire for sexual intercourse that they became impotent. In the *Regimen* of the Hippocratic school males of all species were warmer and drier, while females were colder and moister.[234]

---

230 Avicenna, *Canon of Medicine* 2.3.3; *The General Principles of Avicenna's "Canon of Medicine,"* trans. Mazhar H. Shah (Karachi: Naveed Clinic, 1966), p. 219.

231 Aristotle, *Problemata* 35.1, 4, 5; *Problems,* trans. W. S. Hett, rev. ed., 2 vols. (Cambridge, Mass.: Harvard University Press, 1957-61), 2:253, 255.

232 For a survey of females in medical theory and practice, see Yvonne Knibiehler and Catherine Fouquet, *La femme et les médicins: Analyse historique* (Paris: Hachette, 1983), pp. 15-80.

233 For the inventions early in the seventeenth century, see Anthony Turner, *Early Scientific Instruments: Europe, 1400-1800* (London: Sotheby, 1987), pp. 130-31.

234 Hippocrates, *De aere, aquis, locis* 23, 21, 22; *Regimen* 1.34; cited by Prudence Allen, *The Concept of Woman: The Aristotelian Revolution, 750 BC-AD 1250* (Montreal: Eden, 1985), pp. 48, 95.

Aristotle applied the primary metaphysical opposites of hot and cold to generation, as embodied in male and female. "Male animals are hotter than female ones, since it is on account of coldness and inability that the female is more abundant in blood in certain regions of the body." And, "The opposite of the male is the female, which is female in virtue of its inability to effect concoction, and of the coldness of its bloodlike nourishment." It was Aristotle who decided heat and maleness superior. Females were produced by a deficiency of heat, so they were inferior to males.[235] Galen repeated the reason in considering the utility of bodily parts. "The female is less perfect than the male by as much as she is colder than he." And with emphasis, "The female is less perfect that the male for one principal reason—because she is colder; for if among animals the warm one is more active, a colder animal would be less perfect than the warmer." Again, "Now just as mankind is the most perfect of all animals, so within mankind the man is more perfect than the woman, and the reason for his perfection is the excess of heat, for heat is Nature's primary instrument." For lack of heat the female generative organs could not project externally like those of the male but remained trapped internally, with only imperfect seed and a cavity to receive his perfect seed.[236] The advantage of such female "mutilation" was the gestation of the fetus.[237]

In scholastic thought the category of temperature frequently differentiated the sexes in Albert the Great's deliberation on animals. Temperature governed the intensity of sexual desires and determined the sex of the fetus. Heat meant strength, cold weakness. Heat as determining maleness guaranteed quicker generation and gestation and easier parturition.[238] While the ancient commonplace was still repeated in renaissance commentaries, in the sixteenth century there began a rejection of the physiological inferiority of women as incomplete males. Julius Caesar Scaliger's (1484-1558) *Exercitationes de subtilitate* stated both sexes to be of the same temperature. Women only appeared colder, he wrote. Although most texts still considered females colder and moister than males, with less active semen, after 1580 that condition was no longer considered a determinant of imperfection. Female temperature was reassessed as functional, resulting in wider hips. It

---

235 Aristotle, *De generatione animalium* 765b, 766a, 767a; *Generation of Animals*, trans. A. L. Peck (Cambridge, Mass.: Harvard University Press, 1963), pp. 387, 395; cited by Allen, *Concept of Woman*, pp. 95, 101. See also G. E. R. Lloyd, *Science, Folklore, and Ideology: Studies in the Life Sciences in Ancient Greece* (Cambridge: Cambridge University Press, 1983), pp. 33-34.

236 Galen, *De usu partium* 14.6; trans. May, 2:630, 628, 630; cited by Allen, *Concept of Woman*, p. 187.

237 Galen, *De usu partium* 14.6; trans. May, 2:630.

238 Albert the Great, *Quaestiones super de animalibus* 6.6-13; 5.10; 9.16-17, 24-28; cited by Allen, *Concept of Woman*, pp. 364-66, 368-69.

was decided necessary for lactation. As cooler to the touch, women simply became relegated to the domesticity of child bearing and rearing.[239]

The female touch was not necessarily sexual, however. One renaissance painting of the *Noli me tangere* scene denotes Magdalen as wanton and that is its only rendition by a female artist. Lavinia Fontana (1552-1614) portrays her in a yellow cloak,[240] the attribute of a prostitute in her legal distinction from an honorable woman.[241] It was because the prostitute as impure was stigmatized for social exclusion, like the Jew and the leper, that she was required to wear a visible sign. Her touch polluted, her hand was abominable; consequently, she was untouchable.[242] Although the two figures in the painting remain in the standard positions—Jesus upright, Magdalen debased, she is not untouchable. Jesus does not reciprocate her typical gesture of an outstretched hand but he does touch the rim of her halo with his fingertip. Titian hinted at a similar social status for Magdalen by dressing her in finery that exceeded the Venetian sumptuary laws, from which courtesans were excused. A certain detail of her attire, unlaced sleeves, suggests the early morning hour,[243] so, perhaps, the impetuosity of her love in rushing to the tomb before her toilet was complete. A woman, upon rising, was supposed to wash her arms and face, then lace up tightly the sleeves of her chemise.[244] Laced sleeves was a rule of the God of Love in *Roman de la rose*, the most important medieval literature in the vernacular.[245] Venetian courtesans did wear that basic item: the chests in the bedroom of Julia Lombardo contained sixty-four fine white chemises.[246] Yet Magdalen's attire is relaxed, rather than fashionably rigid. By the implication of her unlaced sleeves, her hands are unwashed. She is proverbially "unprepared": unclean to touch the risen Lord. As Bulwer would note in

---

239 Maclean, *Renaissance Notion of Woman*, pp. 33-36.

240 Lavinia Fontana, Noli me tangere, 1581, Uffizi, Florence; reproduced in Ann Sutherland Harris and Linda Nochlin, *Women Artists: 1550-1950*, exhibition catalogue, Los Angeles County Museum of Art (New York: Alfred A. Knopf, 1976), pl. 7.

241 For yellow for prostitutes, see Barasch, "Renaissance Color Conventions: Liturgy, Humanism, Workshops," in idem, *"Imago hominis": Studies in the Language of Art* (Vienna: IRSA, 1991), p. 173. For the yellow shawl and headdress of prostitutes attributed to Magdalen, although not this particular artistic example, see Lawner, *Lives of the Courtesans*, p. 178, citing Giovanni Girolamo Savoldo's painting of Magdalen with her ointment jar, for which see Pardo, "Savoldo's Magdalen," pp. 67-91. Although by the sixteenth century the insignia was not worn in Venice or many other places, procuresses still wore them, p. 178.

242 Roussiaud, *Medieval Prostitution*, p. 57.

243 Stella Mary Newton Obe, "The Body and High Fashion during the Renaissance," in *Corps à la Renaissance*, ed. Céard et al., p. 28. Titian, Noli me tangere, National Gallery, London; reproduced, figs. 33, 34. For the laws, see Elisabeth Pavan, "Police des moeurs, société, et politique à Venise à la fin du Moyen Âge," *Revue historique* 536 (1980):263.

244 Amanieu de Sescas, "Aissó es l'essenhamen de la donzela," p. 390. For the author, see Bornstein, *Lady in the Tower*, pp. 36-37.

245 Guillaume de Lorris, *Roman de la rose* line 2157.

246 See Cathy Santore, "Julia Lombardo, 'Somtuosa Meretrize': A Portrait by Property," *Renaissance Quarterly* 41 (1988):47-48.

his *Chirologia*, washing the hands before religious exercises, even prayer, was the practice of most nations.[247]

Magdalen holds in those paintings and many others a jar of ointment, so that her touch is at least ambiguous: sexual but soothing. The salving effect of the female hand upon the wounded body was saving. It was not uncontroversial, however, as the fourteenth-century trial of five women for practicing medicine without a license revealed. The lawsuit by the faculty of medicine at Paris against Jacqueline Felice de Almania charged her specifically for touching patients: "that she had practised in Paris and the suburbs, visiting the sick, examining their urine, taking their pulse, and feeling their bodies and members."[248] Yet Pisan counseled all noble women to apply the sense of touch to unfortunate others for their good, if not medically, still compassionately. "Speaking to the poverty-stricken and the ill, touching them and gently comforting them, she will be distributing the greatest charity of all." It was not only by her alms but also by her arms, then, that a woman blessed. The poor, Pisan explained, preferred the visitation of the powerful because they felt despised. If an important personage attended them, they regained self-respect. In that process of elevating lowly persons to dignity, raising them up morally and socially, the presence of the female hand on the skin, and not just her voice in the ear, was "the greatest charity of all." It extended to others the prayer to the Virgin with which Pisan advised women to begin their day: "Please grasp my hand, by your Holy Mercy, to pull me from the swamp of sin and iniquity."[249] The gesture receives confirmation in Agnolo Bronzino's (1503-72) painting of the harrowing of hell, in which a woman, imitating the grip of the risen Jesus on an elderly man, reaches down into the pits to pull another woman to safety.[250]

Yet the grasping female hand was blamed precisely for that universal death and punishment in hell. Death was believed not a natural event but a moral experience. It was the consequence of original sin, the universal human contagion of Adam and Eve's willful grasping of the forbidden fruit. Death was punishment for original sin and so was sexuality—become concupiscent, rather than natural. Although the original sin was spiritual, not carnal—a rational rebellion of pride or disobedience in which sexuality had no part, sexuality became, as its consequence, unruly. The disordered affectivity of fallen humanity was even supposed to be most acutely experienced in sexuality, rather than any other sensibility. As the scholastic scientist Albert the Great argued, "For that pleasure moves more than the rest, touch is more sensitive in the area of the genitals, and the transmission of corrup-

247 Bulwer, *Chirologia*, pp. 29-31.

248 Cited by C. H. Talbot, "Dame Trot and Her Progeny," in *Essays and Studies*, ed. T. S. Dorsch (London: John Murray, 1972), p. 4.

249 Christine de Pisan, *Livre de trois vertus* 1.10, 5; trans. Willard, pp. 88, 78.

250 Bronzino, Christ in limbo, Museo di Santa Croce, Florence; reproduced in McComb, *Agnolo Bronzino*, pl. 36.

tion occurs through that area."[251] Not the genitals, but the fingertips or palms of the hand, had been the classical measure of reaction to tactile stimulation, as in the test of pain from heat or the diagnosis of bodily temperature. Yet the genitals assumed primacy through Augustine's doctrine of original sin, in which sexual intercourse as necessarily lustful became the agent of a transmission that was inherited. Original sin was contracted from parent to child by conception. Although the contamination was not from the act of intercourse but from its voluntary lust,[252] that distinction could be suppressed or forgotten. As Michelangelo poetized, "my sin, in which I was born, just as my father was. . . . my predestined state of wickedness."[253]

Agrippa von Nettesheim proposed that the human fall *was* sexual intercourse, with the serpent symbolic of the penis.[254] The most frequent representation in art was of Eve offering Adam the apple, whose rotundity imitated her breast. The numerous paintings of the fall during the Reformation newly indicated or implied by gesture to the genitals that the original sin was erotic.[255] Or the fig leaf substituted for the hand in the classical pose of Venus Pudica, in which the left hand of the goddess was modestly spread across her genitals.[256] Although the figures of Adam and Eve in the garden were always shown nude, there was strong and increasing emphasis in sixteenth-century art, especially among northern artists, on sexuality in that scene.[257] In Michelangelo's fresco of the Fall on the ceiling of the Sistine Chapel the genitals of neither sex are displayed. Yet the serpent is very much a woman, in its beautiful visage, in its torso with pendant breasts, and

---

251 See Pierre J. Payer, *The Bridling of Desire: Views of Sex in the Later Middle Ages* (Toronto: University of Toronto Press, 1993), pp. 39-60, citing Albert the Great, *De bono* 3.3.14, ad 1.

252 Payer, *Bridling of Desire*, p. 54. See also in general, Peter Brown, *Augustine and Sexuality*, Colloquy, 46 (Berkeley, Calif.: Center for Hermeneutical Studies in Hellenistic and Modern Culture, 1983); Margaret Miles, *Augustine on the Body*, American Academy of Religion Dissertation Series, 31 (Missoula, Mont.: Scholars, 1979).

253 Michelangelo, *Rime* 66; *The Poetry of Michelangelo*, trans. James M. Saslow (New Haven, Conn.: Yale University Press, 1991), p. 162.

254 Agrippa von Nettesheim, *De originali peccato*, Iir; cited by A. Kent Hieatt, "Eve as Reason in a Tradition of Allegorical Interpretations of the Fall," *Journal of the Warburg and Courtauld Institutes* 43 (1980):222; Ewald M. Vetter, "Necessarium Adae peccatum," in *Ruperto-Carola: Zeitschrift der Vereinigung der Freunde der Studentenschaft der Universität Heidelberg e. V.* 18 (1966):155.

255 For collected examples, see Russell with Barnes, *Eva/Ave*, pp. 119, 120, 122, 123, 125, 126. See also Larry Silver and Susan Smith, "Carnal Knowledge: The Late Engravings of Lucas van Leyden," *Nederlands Kunsthistorisch Jaarboek* 29 (1978):244-51. For Adam and Eve in reformation art, see also Harbison, introduction to *Symbols in Transformation: Iconographic Themes at the Time of the Reformation: An Exhibition of Prints in Memory of Erwin Panofsky*, exhibition catalogue, Princeton Art Museum, March 15-April 13, 1969, eds. Hedy Backlin-Landman and Barbara T. Ross (Princeton, N.J.: Art Museum, Princeton University, 1969), pp. 16-18.

256 Clark, *Nude*, pp. 317, 86.

257 Trapp, "Iconography of the Fall," pp. 250, 252, 264. For nude beauty in the scenes, see Frye, *Milton's Imagery and the Visual Arts*, pp. 262-64.

in its shapely limbs.[258] With her right hand Eve gestures obscenely with the shameful middle finger between the tightly pressed calves of her legs.[259] While in this fresco of the Fall her genitals are hidden by those legs, in its adjacent scene of Expulsion from Paradise they are visible as she walks at Adam's side.

The sense of touch acquired a sexual denotation in Christian morality that surpassed its implicit connotation in classical physics by the primary opposites of temperature. Classical philosophers had been vague, perplexed, even confused, about what the sense of touch was. Their influence on medieval and renaissance thinkers varied. For the structure of a sensory organ studied in detail, they relied on Galen; for the function of sensory organs and the entry of sensation into consciousness, Aristotle.[260] That philosopher had inquired importantly in *De anima* about whether touch was a single sense or a plurality of senses. What was the sensory organ for its faculty? Was it the flesh, or in fleshless creatures something analogous? Or was flesh only the medium of touch, with the primary sensory organ different and internal? The other senses, he observed, dealt with singular opposites, while touch dealt with several antithetical pairs: hot and cold, dry and moist, hard and soft, and so on. In considering whether its organ was external or internal, Aristotle thought that "the body must be the naturally cohering medium for the faculty of touch, through which the plurality of sensations is communicated." He concluded that "flesh is the medium for the faculty of touch." The objects of that sense were "the distinctive qualities of body as body" as hot or cold, dry or moist.[261]

In his account of the other senses Aristotle emphasized their objects. For touch he pursued a different policy, stressing a different criterion: contact. The objects of touch were unreliable for identifying and defining that sense because they were extremely varied, so that the task would be laborious. Even knowledge of those objects would still not indicate what united the varieties of touch or why it excluded some kinds of sensory perception. Also, many of the objects apprehended by touch were apprehended by the other senses. So he appropriated the notion of contact, direct contact with the body, as singular in touch. The word *haphē* for "touch" originally meant "contact." In his numerous appeals to the concept Aristotle believed

---

258 Trapp, "Iconography of the Fall," p. 252, suggests that "Michelangelo's Serpent is more woman than her predecessors." For the tradition, see Henry Ansgar Kelly, "The Metamorphoses of the Eden Serpent during the Middle Ages and the Renaissance," *Viator* 2 (1971):301-28; John K. Bonnell, "The Serpent with a Human Head in Art and in Mystery Play," *American Journal of Archaeology* 21 (1917):255-91.

259 See also Steinberg, "Eve's Idle Hand," *Art Journal* 35 (1975-76):130-35.

260 For influence, see J. Playfair McMurrich, *Leonardo da Vinci the Anatomist (1452-1519)*, Carnegie Institution of Washington Publications, 411 (Baltimore, Md.: Williams and Wilkins for the Carnegie Institution of Washington, 1930), p. 215.

261 Aristotle, *De anima* 422b, 423a, 423b; trans. R. D. Hicks (Amsterdam: Adolf M. Hakkert, 1965), pp. 99, 103.

that the other senses—except for taste, which he was forced to include under touch—never operated through direct contact. The perceptual powers of touch he enumerated as: hot and cold, fluid and dry, hard and soft, heavy and light, viscous and brittle, rough and smooth, coarse and fine, and flavor (for taste). His theory departed from previous philosophy, in which all the senses operated by direct contact, with particles streaming from the perceived object into the sensory organs. For Aristotle the organs did not receive particles of matter from the object perceived; they received form without matter. In another comparison Plato had grouped properties as objects of touch as affections common to the entire body perceived without a localized organ. That localized criterion, in which touch operated without any obvious organ, was closer to the modern concept, which by lay definition concerns the powers of feeling the sensible properties of non-sensible bodies. Aristotle, with his preference for immediate tactile contact, finally settled the localized organ for touch in the region of the heart.[262] The peripheral organ for touch, the skin, was perceived by the cool element of earth but it was necessarily conveyed to the common sense in the hottest region of the body. The response of the skin to a wide variety of stimuli communicated various impressions. Undulations of the blood, which was the carrier of soul, conveyed those sensations to the heart, where blood was hottest. There was harbored the vital fire.[263]

Aristotle thought contact the basic property of all living organisms. It was necessary for life. The reaction of the flesh of the skin as sensitive was the universal, fundamental reaction of all matter, not only skin.[264] As he expounded in *De anima*, "An animal, unless it has touch, can have no other sense, the animate body being always, as we have remarked, capable of tactile sensation." And, "Without touch," he wrote, "there can be no other sense." The loss of the sense of touch—and only that sense—necessarily involved the death of the animal. "For it is not possible for anything that is not an animal to have this sense, nor is it necessary for anything that is an animal to have any other sense besides this." An excess of tangible objects was fatal to touch and thus to life. "And it is by this sense that the life of the animal is defined," he concluded, "touch having been proved to be indispensable to the existence of an animal." An excess of tangible qualities destroyed not only the sensory organ but also the animal itself. "For touch

262 Richard Sorabji, "Aristotle on Demarcating the Five Senses," *Philosophical Review* 80 (1971):78, 73-77. For the tactile pairs of opposites, see Aristotle, *De anima* 422b; *De generatione animalium* 329b. The reference is to Plato, *Timaeus* 64a, 65b. For the senses, including touch in the region of the heart, see Aristotle, *De partibus animalium* 656a; *De sensu* 438b.

263 Rudolph E. Siegel, *Galen on Sense Perception: His Doctrines, Observations, and Experiments on Vision, Hearing, Smell, Taste, Touch and Pain, and Their Historical Sources* (New York: S. Karger, 1970), p. 175.

264 Aristotle, *De anima* 413b, 422b; cited by Siegel, *Galen on Sense Perception*, p. 174.

is the one sense that the animal cannot do without." The other senses were the means to its well-being; touch to its very being.[265]

Galen concurred with Aristotle's association of touch and contact. Skin responded to tactile stimulation only through immediate contact with an object, unlike the other senses, which were mediated by a neutral agent, like the air for hearing or smell. In that tradition he considered sensation through concepts of qualities, elements, and humors. But his own anatomical studies of peripheral nerves advanced the knowledge of sensory perception. Although skin transmitted various information about an object, the receptive organ of the hand was supplied by one type of nerve, he believed. Because of the unity of that peripheral sensory nerve, Galen specified the hand as the organ for the perception of all tactile qualities. Touch in his medicine was no longer spread over the skin of the entire body but localized in the hand. There was no need of one organ for apprehension; another for touch—for holding, lifting and transferring objects; yet another for discrimination of the qualities of an object as hot or cold, hard or soft. Merely by grasping, the hand could judge all of the impressions simultaneously. The stimuli received by the skin of the hand, or the tissues beneath it, were transmitted directly through the peripheral nerves to the brain. Although the qualities of touch were still differentiated by elements—the traditional paired opposites, they became classified essentially by psychological principles of immediate recognition or conscious judgment. Simple sensations of touch and temperature were immediately recognizable, while complex sensations such as hard or soft required a conscious judgment based on experience.[266]

Experience, from experiment, furthered the science of touch in renaissance anatomy. In da Vinci's mechanistic physiology there was a process from the impact of stimuli on the sensory organ to the emergence in consciousness in the common sense that derived from movement and percussion. He discussed the distribution of touch over the body: how it clothed all the superficial skin. Touch passed through the perforated nerves and was carried to the common sense. Its nerves proceeded spreading into infinite ramifications in the skin, which encompassed bodies, limbs, and viscera. The perforated nerves carried orders and sensations to the functioning parts, to the extremities of the digits of the fingers. This required time, and he wondered whether an organ player while mentally attending to the sense of hearing was affected by the sense of touch. The hand was the most significant bodily part for touch. Da Vinci performed the Aristotelian experiment of feeling an object with the fingers crossed so that a rounded object when touched seemed double. He performed his own experiment on the spinal cord of a

265 Aristotle, *De anima* 435a-b; trans. Hicks, pp. 161, 163.

266 Siegel, *Galen on Sense Perception*, pp. 174, 175, 176-77. For the localization of touch in the hand, see Galen, *De usu partium* 2.6.

frog, his only certain vivisection, labeling a structure "the origin of the nerves" and "the sense of touch." When he pithed the frog it ceased to show reflexive response to touch, so he surmised that touch was centered in that region of the nervous system, the medulla oblongata and the fourth ventricle, at the end of the spinal cord. In a later experiment he injected the cerebral ventricles with wax to outline their shape. Da Vinci deduced that the nerves that effected the sense of touch united at the end of the spinal cord, from which location the sensation passed into the fourth ventricle. His observation was incompatible with his theory, since the sense of touch would have reached the common sense in the middle, third ventricle before passing through the required *imprensiva*, which he labeled in his drawings as lateral ventricles.[267]

Beyond his innovation, the ordinary classical knowledge was still current in renaissance thought. When Cajetan preached in the Sistine Chapel on immortality, he argued that corporeal actions included the modifications of hot and cold, moist and dry, hard and soft.[268] At the turn of the seventeenth century Cesare Ripa (fl. 1600) would epitomize in his *Iconologia* the tradition. Touch was common to all animals, even with the deprivation of the other senses; it was diffused throughout the entire body, through which it perceived the powers of the objects touched; but it consisted principally in the hands as feeling and taking things.[269] Nothing was explicated in the classical philosophical or medical discussion of touch about sexual contact, however. When a localized organ was specified for the sense of touch, it was the heart for Aristotle and the hand for Galen. The genitals were not at issue, although they were implied in the paired opposites of temperature that touch apprehended: the hot as male, the cold as female. The Christian specification of touch as sexual did have some precedence in Lucretius's *De rerum naturae*, which considered how hot and cold, smooth and rough pricked the senses. He included sexual intercourse among the impinging of objects

---

[267] Kenneth D. Keele, "Leonardo da Vinci's Physiology of the Senses," in *Leonardo's Legacy: An International Symposium*, ed. O'Malley, UCLA Center for Medieval and Renaissance Studies Publications, 2 (Berkeley and Los Angeles: University of California Press, 1969), p. 54; idem, *Leonardo da Vinci's Elements of the Science of Man* (New York: Academic, 1983), p. 230, and for the pithing of the frog, pp. 237-38. For touch, see also McMurrich, *Leonardo da Vinci the Anatomist*, p. 216. Da Vinci, Experiment on the spinal cord of a frog, *The Drawings of Leonardo da Vinci in the Collection of Her Majesty the Queen at Windsor Castle*, ed. Clark and Carlo Pedretti, 2d ed. (London: Phaidon, 1968), 12613v; *Corpus of the Anatomical Studies in the Collection of Her Majesty the Queen at Windsor Castle*, ed. Keele and Pedretti, 3 vols. (New York: Harcourt Brace Jovanovich, 1978-80), 1r; reproduced in Keele, *Leonardo da Vinci's Elements of the Science of Man*, p. 231, fig. 10.1. See also from ed. Clark and Pedretti, 1912r; ed. Keele and Pedretti, 104r, p. 65, fig. 2.27. For the organ player, see Keele, *Leonardo da Vinci's Elements of the Science of Man*, p. 230; O'Malley and Saunders, *Leonardo da Vinci on the Human Body* (New York: Henry Schuman, 1952), pp. 27-28 and reproduced, fig. 56.

[268] Tommaso de Vio, *Oratio* 4, in *Opuscula omnia* 186b.

[269] Cesare Ripa, *Iconologia* 2.

on the body or their issuing from within it. "For touch, so help me the holy power of God," he poetized, "it is touch that is the bodily sense, whether when a thing penetrates from without, or when hurt comes from something within the body, or when it gives forth pleasure in issuing forth by the creative acts of Venus, or when from a blow the seeds make riot in the body itself and confuse the sense by their turmoil." Only strike any part of your body with with a hand as an experiment, he invited.[270]

The identification of the sense of touch as sexual formally originated with Philo in an amplification of the classical topic of the choice of Hercules between virtue and vice.[271] The choice of vice was pleasure,[272] personified as a harlot or a courtesan. Her catalogue of the enticements of the senses to the mind—varied colors, melodious sounds, delicious tastes, and fragrant scents—climaxed in "amours without ceasing, frolics unregulated, chamberings unrestricted." Although she did not state those as "touches," by the rhetorical device of climax that definition was understood, since the other senses had been catalogued. Pleasure was summarized as having told "of the faculties born of touch." Her appearance was meretricious, with cosmetics and ornaments, like bracelets on her wrist, rather than deeds in her hand. She was predictably a bather. "She revels perpetually in the warmth of the bath."[273]

The Christian apologist Lactantius under the topic of touch also treated only sexual pleasure, which he considered the most damaging of sensual allurements.[274] Although he defined "that pleasure which is received from touch" as "a sense of the whole body," he proceeded to condemn as touch "passion alone, which must be especially restrained since it especially harms." The Creator had instilled in the two sexes "the desire of each other and joy in union," more vehemently so in humans than in other animals. Its sole divine purpose was propagation. Just as the eyes were conferred to see the actions necessary to life, so the genitals were given for procreation. That

---

270 Lucretius, *De rerum natura* lines 434-41; trans. W. H. D. Rouse (Cambridge, Mass.: Harvard University Press, 1959), p. 115.

271 Louise Vinge, *The Five Senses: Studies in a Literary Tradition* (Lund: Liber Laromedel, 1975), p. 23.

272 For his severe denunciation of pleasure as evil, see also Richard A. Baer, Jr., *Philo's Use of the Categories Male and Female*, Arbeiten zur Literatur und Geschichte des hellenistischen Judentums, 3 (Leiden: E. J. Brill, 1970), p. 92. See also Genevieve Lloyd, *The Man of Reason: "Male" and "Female" in Western Philosophy* (London: Methuen, 1984), pp. 22-28. For Philo's Eve, see Daniel Bayarin, *Carnal Israel: Reading Sex in Talmudic Culture*, New Historicism, 25 (Berkeley and Los Angeles: University of California Press, 1993), pp. 78-80. For mind vs. sense, see Sharon Lea Mattila, "Wisdom, Sense Perception, Nature, and Philo's Gender Gradient," *Harvard Theological Review* 89 (1996):112-20.

273 Philo, *De sacrificiis Abelis et Caini* 20, 22, 31, 21; trans. Colson and Whitaker, 2:109, 115, 109.

274 Vinge, *Five Senses*, pp. 36, 37, citing Lactantius, *Divinae institutiones* 6.23. For a survey of the senses in patristic literature, see also Ernst von Dobschütz, "Die fünf Sinne im Neuen Testament," *Journal of Biblical Literature* 48 (1929):378-411.

divine law was to be obeyed by their control through modesty and chastity. The devil depraved God's intention toward people by illicit desires, through stirrings of the imagination and stimulations of the genitals. He even established against lawful marriage prostitution and homosexuality. Shameful bodily contamination through sexual contact smeared the mind with filth. Humans were not to transfer their souls to their bodies for death but to bridle pleasure to check any vagrant spirit. They were to strive toward "a blessed and uncorrupted integrity of body" by attaining through virtue the divine likeness.[275] Although fleshly temptations arose from all five senses, sexual temptation was particularly from touch.[276]

Ambrose agreed that the sense of touch was significant in representing "the keenest sort of pleasure," although he did not specify that pleasure as erotic.[277] Augustine was more philosophical than moralistic about touch. Impressions entered the body by the senses, touch "by the sensation of the whole body, what is hard or soft, hot or cold, smooth or rugged, heavy or light." He did typify touch as sexual in his catalogue of the senses as contrary to his love of God. Touch meant "limbs acceptable to carnal embraces." Yet he reasoned by analogy that in loving God he did love "a certain embrace." It was "the embrace of my interior humanity," where "there clings what satiety does not sunder." Since all of his senses strained toward God, he could affirm of an embrace that "this is what I love, when I love my God." He also ascended to the notion that God present with him and within him touched him. "You touched me, and I was impassioned toward your peace."[278] Yet analogy and antithesis remained in tension. In considering in his speculation on the Trinity the prohibition of Jesus to Magdalen, he again explained *Noli me tangere*: "For touch puts a certain end to acquaintance."[279] The knowledge of God was spiritual, not tactile. Medieval doctrine also acknowledged that it was through the senses that the body attained mentally to reason, ultimately to contemplation, of the immaterial and divine truths. Yet people were thought dual in nature—spiritual and corporeal—so that the ill use of the senses corrupted them. When Hugh of St. Victor, in articulating such doctrine, considered the senses, he preached, "Last is touch, which by the softness of various garments, and the filth of various obscenities, often contaminates."[280]

---

275 Lactantius, *Divinae institutiones* 6.23; *The Divine Institutes*, trans. Mary Francis McDonald, Fathers of the Church, 49 (Washington, D.C.: Catholic University of America Press, 1964), pp. 457, 462.

276 Vinge, *Five Senses*, p. 44.

277 Ambrose, *Hexameron* 6.9.64; trans. Savage, p. 275.

278 Augustine, *Confessiones* 10.8.13; 10.6.8; 10.27.38. For sensation in general, see Carol Harrison, *Beauty and Revelation in the Thought of Saint Augustine* (Oxford: Clarendon, 1992), pp. 16-21, 165-66; Miles, *Augustine on the Body*, pp. 9-39.

279 Augustine, *De Trinitate* 1.9.18.

280 Hugh of St. Victor, *Sermones centum* 35, in *Patrologia latina*, 177:985.

Although touch did not always contaminate, it so frequently did that it was considered a dangerous faculty. As Hugh preached, it was among the senses "last." The ranking of touch as the least of the senses was classical. Aristotle had so classified it because touch required actual contact with a material object. It least perceived the form of the object as distinguished from its matter. The descent to touch was from sight, to hearing, to smell, to taste.[281] Thomas Aquinas replicated the order and its argument. Sight was the most spiritual sense because it did not involve physical change in the organ; touch was the least because it did. As he argued, "The hand touching something hot gets hot."[282] Even most renaissance aesthetes, considering the perception of beauty through the senses, admitted only sight and hearing as valuable. They were spiritual senses because they incited the mind to love beauty and so to ascend from the corporal to the incorporeal, thus to the nobility of the mind. Sight was primary: beauty entered through the eyes. Touch was gross, the grossest sense, essentially material and even animalistic. It inflamed the desire for sexual union, thus led to illicit embraces.[283]

As the knight of La Tour-Landry counseled his daughters, a prudent person would touch no object that might harm the soul, for lewd handling stirred the flesh and the blood, precipitating a fall into lechery. Before touching anything, a prudent person would look carefully at her hands, deliberating whether they would incite her to sin, for the folly of mother Eve in touching the fruit had introduced to human nature the vice of lust.[284] The association of touch with the sexual and females with sexual temptation made the custody of that sense of particular importance for women. The household guide *Le ménagier de Paris* advised women to preserve their chastity by guarding the senses, "the hands from foolishly touching."[285] In considering the senses as guardians of the heart the medieval *Ancrene Riwle* for recluses defined "touch, or the feeling that is in every part of the body." Because it was so pervasive, it was the most dangerous. "The fifth of the senses is that of touch. This one is present in all the others, and throughout the body, and therefore it needs the most care." The text adjured the anchoresses by the nails that fixed Christ's hands to the cross: "Keep your hands inside your windows. Touching with the hands, or any other kind of touch between a man and an anchoress is a thing so anomalous, an action so

281 McMurrich, *Leonardo da Vinci the Anatomist*, p. 216.

282 Thomas Aquinas, *Summa theologiae* 1a.78.3; trans. Timothy Suttor (New York: Blackfriars with McGraw Hill, 1970), 11:131. Aquinas believed that only two sensations were distinguished through touch, i.e., temperature and pressure.

283 Kelso, *Doctrine for the Lady*, p. 145. For typical praise of the eyes, consider "the eyes, in which the noblest and most perfect of all the senses resides, through which our intellect gathers, as through windows of transparent glass, everything visible. And furthermore, since through the eyes our faculties are known better than through any of the other senses." Firenzuola, *Delle bellezza delle donne* 1; trans. Eisenbichler and Murray, p. 26.

284 *Livre du Chevalier de La Tour-Landry* 39-46.

285 *Ménagier de Paris* 1.3.

shameful, and a sin so plain, so loathsome to everyone, and so great a scandal." Hands were terribly sinful to avowed ascetics. As the counsel continued, "Not only touching hands, but the mere putting out of the hand, except in case of necessity, is to court God's anger and to invite His wrath." Horror of hands extended beyond their tactile function to even their perception by the nobler sense of sight. "Looking at her own white hands does harm to many an anchoress whose hands are too beautiful because they are too idle. They should scrape up earth every day out of the grave in which they shall rot."[286]

The author who associated touch with sexuality, Philo, developed a more sinister association that would prove fatal to women. Pleasure was a "sorceress," pricking the mind with libidinous desire by her "talismans and witchcraft." Pleasure, with the sense of touch typified as sexual pleasure, was a "lewd dealer in magic."[287] *Malleus maleficarum* imagined woman as the chimera, the classical monster with a lion's visage, goat's belly, and viper's tale. The comparison meant that "a woman is beautiful to look upon, contaminating to the touch, and deadly to keep." Her hands captured sinners. "And her hands are as bands for binding; for when they place their hands on a creature to bewitch it, then with the help of the devil they perform their design." A witch could by prestidigitation so hide a man's genitals that he could not feel them, then restore them to sensation by her touch. Physical contact of the joints or limbs with a witch was to be guarded against. As a precaution at trials for witchcraft, the judge and his assessors "must not allow themselves to be touched physically by the witch, especially in any contact of their bare arms or hands."[288]

Conjuration could be manual, as when it involved during the recitation of a rhyme the placement of the hand against a wall, with each finger representing a devil.[289] Witchcraft was not especially tactile, however, since magic, like sorcery, worked (as believed) more mediately than contactually. Spells, charms, and potions were usual. Touches, despite stated fears of contamination, were unusual. The human dignity of erect bipedality was not initially threatened except by sorcerous laming. Luther believed that witches in their liaison as the devil's whore rendered people lame.[290] But

---

[286] *Ancrene Riwle* 2, 7; *The "Ancrene Riwle" (The Corpus MS.: Ancrene Wisse*, trans. M. B. Salu (London: Burns and Oates, 1955), pp. 21, 49, 51, 180. The pervasiveness of touch was classical. As Cicero wrote, "The sense of touch is evenly diffused over all the body, to enable us to perceive all sorts of contacts and even the minutest impacts of both cold and heat." *De natura deorum* 141; trans. H. Rackham (London: Heinemann, 1933), p. 259.

[287] Philo, *De sacrificiis Abelis et Caini* 26, 28; trans. Colson and Whitaker, 2:111, 113.

[288] Sprenger and Institoris, *Malleus maleficarum* 1.6; 2.1.7; 2.2.4; 3.5; trans. Summers, pp. 46, 47, 228.

[289] Ruth Martin, *Witchcraft and the Inquisition in Venice, 1550-1650* (Oxford: Basil Blackwell, 1989), p. 103.

[290] For Luther, see E. William Monter, *Witchcraft in France and Switzerland: The Boarderlands during the Reformation* (Ithaca, N.Y.: Cornell University Press, 1976), p. 31.

laming was not intended by direct contact but by sympathetic magic. An image was fashioned; its leg broken. An image of wax to cause the downfall of a pope, the seduction of a woman, or the infliction of any bodily harm was commonly pricked with pins, then left where the victim would touch it or pass by it.[291] The ancient origins of the practice—nails driven in dolls—were aimed at immobility, rather than maiming: literally "nailing down" an opponent. In the sole tale of escape from such a binding spell, in a Byzantine miracle, a paraplegic was cured when the nails were withdrawn from a bronze statuette.[292] In another method the position of the arms—up or down—signified favor or death on waxen dolls fashioned by a sorcerer in Marguerite de Navarre's (1492-1549) tale.[293]

Mere restraint of an enemy by such indirect methods became bodily harm through overt touch in early modern trials for formal witchcraft. The allegation became frequent of devil worshippers being in direct, physical contact with their victims: hands pressing a baby on the chest to wound it or on its head to paralyze it. Witches also allegedly touched others dangerously through mediums by smearing them with ointment or beating them with a stick.[294] Yet, in plain contradiction, the very pact with the devil that identified the witch destroyed the human tactile sense. A woman named Antonia anointed a girl, who then died; yet for kissing a demon's foot her own left pinkie was deadened forever.[295] Perussone Gapit, accused of paralyzing a child by the laying on of hands, had a finger so roughly scratched by the devil in the guise of a bear that she feared it would fall off. It was still sore during her interrogation.[296] Such rare examples of diabolical touch from the fifteenth century swelled in the sixteenth century into an institution, by which a mark on the skin became the proof of a pact with the devil. Because of Protestant emphasis on the pact as the essence of the crime, the devil's mark became an inevitable feature of its trials, although it was

---

291 Richard Kieckhefer, *European Witch Trials: Their Foundations in Popular and Learned Culture, 1300-1500* (London: Routledge and Kegan Paul, 1976), pp. 5, 54, 13, 14, 50-55, 59.

292 Christopher A. Faraone, "Binding and Burying the Forces of Evil: The Defensive Use of 'Voodoo Dolls' in Ancient Greece," *Classical Antiquity* 10 (1991):193-94, citing Sophronius, *Narratio miraculorum sanctorum Cyri et Joannis*, in *Patrologia graeca*, 87-3:3625.

293 Marguerite de Navarre, *Heptameron* 1.1. For a waxen figure stuck with needles, see also Guido Ruggiero, *Binding Passions: Tales of Magic, Marriage, and Power at the End of the Renaissance* (New York: Oxford, 1993), pp. 57-58.

294 Kieckhefer, *European Witch Trials*, pp. 48-49, 76, 32. For killing children by touch, see also Christina Larner, "*Crimen exceptum*? The Crime of Witchcraft in Europe," in *Crime and the Law: The Social History of Crime in Western Europe Since 1500*, ed. V. A. C. Gatrell, Bruce Lenman, and Geoffrey Parker (London: Europa, 1980), p. 53.

295 Kieckhefer, *European Witch Trials*, p. 25; Robert Rowland, "'Fantasticall and Devilishe Persons': European Witch-beliefs in Comparative Perspective," in *Early Modern European Witchcraft: Centres and Peripheries*, ed. Bengt Ankarloo and Gustav Henningsen (Oxford: Clarendon, 1990), pp. 162-63.

296 Kieckhefer, *European Witch Trials*, p. 33.

marginal, or even unknown, in Catholic trials. The pact involved a small obscure mark on the skin left by the devil's scratch or bite. Suspects were stripped, shaved, and searched for it by professional "prickers." The method was to probe the skin with needles until a spot insensitive to pain was found.[297] The touch of the devil to a human was anti-tactile: it deadened the basic animate sensation.

Female hands had become suspect and their comportment for good or for evil was of grave concern to moralists. Hands were never to be idle, not only for medieval recluses but also for renaissance ladies. Alberti stated in *Il libro della famiglia* that a wife was to be no idler with her elbows on the windowsill, while her needlework slackened in her lap. "Always keep busy," he ordered.[298] Spinning was also argued as make-work to relieve the tedium of domestic isolation.[299] Raffaela the bawd agreed that handiwork—any piece would do— was for appearance, not for profit, so that visitors to a household would not surprise its women idle.[300] But neither were female hands to be overly mobile. Their gesture in conversation especially was to be guarded, "without excessive motions of the hand."[301] As the medieval writer Francesco Barbaro counseled in *De re uxoria*, "Excessive movement of the hands and other parts of the body cannot be done without loss of dignity, and such actions are always joined to vanity and are signs of frivolity." In gesturing, a woman was to observe decency and merit her dignity.[302] If a lady's hands or fingernails were not nice, she was not to signal with them but rest them calmly.[303]

Female hands were to be occupied usefully at the spindle and distaff. Even when females had no hands they were expected to perform handiwork by the ingenuity of other bodily parts. The renaissance anatomist Alessandro Benedetti (1450?-1512) reported eyewitness of "a woman born without arms who was skilled in using her feet instead of hands for spinning and sewing."[304] Paré recounted in his collection on monsters that

---

297 Monter, *Witchcraft*, pp. 25, 54-55, 57, 60, 61, 144, and especially 157-66. The practice was unknown to the Roman Inquisition. John Tedeschi, "Inquisitorial Law and the Witch," in *Early Modern Witchcraft*, ed. Ankarloo and Henningsen, p. 84.

298 Alberti, *Libro della famiglia* 3, pp. 225-26; trans. Watkins, p. 223.

299 Francesco da Barberino, *Reggimento e costumi di donne*, p. 17; cited by King, *Women of the Renaissance*, p. 79.

300 Piccolomini, *Dialogo de la bella creanza de le donne*, pp. 36-37.

301 Pisan, *Livre de trois vertus* 1.11; trans. Willard, p. 92.

302 Francesco Barbaro, *De re uxoria* 2.3; "On Wifely Duties," trans. Benjamin G. Kohl, in *The Earthly Republic: Italian Humanists on Government and Society*, ed. idem and Ronald G. Witt (Philadelphia: University of Pennsylvania Press, 1987), p. 202; also cited by King, *Women of the Renaissance*, p. 40.

303 *Clef d'amours* lines 2517-20; also cited by Bornstein, *Lady in the Tower*, p. 41 without documentation. The advice reverts to Ovid, *Ars amatoria* 3.275-76.

304 Alessandro Benedetti, *Historia corporis humani, sive anatomice* 1.3, in L. R. Lind, *Studies in Pre-Vesalian Anatomy: Biography, Translations, Documents*, Memoirs of the American Philosophical Society, 104 (Philadelphia, Pa.: American Philosophical Society, 1975), p. 84.

"an armless woman was seen in Paris who cut cloth and sewed and performed several other actions."[305] The city council in Strasbourg allowed a man to display—for a penny a peek—a woman "with no hands and only one foot, but who can still do all sorts of handiwork, like spinning."[306] Textile labor was believed primordial. As Giovanni Boccaccio (1313-75) stated in *De claris mulieribus*, while her husband Adam tilled with the hoe, Eve "discovered the art of spinning with the distaff."[307] A relief by Quercia, from whom Michelangelo derived the erectile posture of Eve at creation, stood her with a spindle while Adam dug with a spade.[308] Scripture said that in the beginning both sexes tailored. "They sewed fig leaves together and made themselves aprons" (Gen. 2:7). Society divided manual labor, however, portioning the industry of cloth to females.[309] In Homeric epic Telemachus ordered Penelope, "But now go to your room; tend to your tasks, the distaff and the loom. . . leave speech to men."[310] The Christian paradigm to sanction that female task was the Virgin Mary, although her handiwork is depicted as allegorical, rather than domestic.[311] The friar Luis de León, who exhorted the perfect wife to "handle the flax and embroider the silks" and so by approval to "upraise to dignity and consideration the virtue of housewifery," thought this female task even divine in sanction. Scripture was so detailed and particular on the duty of married women, he wrote, that

---

305 Paré, *De monstres* 8; *On Monsters and Marvels*, trans. Janis L. Pallister (Chicago: University of Chicago Press, 1982), p. 36.

306 Strasbourg, Archives municipales, Statuten, 21:186; cited by Merry E. Wiesner, "Spinsters and Seamstresses: Women in Cloth and Clothing Production," in *Rewriting the Renaissance*, ed. Ferguson et al., p. 202.

307 Giovanni Boccaccio, *De claris mulieribus* 1; *Concerning Famous Women*, trans. Guido A. Guarino (New Brunswick, N.J.: Rutgers University Press, 1963), p. 2.

308 Jacopo della Quercia, Adam and Eve at work, main portal of San Petronio; reproduced in Beck, *Jacopo della Quercia*, 2:pl. 108. See also Maureen Pelta, "Expelled from Paradise and Put to Work: Recontextualizing Castagno's Adam and Eve," *Journal of Medieval and Renaissance Studies* 25 (1995):73-87; Niccolò de Tommaso, Adam and Eve at work, ex-Convento del T, Pistoia; reproduced in Berenson, *Italian Pictures*, 1:311.

309 For an anthropological introduction, see Annette B. Weiner and Jane Schneider, eds., *Cloth and Human Experience* (Washington, D.C.: Smithsonian Institution Press, 1989), pp. 20-25; eadem, "Cloth and the Organization of Human Experience," *Current Anthropology* 27 (1986):181-82; Schneider, "The Anthropology of Cloth," *Annual Review of Anthropology* 16 (1987):413; Mary Ellen Roach and Joanne Bubolz Elder, "The Language of Personal Adornment," in *Fabrics of Culture*, ed. Cordwell and Schwartz, pp. 7-21; Schwartz, "Uncovering the Secret Vice: Toward an Anthropology of Clothing and Adornment," pp. 23-45. The first eyed needles of bone date from the Aurignacian period, as evidence of sewing, while textile garments and evidence for weaving date to the Neolithic age. Anthropologists of clothing reject the theory of "shame" as the origin of clothing: that Adam and Eve invented it to conceal their genitals, pp. 24, 26.

310 Homer, *Odyssey* 21.377-78, 379-80; *The Odyssey of Homer*, trans. Allen Mandelbaum (Berkeley and Los Angeles: University of California Press, 1990), pp. 438-39.

311 See Robert L. Wyss, "Die Handarbeiten der Maria: Eine iconographische Studie unter Berucksichtung der textilen Techniken," in *"Artes minores": Dank an Werner Abegg*, ed. Michael Stettler and Mechild Lember (Bern: Stämpfli, 1973), pp. 113-88; Irena Turnau, "The Diffusion of Knitting in Medieval Europe," in *Cloth and Clothing in Medieval Europe*, ed. Harte and Ponting, p. 382, and see pp. 373, 384-85, figs. 19.7, 8, 9.

"entering their homes, the Holy Spirit reaches the point of putting the needle into their hands, grasps the distaff for them, and even twirls the spindle in their fingers."[312]

For a woman to reject that religious duty of handiwork meant inversion or misrule, as in Dürer's depiction of an old hag riding backward on a goat, with a distaff perversely between her legs,[313] rather than properly in her arms. An inverted social order is depicted by the woman holding in her hands the symbols of the male order—sword, purse, breeches, while the male is forced to the distaff that should be hers.[314] Or she grasps him by the wrist in control and beats him with the spindle, as he struggles to steady himself from falling to the ground.[315] In the seventeenth century the very sense of touch will be allegorized by Jan Miense Molenaer (b.c.1610-68) as a wife beating her husband on the head with a shoe.[316]

Those were variants on the inversion[317] in which women rode men, reducing them to animal all fours. The famous case was Phyllis riding Aristotle.[318] It was a medieval topic of the power of women, displayed on decorative objects and revived with popularity late in the fifteenth century by printmakers of secular images. According to its legend the philosopher Aristotle succumbed to lust for the beautiful Phyllis, wife of his pupil Alexander the Great. When he propositioned her sexually, she insisted that

---

312 Luis de León, *Perfecta casada* 4, intro., 3; trans. Hubbard, pp. 30-31.

313 Albrecht Dürer, Witch riding on a goat, engraving, c. 1500-1, National Gallery of Art, Washington, D.C.; reproduced in Russell with Barnes, *Eva/Ave*, p. 166. See also Ruth Mellinkoff, "Riding Backwards: Theme of Humiliation and Symbol of Evil," *Viator* 4 (1973):153-76; Natalie Zemon Davis, "The Rites of Violence: Religious Riot in Sixteenth-Century France," *Past and Present* 59 (1973):83-84.

314 Keith Moxey, *Peasants, Warriors, and Wives: Popular Imagery in the Reformation* (Chicago: University of Chicago Press, 1989), p. 104. A wife kicks her husband in the back and threatens him with her distaff while she pulls on a pair of trousers. Master of the Amsterdam Cabinet, Henpecked husband, c. 1475-80, Louvre, Paris; reproduced in J. P. Filedt Kok, *The Master of the Amsterdam Cabinet, or The Housebook Master, ca. 1470-1500* (Princeton, N.J.: Princeton University Press, 1985), p. 195 n. 95. See also Lené Dresen Coenders, "De strijd om de broeck: de verhouding man/vrouw in het begin van de moderne tijd (1450-1630)," *De Revisor* 4 (1977):29-37.

315 Israel von Meckenem, Angry wife, engraving, c. 1495-1503, National Gallery, Washington, D.C.; reproduced in Russell with Barnes, *Eva/Ave*, p. 194.

316 Jan Miense Molenaer, Sense of touch, 1637, Mauritschuis, the Hague; see Schama, *Embarrassment of Riches*, pp. 400-2; reproduced, fig. 142. For the artist's wife, see Juliane Harms, "Judith Leyster: Ihr Leben und ihr Werke," *Oud Holland* 44 (1927):88-96, 113-26, 145-54, 221-42, 275-79; *Judith Leyster: A Dutch Master and Her World*, ed. James A. Welu (New Haven, Conn.: Yale University Press for the Worcester Art Museum and the Frans Halsmuseum, 1993).

317 For the topsy-turvy world in general, see Moxey, *Peasants, Warriors, and Wives*, pp. 101-26. For the topic of the power of women, see Smith, "'To Women's Wiles I Fell': The Power of Woman Topos and the Development of Medieval Secular Art," Ph.D diss., University of Pennsylvania, 1978; Davis, "Woman on Top," in eadem, *Society and Culture in Early Modern France: Eight Essays* (Stanford, Calif.: Stanford University Press, 1975), pp. 124-51; Silver and Smith, "Carnal Knowledge, pp. 251-52.

318 See also Davis, "Woman on Top," pp. 135-36; Moxey, *Peasants, Warriors, and Wives*, p. 103.

he first put on a bridle and allow her to ride around the garden on his back. The moral was that passion overcame reason, reducing a human to a beast in behavior.[319] Both figures are nude in the woodcut by Hans Baldung Grien (d.1545), although she wears a hat as a sign of superiority.[320] Ordinary women could copy Phyllis, as in the coat of arms depicting a wife riding a peasant male who holds a distaff and howls in pain. Another peasant below stands on his head in reversal of social values[321] but also in corruption of all human nature as standing properly on its feet. The correct order was for the male as virtuous to rule the female as vicious, as in Paolo Veronese's (1528-88) fresco where he holds a rod of correction and the reins of a bit which is in her mouth.[322] The female astride the male carnally was the literal inversion. Tomás Sánchez (1550-1610), the primary interpreter of the Tridentine rules on marriage, declared that the woman on top in sexual intercourse committed a mortal sin because she inverted the natural order.[323]

---

319 Russell with Barnes, *Eva/Ave*, p. 149.

320 Hans Baldung Grien, Phyllis riding Aristotle, woodcut, 1513. See James H. Marrow and Alan Shestack, *Hans Baldung Grien: Prints and Drawings* (Washington, D.C.: National Gallery of Art, 1981), p. 171; reproduced, p. 170; Karl Oettinger and Karl-Adolf Knappe, *Hans Baldung Grien and Albrecht Dürer in Nürnberg* (Nürnberg: Hans Carl, 1963), abb. 66. For a variant, see Marianne Bernhard, ed., *Hans Baldung Grien: Handzeichnungen Druckgraphik* (Munich: Südwest, 1978), p. 97. For other examples, see Master MZ, Phyllis riding Aristotle, engraving, c. 1500, Museum of Fine Arts, Boston; reproduced in Russell with Barnes, *Eva/Ave*, p. 149; Lucan van Leyden, woodcut, reproduced in Jacobowitz and Stepanek, *Prints of Lucas van Leyden and His Contemporaries*, p. 145, fig. 49b; Max J. Friedlander, *Lucas van Leyden*, ed. F. Winkler (Berlin: Walter de Gruyter, 1963), pl. 77; Albrecht Dürer, watercolor, Pierpont Morgan Library, New York; reproduced in Charles W. Talbot, Gaillard F. Ravenel, and Jay A. Levenson, *Dürer in America: His Graphic Work* (Washington, D.C.: National Gallery of Art, 1971), cat. no. 29; Peter Flötner, Kunstsammlunger der Veste, Coburg; detail reproduced in Lyndal Roper, *The Holy Household: Women and Morals in Reformation Augsburg* (Oxford: Clarendon, 1989), p. 111.

321 Israel van Meckenem after the Master of the Housebook, Coat of arms with tumbling boy, National Gallery, Washington, D.C.; reproduced in Russell with Barnes, *Eva/Ave*, p. 175. For the continuance of the design, see Linda Stone-Ferrier, "Spun Virtue, the Lacework of Folly, and the World Wound Upside-Down: Seventeenth-Century Dutch Depictions of Female Handiwork," in *Cloth and Human Experience*, ed. Weiner and Schneider, pp. 215-42. The inversion of the sexes at weaving is as ancient as Egyptian practice. See Herodotus 2.35; cited by François Hartog, *The Mirror of Herodotus: The Representation of the Other in the Writing of History*, trans. Janet Lloyd, New Historicism, 5 (Berkeley and Los Angeles: University of California Press, 1988), p. 213; see also Christian Froidefond, *Le mirage égyptien dans la littérature grecque d'Homère à Aristote* (Paris: Gap Ophrys, 1971), pp. 129-36; S. Pembroke, "Women in Charge: The Function of Alternatives in Early Greek Tradition and the Ancient Idea of Matriarchy," *Journal of the Warburg and Courtauld Institutes* 30 (1967):17. The Amerindians were thought to have been Egyptian in origin because they inverted the natural order for weaving. Juan Suárez de Peralta, *Tratado del descubrimiento de las Indias*, p. 5; cited by Anthony Pagden, *The Fall of Natural Man: The American Indian and the Origins of Comparative Ethnology* (Cambridge: Cambridge University Press, 1982), p. 175.

322 Veronese, fresco in the Villa Maser; reproduced in van Marle, *The Development of the Italian Schools of Painting*, 19 vols. (The Hague: Martinus Nijhoff, 1923-38), 2:7, fig. 7.

323 Tomás Sánchez, *De sancto matrimonii disputationum* 9.16.1.3; cited by James A. Brundage, *Law, Sex, and Christian Society in Medieval Europe* (Chicago: University of Chicago Press, 1987), p. 566. See also the position as preventing conception in John T. Noo-

Although the classical exemplar of female labor was noble Penelope, whose fidelity was proved at the loom, even an ignoble woman was expected to tend to her task. In a renaissance drama of Easter the disciple Peter rebuked Magdalen's report of the risen Lord: "That rumor I will not believe. Hurry home and mind your spinning. It is a sin and a shame that females run all over the countryside." He threatened her for disobedience with the sense of touch—a clout on the ear, cheek, and neck.[324] Women collaborated in that valuation, with Pisan concurring that reformed prostitutes should spin. A wise mistress set the example for her household by her practical handiwork. She would even have flax spun for her by poor women in town into tablecloths and towels. As that author exuded, "Having smoothly-woven, fine linens is a well-earned, honest pleasure for any woman who is careful and provident. She can take great pleasure in white, sweet-smelling linens stored in her coffers." They could be used for special guests her husband might invite, to her high praise.[325]

Yet the improper use of the female craft could harm women and their offspring. If seamstresses and women who worked tapestries on their knees crossed their legs habitually during pregnancy, they could form monsters—children born bent with twisted hands and feet. Needles dropped or slipped from female hands could also create monsters. There were horrible tales of females who accidently swallowed needles, which were then urinated, or vomited, or just ejected from their bodily apertures. Or there was the wife of a Jewish cloth merchant, riding on horseback, whose buttock was penetrated by a needle from her pin case and later extracted from her groin rusted. Paré himself extracted a stone like a walnut in which was embedded a sewing needle; after its presentation to the king, he kept it in his study as a token of the monster.[326]

Not all women cared to be praised for their handiness with needlework. The craft expressed the type of femininity as mindless and decorative. Needlework advocated, whether in manuals of female behavior or of embroidery patterns, submissive virtues of chastity, humility, and obedience.[327] Renaissance women learned needlework and spinning as their basic education.[328] Female desire for human dignity through a nobler education formed

---

nan, Jr., *Contraception: A History of Its Treatment by the Catholic Theologians and Canonists*, enlarged ed. (Cambridge, Mass.: Belknap Press, Harvard University Press, 1986), pp. 224-26, 238-41.

324 "Das Erlauer Österspiel" III 1386-89, 1397-1402; cited by Malvern, *Venus in Sackcloth*, p. 38.

325 Pisan, *Livre de trois vertus* 3.10; 2.10; 3.2; trans. Willard, p. 188.

326 Paré, *Des monstres* 11, 17, 32, 4, 15,

327 See Rozsika Parker, *The Subversive Stitch: Embroidery and the Making of the Feminine* (London: Women's Press, 1984), pp. 6, 81. But for an embroidery of the mastery of men by women, as legitimately conducing to marriage, see Smith, "The Power of Women Topos on a Fourteenth-Century Embroidery," *Viator* 21 (1990):203-28.

328 King, *Women of the Renaissance*, pp. 166-67.

around a manual topic of needlework versus knowledge. What were women to have in hand: distaff or book? An artist might portray either item, as in Pontormo's portrait of a woman with her hands resting on a basket of spindles or alternatively his portrait of a woman with a volume of verse.[329] That renaissance topic for female choice was but a variant on the renaissance topic for male choice as arms versus letters: the weapon or the book. Its famous anecdote was Michelangelo's inquiry to Julius II about how to balance the right hand of his statue raised in benediction. When the sculptor asked the pope what to place in its left hand, the model replied, "Put a sword there; I know nothing about literature."[330] For both sexes moral character was defined by the decision of what to take and hold in hand. Both sexes, if the authors were humanists, praised the female choice of books versus needles.

Angelo Poliziano (1454-94) lauded Cassandra Fedele. "But in our age, in which it is rare even for men to excel in letters, you are the only maiden living who handles a book instead of wool, a reed pen instead of make-up, a metal stilus instead of a needle, and who smears not her skin with white lead, but rather paper with ink."[331] Erasmus in his *Christiani matrimonii institutio* acknowledged that the spindle and distaff were the universal female instruments, suitable for spoiling idleness among all classes. Yet, while parents instructed daughters in the art of embroidering silken stuffs, they would do better if they educated them in good letters. The girl who wove was occupied but still free to listen to juvenile fables and to respond with jokes. Yet "she who is intent on her books totally possesses her spirit." Telemachus may have sent Penelope to the spindle and distaff, but the subject to be woven on her tapestries was first read.[332] Erasmus had learned about female erudition personally from such models as Margaret More Roper (1505-44). The introduction to her translation of his meditation on the "Our Father" argued similarly that books absorbed the mind, while handiwork only occupied the fingers, allowing the imagination to

---

329 Pontormo, Woman with basket of spindles, c. 1516-18, Uffizi, Florence; reproduced in Berti, *Pontormo*, pl. XXXI, and detail p. 41, pl. 5; Forster, *Pontormo*, pl. 91. Pontormo, Portait of a lady with a volume of verse, former Yerkes collection; reproduced in Clapp, *Jacopo Carucci da Pontormo*, fig. 131.

330 Vasari, *Vita di Michelangelo*, 1:34-35.

331 Angelo Poliziano to Cassandra Fedele, in eadem, *Epistolae et orationes*, pp. 155-58; trans. King and Rabil, *Her Immaculate Hand*, p. 127; cited also in Anthony Grafton and Jardine, *From Humanism to the Humanities: Education and the Liberal Arts in Fifteenth- and Sixteenth-Century Europe* (London: Duckworth, 1986), pp. 49-50; Jardine, "'O decus Italiae virgo,' or, The Myth of the Learned Lady in the Renaissance," *The Historical Journal* 28 (1985):806; King, "Book-Lined Cells," p. 76; and see eadem, *Women of the Renaissance*, pp. 180-81.

332 Erasmus, *Christiani matrimonii institutio*, in *Opera omnia* (Leiden), 5:663. Cf. *Epistolae* 1233, 4:578-79. See also J. Kelley Sowards, "Erasmus and the Education of Women," *Sixteenth Century Journal* 13 (1982):77-90.

wander.[333] Agrippa von Nettesheim in his declamation on the nobility of women denounced it "male tyranny"—against divine justice and natural law—to deny females the freedom of choice. A woman was shut up in house or convent, "not allowed to wield anything other than needle and thread, as though she were incapable of more lofty activities."[334] Yet the poet Louise Labé (1526?-1566) observed at mid-century that "many women, in order to appeal to those among their friends who were poets, have traded in their baskets and sewing for pens and books."[335]

Not all agreed with the exchange. Federico Luigini argued in *Il libro della bella donna* that the distaff and wheel were not only for plebian but also noble females. While the lowly would find only utility in the skills, the highborn would secure honor.[336] Giovanni Michele Bruto (c.1515-c.1574) also declared in *La institutione di una fanciulla nata nobilmente* "how far more convenient the distaff and spindle, needle and thimble were for them with a good and honest reputation, than the skill of well using a pen."[337] The argument alternated like a shuttle through a warp. An anonymous *Oratione dell'humile invaghito* complained, "Instead of teaching women good and praiseworthy arts we turn them to mechanic exercises. In place of paper and ink we give them needle and thread."[338]

At the close of the century the accomplished author Maria de Zayas y Sotomayor (1590-1650) would plead that "the true cause of women not being learned is not a defect in ability but a lack of application, for if in our upbringing they gave us books and teachers as they place cambric on our sewing cushions and patterns on our embroidery frames, we would be as suited as men are for positions and university chairs." Perhaps, she speculated, women would be even keener than men at learning for being naturally colder, since understanding consisted in moistness.[339] She thus reversed the traditional designation of hot and dry humors—male qualities—as the right combination for intelligence. Books, which had been associated through reading with the sense of sight, became also tactile in value with the mass

---

333 Richard Hyrde, introduction to Margaret More Roper, *A Devout Treatise upon the "Pater noster,"* p. 100.

334 Agrippa von Nettesheim, *De nobilitate*, C7; cited by Maclean, *Renaissance Notion of Woman*, p. 80.

335 Labé, *Debat de Folie et d'Amour* 5.1312-16; *Louise Labé's Complete Works*, trans. Edith R. Farrell (Troy, N.Y.: Whitston, 1986), p. 83. See also Jordan, *Renaissance Feminism*, pp. 175, 182-84.

336 Federigo Luigini, *Il libro della bella donna* 1-3; cited by Kelso, *Doctrine for the Lady*, p. 121.

337 Bruto, *La institutione di una fanciulla nata nobilmente*, ff. 26a-28a; cited by Kelso, *Doctrine for the Lady*, pp. 59-60 (modernized).

338 *Oratione dell'humile invaghito*, ff. D-DZa; cited by Kelso, *Doctrine for the Lady*, p. 18.

339 Maria de Zayas y Sotomayor, "Al que leyre," *Novelas amorosas y ejemplares*, pp. 22-23. For the author, see recently Mercedes Maroto Camino, "Spindles for Swords: The Re/discovery of Maria de Zayas' Presence," *Hispanic Review* 62 (1994):519-36.

production of the quarto edition that rendered them literally "manuals." Knowledge became dependent not on storage in memory but on portage in hand. A renaissance book could be carried about just like the ancient items that had distinguished humanity from other animality by the sense of touch: the tool and the weapon. Yet it was the ancient manual and moral choice for women—needles rather than books—that epitomized in renaissance art the sense of touch.

The iconographic theme of the five senses dated to scattered examples in Romanesque art but from the thirteenth century was more frequently depicted. For want of any classical representation, medieval artists necessarily exercised their ingenuity. The concept originated in microcosmic man with the elements—touch being associated with the earth as Aristotle thought. In versions of the choice of Hercules the Pythagorean fork in the road could include the five senses, beginning with sight and ending with touch. Although in many didactic treatises the senses were so equated with vice and with sin, more often they were considered neutral. Their depiction is absent from the façades of cathedrals, where the virtues and vices battle allegorically for souls. Although the sensory theme was neglected by religious artists, it was incorporated into profane art, with virtually all of its imagery secular. There emerged two particular types: humans holding emblems and animals as symbols. The Latin translation of Aristotle's *Parva naturalia* occasioned historiated initials in which each sense was a human figure holding a significant object. For touch it was the harp, since the plucking of that instrument was in French *toucher.* Since the Latin noun for each of the five senses was masculine in gender, originally they were personified by males.[340]

The animals appeared in French illuminations, with the initial pictorial form of the five senses in manuscripts of Richard de Fournival's thirteenth-century *Bestiare d'amour*, an art of love.[341] Its author observed conventionally that the sense of touch had multiple objects. "But many things serve touch, for with it one feels hot, cold, moist, dry, rough, smooth and many other things." He settled, nevertheless, on a singular animal, "the spider for touch."[342] He probably borrowed from a frequently cited mnemonic verse,

---

340 Carl Nordenfalk, "Five Senses in Late Medieval and Renaissance Art," *Journal of the Warburg and Courtauld Institutes* 48 (1985):1; idem, "Les cinq sens dans l'art du Moyen-âge," *Revue de l'art* 34 (1976):17-21; "Five Senses in Late Medieval and Renaissance Art," pp. 2, 21, 2, 7.

341 Nordenfalk, "Five Senses in Late Medieval and Renaissance Art," pp. 22-23. See also illustration, Besitiaire d'amour, Lombardie, 1300-25, New York, Pierpont Morgan Library, MS. 459, fol. 9v; reproduced, p. 24, fig. 12, and also in H. W. Janson, *Apes and Ape Lore: In the Middle Ages and the Renaissance* (London: Warburg Institute, University of London, 1932), pl. XLIVb.

342 Richard de Fournival, *Li bestiaires d'amours*, p. 36; *Master Richard's "Bestiary of Love" and "Response,"* trans. Jeanette Beer (Berkeley and Los Angeles: University of California Press, 1986), pp. 12, 13.

"The boar excels us in hearing, the lynx in sight, the monkey in taste, the vulture in smell, the spider in touch."[343] It appeared in Thomas of Cantimpré's *De naturis rerum*,[344] although likely cited from a lost encyclopedia or digest.[345] The arachnid, falsely supposed an insect,[346] became fixed as the tactile symbol. In the cloister of the monastery delle Tre Fontane in Rome, on the length of the terrace wall, is a late medieval fresco of didactic subjects, a visual encyclopedia based on French scholastic works. A dandy gestures to medallions about him in which the spider resides in its web for the sense of touch.[347] The secular character of the sensory iconography also rendered it appropriate to buildings that were not ecclesiastical, with the best parallel to that monastic fresco another one on the walls of a medieval castle at Longthorpe near Peterborough. Frescoed above the fireplace in the tower is a royal figure, probably reason, who from his position in the middle of a wheel rotates its spokes with his hand. On the rim of the wheel are depicted the senses, with the spider in its web for touch.[348]

The belief that certain senses were more developed in lower animals than in humans was ancient, although Pliny maintained that humans excelled in touch. "Among the senses, that of touch in man ranks before all the other species, and taste next; but in the remaining senses he is surpassed by many other creatures."[349] Albert the Great agreed that touch was most highly developed in humans,[350] and so did Laurent Joubert (1529-83), the renaissance physician.[351] The choice of the spider for touch was, nevertheless, apt in recognition of its tactile quality. Bartholomaeus Anglicus in *De*

---

343 See Hans Walther, *Initia carminum ac versuum medii aevi posterioris latinorum*, Carmina medii aevi posterioris latina, 1-1 (Göttingen: Vandenhoeck and Ruprecht, 1969), no. 12243; cited by Nordenfalk, "Cinq sens," p. 22.

344 Thomas of Cantimpré, *De naturis rerum* 4.1.

345 Janson, *Apes and Ape Lore*, p. 239.

346 Spiders were not classified as arachnids until the nineteenth century, as differing from insects in two, rather than three, bodily parts and eight, rather than six, legs. However, some scientists in the sixteenth century noted the eight legs. See Paul Delaunay, *La zoologie au seizième siècle*, Histoire de la pensée, 7 (Paris: Hermann, 1962), pp. 224, 226.

347 Nordenfalk, "Cinq sens," p. 25. Fresco, Man and his senses, Monastery delle Tre Fontane, Rome; reproduced, fig. 13; Carlo Bertelli, "L'enciclopedia delle Tre Fontane," *Paragone* 20 (1969):pl. 9, and detail pl. 10.

348 Nordenfalk, "Cinq sens," pp. 24-25. Man and his senses, fresco, school of Peterborough, second quarter of 14th century, Longthorpe Tower, Northants; reproduced, p. 25, fig. 14. See also E. Clive-Rouse and Audrey Baker, "The Wall-Paintings at Longthorpe Tower near Peterborough, Northants," *Archaeologia, or Miscellaneous Tracts Relating to Antiquity*, Society of Antiquaries of London, 96 (Oxford: Charles Batey for the Society of Antiquaries, 1955), pp. 12-13, 42, 44-47, and reproduced, pl. XVII; Margaret Wood, *The English Mediaeval House* (London: Phoenix House, 1965), pp. 399-401, and reproduced, pl. LX; Janson, *Apes and Ape Lore*, reproduced, pl. XLIVa; Vinge, *Five Senses*, reproduced, p. 52, fig. 2; Francis Klingender, *Animals in Art and Thought to the End of the Middle Ages*, ed. Evelyn Antal and John Harthan (London: Routlege and Kegan Paul, 1971), p. 428, pl. 262.

349 Nordenfalk, "Cinq sens," p. 22, citing Pliny, *Historia naturalis* 10.88.191; trans. Rackham, 3:413-15.

350 Albert the Great, *Historia animalium* 21.3.

351 Laurent Joubert, *Traité du ris* 2.6.

proprietatibus rerum typified medieval lore in stating that, among beasts of round bodies, the spider had the best sense of touch, because it felt from the hub of its web a movement even on the farthest thread.[352] For that ability the spider was like the human head of a household. Alberti in *Il libro della famiglia* compared the renaissance patriarch to a spider residing in the hub of his web, alert to any tension on its finest and furthest filaments.[353] The monarch Philip II (1527-98) was compared for his sedentary and static style of government, in retreat in the center of the Iberian peninsula, to a spider motionless in the hub of his web, whose filaments extended almost globally.[354] Alternately, the household of a bachelor was decried as covered in spiders' webs in Bernardino of Siena's (1380-1444) praise for matrimony,[355] with the implication that a good wife would sweep them out with her broom. When the bachelor Michelangelo complained of his confinement at home, ill and aged, he poetized:

> there's little room to fly in my dark tomb,
> where Arachne and a thousand of her workers,
> spinning, make little bobbins of themselves.

Even, "In one of my ears a spiderweb is nested.[356]

The iconographic transference of the five senses from males to females occurred abruptly at the turn of the sixteenth century with a new rule of personification.[357] There was some ancient precedent for the association of women with the spider as the emblem of touch, although not exclusively. Aristotle wrote influentially that spiders divided their labor: the males hunted, while the females spun.[358] Pliny even elaborated the misconception into an exemplar of marital harmony. "People think that it is the female that weaves and the male that hunts, and that thus the married pair do equal shares of service." Not only was the female associated with the singular and spectacular aspect of the spider, but also the very filament of its web was thought to originate in her womb,[359] an organ that males by definition

---

352 Bartholomaeus Anglicus, *De proprietatibus rerum* 18.

353 Alberti, *Libro della famiglia* 3, pp. 215-16.

354 Fernand Braudel, *The Mediterranean and the Mediterranean World in the Age of Philip II*, trans. Siân Reynolds, 2 vols. (New York: Harper and Row, 1972), 2:676; Geoffrey Parker, *Philip II* (London: Hutchinson, 1979), pp. 24-25.

355 Bernardino of Siena, *De honestate coniugatarum*, in *Opera omnia* 2:107-8; cited by Herlihy and Christiane Klapisch-Zuber, *Les toscans et leurs familles: Une étude du catasto florentin de 1427* (Paris: Presses de la Fondation nationale des sciences politiques, 1978), p. 600.

356 Michelangelo, *Rime* 267; trans. Saslow, pp. 452, 453. For the poem in general, see Clement, *Poetry of Michelangelo*, pp. 266-68.

357 Nordenfalk, "Five Senses in Late Medieval and Renaissance Art," p. 7. See also Bloomfield, "A Grammatical Approach to Personification Allegory," *Modern Philology* 60 (1962-63):161-71.

358 Bartholomaeus Anglicus, *De proprietatibus rerum* 18.

359 Pliny, *Naturalis historia* 1.28.84; 11.28.80; trans. Rackham, 3:485. Bartholomaeus Anglicus, *De proprietatibus rerum* 18.

lacked. Although in modern science the liquid silk of the spider is a secretion produced by spinnerets from the abdominal glands of either sex,[360] medieval and renaissance science may have been correct in its sexual connotation.[361] Traditional scientists and artists did correctly associate spiders with tactile values. Spiders perceive and transmit vibrations on their webs for predation, courtship, territorial behavior, and social interaction.[362] So efficient is the web as a method that the spider scarcely ever uses any sense but the one that the action of the web requires: touch. Its feet are observable touching the threads and are so sensitive to their movements that the spider responds to the vibrations of any object in the web and differently to different vibrations: prey, enemy, mate, or neutral object like thistledown blown against it. Because of this delineated sense of touch, of which the web itself becomes an extension, the spider has only limited use for the other senses. Supplementing its tactile sense is a muscular sense. Any vibration in a thread of the web changes its tension, temporarily or permanently, in isolation or in repetition. The spider reacts to the change in tension, with its direction in walking across the web determined by the tensions of the filaments on which it is stepping. The experience is foreign to humans; even among other animals there is no facile comparison in response to the forces in the surface over which it moves. The tactile-muscular ability of the spider defines it as unique among creatures.[363] And it alone has locomotion in all three dimensions.[364]

Although the critical description of a spiderweb dates to the nineteenth century,[365] the depiction of its function for catching flies was as old as the art of the paleolithic cave.[366] The renaissance emblematist Joachim Camerarius (1500-74) depicted violent death as a spider in the center of an orb

---

360 Rainer F. Foelix, *Biology of Spiders* (Cambridge, Mass.: Harvard University Press, 1982), p. 111.

361 For the evolution of the the spinning apparatus from selective presssures associated with reproduction, see Jeffrey W. Schultz, "The Origin of the Spinning Apparatus in Spiders," *Biological Reviews of the Cambridge Philosophical Society* 62 (1987):107, 109.

362 See Friedrich G. Barth, "Spiders and Vibratory Signals: Sensory Reception and Behavioral Significance," in *Spider Communication: Mechanisms and Ecological Significance*, ed. Jerome S. Rovner and Peter N. Witt (Princeton, N.J.: Princeton University Press, 1982), p. 67; W. Mitch Masters, Hubert S. Markl, and Anne J. M. Moffat, "Transmission of Vibration in a Spider's Web," in *Spiders: Webs, Behavior, and Evolution*, Papers Presented at the 1981 Meeting of the American Arachnological Society at the University of Tennessee, ed. William A. Shear (Stanford, Calif.: Stanford University Press, 1986), p. 69.

363 See Theodore Savory, *The Spider's Web* (London: Frederick Warne, 1952), pp. 17, 19-20. For minimal visual abilities of the spider, see Masters et al., "Transmission of Vibrations," p. 49.

364 Foelix, *Biology of Spiders*, pp. 148-58.

365 Foelix, *Biology of Spiders*, pp. 148-58.

366 Klingender, *Animals in Art and Thought*, p. 9, citing Juan Bautista Porcar Ripollés, Hugo Obermaier, and Henri Breuil, *Las pinturas rupestres de la Cueva Remigia (Castellón)* (Madrid, 1936), pl. 71; reproduced also in Erwin Schimitschek, *Insecten in der bildenden Kunst, im Wandel der Zeiten in psychologenetischer Sicht*, Veröffentlichungen Naturhistorisches Museum, 14 (Vienna: Naturhistorisches Museum, 1977), p. 16, fig. 3.

web with insects buzzing about it.[367] Although there were a variety of webs and strategies, such as sheets, meshes, and tubes, renaissance artists depicted the best known, the orbs. With their geometrical construction they were effective and economical traps for prey, the very purpose toward survival of the species.[368] Authors since antiquity were fascinated by the skill of the spider in spinning the warp and weaving the web to trap its prey.[369] Pliny told how the spider set up the threads of the warp from inner material and how "with such careful use of its claw and such a smooth and even thread it spins the warp, employing itself as a weight." He elaborated how "it starts weaving at the centre, twining in the woof in a circular round, and entwists the meshes in an unloosable knot, spreading them out at intervals that are always regular but continually grow less narrow."[370] Michel de Montaigne (1533-92) considered it intelligent. "Why does the spider thicken her web in one place and slacken it in another, use now this sort of knot, now that one, unless she has the power of reflection, and thought, and inference?"[371]

The spider assumed anthropological importance when it became entangled in the web of renaissance argumentation about the definition of human nature by erect bipedality. About the monstrous peoples there had been report of some with spider legs.[372] Erect creatures were not to debase themselves to crawly things. Nor was the tactile emblem of the sense of touch—the spider—to become confused with a gustatory delight. There developed the problem of what the Amerindians did with spiders: as with hands, they ate them. A report from Diego Alvarez Chanca, a physician on board during Columbus's voyages, said that they ate spiders from the ground. "So it seems to me," he wrote, "that their degradation is greater than that of any beast in the world."[373] Such unselective consumption was feared to promote cannibalism, the eating of their own kind. The failure to conform to dietary norms indicated a lack of reason, belonging to the lower species as generated

367 Joachim Camerarius, *Symbolorum et emblematum* 3.119.

368 See Foelix, *Biology of Spiders*, pp. 121-42, 162-67. For the orb, see also William G. Eberhard, "Function and Phylogeny of Spider Webs," *Annual Review of Ecology and Systematics* 21 (1990):341-72.

369 Pliny, *Naturalis historia* 11.28.80-83; e. g., Florence McCullough, *Medieval Latin and French Bestiaries*, Studies in the Romance Languages and Literatures, 33 (Chapel Hill: University of North Carolina Press, 1960), pp. 171-72.

370 Pliny, *Naturalis historia* 11.28.80; trans. Rackham, 3:481.

371 Montaigne, *Essais* 2.12, p. 455; *The Complete Works of Montaigne: Essays, Travel Journal, Letters*, trans. Donald M. Frame (Stanford, Calif.: Stanford University Press, 1967), p. 333.

372 Rudolf Wittkower, "Marvels of the East: A Study in the History of Monsters," *Journal of the Warburg and Courtauld Institutes* 5 (1942): 165, citing Strabo, *Geographica* 2.1.9.

373 Diego Alvarez Chanca in Lionel Cecil Jane, ed., *Select Documents Illustrating the Four Voyages of Columbus*, 1:70; cited by Mary B. Campbell, *The Witness and the Other World: Exotic European Travel Writing, 400-1600* (Ithaca, N.Y.: Cornell University Press, 1988), p. 177. Edition unavailable but verified in Martín Fernandez Navarrete, *Viajes de Cristóbal Colón*, p. 241; also cited by J. H. Elliott, *The Old World and the New, 1492-1650* (Cambridge: Cambridge University Press, 1970), p. 42.

spontaneously.[374] The principal rhetorician against the cause of the Amerindians as human beings, Juan Ginés de Sepúlveda (1498-1573), argued that their mental facility was mechanical, their artistry mimetic, exactly like spiders. In his account of Hernan Cortes's capture of Montezuma, he observed an immense multitude of natives who gave the impression of lacking not only facility and prudence but even ability. "Is it not proof," he asked, "that those are slaves by nature?" Some men did have advantage over others in ability, in talent, strength, and virtue, he insisted. As for the Mexicans, "The fact that some of them appear to have talent for certain works of artifice is no argument for human prudence, moreover, since we see how certain insects, like bees and spiders, produce works that no human ability achieves imitating."[375]

Yet others might have thought such reasoning exemplified the proverb *aranearum telas texere*. As Erasmus explained, it meant spending infinite and anxious effort on something futile. Dialectical reasoning was like such spider webs, which appeared careful and accurate in their construction to trap flies, but were trivial and fragile, easily ripped apart.[376] Montaigne merely reported that "in that world of the new Indies there was found great nations, and in very varied climates, who lived on spiders, made provision of them, and raised and fattened them. . . . They cook them and prepare them with various sauces."[377] In a range of cultures from Africa to Melanesia the spider was not only creative but the very demiurge.[378] The belief was not foreign to the origins of Western civilization either. In his commentary on Plato's *Timaeus* Chalcidius preserved the concept of *hē gemonikon*, the *principale* or original thing of the soul. Its function was that "just as a spider in the middle of its web controls all the warps of the threads by its feet, so that when strokes from small animals rush in from whatever direction, it feels it from the proximate one." So did the soul in the center of the heart retain the warps of the senses, so that whatever was announced in proximity it recog-

---

374 Pagden, *Fall of Natural Man*, p. 87, citing Girónimo Girava, *La cosmographia y geographia*, p. 199; also cited by Elliott, *Old World and New*, p. 45. For spontaneous generation, see Aristotle, *Historia animalium* 539b.

375 Juan Ginés de Sepúlveda, *Democrates segundo, o de las justas causas de la guerra contra los indios*, p. 36; cited by Pagden, *Fall of Natural Man*, pp. 116, 136. See also Raoul MacGregor, "La répresentation des insectes dans l'ancient Mexique," *Entomologiste* 25 (1969):2-8. In modern science spiders, because of their instantaneous reaction to vibration on the web, closely approach being mechanistic animals. Savory, *Spider's Web*, p. 133.

376 Erasmus, *Adagia* 1.4.47; cf. *Parabolae* 616c. See Basil, *Homiliae in Hexameron* 1.2; Diogenes, *Solon* 1.58.

377 Montaigne, *Essais* 1:23, p. 109; trans. Frame, pp. 77-78.

378 André Siganos, *Les mythologies de l'insecte: Histoire d'une fascination* (Paris: Méridiens, 1985), pp. 24-25. For an example, see G. M. Mullet, *Spider Woman Stories: Legends of the Hopi Indians* (Tucson: University of Arizona Press, 1979). See also in general Charles L. Hogue, "Cultural Entomology," *Annual Review of Entomology* 32 (1987):181-99.

nized.[379] That spidery image of the origin of the universe was ideal for the renaissance government of state or household, as in Philip II and Alberti.

But it was classically in the house that spinning was done, precisely in it center, at the hearth where the matron or maiden sat like a spider in the middle of its web.[380] She worked in pious imitation of Minerva, goddess of handiwork, whose frieze on her temple in the Roman imperial fora depicted her with a spindle.[381] The stylization of all female labor on Latin epitaphs was *lanifica*, or "woolworker."[382] An early medieval nun, Leoba, who dreamed a spiritual revelation, had to allegorize her verbal ability into such tactile labor. In her dream she became like a spider, with a purple thread issuing from her mouth. When she tried to draw it out with her hand, it was enormous, endless, as if from her very bowels. When her hand was full of her thread, she rolled it into a ball, until exhausted from the tedious labor she awoke from her dream. An elderly prophetess in the convent interpreted the thread as wise counsels from the heart; the full hand, the execution of words in actions; the ball itself, the mystery of divine teaching ever in motion from action to contemplation.[383]

A renaissance treatise on the perfect wife related the succession of regal spinners from Helen of Troy to Isabella of Spain (1451-1504) as exemplars. Since antiquity, every married woman conducted by the bridegroom to his house had discovered a distaff by the door; so should the contemporary woman continue the tradition and task.[384] The artistic decoration in houses that depicted female pastimes, dating from the fourteenth century, was of women weaving.[385] Francesco del Cossa's (c.1435-c.1477) fresco of the triumph of Minerva in the Palazzo Schifanoia, Ferrara, divides males and females on either side of her chariot. The men hold scrolls; the women, im-

---

379 Chalcidius, *Timaeus a Calcidio translatus commentarioque instructus* 220, in *Stoicorum veterum fragmenta* 2:fr 879, attributing the passage to Chrysippus.

380 Sarah B. Pomeroy, *Goddesses, Whores, Wives, and Slaves: Women in Classical Antiquity* (New York: Schocken, 1975), p. 30. For the labor, see Kate McK. Elderkin, "The Contribution of Women to Ornament in Antiquity," in *Classical Studies Presented to Edward Copps on his Seventieth Birthday* (Princeton, N.J.: Princeton University Press, 1936), pp. 124-43.

381 See P. H. von Blanckenhagen, *Flavische Architektur und ihre Dekoration, untersucht am Nervaforum* (Berlin: Gebr. Mann, 1940), pp. 119, 124-25, 132; reproduced, pls. 40-41.

382 J. P. V. D. Balsdon, *Roman Women: Their History and Habits* (London: Bodley Head, 1962), p. 207; Eva Cantarella, *Pandora's Daughters: The Role and Status of Women in Greek and Roman Antiquity*, trans. Maureen B. Fant (Baltimore, Md.: Johns Hopkins University Press, 1987), pp. 132-33. See also Elizabeth P. Forbis, "Women's Public Image in Italian Honorary Inscriptions," *American Journal of Philology* 111 (1990):493-512.

383 Rudolf of Fulda, *Vita Leobae* 8.

384 Luis de León, *Perfecta casada* 4.

385 Van Marle, *Iconographie de l'art profane*, 1:156-60. For background, see Frances M. Bisioglio, "'Unspun' Heroes: Iconography of the Spinning Woman in the Middle Ages," *Journal of Medieval and Renaissance Studies* 25 (1995):163-76.

plements for the weaving loom and the embroidery frame.[386] Knowledge versus needlework was epitomized. Not only did such artistic representation of female handiwork decorate the interiors of houses but also their actual production filled them. Renaissance women produced at home and for the home the ordinary decoration of textiles, particularly linens for bed and table, cushions and covers for benches, and hangings for walls. More sumptuous embroidery was done in professional workshops,[387] but many women worked for sheer survival in textile labor from its very meanest tasks.[388]

Cesare Vecellio (c.1521-1601) produced a pattern book of renaissance lace, which included among its points and rosettes an insertion depicting a chase. In the middle is a spider web of four concentric rings with a filled center. Ladies with needles were to copy that creature dexterously with their very lives: for pleasure and praise.[389] It was in the imitation of Minerva, and in her rivalry, that women coincided with spiders as symbols of the sense of touch. In the classical myth in Ovid's *Metamorphoses* was a maiden Arachne who, although of humble origins, achieved fame for her skill in spinning and weaving wool. Not only was her finished product a pleasure to see but so was her graceful and deft workmanship. "Whether she was winding the rough yarn into a new ball, or shaping the stuff with her fingers, reaching back to the distaff for more wool, fleecy as a cloud, to draw into long soft threads, or giving a twist with practised thumb to the graceful spindle, or embroidering with her needle: you could know that Pallas had taught her." Yet that divine grace was precisely what Arachne denied and she sullenly, angrily challenged Minerva to a contest at the loom, with anything as forfeit. Both women stretched the warp and wove narrative scenes skillfully with rich threads. Arachne's work was not only flawless; it also depicted the deceptions of the gods toward mortals. Minerva, indignant at the girl's success and blasphemy, tore the web and struck her in the head with the shuttle. To escape the intolerable pain Arachne put a noose around

---

386 Francesco del Cossa, Allegory of March, c. 1470, Palazzo Schifanoia, Ferrara; reproduced in Rosemarie Molajoli, *L'opera completa di Cosmè Tura e i grandi pittori ferraresi del suo tempo: Francesco Cossa e Ercole de Roberti*, Classici dell'arte, 73 (Milan: Rizzoli, 1974), pl. LII, and detail LVI; van Marle, *Iconographie de l'art profane*, p. 158, fig. 146; Herald, *Renaissance Dress*, p. 71, fig. 37. For renaissance women and the image of that goddess, see Francis H. Dowley, "French Portraits of Ladies as Minerva," *Gazette des beaux-arts* 45 (1955):261-86; Wittkower, "Transformations of Minerva in Renaissance Imagery," *Journal of the Warburg and Courtauld Institutes* 12 (1939):194-205; Edgar Wind, *Pagan Mysteries in the Renaissance* (New Haven, Conn.: Yale University Press, 1958), pp. 162-64.

387 Peter Thornton, *The Italian Renaissance Interior: 1400-1600* (London: Weidenfeld and Nicolson, 1991), pp. 77-84.

388 See recently Wiesner, "Spinsters and Seamstresses," in *Rewriting the Renaissance*, pp. 191-205; but for the initial study, Marian K. Dale, "The London Silkwomen of the Fifteenth Century," *Economic History Review* 4 (1933):324-35. For the renaissance industry, see Walter Endrei, *L'évolution des techniques du filage et du tissage du Moyen Âge à la révolution industrielle*, Industrie et artisanat, 4 (Paris: Mouton, 1968).

389 Cesare Vecellio, *Corona delle nobili et virtuose donne*, pp. 8, 3.

her neck. The goddess lifted her hanging body and said pitifully: live but always hang. She sprinkled her with poison until Arachne shriveled into a spider.[390]

Renaissance literature memorialized her, as in William Shakespeare's (1564-1616) allusive verse, "Ariachne's broken woof."[391] Yet Arachne had been praised because she spun a fine thread, Guarino Veronese (1374-1460) recalled. Why should learned women not be praised for their literary style?[392] To write "with slender thread" was proverbial for a simple style. Other analogies for labor borrowed from that craft: "to set up a web," "to weave a small web," and "such is the web now woven."[393] Arachne had also been memorialized in classical art, forever with Minerva on the frieze of her Roman temple.[394] The renaissance artist Frans Floris (1519/20-70) owned a series of eight engravings of human activities, which he commissioned from the engraver Philip Gall and probably hung in Antwerp in the great room of his very house. Each was a female mythological personification, with Arachne for textile labor.[395] Yet with the development of the iconography of the five senses, renaissance women, whether domestically or industrially, became spider women, symbols of touch.

With the invention of printing, from the sixteenth century on the sensory theme was represented predominantly in the graphic arts. Its technique was modern but its spirit medieval. The initial exact illustration of the subject was by Georg Pencz (1500-50), who in the 1540s engraved the five senses

---

390 Ovid, *Metamorphoses* 6.1-145; trans. Frank Justus Miller, rev. G. P. Goold, 2 vols. (London: William Heinemann, 1976-77), lines 17-22, pp. 289-91. For spiders, see also André Sauvage, "Les insectes dans la poésie romaine," *Latomus* 29 (1970):270.

391 William Shakespeare, *Troilus and Cressida* 5.2. See also J. Hillis Miller, "Ariachne's Broken Woof," *Georgia Review* 31 (1977):44-60.

392 Guarino Veronese on the sisters Isotta and Ginevra Nogarola, in the *Opera* of Isotta's work, 1:58-59; cited by Jardine, "Isotta Nogarola," pp. 236-37. See also Guarino, *Epistolario* 697, in 2:293.

393 *Tenui filo*, in Erasmus, *Adagia* 2.6.75; *exordiri telam*, 2.6.68; *tenuem nectis* 2.9.3; *ex tela texitur* 2.1.25; trans. Mynors, 33:327, 325; 34:91; 33:30.

394 P. H. von Blankenhagen, *Flavische Architektur und ihre Dekoration, untersucht am Nervaforum* (Berlin: Gebr. Mann, 1940), pp. 119-20; Wolfgang Schurmann, *Typologie und Bedeutung der stadtrömischen Minerva-Kultbilder*, Rivista di archeologia supplementi, 2 (Rome: Giorgio Bretschneider, 1985):12, 52-53.

395 Philip Galle after Frans Floris, engraving, Arachne, 1574; reproduced in Carl van de Velde, "The Painted Decoration of Floris's House," in *Netherlandish Mannerism*, Papers Given at a Symposium in Nationalmuseum, Stockholm, September 21-22, 1984, ed. Görel Cavalli-Björkman Nationalmusei Skrifserie, 4 (Stockholm: Nationalmuseum, 1985), p. 132, fig. 8; idem, *Frans Floris (1519/20-1570): Leven en werken*, 2 vols., Verhandelingen van de Koninklijke Akademie voor Wetenschappen, Letteren en Schone Kunsten van België, Klasse der Schone Kunsten, 37-30 (Brussels: Paleis der Academiën, 1975), 1:429, pl. 279. Cf. Maarten van Cleve, Arachne, Kupferstichkabinett, Berlin; reproduced in idem, "The Painted Decoration of Floris's House," p. 133, fig. 10; idem, *Frans Floris*, 2:341. For another myth associating Minerva with weaving and the metamorphosis of women, see Francesco Primaticcio (1504-70), Daughters of Minyas, drawing, Nationalmuseum, Stockholm; reproduced in Diane Degrazia, *Correggio and His Legacy: Sixteenth-Century Emilian Drawings* (Washington, D.C.: National Gallery of Art, 1984), p. 237, pl. 75.

as nearly nude females.[396] Although the senses had previously been depicted as males or animals, their femininity was ancient in Philo's commentary on the creation. In humans, he wrote, "mind corresponds to man, the senses to woman." The creation of woman from flesh (Gen. 2:22) meant that "the exact name for sense-perception is 'woman.'" Since males were active, their province was mental; since females were passive, theirs was perceptive.[397] The anatomical literature only incidentally distinguished females from males by touch, because they had softer skin.[398] The renaissance fashion plate, a courtesan, was praised as lovely from every angle. "Your form is majestic straight-on, sideways or in profile." But, underneath it all, she was also as "soft as ravioli."[399] Agrippa von Nettesheim on the excellence of that sex praised the extreme delicacy of the female body, "to touch, her flesh so tender."[400] In Pencz's personification Touch is female. She sits at a ribbon-loom, her head bent over her work, while in the window of her room a spider presides in the hub of its orbicular web. A phrase from the medieval couplet comparing the excellence of animals to humans—"but the spider in touch"—explains the scene.[401] Small oval prints by the French engraver Étienne Delaune (c.1518-83) show the senses as classical women in landscapes with symbolic animals. Touch gestures with her extended arm to a loom idle on the ground.[402]

The allegory of the senses became increasingly popular in Netherlandish art in the last four decades of the century. The initial and most influential treatment was by Floris, as engraved by Cornelis Cort (1533-78), the best craftsman. The method of Pencz in combining women and animals is repeated. Each sense is symbolized by a supernatural female, garbed in a silken tunic over a voluptuous body, who holds an attribute. By her side is an animal, although a nobler sort than those of the medieval menagerie. Touch receives the tortoise, a new symbol of a sensitive creature in a new seaside setting. The animal copies the American variety, a rarity for display in the zoological gardens of renaissance princes. The engraver, apparently on his own initiative, inserted the conventional spider. It hangs its web be-

---

396 Nordenfalk, "Five Senses in Late Medieval and Renaissance Art," p. 10.

397 Philo, *De opificio mundi* 59.165; *Legum allegoria* 2.11.38; trans. Colson and Witaker, 1:131, 249.

398 Schiebinger, "Skeletons in the Closet," p. 50.

399 Andrea Calmo, *Lettere* 4.26; cited by Lawner, *Lives of the Courtesans*, p. 63.

400 Agrippa von Nettesheim, *De nobilitate*, p. 55.

401 Nordenfalk, "Five Senses in Late Medieval and Renaissance Art," pp. 19-20. Georg Pencz, Touch, engraving, 1540s; reproduced, pl. 8e; Adam von Bartsch, *Le peintre graveur*, 21 vols. in 16 (Vienna, 1803-21), 8:353-54; W. L. Strauss, ed., *The Illustrated Bartsch*, 163 vols. (New York: Abaris, 1978-90), 16:124; David Landau, *Catalogo completo dell'opera grafica di Georg Pencz* (Milan, 1978), pp. 135-36 n. 108; Vinge, *Five Senses*, p. 55, fig. 7. Cf. the engraving of Sight; reproduced by Nordenfalk, "Five Senses in Late Medieval and Renaissance Art," pl. 8a; *Illustrated Bartsch*, 8:123.

402 Nordenfalk, "Five Senses in Late Medieval and Renaissance Art," p. 20. Étienne Delaune, Touch, engraving; reproduced, pl. 9e.

tween branches of a tree,[403] in allusion to Pliny's notation that the spider practicing its skill stretched its web between two trees.[404] But the woman as Touch handles no loom. With the index finger of her right hand she points to heaven. A bird on her extended left arm bites her thumb with its beak, causing her to make a pained face, as in late medieval drawing of the nervous system. Pain was a standard medical topic of the sense of touch; but a bird perched on a human hand had a sexual connotation. Its attack is on her chastity: coition is painful. Of the five senses in the series, touch is the only woman who is displayed bare-breasted. Floris's example was developed by several artists, who introduced to the sense of touch new emblems for pain by dangerous reptiles: snake, scorpion, lizard.[405] In a version by Hendrik Goltzius (1558-1617) a snake, twined around a woman's arm like a bracelet, bites her hand, while her other arm is extended as if to ward it off or balance herself. The landscape preserves the spider in the middle of its web spun between two barren branches of a tree.[406]

Biblical scenes became sketched into backgrounds of the senses as moralizing exegesis. Touch was emphatically not the fall: that type was not Adam and Eve handling the forbidden fruit but the angel expelling them from paradise. The sensory repertoire was borrowed by artists and artisans for interior decoration on wainscots, ceilings, furniture, and textiles, especially in the dining hall and bedroom. It delighted and admonished on a cupboard, jewelry case, plaque, on glass, alabaster, or embroidery, even on a royal coffin where the senses are depicted asleep. In engravings after Adam van Noort late in the century Touch in the center of a grouping of the senses extends an arm with the bird, while with the other she gestures to heaven, as a diptych exhorts her prudent use. In another version Touch as a still ideal personification shares a seat with Man. She holds his hand as he lovingly embraces her bare shoulder, while a bird bites the juncture of their hands on the backs.[407] In an engraving from a series by Jan Saenredam (1565-1607)

---

403 Nordenfalk, "The Five Senses in Flemish Art before 1600," in *Netherlandish Mannerism*, ed. Cavalli-Björkman, pp. 135-37. Cornelis Cort after Frans Floris, Touch, engraving, 1561; reproduced, p. 137, fig. 2; F. W. H. Hollstein and Christiaan Schuckman, *Dutch and Flemish Etchings, Engravings, and Woodcuts ca. 1450-1700*, ed. D. De Hoof Scheffer, 41 vols. (Amsterdam: Menno Hertzberger; Roosendaal: Koninklijke van Paal, 1949-92), 5:59; J. C. J. Bierens de Haan, *L'oeuvre gravé de Cornelis Cort graveur hollandais, 1533-1578* (The Hague: Martinus Nijhoff, 1948), p. 211; Velde, *Frans Floris*, 2:fig. 290, and see 1:432; Christopher Brown, *Images of a Golden Past: Dutch Genre Painting of the Seventeenth Century* (New York: Abbeville, 1984), p. 38.

404 Pliny, *Naturalis historia* 11.28.83.

405 Nordenfalk, "Five Senses in Flemish Art before 1600," pp. 138-39, 143. See E. de Jongh, "Erotica en vogelperspectif," *Simiolus* 3 (1968-69):23-74; and *Tot Lering en Vermaak*, Rijksmuseum, Amsterdam, 16 September-15 December, 1976, pp. 167-68.

406 Hendrik Goltzius, Touch, engraving for Philip Galle, c. 1578; reproduced in Walter L. Strauss, *Hendrik Goltzius 1558-1617: The Complete Engravings and Woodcuts*, 2 vols. (New York: Abaris, 1977), 1:89, and see pp. 84-89.

407 Nordenfalk, "Five Senses in Flemish Art," pp. 143-50. Anton Wierix after Adam van Noort, Five senses in a landscape, engraving, before 1591; reproduced, p. 148, fig. 20. A.

after Goltzius an amorous couple embraces a turtle in their laps.[408] The iconography of touch, the sense of the hand, has reverted to the erotic.

The genre of the senses incorporated courtesans, portraying touch frequently as the most insidious.[409] The initial coupling of a woman and the sense of touch had been an allegorical Flemish tapestry in which the lady holds her pennon in her right hand, while with her left fingers she fondles the horn of the unicorn.[410] Josse Badius (1462-1535) in his supplement on foolish women to *Stultiferae naves* explained touch as the most voluptuous of the senses. He illustrated it with a sexual scene of kissing and fondling, emptying a purse, lifting a skirt—all under the fluttering banner of lust emblematized by a goat. In the initial association of the senses with ancient culture the hero of Francesco Colonna's (1432/3-1527) *Hypnerotomachia Poliphili* encountered five nymphs in a pleasance. Aphea, or touch, bore no attribute but reached out to the lover with her hand. The embrace, the motif of the amorous couple, became a standard means of illustrating the tactile sense.[411] In literature the bawd Raffaela frankly proposed that a neglected wife was not endowed with beautiful hands so that she could toy with needle and thread or spin among the cinders. A good female figure included "frankness of arms" that were physically straightforward and morally open. Fair arms should be displayed at table or in games toward amorous opportunities.[412] Others thought bare female arms simply "dangerous."[413] But, even when a woman tended to needlework, her arts of love could be displayed, as in Giambattista Marino's (1569-1625) baroque sentiment. "A dart, a dart, not a needle, she uses in her labor, a new Arachne of love, she whom I adore; so that while she embroiders and adorns the lovely cloth, she pierces and stabs my heart with a thousand points."[414]

Portrayal of the comportment of female hands changed some when a woman took the subject into her own hands. Vecellio, a kinsman of Titian,

---

Collaert after Adam van Noort, Man entertained by the five senses, engraving, late 16th c.; reproduced, p. 149, fig. 21.

408 Jan Saenredam after Hendrick Goltzius, Touch, engraving, Rijksprentenkabinet, Rijksmuseum, Amsterdam; reproduced in *Dutch and Flemish Etchings, Engravings, and Woodcuts*, ed. Hollstein, 25:76-78; Brown, *Images of a Golden Past*, p. 38.

409 Lawner, *Lives of the Courtesans*, p. 198. See also Touch as a vested woman with bird on arm (not pecking her) and turtle at feet in Ripa, *Iconologia* 2.

410 Nordenfalk, "Cinq sens," pp. 25-27; idem, "Five Senses in Late Medieval and Renaissance Art," pp. 7-10. Flemish tapestry, Touch, Musée de Cluny, Paris; reproduced, p. 27, fig. 20; Pierre Verlet and Francis Salet, *The Lady and the Unicorn* (London: Thames and Hudson, 1961), p. 21.

411 Nordenfalk, "Five Senses in Late Medieval and Renaissance Art," pp. 13, 15, 17. Woodcut, Ship of touch, *Stultiferae naves* (Paris, 1500); reproduced, p. 13, pl. 4f. Francesco Colonna, *Hypnerotomachia Poliphili* (Venice, 1499); reproduced, p. 15, pl. 5a.

412 Piccolomini, *Dialogo de la bella creanza de le donne*, pp. 15, 85, 31, 32-33. A woman with thin arms should not wear tight sleeves to display her ugliness, p. 21.

413 Barbaro, *De re uxoria* 2.4; trans. Kohl, p. 205.

414 Giambattista Marino, *Canzoni e madriagli amorosi* 19; cited by Mirollo, *Mannerism and Renaissance Poetry*, p. 156.

had compiled his patterns for noble needlework so that skillful and virtuous ladies might be "accomplishing with the needle what the most excellent painters accomplish with the brush."[415] Sofonisba Anguissola (1532-1625) preferred the brush to the needle. Although she did not execute any Eve, she did donate her self-portrait to the patron of the Sistine Chapel ceiling, Pope Julius II. Letters from her father to Michelangelo indicated that the artist had spoken encouragingly to her, had examined and praised her work, and demonstrated affection to her. Michelangelo had introduced Sofonisba to the art of painting, he wrote, and his influence was visible in her improvement in anatomy and composition. There was a stylistic feature that recurred in most of her portraiture over six decades of production, appearing in her first and last works. Anguissola's mark was her position and stylization of the human hands, which she characterized with the thumb and index finger in the shape of a squared letter *U*. She early experienced problems with anatomy and drew hands imprecisely. By mid-century she resolved her difficulty, as she replaced the elongated fingers she had copied from her initial master with forms that were solid and correct. It was from Michelangelo that she had learned how to draw hands that were anatomically correct.[416] In the next century François Poullain de la Barre (1647-1725) would argue for the equality of the sexes that women themselves were capable of anatomizing. "They too have eyes and hands; may they not. . . perform dissections of a human body and consider the symmetry, and structure thereof?"[417] Although women had been licensed since early in the fourteenth century to practice surgery,[418] and the first official dissection in western civilization was on female corpses,[419] Anguissola did not take up the knife as well as the brush.

---

[415] Vecellio, *Corona delle nobili et virtuose donne*; *Pattern Book of Renaissance Lace: A Reprint of the 1617 Edition of the "Corona delle nobili et virtuose donne"* (New York: Dover, 1988), p. 3.

[416] Ilya Sandra Perlingieri, *Sofonisba Anguissola: The First Great Woman Artist of the Renaissance* (New York: Rizzoli, 1992), pp. 74, 67-69, 129-30, 44-199 passim, 49, 73. See also Tolnay, "Sofonisba Anguissola and Her Relations with Michelangelo," *Journal of the Walters Art Gallery* 4 (1941):115-19. For reproductions, see also Flavio Caroli, *Sofonisba Anguissola e le sue sorelle* (Madrid: A. Mondadori, 1987). See in general Claire-Lise Schwok-Bionda, "Autour de Sofonisba Anguissola et de ses soeurs," *L'Oeil* 467 (1994):32-37; María Kusche, "La antigua galería de retratos del Pardo: Su importancia para la obra de Tiziano, Moro Sánchez Coello, y Sofonisba Anguissola y su significado para Felipe II, su fundador," *Archivo español de arte* 65 (1992):11-14; Sharlee Mullins Glenn, "Sofonisba Anguissola: History's Forgotten Prodigy," *Women's Studies* 18 (1990):295-308; Kusche, "Sofonisba Anguissola en España: Retratista en la corte de Felipe II junto a Alonso Sánchez Coello y Jorge de la Rua," *Archivo español de arte* 52 (1989):391-420; and for her biography, Fredrika H. Jacobs, "Woman's Capacity to Create," *Renaissance Quarterly* 47 (1994):74-101.

[417] François Poullain de la Barre, *De l'égalité des deux sexes*, pp. 59-62; cited by Schiebinger, *Mind Has No Sex?*, p. 176.

[418] A. L. Wyman, "The Surgeoness: The Female Practitioner of Surgery, 1400-1800," *Medical History* 28 (1984):24-32.

[419] Pouchelle, *Body and Surgery*, p. 82.

Hands were a renaissance introduction to portraiture. At the turn of the fifteenth century in France and the Low Countries, later in Italy and Germany, one or both hands were included frequently on figures displayed to the waist. For such half-length portraits, the principal problem of composition was its very justification: why sever the figure, amputating the lower half? Artistic solutions were the assertion of the actual picture frame, the use of a framing structure, or most commonly of a parapet along the lower edge. On that ledge the sitter might rest the arms, one or both hands, or an elbow. It was Rogier van der Weyden (c.1400-64) who perfected the system, which became widely imitated, of sitters resting their folded hands on the lower edges of the frame or on unseen horizontal surfaces at that level. The devices acted as if window frames, so that the lower closure of the picture was justified and acceptable. Even a dog might place his paw there, as in a portrait by Bronzino, perhaps in mockery of the device. Yet such devices necessitated some foreshortening of the arms and hands. With the development and acceptance of the convention, compositions were terminated not by artificial contrivances but by artistic designs. The hands became a convenient place for closure, with the careful arrangement of the limbs balancing and completing the composition.[420]

Yet hands were so difficult to draw that their inclusion in portraiture figured in the price of the commission. Some artists devised ways partly to conceal one or both hands. The long sleeves in dress that were fashionable clothed them almost to the knuckles. Another reason for hiding the hands was compositional. Although the hands were the most important and expressive area of the body after the face, they also occupied approximately the same area as it did. Of the same high skin tone as the face, hands might further distract attention from its primacy. In half-length portraits a hand could be covered with a glove or drapery to compress its area. In fuller depictions of the figure hands could be placed a greater distances from the face, so that their concealment was less urgent. One treatise advised the artist not to tell the sitter when he was about to draw the hands, because, so prompted, the sitter would give the hand an affected pose. The portraitist should rather be attentive to good grace in the hand and seize that moment to delineate it.[421]

Anguissola's artistic concentration on the exactitude of the human hand was a personal signature but it also exemplified renaissance attention to tactile values. There were senses of touch, both scientific and moral, from experience and from custom. The oddity about Eve's palm on the Sistine Chapel ceiling was that Michelangelo did not paint her anatomically.

---

[420] Lorne Campbell, *Renaissance Portraits: European Portrait-Painting in the Fourteenth, Fifteenth, and Sixteenth Centuries* (New Haven, Conn.: Yale University Press, 1990), pp. 61, 69, 72-75.

[421] Campbell, *Renaissance Portraits*, pp. 141, 157, 95, 96, 178, citing Nicholas Hilliard, *A Treatise Concerning the Arte of Limning*, p. 114.

Unlike Anguissola's sittings, there are no extant drawings by him of women from life: his studies of females were all drawn from males.[422] He simply transferred the dignity of the one sex to the other.

[422] See Clark, *Nude*, p. 251. For the virtual interchangeability of language for male and female in his poetry, see Saslow, *Poetry of Michelangelo*, pp. 49-50.

CHAPTER THREE

GOD'S HAND

The divine hand in Michelangelo's frescoes on the Sistine Chapel ceiling gestures toward his human creatures to command an erect posture with able hands. Adam and Eve are not about to touch God. Contemporary viewers would have known the basic doctrine. As John Calvin (1509-64) conventionally declared, God "cannot be touched by human hands."[1] Yet Calvin emphatically believed that human hands could be touched by divine ones, by the initiative of grace, although not in mutuality. As he commented on Genesis, that "wonderful maker" and "universal architect," to manifest his infinite wisdom, created everything with a certain reason and design.[2] Elaborating on that design in his *Institutio christianae religionis*, Calvin displayed the structure of the human body: how the keenest acuity was needed "to weigh, with Galen's skill, its articulation, symmetry, beauty, and use." He appealed to the consummate teleology, for Galen exalted the purpose in the structure and function of the human body:[3] an argument from divine design exemplified in his *De usu partium* by the hand. Calvin compatibly wrote of a universal acknowledgement that "the human body shows itself to be a composition so ingenious that its Artificer is rightly judged a wonder-worker." People found God not only in the soul but a hundred times over in the body. They experienced his "exquisite workmanship" in its individual members, not only in the senses of the dominant head but "even to their very toenails." The testimonies affirming the divine majesty in the universe were not only traceable by the eyes but also "signified with the fingers."[4] The artifice of God was superior to that of humans, for, while craftsmen needed their work before their very eyes, he worked in the dark and in secret within the maternal womb. His skill sparkling in the figure of the human body was inestimable. Calvin invited people to inspect their own fingernails. No detail of a single part could be altered or demonstrated as unsuitable. No embroiderer in gold could achieve

---

1 John Calvin, *Institutio christianae religionis* 2.14.2.

2 Calvin, *Commentarii in quinque libros Mosis* ad Gen. 1:14; argumentum, in *Opera omnia* (Brunswick), 51:10; ad Gen. 1:4. See also *Institutio christianae religionis* 1.1.4.

3 See R. J. Hankinson, "Galen and the Best of All Possible Worlds," *Classical Quarterly* 39 (1989):206-27.

4 Calvin, *Institutio christianae religionis* 1.5.2, 4, 9; *Institutes of the Christian Religion*, trans. Ford Lewis Battles, 2 vols., Library of Christian Classics, 20-21 (Philadelphia, Pa.: Westminster, 1960), 1:53-54, and my translation. Unless otherwise noted, all translations of Calvin, not only of *Institutio christianae religionis* but also of his other works, are my own.

with diligence and cunning a fraction of such a manifold and varied web.[5] The skill of God the Creator surpassed Arachne at the loom.

Calvin praised fingernails as "mirrors of God's providence, in which we see marvelous workmanship, for they serve to put the hands to work, to strengthen them and to teach how to bend the fingers and to hold what is necessary."[6] Although the teleology was "Galen's skill,"[7] the metaphor of the mirror was Calvin's argument. The very pagans, he wrote, had been constrained to acknowledge a sovereign deity, "convinced by only a human fingernail." The context of his apologetic was his condemnation of philosophical and clerical speculation, in favor of the ordinary observation of even uneducated persons.[8] Plato had ridiculed the gods in making the human fingernail as "bad workmen," and Aristotle had failed to understand its providential usage.[9] With the metaphor of the mirror Calvin distanced the design of the human body not only from such vain speculation but also from occult knowledge and evil purpose: catoptromancy. Fingernails were indeed used as mirrors, but for magic. John of Salisbury related in *Policraticus* his youthful experience as a student whose clerical master was an adept at divination by crystal-gazing. His teacher initiated him into the occult by anointing his fingernails with holy chrism so that images would appear reflected in thèm and impart secrets. Spirits were believed to appear to a virgin boy in such a reflective surface, although the practice was thought to be punished by blindness.[10] *Malleus maleficarum* also reported how witches enticed virgin boys and girls into their power by such reflections.[11] The parings of fingernails were believed abodes of evil, incapable of serving God.[12] As such they figured in sorcery. A sorceress prescribed for uxorial love sticking the clippings of the husband's nails inside a hen's heart, then placing them in the wife's vagina.[13] A treatise on

5 Calvin, in Ps. 139:15. For uterine life, see in Ps. 71:6; 139:13. For admiration of the providential and wise design of the fetus, see also Galen, *De usu partium* 15.4-7; Realdo Columbo, *De re anatomica* 12. For embyological knowledge from antiquity through the sixteenth century, see Howard B. Adelman, ed., introduction to *Embryological Treatises of Hieronymus Fabricius* (1533c.-1619), pp. 36-70.

6 Calvin, *Sermons sur le livre de Iob* 39, in *Opera omnia* (Brunswick), 33:488; cited by William J. Bouwsma, *John Calvin: A Sixteenth Century Portrait* (New York: Oxford University Press, 1987), p. 134.

7 Galen, *De usu partium* 1.6-11.

8 Calvin, *Sermons sur le livre de Iob* 39, in *Opera omnia* (Brunswick), 33:488.

9 Galen, *De usu partium* 1.8.

10 See Richard Kieckhefer, *Magic in the Middle Ages* (Cambridge: Cambridge University Press, 1990), pp. 151, 158-59, citing John of Salisbury, *Policraticus* 2.28.

11 Jacob Sprenger and Heinrich Institoris, *Malleus maleficarum* 2.1.13.

12 Kurt Seligmann, *The History of Magic and the Occult* (New York: Harmony, 1975), pp. 16-19.

13 Kieckhefer, *European Witch Trials: Their Foundations in Popular and Learned Culture, 1300-1500* (London: Routledge and Kegan Paul, 1976), p. 58. For fingernails in sorcery, see also Lyndal Roper, *Oedipus and the Devil: Witchcraft, Sexuality, and Religion in Early Modern Europe* (London: Routledge, 1994), pp. 188, 189.

female beautification counseled against manicuring on Thursday at sunrise as apotropaic.[14] Yet, in the conceptual opposition that so typified thought on sensation, nail parings were a classical cure for fever.[15] The recipe of Ambroise Paré (1510-90) against quartan fever was to place the parings in a linen cloth tied around the neck of a live eel and to throw it back into the water.[16] And they seem to have been collected as a relic. Aldebert, a popular holy man wandering in eighth-century Gaul, was accused by Boniface of distributing his clippings to his disciples as relics.[17]

Calvin admired fingernails toward belief in their divine design. The glory of God flashed in the human body. Although the divine image was primarily in the mind and heart or in the soul and its faculties, "yet there was no part of man, not even the body itself, in which some sparks did not glint."[18] Calvin acknowledged the classical topic of human dignity by erect bipedality. "I do not deny, indeed," he wrote, "that our outward form, in so far as it distinguishes and separates us from brute animals, at the same time more closely joins us to God." He even quoted with tolerance the familiar passage from Ovid's *Metamorphoses*—providing, he added, that the divine image conspicuous in such external marks as the uplifted countenance be understood as spiritual. Calvin argued as too gross a conception Andreas Osiander's (1498-1552) extension of the divine image to the human body. Yet Calvin remained convinced that the persuasion of God's existence was "naturally inborn in all, and is fixed deep within, as it were in the very marrow."[19] The marrow was philosophically and medically the primary living tissue. In Plato's *Timaeus* the demiurge had begun with the creation of marrow, from the smoothest and shapeliest of the basic triangles of all four elements, combined in proper proportion. He then molded the marrow into a

---

14 Marie-Claude Phan, "Pratiques cosmétiques et idéal feminin dans l'Italie des quinzième et seizième siècles," in *Les soins de beauté: Moyen Âge, début des temps moderns*, Actes du troisième colloque international Grasse (26-28 avril 1985), ed. Denis Menjot (Nice: Université de Nice, 1987), p. 112, citing *Amira* without reference.

15 Pliny, *Naturalis historia* 28.23-86.

16 Ambroise Paré, *Des monstres* 32.

17 Patrick J. Geary, "The Ninth-Century Relic Trade: A Response to Popular Piety," in *Religion and the People, 800-1700*, ed. James Obelkevich (Chapel Hill: University of North Carolina Press, 1979), p. 10. Nail clippings of Jesus as relics are mentioned by Carlos M. N. Eire, *War Against the Idols: The Reformation of Worship from Erasmus to Calvin* (Cambridge: Cambridge University Press, 1986), p. 16.

18 Calvin, *Institutio christianae religionis* 1.15.3; trans. Battles, 1:188, with my change of "glow" to glint, since *mico* is intermittent, not steady, light. For light transmitted from the soul to the body, diffused among its limbs and senses and shining forth in action, word, and gesture, see also Bernard of Clairvaux, *Sermones in Cantica canticorum* 85.11. See also "the splendor of the celestial majesty shining through bodies." Marsilio Ficino, *Commentariorum in "Convivo" Platonis* 2.6; *Commentary on Plato's "Symposium" on Love*, trans. Sears Jayne, 2d rev. ed. (Dallas, Tex.: Spring, 1985), p. 52. See also 5.5; 6.2.

19 Calvin, *Institutio christianae religionis* 1.3.3; trans. Battles, 1:46. Against Osiander see also *In libros Mosis* ad Gen. 1:26. See also Charles Partee, *Calvin and Classical Philosophy*, Studies in the History of Christian Thought, 14 (Leiden: E. J. Brill, 1977), p. 53.

sphere to contain the divine seed, the vessel of which was in the head. Other parts of the marrow he divided into long shapes for enclosure in the vertebrae and the spine and other bones. Bone was formed next from the marrow and from earth refined and hardened. The spinal column was constructed purposively of flexible vertebrae to protect the divine seed in a bony enclosure. The structure was then clothed in flesh to protect the skeleton, which otherwise would have been too brittle, too stiff, and liable to decay from fluxes of temperature.[20] Belief in the existence of God was for Calvin thus implanted in humans with the creation of their erect skeleton. Belief was structural to people, deeply within their marrow.

The introduction to Calvin's commentary on Genesis was an argument from design in which the senses figured immediately and importantly. "With the eyes we indeed perceive the world, with the feet we tread the earth, with the hands we gently touch innumerable aspects of the work of God; we inhale a sweet and pleasant scent from herbs and flowers; we enjoy enormous goods. But in these very things of our acquaintance there is contained an infinity of divine power, goodness, and wisdom, which absorbs all our senses." Yet Calvin projected that sensual absorption onto humanity only as primordially created, while he greatly depreciated the sensory powers of humanity as since then fallen. The image of God related to the original perfection of the wholesome nature, "when Adam was endowed with right discernment, had disposition ordered toward reason, all his senses healthy and orderly, and truly excelled in all goods." While the divine image principally and eminently was seated in the mind and heart, "yet there was no part of him in which some sparks of it did not shoot." The original senses were all quickly compliant to reason, and there was a corporeal symmetry of their order. The physical body itself was without defect. While Adam did lose one rib, that was only so that he might embrace in Eve a piece of himself.[21]

"Now God's image is the perfect excellence of human nature which shone in Adam before his defection," he explained, "but was subsequently so vitiated and almost blotted out that nothing remains after the ruin except what is confused, mutilated, and disease-ridden." Although the image of God was not destroyed and abolished, it was so corrupted that its remains were a "frightful deformity,"[22] a "deformity throughout that appears ugly."[23] Calvin expressed that lapse not only as a general corruption but also in language specifying the moral fall as a physical fall. Adam primordially "stood." His

---

20 Plato, *Timaeus* 91b. See James Longrigg, *Greek Rational Medicine: Philosophy and Medicine from Alcmaeon to the Alexandrians* (London: Routledge, 1993), pp. 130-35.

21 Calvin, *In libros Mosis* argumentum; ad Gen. 1:26; and see *Institutio christianae religionis* 1.15.8; ad Gen. 2:16; 2:21. For Eve from Adam's rib, see also *Institutio christianae religionis* 4.19.35.

22 Calvin, *Institutio christianae religionis* 1.15.4; trans. Battles, 1:190, 189. For the human condition after the fall, see also in Ps. 8:5.

23 Gen. 1:26 cf. "mutilated."

fall threw, hurled, cast down himself and his universal posterity to a debased position. There resulted in humans "feebleness." A person was menaced by his own body as a lurking-place of a thousand diseases, whose cause and fomation was within him. That debility extended to the sense of touch, as experienced essentially in temperature. "For what else would you call it," Calvin asked, "when he neither freezes nor sweats without danger?" Such weakness of even the body and its senses implied the delusion of esteeming the soul and its powers.[24] The once perfect body had become a mass of vices.[25]

Original sin was "a hereditary depravity and corruption of our nature." There was morally in humans a fallen state comparable physically to skeletal "crookedness."[26] Although Calvin's word *pravitas* morally means "depraved, vicious, or perverse," primarily it means "crookedness, irregularity, deformity": as if all people were cripples. In the primordial lapse from faith and obedience this depravity was diffused not only in the soul but also in the body.[27] It was especially manifested in weak bones. While the flesh was the tender part of the bodily system, the bones were the strongest parts of the human frame. "A blow to the bones," Calvin wrote, "is felt more than if a sword should stab through the internal organs or other pliable parts of the body." Bones were thus a metaphor for strength and power. When they dried up, vigor was wasted.[28] Bent or broken bones meant serious debility.

He instructed in his dedicatory letter to *Institutio christianae religionis* that faith should appropriately recognize salvation in Christ as metaphorically a restoration of the senses and parts of the body. Humans were "lame, to be made straight by him."[29] The method to be used "until the crooked is made straight again" was "clemency," the very subject of Calvin's initial publication.[30] The beginning of salvation was restoration in Christ to true and solid integrity as wholeness. Concerning dedication to spiritual living in holiness and righteousness, Calvin wrote that "no one in this earthly prison of the body has sufficient strength to press on with due eagerness, and weakness so weighs down the greater number that, with waddling, and

---

24 Calvin, *Institutio christianae religionis* 1.2.3; 1.15.8; 1.1.1; 1.17.10; 1.1.2; trans. Battles, 1:223.

25 Calvin, in Col. 2:11.

26 Calvin, *Institutio christianae religionis* 2.1.8; 1.1.1; trans. Battles, 1: 251. The notion that Adam's sin was gluttony is dismissed at 2.1.4.

27 Calvin, *In libros Mosis* ad Gen. 3:6.

28 Calvin, in Ps. 6:2; 42:11; 14:5; 22:17; 102:3. For bones dried up by melancholy, see in Is. 66:14; for medical bodily moisture dried by grief, in Ps. 22:15.

29 Calvin, "Praefatio ad regem Galliae," *Institutio christianae religionis*, in *Opera omnia* (Brunswick), 2:13; trans. Battles, 1:13.

30 Calvin, *Commentarius in Senecae "De clementia"* 2.7.5; *Calvin's Commentary on Seneca's "De clementia,"* trans. Battles and André Malan Hugo, Renaissance Society of America, Renaissance Text Series, 3 (Leiden: E. J. Brill for the Renaissance Society of America, 1969), p. 379. Seneca's treatise is discontinued here.

limping, and even creeping along the ground, they move at a feeble rate."[31] He himself experienced this debility from "gout" (arthritis). Calvin wrote personally of the onset of an acute pain seizing his calves, which developed into diseased joints from his feet to his knees. It rendered him inactive, and, even when the sharp pains subsided, he only crept with difficulty from bed to table. Once he had to be carried to the church for preaching.[32]

Yet the scriptural prophecies afforded consolation and hope. On the promise of God gathering the lame (Mic. 4:6) Calvin explained that the Hebrew word meant "side," metaphorically those who walked on only one side as "maimed and weak." The verse prophesied that the Church as afflicted by God's hand would be strengthened and invigorated. The maimed should not despair, for they would experience something like a resurrection. On another verse of salvation for the lame (Zeph. 3:19) he compared a "mutilated and broken" Church to a person "with dislocated limbs. . . useless as to any work." It was even "prostrate and fallen. . . scattered here and there, like a mangled body of a man, an arm here and a leg there." Again, God would renew that body as in a resurrection.[33] It was the state of being strangers to Christ that made people "lame," that is, "lacking in every capability of doing good." Only Christ could restore limpers to true health. The human members were too lively under the impulse of sinful passion: "the hands too prompt to theft, plunderage, cruelty; the feet swift to do harm." Once wickedness possessed the mind it dragged the hands and feet with it.[34] The hands were disobedient to the mind, because the mind was impure. "We provoke our senses to evil by unbridled license," he wrote. Yet, since the hands had no movement of their own, they should not be punished by deliberate mutilation.[35]

Although the limbs were as good as dead—destitute, corrupt, polluted, there was a remedy: recreation in Christ. The gospel documented his restoration of "whole powers to the mutilated and the lame" as bodily tokens of spiritual blessings.[36] In imitation the apostolic cure of the man lame from birth was a perfect healing. It was a difficult miracle, Calvin commented, because it was not just a matter of legs out of joint, or a casualty of disease, but a natural defect. Since the man had to be carried, he was not a slight halter but a paralyzed invalid, as if his legs were dead. Upon cure, he

---

31 Calvin, *Institutio christianae religionis* 1.15.4; trans., Battles, 1:689, with my change of "wavering" to waddling.

32 Émile Doumergue, *Jean Calvin: Les hommes et les choses de son temps*, 7 vols. (1899; rpt. Geneva: Slatkine, 1969), 3:521-22, citing Letter to physicians of Montpellier, 8 February, 1564, in *Opera omnia* (Brunswick), 20:252-54; Letter to Théodore de Bèze, 7 October, 1561, in 19:30; Letter to Heinrich Bullinger, 27 December, 1562, p. 602.

33 Calvin, in Mic. 4:6; Soph. (Zeph.) 3:19.

34 Calvin, in Is. 35:5; 9:17.

35 Calvin, *Commentarius in harmoniam evangelicam* ad. Matt. 5:29, cf. 6:22.

36 Calvin, in Is. 35:5.

settled on his feet, leaped up, and walked joyfully to the temple.[37] Calvin characterized the world as a "slippery place" for everyone. But the hand of God reached under the faithful to steady them when they stumbled or to raise them when they fell, while the ungodly strolled leisurely but presumptuously as if on ice: headed for a sure fall.[38]

Calvin compared limping to the mental fluctuation in persons that tended to deviation from the straight moral path.[39] More gravely he defined the lame person as "one so stripped of power as wholly to fail in himself."[40] That variance corresponded to the theological usage of the metaphor of limping in a scale from slight, to severe, to total disability. The notion that humanity was lame was not strictly scriptural. There was no indication in Genesis that the cursed and banished Adam and Eve limped from the garden of paradise. Artists depicted them as leaving it still on their own two feet, although their heads might be bowed and their shoulders hunched in shame, as in Michelangelo's cringing Eve on the Sistine Chapel ceiling. The notion of the moral fall as a physical fall necessarily implied the classical topic of erect bipedality. Hesiod had poetized the golden age of immortality as one of "legs and arms never failing." With the appearance of death, as in the Homeric verses, the knees bent and yielded; the human body collapsed to the earth.[41]

Firm feet could be a metaphor for the dignity of human nature but they were not always honorable. The head was usually considered the noblest part of the body, with the brain as the seat of rationality and intellection and with luminous eyes for the primary sense of sight. As Marsilio Ficino (1433-99) extolled it, "Nature has given to those parts of the body below the head only the power of touch, but she has furnished the head alone with the powers of all the senses." Lest anyone doubt, "let them always remember, too, that we never think with feet or hands, but only with the head." The moral served to instruct the head of state or Church that he should surpass the laity, as if bodily limbs, in mental virtues In the metaphor of the body politic the feet were the lowliest people in society, the laborers. Feet were variously deprecated. There was the Christian practice since antiquity of stretching out the feet of the dying in the belief that the soul escaped the body from the toes upward, exiting through the mouth.[42] There was the devil in the sixteenth century who admitted under exorcism that he had en-

---

[37] Calvin, in Acta 3:2.

[38] Calvin, in Ps. 73:18; cf. 121:3.

[39] Calvin, in Heb. 12:13.

[40] Calvin, in Zeph. 3:19.

[41] Hesiod, *Opera et dies* lines 109-15; trans. H. G. Evelyn-White (Cambridge, 1914; rpt. 1977), p. 11; cited by Mirko D. Grmek, *Diseases in the Ancient Greek World*, trans. Mireille Muellner and Leonard Muellner (Baltimore, Md.: Johns Hopkins University Press, 1989), pp. 5, 20, without reference to this argument.

[42] See Alfred C. Rush, *Death and Burial in Christian Antiquity*, Studies in Christian Antiquity, 1 (Washington, D.C.: Catholic University of America Press, 1941), pp. 91-92, 109-10.

tered into the human body through the feet, creeping to the brain, and that he would depart it again through the feet.[43] Giovanni Pico della Mirandola (1463-94), discoursing on human dignity, despised feet even metaphorically. "Surely the foot of the soul is that most contemptible part by which the soul rests on matter as on the soil of the earth, I mean the nourishing and feeding power, the tinder of lust and the teacher of pleasurable weakness." There was no ascent to divinity by foul feet.[44] As Erasmus (1469?-1536) stated the commonplace, "In the head is reason, in the feet emotion."[45] Calvin similarly commented, "Feet metaphorically means all affections and cares by which we contact the world. For if the Spirit occupied all our parts, we would have nothing more of the filths of the world. Certainly now by that part [feet] we are carnal, creeping on the ground, or at least sticking our feet in the mud; and to that extent we are unclean."[46] Human afflictions were deep and dangerous muck, "for if someone fixes his foot on solid ground he can raise himself, as we see many who emerge from water with a thrust; but he who sticks in the mud perishes."[47] Michelangelo testified how as an artist his soul could arise to beauty through his eyes but how his feet were hindered from transporting his arms and hands there.[48] And, despite his praise of the noble head, Ficino confessed himself in prayer a limping lover of God, who implored the divine hand to be outstretched toward him.[49]

Limpers, as heroes and anti-heroes, had a lineage deriving from the ancient epics. The significance of the debility was sexual, either generative or impotent. The concept may have originated in a Near-Eastern mythology of sacral kingship that demanded death for fertility but substituted laming by hamstringing or dislocation of the thigh. Christian literature frequently portrayed its anti-heroes as limpers, such as the maimed and sterile fisher king of the Grail legends or the very devil.[50] Limping became the human condition in the lament of Bernard of Clairvaux, the most popular of medieval spiritual writers. As he interpreted in his *Sermones super Cantica canticorum*, with original sin Adam lost his "uprightness," although the soul in its grandeur retained the divine image. "But he limps, as it were, on one foot, and has become an estranged son." No longer proudly erect, in its debility humanity limped away from the path, just as Calvin repeated. A

43 Paré, *De monstres* 32.

44 Giovanni Pico della Mirandola, *Oratio de dignitate hominis* 11; "On the Dignity of Man," trans. Elizabeth Livermore Forbes, in *The Renaissance Philosophy of Man*, in Ernst Cassirer et al. (Chicago: University of Chicago Press, 1948), p. 229.

45 Erasmus, *Ecclesiastes, sive de ratione concionandi*, in *Opera omnia* (Leiden), 5:791.

46 Calvin, in John 13:9.

47 Calvin, in Ps. 69:2.

48 Michelangelo, *Rime* 166.

49 Ficino, *Epistolae* 1.116.

50 Peter L. Hays, *The Limping Hero: Grotesques in Literature* (New York: New York University Press, 1971), pp. 17-27, 8, 65-66, 68-69.

disabled humanity was disturbed and wrenched from the rectitude of the divine image. It became bent to the ground and it brooded over the earth.[51] Dante venturing his pilgrimage was a limper: he hobbled from the perilous pass toward the blessed summit like a man wounded in his left foot. A medieval tradition about lameness developed from Aristotelian physics, in which movement originated on the right, so that the left was stationary. A scholastic analogy applied walking to the faculties of the soul: the intellect was like the right foot, which struck forward; the will, like the left, which dragged behind. Limping represented the instability of the intellect and the will, which disabled humanity toward its divine destiny. From original sin the right leg or intellect was wounded by ignorance; the left or will, by concupiscence. The posterity of Adam was afflicted with such limping in its inability to order appetite to mind.[52] The ascetic accusation that Francesco Petrarca (1304-74) was dragging his feet in renouncing his poetic art implied the weakness of the will to achieve what the intellect understood as good.[53] The experience of Ignatius Loyola (1491-1556), an actual limper from wounds in battle to both legs, became a moral for everyone's debility: when he fell, the fortress surrendered to the enemy. His will was shattered, just as his leg bone needed resetting, while his intellect was badly injured but still able to grope while dragging the destroyed limb.[54] Michelangelo poetized how he shifted back and forth between the right and the left foot, searching for salvation, only to get lost on its path. He was "hobbling," he said.[55] The metaphor will still be current in John Donne's (1573-1631) universal anatomy:

> Then, as mankinde, so is the worlds whole frame
> Quite out of oiynt, almost created lame.

The poet exclaimed, "How lame a cripple this world is."[56]

---

[51] Bernard of Clairvaux, *Sermones super Cantica canticorum* 80.2.4; *On the Song of Songs*, trans. Irene Edmonds, Cistercian Fathers Series, 40 (Kalamazoo, Mich.: Cistercian, 1980), 4:149; also cited by Anthony K. Cassell, "Failure, Pride, and Conversion in 'Inferno' I: A Reinterpretation," *Dante Studies* 74 (1976):19 n. 2.

[52] John Freccero, "Dante's Firm Foot and the Pilgrim without a Guide," *Harvard Theological Review* 52 (1959):251-68; rpt. in idem, *Dante: The Poetics of Conversion*, ed. Rachel Jacoff (Cambridge, Mass.: Harvard University Press, 1986), pp. 29-54.

[53] Nancy H. Rosenberg, "Petrarch's Limping: The Foot Unequal to the Eye," *Modern Language Notes* 77 (1962):101-2.

[54] Luis Gonçalves da Câmara, *Acta patris Ignatii* 1.2. Marjorie O'Rourke Boyle, *Loyola's Acts: The Rhetoric of the Self*, New Historicism, 36 (Berkeley and Los Angeles: University of California Press, 1997), pp. 22, 29-33, 42-44.

[55] Michelangelo, *Rime* 162, 175; *The Poetry of Michelangelo*, trans. James M. Saslow (New Haven, Conn.: Yale University Press, 1991), p. 175.

[56] John Donne, "The First Anniuersarie: An Anatomy of the World, Wherein, By Occasion of the Untimely Death of Mistris Elizabeth Drury the Frailty and Decay of This Whole World is Represented" lines 191-92.

Lameness was defective. As the late medieval physician Henri de Mondeville epitomized the disability, "the lame man, an imperfect man."[57] Then there was the anecdote from Michel de Montaigne (1533-92) of the man on the scaffold about to be hanged, who was offered his life in exchange for marrying a wench. "'Tie up, tie up!" he said. "She limps."[58] The failure of physical rectitude was blamed in deformed persons from values of strength and beauty. They lacked the upright deportment required by social custom.[59] Calvin acknowledged that lameness was caused physically, by dislocation or disease of the bones.[60] But he thought that curvature of the spine, as in the woman with the "spirit of infirmity," could be beyond ordinary medical disease—a diabolical work.[61] A sorceress testified how a lame man had begged her for a cure: she boiled herbal water and splashed it onto the street so that the next passerby would contract the debility instead of him.[62] Other unfortunates resorted to doctors, or to saints.

Yet all bodily instability of all persons was in renaissance manners supposed to be strictly under control. As Giovanni Della Casa's (1503-56) manual on civility pronounced, it was bad manners to mimic or to mock a lame or hunchbacked person. Worse, it was "not proper" for anyone even to "tremble or shake."[63] The most popular interpretation of the mark of Cain as vice was not a brand or a blemish but a spastic trembling of the body, so that he could not steady or even uphold his limbs.[64] When at the turn of the fifteenth century the Swiss authorities tried to capture a member of a diabolical sect, their hands were reported to tremble uncontrollably[65] just from proximity to evil. Trembling was classically associated with madness.[66] Leonardo da Vinci (1452-1519) noted it of senseless persons, whose gestures did not act with the permission of the soul, like shiverers, paralytics,

---

57 Henri de Mondeville, *Chirurgia*, p. 198; cited by Marie-Christine Pouchelle, *The Body and Surgery in the Middle Ages*, trans. Rosemary Morris (London: Polity, 1990), p. 86. For the lame as ugly and shameful, causing derision, see Eddie R. Lowry, *Thersites: A Study in Comic Shame* (New York: Garland, 1991), pp. 94-105.

58 Michel de Montaigne, *Essais* 1.14, p. 52; *The Complete Works of Montaigne: Essays, Travel Journal, Letters*, trans. Donald M. Frame (Stanford, Calif.: Stanford University Press, 1967), p. 34.

59 Georges Vigarello, "The Upward Training of the Body from the Age of Chivalry to Courtly Civility," trans. Ughetta Lubin, in *Fragments for a History of the Human Body*, ed. Michel Feher with Ramona Nadaff and Nadia Tazi, 3 vols. (New York: Zone, 1989), 2:149.

60 Calvin, in Ps. 35:15.

61 Calvin, *In harmoniam evangelicam* ad Luke 13:10

62 See Kieckhefer, *European Witch Trials*, p. 56.

63 Giovanni della Casa, *Galateo* 189-90, 322; trans. Konrad Eisenbichler and Kenneth R. Bartlett, Centre for Reformation and Renaissance Studies Translation Series, 2 (Toronto: Centre for Reformation and Renaissance Studies, 1986), p. 60.

64 Ruth Mellinkoff, *The Mark of Cain* (Berkeley and Los Angeles: University of California Press, 1981), pp. 40-57.

65 Kieckhefer, *European Witch Trials*, p. 20; Sprenger and Institoris, *Malleus maleficarum* 2.1.1; 2.1.2.

66 G. E. R. Lloyd, *Science, Folklore, and Ideology: Studies in the Life Sciences in Ancient Greece* (Cambridge: Cambridge University Press, 1983), p. 169.

epileptics, and buffoons.[67] Calvin commented on the forcible convulsions that threw a lunatic, epileptic, or dizzy person to the ground inert—as if dead.[68] Those who were unable to control their gait and posture were simply insane, like the demoniac in Raphael's (1483-1520) scene of the transfiguration whose legs are askew and whose arms are wild. Pieter Brueghel the Elder's (c.1525-69) painting of Dulle Grete (Mad Meg) portrays her wide striding gait with splayed legs.[69] Lame legs were not a horrible defect or casualty in comparison with other disabilities and diseases, however. A great wound to the foot was considered less injurious than a speck of dust in the eye, because of the greater nobility of the sense of sight than touch. A single grain of corrosive matter was more harmful to the eye than a hundred to the foot.[70] Yet the most miraculous case of surgery ever performed was on a leg, by the very patron saints of medicine, Cosmas and Damian. They amputated the lower leg of a wounded man and the matching limb of a corpse, then exchanged the two parts by transplant.[71]

Protestant reformers, to emphasize human incapacity against efforts to merit salvation, exceeded the Catholic metaphor of fallen humanity as a limper. They lowered people still further onto all fours. Quadrupeds had been a patristic comparison for certain immoral persons, like gluttons who unduly bent prone over the table while eating. Ambrose in his homilies on Genesis had observed real quadrupeds as lacking in the ability to stand erect, and so seeking sustenance in the earth toward which they inclined. He thus enjoined humans, "Take care not to be bent over like cattle. See that you do not incline—not so much physically as they do, but morally.

---

[67] Kenneth D. Keele, *Leonardo da Vinci's Elements of the Science of Man* (New York: Academic, 1983), pp. 160, 162, citing *The Drawings of Leonardo da Vinci in the Collection of Her Majesty the Queen at Windsor Castle*, ed. Kenneth Clark and Carlo Pedretti, 2d ed. (London: Phaidon, 1968), 19019v; *Corpus of the Anatomical Studies in the Collection of Her Majesty the Queen at Windsor Castle*, ed. Keele and Pedretti, 3 vols. (New York: Harcourt Brace Jovanovich, 1978-80), 39v; *Treatise on Painting*, 1:408.

[68] Calvin, *In harmoniam evangelicam* ad Mark 9:17.

[69] See Sander L. Gilman, *Seeing the Insane: A Cultural History of Madness and Art in the Western World* (New York: John Wiley and Sons and Brunner/Mazel, 1982), pp. xii, 24, 48. Raphael, Transfiguration, Madrid; reproduced, p. 25, pl. 33. See also Herbert von Einem, *"Die Verklärung Christi" und die "Heilung des Besessenen" von Raffael*, Akademie der Wissenschaften und der Literatur in Mainz, Abhandlungen der Geistes-und Socialwissenschaftlichen Klasse, 5 (Wiesbaden: Franz Steiner, 1966). Pieter Breughel the Elder, Dulle Grete, Pinacoteca, Vatican; reproduced in Gilman, *Seeing the Insane*, p. 47, pl. 58.

[70] See Pouchelle, *Body and Surgery*, p. 119. For facial ugliness as surpassing manual ugliness, and disease in the entrails as worse than in the feet, see Ficino, *Epistolae* 3.59.

[71] *Kosmas und Damian*, miracle 48. See also Owsei Temkin, *Hippocrates in a World of Pagans and Christians* (Baltimore, Md.: Johns Hopkins University Press, 1991), pp. 166-67. For artistic examples, see Fra Angelico, c. 1438-40, San Marco, Florence; reproduced in Umberto Baldini, *Beato Angelico* (Florence: D'Arte il Fiorino, 1986), p. 192; Francesco Pesellino (1422-57), Louvre, Paris; reproduced in Hans Schadewaldt, "From Prehistory to the End of the Fifteenth Century," in *Medicine in Art: A Cultural History*, ed. Jean Rousselot (New York: McGraw Hill, 1967), p. 117; Anneliese Wittmann, *Kosmas und Damien: Kultausbreitung und Volksdevotion* (Berlin: Erich Schmidt, 1967), frontispiece and passim.

Have regard for the conformation of your body and assume in accordance with it the appearance of loftiness and strength."[72] The comparison of human vices and animal traits was a moral commonplace. Loyola's *Exercitia spiritualia* illustrates the sinner laden with a basket of such vicious beasts crawling toward hell.[73] But the reformed metaphor debased humanity itself, not only a particular sinner, to a quadruped.

Calvin appealed to a comparison in Augustine's writings of the human will as a horse pricked to the command of its riders, God or the devil. "'If God sits astride it,' he says, 'then as a moderate and skilled rider, he guides it properly, spurs it if it is too slow, checks it if it is too swift, restrains it if it is too rough or wild, subdues it if it balks, and leads it into the right path.'" Not so with the contending rider. "'But if the devil saddles it, he violently drives it far from the trail like a foolish and wanton rider, forces it into ditches, tumbles it over cliffs, and goads it into obstinacy and fierceness.'"[74] Augustine had proposed no such bestial example; Calvin but varied a *Hypomnesticon* falsely attributed to him.[75] That text but varied Plato's metaphor of the charioteer driving two opposite horses,[76] by substituting one horse with two opposite charioteers. Calvin expressed some reservation about the comparison. "Since a better comparison does not come to mind, we shall be satisfied with this one for the present."[77] Martin Luther (1483-1546) had already cited it famously in his forensic challenge to Erasmus, *De servo arbitrio*, on the bondage of the will. Only for Luther the quadruped was not so noble as Calvin's steed—merely a beast of burden. A human was a stupid pack animal for the mastery of whose will God and Satan contended. "If God mounts it, it wills and gallops off to wherever God wills, as the psalm says: I have become like a beast of burden, and I am ever with you [Ps. 73:22-23]. If Satan takes to the saddle, it wills and gallops off to wherever Satan wills." Nor could it prefer or encourage a choice of riders. "Nor does it have the choice to goad either rider or to prefer one, but the riders themselves contend for the procurement and possession of it."[78] The ritual substitution of human beings for beasts of

---

72 Ambrose, *Hexameron* 6.3.10; *Hexameron, Paradise, and Cain and Abel*, trans. John J. Savage, Fathers of the Church, 42 (New York: Fathers of the Church, 1961), p. 233.

73 Reproduced in René Fülöp-Miller, *The Power and Secret of the Jesuits*, trans. F. S. Flint and D. F. Tait (London: G. P. Putnam's Sons, 1930), pl. 8; cited by Samuel S. Chew, *The Pilgrimage of Life* (New Haven, Conn.: Yale University Press, 1962), pp. 251-52.

74 Calvin, *Institutio christianae religionis* 2.4.1; trans. Battles, 1:309.

75 Pseudo-Augustine, *Hypomnesticon* 3.11.20. Identified by Battles, trans., p. 309 n. 3, and by other sources.

76 Plato, *Phaedrus* 246a.

77 Calvin, *Institutio christianae religionis* 2.4.1; trans. Battles, 1:309-10.

78 Martin Luther, *De servo arbitrio*, p. 126. For comparative analysis, see Boyle, "Luther's Rider-gods: From the Steppe to the Tower," *Journal of Religious History* 13 (1985):260-85.

burden had in the carnival celebrations of late medieval Germany symbolized an inversion of the social order.[79]

Postural debasement could be a gesture of penitence. The medieval monk Peter the Chanter had supposed that, just as in copulation people laid down meanly like animals, so in repentance for sin they should fall down to the position of quadrupeds.[80] Yet a sinful humanity could be pressed still further toward the ground, and Calvin did so with the lowliest of animal similes. Except for Christ as mediator, he wrote, the divine majesty was too lofty to be attained by mortals, who were "like bare worms crawling upon the earth."[81] The simile was not exclusively Protestant. The charismatic nun Teresa of Avila (1515-82), who founded her cloistered order to pray for the conversion of Calvin's partisans, employed it of her interior castle. In its principal palace, where transpired the most secretive affairs between God and the soul, he communicated with people only as "stinky worms."[82] Women, because of their phlegmatic and mucous humor, were more susceptible than men to the worms that infested the body through poor digestion. There was reported during the period of the Council of Trent a certain woman who spewed from her navel menstrual blood and live worms.[83]

The notion of females as wormy reverted to Eve's debasement and curse. Calvin believed that in her lapse from faith and obedience depravity was diffused not only in her soul but through all parts of her body.[84] A creeping Eve was unique to the iconography of the cathedral of Autun, where she was portrayed on a lintel horizontally: on her knees and elbow, cheek in hand in a gesture of grief, extending her free arm backwards to take the apple from the serpent. In other medieval scenes of the primordial temptation Eve had been standing or seated. She became at Autun an exemplary image of the sinner cursed to creep like the serpent on belly and breast. The common medieval ritual for public penitence ordered that the designated sinners prostrate themselves before the bishop outside the church. They were then led inside where they prostrated themselves again, specifically "on knees and elbows," so that Eve crawling on the lintel of the cathedral may figure the actual liturgical practice. The debasement of Adam's soul in the dust, with his

---

79 Keith Moxey, *Peasants, Warriors, and Wives: Popular Imagery in the Reformation* (Chicago: University of Chicago Press, 1989), p. 101.

80 Peter the Chanter, *De penitentia et partibus eius* lines 2343-46.

81 Calvin, *Institutio christianae religionis* 2.6.4. Cf. Philosophers imagining sensory perception as crawling on the ground, 2.2.2. For humans as earthworms, see also Calvin, in Ps. 8:4.

82 Teresa of Avila, *Castillo interior* 6.4.10.

83 Piero Camporesi, *The Incorruptible Flesh: Bodily Mutation and Mortification in Religion and Folklore*, trans. Tania Croft-Murray and Helen Elsom, Cambridge Studies in Oral and Literate Culture, 17 (Cambridge: Cambridge University Press, 1988), pp. 82, 114, citing Giovan Battista Condronchi, *De morbis*, p. 29.

84 Calvin, *In libros Mosis* ad Gen. 3.6.

belly on the ground like the cursed serpent, had been expressed by Ambrose in considering the fall of humans from the erect posture of contemplation.[85] Gregory the Great had concurred about the purpose of the creation of humans as a "mind standing upright" toward full contemplation, without any deflection by corruption. But, since Adam had moved the foot of his will from the native firmness of his stance toward guilt, he fell instantly from loving his Creator to loving himself. He could no longer stand up by himself because he had collapsed below himself. No longer upheld by the solidity of his original stance, he was constantly changing with the motion of varying desires. "For because the mind was unwilling to stand firm while it could, now it cannot stand even when it wants to."[86]

The belief that a decaying human spine or spinal medulla could give birth to a serpent was as old as Pliny's natural history. In the sixteenth century Giambattista Della Porta (1535?-1615) was still teaching in his natural magic that serpents were born from human marrow.[87] The worm was the ancient prototype of the creatures who were ritually unclean because they swarmed.[88] In science worms were disparaged because they were believed to reproduce by the lowest method, spontaneous generation. From dew, mud and dung, wood, hair, flesh, and residues—either voided or internal—emerged certain creatures, like flies and fleas, eels, and grubs. An example was the helminths, or intestinal worms, in the three types of flat worm, round worm, and ascarid.[89] Worms even became an anthropological test of human nature. In the condemnation of the Amerindians as "bestial" the spiders they ate were consumed with worms.[90] Worms were within bodies not only by the voluntary choice of diet, however, but also by the natural corruption of the flesh from diet. Putrefaction was not only a process of tissues decaying after death but also one concurrent with life, as inherent to its corruption. The flesh was food for worms: its interior hosted swarms feed-

---

85 O. K. Werckmeister, "The Lintel Fragment Representing Eve from Saint-Lazare, Autun," *Journal of the Warburg and Courtauld Institutes* 35 (1972):1-30, citing *Ordo L* 18.29; Ambrose, *De paradiso* 15.74. Eve, lintel fragment from S. Lazare, Musée Rolin, Autun; reproduced, pls. 1 a-c; Clark, *The Nude: A Study in Ideal Form*, Bollingen Series 35-2 (New York: Pantheon, 1956), p. 314, fig. 252.

86 Gregory the Great, *Moralia in Job* 8.9.19; cited by Werkmeister, "Lintel Fragment," p. 25. Cf. Belief stands, doubt wobbles, unbelief falls. Augustine, *Sermo* 250.2.

87 Camporesi, *Incorruptible Flesh*, pp. 78, 82, without documentation for Pliny, but citing Giambattista Della Porta, *Della magia naturale* 20.

88 Mary Douglas, *Purity and Danger: An Analysis of the Concepts of Pollution and Taboo* (London: Ark, 1984), p. 56.

89 For worms, see Aristotle, *Historia animaliarum* 521a. D. M. Balme, "Development of Biology in Aristotle and Theophrastus: Theory of Spontaneous Generation," *Phronesis* 7(1962):91-104.

90 Diego Alvarez Chanca, in Martín Fernandez de Navarrete, *Viajes de Cristóbal Colón*, p. 241. Spiders, however, were not among the insects spontaneously generated. Aristotle, *Historia animalium* 551a; *De generatione animalium* 721a.

ing on the intestines. Death merely manifested what was concealed by the envelope of skin during life.[91]

Multiple tiny parasites—fleas, lice, grasshoppers, mosquitoes, gnats, hornets, wasps, flies, bedbugs, and caterpillars—drew human blood, causing sores or ulcers. But it was worms that supremely harassed people for centuries: sometimes they were endemic, sometimes so virulent and malignant as to be epidemic. The very notion of putrefaction was associated with the smell they produced. They were believed to be born in the stomach from the cold foods that required slow digestion. In the stomach they began to devour the morsels of food there to deprive the victim of nourishment. Medical accounts recorded the clinical signs of infestation, from glazed eyes to chattering teeth. But worms were not satisfied with the contents of the human stomach; they intended maliciously on the heart. In the process of worming their way to it their fumes created fevers, the weakening and failing of the pulse, and mental disorders. Pain and palpitation of the heart affected the stability of the total person: dizziness, epileptic seizure, convulsion. There were awful "twistings and turnings." The bodily contortions from worms could be extreme: to the report that some boys "even reached the napes of their necks with their heels." Worms caused trembling, fainting, and death: autopsy frequently revealed a double-headed worm attached to a boy's heart.[92]

Calvin himself itched from intestinal parasites. They so aggravated his sore hemorrhoids that in his sleep he scratched at them with his fingernails, worsening his condition.[93] He acknowledged by the current science of their origin that even the worms that nibbled metaphorically at the hearts of unbelievers were "formed out of the earth." Their effect was "an awful and horrible fear and restlessness."[94] When Calvin considered the case of Herod, persecutor of the apostles, as "eaten by worms" (Acts 12:23), he interpreted that as "a lousy disease [pediculosis]. . . corrupt with stench and rottenness," which reduced him "like a living cadaver." Since Herod loathed lice and worms, it was fitting for God to punish his pride and cruelty with such ignominy. "And this stinking putridity burst forth from his own body, which consumed him by gnawing away at it."[95] Of course, everyone was covered with worms in death.[96] By the word "worm" in the verse "But I am a worm and not a man" (Ps. 22:6) the psalmist declared and lamented the misery of his condition, in hope that God would extend his hand and save

---

91 Camporesi, *Incorruptible Flesh*, pp. 77-78.

92 Camporesi, *Incorruptible Flesh*, pp. 80, 114, 112. For the attachment to the heart, see Alessio Piemontese, *Secreti* 1.

93 Doumergue, *Jean Calvin*, 3:516.

94 Calvin, in Is. 66:24.

95 Calvin, in Acta 12:23. See also "the heart and life of a great and triumphant emperor is the breakfast of a little worm." Montaigne, *Essais* 2.12, p. 462; trans. Frame, p. 339.

96 Calvin, in Is. 14:11.

his abasement.[97] The prophet also bewailed as a worm the "abject and despised" condition of Israel, as if it were "no one." He equated it with "dirt and rottenness."[98]

In preaching on the phrase "man, who is a worm" (Job 25:6), Calvin generalized. "Now we come to humans. What are they? What can they do? What is their power? About what can they vaunt? They are nothing but worms and rot and still they wish to justify themselves?" To practice and apply that scripture meant that before God people were unable to proffer anything praiseworthy. "Humans are here declared void of all good, and that there is not a single drop of justice by which they can valorize themselves; but they pass condemnation knowing that there is in them nothing but every poverty and misery." If this teaching were well known, Calvin continued, there would not be such war and dispute with the papists over free will, as if people had some power to dispose themselves toward God. It was true, he conceded, that Catholics well acknowledged that humans were infirm and incapable without grace. But why bother with such acknowledgement, he complained, since they attributed to themselves preparations for and cooperations with grace, so that they were, in short, its companions. In conscience people should humble themselves before God as "only worms and rot, with nothing in us but infection and stink throughout."[99]

For Calvin the fall of original sin was not from pride but from unbelief.[100] In that unbelief humans prostrated themselves before idols in fallen bodily postures, as if they were quadrupeds or worms. "It is worship of God alone that renders men higher than the brutes, and through it alone they aspire to immortality," he wrote. In the absence of religion people were not superior to the beasts but even more miserable.[101] Calvin thus replicated Lactantius's ancient apologetic against idolatry: that it debased the human dignity of an erect posture.[102]

Yet idolatry manifested a desire to touch God, a desire that displayed the contradiction marking sensation as humanly analogous or antithetical to the divine. The conflict was vividly portrayed in the scriptural counterparts of Magdalen and Thomas—the one forbidden, the other invited to touch their risen Lord. The pericopes, unique to the gospel of John, were successive in it, so that exegetes could not fail to remark the contrast. The gospel announced that, when Magdalen went to tell the disciples, she said, "I have seen the Lord" not "I have touched the Lord." Yet if the devout flirted with the hope that she had indeed touched him (behind the scenes), they reveled in their imaginations about the disciple who certainly had. As Erasmus

97 Calvin, in Ps. 22:6.
98 Calvin, in Is. 41:14.
99 Calvin, *Sermons sur le livre de Job* 94 ad Job 25:6.
100 Calvin, *In libros Mosis* ad Gen. 3:6. From unbelief arose pride and ambition.
101 Calvin, *Institutio christianae religionis* 1.3.3; 3.20.22; trans. Battles, 1:47; 2:880.
102 Lactantius, *De opificio Dei* 10, discussed above in chapter one, pp. 37-38.

paraphrased that pericope, the testimony of the other disciples was insufficient for Thomas, whose faith demanded certification by all of his own senses. So Jesus invited him to "put your finger here in the wounds from the nails, and look at the actual marks of the metal; bring your hand to my side and touch the wound from the spear." Thomas did so and believed. Erasmus explained, "The touch of the body that had hung dead on the cross a little while ago gave witness that a real person had risen again." Jesus rebuked Thomas for believing because of the senses of sight, hearing, and touch; he pronounced blessed those who would believe while deprived even of sight.[103] The preacher for the Sistine Chapel, Tommaso da Vio, Cajetan (1469-1534), also moralized. Jesus' command to Thomas to put his fingers into the wound demanded interiority, not superficiality, of belief.[104]

Calvin reprimanded Magdalen as superstitious and carnal, an example of the error of the human mind through sensory perception. He was also unsympathetic toward Thomas as dull and obstinate, "even to probing Christ by touch." The disciple's demand to touch was a natural wickedness with no relationship to faith. His was a "sensual judgment." Unsatisfied with the sight of the wounds, Thomas wanted "his hand also as witness" by "probing by hand and examining by touch" the wound in his side. Instead of being overwhelmed with shame and wonder at the vision of the risen Lord, "unconscious of any guilt, he boldly and intrepidly thrusts his hand." Jesus was desirous to promote and confirm faith and so he displayed his wounds temporarily for instruction, until all the disciples might be convinced. Yet he blamed Thomas for the need to be drawn impetuously to faith "by sensual experience, which would shrink back by the nature of faith." It was not by touching, however, that Thomas believed but by being jolted awake in recalling doctrine. "For faith can never endure from the naked experiences of things," Calvin stated. Jesus thus blamed Thomas for regarding faith as bound to the senses.[105]

The skeletal structure of humans that had manifested in its erectness a divine design had become since the fall twisted. The marrow of human bones, with its deep persuasion of the divine existence, was hidden.[106] Now for Calvin "an itching pride in the marrow of humans tickles with its allurements."[107] Instead of faith embedded in the marrow, as at creation, arro-

---

103 Erasmus, *Paraphrasis in evangelium Joannis*, in *Opera omnia* (Leiden), 7:645; *Paraphrase on John*, trans. Jane E. Phillips, *The Collected Works of Erasmus* (Toronto: University of Toronto Press, 1991), 46:220. For some patristic exegesis as background, see John Chrysostom, *Homilia* 87; Augustine, *In Iohannis homilia* 121.3; Gregory the Great, *Homilia* 26.

104 Tommaso de Vio, *In quatuor evangelia*, p. 497.

105 Calvin, in John 20:11, 20-29. Cf. his exegesis of the Roman centurion who did not desire Jesus' "touch" on his servant but for whom his mere word sufficed. *In harmoniam evangelicam* ad Matt. 8:10.

106 Calvin, in Heb. 4:12.

107 Calvin, *Institutio christianae religionis* 2.1.2.

gance was deeply fixed there.[108] Faith originated not in human experience but in the divine word.[109] It was the reading of scripture that vividly affected a person, adhering properly to the "marrow."[110] It was consequent of such Calvinist belief that the relic of Thomas's bold finger, in repository in the cathedral in Soissons, was destroyed by the Huguenots when they despoiled its sacristy.[111]

Yet others were fascinated by the pericope of Thomas the doubter. Margherita Colonna, an ascetic, and her brother Giacomo, a cardinal, so fervently debated whether or not Thomas had actually put his finger in Christ's wounds at the divine invitation that they became ecstatic.[112] Scenes of disciple's incredulity dated from the fourth century, such as the mosaic in S. Apollinare Nuovo, Ravenna. Most depict Jesus uncovering the wound in his side by parting his garment, while Thomas ventures toward it with his index finger.[113] Andrea del Verrocchio (1435-88) in a novel arrangement places the figures on the diagonal but represents their hands traditionally. Jesus blesses Thomas overhead and parts his own garment to reveal his wound, while the disciple tends his fingers toward it. Their hands, although visually focal, are only finished sculpturally on the sides that are visible to observers from the street.[114] In a painting by Giovanni Battista Cima da Conegliano (1459c.-1517/8) the disciple just touches his index finger to the wound; in another version, his middle finger, but with Jesus taking him by the wrist.[115] The iconography of the grasp by the wrist dated from the thir-

---

108 Calvin, *In harmoniam evangelicam* ad Luke 18:9.

109 Calvin, in John 20:29.

110 Calvin, *Institutio christianae religionis* 1.8.1.

111 Louis Réau, *Histoire du vandalisme: Les monuments détruits de l'art français*, 2 vols. (Paris: Hachette, 1959), 1:74.

112 Livario Oliger, "B. Margherita Colonna," *Lateranum* n.s., 1-2 (1935); cited by Robert Brentano, *Rome before Avignon: A Social History of Thirteenth-Century Rome* (New York: Basic Books, 1974), pp. 174-79.

113 Gertrud Schiller, *Ikonographie der christlichen Kunst*, 2d ed., 3 vols. (Gütersloh: Gerd Mohn, 1969), 3:108-14, 446-55; Angelo Maria Raggi, in *Bibliotheca sanctorum*, 12 vols. (Rome: Istituto Giovanni XXIII nella Pontificia università lateranense, 1961-68), 12:539-44.

114 Charles Seymour, *The Sculpture of Verrocchio* (London: Studio Vista, 1971), p. 59. Andrea del Verrochio, Incredulity of St. Thomas, bronze, ?1479-83, Or S. Michele, Florence; reproduced, pp. 163-64, pls. 63-78; p. 59, figs. 74, 76; Curt Sachs, *Das Tabernakel mit Andreas del Verrocchio Thomasgruppe an Or San Michele zu Florenz: Ein Beitrag zur Florentiner Kunstgeschichte*, Zur Kunstgeschichte des Auslandes, 23 (Strassburg: J. H. E. Heitz, 1904), pl. 1, and see pp. 36-39; Schiller, *Ikonographie der Kunst*, 3:455, fig. 367. For the rationale of the commission, see Andrew Butterfield, "Verrocchio's Christ and St. Thomas: Chronology, Iconography, and Political Context," *Burlington Magazine* 134 (1992):225-33.

115 Cima da Congeliano, Incredulity of St. Thomas, 1502-9, National Gallery, London; reproduced in Peter Humfrey, *Cima da Conegliano* (Cambridge: Cambridge University Press, 1983), pl. 120, and see pp. 110-11; Luigi Menegazzi, *Cima de Conegliano* (Treviso: Canova, 1981), fig. 109, and see pp. 117-18; Jill Dunkerton, Susan Foister, Dillian Gordon, and Nicholas Penny, *Giotto to Dürer: Early Renaissance Painting in the National Gallery* (New Haven, Conn.: Yale University Press with National Gallery Publications, London, 1991), p. 66, fig. 72. Cima da Congeliano, Incredulity of St. Thomas, 1504-5, Galleria dell'Accademia,

teenth-century church of St. Thomas in Strasbourg and it was explored by northern artists. With that human-to-divine contact, Jesus' wound was believed to bleed anew, so that by legend the disciple's hand was forever stained red with his master's blood.[116] The Master of the Bartholomew Altar (c.1450-1510) elevates the scene to heaven, as witnessed by God the Father with uplifted hands, angels, and saints, like Magdalen with her jar of ointment open. Jesus grasps Thomas by the wrist, placing his index and middle fingers to the hilt into the gaping wound, while the disciple's thumb is pressed against his breast.[117] Their hands are central to the composition.[118] Hans Baldung Grien (d.1545) repeats the tactile and manual motif,[119] as does Albrecht Dürer (1471-1528).[120]

But it was Michelangelo Merisi da Caravaggio (1573-1610)[121] who at the end of the century pressed the sense of touch to experiential realism. In his painting the risen Jesus is no longer guiding Thomas manually. The guiding of hands was for mere children. Caravaggio portrayed that pedagogy in his painting of Matthew composing his gospel, where an angel's hand rests on the back of the evangelist's hand as he writes.[122] In his paint-

---

Venice; reproduced in Humfrey, *Cima de Conegliano*, pl. 120, and see pp. 151-52; Menegazzi, *Cima de Conegliano*, fig. 110, and see pp. 118-19.

[116] Réau, *Iconographie de l'art chrétien*, 6 vols. (Paris: Presses universitaires de France, 1955-59), 3-3:1269.

[117] Master of the Bartholomew Altar, Wallraf-Richartz Museum, Cologne; reproduced in Otto H. Förster, *Das Wallraf-Richartz-Museum in Köln*, 2 vols. (Cologne: M. Dumont-Schauberg, 1961), 1:pl. 64; Alfred Stange, *Deutsche Spätgotische Maleri 1430-1500*, vol. 3 of *Deutsche Malerei des Mittelalters*, 3 vols. in 1 (Königstein im Taunus: Karl Robert Langewiesche Nachfolger Hans Köster, 1965), pl. 57; Schiller, *Ikonographie der Kunst*, 3:454, fig. 364.

[118] Lola Sleptzoff, "Le motif de la main dans la peinture allemande, 1420-1520," in *Norms and Variations in Art: Essays in Honour of Moshe Barasch* (Jerusalem: Magnes Press, Hebrew University, 1983), p. 79.

[119] Hans Baldung Grien, Incredulity of St. Thomas, 1512, Kupferstichkabinett, Strassburg; reproduced in Marianne Bernhard, *Hans Baldung Grien: Handzeichnungen Druckgraphik* (Munich: Südwest, 1978), p. 144.

[120] Reproduced in Walter F. Friedlander, *Caravaggio Studies* (Princeton, N.J.: Princeton University Press, 1955), p. 163, fig. 89, with reference to Caravaggio.

[121] Michelangelo Merisi da Caravaggio, Incredulity of St. Thomas, 1599, Sanssouci-Staatliche Schlösser und Gärten, Potsdam; reproduced in Maurizio Marini, *Caravaggio: Michelangelo Merisi da Caravaggio "pictor praestantissimus,"* Quest'Italia, 117 (Rome: Newton Compton, 1987), p. 177, pl. 36, and detail p. 176; Alfred Moir, *The Italian Followers of Caravaggio*, 2 vols. (Cambridge, Mass.: Harvard University Press, 1967), 111:pl. 24, and see p. 110; Howard Hibbard, *Caravaggio* (New York: Harper and Row, 1983), p. 167, fig. 104, and see pp. 167-68, 311; Roger Hinks, *Michelangelo Merisi da Caravaggio: His Life—His Legend—His Works* (London: Faber and Faber, 1953), pl. 28, and see pp. 103-4; Walter F. Friedlander, *Caravaggio Studies* (Princeton, N.J.: Princeton University Press, 1955), pl. 22, and see pp. 161-62; Schiller, *Ikonographie der Kunst*, 3:455, fig. 369.

[122] See Irving Lavin, "Divine Inspiration in Caravaggio's Two 'St. Matthews,'" *Art Bulletin* 56 (1974):77-78, without reference to his Doubting Thomas. Caravaggio, St. Matthew composing his gospel, destroyed, formerly Kaiser-Friedrich Museum, Berlin; reproduced, p. 60, fig. 1. For the hand used for leading and polite guidance, see also Barasch, *Giotto and the Language of Gesture* (Cambridge: Cambridge University Press, 1987), pp. 134-36.

ing of Thomas's incredulity Jesus with a visible nail mark on his hand holds Thomas's wrist. The disciple lifts the upper flap of flesh and probes his index finger past the first joint into the sacred wound. In the sleeve of his own robe there is a similar horizontal slit. The disciple's brow is furrowed, his eyes are wide open in amazement. Two disciples witness the experiment. But it is the involvement of Jesus himself that distinguishes the portrayal. No longer aloof and authoritative, but intimate and involved, he gazes down intently at the hand exploring his wound.

The practice of poking fingers into sacred or solemn places was as old as the impressions into the clay of the prehistoric cave at Gargas.[123] Arcaulf, a bishop of Gaul who was shipwrecked off the west coast of Britain late in the seventh century, narrated to his host Adamnan, abbot of the monastery of Iona, a similar tale about his pilgrimage. He told how the marble column where George the confessor had been flogged preserved a remarkable impression. An unbeliever had thrust at the saint's image on the column with his lance, which penetrated the marble as if it were snow. As his horse collapsed dead beneath him, in falling "he placed his hands against the marble column, and his fingers sank into it as if it were fine dust or mud and remained fast." Just as the lance had penetrated the impenetrable, so did his fingers. The hardened man was unable to withdraw them but in his fright he softened in penitence, until by divine mercy he was released. "Wonderful to relate, to this day there remain in the marble column the prints of his ten fingers inserted up to the roots, and into their place the holy Arculf inserted his own ten fingers they likewise penetrating up to the roots."[124]

Digital insertion was also a test of truth. There was erected at Rome in the portico of the church of S. Maria in Cosmedin a round stone with a hole that gobbled the fingers of liars or perjurers. Oaths had been taken on stones since classical antiquity—from pebbles held in the hand to monoliths touched.[125] The adage "to swear by Jupiter the stone" meant an oath of special sanctity, as derived from the ancient ritual of making treaties by holding stones. Even Augustine considered such an oath valid. If a Christian swore to a pagan by the stone and failed to perform his promise, he perjured himself. The adage literarily meant with all solemnity or with special empha-

---

123 Frequently reported, e.g., Claude Barrière, *L'Art pariétal de la grotte de Gargas: Palaeolithic Art in the Grotte de Gargas*, trans. W. A. Drapkin, 2 vols., Mémoires de l'Institut d'art préhistorique de Toulouse, 3, British Archaeological Reports Supplementary Series, 14 (Oxford: British Archaeological Reports, 1976), especially p. 518.

124 Adamnan, *De locis sanctis* 3.4.13; trans. Denis Meehan, Scriptores latini hiberniae, 3 (Dublin: Dublin Institute for Advanced Studies, 1958), pp. 113, 115; cited by Mary B. Campbell, *The Witness and the Other World: Exotic European Travel Writing, 400-1600* (Ithaca, N.Y.: Cornell University Press, 1988), p. 39.

125 John Webster Spargo, *Virgil the Necromancer: Studies in Virgilian Legend*, Harvard Studies in Comparative Literature, 10 (Cambridge, Mass.: Harvard University Press, 1934), pp. 214-15.

sis.[126] Stones with holes in them were believed especially efficacious for truth. The Roman church with the famous stone "mouth of truth" was erected on or near the site of the Forum Boarium, where cattle traders had raised temples to Truth-Telling and Fair-Play and also to Chastity. It was near the supposed site of the Ara Maxima of Hercules, where the most solemn oaths were sworn, for he was the god of oaths, of the plight of troths, and of the sanctity of pledges. A fourteenth-century poem by a minstrel, Klingsor, recounted the legend of a Roman statue devised by Vergil that bit off the fingers of perjurers. An emperor who suspected his wife of adultery said she could exonerate herself by putting two fingers into the mouth of the image while asserting her innocence. If she lied, its mouth would close on her hand. She advised her lover to dress in rags as a fool and to mingle with the spectators, then embrace her with both arms and kiss her as she approached the test. On the stone she swore that only her husband and that fool had embraced her. The image shattered into a thousand pieces.[127] The initial depiction of the legend was a print by Lucas van Leyden (1491-1533), in whose novel interpretation the statue is a lion.[128] The empress kneels before it, raising her right hand in an oath, while inserting the fingers of her left hand but only to the second joints.

The iconography of doubting Thomas, testing the truth with his finger, displayed a progression in the exploration of the sense of touch toward the divine: from reverential demurral to experiential knowledge. The tentative extension of the disciple's finger at a distance yielded in late medieval art to the coercive gesture of Jesus in grasping his wrist to guide his fingers into the wound. The climax was Caravaggio's remarkable portrayal of Jesus' intentness on the tactile evidence of his own body. The iconography of faithful Magdalen in the *Noli me tangere* scenes displayed the reverse tendency. The expansive gesture of her out-flung arms, which climaxed in Michelangelo's cartoon executed by Jacopo da Pontormo (1494-1557), abated in Agnolo Bronzino's (1502-72) version. Although her arms are still outstretched, she loses her erect stance. Magdalen is bent in the middle, about to genuflect.[129] In Antonio da Correggio's (c.1489/94-1534) painting she is seated on her haunches, while Jesus stands pointing to heaven and gesturing

---

[126] Erasmus, *Adagia* 2.6.33, in *Opera omnia* (Leiden), 2, citing Augustine, *Sermones* 180.13.

[127] Spargo, *Virgil the Necromancer*, pp. 214-15, 36-37, and for later legends, pp. 207-27.

[128] Lucas van Leyden, woodcut, Mouth of truth, c. 1512, Museum of Fine Arts, Boston; reproduced in Ellen S. Jacobowitz and Stephanie Loeb Stepanek, *Prints of Lucas van Leyden and His Contemporaries* (Princeton, N.J.: National Gallery of Art, Washington, with Princeton University Press, 1992), p. 123, and see p. 121.

[129] Agnolo Bronzino, Noli me tangere, Louvre, Paris; reproduced in Arthur McComb, *Agnolo Bronzino, His Life and Works* (Cambridge, Mass.: Harvard University Press, 1928), pl. 41, and see his comment about "her body bowed down," p. 75.

down to her. She no longer extends her arms to touch him.[130] In Federico Barocci's (1532-1612) painting toward the end of the century she is seated with one hand musingly to her head, the other symbolically on her jar of ointment.[131] She is not about to touch him.

Such inconsistency, even contradiction, about the human sense of touch toward the divine reality could mingle in a single person. Calvin evidenced such tactile confusion. In criticizing Thomas's unbelief, he wrote *palpo* to derogate the disciple's sensual experiment. The verb means "to stroke, to touch softly, to pat." Yet in the argument from design in his commentary on Genesis he had used the same verb to explain the universal human feeling of the multiform universe: "with the hands we gently touch."[132] In his *Institutio christianae religionis* he cited Paul on how the blind could even discover God by "patting," a gentle image of lightly touching his contours, manifest in creation, with the human fingertips.[133] In commenting on the specific verse of Acts 17:27, he wrote that "the goodness of God is especially noteworthy, because he so familiarly insinuates himself that he is also able to be patted by the blind."[134] The fault of Thomas, the doubter and experimenter, was that he had the plain evidence of the sense of sight yet demanded the added testimony of touch.

Yet Christians in the sixteenth century, deprived of the visual presence of their risen Lord, could like blinded creatures grope about the universe with the sense of touch to feel for the faint contours of the divine face. Although they could not so worship God with their hands, neither should their hands be idle. Calvin stated, "We do not say that religion and sanctity consist in the external, in adoring God with the eyes, hands, or feet; but we say that external service is an appendage and accessory of spiritual service."[135] The gestures customarily observed in prayer were exercises toward reverence. The ceremony of raising the hands was universal in time and space and still in practice, he observed. Yet there was naturally instilled in humans the principle that "their prayers are lawful only when their minds are

---

130 Correggio, Noli me tangere, c. 1520, Prado, Madrid; reproduced in Giuliano Ercoli, *Arte e fortuna del Correggio* (Modena: Articoli, 1982), pl. XXXVI, and detail XXXVII; Stefano Bottari, *Correggio*, Collana d'arte, 1 (n. p.: G. Barbèra, n. d.), pl. XIII; Cecil Gould, *The Paintings of Correggio* (London: Faber and Faber, 1976), pl. 98, and see pp. 224-26; Corrado Ricci, *Antonio Allegri da Correggio: His Life, His Friends, and His Time*, trans. Florence Simmonds (London, 1896), pp. 234-35.

131 Federico Barocci, Noli me tangere, Uffizi, Florence; reproduced in Andrea Emiliani, *Federico Barocci (Urbino 1535-1612)*, 2 vols. (Bologna: Nuova alfa, 1985), 2:238, and see pp. 238-49, figs. 491-523; Harold Olsen, *Federico Barocci* (Copenhagen: Munksgaard, 1962), pp. 184-85, pl. 57, and see p. 183.

132 Calvin, *In libros Mosis* argumentum.

133 Calvin, *Institutio christianae religionis* 1.5.3.

134 Calvin, in Acts 17:27. Yet in his commentary in Is. 59:10 all humans pat desperately in the dark for the wall of a constricted labyrinth, unable to locate its exit.

135 Calvin, *Response à un certain holandois*, in *Opera omnia* (Brunswick), 9:597; cited by Eire, *War Against the Idols*, p. 259.

uplifted." So the rite of uplifted hands reminded people of their extreme distance from God, unless they should also elevate their thoughts. "But how rarely is there one who, in raising up his hands, is not aware of his own apathy, since his heart stays on the ground?"[136] Hands could never touch God for Calvin but they might signify the desire to do so, not physically but mentally.

Yet others wanted to touch God manually, as had Magdalen and Thomas, at least imaginatively. Devotion to the infant Jesus was one opportunity for the expression of that desire, since in his vulnerability he had to be handled by adult humans. Was he not most frequently portrayed in the arms of his adoring but capable mother? Perhaps she might lend him during prayer to her devotees. A popular book of meditations promoted the practice of fondling the infant Jesus. "His benignity will patiently let Himself be touched by you as you wish and will not attribute it to presumption but to love."[137] Hagiography recounted how the saints cuddled him, nursed him, bathed him.[138] Margery Kempe (b.c.1373), a bourgeois wife, demonstrated a tactile female devotion. In her meditation she swaddled Jesus with fair white cloths, assuring him that she would not bind him tightly.[139] There was even a cult of nuns playing with baby dolls, as if they were Jesus, a devotional practice that became a commercial business. The dolls were idols, Girolamo Savonarola (1452-98) criticized. Yet they were but the realistic conclusion of the imaginative prayer proposed in such popular books as the meditations ascribed to Bonaventure or Ludolph of Saxony's life of Christ. They urged the devout to receive and hold the infant Jesus in their arms, to kiss him, then return him to his mother's embrace.[140] Such pious authors and actors extended meditatively what had commonly been an actual ritual in classical antiquity, the dressing and bathing of religious statues.[141]

Devotion to the gaping wounds of Christ crucified was another access to tangible experience of the divine. There was ordinary prayer to the single

---

136 Calvin, *Institutio christianae religionis* 3.20.33; 3.20.16; 3.20.5; 3.20.16; trans. Battles, 2:873.

137 Pseudo-Bonaventure, *Meditationes vitae Christi* 7; *Meditations on the Life of Christ: An Illustrated Manuscript of the Fourteenth Century*, trans. Isa Ragusa and Rosalie B. Green (Princeton, N.J.: Princeton University Press, 1961), p. 39.

138 David Herlihy, *Medieval Households* (Cambridge, Mass.: Harvard University Press, 1985), pp. 120, 126, 125. See also Shulamith Shahar, "Infants, Infant Care, and Attitudes toward Infancy in the Medieval Lives of Saints," *Journal of Psychohistory* 10 (1982-83):283-91.

139 *The Book of Margery Kempe* 1.6, 86

140 Christiane Klapisch-Zuber, "Holy Dolls: Play and Piety in Florence in the Quattrocento," in eadem, *Women, Family, and Ritual in Renaissance Italy*, trans. Lydia Cochrane (Chicago: University of Chicago Press, 1985), pp. 324, 323, citing Girolamo Savonarola, *Predica* 14 in idem, *Prediche sopra Amos e Zaccaria*; Pseudo-Bonaventure, *Meditationes* 60; Ludolf of Saxony, *Vita Jesu Christi*, 1:77-78.

141 For the ancient practice, see Barasch, *Icon: Studies in the History of an Idea* (New York: New York University Press, 1991), pp. 34-36.

parts of his body, much like Magdalen's inquiry about his hands in the drama. An elaborate fifteenth-century prayer carried an indulgence of three hundred days for each of his fifteen limbs.[142] It was his suffering body that was most attended, as in Juan Manuel's medieval *Libro de los estados*, which considered the pain in its every part: eyes, hair, cheeks, neck, side, arms, shoulders, legs, hands, feet.[143] A rhythmic prayer attributed to Bernard of Clairvaux was the earliest example of such meditation. It proceeded like the description of a beautiful woman by the topic of *effictio*, only in reverse: from feet to knees, hands, side, breast, heart, face. The stanzas on the hands considered them as fatigued in their extension, cruelly punctured with nails, and profusely bleeding. The author prayed Jesus to draw him with his arms and defend him in danger.[144]

Meditation on his wounds dwelled on the puncturing, nail by nail, of his hands and feet. Although there was no scriptural description of the fastening of Jesus to the cross, patristic authors had invented the nails by inference: reading backward from the reference in the story of Thomas and forward by prophecy from Ps. 21:17. In a dialogue attributed to Anselm, Mary explained how the executioners "drove in first one nail so thick that it filled the wound it caused, and no blood could flow. Then they took ropes and dragged the other arm of my son Jesus and drove in a second nail. After this they dragged his feet with ropes and drove in one very sharp nail, and he was so stretched that all his bones appeared."[145] In the popular version attributed to Bonaventure, Jesus voluntarily "opens those royal arms, and, extending His most beautiful hands, stretches them up to His crucifiers." The soldiers "taking his arms, violently extended them, and most cruelly fixing them to the cross." The soldier behind took his right hand and firmly affixed it, while the soldier on the left side took his left hand. He "pulls and extends it as far as possible, puts in another nail, drives it through, and hammers it in." The ladders were removed, and Jesus "hangs with the weight of His body pulling Him down, supported only by the nails transfixing His hands." Indeed, "those three nails sustain the whole weight of his

---

142 Sixten Ringbom, *Icon to Narrative: The Rise of the Dramatic Close-Up in Fifteenth-Century Devotional Painting*, Acta academiae Åboenis, A-31 (Åbo: Åbo Akademi, 1965), p. 49 n. 53.

143 Juan Manuel, *Libro de los estados* 1.57; cited by J. N. Hillgarth, *The Spanish Kingdoms*, 2 vols. (Oxford: Clarendon, 1976-78), 1:148.

144 Inter Bernard of Clairvaux, *Rythmica oratio ad unum quodlibet membrorum Christi patientis et a cruce pendentis*, in *Patrologia latina*, 184:1319-23; cited by Ringbom, *Icon to Narrative*, p. 49 n. 58. The poem is not in the modern critical edition.

145 F. P. Pickering, *Literature and Art in the Middle Ages* (Coral Gables, Fla.: University of Miami Press, 1970), pp. 253, 272, 238-39, citing Pseudo-Anselm, *Dialogus cum B. V. Maria* 10. For the hands of Christ in his passion, see also Karl Gross, *Menschenhand und Gotteshand in Antike und Christentum*, ed. Wolfgang Speyer (Stuttgart: Anton Hiersemann, 1985), pp. 449-53.

body."[146] A female mourner in Hugo van der Goes's (1435?-82) painting of the Lamentation clutches in her hands the very nails plucked from his pierced palms. (The other panel of the diptych shows Eve plucking the forbidden fruit from the tree and Adam with an outstretched hand).[147] Yet not only pious prayers but also sorcerous spells called on Christ's wounds and nails.[148] Calvin wrote against seeking grace in those nails. And he complained in his inventory of relics that they were ubiquitous: one on the crown of Constantine, others multiplied in fourteen locations.[149]

A broadsheet with a pictorial facilitation for prayer associated Christ's wounds in a marginal note with the sense of touch.[150] The consideration of the sense of touch in *Ancrene Riwle* asserted that Christ suffered in that sense more than in any other, so that he might comfort others in pain and divert them from pleasure. He felt the pain not only localized in his wounds but throughout his body; indeed, it penetrated and pierced his soul. He suffered most in the sense of touch because his flesh was exceptionally sensitive, as born from a tender maiden. The ascetic counsel adjured the anchoresses by the nails that fixed his hands to the cross to keep their hands to themselves inside their windows. It blamed touching with the hands or any other part between a man and an anchoress shameful and scandalous. When the women were tempted to sensuality, they should invest their feeling in Christ. "Touch Him with as much love as you sometimes feel for a man."[151] The medieval monk John Whiterig, meditating on Christ's affliction in the five senses, associated touch with "fierce pain in the head, for the crown of thorns pierced it so grievously." He noted more usually the piercing with sharp nails of the hands that had fashioned the universe.[152] The pain of Jesus' suffering was believed tactile, since the existence of separate receptors in the skin for pain was then unknown. Tactile sensations—touch and temperature—resulted medically from moderate

---

[146] Pseudo-Bonaventure, *Meditationes vitae Christi* 68; trans. Ragusa and Green, pp. 333-34; cited also by Pickering, *Literature and Art*, pp. 240-42.

[147] Hugo van der Goes, Lamentation, Kunsthistorisches Museum, Vienna; reproduced in Friedrich Winkler, *Das Werk des Hugo van der Goes* (Berlin: Walter de Gruyter, 1964), pl. 23, and for the diptych, see pp. 37-45; Barasch, "The Crying Face," *Artibus et historiae* 15 (1987):28, fig. 9.

[148] Kieckhefer, *European Witch Trials*, p. 34.

[149] Calvin, *In harmoniam evangelicam* ad Matt. 14:36; *Traité des reliques*, pp. 60, 61.

[150] Passionis Jesu Christi via contemplationis et meditationis quadruplex, woodcut broadsheet of the crucifixion (Augsburg: Ludwig Hohenwang, c. 1477); reproduced in David Freedberg, *The Power of Images: Studies in the History and Theory of Response* (Chicago: University of Chicago Press, 1989), p. 176, fig. 96.

[151] *Ancrene Riwle* 2, 7; *The "Ancrene Riwle" (The Corpus MS.: Ancrene Wisse)*, trans. M. B. Salu (London: Burns and Oates, 1955), pp. 51, 180.

[152] John Whiterig, *The Monk of Farne* 14; cited by Kieckhefer, *Unquiet Souls: Fourteenth-Century Saints and Their Religious Milieu* (Chicago: University of Chicago Press, 1984), p. 103.

stimulation of the sensory nerves in the skin, while pain was thought to be provoked by a violent irritation to the same nerves.[153]

Prints of only the wounded hands or feet of Jesus circulated. Johannes Molanus (1533-85) considered them permissible, not against scripture. The countenance of Christ was not impaired in them, he decided, just because it was cut up and separated into parts. The practice was "popular," but such simplicity was not disagreeable to God, since it fostered a singular meditation on the blessed wounds.[154] Such meditation was marked by a vivid realism. Sixteenth-century devotional poetry in French could observe each detail with precision: the nail piercing the delicate hand, exposing the tendon, the nerve, and the vein in "the strange incision of this anatomy."[155] When Michelangelo gave Vittoria Colonna (1492-1547) a drawing of the crucifixion, she examined it with a magnifying glass and a mirror for mistakes (although she found none).[156] As she reflected traditionally on the crucified hand in "The Triumph of Christ's Cross":

> and wounded was the hand that guides heaven,
> and gives light to the sun, life to mortals,
> virtue below, and eternal glory above.

The cross should be worshipped, she thought, "with clasped hands."[157]

Others desired Jesus' wounded hands to clasp them. The medieval ascetic Angela of Foligno, who stripped naked before a crucifix and dedicated to it each of her bodily members, desired its outstretched arms to embrace her soul.[158] The renaissance courtesan Gaspara Stampa (c.1523-c.1554) also poetized:

> And I pray that you'll extend your hand to me

---

153 Rudolph E. Siegel, *Galen on Sense Perception: His Doctrines, Observations, and Experiments on Vision, Hearing, Smell, Taste, Touch, and Pain, and Their Historical Sources* (New York: S. Karger, 1970), pp. 181, 191.

154 Freedberg, "The Hidden God: Image and Interdiction in the Netherlands in the Sixteenth Century," *Art History* 3 (1982):136, 148 n. 35, citing Johannes Molanus, *De historia ss. imaginum et picturarum pro vero eorum usu contra abusus*, p. 93.

155 Gabrielle de Coignard, *Oeuvres chrestiennes*, in Terence C. Cave and Michel Jeanneret, *Metamorphoses spirituelles: Anthologie de la poésie religieuse française, 1570-1630* (Paris: José Corti, 1972), p. 141. For treatments of hands, see also pp. 143-46.

156 See Robert J. Clements, *The Poetry of Michelangelo* (New York: New York University Press, 1965), p. 278. For the design, see Guido Cimino, *Il crocifisso di Michelangelo per Vittoria Colonna (Storia di un ritrovamento)* (Rome: Edizioni cremonese, 1967); Francesco Negi Arnoldi, "Origine e diffusione del crocifisso barocco con l'immagine del Cristo vivente," *Storia dell'arte* 20 (1974):57-80. For Michelangelo's drawings of the crucifixion, see Clark, *Nude*, pp. 253-56; Frederick Hartt, *Michelangelo*, 3 vols. (New York: Harry N. Abrams, n. d.), 3:216. For the crucifix in the sixteenth century, see Paul Thoby, *Le crucifix, des origines au Concile de Trente: Étude iconographique* (Nantes: Bellanger, 1959), pp. 215-31; idem, *Supplément* (Nantes: A. Bellanger, 1963), pp. 39-41.

157 Vittoria Colonna, *Rime spirituali disperse* 36; trans. Joseph Gibaldi, in *Women Writers of the Renaissance and Reformation*, ed. Katherina M. Wilson (Athens: University of Georgia Press, 1987), p. 43.

158 Angela of Foligno, *De vere fidelium experientia* 11, 66, 151.

And pull me from this stormy sea, whence I
Could never rise through efforts of my own.[159]

Michelangelo's serial drawings of the crucifixion depict outstretched arms, just as he poetized. He was converting, he wrote, from the arts of sculpture and painting toward "that divine love that opened his arms on the cross to take us in." So he prayed,

O Lord, in my last hours,
stretch out toward me your merciful arms,
take me from myself and make me one who'll please you.

The promise of the grace of repentance and the hope of salvation resided for Michelangelo in "your nails and both of your palms."[160]

As if to facilitate meditation on a tactile salvation, there were crucifixes made with moveable arms, not just by artisans but by no less a sculptor than Donatello (?1386-1466) for S. Croce in Florence. The arms were attached to the torso by ball-and-socket joints, and sometimes, when the limbs moved, the wound in the side bled through a connected vessel. In medieval religion such crucifixes functioned principally in the liturgical dramas of Holy Week, as in Benedictine abbeys. After the procession on Good Friday with the crucifix, its body was detached from the cross. The arms were changed in position from extended across to down at the sides, until they would be unwrapped from the shroud on Easter in victory. The crucifix with moveable arms may have been the exemplar for literary and artistic images of Christ leaning from the cross to embrace people. As Caesarius of Heisterbach recounted the miracle of a medieval monk before a crucifix, "Then He withdrew his most merciful arms from the cross, embraced his servant, drawing him to his breast as one being dear to him, in sign of mutual friendship. He clasped him close; and by that embrace destroyed his strongest temptations."[161] Yet tactile values were not straightforward. Crucifixes were also alleged to be mutilated by male wizards, who removed or

---

159 Gaspara Stampa, *Rime varie* 309; trans. Frank J. Warnke, in idem, *Three Women Poets: Renaissance and Baroque: Louise Labé, Gaspara Stampa, and sor Juana Inés de la Cruz* (Lewisburg, Pa.: Bucknell University Press, 1979), p. 79; idem, in *Women Writers*, p. 20.

160 Michelangelo, *Rime* 285.13-14; 161.15-17; 290.5; trans. Saslow, pp. 476, 317, 484. He also notes the similarity of the literary arms outstretched to the drawings of the crucifixion, p. 477 n. 14, as does Michael Hirst, *Michelangelo and his Drawings* (New Haven, Conn.: Yale University Press, 1988), pp. 57-58. For *Rime* 285 and its variants, see also Glauco Cambon, *Michelangelo's Poetry: Fury of Form* (Princeton, N.J.: Princeton University Press, 1985), pp. 133-34; for *Rime* 161, see also Clements, *Poetry of Michelangelo*, p. 125. Michelangelo punned on "arm" in epitaphs for Cecchino Bracchi in *Rime* 184, 212, 213, 217, 221, 222.

161 G. Taubert and J. Taubert, "Mittelalterliche Kruzifixe mit schwenkbaren Armen: Ein Beitrag zur Verwendung von bildwerken in der Liturgie," *Zeitschrift für Deutschen Vereins für Kunstwissenschaft* 23 (1969):79-121; Freedberg, *Power of Images*, pp. 286-87, 294, 305-6, citing Caesarius of Heisterbach, *Dialogus miraculorum* 8.13, 16.

shortened the arm to procure invulnerability in that limb. Some carried the severed arms about them to protect their own bodies.[162]

While many reproached Thomas, the incredulous disciple with the bold finger, other devout persons dared to press their entire bodies right into the wounds of Jesus. As Bonaventure counseled a Franciscan nun, she should draw close to Christ crucified—and much more. "And be not content, as the blessed apostle Thomas was, merely to see in his hands the print of the nails or to thrust your hand into his side," he wrote, "but rather go right in, through the opening in his side, to the very heart of Jesus." There she would be transformed by love, fastened by nails, pierced by the lance, and wounded by the sword, to her own personal crucifixion.[163] Catherine of Siena advised not merely penetrating those wounds toward death but living there in residence. "Make his wounds your home."[164] Such piety was not just the devotion of ascetic and charismatic women. As sophisticated a humanist as Petrarch also sought repose there, "in whose holy wounds I pray you to quiet my heart."[165]

The sublime experience was the spiritual embrace of Juan de Ypes y Álvarez (1542-91), or John of the Cross. Although, like Calvin, he dared not in the austere purity of his faith to touch God, he was intimately touched by him. The notion of a spiritual touch was not novel. Origen had commented on the scriptural Song of Songs how "Christ became the object of each sense of the soul." He was light to illuminate, word to be heard, bread to be tasted, unction to be smelled. "He became the Word made flesh palpable and perceptible, so that the interior person can take hold of the Word of life."[166] Even Ficino, who banished touch from the realm of the intellect, appealed metaphorically to that sense to express contact with God, who existed beyond the intellect. It was "a touch that surpasses understanding, a unifying touch so to speak, that surpasses the intellect and unites the soul itself to the universal unity and goodness, not by the fictive link of the intellect but by the true union of the substance itself." This union resulted in joy, "an intense pleasure, intrinsic, universal, like that of a taste and touch superior to the intellect, savoring intimately and touching a sweetness itself superior to the intelligible." Such substantive delectation was like that of

---

162 Sprenger and Institoris, *Malleus maleficarum* 2.1.16.

163 Bonaventure, *De perfectione vitae ad sorores* 6.2; cited in translation by John Moorman, *A History of the Franciscan Order: From Its Origins to the Year 1517* (Oxford: Clarendon, 1968), pp. 260-61.

164 Catherine of Siena, *Epistolario* 70; cited by Kieckhefer, *Unquiet Souls*, p. 109.

165 Petrarch, *Canzoniere* 366.46-52; *Petrarch's Lyric Poems: The "Rime sparse" and Other Lyrics*, trans. Robert M. Durling (Cambridge, Mass.: Harvard University Press, 1976), p. 579; cited in Boyle, *Petrarch's Genius: Pentimento and Prophecy* (Berkeley and Los Angeles: University of California Press, 1992), pp. 151-52.

166 Origen, *Commentarium in Canticum canticorum* 2; cited by Karl Rahner, "Le début d'une doctrine des cinq sens spirituels chez Origène," *Revue d'ascétique et de mystique* 13 (1932):120.

touch; yet "not of a contiguous object, as in the senses, but of deeply penetrating and being penetrated."[167]

It was by the sense of touch that John of the Cross expressed his own supreme and rare experiences.[168] Unlike Ficino, who only described the natural ascent of the mind to the contemplation and love of God beyond that mind, John of the Cross witnessed to the supernatural embrace of the soul by God. In his Trinitarian romance on the verse "In principio erat Verbum" (John 1:1) he poetized the Son speaking of the Father's gift to him of the creation.

"And I shall hold her in my arms,
To burn there in your love. . ."

It was the just among humans who formed the embraceable body of his bride,

Whom He would gather up
Tenderly into His arms,
There to give her His love;
And thus would bear her to the Father
United into one.

Where she would joy with that same joy
Possessed by God Himself;
For as the Father and the Son
And He who issues from them

All live within each other,
So also would the Bride;
Absorbed, immersed within her God

167 Ficino, *Theologia platonica* 12.3, p. 165; 18.8.1.

168 Rahner, "La doctrine des 'sens spirituels' au Moyen Âge en particulier chez saint Bonaventure," *Revue d'ascétique et de mystique* 14 (1933):295-96. For touch as conveying union, see also Elizabeth Teresa Howe, *Mystical Imagery: Santa Teresa de Jesús and san Juan de la Cruz*, American University Studies, series 2, 76 (New York: Peter Lang, 1988), pp. 182-83, 190-91. There is an indiscriminate collection of citations on the sense of touch in the apologetic work by Auguste Poulain, *The Graces of Interior Prayer: A Treatise on Mystical Theology*, trans. Leonora L. Yorke Smith, 6th ed. (London: Kegan Paul, Trench, Treubner, 1911), pp. 89-90, 92-95, 102-12. Scholarship commonly understands union in John of the Cross intellectually, by resort to his acceptance of the Aristotelian epistemological principle that there is nothing in the intellect that was not first in the senses, in *Subida de monte Carmelo* 1.3.3; 2.12.4. E. g., Steven Payne, *John of the Cross and the Cognitive Value of Mysticism: An Analysis of Sanjuanist Teaching and its Philosophical Implications for Contemporary Discussion of Mystical Experience*, Texts and Studies in the History of Philosophy, 37 (Dordrecht: Kluwer, 1990), p. 20; Howe, *Mystical Imagery*, p. 183. Yet John of the Cross did not identify touch as intellectual or even cognitive. He wrote of a mystical theology, called contemplation, as the science of love—a knowledge through love—but it was love, symbolized by touch, that was unitive. Contemplation was an effect of union, not its identity. John of the Cross, *Comentario* 27.

She would live His very life.[169]

There was nothing intellectualist about that concept of the unification of the just persons as "bride" with the unified persons of the Trinity. It transcended the contemplative tradition. The poetic concept was the Son gathering and carrying in his arms the bride to the Father "united into one." The bride would there enjoy the divine joy of living within God just as God enjoyed his personal life. The concept was ultimately ontological, as expressed in affective and tactile terms. The initial human experience of the union was in the incarnation when

His arms embraced closely
The Bride He brought in,
Whom the radiant mother
Laid down in a crib.[170]

Jesus was the just man whom the Son intimately embraced in union as his bride in the incarnation. (And his mother by imitation took him into her own arms.)

The embrace unto divinization of other just persons was revealed by John of the Cross in his lyric poetry. It was preceded by a lesser union of love, which he described as a wounding. In the poem "Noche oscura" he related how,

With his unhurried hand
He wounded my neck
And all my senses suspended there.[171]

The wound was literally inflicted by God "with his serene (*sereno*) hand." Since it transpired at dark of night, there was allusion to "the night dew (*el sereno*)." And that allusion trailed the scriptural metaphor of dew as divine grace, blessing, provision, manna, and erotic love (Song 5:2).[172] In his poem "Llama de amor viva" John of the Cross resorted to another element, that of fire.

O living flame of love,
How tenderly you wound
And sear my soul's most inward centre!
....
O cautery that heals!
O consuming wound!
O soothing hand! O touch so fine and light

---

169 John of the Cross, "'In principio erat Verbum' acerca de la Santísima Trinidad" 3, 4; Gerald Brenan, *St. John of the Cross: His Life and Poetry, with a Translation of his Poetry by Lynda Nicholson* (Cambridge: Cambridge University Press, 1973), pp. 193, 197.

170 John of the Cross, "'In principio erat Verbum'" 9; trans. Nicholson, p. 205.

171 John of the Cross, "Noche oscura" lines 32-35; trans. Nicholason, p. 147.

172 Gen. 27:28; Ex. 16:13-14; Num. 11:9; Deut. 32:2; 2 Sam. 1:21; 1 Kings 17:1; Job 29:19; 38:28; Ps. 110:3; 133:3; Is. 18:4; 26:19; Hos. 14:5; Mic. 5:7; Hag. 1:10; Zech. 8:12.

That savors of eternity
And satisfies all dues;
Slaying, you have converted death to life.[173]

The cautery was literally "smooth, soft, delicate, mellow" (*suave*). The hand was "soft, tender, mild, bland" (*blanda*); its touch "delicate, gentle, refined" (*delicado*). And it savored not of "eternity," as the suspension of temporality, but literally of an ontological state, "eternal life." Again, the tactile connoted the affective, and both meanings tended toward the ontological. In his prose commentary he explained initially that the poem was about divine union, with the flame as a metaphor for the Holy Spirit. On the second stanza he commented that the hand was the Father, the touch the Son, and the wound the Spirit. The hand was "the merciful and omnipotent Father." Because he was rich and powerful, he was generous and giving of graces to the soul, especially the merciful touch of the Son. That Son was the delicate touch, who in his divine nature subtly penetrated the substance of the soul with delights. That immensely subtle and delicate touch refined, polished, and purified the substance of the soul with its ineffable divine substance. Sensual activity, being merely natural, could not attain to the supernatural spirit. It required restraint, then abandonment. Yet conversely, the spirit could overflow into the senses.[174]

It was in his *Cántico espiritual* that John of the Cross revealed—beyond such affective touches, however substantive— the ontological union of the full embrace. Commenting on the hand of the bridegroom on the latch of the beloved's door (Song 5:4), he explained "the divine touch." The lover's touch was his love; his hand, his mercy. The hand was the manner by which he penetrated the soul according to its perfection of spiritual heat. The womb of the beloved that trembled at his touch was "the will," in which the touch was given. The Son's promise in the romance, to gather the bride into his arms and bear her to the Father for a unitive experience of the Trinitarian life and love, was poetically fulfilled in the spiritual canticle. The soul, after searching the woods and thickets planted by her beloved's hand, entered the amorous pleasance to repose:

Her neck reclined
To rest upon the Loved One's gentle arms.[175]

As explained in the prose commentary, the entry into the pleasance represented the rescue of the bride from sensual and diabolical hands. The bridegroom held her now like the shepherd who set the stray lamb on his shoul-

[173] John of the Cross, "Llama de amor viva" lines 1-3, 7-12; trans. Nicholson, p. 163.

[174] John of the Cross, *Commentario* 1, 2. Cf. *molli brachio, levi brachio,* "with a gentle touch, a light touch," as meaning work not taken seriously. Erasmus, *Adagia* 1.4.27; *The Collected Works of Erasmus*, trans. Margaret Mann Phillips (Toronto: University of Toronto Press, 1971), 31:339.

[175] John of the Cross, *Cántico espiritual* 25.6; 22.139-40; trans. Nicholson, p. 157.

ders (Luke 15:4-5), or the woman who found the drachma and lifted it high for all to see and rejoice (vv. 8-9). "And it is wonderful to see his pleasure in carrying the rescued, perfected soul on his shoulders, held there by his hands in this desired union." Then, "he takes her now in his arms. . . as though she were placed in the arms of her bridegroom." There she "experiences an intimate spiritual embrace, which is a veritable embrace, by means of which she lives the life of God."

What transpired was the substantial transformation of the soul in God. The embrace as the supreme touch, divine to human, was no revival of the classical topic of human dignity by erect posture. Rather, it reversed it, just as John of the Cross inverted the classical order of the valuation of the senses by ascribing the primacy to touch, rather than to sight. The human soul was metaphorically not upright before God, on its own two feet. The very neck that purposed anatomically to hold up the head was "wounded" by the divine touch and it "reclined" on God.

Precisely how it reclined would have provided a classical medical diagnostic, since the healthy position, in which most people relaxed, was to lie on the side. "But to lie on the back, with the arms and the legs stretched out is less good," Hippocrates considered.[176] Yet the neck inclined backwards was the convention since classical antiquity for both sexual coition and spiritual union. It signified an excess of pleasure, or ecstasy, as in the Dionysiac processional. The maenads in their nocturnal dancing were depicted with their faces heavenward, their necks hyperextended backwards, as if dislocated from the rest of the body. The classical form was revived in sixteenth-century art. The neck thrown back translated religious ecstasy as pleasurable love or as fainting, as in portrayals of Mary Magdalen. The neck was also exaggerated downwards to express submission, as in the figure of the archangel Gabriel in scenes of the annunciation (or in the recommended posture for women before the Eucharistic elevation). The pose also signified extreme sadness—from Niobe weeping to Christ crucified or deposed, with his head drooping.[177]

In John of the Cross' poetry, just as the neck was disabled, so were the hands that the upright posture enabled to act unengaged. Only the gentle arms of the divine lover appeared in his verse. In his prose commentary he explained the reclined posture of the bride. "To recline the neck on the arms

---

176 Hippocrates, *Prognostics* 3; *Hippocrates*, trans. W. H. S. Jones, 6 vols. (New York: G. P. Putnam's Sons, 1923), 2:13.

177 See L. P. Fischer, "L'esthétique du cou humain adulte à travers l'histoire de l'art," in *Conférences d'histoire de la médicine, Cycle 1990-1991* (Lyon: Collection fondation Marcel Mérieux, 1991), pp. 43-44; Barasch, "The Tossed-Back Head: The Ambiguity of a Gesture in Renaissance Art," in idem, "Imago hominis": Studies in the Language of Art (Vienna: IRSA, 1991), pp. 152-60; rpt. from *Spiegel und Gleichnis: Festschrift für Jacob Taubes*, ed. U. Bolz and W. Hubener (Würzburg, 1983), pp. 11-22. Although Barasch quotes John of the Cross's oxymorons, such as divine light as dark night, he omits the verse about the neck.

of God is to have her strength, or, better, her weakness, now united to the strength of God, because the arms of God signify the strength of God " That posture was appropriately designated the state of spiritual marriage, "for now God as the soul's strength and sweetness" sheltered it from evil and habituated it to the enjoyment of good. The bed upon which the soul reclined was the very bridegroom.[178]

John of the Cross developed the marital theme, with the voice of the bridegroom speaking.

"Beneath the apple tree,
There was your betrothal to me sealed.
There I gave my hand to you
And you were healed
Where once before your mother was defiled."[179]

Allusion was to the tree of Eden, by which human nature was depraved and lost by Adam's grasp, and to the tree of the cross, by which it was redeemed and restored by Christ's arms. The maternal reference was not to Eve; it was, rather, a personification of the original human nature as violated in both parents, male and female. John of the Cross explained the bridegroom's giving of his hand to the bride as favor and help, which raised her from her miserable and low state to his company and contract.[180] Matrimony had classically been signified by the joining of the right hands of the betrothed couple (*dextrarum iunctio*).[181] The circular wedding band was the abiding symbol of that union, and clasped hands were specifically reproduced on rings called *fede* for "faith."[182] As a renaissance courtier affirmed, the tongue of a lover might lie, but a pledge in hand was infallible proof.[183] Clasped hands endured as the renaissance emblem of uxorial fidelity.[184] It was even believed that touch was the primordial sign of social union. "God instituted

---

[178] John of the Cross, *Commentario* 22; *Selected Writings*, trans. Kieran Kavanaugh (New York: Paulist, 1987), pp. 256, 258, 259.

[179] John of the Cross, *Cántico espiritual* 25.6; trans. mine; 23.141-45; trans. Nicholson, p. 157.

[180] John of the Cross, *Commentario* 23.

[181] See Susan Treggiari, *Roman Marriage: "Iusti coniuges" from the Time of Cicero to the Time of Ulpian* (Oxford: Clarendon, 1991), pp. 149-51, 164-65; Gross, *Menschenhand und Gotteshand*, pp. 391-93; Jean-Claude Schmitt, *La raison des gestes dans l'Occident médiéval* (Paris: Gallimard, 1990), p. 329.

[182] Gerald Taylor and Diana Scarisbrick, *Finger Rings from Ancient Egypt to the Present Day* (London: Lund Humphries for the Ashmolean Museum, Oxford and the Worshipful Company of Goldsmiths, 1978), pp. 71-72.

[183] Stefano Guazzo, *Civil conversatione* 4.

[184] Seymour Slive, *Frans Hals*, 2 vols. (London: Phaidon, 1970), 1:180; H. Diane Russell with Bernadine Barnes, *Eva/Ave: Woman in Renaisance and Baroque Prints* (Washington, D.C.: National Gallery of Art with the Feminist Press at City University, New York, 1990), p. 64.

society in the first couple, who walked 'arm in arm' so that they might live 'as one.'"[185]

So were other relationships given by hand. Fides, the Roman personification of good faith or mutual trust, had as her symbol covered hands. A sacrificer to her cult was required to have his hand covered with a white cloth,[186] like a Catholic woman about to receive the Eucharist. A kiss to the hand was supplicatory, although renaissance manners denounced it as "a silly habit." More solemn was the handshake.[187] Joined hands were a symbol of faith sworn.[188] The giving of hands was even appropriated for evil compact. When a bawd desired a wife's confidence, this dialogue ensued:

> Raffaela. "Give me your hand."
> Margherita. "Here it is. Now speak."[189]

Other examples were the ancient swearing of oaths on stones, from which developed digital insertion as a test of truth, and the feudal gesture of commendation, from which developed the liturgical usage of hands joined at the palms. Grasping a wrist meant power, either to rescue or to rape. In the common organic metaphor of the body politic the arms or hands were assigned to the militant, who executed by force the power that descended from the ruler as head.[190]

Some people took the arms, hands, and fingers of John of the Cross in a crude sense: literally they took them. His corpse was cannibalized. At his death crowds gathered in the streets after midnight during a downpour, then broke forcibly into the priory. Not only did they kiss his dead hands and feet but also one devotee bit off his toe, while others tore off his fingernails. The scene was repeated at his funeral. Soon his corpse was minus an arm, a foot, and several fingers. The remaining limbs were finally severed by ecclesiastical permission, with the other arm dispatched to Medina del Campo and the fingers dispersed about.[191] There was nothing novel in such sensual

---

185 Martin Le France, *Champion des dames*, pp. 185-86; cited by Constance Jordan, *Renaissance Feminism: Literary Texts and Political Models* (Ithaca, N.Y.: Cornell University Press, 1990), p. 93, who comments that the idea was reflected in Justianian's *Digests*.

186 *Oxford Classical Dictionary*, p. 436; Gross, *Menschenhand und Gotteshand*, p. 387.

187 Gerhard Neumann, *Gesten und Gebärden in der griechischen Kunst* (Berlin: Walter de Gruyter, 1965), pp. 49-58; Carl Sittl, *Die Gebärden der Griechen und Römer* (1890; rpt. New York: G. Olms, 1970), pp. 79, 166. My citation is from *Galateo* 129; trans. Eisenbichler and Bartlett, p. 23. For the handshake, see also Barasch, *Giotto and the Language of Gesture*, pp. 128-33; Gabriel Herman, *Ritualised Friendship and the Greek City* (Cambridge: Cambridge University Press, 1987), pp. 41-72.

188 Guy de Tervarent, *Attributs et symbols dans l'art profane, 1450-1600: Dictionnaire d'un langage perdu*, Travaux d'humanisme et Renaissance, 29, 2 vols. (Geneva: E. Droz, 1958-59), 2:258-60.

189 Alessandro Piccolomini, *Dialogo de la bella creanza de le donne*, p. 13.

190 For the metaphor, see Pouchelle, *Body and Surgery*, pp. 109-16. A principal source was John of Salisbury, *Policraticus* 5.2; 6.20, 24, 25. For another example of the knights as hands, see Peter the Chanter, *De penitentia et partibus eius* lines 2011-65, especially 2058-60.

191 Brenan, *St. John of the Cross*, p. 83.

devotion. Mary Magdalen had lost a bit of bone from her arm when Hugh of Lincoln chewed it off her relic. To her outraged devotees he explained that, if he could eat Christ's body in the Eucharist, he could gnaw at Magdalen's arm.[192] Teresa of Avila suffered a similar amputation. When the architect of her posthumous convent was shown her arm for veneration, he plucked off a fingernail the size of a chickpea, wrapped it in paper, and hid it in his book of devotions.[193] Hands were realistic substitutes for social relationships.

Social reciprocity had been since the archaic age a matter of handing: giving, receiving, and returning manually and mutually. The concept of *charis* (grace) governed ancient life. The word was literally rooted in "pleasure," specifically the pleasure that brought enjoyment. Its divine dispensers were the Charites, or Graces, and the pleasure they bestowed was never private, always mutual. Aristotle recognized their social importance of bonding through pleasure in his ethics, by observing that they presided over free exchange and gift-giving.[194] From their obscure origin as stones plunged from the sky, worshipped in cult and honored in contest,[195] the Graces were developed artistically into sculpture of three maidens in the round and in relief . The complex pose of three nude figures interlaced may have been derived from choreography, excerpted from a frieze of a row of dancers with their arms on each other's shoulders.[196] The renaissance recovery of the classical nude form seems to have been a miniature of them in Jean duc de Berry's *Très riches heures*. A Hellenistic fragment in the Sienese collection of Francesco Cardinal Piccolomini (Pope Pius III, d. 1503) was certainly influential.[197] In renaissance culture the Graces claimed

---

[192] Adam of Eynsham, *Magna vita sancti Hugonis* 5.15; cited by Carolyn Walker Bynum, "The Female Body and Religious Practice in the Later Middle Ages," in *Fragments for a History of the Human Body*, ed. Feher, 1:164.

[193] Luis Cervera Vera, *Complejo arquitectónico del monasterio de San José en Avila* (n. p.: Ministerio de cultura, 1982), p. 60; idem, "Las obras y trabajos de Francisco de Mora en Avila," *Archivo español de arte* 60 (1987):402-4.

[194] Bonnie MacLachlan, *The Age of Grace: "Charis" in Early Greek Poetry* (Princeton, N.J.: Princeton University Press, 1993), pp. 4-5, 147, citing Aristotle, *Ethica nichomachea* 1133a. For their ancient history, see also Karl Deichgräber, *Charis und Chariten, Grazie und Grazien* (Munich: Ernst Heimeran, 1971); Erkinger Schwarzenberg, *Die Grazien* (Bonn: Rudolf Habelt, 1966). The experience of grace was also an encounter with beauty. MacLachlan, *Age of Grace*, p. 5.

[195] Pausanias, *Descriptio Graeciae* 7.22.4; 9.24.3; 9.27.1; 9.38.1 and many other authors, cited by Freedberg, *Power of Images*, p. 66. For the competitions in their honor, see John Buchler, "The Charitesia at Boiotian Orchomenos," *American Journal of Philology* 105 (1984):49-53.

[196] Clark, *Nude*, pp. 90-91

[197] Statue group, Roman copy of a Hellenistic original, Piccolomini library, cathedral, Siena; reproduced frequently, e. g., in Phyllis Pray Bober and Ruth Rubenstein, *Renaissance Artists and Antique Sculpture: A Handbook of Sources* (London: Harvey Miller with Oxford University Press, 1986), pl. 60; Clark, *Nude*, p. 385.

the devotion of many eminent painters.[198] Raphael has them handle virtuously the golden apples of the garden of the Hesperides,[199] while for Sandro Botticelli (1444?-1510) they dance about Venus in his Primavera,[200] and for Correggio they curve as the very sign of feminine grace[201] to symbolize concord.[202] In Giovanni Paolo Lomazzo's (b.1538) *Trattato dell'arte de la pittura* the subject retained its classical meaning of mutuality. Grace disposed one "to receive gifts cheerfully, to give rewards willingly, bestow with a majesty, requite with a bounty, and obtain all suits with fortunate success."[203]

---

198 For listings, see Jane Davidson Reid with Chris Rohmann, *The Oxford Guide to Classical Mythology in the Arts*, 2 vols. (New York: Oxford University Press, 1993), 1:474-76; Tervarent, *Attributes et symbols dans l'art profane*, 1:177-80; W. Deonna, "Le groupe de trois Grâces nues et sa descendance," *Revue archéologique* 31 (1930):308-12. The artists include Francesco del Cossa (c. 1435-c. 1477), Andrea Mantegna (1431-1506), Baldassare Peruzzi (1481-1536), Pinturicchio (1454-1513), Domenico Beccafumi (1486-1551), Lucas Cranach (1472-1553), Baldung Grien (1484/85-c.1562), Sodoma (1477?-1549), Cecchin Salviati (1510-63), Francesco Primaticcio (1504-70), Jacopo Tintoretto (1518-94), Hendrik Goltzius (1558-1617). To be added to their lists is Jacopo Pontormo, Studies for the Three Graces, 1540-49, Uffizi, Florence; reproduced in *Pontormo: Drawings*, ed. Salvatore S. Nigro (New York: Harry N. Abrams, 1992), pl. 63(3) and 64(1); Janet Cox-Rearick, *The Drawings of Pontormo*, 2 vols. (Cambridge, Mass.: Harvard University Press, 1964), 2:fig. 310, and see 1:292-93; Anna Forlani-Tempesti, *Disegni del Pontormo nel gabinetto di disegni e stampe degli Uffizi*, exhibition catalogue, Milan, Pinacoteca di Brera, aprile-maggio 1970 (Florence: Centro Di, 1970), pl. 26; Clark, *Nude*, p. 336. Albrecht Dürer copied them perversely as elemental in his engraving Four witches, 1497, Metropolitan Museum of Art, New York; reproduced in Russell with Barnes, *Eva/Ave*, p. 463, fig. 1. See Eugene J. Dwyer, "The Subject of Dürer's Four Witches," *Art Quarterly* 34 (1971):456-73. See also in general Bober and Rubenstein, *Renaissance Artists and Antique Sculpture*, pp. 95-97; Jean Seznec, *The Survival of the Pagan Gods: The Mythological Tradition and Its Place in Renaissance Humanism and Art*, trans. Barbara F. Sessions, Bollingen Series 38 (New York: Pantheon, 1953), pp. 207-9.

199 Raphael, Three graces, 1504-5, Musée Condé, Chantilly; reproduced in Leopold D. Ettlinger and Helen S. Ettlinger, *Raphael* (Oxford: Phaidon, 1987), p. 29, fig. 16; Jean-Pierre Cuzin, *Raphaël: Vie et oeuvre* (Paris: Office du livre, 1983), pp. 56, 58, 62; *The Complete Paintings of Raphael* (New York: Harry N. Abrams, 1966), pl. V; Clark, *Nude*, p. 106, fig. 81. Cf. Raphael, Three Graces for the wedding of Cupid and Psyche, 1518, Windsor, Royal Collection 12754; reproduced in Paul Joannides, *The Drawings of Raphael with a Complete Catalogue* (Berkeley and Los Angeles: University of California Press, 1983), pl. 43.

200 Botticelli, Primavera, Uffizi, Florence. See also E. H. Gombrich, "Botticelli's Mythologies: A Study in the Neoplatonic Symbolism of His Circle," *Journal of the Warburg and Courtauld Institutes* 8 (1945):32-40; Edgar Wind, *Pagan Mysteries in the Renaissance* (New Haven. Conn.: Yale University Press, 1958), pp. 103-6; Clark, *Nude*, pp. 97-98, 101.

201 Correggio, Graces, fresco, Camera di san Paolo. Clark, *Nude*, p. 133.

202 Erwin Panofsky, *The Iconography of Correggio's Camera di san Paolo*, Studies of the Warburg Institute, 26 (London: Warburg Institute, University of London, 1961), pp. 56-58, and reproduced, fig. 26; Francesco Barocelli, *Il Correggio e la Camera di san Paolo* (Milan: Electa, 1989), p. 137, pl. 96; Giuliano Ercoli, *Arte e fortuna nel Correggio* (Modena: Artioli, 1982), p. 127, pl. XXV; Roberto Longhi, *Il Correggio nella camera di San Paolo*, ed. A. Ghidiglia Quintavalle (Milan: Silvana editoriale d'arte, n. d.), pp. 86-88.

203 Giovanni Paolo Lomazzo, *Trattato dell'arte de la pittura* 2.3; *A Tracte Containing the Artes of Curious Paintinge (1598)*, trans. Richard Haydocke, The English Experience, 171 (New York: Da Capo, 1969), p. 46 (modernized). For *grazia*, see also David Summers,

In literature the Graces decorated François Rabelais's (c.1490-1553) fountain for the abbey of Thélème[204] and they were celebrated by William Shakespeare (1564-1616), Edmund Spenser (c.1552-99), and John Milton (1608-74).[205] Their triad could exemplify a secular civility, as in Spenser's verse,[206] or be captioned in a hybrid emblem book with a scriptural verse (1 John 4:8) for divine charity, God as love.[207] As the antique group that most engaged allegory, the Graces were especially moralized by Ficino as exemplary of the Neoplatonist doctrine of love. While for the Neoplatonists they meant love, for the Stoics they meant liberality.[208] In the eclecticism of renaissance thought the traditions could be combined. Agnolo Firenzuola (1493-c.1545), writing on female beauty, explained them essentially. "Metaphorically, those Graces signify nothing more than the combined rewards given by grateful people in return for benefits already received." Their association with love was consequent. "Because in affairs of the heart and matters of love many benefits accumulate between the lovers, and they reward each other for them, all day long, the Graces were assigned as servants to beautiful Venus."[209] Grace could be distinctively bestowed on women, as in praise of Magdalen's election as the first apostle. "And so women announced the triumph of the resurrection, for Christ knew that above all grace was the grace of a woman."[210]

Michelangelo and the Language of Art (Princeton, N.J.: Princeton University Press, 1981), p. 58.

[204] François Rabelais, *Gargantua* 55, as borrowed from Francesco Colonna, *Hypnerotomachia Poliphili*.

[205] See John M. Wallace, "*Timon of Athens* and the Three Graces: Shakespeare's Senecan Study," *Modern Philology* 83 (1986):349-63; Mark Archer, "The Meaning of 'Grace' and 'Courtesy': Book VI of *The Faerie Queene*," *Studies in English Literature, 1500-1900*, 27 (1987):17-34; Patrick Cheney, "Spenser's Dance of the Graces and Tasso's Dance of the Sylvan Nymphs," *English Language Notes* 22 (1984):5-9; Stella P. Revard, "'L'allegro' and 'Il penseroso': Classical Tradition and Renaissance Mythography," *Publications of the Modern Language Association* 101 (1986):338-50.

[206] Edmund Spenser, *Faerie Queene* 6.10.23; cf. *Shepheardes Calendar*, April 109; cited by Wind, *Pagan Mysteries in the Renaissance*, pp. 33-34.

[207] Three Graces, in *Mikrocosmos, Parvus mundus* (Antwerp: Geerhardt de Jode, 1579); reproduced in Russell with Barnes, *Eva/Ave*, p. 92, fig. 18.

[208] Wind, *Pagan Mysteries*, pp. 31, 39-48, 71-73.

[209] Firenzuola, *Della belleza della donne* 1; *On the Beauty of Women*, trans. Eisenbichler and Jacqueline Murray (Philadelphia: University of Pennsylvania Press, 1992) p. 35. Consider also "the graces given for benefits received, that make he who gives them feel grateful and appreciated." For female grace in particular, see Ruth Kelso, *Doctrine for a Lady of the Renaissance*, 2d ed. (Urbana: University of Illinois Press, 1978), pp. 197-200, 145. For some other renaissance concepts of grace, see Baldassare Castiglione, *Cortegiano* 1.14, 24; 2.7; 4.5; and see Eduardo Saccone, "'Grazia,' 'spezzatura,' 'affettazione' in the *Courtier*," in *Castiglione: The Ideal and the Real in Renaissance Culture*, ed. Robert W. Hanning and David Rosand (New Haven, Conn.: Yale University Press, 1983), pp. 45-67; Giovanni della Casa, *Galateo* 288-89.

[210] Guillaume Pepin (c. 1465-1533), *Rosareum aurem B. Mariae virginis*, p. 353; cf. *Conciones quadragesimales*, p. 434; cited by Larissa Taylor, *Soldiers of Christ: Preaching in Late Medieval and Reformation France* (New York: Oxford, 1992), p. 175.

It was the Stoic interpretation of liberality that explained the values of the Graces as tactile. Seneca interpreted in *De beneficiis* "why they have their hands interlocked." The different explanations were that one bestowed, one received, and one accepted a benefit; or that they represented classes of benefactors as earners, returners, and simultaneous receivers and returners. He developed the argument. "Why do the sisters hand in hand dance in a ring which returns upon itself? For the reason that a benefit passing in its course from hand to hand returns nevertheless to the giver; the beauty of the whole is destroyed if the course is anywhere broken, and it has most beauty if it is continuous and maintains an uninterrupted succession."[211] As the adage acknowledged, *gratia gratiam parit*, or "one favor begets another." That mutual favoring was tactile. Another adage, *manus manum fricat*, or "one hand rubs another," so explained mutual convenience. Then there was the saying *senes mutuum fricant* for "old men rub one another," in recognition that "beasts must be rubbed down by someone else because they have no hands." In the sum of manual mutuality: *fricantem refrica*, or "you scratch my back and I'll scratch yours," an adage related to "one hand washes the other."[212] Erasmus, who compiled these classical sources, compared the pagan Graces with the Christian Holy Spirit in his treatise on marriage. His moral was that spouses should not desire in human benevolence a union of corporeal pleasure but aspire in heavenly inspiration to the gift of charity, as more properly binding the mind to God.[213]

The symbolism of hands as grace, for social favor toward social bond, depended on their primary sense as executors of power. Although one pair of human hands should act toward another benevolently, that graciousness implied their basic ability to act. The adage *ambabus manibus haurire*, "to take with both hands," meant to do something with all one's might. To act *manibus pedibusque*, "with hands and feet," added diligence and speed. And there was *multae manus onus levius reddunt*, or "many hands make light work." People who failed to act were *compressibus manibus*, "with folded hands," idlers who lamented their lot anxiously but remained inactive.[214] Hands were properly agents of deeds, and their power was vigorously defended or denied during the sixteenth century in the theological controversy about will and grace. The principal scripture adduced in favor of free choice in the conflict between Erasmus and Luther was metaphori-

211 Seneca, *De beneficiis* 1.3.2-4; *Moral Essays*, trans. John W. Basore, 3 vols. (Cambridge, Mass.: Harvard University Press, 1963-64), 3:13, 14. See also Wind, *Pagan Mysteries*, pp. 32-33.

212 Erasmus, *Adagia* 1.1.34, 33; 1.7.98, 99; trans. Phillips, 31:83, 82; trans. R. A. B. Mynors, 32:126. Cf. for "open-hearted goodwill," *nudae gratiae*, or "naked are the graces," *Adagia* 2.7.50; trans., Mynors, 34:25.

213 Erasmus, *Institutio matrimoniis christiani*, in *Opera omnia* (Leiden), 5:619.

214 Erasmus, *Adagia* 1.9.16; 1.4.15; 2.3.95; 2.1.23; trans. Mynors, 32:189-90; trans. Phillips, 31:332; trans. Mynors, 33:187, 29-30.

cally manual. "God from the beginning constituted man, and left him in the hand (*manu*) of his counsel. He added his commands and precepts: If you wish to keep the commandments and to keep pleasing fidelity forever they will keep you. He has set before you fire and water; to whichever you will, stretch our your hand (*porrige manum tuum*). Before man life and death, good and evil; what pleases him will be given him (Ecc. 15:14-17 Vulg.)." Erasmus argued that, if there was no moral freedom of choice, then scripture was promoting a false model: a person with his right arm tied was ordered to extend it, when only his left arm was free. Luther rejoined concerning merit toward grace that people were captive with "both arms tied."[215] Calvin thought that the neglect of those natural means placed in human hands was tempting God, as if one were to sever a man's arms and hands and then order him to work. But the means toward righteousness and salvation were not in human hands, he stated.[216]

In whose hands did power reside? in whose hands lay the initiative toward grace? and which hand chose, the right or the left? The polarity of beliefs was exemplified and epitomized by the Carmelite companions, John of the Cross and Teresa of Avila. He believed that the just person as a spiritual bride reposed in the arms Christ the lover, who had mercifully extended his hand to uplift its fallen and miserable state to his divine embrace. She believed that the initiative toward spiritual union was within human grasp. Teresa of Avila frankly asserted in her *Castillo interior*, "May it please his Majesty to give us the grace to merit to arrive at this state; for it is in our hand, if we will."[217] The human hand was a patristic metaphor for merit, as in Ambrose's commentary on Genesis.[218] The semipelagian belief of Teresa of Avila was classical, as ancient as the adage *manum admoventi fortuna est imploranda*, or "set your hand to the work before you appeal to Fortune." As Erasmus explained, "The lesson of the adage is that, while we ought to trust in divine help, we should strive none the less, as far as in us lies, by our own efforts; otherwise heaven will not listen to the prayers of indolent and lazy men." The adage recommended an even balance of dependence and duty. Erasmus cited Aeschylus: "When a man makes an effort himself, then god too takes a hand." This was because "God loves to help the man who helps himself." A complementary adage was "Invoke Minerva, but use your own strength too." It similarly "warns us not to relax our efforts in reliance on divine assistance." That adage Erasmus considered especially appropriate to women, since Minerva was patron of their wool work. Both adages originated in the story of a carter whose ass was stuck in the mud; he merely

[215] Erasmus, *De libero arbitri, diatribē sive collatio*, pp. 19, 33; Luther, *De servo arbitrio*, pp. 156, 170.

[216] Calvin, *In harmoniam evangelicam* ad Matt. 4:7.

[217] Teresa of Avila, *Castillo interior* 5.3.7.

[218] Ambrose, *Hexameron* 6.8.53.

appealed for help to a god. God replied that heaven would help him, but only when he put his own hand first to relieving the distress of the beast.[219] Teresa of Avila aspired to do "everything that we are able to do on our part," even "the tiny thing that was in me," defined as the perfect observance of the evangelical counsels. That aspiration coincided with the semipelagian premise toward grace of doing what was within one's power (*facere quod in se est*). "Let us endeavor to do what is in ourselves," she urged. She insisted on merit, even "meriting more and more," as initially within the grasp of her free will to act.[220] Opposition to free will in the human hand was expressed manually by Montaigne in his "Apologie de Raymond Sebond," where he cited Plutarch's *Moralia*. "He will rise, if God by exception lends him a hand; he will rise by abandoning and renouncing his own means, and letting himself be raised and uplifted by purely celestial means."[221]

The concept of will was also traditionally expressed in terms of handedness: not only in whose palm—divine or human—was the power to act but also in which hand it was—right or left, as symbolic of good and evil. The right was the favored side. From a primitive dualism that associated the right with the sacred,[222] the Greek medicine and philosophy that established norms of Western culture determined it as the side of life and light, the male and the good.[223] As Augustine moralized on adversity and prosperity, "What is, on the left hand? Temporal, mortal, bodily. . . . What ought they to have set on the right hand? God, eternity, the years of God which fail not."[224] The testimony of fidelity and of health was offered through the sign

---

219 Erasmus, *Adagia* 2.2.81; 1.6.18; trans. Mynors, 33:118-19; 32:15.

220 Teresa of Avila, *Vida* 32.4-5; *Castillo interior* 2.1.8; 3.3.1; 3.1.7; 3.2.8; 4.1.7; 4.2.9; 4.3.3; 4.3.5; 5.1.2; 7.2.8 For an analysis of her semi-pelagianism, see Boyle, *Divine Domesticity: Augustine of Thagaste to Teresa of Avila*, Studies in the History of Christian Thought, 74 (Leiden: E. J. Brill, 1997), pp. 227, 250-55.

221 Montaigne, *Essais* 2.12, p. 604; trans. Frame, p. 457.

222 The basic argument is Robert Hertz, *Death and the Right Hand*, trans. Rodney and Claudia Needham (Glencoe, Ill.: Free Press, 1960), pp. 89-113. For recent anthropology, see Serge Tcherkézoff, *Dual Classification Reconsidered: Nyamwezi Sacred Kingship and Other Examples*, trans. Martin Thom (Cambridge: Cambridge University Press, 1987). For the favoring of the right and the evolutionary emergence of bipedality, see Michael C. Corballis, *The Lopsided Ape: Evolution of the Generative Mind* (Oxford: Oxford University Press, 1991), pp. 102; idem, "Laterality and Human Evolution," *Psychological Review* 96 (1989):492-505. Against the left hand employed alone in gesture, see Quintilian 11.3.114; against left-handedness, see Bulwer, *Chirologia*, pp. 233-38.

223 Geoffrey Lloyd, "Right and Left in Greek Philosophy," in *Right and Left: Essays on Dual Symbolic Classification*, ed. Rodney Needham (Chicago: University of Chicago Press, 1973), pp. 167-86. Cf. the religious rules in Islam and Hinduism about using the right hand only for eating, the left only for excretory and sexual purposes. V. Reynolds and R. E. S. Tanner, *The Biology of Religion* (London: Longman, 1983), p. 230.

224 Augustine, *Enarrationes in psalmos* 143.18; *Expositions on the Book of Psalms*, trans. C. Marriott and H. Walford (Oxford, 1857), 6:312; cited by D. J. MacQueen, "St. Augustine's Concept of Property Ownership," *Recherches augustiniennes* 8 (1972):201. See p. 202 n. 55 for the dualism of the right for prosperity, the left for adversity.

of the right hand.[225] From infancy there was the medical practice of liberating the right hand first from the swaddling cloths, lest it be weaker than the left hand for lack of exercise, and left-handedness result.[226] The right hand was believed more agile and mobile because it was warmer, from the influence of the heart. Males alone were believed to be ambidexterous (like the expert Scythian archers) because they were elementally hotter than females.[227] It was not until the seventeenth century that Germain Poullain de la Barre (1647-1725), arguing that women had the same sensory organs as men, asserted that their hands were just as dexterous.[228]

Yet, although symbolically males tended to be right and females left, both sexes were required to choose morally and correctly between the right and the left, or good and evil. As in the adage, *omni pede standum*, "one must put one's best foot forward,"[229] and that was undoubtedly the right foot on the right path. The choice of Hercules between virtue and vice became illustrated by the Pythagorean *Y* as a fork in the road, whose branches tended toward the right or left.[230] In Christian iconography that branching was superimposed on the cross, with Jesus inclining his head in his redemptive death voluntarily toward the right, or the good.[231] Contrarily, the devil's mark on the alleged witch was often made with the nails or claws of his left hand and on the left side of her body.[232] Margarida Lourenço confessed be-

---

225 Isidore of Seville, *Etymologiae* 11.1.66.

226 Soranus, *Gynaecia* 2.19.42; cf. Plato, *Leges* 794d. See also Lloyd, *Science, Folklore, and Ideology*, pp. 175-76.

227 Aristotle, *De anima* 432; *Problemata varia anatomica*, p. 32. See also Lloyd, *Science, Folklore, and Ideology*, p. 30, citing Aristotle, *Historia animalium* 497b, cf. *Ethica nichomachea* 1134b, *Magna moralia* 1194b. For the Scythian archers, see Plato, *Leges* 795a; cited by Edith Hall, *Inventing the Barbarian: Greek Self-Definition through Tragedy* (Oxford: Clarendon, 1989), p. 139 n. 108.

228 François Poullain de la Barre, *De l'égalité des deux sexes*, p. 60; cited by Londa Schiebinger, "Skeletons in the Closet: The First Illustrations of the Female Skeleton in Eighteenth-Century Anatomy," *Representations* 14 (1986):46. For the female as rarely ambidexterous, see Hoffman, *De generatione hominis*, pp. 3-4; cited by Ian Maclean, *The Renaissance Notion of Woman: A Study in the Fortunes of Scholasticism and Medical Science in European Intellectual Life* (Cambridge: Cambridge University Press, 1980), pp. 32, 35.

229 Erasmus, *Adagia* 3.1.34; trans. Mynors, 34:194.

230 Xenophon, *Memorabilia* 1.2.21-34. See G. Karl Galinsky, *The Herakles Theme: The Adaptations of the Hero in Literature from Homer to the Twentieth Century* (Oxford: Basil Blackwell, 1971), pp. 64-68; Panofsky, *Hercules am Scheideweg: Und andere antike Bildstoffe in der neueren Kunst*, Studien de Bibliothek Warburg, 18 (Leipzig: B. G. Teubner, 1930).

231 Wolfgang Harms, "*Homo viator in bivio*": *Studien zur Bildlicheit des Weges*, Medium aevum, philologischen Studien, 21 (Munich: Wilhelm Fink, 1970), pp. 57-98, and see also *Y*-Form crucifix as vegetation, miniature, codex from southeast Germany, c. 1230, pl. 9.

232 Norman Cohn, *Europe's Inner Demons: An Enquiry Inspired by the Great Witch-Hunt* (London: Chatto Heinemann for Sussex University Press, 1975), p. 100.

fore the Inquisition that, when the devil had extracted blood with a lancet so as to write her name in his book, it was from her left arm.[233]

Handedness not only symbolized choice but also fate, its reverse. In the popular science of chiromancy, or palm-reading, the human hand mediated between the intellectual macrocosm in the head and the material macrocosm in the body. The hand was the active force through which the mind manifested itself, second only to it in the microcosmic hierarchy. The hand bore macrocosmic imprints of character and destiny. The left hand, since it worked less, was believed to preserve those signs for reading better than the right hand. The left inscribed the primitive destiny allotted by the stars at birth; the right, those changes a person effected by his will and his work. The left thus displayed natural disposition; the right, the human product of those gifts. Judgment was made by consulting the length of lines, the depth of engraving, their color and continuity.[234] As Firenzuola advised on manual beauty, the lines should be clear and distinct, well marked, not mixed or crossed. The mounds of Jupiter, Venus, and Mercury should be quite distinct, but not too elevated. The line of the intellect should be deep and clear and uncrossed by any other line. The hollow between the index finger and the thumb should be well set, unwrinkled, and vivid.[235] A book like *Chyromantie ac physionomiae Anastasis* by Bartolomaeus della Rocca, called Cocles (1467-1504), discoursed from its principles to its practices.[236] He was accurate in chiromancy, fatally so, according to an anecdote. Cocles read the palm of the ruler of Bologna, Giovanni Bentivoglio, and predicted his exile, then death in battle. The enraged Bentivoglio had the chiromancer murdered. Pope Julius II did take Bologna.[237]

Morality devolved about hands, and Calvin was exemplary of manual values. No one, he avowed, could presume to touch God, but God could initiate to touch people. He touched Calvin with a force that was less intimate than his unitive embrace of John of the Cross but more influential. Calvin knew well the convention of God's hand. In scripture it was synonymous with force; literally, God was "armed," and that signified his dominion and power. Christian iconography since the fourth century had depicted an active deity, creating and sustaining life, protecting and

---

233 Francisco Bethencourt, "Portugal: A Scrupulous Inquisition," in *Early Modern European Witchcraft: Centres and Peripheries*, ed. Bengt Ankarloo and Gustav Hennigsen (Oxford: Clarendon, 1990), pp. 417-18.

234 Seligmann, *Magic, Supernaturalism, and Religion* (New York: Pantheon, 1973), pp. 266-71. See also Lynn Thorndike, *A History of Magic and Experimental Science*, 8 vols. (New York: 1923-58), 4:64, 117, 143, 165, 278, 294, 324, 462, 528; 5:673-78.

235 Firenzuola, *Della belleza delle donne* 2.

236 Thorndike, *History of Magic and Experimental Science*, 5:50-68. For an example of criticism of chiromancy, see Heinrich Cornelius Agrippa von Nettesheim, *De incertitudine et vanitate scientiarum* 35.

237 Walter Sorrell, *The Story of the Human Hand* (Indianapolis, Ind.: Bobbs-Merrill, 1967), p. 29.

liberating the faithful with his hand.[238] As Calvin explained, the phrase "'the hand of God,' as is well enough known is taken by metonymy for power."[239] For Calvin "the rule of piety is that God's hand alone is the judge and the governor of fortune, good or bad, and that it does not rush about with heedless force, but with most orderly justice deals out good as well as ill to us." Against belief in mere fortune he argued that even inanimate objects did not exercise power "except as directed by God's ever-present hand." What seemed but chance, faith recognized as divine impulse. "Whatever changes are discerned in the world are produced from the secret stirrings of God's hand." Even evil was under that power. The devils were restrained by God's hand as by a bridle, so that they could not lift a finger toward the execution of their will except by his command. When Adam fell, it was by divine permission. "What else, I ask, is the permission of him, who has the right of prevention, and in whose hand (*manu*) the matter is placed, than the will?" The hand of God stretched forth was his purpose.[240] As Calvin commented on Is. 14:27, when the Lord spoke his counsel he showed his hand, so that its power was hallowed and incapable of voiding.[241] When persons acknowledged that power of God they were led as by the hand to faith.[242]

Even from the first act of creation the Lord "holds in his hand the light" and "he stretches out toward us his hand in a certain manner" for our enjoyment of its brightness. At his rest on the seventh day "the last touch" was placed by God on his work so that it would not lack perfection.[243] As Giorgio Vasari (1511-74) similarly wrote of Michelangelo's frescoed Creation of Light on the Sistine Chapel ceiling, "His Majesty with open arms supported on himself alone demonstrates both love and craft." Michelangelo the artist also put "the finishing touch" of perfection on his own work.[244] The adage *summam manum addere*, "to add the final touch," was the language of craftsmen, who worked from the initial mock-up to the last polish-

---

238 Martin Kirigin, *La mano divina nell'iconografia cristiana*, Studi di antichità cristiana, 31 (Vatican City: Pontificio istituto di archeologia cristiana, 1976), pp. 21, 96-110; L. H. Grondijs, *De Icononographie van Schepping en Godsverschijningen* (Amsterdam: Elsevier, 1942), pp. 81-109; Schmitt, *Raison des gestes*, pp. 93-133.

239 Calvin, in Ps. 78:42. He characteristically uses *virtus* for divine power. For the hand as dominion and power, see also in Ps. 49:15; for government, in Ps. 73:1.

240 Calvin, *Institutio christianae religionis* 3.7.10; 1.16.2; 1.16.9; 1.17.11; 1.18.1; trans. Battles, 1:701, 199, 210; *In libros Mosis* ad Gen. 3.1; *Institutio christianae religionis* 1.17.14. For permission and will, see also in Ps. 115:3. For the medieval theological question of absolute versus ordained power, see David C. Steinmetz, "Calvin and the Absolute Power of God," *Journal of Medieval and Renaissance Studies* 18 (1988):65-79. For examples of the divine hand stretched forth, see Calvin, *In harmoniam evangelicam* ad Luke 1:7; 10:19; Matt. 4:13; 11:28; 14:16, 28; in Ps. 40:5; 48:10; 73:23; in Is. 1:25; 9:12, 17, 21.

241 Calvin, in Is. 14:27.

242 Calvin, *In harmoniam evangelicam* ad Mark 3:23.

243 Calvin, *In libros Mosis* ad Gen. 1.3; 1.16; 2.2.

244 Giorgio Vasari, *Vita di Michelangelo*, pp. 40, 37; trans. mine.

ing.[245] But Augustine had explained of the creation of humans in the divine image that God did not work as did artisans, who shaped earthly material with human hands. As he stated in *De civitate Dei*, "The hand of God is the power of God, who produces even visible things in an invisible way."[246]

Calvin wrote traditionally of God as an artisan, as in the iconography of the creation of Adam and Eve. The elect were "the works of his hand," whom he formed from the beginning, more assiduously adorned, then polished to the highest perfection.[247] But the arms of God was a figure of speech, *anthropopatheia*. Calvin modified the manual metaphor by the phrase "in a certain degree" (*quodammodo*), in the belief that it was not to be interpreted literally but as a simile. He complained that the anthropomorphites had imagined from such a passage that God was corporeal: that he possessed the hands and feet scripture frequently ascribed to him. Calvin refuted their opinion by an argument from the classical rhetorical principle of accommodation. "For who even of the slightest wit does not know that God, as wet-nurses are wont to do with infants, in a certain measure (*quodammodo*) stutters to us? Such forms of speaking do not so much express fluently what God may be, as they accommodate the conception of him to our tenuity."[248]

Calvin also knew the classical convention of the hand as power. He had explained it professionally in his initial text, a commentary on Seneca's *De clementia*, which contributed to his understanding of divine authority as tactile. Its imperial prosopopoeia declared that the emperor ruled by divine election.[249] "I of all mortals have found favor with Heaven and have chosen to serve on earth as vicar of the gods. I am the arbiter of life and death for the nations; it rests in my hand (*in manu mea*) what each man's fortune and state shall be." Calvin's commentary began with a familiar letter to Cicero, citing, "How far you desire to put him under an obligation rests in your hand." Cicero himself expressed the meaning of the phrase "beautifully" in *De officiis*, Calvin thought, to the effect that what is received on the spot, or

---

245 Erasmus, *Adagia* 1.2.34; trans. Phillips, 31:176.

246 Augustine, *De civitate Dei* 12.12; *The City of God against the Pagans*, trans. Henry Bettenworth, 7 vols. (Cambridge, Mass.: Harvard University Press, 1963-72), 4:115.

247 Calvin, *In harmoniam evangelicam* ad Matt. 13:12; cf. in Is. 64:8; in Ps. 57:1.

248 Calvin, *Institutio christianae religionis* 3.24.17; 1.13.1. See also in Is. 49:16. For scripture as divine baby-talk, see also Erasmus, *Enchiridion militis christianis*, in *Ausgewählte werke*, p. 34. For the incarnation as divine baby-talk, see Augustine, *Enarrationes in psalmos* 30(2-1).9; 33(1).6; 109.12; 119.2; 130.9-14; *In evangelium Iohannis tractatus* 35.3. For the human body and the image of God, see also Mary Potter Engel, *John Calvin's Perspectival Anthropology*, American Academy of Religion Academy Series, 52 (Atlanta, Ga.: Scholars, 1988), pp. 42-47. Erasmus also criticized the "anthropomorphites who think God is corporeal in human species, when they read that man is created in the image of God, especially when scripture throughout attributes to God human members—face, mouth, eyes, ears, hands, arms, feet." *Ecclesiastes* 1037.

249 See J. Rufus Fears, "Nero as the Vicegerent of the Gods in Seneca's *De clementia*," *Hermes* 103 (1975):486-96.

"in the hand," is so much more satisfying. "Therefore," he explicated, "we elegantly say a thing which is certain 'rests in our hand,' as if grasped by the hand. One also says, 'in the hands,' and 'to the hand,' and 'before the hands,' and 'under the hand,' and 'within the hands.'" Since the last two examples were rarer, he supplied citations from Seneca and Suetonius; but he allowed Vergil the last word on the diction of *in manu mea*:

> All else, with what wide ruin it lies smitten,
> Is before your eyes and within your hands.

"In other words," Calvin continued, "Nero says it is easy for him to make rich whom he will and also to impoverish whom he will." The words "hand" could also be interpreted as "sway" or "arbitrage," as had Suetonius in his *Nero*. "'He had done all things that were necessary, by way of preparation, but the issue of the approaching trial was in the hand of fortune.'" The meaning was the same. The ruler was the instrument of Fortune, who by her hand and ministry turns everything topsiturvy."[250] Seneca's expression "in my hand" belonged to religious and juridical vocabulary. It expressed the basis of the will of the ruler in divine favor and in relation to divine power.[251]

In his scholarship Calvin commented on the classical ruler, who by his metaphorical hand as vicegerent of the god displayed and effected the divine will. In his correspondence Calvin revealed his personal experience of the divine will as "hand." He acknowledged from experience that people were not allowed to foresee much, so that the Lord would the better provide everything. "When I promised myself complete calm, there appeared on the doorstep what I had least expected. In contrast, when I mulled over an unpleasant spot, a feather bed was arranged for me beyond imagination. And all these things are the hand (*manus*) of the Lord, which if we commit ourselves to it will be solicitous for us."[252] The providential hand of God was not always obvious to Calvin, however. The very order of creation displayed his paternal solicitude through human formation, provision, even abundance. Yet, he thought that "the fact that he often holds his hand as if it were closed ought to be imputed to our sins."[253]

Another decisive personal revelation was manual. No one knew of his authorship of *Institutio religionis christianae*, Calvin divulged—not in any town, not even in Geneva—until the hand of God intervened. It so acted

---

250 Calvin, *In "De clementia"* 1.1, 2, citing Cicero, *Epistulae familiares* 8.6.1; *De officiis* 2.17.60; Seneca, *Epistulae morales* 71.1; Suetonius, *Augustus* 49.3; Vergil, *Aeneid* 11.310-11; Suetonius, *Nero* 23.3; trans. Battles and Hugo, pp. 19, 33,

251 Bernard Morturex, *Recherches sur le "De clementia" de Sénèque: Vocabulaire et composition*, Collection Latomus, 128 (Brussels: Latomus, 1973), pp. 16, 17.

252 Calvin, Letter to François Daniel (no. 457), in *Correspondance des réformateurs*, 3:156-58.

253 Calvin, *In libros Mosis* ad Gen. 1.26.

through Guillaume Farel (1489-1565), who retained Calvin in that city, not so much by counsel and exhortation as by "a fearful obligation calling God to witness it, as if God from heaven had taken hold of me with a forcible hand."[254] Human hands could be agents of the divine hand. A scriptural type was Jacob seeking his father's blessing as a recognition of "grace deposited in the hand of his blessing father." This was so, Calvin explicated, because "when the Lord sees us crawling on the earth, through the hand of men he leads us to him."[255] Calvin hoped that his own hands, with which he wrote, would be invested with spiritual power. In the dedicatory letter for his commentary on Genesis to Henry, duke of Vendome, he exhorted the future king of France (Henry IV) to a boldly Christian discipleship. Calvin inscribed to him that publication "so that God, as if by taking hold of you with his hands in a re-creation, made claim on you for himself (*si Deus quasi inecta manu de integro sibi te vendicet*)."[256] The desired act replicated Calvin's own experience of being stayed at Geneva by Farel: *inicere manum*.

Calvin had explained the repeated phrase *inicere manum* in his commentary on Seneca's *De clementia* at the line "lay a restraining hand upon himself." It meant "to bring his emotions under control, and keep them within measure." Calvin cited Vergil, "'The Fates have laid their restraining hand./ They have got what is owed them.'" He also cited Servius's commentary. "'The author has used a legal term. For it is called a 'laying on of hands' whenever, waiting for no authority of the judge, we claim what is owed us.'" Ovid's amatory verse confirmed that interpretation. "'And I shall say, they are mine; and lay my hand upon them'"; also, "'I shall lay my hands of rulership upon my rights.'" Calvin added that the jurisprudent Guillaume Budé (1468-1540) had explained the expression "properly and carefully" as a legal term. But he was mistaken, thought Calvin, in supposing that there was no ancient authority for the recent employment of *inicere manum* as the equivalent of *affere* or *inferre manum*. Horace had so used it in the verse "lest he lay rude hands on thee."[257]

That imposition of hands also figured in Calvin's commentary on Seneca's line "which loves peace and stays the hand." Calvin instructed that "hand" was to be understood as "violence," as in Cicero's use of "force and

---

[254] Calvin, *In librum Psalmorum commentarius* intro., in *Opera omnia* (Brunswick), 31:23, 26.

[255] Calvin, *In libros Mosis* ad Gen. 27:12.

[256] Calvin, Letter to Henri de Navarre, July 1563, in *Opera omnia* (Brunswick), 20:117.

[257] Calvin, *In "De clementia"* 1.5.4, citing Vergil, *Aeneid* 10.419; Ovid, *Amores* 1.4.40; 2.5.30; Horace, *Carmina* 1.17.25; cf. Curtius 10.1.37; trans. Battles and Hugo, pp. 115, 117. For Budé on *manus iniectio*, see *Annotationes in "Pandectas"*, in *Opera omnia*, 3:81b-82c. For *manus iniectio* as a legal term, see Alan Watson, *Law of Succession in the Later Roman Empire* (Oxford: Clarendon, 1971), pp. 166-67; Francis Zulueta, *The Institutes of Gaius, Part II: Commentary*, 2 vols. (Oxford: Clarendon, 1953), pp. 242-47.

hand" (main force).[258] The term *manus iniectio* was a legal term, as in Gaius's own *Institutio*, for claim by seizure.[259] Calvin believed that the pride of the flesh was so "violent" that people never submitted themselves to God "unless subjected violently."[260] Calvin's employment of the term concerning his charge to stay at Geneva occurred in a letter to François Daniel, who was his friend at Orléans during his study there for a law degree.[261] The two aspirant lawyers would have understood its exact legal sense: Calvin declared that God had forcefully claimed him by hand.

Calvin explained how fathers and teachers, when their words were not satisfactorily effective, would arrest their children or students by such manual seizure (*manu . . . iniecta*) to compel them to obey. "Thus the Lord does to his ministers, who sometimes wish to give up on everything, because they suppose themselves deluded in its work. He retains them as if by manual seizure (*manu iniecta*) so that they may continue in their office." Anyone who served God faithfully understood and experienced that as necessary. There was no graver temptation to faith than its failure, Calvin wrote. "This manual apprehension (*manus apprehensio*) was thus extremely necessary, because not only are we too flexible and fickle toward harm, but even more naturally bent to evil, even if no one impels us." Add custom to nature and "we are hardly our own masters." Thus he counselled prayer that God "not only with his word but even with the seizure of his hand (*iniecta manu*) might retain us." Calvin believed that God taking hold of a person's hand was a sign of his favor.[262]

Not only providential intervention by others, such as Farel toward Calvin, but deliberative self-knowledge handed people over to God. As the initial section of *Institutio christianae religionis* declared its premise, "The knowledge of ourselves not only arouses us to seek God, but also, as it were (*quasi*), leads us by the hand (*manu*) to find him."[263] Such self-knowledge was the classical acknowledgement, proverbial since the Delphic oracle, of the immense distinction in status between gods and mortals. It implied the prudence of humans not exceeding their proper nature.[264] Concerning self-knowledge toward divine knowledge, Calvin clarified that it was not merely

---

[258] Calvin, *In "De clementia"* 3.1.3, citing Cicero, *De officiis* 1.22.76; *In Verram* 2.4.65.146; trans. Battles and Hugo, pp. 85-87. Calvin comments that "the opposite expression is 'to come hand to hand' (*ad manus venire*)"; trans., p. 87.

[259] Gaius, ed. Zulueta, 2:242-47.

[260] Calvin, *In harmoniam evangelicam* ad Luke 1:12. For divine violence in subduing people to repentance, see also ad 15:15.

[261] For Daniel, see Quirinus Breen, *John Calvin: A Study in French Humanism* (Grand Rapids, Mich.: Wm. B. Eerdmans, 1931), p. 43.

[262] Calvin, in Is. 65:2; 41:13; 42:6.

[263] Calvin, *Institutio christianae religionis* 1.1.1; trans. Battles, 1:37.

[264] Jean Defradas, *Les thèmes de la propagande delphique* (Paris: C. Klincksieck, 1954), pp. 277-80, 286, 284. See also Plato, *Phaedrus* 229d-230a, *Timaeus* 29c-d. For its assimilation and alteration in Christian tradition, see Pierre Courcelle, *Connais-toi, toi-même de Socrate à saint Bernard*, 3 vols. (Paris: Études augustiniennes, 1974-75).

a cognitive and intellectual experience. Calvin thought that grace as animating a person was felt within, a "quickening," as in the basic life of vegetation. A comparison between the divine majesty and human lowliness was fully a matter of being "touched" and "affected." As he wrote, "Man is never sufficiently touched and affected (*tangi et affici*) by the awareness of his lowly state until he has compared himself with God's majesty."[265] Although Calvin's anthropomorphic language was carefully qualified (*quodammodo*, *quasi*), it was employed. Knowledge had been classically and traditionally compared to the action of the eye, or sight. In comparing it to the passion of the hand, or being led, Calvin departed from the contemplative norm. His concept of self-knowledge as leading a person by the hand to God coincided with the iconography of guidance, as in Caravaggio's painting of the angel of inspiration holding the hand of Matthew as he inscribes his gospel.[266]

Calvin understood the body as composed of nerves, joints, and ligatures that derived their vitality, as in Galen's medicine, solely from the head.[267] He thus could acknowledge the primacy in the sensorium of sight, which was situated in the head.[268] The eyes acted as guides for the other senses.[269] Calvin repeated the classical hierarchy of the human senses in commenting on the Pauline comparison between the more and the less dignified members of the human body (1 Cor. 12:15, 21). "For the eye obtains a higher grade of honor in the body than the hand: and the hand than the foot. Truly if a hand stirred by envy should refuse to do its duty, would nature suffer this? would the hand be heeded so that it might withdraw from the rest of the body?" He explained how Paul enjoined the more dignified parts not to despise the lesser, since all were needed. "The eye surpasses the hand, but nevertheless cannot despise it or insult it as if useless."[270] But that was in commenting on a scriptural argument for the cooperation of the members of the Church, which were like the parts of a body in their variety of gifts and offices. Calvin had also explained on Seneca that the conventional preference for the head, as a model for the ruler, was derived from medical opinion. "Although they [the physicians] agree that a mutual sympathy inheres in all the members of the body, still consider the head as the particular seat of life, inasmuch as from it all the nerves take their origin."[271]

In commenting on that scriptural verse, Calvin repeated the classical hierarchy of sight over touch that Paul had employed. But Calvin departed

---

265 Calvin, *Institutio christianae religionis* 1.13.13; 1.2.3; trans. Battles, 1:39.

266 See Lavin, "Divine Inspiration in Caravaggio," pp. 77-78; Barasch, *Giotto and the Language of Gesture*, pp. 134-36.

267 Calvin, in Col. 2:19. For the head and the heart as the vital parts, see also in Is. 1:5.

268 Bouwsma, *John Calvin*, p. 72.

269 Calvin, in Ps. 36:1.

270 Calvin, in 1 Cor. 12:15, 21.

271 Calvin, *In "De clementia"* 2.2.1; trans. Battles and Hugo, p. 349.

from that hierarchy, canonized by Augustine's intellectualist philosophy, in ignoring his correlative doctrine of the beatific vision. Commenting on the verse about the vision of God (1 John 3:2), Calvin complained that Augustine had tortured himself exquisitely about it yet failed to profit. Instead of such a contest over how God might be seen, Calvin emphasized the peace and sanctification without which he would not be seen.[272] In his revision of the contemplative ideal, to behold the face of God was not to contemplate his truth; rather, it was to believe his paternal favor.[273] Calvin thus importantly altered the tradition since Augustine of explaining the divine-human relationship by a facultative psychology. He resorted, rather, to social relationships. In defining the difference between a brutish and a human life, Calvin did not honor the classical norm of intellection. He determined the vital distinction as familial, both affectively and legally. Even brutish persons knew, he wrote, that they were "created for a nobler and higher end." As Calvin redefined that purpose, "And what end shall we find, except that of honoring God and of allowing ourselves to be governed by him, like children by a good father, to the end that after having finished the voyage of this corruptible life, we should be received into his eternal inheritance? Behold, the principal, and even the entire matter."[274] It was relational, not intellectual; social, not psychological.

In explicating that end, Calvin appropriated and dignified the sense of touch. He conferred on divine providence only eyes but also hands (and feet), as having equally important roles as sight. As he explained in *De aeterna Dei praedestinatione*, "We mean by providence not an idle observation by God in heaven of what goes on in earth, but His rule of the world which He made; for He is not the creator of a moment, but the perpetual governor. Thus the providence we ascribe to God belongs not less to his hands than to his eyes (*non minus ad manus quam ad oculos*)."[275] The hands of providence would prove to be the very hands of Christ and of his appointed ministers, angelic and human. In the initial book of *Institutio christianae religionis* Calvin stated traditionally the purpose and end of human existence as contemplative. He wrote of aspiring to "the clean con-

---

[272] Calvin, *Commentarius in epistolas catholicas* ad loc. Calvin is characteristically anti-speculative, e. g., in Phil. 1:10; in 1 Tim. 1:3. Against curious disputation about paradise, see *In harmoniam evangelicam* ad Luke 23:43. For further criticism of Augustine as "customarily too much the Platonist rapt to ideas," see in John 1:3.

[273] Calvin, in Ps. 17:15.

[274] Calvin, *Quatre sermons traictants de matières fort utiles pour nostre temps: De souffrir persecution*, in *Opera omnia* (Brunswick), 8:396-97. Calvin also summarized other authors' definitions of beatitude, e. g., in Heb. 4:10; in Col. 1:5; in John 11:25; in Gal. 2:19; in Eph. 4:18.

[275] Calvin, *De aeterna Dei praedestinatione*, in *Opera omnia* (Brunswick), 8:347; *Concerning the Eternal Predestination of God*, trans. J. K. S. Reid (London: James Clarke, 1961), p. 162, with my change of his "not only to his eyes but to his hands," since Calvin's comparison is more emphatic.

templation of God (*sinceram contemplationem Dei*)" through the Word and not just the world. He hoped that "the solid religion of the Word may occupy our minds, wherein shines the Spirit who makes us contemplate (*contemplare*) there the face of God."[276] Initially Calvin did not realize or acknowledge that contemplation and the Word were fundamentally disparate. Contemplation (*theoria*) was not a scriptural word or concept, so that to contemplate scripture was foreign to its very principle. So familiar was the insinuation of the Greek philosophical ideal to Christian scriptural exegesis that Calvin not only assumed their compatibility and coincidence but also accepted the apparently universal Catholic substitution of intellection for the very different ways in which scripture revealed the human end. However, by the climax and completion of that text in book four Calvin had advanced to a more scriptural mode of understanding. He asserted the human end not as intellectual on an ocular model but as possessive on a tactile model.

Calvin's own purpose he declared as "traditional," in the meaning of tradition as handed on, "hand to hand" serially.[277] His *Institutio christianae religionis* was a tactile task, right from "when I first set my hand (*manum*) to this work." As he elaborated in its dedicatory epistle to Francis I, "My purpose was solely to transmit (*tradere*) certain rudiments by which those who are touched (*tanguntur*) with any zeal for religion might be shaped (*formarentur*) to true godliness (*religio*)." He thus set his hand to the page, to hand on to touched persons some basics by which they might be shaped, as if sculptured, to religion as "binding." His opponents had misrepresented the evangelical purpose with lies and subtleties and slanders about the activity of evangelical hands, whose violence allegedly inverted the proper order of doctrine into a topsy-turvy world, dizzily on its head, rather than stably on its feet. "It is as if this doctrine looked to no other end that to wrest (*extorqueat*) scepters from the hands (*e manibus*) of kings, to cast down (*praecipitet*) all courts and judgments, to subvert (*suvertat*) all orders and civil governments, to disrupt (*perturbat*) the peace and quiet of the people, to abolish (*abroget*) all laws, to scatter (*dissipet*) all lordships and possessions—in short, to turn (*volvat*) everything upside down (*sursum deorsum*)." Calvin petitioned the king to "take up" (*suscipere*) an inquiry, since until now the case of the persecuted evangelicals had been badly "handled" (*tractata*), even "tossed about" (*exagitata*). He repeated the legal phrase for God seizing him through Farel to stay at Geneva. Calvin complained that his detractors had seized (*manum iniiciunt*) the reformed believers with accusations of arrogance and presumption. He explained his personal purpose as manual, as also handling. "I embrace (*complector*) the common cause of all believers, that of Christ himself." If

276 Calvin, *Institutio christianae religonis* 1.6.3; 1.9.3.

277 For the meaning of tradition, see Calvin, in Ps. 44:1.

his interpretation in the *Institutio christianae religionis* were measured by the rule of faith, that is scripture, then he was certain that "victory is in our hands (*in manibus*)."[278]

In so embracing the cause of Christ, Calvin imitated his singular hands. Although angelic,[279] and merely human, hands could be divine agents, they did no work without divine direction. So Calvin instructed that faith should tend from such intermediates as himself toward Christ as the sole mediator "that we may wholly depend upon him, lean upon him, be brought to him, and rest in him." Against the veneration of the saints he cited Ambrose on a manual Christ. "'He is our right hand, through which we offer ourselves to the Father. Unless he intercedes, there is no intercourse with God either for us or for all saints.'"[280] Calvin considered the hands of Christ, how the gospel testified to their healing touch. His commentary on the tactile cure of the leper was especially remarkable, since the medieval iconographic tradition had ruined the sense of the pericope. Scripture read: "And he stretched out his hand and touched him, saying, 'I will; be clean.' And immediately the leprosy was cleansed" (Matt. 8:3). Art did not portray Christ touching the unclean man humanly, however, but merely blessing him hieratically from a safe distance.[281] A contemporary example was in the Sistine Chapel, a fresco by Cosimo Rosselli (1439-1507) in which Christ extends his palm toward the leper and blesses him with his right hand. The leper kneels with his arms receptively open and up. The interpretation is sacrificial and priestly, just as Pope Sixtus IV himself understood it in his *De sanguine Christi*.[282] The iconographic tradition was a scene after the

---

278 Calvin, *Institutio christianae religionis* praef., in *Opera omnia* (Brunswick), 30:10, 11, 13; trans. Battles, pp. 9, 10, 11, 13.

279 Calvin, *Institutio christianae religionis* 3.20.23. For angels as custodians, see *In harmoniam evangelicam* ad Matt. 4:6.

280 Calvin, *Institutio christianae religionis* 1.14.12; 3.20.1, citing Ambrose, *De Isaac vel anima* 8.75; trans. Battles, 1:172; 2:879.

281 For collected illustrations, see László Kátó, *Horn, Clapper, and Bell* (Montreal: Institute of Microbiology and Hygiene, 1976), pp. 6, 20, 34, 35, 100, 104, 105; William B. Ober, "Can the Leper Change His Spots? The Iconography of Leprosy," *American Journal of Dermapathology* 5 (1983):49, 53, 54, 55; Schiller, *Ikonographie der christlichen Kunst*, 1:462-63, figs. 530-35. For general background, see Saul Nathaniel Brody, *The Disease of the Soul: Leprosy in Medieval Literature* (Ithaca, N.Y.: Cornell University Press, 1974), and especially on art, pp. 48, 50, 51, and ill. 5, 6; Françoise Bériac, *Histoire des lépreux au Moyen Âge: Une société d'exclus* (Paris: Imago for Centre national des lettres, 1988); Peter Richards, *The Medieval Leper and his Northern Heirs* (Cambridge: D. S. Brewer, 1977); Laurence Wright, "'Burning' and Leprosy in Old French," *Medium Aevum* 56 (1987):101-11; Luke Demaitre, "The Description and Diagnosis of Leprosy by Fourteenth-Century Physicians," *Bulletin of the History of Medicine* 59 (1985):327-44; Michael Dols, "The Leper in Medieval Islamic Society," *Speculum* 58 (1983):891-916.

282 Cosimo Rosselli, Healing of the leper (lower right corner of Sermon on the Mount), fresco, Sistine Chapel; reproduced in Leopold D. Ettlinger, *The Sistine Chapel before Michelangelo: Religious Imagery and Papal Primacy* (Oxford: Clarendon, 1965), pl. 11, and see pp. 89-90. Ober, "Iconography of Leprosy," p. 175, fig. 23, with detail p. 176, fig. 24. For the rationale of the cure of the leper in the papal chapel, see the legendary leprosy of

cure, as if to depict Christ touching such an impure person would be scandalous morally, repulsive aesthetically, and dangerous medically. The divine hands do not artistically touch the leprous hands.

Nor did the evangelical literature improve the interpretation of the pericope. The depiction of Jesus healing the leper in Geiler von Kaysenberg's *Evangelium* has Jesus standing, inclining toward him with extended hands; the leper sits holding a bowl in his right hand with his left outstretched.[283] But they do not touch. This lack of contact in the iconographic tradition reflected the list of prohibitions against a leper touching: forbidden to touch a well or even its rope, unless wearing gloves; forbidden to touch any object in bargaining, until purchased; forbidden to touch children or to hand them anything; forbidden to touch ecclesiastical vessels. Protective gloves could be required as an item of the leper's distinctive costume.[284] Yet the first published illustration of a human person actually touching a leper dated to the same year as Roselli's fresco, in a woodcut of *Regimen sanitatis* where an examining physician touches the leper's bare chest with his hand.[285]

There was a fragment of a gospel book dating to the ninth century from Calvin's territory, from Hautvillers or Reims, that shows Christ touching the leper's chin.[286] Whether or not Calvin knew such a rarity, he did know scripture and he did not shrink from an interpretation of Jesus touching the leper. Although according to the law the touch of the leper was contagious, Calvin affirmed that in Christ there was "a purity that absorbed all uncleanness and pollution, so that in touching the leper he was neither contaminated nor did he transgress the law." The incident became for Calvin the premise for an analogy with the very incarnation. "For taking up our flesh not only did he dignify the hand with his contact, but in one and the same body he grew together with us, so that we might be flesh of his flesh (Gen. 2:2)." Scriptural reference was to the divine commandment of the carnal

---

Constantine, who in exchange for a cure granted Pope Sylvester II temporal dominion (Donation of Constantine). See Brody, *Disease of the Soul*, pp. 57-59; Stephen R. Ell, "Leprosy and Social Class in the Middle Ages," *International Journal of Leprosy and Other Mycobaterial Diseases* 56 (1986):303-5. Cf. Botticelli, fresco, Purification of the leper, Sistine Chapel; reproduced, Ober, "Iconography of Leprosy," p. 177, fig. 25, and see pp. 176-78; Ettlinger, *Sistine Chapel*, pl. 9. See also in general John Monfasani, "A Description of the Sistine Chapel under Pope Sixtus IV," *Artibus et historiae* 7 (1983):9-18.

283 Jesus healing the leper, Johann Geiler von Kaysenberg, *Evangelium* (Strassburg, 1515); reproduced in Kátó, *Horn, Clapper, and Bell*, p. 6.

284 Brody, *Disease of the Soul*, pp. 66, 67, 78.

285 Ober, "Iconography of Leprosy," p. 178; reproduced, Two physicians examine a leper, woodcut, from *Regimen sanitatis* (Ulm: Conard Dinckmut, 1482), p. 178, fig. 27. See also Leprosy diagnosed by a committee, woodcut, H. von Gersdorff, *Feldtbuch der Wundtarztney* (Strassburg: J. Schott, 1517); reproduced, p. 179, fig. 29. For a medieval example in manuscript, where the doctor touches the leper's spotted face with his hands, see Physician examining a leper, marginal sketch, early 13th century, Trinity College, Cambridge MS. 0.1.20, fol. 262e; reproduced, p. 179, fig. 28.

286 Sketch, second half of ninth century, Hautvillers or Reims, fragment of a gospel book; reproduced in Schiller, *Ikonographie der christlichen Kunst*, 1:532.

union of Adam and Eve. Thus the incarnation was metaphorically in Calvin's exegesis, as in John of the Cross's lyric, marital and sexual. In assuming human flesh, Calvin continued, God did more than extend his arm to people: he descended from heaven to hell. "Yet nevertheless, he did not contract any stain but, retaining integrity, he emptied out all our defilements and filled us with his sanctity." Although Jesus could have healed the leper by his word alone, by the touch of his hands he applied the feeling of pity. The gesture should not be astonishing, thought Calvin, since God willed to put on human flesh so that he might purge us from all sins. "The extension of his hand was a sign and signal of immense grace and goodness." The text should not be read sluggishly and frigidly but with great amazement "that the son of God did not abhor conversation with a leper but should even reach out to touch that uncleanness."[287]

In his exegesis of the pericope of the transfiguration Calvin explained that Jesus raised up the prostrate disciples to fulfill his duty. He descended to them that they might proceed to the sight of God fearlessly, for his majesty was so completely terrible that it was remote from all flesh. "Not by his familiar speech alone is the heart consoled, but by his touch is it confirmed." The paralytic in the gospel (John 5:3) was cured "as by a hand from heaven openly thrust forth," which manual extension made God plainly present. Although the open hand of a healing God publicized his presence among people, its initiative was both secret and surprising. "Truly beyond expectation he displayed a hand drawn forth from hidden places how much his goodness surpasses the straights of our faith."[288] Calvin's insistence on an open palm deliberately proffered from a secret place related to his apologetic against the notion of an idle God. As Erasmus explained the adage *manum habere sub pallio*, to "have one's hands in one's pockets," literally "under one's cloak," it was used of lazy and spiritless persons. The expression originated in "the use of gesture in speaking." Quintilian had criticized orators who never exerted themselves to their subject by speaking with gestures but soberly kept their hands under their cloak.[289] The artistic motif of the slack or hidden hand signified the fool[290] and the idler; by the sixteenth

[287] Calvin, *In harmoniam evangelicam* ad. Matt. 8:3. Modern exegesis interprets the pericope more as a ritual purification than a medical healing. See Carl R. Kazmierski, "Evangelist and Leper: A Socio-cultural Study of Mark 1.40-45," *New Testament Studies* 38 (1992):37-50; Howard Clark Kee, *Miracle in the Early Christian World* (New Haven, Conn.: Yale University Press, 1983), pp. 10-11. See also Calvin's exegesis of Christ touching the coffin of the son of the widow of Naim as a sign of his willingness to descend to the grave to vivify believers. *In harmoniam evangelicam* ad Luke 7:11.

[288] Calvin, *In harmoniam evangelicam* ad Matt. 17:5.

[289] Erasmus, *Adagia* 2.10.31; trans. Mynors, 34:139-40.

[290] D. J. Gifford, "Iconographical Notes Towards a Definition of the Medieval Fool," *Journal of the Warburg and Courtauld Institutes* 37 (1974):336-42.

century it indicated a particular idler, the pauper.[291] Calvin insisted that, even when the divine hands were hidden, they were never idle. Governance, not fortune, ruled the universe. An idle God was himself the invention of fools.[292] Calvin affirmed the "paternal care of God who has embraced us before we were born."[293] The active exposition of the hidden hands of God was principally the work of Christ. "For Christ is the image, in which not only his breast renders God to our sight but his hands and also his feet. I call 'breast' that secret love by which we are embraced (*complexus*) in Christ: through the hands and also the feet, which I understand as the exposure to our eyes of his works."[294]

Calvin commented on how Jesus cured by the imposition of his hands. The act was proper and reasonable, he thought, since by law imposition was a sign of reconciliation and also a rite of consecration. It was further a means of conferring the gifts of the Spirit, as when Jesus blessed the children (Matt. 19:13, 15). The ceremony was doubtless one that Christ frequently and habitually used, Calvin supposed. Although he could have accomplished his will without lifting a finger, a liberal use of external signs was useful to people. Calvin then offered an interpretation that signaled his own understanding of salvation. "But I interpret the hands of Christ imposed on the sick simply that he, commending them to the Father, procured grace and deliverance from their diseases."[295] By that interpretation Calvin affirmed not only the active hands of Jesus but also the Son as procuring with them favor and freedom from the hand of the Father. The belief was patristic,[296] and Calvin himself cited it from Ambrose against the veneration of the saints for the sole mediation of Christ. Again, "'He is our right hand, through which we offer ourselves to the Father.'"[297]

The manual collaboration of Father and Son was current in such devotion as Vittoria Colonna's verse.

> The great Father draws the soul to heaven,
> bound with string of love, and the knot is tied,
> by his dear Son's hand; and so lovely a manner,
> no less than the act itself contents the heart.[298]

---

[291] Susan Koslow, "Frans Hals's Fisherboys: Exemplars of Idleness," *Art Bulletin* 67 (1975):421-25.

[292] Calvin, *Institutio christianae religionis* 1.4.2; 1.2.2; in Ps. 14:1. For general theological background, see B. A. Gerrish, "'To the Unknown God': Luther and Calvin on the Hiddenness of God," in idem, *The Old Protestantism and the New: Essays on the Reformation Heritage* (Chicago: University of Chicago Press, 1982), pp. 131-49.

[293] Calvin, *In harmoniam evangelicam* ad Matt. 26:39.

[294] Cavin, *In libros Mosis* argumentum ad Gen., in *Opera omnia* (Brunswick), 23:11.

[295] Calvin, *In harmoniam evangelicam* ad Luke 4:39; Matt. 19:13, 15; Mark 7:32.

[296] Gross, *Menschenhand und Gotteshand*, pp. 445-47.

[297] Calvin, *Institutio christianae religionis* 3.20, citing Ambrose, *De Isaac vel anima* 8.75; trans. Battles, 2:289;

[298] Colonna, *Rime spirituali* 73; trans. Gribaldi, in *Women Writers*, p. 41.

As Calvin himself wrote, "For Christ is the image, in which not only his breast renders God to our sight, but his hands and also his feet. I call 'breast' that secret love by which we are embraced (*complexus*) in Christ: through the hands and also the feet, which I understand as the exposure to our eyes of his works."[299] The breast of Christ was God's secret embrace of believers; his hands (and feet) were the open and visible embrace. Manual examples in scripture were the imposition of his hands on people, by which Jesus commended the sick to the Father and thus procured for them grace and deliverance.

The supreme manual exemplar was when Jesus crucified delivered his own spirit into his Father's hands. That was for Calvin the saving act by which all believers were handed over to God. God "embraced in favor (*favore suo complecti*) those whom he had loved before the creation of the world," he wrote, but he "revealed his love when he was reconciled to us by Christ's blood."[300] The gospel verse "Into thy hands I commend my spirit" included the commission of all believers to God. "Christ did not commend his soul to the Father with private regard to himself, but all souls of his faithful people as if embraced into a packet (*fasiculo complexum*)."[301] The crucified Christ did more than give a helping hand, as in the adage *dare manum*, which Calvin knew meant to help a shipwrecked voyager or a pokey child.[302] His verb *complector* properly meant that Jesus had entwined himself around believers, like the artistic Graces interlinking their arms. He did it so that, together with him, they might be saved. Jesus' dying prayer was decisive. "By this prayer he reserved the right of saving all souls. Not only does the heavenly Father for his sake deem them worthy of his charge; but resigning his portions to him, he commits their salvation to him." At his own death each Christian should thus commend himself to that guardian of those whom the Father has handed to him.[303] For Calvin the crucified Christ committed his soul into the hands of the Father and, in so doing, embraced his arms around, bundling them up, the souls of all believers. The Father in reciprocity handed back to the Son their salvation. Calvin's soteriology as a manual deliverance of the faithful from Son to Father, then Father to Son, was fundamental and essential to his doctrine of election.

In his articulation of the creedal affirmation of the communion of saints in *Institutio christianae religionis* Calvin asserted election as a divine secret. It was not for people to distinguish the reprobate from the elect. Conviction of membership in the Church was not a matter of sensual perception.

---

299 Calvin, *In libros Mosis* argumentum ad Gen., in *Opera omnia* (Brunswick), 23:11.

300 Calvin, *Institutio religionis christianae* 2.17.2; trans. Battles, 1:530.

301 Calvin, *In harmoniam evangelicam* ad Luke 23:46.

302 Calvin, *In "De clementia"* 2.6.2.

303 Calvin, *In harmoniam evangelicam* ad Luke 23:46. For God as the custodian to whom the faithful yield their souls in death, see in John 19:30. For the hand of the Father present at the scene of the crucifixion in art, see Kirigin, *Mano divina*, pp. 178-83.

To embrace (*ad amplexandam*) the unity of the Church by the sharing of individual benefits "there is no need to perceive the Church with the eyes or to pat it with the hands (*manibus palpare*)." It was rather for human faith "to establish (*statuere*) with certainty in our minds that all those who, by the clemency of God the Father through the efficacy of the Holy Spirit should come into the participation of Christ are segregated into the personal fund (*peculium*) and personal possession (*propriam possessionem*) of God."[304] Calvin's terminology was jurisprudential. The very title of his text as *institutio*, although polysemous, resonated with its usage as the title of important legal compilations. In Roman civil law *institutio* was also a particular and basic term, as in Gaius's *Institutiones*[305] and Justinian's *Institutiones*.[306] It meant the institution of an heir, by the solemn form, "Titius heres esto." In designating sons in power as heirs, they had to be instituted or disinherited by name in the will, or else the will was void. Inheritance was that portion of the property of the deceased that came to the heir; it could be divided among heirs in any share or proportion, traditionally into twelfths.[307]

When Calvin titled his work *institutio* he generally meant "instruction," specifying that he was arranging the Christian religion according to a "simple and . . . elementary form of teaching (*simplicem et . . . rudem formam docendi*)."[308] The order of teaching was commonly distinguished from the order of discovery, which would have been the first part of rhetoric, or invention (*inventio*). The word *institutio* primarily meant not instruction, however, but "disposition, arrangement," which was the third classical part of rhetoric. As Calvin epitomized true eloquence, it consisted in "the prudent invention of subjects, ingenious disposition, and elegant speaking."[309] Erasmus had compared disposition or order in speech to the nerves in an animate body, connecting its parts.[310] As Pierre de Ronsard (1524-85) would define its contemporary usage in *L'art poétique*, disposition was "an elegant

304 Calvin, *Institutio christianae religionis* 4.1.3. For the efficacy of the Spirit, see 3.1.1.

305 For Gaius on the institution of the heir, see Zulueta, *Institutes of Gaius*, 2:91-93.

306 Justinian, *Institutiones* 1.14.3; cf. *Digest* 28.5.

307 For the institution of the heir, see Watson, *Law of Succession*, pp. 40-51; and for inheritance, pp. 1-7. A primary text on the institution of heirs is Justinian, *Digest* 28.5.

308 Calvin, *Institutio christianae religionis* praef., in *Opera omnia* (Brunswick), 2:9; trans. Battles, 1:9. For the different use of "institutes" in modern literary criticism to describe a genre of ideal portraits of a society, institution, or occupation, see Thomas M. Greene, "The Flexibility of the Self in Renaissance Literature," in *The Disciplines of Criticism*, ed. Peter Demetz, idem, and Lowrey Nelson, Jr. (New Haven, Conn.: Yale University Press, 1968), p. 250.

309 Calvin, in 1 Cor. 1:17. Calvin was well disposed toward rhetoric by his acceptance in his commentary ad loc. of Erasmus's correction of the paradigmatic *verbum* of John 1:1 to *sermo*. Théodore de Bèze also followed Erasmus's correction in his translation. Boyle, "*Sermo*: Reopening the Conversation on Translating Jn 1,1," *Vigiliae christianae* 31 (1977): 161.

310 Erasmus, *Ecclesiastes* 861.

and perfect collocation and ordering of the subjects invented."[311] Calvin's text was a pedagogical organization.[312] But Calvin's rhetorical arrangement climaxed in the legal meaning of institution. And so very ingeniously did he argue the case of how the children in the authority of the Father were "instituted" as legal heirs by their adoption as brothers of Christ. Calvin also explained how they thus passed legally from divine ownership to divine possession as a "personal fund." It was the precise function of the Son as mediator, he taught in *Institutio christianae religionis*, to make people inheritors: "to make the children of men, children of God; of the heirs of Gehenna, heirs (*haeredes*) of the Heavenly Kingdom."[313] His very text *Institutio christianae religionis* concerned the "institution" of heirs through Christ.

Calvin's knowledge of the legal inheritance of property had been expertly demonstrated in his commentary on Seneca's *De clementia* at the phrase "on being recorded as co-heir." He had explained in professional detail, by reference to Justinian's *Digest*, the distinction between the recorded heir (*heres scriptus*) and the named heir (*heres nuncuptatio*). Calvin considered the case of a somewhat obscure naming or recording of an heir in a will, whether it could be settled according to the common practices. He stated his own conclusion on the question. "Therefore a recorded heir is one whom the testator has recorded with his own hand; a named heir, one whose name the testator dictated to a receiving scribe." He supported his legal opinion with Suetonius's example of Anthony naming Cleopatra's children as heirs. He also cited Juvenal and Pliny as literary witnesses to the usage of naming heirs by dictation.[314] Calvin applied his knowledge of the law of inheritance to the ordinances for Geneva, for which he drafted one on complaints of heirs against heirs.[315] When he composed his own last will and testament, he used precisely the legal term *institutio* that was the profound meaning of his *Institutio christianae religionis*. Calvin established his legal will on his personal inheritance of eternal life through Christ, "having no

---

311 "une elegante et parfaicte collocation et ordre des choses inventées." Pierre de Ronsard, *L'art poétique*, in *Oeuvres complètes*, 2:1001. See also Quintilian, *Institutiones oratoriae* 7.1.1.

312 See also Bouwsma, *John Calvin*, p. 5.

313 Calvin, *Institutio christianae religionis* 2.12.2; trans. Battles, 1:465. For reward as "inheritance," see 3.18.2.

314 Calvin, *In "De clementia"* 1.16, citing Justinian, *Digest* 37.11.8; 28.1.21 (cf. 28.5); Suetonius, *Augustus* 17.1; Juvenal, *Saturae* 3.161, 6.218.; trans. Battles and Hugo, p. 259. For the French customary law of inheritance, see Emmanuel Le Roy Ladurie, "Family Structures and Inheritance Customs in Sixteenth-Century France," trans. Patricia M. Rannum, in *Family and Society*, ed. Robert Forster and Orest Ranum (Baltimore, Md.: Johns Hopkins University Press, 1976), pp. 75-103; rpt. from *Annales* 27 (1972):825-46. For an introduction to the canon law of inheritance, see Harold J. Berman, *Law and Revolution: The Formation of the Western Legal Tradition* (Cambridge, Mass.: Harvard University Press, 1983) pp. 230-37.

315 Calvin, *Fragments des travaux relatifs à la législation civile et politique*, in *Opera omnia* (Brunwsick), 10-1:143.

other hope or refuge than by his gratuitous adoption, on which my entire salvation is founded." As for instituting his family as heirs, "Concerning the little good that God has given me here to dispose of, I name and institute (*institue*) for my sole inheritor my well loved brother, Antoine Calvin."[316]

Calvin interpreted scripture in his *Institutio christianae religionis* according to his learning, and his knowledge was of the humanities and the law. The academic study of the law in his native France was divided between medieval tradition and renaissance innovation. The tradition had adapted Roman civil law to contemporary circumstances by glosses and commentaries on the glosses. The innovation, headed by Budé, recovered the foundations of Roman civil law as a source of ancient customs, institutions, and wisdom. After a degree in the humanities at the University of Paris, Calvin began the study of the law in obedience to his father. At the University of Orléans, where he matriculated, the doctors of the law were conservatives, who used Accursius's scholastic *Magna glossa* and the commentary on it by Bartole da Sassoferrato (1314-57). Calvin was subsequently attracted to the faculty of law at Bourges by the appointment there of Andrea Alciati (d.1550), famous as an emblematist but also a jurisconsult, who was doctor of laws from Bologna and a practitioner at Milan.[317] Calvin was himself finally early in 1531 *licencié-es-lois*, probably from the University of Orléans.[318]

Calvin's knowledge of Roman civil law was professional, and he preferred the new direct method on the sources to the mediate usage of the medieval tradition. In his commentary on Seneca's *De clementia*, written in the year after receiving his law degree, he employed primary legal texts. His principal source was the compiled *Corpus iuris civilis*, which he cited at least eighty-six times; but also Justinian's *Digest* forty-nine times, *Codex* thirteen times, his *Institutiones* twice, and *Novellae* once. Calvin appealed on legal procedure to Cicero, Quintilian, and the Greek orators. Among contemporary sources he used Budé's texts on Justinian's digest, titled *Annotationes in Pandectas* and *Annotationes reliquae (posteriores) in Pandectas*,

---

316" Testament de Calvin," in *Opera omnia* (Brunswick), 20:297, 300.

317 For Calvin's studies of the humanities and the law, see Breen, *John Calvin*, pp. 15-52, 139; Thomas F. Torrance, *The Hermeneutics of John Calvin* (Edinburgh: Scottish Academic Press, 1988), pp. 79-132. For context on jurisprudence in French universities, see also Peter Stein, "Legal Humanism and Legal Science," in idem, *The Character and Influence of the Roman Civil Law: Historical Essays* (London: Hambledon, 1988), pp. 91-100; Donald R. Kelley, *The Foundations of Modern Historical Scholarship: Language, Law, and History in the French Renaissance* (New York: Columbia University Press, 1970), pp. 53-80, 87-103; and for a sample of its practice, Michael L. Monheit, "Guillaume Budé, Andrea Alciati, Pierre de l'Estoile: Renaissance Interpreters of Roman Law," *Journal of the History of Ideas* 58 (1997):21-40.

318 T. H. L. Parker, *John Calvin: A Biography* (London: J. M. Dent, 1975), p. 159, according to an affadavit dated 14 February 1532.

which had been decisive for his own methodological change from the medieval tradition to the renaissance innovation.[319] Calvin appropriated Budé's annotations as the very model for his commentary on Seneca.[320] He also cited Alciati and Johann Ulrich Zasius.[321]

Although Calvin apparently did not practice in the courts, his knowledge of the law endured. The legal knowledge early displayed in his commentary on Seneca was later reflected in his politics.[322] He also established new ordinances for Geneva, which had been by statute under canon law. Repugnant to that, he sought to unify Roman civil law with the customary law of Geneva, as reflected in its franchises and edicts.[323] In his contributions to its codification he demonstrated a foundation in the *Corpus iuris civilis* for laws of contract and of property and for judicial procedure.[324] Calvin was capable of applying civil law not only to the interpretation of classical literature but also to contemporary life.

Even Calvin's understanding of the scriptural function of the law,[325] which Luther firmly opposed to grace, was positive, in imagining order and structure, including the structure of divine love in the acts of creation and redemption.[326] Calvin's mentality toward the sacred and the secular was not strictly dichotomous, and he usefully appropriated civil law as a proper discipline for the understanding of God.[327] As he stated in *Institutio christianae religionis*, "We fancy no lawless (*exlegem*) God who is a law unto himself (*sibi ipsi lex*)." Indeed, the divine will was "the law of all laws." In considering secular truth as spiritual gift, Calvin asked, "Shall we deny

---

319 Battles, introduction to *In "De clementia,"* p. 140. For Calvin's interest in fundamental legal questions in the commentary, see also Breen, *John Calvin*, pp. 61, 62; and for Budé's influence, pp. 44, 140.

320 Breen, *John Calvin*, p. 96; and for Budé himself, see pp. 113-24.

321 Battles, introduction to *In "De clementia,"* p. 140.

322 Breen, *John Calvin*, pp. 141-45; Oberman, *"Initia Calvini": The Matrix of Calvin's Reformation*, Mededelingen van de afdeling Letterkunde, nieuwe Reeks, 54-4 (Amsterdam: Koninklijke Nederlandse Akademie van Wetenschappen, 1991), pp. 36-38.

323 Josef Bohatec, "Calvin et la procédure civile à Genève," *Revue historique de droit français et étranger* 62 (1938):229-32, 294.

324 Harro Höpfl, *Christian Polity of John Calvin* (Cambridge: Cambridge University Press, 1982), p. 6; Alister E. McGrath, *A Life of John Calvin: A Study in the Shaping of Western Culture* (Oxford: Basil Blackwell, 1990), p. 59.

325 For a systematic theological exposition, see I. John Hesselink, *Calvin's Concept of the Law*, Princeton Theological Monograph Series, 20 (Allison Park, Pa.: Pickwick, 1992).

326 Edward A. Dowey, "Law in Luther and Calvin," *Theology Today* 41 (1984):153.

327 Tradition has denied his usage of Roman civil law in theology, as if his religious conversion erased his secular learning. Arguments that the concepts of the divine majesty and of the divine transcendence of the law owed to secular legal theory have been dismissed, influentially so by François Wendel, *Calvin: Sources et évolution de sa pensée religieuse* (Paris: Presses universitaires de France, 1950), p. 126. Although it has been allowed that Calvin's legal study influenced his emphasis on clarity, brevity, and architectonic principle in *Institutio christianae religionis*, its "content and purpose, which are almost wholly biblically grounded" have been stated as quite different by Basil Hall, "John Calvin, the Jurisconsults, and the *jus civile*," *Studies in Church History* 3 (1966):216.

that the truth shone upon the ancient jurists who established civic order and discipline with such great equity?" He honored jurisprudence first in his list of worthy secular disciplines; beneath it in distinction were philosophy, rhetoric, medicine, and mathematics.[328] Calvin lauded all the disciplines of solid erudition with true method as usefully proceeding from the Holy Spirit. Reason rendered a human better than a beast, he conceded. But "how much honor do the liberal teachings merit, which so refine a person to render him truly human!" he exclaimed. Calvin reserved his supreme praise for the law. "Who would not extol with the highest praises jurisprudence, by which republics, sovereignties, and reigns are sustained?"[329] Calvin also instructed on a Christian resort to the secular legal system, as guided by charity.[330] In his dedicatory letter to *Institutio christianae religionis* he declared that he himself was taking up "the common cause of all believers, that of Christ himself," a legal case.[331] It was in Calvin's appropriation of jurisprudence, subordinating philosophy to it, that he achieved an authentically scriptural interpretation of the human end as possession (adoptive inheritance), in distinction to the philosophical tradition of the human end as intellection (beatific vision).

Exactly how Calvin's readers comprehended his theology of inheritance would have depended on the reception of Roman civil law. He himself had contributed an ordinance for Geneva on the complaints of heirs against heirs.[332] The civil edicts composed by the jurist Germain Colladon had dispositions on persons and goods, including wills and "the institution of heirs" as legal categories. Concerning the form of a valid will, the edicts did not juridically demand the institution of heirs, however.[333] Calvin in his own will, however, used the legal formula: *ie nomme et institute*.[334] His

328 Calvin, *Institutio christianae religionis* 3.23.2; 2.2.15; trans. Battles, 2:920; 1:274.

329 Calvin, in 1 Cor. 1:17, 20.

330 Joseph Allegretti, "'In All This Love Will Be the Best Guide': John Calvin on the Christian's Resort to the Secular Legal System," *Journal of Law and Religion* 9 (1991):1-16. For Calvin on civil law and ethics, see Ralph Hancock, *Calvin and the Foundations of Modern Politics* (Ithaca, N.Y.: Cornell University Press, 1989), pp. 82-99.

331 Calvin, *Institutio christianae religionis* praef., in *Opera omnia* (Brunswick), 2:11; trans. Battles, 1:11. For Luther's *De servo arbitrio* as a legal case composed as forensic rhetoric, see Boyle, *Rhetoric and Reform: Erasmus' Civil Dispute with Luther*, Harvard Historical Monographs, 71 (Cambridge, Mass.: Harvard University Press, 1983).

332 Calvin, *Législation civile et politique*, in *Opera omnia* (Brunswick), 10-1:143.

333 Erich-Hans Kaden, *Le jurisconsulte German Colladon ami de Jean Calvin et de Théodore de Bèze*, Mémoires publiés par la Faculté de droit de Genève, 41 (Geneva: Librairie de l'Université, 1974), pp. 115, 123. His source is *Edits civils de la République de Genève* (Geneva: Société des libraires et éditeurs de la Suisse romande, Geneva, 1707), which was unavailable to me. Although social reproduction depended largely on inheritance, there has been little research by either legal or social historians on the actual practices and processes. For this criticism, see also Thomas Kuehen, "Law, Death, and Heirs in the Renaissance: Repudiation of Inheritance in Florence," *Renaissance Quarterly* 45 (1992):485. The social model at Geneva included women since equal inheritance was practiced. E. William Monter, "Women in Calvinist Geneva (1550-1800)," *Signs* 6 (1980):202.

334 Calvin, "Testament," in *Opera omnia* (Brunswick), 20:300.

theological concept of adoption was a more complicated, perhaps vacuous, social model, since adoption had been abandoned. Adoption had been a practical Roman strategy for obtaining heirs, thus prolonging the lineage, in a society threatened by high rate of infant mortality.[335] Yet Catholicism discouraged adoption, although it did not canonically prohibit it, because its concern with the temporal inheritance of goods competed with the spiritual inheritance of the good as salvation.[336] Medieval society did not practice adoption, and the estates of heirless couples devolved to the Church as an acquisition of property.[337]

In the sixteenth century in Calvin's native France adoption was in disuse. French customary law either forbade adopted children the same rights of inheritance, especially through intestate succession, as legitimate biological children or it proscribed adoption altogether. Gallican jurists, commenting on its disappearance, pronounced adoption "unnatural" and "un-Christian." Preferring blood ties to legal ties, they rejected it as a foreign, Roman method. Popular prejudice considered adoption a public admission of sterility or infertility, a challenge to the divine will manifest in natural causality, and a disruption of the inheritance of collateral heirs that compromised the purity of the bloodline. In actual practice, circumventing the written law by improvised strategies, some artisans and merchants in Paris and Lyon did adopt children, according to contracts from the registers of notaries.[338] Unless adoption was also revived in the reformed practice, Calvin's concept would not have had a social model. Yet Théodore de Bèze (1519-1605), successor to Calvin, testified in his *Tractatio de repudiis et divortis* that adoption had ceased to be practiced in Geneva.[339] So, Calvin's congregation had no practical analogy for his doctrine. Repudiating the judgment of the Gallican jurists, among whom he had studied, indeed of the civil law codes of most western European countries, Calvin reverted to the Roman model. Although he might have agreed that adoption was unnatural, he certainly disagreed that it was un-Christian. Adoption was his very definition of Christian.

---

335 See Mireille Corbier, "Divorce and Adoption as Roman Familial Strategies (Le divorce et l'adoption 'en plus')," in *Marriage, Divorce, and Children in Ancient Rome*, ed. Beryl Rawson (Oxford: Clarendon Press for the Humanities Research Centre, Australian National University, Canberra, 1991), pp. 63-76; Suzanne Dixon, *The Roman Family* (Baltimore, Md.: Johns Hopkins University Press, 1991), pp. 112-13.

336 Kristen E. Gager, *Blood Ties and Fictive Ties: Adoption and Family Life in Early Modern France* (Princeton, N.J.: Princeton University Press, 1996), p. 3.

337 Jack Goody, *The Development of the Family and Marriage in Europe* (Cambridge: Cambridge University Press, 1983), pp. 98-102.

338 Gager, *Blood Ties and Fictive Ties*, pp. 51-56, 3-6, 60, 8-9, 15, and for the Catholic rejection of adoption, pp. 41-47.

339 Théodore de Bèze, *Tractatio de repudiis et divortis*, p. 204; cited by Natalie Z. Davis, "Ghosts, Kin, and Progeny: Some Features of Family Life in Early Modern France," *Daedalus* 106 (1977):113 n. 56.

Despite customary law and Catholic ideology, and parallel to Roman civil law, adoption would have had for Calvin's congregation a scriptural model. Adoption was ancient for the relationship between God and Israel. The concept was not sacral in origin but secular: the scriptural formulas were borrowed from Near-Eastern texts.[340] Filial adoption for inheritance was also an aspect of Pauline soteriology (Rom. 8:14, 23, 9:4; Gal. 4:6-7; Eph. 1:5). Calvin explicated adoption from those several Pauline texts but he thought it not restricted to them. Rather, it was fundamental to the very gospels, even though they did not cite that word or concept. In his argument to his commentary on the synoptic gospels Calvin declared that "gratuitous adoption" was revealed by the incarnation, in Christ becoming a brother with humans. And in his exegesis he repeated his belief in adoption, even when the word did not appear in the text. In sum, he declared, "For the key to the kingdom of heaven is the gratuitous adoption of God, which we conceive from the word."[341]

Roman civil law was appropriate for such an urban culture as Geneva, since it concerned both concepts of property useful to a commercial and manufacturing elite and methods for the protection and management of possessions useful to technicians.[342] Calvin must have been convinced that its jurisprudence, which was in revival and reception—and that by his own hand, could still be effective for Christian instruction. In his description of the elect he immediately signaled legal usage with the verb *statuere*. Christians were not merely to "establish" the meaning of election with certainty in their minds, they were to "hold it to be the law": as a statute. He declared that the elect were those "in the personal fund (*peculium*) and personal possession (*personam possessionem*) of God." The terms *possessio* and *peculium* had definite legal meanings. Absolute ownership with power of disposal at will was dominion (*dominium*), and God absolutely had dominion over everyone. As Calvin wrote, "The perfect plenitude of all dominion (*dominium*) is to be found in the one God."[343] Possession differed (although under certain conditions possession could result in eventual ownership). A person might own a thing and not possess it or possess it but

[340] Janet L. R. Melnyk, "When Israel Was a Child: Ancient Near Eastern Adoption Formulas and the Relationship between God and Israel," in *History and Interpretation: Essays in Honour of John H. Hayes*, ed. M. Patrick Graham, William D. Brown, and Jeffrey K. Kuan, Journal of the Society of Old Testament Studies Supplement, 173 (Sheffield: Journal of the Society of Old Testament Studies, 1993), pp. 245-59.

[341] Calvin, *In harmoniam evangelicam* argumentum, in *Opera omnia* (Brunswick), 23:1. For adoption, see ad Luke 11:27; Matt. 3:2; 22:30; in Ps. 46:7; 103:13; in Is. 43:1, 21; in Rom. 1:7; 8:17, 23, 29; in Gal. 3:26; in 1 Cor. 1:20; in Col. 3:22; in 1 Thess. 5:24; in 2 Thess. 2:14; in 1 Pet. 1:6; 1 John, argumentum, 3:1.

[342] For he general suitability of Roman law to a late medieval urban culture, see Gerald Strauss, *Law, Resistance, and the State: The Opposition to Roman Law in Reformation Germany* (Princeton, N.J.: Princeton University Press, 1986), p. 60.

[343] Calvin, in Ps. 136.1.

not own it.[344] Dominion was legal sovereignty; possession, factual sovereignty.[345] Possession in a non-technical sense meant actual physical control over a thing or person in fact and intention. It could be exercised directly or through another person. In a more technical sense possession meant "that kind of control over a thing for the benefit of which the possessory interdicts were intended."[346]

Calvin not only knew the legal theory of possession but he also applied it to Geneva's ordinances concerning possessions and concerning lawsuits on possessions.[347] Concerning possessory complaints he distinguished between the right and the cause. Right was based on the right of the acquisition of property by inheritance, sale, or gift. For proof of the right of possession the possessor had to valorize his title.[348] In refined classical law the acquisition of possession required physical control (*corpus*) and requisite intention (*animus*). There were various means for citizens to acquire property, such as a formal act of transfer (*mancipatio*), or possession of it for a certain uninterrupted period of time (*usucapio*), or the capture of a wild animal (*occupatio*). The legality of *traditio*, the voluntary transfer of the thing by delivery, usually physical delivery,[349] based Calvin's soteriology.

The election of the children of Abraham as a *peculium* Calvin had indicated in his exegesis of Ex. 19:5 as an "acquisition" (*acquirert*). The new election by adoption in Christ was a certain type of acquisition, a *traditio*, or the voluntary physical delivery of a thing. Christ crucified had accomplished this when he handed over to the Father his soul with the souls of believers. Calvin called them a "bundle" in hand.[350] That concept he derived from scripture (1 Sam. 25:29), and in a sermon on that pericope he explained "bundle" as a similitude for divine providence. It was, he preached, "as if God wrapped those of whom he had custody in a bundle, just like hiding some precious gem in a more pure and holy place." Thus God was said to have the souls of his elect compacted in a bundle so that he might protect them securely by his providence. "We ourselves and everything that

[344] See Thomas Collett Sanders, ed., *The Institutes of Justinian* (London: Longmans, Green, 1922), pp. xlix, 1, without reference to Calvin.

[345] J. A. C. Thomas, *Textbook of Roman Law* (Amsterdam: North Holland, 1976), p. 138.

[346] For possession in general, see Watson, *The Law of Property in the Later Roman Republic* (Oxford: Clarendon, 1968), pp. 81-90.

[347] Calvin, *Législation civile et politique*, in *Opera omnia* (Brunswick), 10-1:140, 141.

[348] Bohatec, "Calvin et la procédure civile," pp. 251-81, especially p. 254. For inheritance, see p. 257. For introduction to the canon law of property, see Berman, *Law and Revolution*, pp. 237-45.

[349] For the acquisition of ownership, see Justinian, *Digest* 41. For an explanation, see Watson, *Law of Property*, pp. 16-80, with *traditio* at pp. 61-62, and as transfer of possession, p. 81.

[350] Calvin, *In harmoniam evangelicam* ad Luke 23:46.

is ours repose in the hand of God," Calvin explained, in a hiding place where we cannot be snatched.[351]

But the secret bundle of the elect, like some precious gem, was not only acquired and sequestered: it was also traded. Christ crucified traded it to the Father by the Roman property law of *traditio*. Salvation was thus like the delivery of a package, a voluntary gift as a legal transaction. Calvin stated the purpose of his *Institutio christianae religionis* as a literary imitation of that incorporating act. "My purpose was solely to transmit (*tradere*)."[352] Calvin's imitation of Christ was a literary imitation of *traditio* as a legal act. The legal concept encompassed rights of both ownership and possession, as in the sale of goods. Christ crucified embraced all believers in his arms and delivered them together with his own spirit into his Father's hands. God's possession and retention of his elect was legally his sufficient physical control over them as owned property. The elect and the reprobate were both *owned* by God, but only the elect were *possessed* by him. And that possession was in, through, and by the Son's willed legal transfer by delivery: hand to hand. The Father who thus possessed the elect then handed them back to the Son. That transfer made them his "personal fund" (*peculium*).

The word *peculium*, from which the notion of what is "particular" and even "peculiar" to a person derives, has been translated in Calvin's text as "property."[353] Calvin accepted that general translation in his commentary on Num. 32:1, where he followed the Vulgate version of the Israelite ownership of a flock of sheep.[354] He stated in *Institutio christianae religionis* that God had chosen the Jews "as his particular flock (*gregem peculiarum*)." Calvin's philology in his description of the elect resonated with such ovine reference. The article of the creed about the communion of saints meant in sum, he wrote, that each Christian "should behave like a sheep of the flock."[355] Calvin also commented on Ps. 135:4 concerning God's election of Abraham's children "as his peculiar (*peculiarem*) people." This was "not that they excelled by their personal virtue, but because but a gratuitous favor the heavenly father has embraced (*complexus*) them." The ancient law has been superseded, Calvin explained, and today "he adopts (*adoptat*) them into his flock and incorporates them into the body of his only-begotten

---

351 Calvin, *Homiliae in primum librum Samuelis*, in *Opera omnia* (Brunswick), 30:552-54. The scriptural simile has been considered a purse holding precious objects for safe keeping and also, even more suggestively, the bag holding pebbles that shepherds used to count the sheep and the goats in the flock. Peter R. Ackroyd, *The First Book of Samuel* (Cambridge: Cambridge University Press, 1971), p. 198.

352 Calvin, *Institutio christianae religionis* praef., in *Opera omnia* (Brunswick), 2:10; trans. Battles, 1:9.

353 Trans. Battles, 2:1016.

354 Calvin, *Mosis reliqui libri quatuor in formam harmoniae* ad loc.

355 Calvin, *Institutio christianae religionis* 1.6.1; 4.1.3.

Son."[356] But the Israelites had initially been selected above all others "as a *peculium* to him" and adopted as children.[357]

Calvin knew that peculiarity was not just a matter of herds. Exodus 19:15 declared the divine promise: "Now, therefore, if you will obey my voice and keep my covenant, you shall be my own possession among all peoples, for all the earth is mine." That pericope was decisive to Calvin's ecclesiastical and civic foundation, continuing "and you shall be to me a kingdom of priests and a holy nation" (v. 16). He considered the meaning of that promise of peculiarity. "For he had not willed to discharge himself toward them by a single act of affability but to procure (*acquireret*) them as his peculiar (*peculiarem*) people. That exceptional case he proposed under the Hebrew word meaning "whatever things are most precious, as whatever is hoarded in a treasure chest." Calvin allowed that the noun *peculium*, by which the Vulgate translation had rendered the Hebrew, did not square badly, because from the immediate context it noted the separation of that people from all others. They were the Lord's "share" (*portio*), his "cord" (*funiculus*), "by gratuitous adoption."[358]

The concept of the peculiar people as a precious treasure was emphasized in Calvin's commentary on the prophecy "'They shall be mine, says the Lord of hosts, my special possession on the day when I act, and I will spare them as a man spares his son who serves him (Mal. 3:7).'" The following verse explicated that the righteous and the reprobate would then be distinguishable. As Calvin interpreted the prophecy, "Therefore, on the day he gathers (*colligit*) his Church, then we shall appear to be his *peculium*." He explained the term. "By the noun *peculium* God rightly judges that the lot of the pious is different from the rest of the world by chance; as if he said, now they are so commingled one with the other that those who cherish me seem no more my own than the others, but then they will be a *peculium* to me." The worldly mix of the righteous and the wicked pertained only to external affairs. "For we know," wrote Calvin, "by this law that we have been divinely elected before the creation of the world so that we should be as if (*quasi*) a *peculium* to him." Although in affliction the promise seemed false, nevertheless, Calvin affirmed that "the faithful are as if a *peculium* to God, that is they are to him for a price (*in pretio*), and that he bestows (*prosequitur*) on them a singular love, as if they were his inheritance (*quasi suum hereditatem*)."[359] The scriptural concept was the personal ownership of property: flocks, treasures, and, finally with Calvin's interpretation as *pretium*, money.

---

[356] Calvin, in Ps. 135:4.

[357] Calvin, in Rom. 9:4.

[358] Calvin, *Mosis reliqui libri quatuor in formam harmoniae* ad. loc. For his knowledge of Hebrew, see Breen, *John Calvin*, pp. 63-65.

[359] Calvin, in Mal. 3:7.

The origin of the term *peculium* was indeed "flock." The printer Robert Estienne's (1503-59) *Thesaurus linguae latinae* recorded its etymology: "'peculium' was from 'pecus' (herd)." But he elaborated that among most authors *peculium* was patrimony, the money of the head of household, because it consisted of his whole substance including herds. He quoted the jurists knowledgeably, for Estienne was the son-in-law of Budé and he relied on his annotations of Justinian's *Digest* for legal terminology. Estienne's *Dictionarium latinogallicum* defined *peculium* directly, that is, legally. It was "the money or other item that the master gives to his slave for trade."[360] Calvin in his exegesis of *peculium* as a flock or treasure had stated that the election as a divine *peculium* was a "law." And when he interpreted the faithful in relation to God as "his inheritance (*suum hereditatem*)" that referred to a particular legal type. In Roman civil law there were different types of heirs; *heres suus* was "someone subject to the deceased's parental power (*patria potestas*)."[361] When Calvin considered the Judaic election and inheritance his language could be qualified—"as if (*quasi*)."[362] But Christian election and inheritance were denotative. Calvin's choice of the term *peculium* to define the elect in *Institutio christianae religionis* was deliberate. It had not appeared in the edition of 1536, which only discussed the communion of saints concerning the mutual sharing of individual gifts.[363] The *peculium* was an exact term of Roman civil law, frequently discussed concerning its holders, as in Justinian's own *Institutiones*.[364] Its legal sense provided the foundation and rationale of Calvin's doctrine of election, as involving a lawful transaction of property, the elect, between Father and Son.

Roman property law was established on the distinctive juridical principle of paterfamilial authority (*patria potestas*). The male head of household had absolute sole rights of ownership of the property of his family (spouse and children), and of both the property and persons of his slaves and their children.[365] Only two conditions released them from that power, allowing

---

360 Robert Estienne, *Thesaurus linguae latinae*, 3:477. "L'argent ou autre chose que le maistre baille a son serf pour trafiquer." *Dictionnaire latinogallicum*, p. 523. The ancient meanings of *haereditas* as *pecunia* and of *pecunia* as total possessions, rather than just money, were derived from *pecus*. See Erasmus, *Ecclesiastes* 922, which repeats Cicero, *Topica* 6.29; Varro, *De lingua latina* 5.

361 For the meaning of *heres suus*, see Justinian, *Digest*, p. xix.

362 Calvin, in Mal. 3:7.

363 See Calvin, *Institutio christianae religionis* (1536) 2.4.30. For the bestowal and sharing of gifts in the Church, see also in Rom. 12:6.

364 For legal definitions, see *Vocabularium iurisprudentiae romanae*, ed. Otto Gradenwitz, Bernard Kuebler, E. T. Schulze, Rudolf Helm et al. (Berlin: Georgius Reimeri, 1903), 4:cols. 573-75, and for places in disputed cases, cols. 575-79.

365 For *patria potestas*, see Gaius, *Institutio* 1.55, and Zulueta, ed. *Institutes of Gaius*, 2:29-30; Jane F. Gardner, *Being a Roman Citizen* (London: Routledge, 1993), pp. 52-83; W. K. Lacey, "*Patria potestas*," in *The Family in Ancient Rome: New Perspectives*, ed. Rawson (London: Croom Helm, 1986), pp. 121-44; P. Voci, "Storia della *patria potestas* de Augusto a

them legal capacity: the death of the head of household and their emancipation or manumission.[366] The *eman*cipation of sons and the *manu*mission of slaves literally meant a release or dismissal from the paterfamilial hand; it implied the basic concept of "hand" (*manus*) as power. Legally "hand" (*manus*) explicitly denoted a husband's authority over a wife, and the marriage of a daughter was called "hand" (*manus*) in the original Roman practice.[367] Property was invested in the head of household absolutely. Everything was acquired for him; he could exchange acquisitions within the family, or give them to an outsider, or sell them. It passed to the father through personal acts and through the acts of the persons in his authority, such as slaves in usufruct or free persons possessed in good faith.[368] The paternal usufruct of all of a child's goods still prevailed in the civil edicts of 1568 composed for Geneva, although there was also real emancipation, as in the case of marriage, and tacit emancipation for a son.[369]

Calvin knew and understood the principle of paterfamilial authority. He employed it in his *Institutio christianae religionis* to argue for the superiority of the male sex to the female. "The superiority of the male sex is conceded," he wrote, "in the fact that children are reckoned noble or ignoble from their father's status, conversely, in slavery, 'the offspring follows the womb,' as lawyers say."[370] Calvin's latter reference was to the law of the paterfamilial possession of a child born to a woman who was his slave. Even if the child's father were freeborn or manumitted, the child followed the enslaved status of his mother. By right the child was property belonging to her owner, not to herself or her mate.[371] He also explicated in his commentary on Ex. 21:1-6 on the right of the lawful master, not the husband, to the enslaved wife and children. It was a case in which "the sanctity of marriage yielded to private right."[372] Calvin also wrote of slaves during the Roman empire, "whose condition of living was such that they might acquire noth-

---

Diocleziano," *IURA* 31 (1980):37-100; Watson, *Rome of the Twelve Tables: Persons and Property* (Princeton, N.J.: Princeton University Press, 1975), pp. 47-51; J. A. Crook, "*Patria potestas*," *Classical Quarterly* 17 (1967):113-22; Barry Nicholas, *An Introduction to Roman Law* (Oxford: Clarendon, 1962), pp. 65-69.

366 For emancipation and manumission, see Justinian, *Digest* 1.7; 40.1-9; and for manumission, Thomas E. J. Wiedemann, "The Regularity of Manumission at Rome," *Classical Quarterly* 35 (1985):162-75.

367 See Zulueta, ed., *Institutes of Gaius*, 2:34-40. See also Treggiari, *Roman Marriage*, pp. 16-34; Watson, *Rome of the Twelve Tables*, pp. 9-19, 47-51.

368 Justinian, *Institutiones* 2.9. For Calvin on usufruct, see *Législation civile et politique*, in *Opera omnia* (Brunswick), 10-1:130.

369 See Kaden, *Germain Colladon*, pp. 122-23, 125.

370 Calvin, *Institutio christianae religionis* 2.13.3, citing Justinian, *Institiones* 1.3, 4; *Digest* 1.5.5, 2.; trans. Battles, 1:479, and see n. 6. For a different aspect of the question of sexual equality, see John L. Thompson, "*Creata ad imaginem Dei, licet secundo gradu*: Woman as the Image of God according to John Calvin," *Harvard Theological Review* 81 (1988):125-43. For Calvin on masters toward slaves concerning distributive right, see in Col. 4:1.

371 For this law, see Treggiari, *Roman Marriage*, p. 53.

372 Calvin, *Commentarius in Exodi* ad 21:1-6, in *Opera omnia* (Brunswick), 24:701.

ing for themselves, but with their entire labor, zeal, and industry unto death were given over (*addicti*) to their owners." More important than Calvin's knowledge of that historical parental power was his application of it to the contemporary relationship of God to believers. "God by his right lays legal claim to everything of ours and he possesses us by personal obligation for debt and by right of ownership (*nexoque et mancipio*)."[373]

Sons and daughters in Roman civil law could not own any property while in the father's power. To ease their situation practically, the father permitted them to have a "personal fund" (*peculium*). That was originally allowed to slaves as if "pocket money," but by the late republic it became customary to give a personal fund also to sons and daughters. It could be a lump sum of money. Often it was a commercial or industrial business, or a stock-in-trade. Or it was a small separate property, such as a farm, for usufruct through transactions to generate income. Legally its assets and acquisitions belonged as property to the father; but by his permission the son or daughter, or the slave, had the agency, disposition, and management of it. A child, and certainly a slave, kept accounts, unless he wished to be thoroughly deplored. A third party could sue the child or slave, as if the personal fund were his property and not that of the father. But, if the child or slave died while still in paterfamilial power, the personal fund reverted to the father or master. In law the personal fund belonged to the father; in practice it was not usually interfered with, as if it were the private property of the son.[374]

In Calvin's theology it was the Father from whom all benefits derived, but the Son through whom the elect entered into their inheritance of them. "Christ bestows on us something of what he has acquired (*acquisivit*)."[375] And, "Christ is the heir of all the goods of God," he explained, "because the adoption, which we have obtained by his grace, restores the possession of the inheritance (*haereditatis possessionem*), from which we were in Adam cut off."[376] Calvin understood Christian faith in social terms of familial relationships, such as filial piety and fraternal exchange, but precisely as de-

---

373 Calvin, *In harmoniam evangelicam* ad. Luke 17:7. The context is his argument against condign merit.

374 Sandars, ed., *Institutes of Justinian*, p. 158 at 2.9.1; Kruger, ed. *Justinian's Institutes.* See Justianian, *Digest* 15.1, and the definition, pp. xxiii-xxiv. For *peculium*, see Gardner, *Roman Citizen*, pp. 56-62; Watson, "Thinking Property at Rome," *Chicago Kent Law Review* 68 (1993):1356; Aaron Kirschenbaum, *Sons, Slaves, and Freedmen in Roman Commerce* (Jerusalem: Magnes, 1987), pp. 31 n. 1, 39, 209; Treggiari, *Roman Marriage*, pp. 124, 363, 381, 445-46; Nicholas, *Introduction to Roman Law*, pp. 68-69; Thomas, *Textbook of Roman Law*, pp. 239-43; David Daube, *Roman Law: Linguistic, Social, and Philosophical Aspects* (Edinburgh: Edinburgh University Press, 1969), p. 83. The translation of *peculium* as "personal fund" follows the practice of *Justinian's Institutes*, trans. Peter Birks and Grant McLeod (Ithaca, N.Y.: Cornell University Press, 1987); *The Institutes of Gaius*, trans. W. M. Gordon and O. F. Robinson (Ithaca, N.Y.: Cornell University Press, 1988).

375 Calvin, *Institutio christianae religionis* 2.17.2; trans. Battles, 1:530

376 Calvin, in Rom. 4:13.

fined by property law. He so understood it not because he was a legalistic, rather than affective, personality, but because the family was historically defined in terms of property law. A basic concept of divinity for Calvin was ownership (*dominium*). As the rhetorical repetition of his *Institutio christianae religionis* epitomized his doctrine, "We are not our own, but the Lord's. . . we are not our own. . . we are not our own. . . . We are God's. . . we are God's. . . we are God's."[377] And as he simply wrote, "We are the inheritance of the Lord. . . we are the personal fund (*peculium*) of the Lord." For that reason Christians could never be in bondage to other persons.[378] But the particular status of the elect was for Calvin beyond basic ownership. It was possession, which meant an intended physical control. Calvin not only knew the theory and law of possession but he also personally applied it to Geneva's ordinances. Possession was physical: "hands on" the goods. The hands by which God acquired and possessed his elect as property were the very hands of Christ, once crucified, now governing and judging people by delegation at the Father's own right hand.

The concept of God as a possessor of persons was not original. Plato had affirmed it, precisely in his *Laws*, in his discussion of divine providence, a subject that could well have arrested Calvin's notice.[379] It occurred in Plato's argument against the capital crime of censuring the gods as idle and indolent for their neglect of humans,[380] again a favorite apologetic of Calvin's.[381] Plato wrote, "We affirm that all mortal creatures are possessions of the gods, to whom belongs also the whole heaven."[382] Plato's term for possessions was *ktamata*, which lexically means "anything gotten, a piece of property, a possession." It was frequent in the plural form, as "possessions." Since Homer's epics it meant "heirlooms" but also "all kinds of property," such as money, chattels, land. Budé defined it in his commentary on the Greek language as "goods and securities" (*bona et pignora*). He also discussed it as a synonym of *chrēmata*, citing Cicero on its

---

377 Calvin, *Institutio christianae religionis* 3.7:1; trans. Battles, 1:690.

378 Calvin, in 1 Cor. 1.13.

379 For an introduction to Calvin on providence, see Susan E. Schreiner, *The Theater of His Glory: Nature and the Natural Order in the Thought of John Calvin*, Studies in Historical Theology, 3 (Durham, N.C.: Labyrinth, 1991).

380 For the argument against the gods as idle, see R. F. Stalley, *An Introduction to Plato's "Laws"* (Oxford: Basil Blackwell, 1983), pp. 175-76. For George of Trebizond's (1396-c. 1472) translation of Plato's *Leges*, see James Hankins, *Plato in the Italian Renaissance*, 2d rev. ed., 2 vols., Columbia Studies in the Classical Tradition, 17 Leiden: E. J. Brill, 1991), 1:180-84; 2:429-31. Johannes Cardinal Bessarion treated of the passage on the providence of God, against idleness, in *In calumniatorem Platonis* 2.8-10. For Bessarion versus Trebizond in general, see Hankins, *Plato in the Italian Renaissance*, 1:236-63. Hankins also compares the function of the maintenance of the law by the nocturnal council in Plato's *Leges* and the consistory in Calvin's Geneva, p. 175.

381 Calvin, *De aeterna Dei praedestinatione*, in *Opera omnia* (Brunswick), 8:347; against the idle god of Epicurus, see in Ps. 44:23.

382 Plato, *Leges* 902b; *Laws*, trans. R. G. Bury, in *Plato*, 2 vols. (Cambridge, Mass.: Harvard University Press, 1942), 2:361.

usage for money and other items gained as inheritance.[383] Calvin considered Plato among the philosophers "the most religious of all and the most circumspect."[384] But he varied Plato on divine possession by applying the distinction of Roman civil law between dominion and possession. For Plato the gods possessed everyone; for Calvin God owned everyone but possessed only the elect.

Possession could in Roman civil law be exercised either directly or through another person.[385] In Calvin's doctrine the Father exercised his possession of the elect through the Son's hands, precisely as if the elect were a personal fund. Calvin affirmed, "The first step to piety is to recognize that God is a father to us—to watch over us, to guide and cherish us, until he gathers us into the eternal inheritance of his kingdom."[386] The meaning of a Christian was to call God "Father."[387] The appellation "Father" was allowed the faithful by the prayer of Jesus, and Calvin explicated its meaning. "The name father is attributed to him; therefore, in this epithet Christ lavishes upon us now a sufficiently abundant subject for trust." And when the prayer designated the paternal site as "in heaven," scripture signified that "everything is under his rule, that the world and whatever is in it is contained in his hand (*manu*), that his energy is everywhere diffused, everything ordered together by his providence."[388]

Pious persons acknowledged "that they owe everything to God, that they are nourished by his fatherly care, that he is the Author of their every good, that they should seek nothing beyond him." They should seek and depend on all things from him, wrote Calvin, and gratefully "credit" all gifts received to his "account." Calvin continued, "Since you are his handiwork, you have been made over (*addictum*) and bound (*mancipatum*) to his command by right (*iure*) of creation, that you owe your life to him."[389] People were personally vacuous: "empty of good to be filled by him". Emphatically Calvin expounded at the outset of *Institutio christanae religious* that "the mighty gifts (*dotes*) with which we are endowed are hardly from ourselves; indeed, our very being is nothing but subsistence in the one God." The poverty of humanity disclosed the infinitude of benefits that resided in God, "the perfect affluence (*affluentia*) of all goods." And, "There is nothing of our own, but that we hold on sufferance whatever God has bestowed

383 Budé, *Commentarii linguae graecae*, in *Opera omnia* 4:46, 351.

384 Calvin, *Institutio christianae religionis* 1.5.11; trans. Battles, 1:64.

385 Watson, *Law of Property*, p. 81.

386 Calvin, *Institutio christianae religionis* 2.6.4; trans. Battles, 1:347. For a systematic theology of the divine paternity, see also Gerrish, *Grace and Gratitude: The Eucharistic Theology of John Calvin* (Minneapolis, Minn.: Fortress, 1993), pp. 23-29.

387 Calvin, in Gal. 4:6.

388 Calvin, *In harmoniam evangelicam* ad Matt. 6:9.

389 Calvin, *Institutio christianae religionis* 1.2.1, 2; trans. Battles, 1:41. Calvin's philology of *addictum* meant a person given up or made over as a servant to a creditor; *mancipatum* was a sale. For persons as not their own masters but belonging to God, see 3.7.1.

on us. Hence we are ever dependent on him." Because of such absolute dependency, explained Calvin, "he warns us and he urges us to seek him in our every need, as children are wont to take refuge in the protection of parents whenever they are troubled by any anxiety."[390]

That filial piety depended on incorporation into Christ. "For he is not a Father to them unless they recognize Christ to be their true brother."[391] As Calvin emphasized, "The cause and the root of adoption is Christ, because God is not a Father except to those who are members and brothers of his only-begotten Son."[392] Christians could only pray "our Father" through the Son. Explicating that prayer, Calvin stated that it would be "folly, yes indeed insane arrogance, to invoke God as Father, unless in so far as we acknowledge that we are engrafted into the body of Christ as sons."[393] He concluded that there was "no other way of praying than to approach God reliant on the mediator."[394]

Christ was that mediator, and the exact function of the mediator was to make people "inheritors." All Christian prayer was only in the name of Christ. "We ought to offer all prayer to God in Christ's name, as it cannot be agreeable to him in any other name. For in calling God 'Father,' we put forward the name 'Christ.'" It would be rash for a person to arrogate the honor of a son of God, he continued, "unless he had been adopted as children of grace in Christ." Calvin explained adoption: "He, while he is the true Son, has of himself been given us as a brother that what he has of his own by nature may become ours by benefit of adoption if we embrace this great blessing with sure faith."[395] Faith ensured the possession of the promises of the gospel, for there was a legal distinction between their donor and the recipient.[396] Faith felt assured that "God will be a propitious Father where Christ is recognized as brother and propitiator."[397]

There was a benevolent exchange in the incarnation by which Christ, in assuming human poverty, transferred his wealth to humans. Through their adoption as sons by participation in Christ, believers shared his inheritance from the benevolent Father. "For when the Father gives him to us for possessing (*possidendum*), he also communicates his very self in him; this

---

390 Calvin, *Institutio christianae religionis* 1.1.1; trans. Battles, 1:35 and mine; 2.1.1, 3.20.34; trans. Battles, 1:242; 2:897.

391 Calvin, *Institutio christianae religionis* 3.20.21; trans. Battles, 2:879.

392 Calvin, in 2 Cor. 1:20.

393 Calvin, *Institutio christianae religionis* praef., in *Opera omnia* (Brunswick), 2:13; trans. Battles, 1:13; *In harmoniam evangelicam* ad Luke 1:32, 35. For grafting, see also in Rom. 6:5.

394 Calvin, *In harmoniam evangelicam* ad Matt. 6:9.

395 Calvin, *Institutio christianae religionis* 1.2.1; 2.12.2; 3.24.36; trans. Battles, 2:899. For adoption, see 3.6.2; for sharing in Christ, 3.3.9; 3.11.10.

396 Calvin, in Rom. 4:3.

397 Calvin, *Institutio christianae religionis* praef., in *Opera omnia* (Brunswick), 2:13; trans. Battles, 1:13. For the Father propitious to people only in Christ, see also in 2 Cor. 1:20.

truly diffuses the participation in all goods."[398] The goods that the Father bestowed on his only-begotten Son were "not for his private use, but that he might enrich poor and needy men." The means of the reception of such goods by humans was the Holy Spirit of adoption, as the bond that tied persons to Christ. And Christ was the minister and steward of the Father's liberality. "For in Christ he offers . . . all wealth in place of our neediness, in him he opens up to us the heavenly treasures." The fullness of the Father's bounty was in Christ, and to ignore it was as profitless as neglecting a buried treasure.[399] Calvin advised, "Since scripture throughout admonishes us of our nakedness and want, and in Christ pronounces the recovery of what we have let go of in Adam, let us, emptied of all self-trust, offer ourselves to Christ so that he may fill us with his riches."[400] All blessings had been committed to the hand of Christ so that he might extend them to believers.[401] "Such is the nature of his rule, that he shares with us all that he has received from the Father. . . . He enriches us with his wealth." Although Calvin taught that faith assured not prosperity (*prosperitas*) but favor (*favor*),[402] nevertheless Christians should confidently expect "prosperous things (*prospera*)" from him in whom "treasures (*thesauri*) are hidden."[403]

Calvin testified that God "ever extends his hand to help his own," who experienced that assistance through prayer.[404] He instructed as a consideration in prayer that "with full and solid trust we may lie down (*recumbamus*) on him; assuredly his love toward us is paternal, and his immense power."[405] A believer should repose wholly in God with contentment. "God is proposed to the faithful as a guardian (*custos*), so that securely in his providence they may lie backwards (*recumbant*)."[406] Calvin advised the same attitude toward Christ as the mediator. "Depend on him, lean upon him, be brought to him, and rest in him (*ab eo proprusus pendeamus, in eo recumbamus, ad eum feramur et ipso acquiescamus*)."[407] The place where the believer laid back on him was his "breast," which Calvin had explained as "that secret love by which we are embraced (*complexus*) in

---

398 Calvin, in 1 Cor. 1:9.

399 Calvin, *Institutio christianae religionis* 3.1.1; 3.1.2; 4.17.2; 3.20.1; trans. Battles, 1:537; 2:850. For Christ as rich with gifts to enrich people, see also in Is. 11:2. For human poverty, see also *Institutio christianae religionis* 1.1.11. For the Holy Spirit of adoption, see also in John 6:40; 9:37; in Phil. 1:7.

400 Calvin, *In libros Mosis* ad Gen. 3.6.

401 Calvin, in John 6:11.

402 Calvin, *Institutio christianae religionis* 2.15.4; 3.2.28; trans. Battles, 1:499.

403 Calvin, *Institutio christianae religionis* praef., in *Opera omnia* (Brunswick), 2:13; trans. Battles, 1:13.

404 Calvin, *Institutio christianae religionis* 3.20.3; trans. Battles, 2:852.

405 Calvin, *In harmoniam evangelicam* ad Matt. 6:9; cited by Oberman, Laidlaw Lectures, Knox College, University of Toronto, October 1994.

406 Calvin, in Ps. 4:6, 121:3.

407 Calvin, *Institutio christianae religionis* 1.14.12; trans. Battles, 1:172.

Christ."[408] In contrast, the reprobate, who were oppressed, rather than embraced, by the hand of God, would find no rest, only pain. Theirs was a bed too short and narrow for stretching out their limbs or for lifting their head, with a blanket too skimpy for covering them.[409]

The posture of reclining backward on God departed radically from the classical position of humans on their own two feet contemplating the gods. Now there was a horizontal passion, rather than a vertical stance. This reversal of bodily position signified a rectitude or straightness that was truly religious, rather than ideally contemplative. And, instead of a fallen humanity slithering on its belly like a worm, in faith in God it rested on its back. In John of the Cross's poetry that spiritual repose was a marital union; in John Calvin's prose it was a filial or fraternal bond. Calvin could have exploited the erotic analogy, since he considered marital union as the most sacred of bonds among humans, surpassing even filial piety.[410] And in his exegesis of Jesus' imposition of hands on the leper he had compared the incarnation to Eve's formation from Adam as "flesh of his flesh" in etiology of sexual intercourse (Gen. 2:23-24).[411] But he preferred as the model of dependency sons leaning on fathers[412] and brothers upon brothers.

Calvin explicated the security of that reclining position in his comment on the divine promise "And I give them eternal life, and they shall never perish, and no one shall snatch them out of my hand" (John 10:28). The certainty and security of being in Christ's sheepfold rested on a foundation, he stated. "It is assuredly because he himself will be the faithful guardian (*custos*) of our salvation, for he testifies that it is in his hand (*in manu sua*). Christ added that they would be safely guarded by his Father's power. Thus there was "solid certainty of the salvation by the elect." And as Calvin defined its legal basis, "Our salvation is certain because it is in the hand (*manu*) of God. . . who has us under the guardianship (*tutela*) of his hand (*manus*)."[413] Guardianship (*tutela*) was an institution under Roman civil law intended to protect the property of those persons considered incapable of fully managing their affairs: children under the age of puberty, women, lunatics, and prodigals. The father or the law appointed another person, usually an agnate, to act as tutor.[414] Calvin commented that the relation of a person under age to his tutor resembled slavery, since he was under his government. The period of guardianship lasted only until the father ap-

408 Calvin, *In libros Mosis* argumentum ad Gen., in *Opera omnia* (Brunswick), 23:11.

409 Calvin, in Is. 28:20.

410 Calvin, *In libros Mosis* ad Gen. 2:24; *In harmoniam evangelicam* ad Matt. 19:4.

411 Calvin, *In harmoniam evangelicam* ad Matt. 8:3.

412 For the experience of fatherhood, or having progeny, see Calvin, in Ps. 127:3.

413 Calvin, in John 10:28. For divine guardianship, see also in Ps. 23:1; in Is. 43:1.

414 Watson, *Rome of the Twelve Tables*, pp. 71-80; Gardner, *Roman Citizen*, pp. 89-91. For guardianship of girls and women in Gaius, see Zulueta, ed., *Institutes of Gaius*, 2:44-52. For *tutela* in general, see Justinian, *Digest* 26, 27.

pointed the time of its end, he explained, and there were various legal methods for terminating tutelage, as enumerated by lawyers. For the ancient believers the law was their tutor, but God ended that guardianship with the advent of Christ.[415]

The legal institution of guardianship was practiced in Geneva; a regulation stipulated its usage.[416] Extant later in Calvin's own hand was a fragment about *tutelle* in the ordinances he drafted for the city. "Further, action against tutors for poor administration of the guardianship, concerning the things comprised in the guardianship, has only five years after the pupil will have passed the age of minority."[417] An emancipating father could himself act as tutor until the child attained legal age,[418] so that Calvin's designation of the Father's role as tutor was socially conceivable. Calvin likely intended by God's double "manual" powers as father and tutor to emphasize the security of the elect. As he wrote, believers reconciled to the Father through Christ were "secure from all fear, since their salvation has been deposited in his hand and custody."[419]

The position of the risen Christ at the right hand of the Father also held the Church. "Surely the church of Christ has lived and will live so long as Christ reigns at the right hand of his Father (*ad dexteram Patris*). It is sustained by his hand (*cuius manu sustinetur*); defended by his protection; and is kept safe by his power." The Son's station at the right hand of the Father meant delegation, "through whose hand he wills to reign."[420] Calvin considered the position of Christ at the right hand of the Father in solemn possession of the government entrusted to him. "Hence arises a wonderful consolation: that we perceive judgment to be in the hands of him who has already destined us to share with him the honor of judging." Calvin was confident that Christ would not condemn those he received into his "trust and clientele (*fidem clientelamque*)." It was "through the hand of Christ" that God would deliver the church as the covenant by which he adopted (*adoptaverat*) his elect." Upon the ascension of Christ to the right hand of the Father, believers received the "inheritance" (*haereditatem*) through "adoption" (*nos sibi fratres adoptavit*). Calvin cited scripture: "For if brothers, then also fellow heirs (*consortes haereditatis*) with him" (Rom.

---

415 Calvin, in Gal. 4:1.

416 "Règlement sur les tutelles" (1536), in *Les sources du droit du canton du Gèneve*, ed. Rivoire et van Berchen, 2:310-11.

417 Calvin, *Législation civile et politique*, in *Opera omnia*, 10-1:143. See also Bohatec, "Calvin et la procédure civile," pp. 292-93.

418 Gardner, *Roman Citizen*, p. 66.

419 Calvin, *In harmoniam evangelicam* ad Luke 1:74. For God as the "custodian" of the life of believers, see ad Matt. 10:29. For the incarnation as the deposit of a treasure in the Virgin's womb as "a kind of custody," see ad Luke 1:26.

420 Calvin, *Institutio religionis christianae* praef., in *Opera omnia* (Brunswick), 2:22; trans. Battles, p. 24. For Christ at the right hand of the Father, see also 2.15.4; 2.16.5; in Heb. 1:4.

8:17).[421] And that portion of the inheritance for each believer was the very possession of God.[422]

Calvin's was a manual theology, which originated with creation and providence, by and in God's hand; it then transmitted election, by Christ's hand delivering the faithful into the Father's hand; and it ended with the Father returning them to Christ's hand for incorporation into his body and inheritance by adoption. The Church was collected manually (in Calvin's usual verb, *colligere*). It consisted of human embracers of the divine embrace and of one another. It originated in those who "by faith having embraced (*amplexi*) the promise offered them were aggregated into the family of God, so that they might have a common life in Christ."[423] Calvin coherently retained as the sole apostolic ceremony the imposition of hands for the ordination of ministers.[424] But the consequence of the divine-human embrace for all believers, and not just ministers, was social reciprocity. "The saints are gathered (*aggregari*) into the society of Christ on the principle that whatever benefits God confers upon them they should in turn share with one another." Calvin instructed that they should not disturb the political order, which allowed the distinct and personal ownership of private property by an individual, as peace required. But they should share benefits, in the conviction of God as their common Father and Christ as their common head, with whom they were united in fraternal love.[425] Considering the necessity of the brethren, "whatever benefits of God are ours at hand (*ad manum*) invite us to benificence."[426]

Calvin wrote that "the duties of fraternal charity fall under all the senses"[427] but he especially promoted tactile values. Christians for Calvin should be "handy" for one another. Believers should imitate the outstretched hand of God.[428] The recognition of fraternity with Christ meant

---

421 Calvin, *Institutio christianae religionis* 2.16.15; trans. Battles, 1:524; 2.16.17, trans. mine; 2.6.4; 2.12.2; trans. Battles, 1:251, 465. For the ascension of Christ as purposed for common inheritance, see also in John 14:2.

422 Calvin, in Ps. 16:5.

423 Calvin, *In libros Mosis*, argumentum ad Gen., in *Opera omnia* (Brunswick), 23:11.

424 Calvin, *Institutio christianae religionis* 4.3.16. See also 4.4.14; 4.19.6. For background, see Gross, *Menschenhand und Gotteshand*, pp. 102-32; François Garnier, *Le langage de l'image au Moyen Âge: Signification et symbolique*, 2 vols. (Paris: Léopard d'or, 1982-89), 1:196-97; Barasch, *Giotto and the Language of Gesture*, pp. 117-27. For the imposition of hands, see also Calvin, in 1 Tim. 4:14; in 2 Tim. 1:6.

425 Calvin, *Institutio christianae religionis* 4.1.3; trans. Battles, 2:1014. He also allows private property against the overthrow of the political order in *In harmoniam evangelicam* ad Luke 3:10; in John 19:27. For the legitimate use of worldly goods, see *In harmoniam evangelicam* ad Matt. 13:44. See also Richard B. Schlatter, *Private Property: The History of an Idea* (New Brunswick, N.J.: Rutgers University Press, 1951), pp. 77-123, with Calvin especially at pp. 101-4. Against the ascetical poverty of the monastic vow, see also Calvin, *In harmoniam evangelicam* ad Luke 14:33.

426 Calvin, *In harmoniam evangelicam* ad Luke 3:10.

427 Calvin, *In harmoniam evangelicam* ad Matt. 23:23.

428 Calvin, in James 1:8.

"to extend our hand (*manum porrigere*) to one another and to help one another." That phrase in his *Institutio christianae religionis* replicated what the hand of Christ had done for believers in Calvin's exegesis. A Christian extended his hand to other believers by commending them to the Father, just as Christ in the gospels had done so by the imposition of his hands on the sick. God not only stretched out his hand in invitation to people but he also embraced believers as a solicitous father.[429] As Father, God "embraces (*complectitur*) his whole household." So Calvin enjoined the Christian to "embrace (*complectantur*) all who are his brothers in Christ."[430] As "connected together in hope of one inheritance, they ought to embrace one another spontaneously and reciprocally."[431] Calvin's theology was a gracious one of hands joined and arms entwined—divine to human, human to divine, human to human—an embodiment of the Graces as gratuity and as reciprocity. The Graces belonged to his culture. The most touching of the tactile Graces in renaissance art was a marble sculpture in the round by Germain Pilon (c.1531-90) for the tomb of Henry IV of France, to whom as a boy Calvin had dedicated his commentary on Genesis. With their shoulders touching and their arms linked in reciprocal generosity, those Graces bear on their heads as caryatids a funereal urn containing the king's heart.[432] Calvin placed himself firmly in the social and religious circle of embracing when he declared to Francis I that "I embrace (*complector*) the common cause of all believers, that of Christ himself."[433]

A Christian was not to be stingy or greedy, with his hand tightly shut, as in the adage *in sinu manum habere*, "to have one's hand in one's bosom."[434] A particular case of holy handiness was almsgiving to the poor.[435] Calvin deplored the rude practice of his contemporaries, whom he considered far removed from the gentleness of even the pagan philosophers. "If at any time such persons come to give alms to a poor man, then as if it were beneath their dignity to hand it to him, they fling it down by way of in-

---

429 Calvin, in Is. 65:2.

430 Calvin, *Institutio christianae religionis* 3.20.38; trans. Battles, 2:901.

431 Calvin, argumentum in Rom., in *Opera omnia* (Brunswick), 49:6.

432 Germain Pilon, marble sculpture, Tomb of the heart of Henry IV, 1559-63, Louvre, Paris. See Reid with Rohmann, *Oxford Guide to Classical Mythology in the Arts*, 1:475; Tervarent, *Attributes et symbols dans l'art profane*, 1:179; Michèle Beaulieu, *Description raisonnée des sculptures du Musée du Louvre*, vol. 2: *Renaissance française* (Paris: Réunion des musées nationaux, 1978), pp. 126-28, and reproduced, p. 127, fig. 197; Anthony Blunt, *Art and Architecture in France, 1500 to 1700*, 2d ed., Pelican History of Art, Z4 (Harmondsworth, Middlesex: Penguin, 1970), pp. 85-86, and reproduced, pl. 60.

433 Calvin, *Institutio christianae religionis* praef., in *Opera omnia*, 2:11; trans. Battles, 1:11.

434 Erasmus, *Adagia* 2.10.32; trans. Mynors, 34:140.

435 Calvin, *Institutio christianae religionis* 3.20.29. For poor relief in Geneva, see Jeannine E. Olson, *Calvin and Social Welfare: Deacons and the "Bourse française"* (Selinsgrove, Pa.: Susquehanna University Press, 1989). For the dispensation of ecclesiastical possessions, see also Calvin, *Institutio christianae religionis* 4.4.6-8.

sult."[436] Charity in Calvin's doctrine was to be hand to hand, not hand to foot. Almsgiving was also to be done without the left hand knowing what the right hand was doing; that is, secretly, with God as the only witness and him served with a pure conscience.[437]

But, if the poor were embraced into the divine and human circle of love, the reprobate were excluded: as if God crushed them beneath his fingers or opened his palm and let them drop into the abyss. Calvin did write about the hand of God crushing the wicked.[438] The classical ideal of nurturing had been the child safely held in the mature adult hand. An angry wet nurse who let a crying newborn drop from her hands was compared to an enraged maniac.[439] Christians in the sixteenth century could be terrified of falling from, or being dropped from, the security of God's almighty grasp. Teresa of Avila advised the soul to petition God diligently always to hold it "in his hand," for, if he ever should let go of it, it would drop into "the abyss." Even in her spiritual marriage the soul was insecure about "falling," except when his Majesty held it "in his hand" so it did not offend him.[440] The merciful arms of Christ extended on the cross did not embrace everyone, as graphically depicted later by the Jansenist crucifix, which constricts his arms narrowly to signify that the elect will be few.[441] In the iconoclastic reformed church of Geneva there were no crucifixes, no crosses even,[442] no arms to see and by which to imagine a saving embrace. The embrace was a matter of faith. As for those who despised Christ because his external human form did not correspond to the desires of the flesh, Calvin was censorious. "It is not permitted us to imagine a Christ who corresponds to our genius, but it is simply necessary to embrace him as he is offered by the Father."[443]

Calvin's choice of a tactile model for Christian salvation and society was theoretically more comprehensive than the Catholic culture of visualization or the Lutheran culture of aurality-orality. What of the blind and the deaf-mute? What insight into a beatific vision could a blind person imagine? Or what was the hope of justification by faith for a deaf person, when faith came from hearing the Word? But both the blind and the deaf could use their hands to compensate for their disability, by patting, as Calvin liked to say, or by gesturing. Touch was, as Aristotle had defined it, the basic sense,

436 Calvin, *In "De clementia"* 2.6.2; trans. Battles and Hugo, p. 373.

437 Calvin, *In harmoniam evangelicam* ad Matt. 6:3.

438 Calvin, in Ps. 14:5. For the hand of God punishing the wicked, see in Ps. 38:2.

439 See Soranus, *Gynaecia* 2.19.68.

440 Teresa of Avila, *Castillo interior* 5.4.9; 7.3.9.

441 So-called Jansenist crucifix, 1764, Musée des arts et traditions populaires, Paris; reproduced in François Lebrun, "The Two Reformations: Communal Devotion and Personal Piety," in *A History of Private Life*, vol. 3: *Passions of the Renaissance*, ed. Roger Chartier (Cambridge, Mass.: Belknap Press, Harvard University Press, 1989), p. 97.

442 Giuseppe Scavizzi, *The Controversy on Images from Calvin to Baronius*, Toronto Studies in Religion, 14 (New York: Peter Lang, 1982), p. 206.

443 Calvin, *In harmoniam evangelicam* ad Mark 3:17.

the common denominator of animation. Lack sight, lack hearing, yet life endured; lose "contact," and death ensued.[444] Yet Calvin applied the sense of touch ultimately to select and to exclude. The divine promise concerning the crucifixion became selective and exclusionary. The verse "And lifted up I shall draw all things to myself (John 12:32)" was about collecting (*colligenda*) the Church, he wrote. But he qualified the promise. "The saying 'all' which he employs must be understood to refer to the children of God, who are from his flock (*ex grege*)."[445] Only the elect were possessed intentionally and contactually in the divine hand as God's personal fund. Calvin taught that believers experienced the outstretched hand of God to raise them up, while the reprobate were left in total despair. He depicted unbelievers as withdrawing from God's hand.[446]

The inheritance of heaven belonged only to the children of God through adoption. That adoption was "possession itself." As Calvin explained, under the law of the ancient testament the fathers in faith were certain of their adoption but did not yet "by their right" fully enjoy it. Thus, "by adoption (as in Rom. 8:23) 'redemption' is taken hold of (*capitur*), for the very possession (*ipsa possessione*)."[447] Through faith "those adopted by God as his children come to possess the Heavenly Kingdom." And sin, thought Calvin, was "just cause for his disowning (*abdicatio*) us and not regarding or recognizing us as his sons."[448] Abdication was the legal act of disinheriting an heir.[449] Nevertheless, the benefits of the Father were bestowed on believers through the Son; and mysteriously "by a mutual participation in power the Son himself is the author of them." This was "practical knowledge" Calvin asserted, more sure and solid than "idle speculation." In the perception of that truth "does the pious mind perceive the very presence of God (*Deum praesentissimum*), and almost touches him (*et paene attrectat*), when it feels itself quickened, illuminated, preserved, justified, and sanctified."[450] Calvin's tactile verb *attrecto* was frequently used of an unlawful manner, like attempting to touch an untouchable. But if the reach of a religious mind to "almost touch" God was speculatively conceivable, the powerful grasp by which God embraced and held believers was practically jurisprudential.

And if legally God could amass and acquire the elect as if they were a personal fund—money, business, land—what could the elect not do in imitation? Calvin did write of the elect in joyful progress to perfection in inexhaustible riches of divine bounty, while the reprobrate plunged from bad

444 Aristotle, *De anima* 435ab, discussed above in chapter two, pp. 142-43.
445 Calvin, in John 12:32.
446 Calvin, *In harmoniam evangelicam* ad Luke 1, 13, 38.
447 Calvin, in Gal. 4:6.
448 Calvin, *Institutio christianae religionis* 3.2.1.; 2.6.1; trans. Battles, 1:543, 341.
449 Justinian, *Codex* 6.31.6; 6.8.47, and other references in the lexicon.
450 Calvin, *Institutio christianae religionis* 1.13.13; trans. Battles, 1:138.

to worse, languishing in their poverty.[451] But he meant spiritual, not material, goods. It was not Calvin's theological argument that the elect should or would prosper financially by the business of their hands, although capitalist enterprisers may have inferred that. He did not think human nature industrious but, rather, in its depravity conversely inclined to "sluggishness" (*pigrities*) and "laziness" (*inertia*).[452] Lethargy affected even the people of God.[453] He acknowledged his own "habitual sloth," even "timidity and shyness."[454]

Calvin suffered from a complex of physical diseases[455] that were diagnosed in sixteenth-century medicine as slothful, or phlegmatic, in origin: kidney stones, arthritis, catarrh, pleurisy, bronchitis, and pulmonary tuberculosis. The precipitation of phlegm, as excreted in an abnormal mixture of the humors or by excessive heat, was in Galen's prevalent doctrine a personal, constitutional disposition. Kidney stones were thought to be the sticky and heavy phlegm of the blood consolidated in the flesh of the kidney, from which organ they migrated to deposit in the urinary tract. The chalky stones that formed around arthritic joints were from the same thick and sticky phlegm. The abundance of phlegm also rendered a person susceptible to respiratory diseases. Catarrh was a respiratory infection that discharged mucous secretions. An accumulation of phlegm obstructed the bronchial tubes; and lung disease could be phlegmatic, with the symptoms of shallow respiration and mucous discharge.[456] Calvin wrote of his lungs "so loaded with phlegm that respiration is difficult and short."[457] Even the hemorrhoids that tormented him were considered a natural means of purging excessive phlegm. Chronic illness would have left Calvin sensitive to the touch. He wrote knowledgeably of "the sick person with sores all over his

---

451 Calvin, *In harmoniam evangelicam* ad Matt. 13:12.

452 Calvin, *Institutio christianae religionis* 1.13.1. See also in Is. 55:1.

453 Calvin, in Ps. 49:14.

454 Letter to Christopher Libertet, 11 September 1535, in *Opera omnia* (Brunswick), 10:51; cited by Bouwsma, *John Calvin*, p. 30, and for human indolence, see also p. 175. For timidity and shyness, see the prefatory letter to his commentary on the psalms, 22 July 1557, in *Opera omnia* (Brunswick), 31:25. Sluggishness is also acknowledged as a frequent metaphor in Calvin by Margaret Miles, "Theology, Anthropology, and the Human Body in Calvin's *Institutes of the Christian Religion*," *Harvard Theological Review* 74 (1981):306, with a single reference to *Institutio christianae religionis* 1.15.3, which is not relevant.

455 For description and documentation, see Doumergue, *Jean Calvin*, 3:509-26. For catarrh, see pp. 513, 514; pleurisy, bronchitis, and pulmonary tuberculosis, pp. 515-16, 519, 524-25; hemorrhoids, p. 516. A recent article based on it, which purports to be a clinical analysis, does so with reference to modern, not historical, diagnosis. Charles L. Cooke, "Calvin's Illnesses and Their Relation to Christian Vocation," in *Calvin Studies IV*, ed. John Leith and W. Stacy Johnson (Davidson, N. C.: Davidson College, 1988), pp. 41-52. For the kidneys as the seat of the divine tribunal, see Calvin, in Ps. 139:13.

456 For these phlegmatic diseases, see Siegel, *Galen's System of Physiology and Medicine: An Analysis of his Doctrines and Observations on Blood Flow, Respiration, Humors, and Internal Diseases* (Basel: S. Karger, 1968), pp. 322-30.

457 Calvin, Letter to Bullinger, 6 April 1564, in *Opera omnia* (Brunswick), 20:283; cited by Doumergue, *Jean Calvin*, 3:524.

body who dreads every touch of even the most tender physician."[458] And he understood about making and arranging a bed softly so that the invalid might lie in it more comfortably.[459]

His phlegmatic constitution he judged typical of the the corruption of the entire era as "listlessness" (*ignavia*).[460] The exemplars of sloth in early modern culture were the glass men, individuals convinced that their bodies were made of glass in whole or in part. Terrified of being broken, they avoided all physical contact with persons or objects, even to sitting on a chair, lest their buttocks shatter. To venture socially into the streets courted being fractured by falling roof-tiles. Although the delusion was in some seventeenth-century texts diagnosed as melancholic,[461] originally such a case would have been understood as phlegmatic.[462] Calvin alluded in *Institutio christianae religionis* to that same phenomenon of tactile fear as a common experience. As he catalogued secular menaces, "Go through the city streets, you are subject to as many dangers as there are tiles on the roofs."[463] For Calvin all persons were by nature dangerously subject to breakage. The brevity of life and the fragility of glass was a moral comparison, from Augustine's preaching[464] to Vannochio Biringuccio's (1480-1539?) pyrotechnics. As that head of the papal foundry, in the first handbook on metallurgy, wrote about glass, "Considering its brief and short life, owing to its

---

458 Calvin, Letter to the king of England, dedicatory epistle to his *Commentarius in epistolas catholicas*, 24 January 1551, in *Opera omnia* (Brunswick), 14:31.

459 Calvin, in Ps. 41:3.

460 Calvin, Letter to the senate of Frankfort, dedication to his *In harmoniam evangelicam*, 1 August 1555, in *Opera omnia* (Brunswick), 15:710.

461 For the diagnosis of the glass men as melancholics, see Gill Speak, "*El licenciado Vidriera* and the Glass Men of Early Modern Europe," *Modern Language Review* 85 (1990):850-65, citing the fear of falling roof tiles from Cervantes, *El licenciado Vidriera*. The metamorphosis into glass has also been diagnosed as a melancholic delirium by Michel Foucault and other authors, cited by J. R. Sampayo Rodriguez, *Rasgos erasmistas en "La locura del licenciado vidriera" de Miguel de Cervantes*, Problemata semiotica, 10 (Kassel: Riechenberger, 1986), pp. 116-17. Since the protagonist dries up in his bones, Cervantes probably meant melancholy, which was a dry humor. See Cervantes, *Licenciado vidriera*, p. 34.

462 There was a development of the medieval vice of *acedia*, or sloth, into melancholy, so that the concepts are not unrelated. See Siegfried Wenzel, *The Sin of Sloth: "Acedia" in Medieval Thought and Literature* (Chapel Hill: University of North Carolina Press, 1960); Reinhard Kuhn, *The Demon of Noontide: Ennui in Western Literature* (Princeton, N.J.: Princeton University Press, 1976), pp. 3-98, 373-76; Roger Caillois, "Les démons de midi," *Revue de l'histoire des religions* 115 (1937):142-73; 116 (1937):54-83, 143-85; Stanford M. Lyman, *The Seven Deadly Sins: Society and Evil* (New York: St. Martin's Press, 1978), pp. 5-18. For the exchangeable iconography of sloth and of melancholy, as in the the figure of the sleepy person, see Raymond Klibansky, Panofsky, and Fritz Saxl, *Saturn and Melancholy: Studies in the History of Natural Philosophy, Religion, and Art* (London: Thomas Nelson and Sons, 1964), 298, 299, 300 n. 6.

463 Calvin, *Institutio christianae religionis* 1.17.10; trans. Battles, 1:223.

464 Augustine, *Sermo* 18.7; cited by Mary Luella Trowbridge, *Philological Studies in Ancient Glass*, University of Illinois Studies in Language and Literature, 13 (Urbana: University of Illinois, 1928), p. 165.

brittleness, it cannot and must not be given too much love, and it must be used and kept in mind as an example of the life of man and of the things of this world which, though beautiful, are transitory and frail."[465] Yet the glass men were not universally meditative on the fragility of life; they were personally and really frightened of breakage by any physical contact. They were terribly anti-tactile. And neither the emotion of fear nor the metaphor of glass was associated traditionally with the humoral black bile that caused melancholy.

Hippocrates initially used the term "glassy" in medicine to describe the urine from an acute malady in crisis. Praxagoras referred more influentially to a fever from a cold and moist humor that he called "vitreous phlegm (*vitrea pituita*)." In Galen's medicine that "glassy" humor was frequently and consistently defined as "phlegm."[466] A phlegmatic humor produced a general sluggishness and laziness of mind, with such parallel physical symptoms as a droopy head.[467] The physical pull of phlegm downward was typified by its diagnosis as the cause of epilepsy, the falling sickness.[468] The phlegmatic humor morally designated laziness, somnolence, and a feminine softness (because females were cold and wet).[469] Phlegm originated in cold and it made the body colder.[470] Because phelgm was an exceedingly cold humor, as in the modern association of secreted mucus with "a cold," it produced fear. That was evidenced in the phlegmatic's notable pallor, the discoloration of his skin.[471] The adage *ignavi vertitur color*, "the coward

---

465 Vannochio Biringuccio, *De la pirotechnia* 2.14; *The "Pirotechnia" of Vannoccio Biringuccio*, trans. Cyril Stanley Smith and Martha Teach Guidi (Cambridge, Mass.: MIT Press, 1959), p. 132.

466 See Hippocrates, *Coan Prognosis* 3.146; cf. 18.352; Praxagoras through Galen, *De alimentorum facultatibus* 1.12, ed. Kuhn, 6:509; Galen, *De sympomatum causis* 7, ed. 7:137-38; *De differentiis febrium* 6, p. 347; *De inaequali intempere* 8, p. 749; *De locis affectis* 5, ed. 8:81-82; *De humoribus* 1.1; 3.4, ed. 16:11, 367; *Predictionum* 2.36, p. 584; *Hippocratis Epidemiorum commentarius* 3.21, ed. 17:429; *Hippocratis Epidemiorum VI et Galeni in illum commentarius* 1.9; 2.41, ed. 17:848, 979. The references to the Hippocratic and Galenic usage of "glassy", verified in these texts, are listed under *hyalōdē* in Trowbridge, *Philological Studies*, p. 47, and see pp. 28, 45. For texts, see also Durling, *A Dictionary of Medical Terms in Galen*, Studies in Ancient Medicine, 5 (Leiden: E. J. Brill, 1993), p. 316. For an introduction to Galen's humoral theory, see James R. Irwin, "Galen on Temperaments," *Journal of General Psychology* 36 (1947):45-64; Jacob van Wageningen, "De quattuor temperamentis," *Mnemosyne* 46 (1918):374-82.

467 For Galen descriptively on phlegm, see Siegel, *Galen's System of Physiology and Medicine*, pp. 217, 322-33.

468 For epilepsy from phlegm, see Tempkin, *The Falling Sickness: A History of Epilepsy from the Greeks to the Beginnings of Modern Neurology*, 2d ed. rev. (Baltimore, Md.: Johns Hopkins University Press, 1971), pp. 52, 63, 124, 126.

469 E.g., Albert the Great, *De animalibus* 70.1.2.

470 Siegel, *Galen's System of Physiology and Medicine*, p. 336. For fear producing cold and pallor in renaissance thought, see Ficino, *Theologia platonica* 13.4, 5.

471 Galen, *De alimentorum facultatibus* 1.12; *De symptomatum causis* 7; *De differentiis febrium* 6; *De inaequali intemperie* 8; *De locis affectis* 5; *Praedictionum* 2.36; *Hippocratis Epidemiorum VI et Galeni in illum commentarius* 1.9. See also Siegel, *Galen's System of Physiology and Medicine*, p. 324. Aristotle, *Physiognomics* 809a. For phlegm as cold, see

changes color," referred to the face of the timid person going white as its blood retreated to the vital organs.[472] Phlegmatics were naturally "timid."[473] Conversely, a cold temperature made people fearful, as ancient an effect as the "cold terror" that gripped Homeric soldiers on night watch.[474] The commonplace persisted in sixteenth-century belief. Montaigne wrote of fear so constricting the heart that it froze.[475]

Calvin described how fear altered the human bodily posture from its erect stance: the spine bowed and crouched, like a bird, threatened by the fowler's net, that lay flat on the ground without ruffling a feather.[476] He characterized all humans in their depravity as phlegmatic—sluggards. But he stated the remedy as a divine elevation of the mind above secular matters and not necessarily as business opposed to lethargy. "But because he [God] sees that our slow minds sink down upon the earth, and rightly, in order to shake off our sluggishness and inertia he raises us above the world."[477] Thus the scripture of Jesus touching the leper was not to be read "frigidly," or phlegmatically, but amazingly.[478] When Calvin argued that Jesus was truly human he wrote that "he suffered cold,"[479] although there was no scriptural text for that assertion. He did not suggest that Jesus suffered from the heat, although that was more climactically probable. Calvin knew the geography. He wrote of Palestine as a warmer region than "our dense and cold air" of Geneva.[480] "Cold" was simply his shorthand for the human condition as phlegmatic.

It was a condition he acutely suffered. Calvin's sense of suffocation, groping for safe exit in the labyrinth of life,[481] may have expressed his very real fear of respiratory compression and collapse for lack of breath in clean air. He was tubercular.[482] But suffocation was also a phlegmatic condition.

Irwin, "Galen on Temperaments," pp. 58-59; Lloyd, "The Hot and the Cold, the Dry and the Wet in Greek Philosophy," *Journal of Hellenic Studies* 84 (1964):101, 103, 104.

472 Erasmus, *Adagia* 1.2.89; trans. Phillips, 31:220.

473 Albert the Great, *De animalibus* 70.1.2; cited by F. M. Barbado, "Le physionomie, le tempérament, et le charactère d'après Albert le Grand et la science moderne," trans. R. P. L. Dumeste, *Revue thomiste* 36 (1931): 337.

474 Homer, *Iliad* 9.2; cited by Lloyd, "Hot and Cold, Dry and Wet," p. 101; *The Iliad of Homer*, trans. Richmond Lattimore (Chicago: University of Chicago Press, 1962), p. 198. For further examples, see Ficino, *Theologia platonica* 13.4, p. 232; Sprenger and Institoris, *Malleus maleficarum* 1.2.

475 Montaigne, *Essais* 1.18, p. 75.

476 Calvin, in Ps. 57:6.

477 Calvin, *Institutio christianae religionis* 1.13.1; trans. Battles, 1:121.

478 Calvin, *In harmoniam evangelicam* ad Matt. 8:3. For Calvin's language of frigidity, see also Bouwsma, *John Calvin*, p. 174.

479 Calvin, *Institutio christianae religionis* 2.13.1. He also hás Lazarus wasting away in "cold," although scripture does not mention temperature. *In harmoniam evangelicam* ad Luke 16:19.

480 Calvin, *In harmoniam evangelicam* ad Matt. 15:32.

481 Bouwsma, *John Calvin*, p. 47.

482 Calvin, in Ps. 69:1.

As Ficino explained it in his treatise on the health of the learned, "Suffocation is something that results from the overabundance or putrefaction of any humor, especially from the immoderate increase or putrefaction in some way of phlegm, so that phlegm has not without cause been called 'the attacker of life.'"[483] Suffocation also related humorally to cold temperature. As Paré explained the relation, "Extreme cold, whether by the surrounding air or by application of cold and stupefactive repercussive remedies, makes a cold irregular temperature so great that the spirits are suffocated and extinguished." The spiritually destitute part of the body then mortified, as in persons "who walk through snows and ices, for by the extreme cold they lose some of their members and quite often their lives," like soldiers in the mountainous passes of Piedmont during winter. Paré cited the aphorisms of Hippocrates about frigid temperature. "Cold is contrary and hostile to the bones, teeth, nerves, to the brain, to the marrow of the back, generally to our life (which consists in warmth and humidity), because it makes spasms or convulsions or other movements against our will, disordered agitation of the whole body (which we call chills), and consequently by its great violence is often times the cause of our death."[484]

It was cold for Hippocrates that penetrated the spinal marrow to cause the severe phlegmatic disease of dropsy.[485] Calvin thought that it was in the very spinal marrow that belief in the existence of God had been implanted at creation.[486] The human figure, as spinally diseased since its fall from the original erect posture, was thus morally dropsical. It was subject to the disorder of convulsions and chills and, from extreme exposure to the cold, also to suffocation—with physical mortification requiring amputation as a symptom of spiritual death. It was thus that Calvin compared even the Church to an amputee, whose limbs had been severed and scattered, until the healing touch of Christ should restore its bodily integrity in a kind of resurrection.[487] Calvin was medically knowledgeable about gangrene, a usual cause of amputation, quoting Galen and other authors on its etiology. He described how from an inflammation of a member of the body the gangrene spread, creeping into adjacent areas, consuming like a fire the flesh, nerves, and bones. Unless the infection was cut immediately, the hand would cause

---

[483] Ficino, *De vita* 2.2; *Marsilio Ficino: Three Books on Life*, trans. Carol V. Kaske and John R. Clark, Medieval and Renaissance Texts and Studies, 57; Renaissance Text Series, 11 (Binghamton, N.Y.: Medieval and Renaissance Texts and Studies, 1989), p. 169.

[484] Paré, *Chirurgie* 7.5, 6, citing Hippocrates, *Aphorisms* 5.18; *Ten Books of Surgery with the Magazine of the Instruments Necessary for It*, trans. Robert Whitelinker and Nathan Womack (Athens: University of Georgia Press, 1969), pp. 127, 128. For suffocation from cold, see also the testimony of the physician at the French court, Laurent Joubert, *Traité du ris* 1.12.

[485] Hippocrates, *De internis affectibus* 13. For Galen on dropsy as a phlegmatic disease, see Siegel, *Galen's System of Physiology and Medicine*, pp. 332-40.

[486] Calvin, *Institutio christianae religionis* 1.3.3.

[487] Calvin, in Mic. 4:6; Soph. (Zeph.) 3:19.

the loss of the arm, and the foot of the whole leg. By depriving the limb of heat and vital energy, it eventually caused nekrosis unto mortification, as in St. Anthony's fire (ergotism). In Calvin's comparison its destructive "contagion" had caused the horrible extinction of the gospel by the papists, because of the inertia of their pastors.[488] Calvin's moral judgment of human nature and character had its medical science in humoral theory, in temperature as the classical subject of the sense of touch.

To venture through the city streets, as Calvin indicated, was perilous, because it risked exposure to personal breakage by contact. Yet not to frequent the city streets was to withdraw into the vice of sloth. Tactile values were fraught with ambiguity. Avarice had also been caricatured as handy, as in Prudentius's description of a greedy sinner by the deformities of leprous hands, "who in his greed crooks his hands and draws them close, his palm doubled, his fingernails like hooks, and cannot relax the tendons."[489] There was a proverb for tenacity in safeguarding one's possessions, *toto corpore, omnibus unguiculis*, "with the whole body, with all one's nails (claws)." And it was also proverbial to associate avarice with dirty fingernails: a greedy person was morally "sordid."[490] Calvin instructed against avarice,[491] which he expressed by the vernacular phrase *prendre et ravir à toutes mains*, "to take and abduct with full hands."[492] He especially forbade avarice among the clergy. Although he allowed the imposition of hands upon ministers (*manus impositio*), he rejected any consequent ministerial seizure of property by hands (*manum iniectio*). Calvin had himself been legally seized by God (*manum inectio*) as his personal property, but he forbade the clergy so to act against the property of others. They were to resist "filthy lucre. . . not only to lay hands on (*manibus inicere*) villages and castles, but to carry off vast provinces, finally to seize whole kingdoms!"[493]

All goods descended from God as their author. Against grasping them Calvin wrote, "For it is of great importance that we touch (*attingere*) nothing of God's goods without his permission; for we cannot enjoy anything with a good conscience, except we receive it as from the hand (*manu*) of God."[494] Believers were essentially not to handle human goods but to em-

---

488 Calvin, in 2 Tim. 2:17, citing Galen, *De methodo medendi* 2.1, ed. Kuhn, 11:1-146; *De tumoribus praeter naturam* 6, 8, ed. 7:705-52; Paulus Aeginata, *Opera* 4.19; Aetius 14; Celsus, *De medicina* 5.26-31; Calvin, *Sermons sur la seconde epistre à Timothée* 12, in *Opera omnia* (Brunswick), 54:155. See also W. G. Spencer, appendix I, "On the Meaning of the Word 'Cancer' in Celsus and His References to Malignant Disease," in Celsus, *De medicina*, trans. idem, 3 vols. (Cambridge, Mass.: Harvard University Press, 1971), 3:589-92.

489 Brody, *Diseases of the Soul*, p. 131, citing Prudentius, *Peristephanon*.

490 Erasmus, *Adagia* 1.4.22; 4.1.82; trans. Phillips, 31:337.

491 Calvin, *Institutio christianae religionis* 3.10; *In harmoniam evangelicam* ad Luke 12:13, 15; 14:14.

492 Calvin, in Is. 9:20.

493 Calvin, *Institutio christianae religionis* 4.5.18; trans. Battles, 2:1101.

494 Calvin, *In libros Mosis* ad Gen. 1:28.

brace divine promises. Calvin wrote against covetousness, enjoining as the only method for its correction "to embrace (*amplectimur*) the promises of God, by which he testifies that he will have our care."[495] The remedy for the fall by touch, the primal parental grasp, was to be raised up by clasping socially the divine hands reaching down.

The culture of the sixteenth century generously encompassed the rhetorical hand of God in Michelangelo's art and the jurisprudential hand of God in Calvin's doctrine. For both, God was not an idler in the heavens to be contemplated by humans created erect to gaze up in wonder. He was active with his hands to be imitated in artistic design or social reciprocity. The image of God in humans was by tradition in the soul, but in Michelangelo's renaissance icon and in Calvin's reformation iconoclasm that image was surfacing in the body. The imitation of God was in the hand.

---

[495] Calvin, *In harmonia evangelicam* ad Matt. 6:26.

PRIMARY SOURCES

Achellini, Alessandro. *Annotationes anatomicae.* Bologna, 1520.

Acosta, José de. *Historia natural y moral de las Indias.* Edited by José Alcina Franch. Madrid: Historica, 16, 1987.

Acta sanctorum. Edited by Joanne Carnandet. New ed. 69 vols. in 70. Paris: V. Palme, 1863-1940.

Adam of Eynsham. *Magna vita sancti Hugonis. Life of Hugh of Lincoln.* Edited by Decima L. Douie and Hugh Farmer. London: Nelson, 1961-62.

Adamnan. *De locis sanctis.* Edited by Denis Meehan. Scriptores latini hiberniae, 3. Dublin: Dublin Institute for Advanced Studies, 1958.

Aelian. *De natura animalium.* Edited by A. F. Scholfield. 3 vols. Cambridge, Mass.: Harvard University Press, 1971.

Agrippa von Nettesheim, Heinrich Cornelius. *De incertitudine et vanitate scientiarum.* Edited by Catherine M. Dunn. Renaissance Editions, 4. Northridge: California State University Press, 1974.

——. *De nobilitate et praecellentia foeminei sexus.* Edited by Charles Béné. Geneva: Droz, 1990.

——. *De originali peccato.* Cologne, 1532.

Albert the Great. *Opera omnia.* Edited by Augustus Borgnet. 18 vols. Paris, 1890-99.

——. *De animalibus.* Edited by Hermann Stadler. 2 vols. Beiträge zur Geschichte der Philosophie des Mittelalters, Texte und Untersuchungen, 15-16. Münster: Aschendorff, 1916-20.

Alberti, Leon Battista. *Opere volgare.* Edited by Cecil Grayson. 3 vols. Bari: Gius. Laterza e Figli, 1973.

Aldhelm. *De virginitate.* In *Opera*, pp. 209-323. Edited by Rudolf Ehwald. Monumenta germaniae historica, auctores antiquissimi, 15. Berlin: Weidmann, 1919.

Aldrovandi, Ulisse. *De piscibus libri V et de cetis liber unus.* Bologna, 1613.

——. *Musaeum metallicum in libros IIII distributum.* Bonn: Iohannes Baptista Ferronus, 1648.

Alessio Piemontese. *Secreti.* Venice, 1555.

Alfonso, Pedro. *Disciplina clericalis.* Edited by Maria Jesús Lacarra. Zaragoza: Guara, 1980.

Amanieu de Sescas. "Aissó es l'essenhamen de la donzela." In Manuel Mila y Fontanels, *Obras.* Vol. 2: *De los trovadores en España*, pp. 388-404. Edited by C. Martinez and F. R. Manrique. Barcelona: Consejo superior de investigaciones científicas, 1966.

——. "Aissó es l'essenham de la donzela." In *Testi didattico-cortesi di provenza*, pp. 229-89. Edited by Giuseppe E. Sansone. Bari: Adriatica, 1977.

Ambrose. *Opera.* Edited by Karl Schenkl et al. 7 vols. Corpus scriptorum ecclesiasticorum latinorum, 32, 62, 64, 73, 78-79, 82. Vienna, 1897.

Amira. Inter Leon Battista Alberti, *Opere volgare.* Vol. 5:269-94. Edited by Anicio Bonucci. 5 vols. Florence, 1843-49.

Anaxagoras. *The Fragments of Anaxagoras.* Edited by David Sider. Beiträge zur klassischen Philologie, 118. Meisenheim am Glan: Anton Hain, 1981.

(Ancrene Riwle). The English Text of the "Ancrene Riwle": "Ancrene Wisse" Edited from MS. Corpus Christi College, Cambridge, 402. Edited by J. R. Tolkien. Early English Text Society, 249. London: Oxford University Press, 1962.

Angela of Foligno. (*Librum de vere fidelium experientia.*). *Le livre de l'expérience des vrais fidèles.* Edited by M.-J. Ferré. Paris: E. Droz, 1927.

Anselm (pseudo). *Dialogus S. Anselmi cum B. V. Maria.* In *Patrologia latina*, 159:271-90.

Aretaeus. *De causis et signis acutorum morborum libri II.* In *Aretaeus.* Edited by Karl Hüde. Corpus medicorum graecorum, 2. Leipzig: Teubner, 1923.

Aristotle. *Opera.* Edited by Immanuel Bekker. 11 vols. Oxford, 1837.

——. *De anima.* Edited by W. D. Ross. Oxford: Clarendon, 1956.

——. *Parva naturalia.* Edited by W. D. Ross. Oxford: Clarendon, 1955.

——. *Politica.* Edited by W. D. Ross. Oxford: Clarendon, 1957.

——. *Problemata.* Edited by Pierre Louis. 3 vols. Paris: Belles lettres, 1991.

Arnold of Villanova. *Opera omnia.* Basel, 1585.

——. A Critical Edition of "Le regime tresutile et très profitable pour conserver et garder la santé du corps humain" [*Regimen sanitatis*] with the commentary of Arnoul de Villeneuve. Edited by Patricia A. Willet. Ph. D diss., University of North Carolina at Chapel Hill, 1974.

Athenaeus. *Deipnosophistae.* Edited by Georg Kaibel. 3 vols. Leipzig: B. G. Teubner, 1887-1962.

Augustine. *Opera.* In *Patrologia latina*, 32-47.

——. *De civitate Dei.* Edited by Bernard Dombart and Alphonse Kalb. 2 vols. Corpus christianorum series latina, 47-48. Turnhout: Brepols, 1981.

——. *De diversis quaestionibus octoginta tribus.* Edited by Almut Mutzenbecher. Corpus christianorum series latina, 14A. Turnhout: Brepols, 1975.

——. *De Trinitate libri XV.* Edited by W. J. Mountain. 2 vols. Corpus christianorum series latina, 50-50A. Turnhout: Brepols, 1968.

——. *Enarrationes in psalmos.* Edited by Eligius Dekkers and Iohannes Fraipont. 3 vols. Corpus christianorum series latina, 50-50A. Turnhout: Brepols, 1956.

——. *In evangelium Iohannis tractatus CXXIV.* Edited by Radbodus Willems. Corpus christianorum series latina, 36. Turnhout: Brepols, 1956.

Augustine (pseudo). *Hypomnesticon.* In *Patrologia latina*, 45:1611-64.

——. *Les "meditations" de sainct Augustin.* Translated by P. Tamisier. Lyon, 1587.

Avicenna. (*Kuliyat-e-Qanum*). *Canon of Medicine.* Translated by Mazhar H. Shah. In *The General Principles of Avicenna's "Canon of Medicine."* Karachi: Naveed Clinic, 1966.

Banister, John. *The Historie of Man.* London, 1578. Rpt. The English Experience, 122. New York: Da Capo, 1969.

Barbaro, Francesco. *De re uxoria.* Edited by Attilio Gresotto. In *Atti e memorie delle Reale accademie di scienza, lettere, ed arte di Padova*, 32 (1915):6-105.

Barberino, Francesco da. *Reggimento e costumi di donne.* Edited by Giuseppe E. Sansone. Filologia romanza, 2. Turin: Loescher-Chiantore, 1957.

Bartholomaeus Anglicus. *De proprietatibus rerum.* Frankfurt: Steinius, 1601. Rpt. Frankfurt: Minerva, 1964.

Bartolommeo della Rocca (Cocles). *Chyromantie ac physionomie Anastasis cum approbatione magistri Alexandri de Achillinis.* Bologna: Iohannes Antonii de Benedictis, 1504.

Basil of Caesarea. *Epistolai.* In *Patrologia graeca*, 32:219-1112.

——. (*Homilia IX in Hexaemeron*). *Homélies sur l'hexaéméron.* Edited by Stanislaus Giet. 2d ed. Sources chrétiennes, 26b. Paris: Cerf, 1968.

Bede. *Hexameron.* In *Patrologia latina*, 91:1-190.

Bede (pseudo). *De mundi coelestis terrestrisque constitutione liber.* In *Patrologia latina*, 90:881-910.

Belon, Pierre. *De aquatilibus libri duo cum iconibus.* Paris, 1553.

——. *L'histoire naturelle des estranges poissons marins, avec la vraie peincture et description du daulphin, et de plusieurs autres de son espece.* Paris: R. Chaudiere, 1551.

Benedetti, Alessandro. *Historia corporis humani, sive anatomice*. Venice: Bernardino Guerraldo, 1502.

Berengario da Carpi, Jacopo. (*Isagogae breves*). *A Short Introduction to Anatomy*. Edited by L. R. Lind. Chicago: University of Chicago Press, 1959. Rpt. New York: Klaus, 1969.

Bernard of Clairvaux. *Opera omnia*. Edited by Jean Leclercq, H. Rochais, and C. H. Talbot. 8 vols. Rome: Cistercienses, 1955-77.

Bernard of Clairvaux (pseudo). *Rythmica oratio ad unumquodlibet membrorum Christi patientis et a cruce pendentis*. In *Patrologia latina*, 184:1319-23.

Bernardino of Siena. *Opera omnia*. Edited by Pacificus M. Perantonus. 9 vols. Florence: Ad Claras Aquas, 1950-65.

Bessarion, Iohannes. *In calumniatorem Platonis*. Edited by Ludwig Mohler. 2 vols. In vol. 2 of Mohler, *Kardinal Bessarion als Theologe, Humanist, und Staatsmann*. Aalen: Scientia, 1967.

Bèze, Théodore de. *Tractatio de repudiis et divortis*. Geneva, 1573.

——. Translator. Biblia sacra, sive Testamentum vetus ab Im. Tremellio et Fr. Junio ex Hebraeo Latine redditum, et Testamentum novum a Theod. Beza e Graeco in Latinum versum. London, 1656.

Biblia pauperum: Facsimile Edition of the Forty-Leaf Blockbook in the Library of the Esztergom Cathedral. Edited by Elizabeth Soltész. n. p.: Corvina, 1967.

Biringuccio, Vannuccio. *De la pirotechnia*. Venice: Venturino Roffinello, 1540.

Boccaccio, Giovanni. *De claris mulieribus*. Berne: Mathias Apiarius, 1539.

Boethius. *Philosophiae consolationis, libri quinque*. Edited by Karl Buchner. Heidelberg: Carl Winter, 1947.

Bonaventure. *Opera omnia*. 11 vols. Quaracchi: Collegium S. Bonaventurae, 1882-1902.

Bonaventure (pseudo). (*Meditationes vitae Christi*). *Meditations on the Life of Christ: An Illustrated Manuscript of the Fourteenth Century*. Edited by Isa Ragusa and Rosalie B. Green. Princeton, N.J.: Princeton University Press, 1961.

Bonvesin da Riva. *De quinquagenta curialitibus ad mensam*. Edited by Immanuel Bekker. In *Opuscula academica berolinensia: Gesammelte Abhandlungen zur Klassischen Altertumswissenschaft Byzantinistik und Romantischen Philolgie, 1826*. Vol. 2: *Aus den Monatsberichten der Preussischen Akademie der Wissenschaften 1842-1871*, pp. 86-90. Leipzig: Zentralantiquariat der Deutschen Demokratischen Republik, 1974.

Borghini, R. *Il riposo*. Florence, 1584. Appendix II of Charles Avery, *Giambologna: The Complete Sculpture*, pp. 250-51. Oxford: Phaidon Christie's, 1987.

De bouc van seden. In *Denkmäler altniederländischer Spracheund Literatur*, 2:561-99. Edited by Eduard Kausler. 3 vols. Tübingen, 1840-66.

Boursier, Louise. *Observations diverses, sur le sterilité, perte de fruict, foecondité, accouchements, et maladies des femmes, et enfants nouveaux naiz*. Paris: A. Saugrain, 1609.

Brandolino, Aurelio. *De humanae vitae conditione et toleranda corporis aegritudine*. Basel: R. Winter, 1543.

Brant, Sebastian. *The Ship of Fools*. Translated by Alexander Bradley. Edited by T. H. Jamieson. Edinburgh, 1874.

Bruto, Giovanni Michele. *La institutione di una fanciulla nata nobilmente*. Antwerp: I. Bellère, 1555. Rpt. Antwerp: Vereenigung der Antwepsche Bibliophielen, 1954.

Budé, Guillaume. *Opera omnia*. 4 vols. Basle, 1557. Rpt. Farnsborough, Hants: Gregg, 1969.

——. *Annotationes in quatuor et viginti "Pandectarum" libros*. Paris: Ascensiana, 1508.

Bulwer, John. *Anthropometamorphosis: Man Transform'd, or the Artificiall Changling*. London: William Hunt, 1653.

——. *Chirologia, or the Natural Language of the Hand and Chironomia, or the Art of Manual Rhetoric*. Edited by James W. Cleary. Carbondale: Southern Illinois University Press, 1974.

Buridan, Jean. *Quaestiones octo "Physicorum" libros Aristotelis*. Paris, 1509. Rpt. Frankfurt: Minerva, 1964.

Caesarius of Heisterbach. *Dialogus miraculorum*. Edited by Joseph Strange. 2 vols. Cologne, 1851.

Calmo, Andrea. *Le "Lettere" di Andrea Calmo*. Edited by Vittorio Rossi. Turin, 1888.

Calvin, John. *Opera quae supersunt omnia*. Edited by Eduard Reuss, Eduard Cunitz, and Johann Wilhelm Baum. Corpus reformatorum, 29-87. 59 vols. in 26. Brunswick: C. A. Schwetschke, 1863-1900.

——. *Commentarii in Epistolam ad Hebraeos*. Edited by T. H. L. Parker. In *Opera omnia*, 19. Geneva: Droz, 1996.

——. *Commentarii in Evangelium Joannis: Prima pars*. Edited by Helmut Feld. In *Opera omnia*, 11-1. Geneva: Droz, 1996.

——. *Commentarii in secundam Pauli Epistolam ad Corinthios*. Edited by Helmut Feld. In *Opera omnia*, 15. Geneva: Droz, 1994.

——. *Commentarii in Pauli Epistolas ad Galatas, ad Ephesios, ad Philippenses, ad Colossenses*. Edited by Helmut Feld. In *Opera omnia*, 16. Geneva: Droz, 1992.

——. (Commentarius in *De clementia* Senecae). *Calvin's Commentary on Seneca's "De clementia."* Edited by Ford Lewis Battles and André Malan Hugo. Renaissance Society of America, Renaissance Text Series, 3. Leiden: E. J. Brill for the Renaissance Society of America, 1969.

——. (*Excuse a messieurs le Nicodemites, Petit traicté, Traité des reliques*). In *Three French Treatises*. Edited by Francis M. Higman. London: Athlone Press, University of London, 1970.

——. *Institution de la religion chrestienne: Texte de la première édition française (1541)*. 2 vols. Paris: Champion, 1911.

Camerarius, Joachim. *Symbolorum et emblematum*. Nuremberg, 1590.

Cardano, Girolamo. *Opera omnia*. Edited by Carolus Sponius. 10 vols. Leiden: Huguetan, 1663.

Cartas dos primeiros jesuitas do Brasil. Edited by Serafim Leite. 3 vols. Sao Paolo: Comissco do IV centenario da cidade do Sao Paolo, 1954.

Cassius Dio. *Historia romana*. Edited by Johannes Melber. 3 vols. Leipzig: Teubner, 1890-1928.

Castiglione, Baldassare. *Il libro del cortegiano*. Edited by Vittorio Cian. 4th ed. Florence: Sansoni, 1974.

Catherine of Siena. *"Epistolario" di s. Caterina da Siena*. Edited by Eugenio Dupré Theseider. Rome: Istituto storico italiano, 1940.

Cavendish, Henry. "Some Attempts to Imitate the Effects of the *Torpedo* by Electricity," Royal Society of London, *Philosophical Transactions* 66 (1776):196-225. Rpt. in *The Electrical Researches Written between 1771 and 1781*. Edited by J. Clerk Maxwell. Cambridge, 1879.

Celsus. *De medicina*. Edited by W. G. Spencer. 3 vols. London: William Heinemann, 1948-53.

Cennini, Gennino. *Il libro dell'arte*. Edited by D. Thompson Jr. New Haven, Conn.: Yale University Press, 1932.

Cereta, Laura. *Epistolae*. Edited by J. G. Tomasini. Padua, 1640.

Cervantes, Miguel de. *El licenciado vidriera*. Edited by Narciso Alonso Cortés. Valladolid: Castellana, 1916.

Chalcidius. *"Timaeus" a Calcidio translatus commentarioque instructus*. Edited by J. H. Waszink. Vol. 4 of *Plato latinus*. Edited by Raymond Klibansky. London and Leiden: Warburg Institute and E. J. Brill, 1962.

Chanca, Diego Alvarez. (*Opus*). In Martín Fernandez de Navarrete, *Viajes de Cristóbal Colón*. Madrid: Calpe, 1922.

Chauliac, Guy de. *Chirurgia magna*. Darmstadt: Wissenschaftliche Buchgesellschaft, 1976.

——. *La grande chirugie*. Edited by E. Nicaise. Paris, 1870.

Christine de Pisan. "Le livre de dit de Poissy." In *Oeuvres poétiques de Christine de Pisan*, 2:159-222. Edited by Maurice Roy. 3 vols. Paris, 1886-96.

La clef d'amours. Edited by Auguste Doutrepont. Halle, 1890.

Cicero. *De finibus bonorum et malorum*. Edited by C. F. W. Müller. Leipzig: B. G. Teubner, 1908.

——. *De inventione, De optimo genere oratorium, Topica*. Edited by H. M. Hubbell. Cambridge, Mass.: Harvard University Press, 1949.

——. *De legibus*. Edited by Clinton Walker Keyes. Cambridge, Mass.: Harvard University Press, 1961.

——. *De natura deorum*. Edited by H. Rackham. Cambridge, Mass.: Harvard University Press, 1961.

——. *De oratore*. Edited by Augustus S. Wilkins. In *Rhetorica*, vol. 1. Oxford: Clarendon, 1902.

——. *Epistolae ad familiares*. Edited by D. R. Shackleton Bailey. Stuttgart: Teubner, 1988.

——. *Orationes*. Edited by Albert Curtius Clark. Oxford: Clarendon, 1909.

——. *Orator*. Edited by Otto Jahn and Wilhelm Kroll. Berlin: Weidmann, 1958.

Coignard, Gabrielle de. *Oeuvres chrestiennes*. Tournon: Pour Jaques Favre libraire en Avignon, 1595.

Colonna, Francesco. *Hypnerotomachia Poliphili*. Edited by Giovanni Pozzi and Lucia A. Ciapponi. 2 vols. Medioevo e umanistica, 38-39. Padua: Antenore, 1980.

Colonna, Vittoria. *Rime*. Edited by Alan Bullock. Scrittori d'Italia, 270. Rome: Gius. Laterza e Figli, 1982.

Columbo, M. Realdo. *De re anatomica libri XV*. Venice, 1559. Rpt. Brussels: Culture et civilisation, 1969.

Condivi, Ascanio. *Vita di Michelangelo*. In *Le vite di Michelangelo scritte da Giorgio Vasari e da Ascanio Condivi*. Edited by Carl Frey. Sammlung ausgewählter Biographien Vasari's, 2. Berlin, 1887.

Condronchi, Giovan Battista. *De morbis qui Imolae, et alibi communiter hoc anno MDCII vagati sunt*. Bologna, 1603.

The Cornish Mystery-Play of the Three Maries. In *Everyman and Other Interludes*, pp. 120-27. London: J. M. Dent and Sons, 1948.

Correspondance des réformateurs dans les pays de langue française. Edited by A.-L. Herminjard. Nieuwkoop: B. de Graaf, 1965.

"La cour d'amour." Edited by L. Constans. In *Revue des langues romanes* 6 (1881):157-79, 209-20, 261-76.

Cyprian. *Opera*. Edited by R. Weber, M. Bévenot, M. Simonetti, and C. Mareschini. 2 vols. Corpus christianorum series latina, 3-3A. Turnhout: Brepols, 1972-76.

Dante Alighieri. *La "Commedia" secondo l'antica vulgata*. Edited by Giorgio Petrocchi. 4 vols. Milan: Mondadori, 1966-68.

Della Casa, Giovanni. *Galateo, overo de' costumi*. Edited by Emmanuela Scarpa. Ferrara: Franco Cosimo Panini, 1990.

Dioscorides. *De materia medica*. Edited by Max Wellmann. 3 vols. Berlin: Weidmann, 1958.

Donati, Marcello. *De medicina historia mirabili*. Mantua: F. Osanam, 1586.

Donne, John. *The Anniversaries*. Edited by Frank Manley. Baltimore, Md.: Johns Hopkins University Press, 1963.

Edits civils de la République de Genève (1568). Geneva: Société des libraires et éditeurs de la Suisse romande, Geneva, 1707.

Edwardes, David. *Introduction to Anatomy 1532*. Edited by C. D. O'Malley and K. F. Russell. Stanford, Calif.: Stanford University Press, 1961.

Empedocles. In *Die Fragmente der Vorsokratiker*. Edited by Hermann Diels. 5th ed. Berlin: Weidmann, 1934.

Erasmus. *Opera omnia*. Edited by Johannes Clericus. 11 vols. Leiden, 1703-6.

——. *Opera omnia*. Amsterdam: North Holland, 1971-.

——. *Ausgewählte Werke*. Edited by Hajo Holborn with Annemarie Holborn. Munich: C. H. Beck, 1964.

——. *De libero arbitrio, diatribē sive collatio*. Edited by Johannes von Walter. Quellenschriften zur Geschichte der Protestantismus, 8. Leipzig: A. Deichert, 1910.

Erastus, Thomas. *De occultis pharmacorum potestatibus*. Basel, 1574.

"Die Erlauer Österspiel" III. In *Das Drama des Mittelalters*, pp. 205-60. Edited by Eduard Hartl. Leipzig: Wissenschaftliche Buchgesellschaft, 1937.

Estienne, Henri. *Dialogue du nouveau langage français, italianisé*. 2 vols. Paris, 1597.

Estienne, Robert. *Dictionnaire latinogallicum*. Paris: Robert Estienne, 1538.

——. *Thesaurus linguae latinae*. 4 vols. Basel: Thurnisiorum, 1740-43. Also, rpt. Brussels: Culture et civilisation, 1964-.

Euripides. *Tragoedia*. Edited by August Nauck. 3 vols. 3d ed. Leipzig, 1869-81.

Fabricius, Hieronymus. (*De formatione ovi et pullae, De formato foetu*). *The Embryological Treatises of Hieronymus Fabricius of Aquapendente: The Formation of the Egg and of the Chick (De formatione ovi etpullae), The Formed Fetus (De formato foetu)*. Edited by Howard B. Adelman. 2 vols. Ithaca, N.Y.: Cornell University Press, 1967.

Fedele, Cassandra. *Epistolae et orationes*. Edited by J. F. Tomasini. Padua, 1636.

Fernel, Jean. *Universa medicina*. Geneva: J. Stoer, 1580.

Ficino, Marsilio. *Opera omnia*. 2d ed. 2 vols. Basle, 1561. Rpt. in Monumenta politica et philosophica rariora, series 1, 7-10. Turin: Bottega d'Erasmo, 1959.

——. (*Commentarius in "Phaedrum" Platonis*). *Marsilio Ficino and the Phaedran Charioteer*. Edited by Michael J. B. Allen. Publications of the Center for Medieval and Renaissance Studies, UCLA, 14. Berkeley and Los Angeles: University of California Press, 1981.

——. (*Commentarius in "Symposium" Platonis*). *Commentaire sur le "Banquet" de Platon*. Edited by Raymond Marcel. Paris: Belles lettres, 1956.

——. (*De vita*). *Marsilio Ficino: Three Books on Life*. Edited by Carol V. Kaske and John R. Clark. Medieval and Renaissance Texts and Studies, 57; Renaissance Texts Series, 11. Binghamton, N.Y.: Medieval and Renaissance Texts and Studies, 1989.

——. *Lettere I: Epistolarum familiarum liber 1*. Edited by Sebastiano Gentile. Florence: L. S. Olschki, 1990.

——. (*Theologia platonica*). *Théologie platonicienne de l'immortalité des ames*. Edited by Raymond Marcel. 3 vols. Paris: Belles lettres, 1964.

Firenzuola, Agnolo. *Delle bellezze delle donne*. In *Opere*, pp. 713-89. Edited by Delmo Maestri. Turin: Unione Tipografico-Editrice, 1977.

Firmicus Maternus. *Matheseos libri VIII*. Edited by W. Kroll, F. Skutsch, and K. Ziegler. 2 vols. Stuttgart: B. G. Teubner, 1968.

Fonte, Moderata. *Il merito delle donne*. In *Donne e società nel seicento: Lucrezia Marinella e Arcangela Tarabotti*, pp. 159-96. Biblioteca di cultura, 167. Rome: Bulzoni, 1979.

Foxe, John. *The Acts and Monuments*. Edited by Stephen Reed Cattley. 8 vols. London, 1843-49.

Francisco de Vitoria. *Comentarios a la Secunda secundae de Santo Tomás (1534-37)*. Edited by Vicente Beltran de Heredia. 6 vols. Biblioteca de teólogos españoles, 2-7. Salamanca, 1932-52.

——. *Relectio de Indis: Carta Magna de los Indios: 450 aniversario, 1539-1989*. Edited by L. Pereña. Corpus hispanorum de pace, 27. Madrid: Consejo superior de investigaciones científicas, 1989.

Galen. *Opera*. Edited by Karl Gottlob Kuhn. 22 vols. in 20. Medicorum graecorum opera quae exstant, 1-20. Leipzig, 1821-33.

——. *Peri chreias moriōn, De usu partium libri XVII*. Edited by George Helmreich. 2 vols. Leipzig: B. G. Teubner, 1907-9.

——. *Galen on Anatomical Procedures: The Later Books*. Edited by M. C. Lyons and B. Towers. Cambridge: Cambridge University Press, 1962.

——. *Galen on Respiration and the Arteries: An Edition with English Translation and Commentary of "De usu respirationis," "In arteriis natura sanguis contineatur," "De usu pulsuum," and "De causis respirationis."* Edited by David J. Furley and J. S. Wilkie. Princeton, N.J.: Princeton University Press, 1984.

——. *Galen on the Usefulness of the Parts of the Body: Peri chreias moriōn, De usu partium*. Edited by Margaret Tallmadge May. 2 vols. Ithaca, N.Y.: Cornell University Press, 1968.

——. *In Hippocratis prorrehticum I comm. III*. Edited by H. Diehls. *De comate secundum Hippocratem*. Edited by J. Mewaldt. *In Hippocratis prognosticum*. Edited by J. Heeg. Corpus medicorum graecorum, 5.9.2. Leipzig: B. G. Teubner, 1915.

——. *Quod animi mores*. In *Scripta minora*, 2. Edited by J. Marquardt, I. Müller, and G. Helmreich. 3 vols. Leipzig, 1884-83.

Gemma, Cornilius. *De naturae divinis characterismis*. 2 vols. in 1. Antwerp: Christopher Plantinus, 1575.

Geoffrey of Vinsauf. *Poetria nova*. In *Les arts poétiques du douzième et du treizième siècle: Recherches sur la technique littéraire du Moyen Âge*, pp. 197-262. Edited by Edmond Farel. Paris: Honoré Champion, 1923.

Gesner, Konrad. *Historiae animalium liber IIII qui est de piscium et aqualtilium animantium natura, cum iconibus singulorum ad vivum expressis fere omnibus DCCVI*. Zurich, 1558.

Ghiberti, Lorenzo. *I commentarii*. Edited by von Schlosser. Berlin, 1912.

Giraldi Cintio, Giovanbattista. *Gli Hecatommithi*. Venice, 1608.

Girava, Girónimo. *La cosmographia y geographia*. Venice, 1570.

Gonçalves da Câmara, Luis. *Acta patri Ignatii*. Edited by Dionisio Fernandez Zapico and Cándido de Dalmases. Monumenta historica societatis Iesu, 66. Rome: Monumenta historica societatis Iesu, 1943.

Gregory of Nyssa. *De hominis opificio*. In *Patrologia graeca*, 44:123-256.

Gregory the Great. *Opera*. In *Patrologia latina*, 75-78.

——. *Moralia in Iob*. Edited by Mark Adriaen. 3 vols. Corpus christianorum series latina, 143, 143a, 143b. Turnhout: Brepols, 1979-85.

Guarino, Antonio. *La coerenza di Publio Mucio*. Naples: Jovene, 1981.

Guarino da Verona. *"Epistolario" di Guarino Veronese*. Edited by Remigio Sabbadini. 3 vols. Venice: A Spese della Società, 1915.

Guazzo, Stefano. *La civil conversatione*. Venice: Salicato, 1548.

Guerrero, Francisco. *El viaje de Hierusalem*. Edited by R. P. Caliroft. Exeter: University of Exeter Press, 1984.

Guglielmo Ebreo Pesaro. *De practica seu arte tripudii: On the Practice or Art of Dancing*. Edited by Barbara Sparti. Oxford: Clarendon, 1993.

Guillaume de Lorris and Jean de Meun. *"Le roman de la rose" par Guillaume de Lorris et Jean de Meun*. Edited by Felix Lecoy. 3 vols. Paris: Champion, 1966-75.

Herodotus. *Historiae.* Edited by Carolus Hude. Oxford: Clarendon, 1908.

Hesiod. *Theogonia, Opera et dies, Secretum.* Edited by Friedrich Solmsen. *Fragmenta selecta.* Edited by R. Merkelbach and M. L. West. 3d ed. Oxford: Clarendon, 1990.

Hilliard, Nicholas. *A Treatise Concerning the Arte of Limning.* Edited by R. K. R. Thornton and T. G. S. Cain. Ashington: Mid Northumberland Arts Group, 1981.

Hippocrates. (*Opera*). *Ouevres complètes.* Edited by Emile Littré. 10 vols. Paris, 1839-61.

Hoffman, Caspar. *De generatione hominis libri quatuor: Contra Mundinum Mundinium.* Frankfurt: Wechelian, Clement Schleichius, and Petrus de Zetter, 1629.

Hollanda, Francisco de. *Diálogos de Roma (da pintura antiga).* Edited by Manuel Mendes. Lisbon: Sá da Costa, 1955.

Homer. *Opera.* Edited by David B. Monro and Thomas W. Allen. 4 vols. 2d and 3d eds. Oxford: Clarendon, 1919-20.

Horace. *Opera.* Edited by Edward C. Wickham and H. W. Garrod. Oxford: Clarendon, 1912.

Hugh of St. Victor. *Sermones centum.* In *Patrologia latina*, 177:899-1210.

Isidore of Seville. *Etymologiarum, sive originum libri XX.* Edited by W. M. Lindsay. 2 vols. Oxford: Clarendon, 1911.

Jacobus da Voragine. *Legenda aurea.* Edited by Theodore Graesse. Rpt. Osnabrück: Otto Zeller, 1965.

Jerome, (*Epistolae*). *Lettres.* Edited by Jerome Labourt. 6 vols. Paris: Belles lettres, 1949-58.

John Chrysostom. *Omnia quae extant opera juxta Benedictiorum versionem.* Edited by A. B. Caillau and M. N. S. Guillon. Paris, 1835-43.

John of Salisbury. *Policratici, sive De nugis curialium et vestigiis philosophorum.* Edited by Clemens C. I. Webb. Oxford: Clarendon, 1909.

John of the Cross. *Vida y obras de San Juan de la Cruz.* Edited by Crisógono de Jesús Sacramentado. Biblioteca de autores cristianos. 7th ed. Madrid: Editorial catolica, 1973.

——. *Obras de san Juan de la cruz.* Edited by Silverio de santa Teresa. Biblioteca mística carmelitana, 10-14. 5 vols. Burgos: Monte Carmelo, 1929-51.

Joubert, Laurent. *Traité du ris: contenant son essence, ses causes, et mervelheus essais curieusement recherchés, raisonés, et observés.* Paris: N. Chesneau, 1579.

Journals and Other Documents on the Life and Voyages of Christopher Columbus. Edited by Samuel Eliot Morison. New York: Heritage, 1963.

Justinian. (*Tituli totius omnium digestorum, seu pandectorum*). *The Digest of Justinian.* Edited by Theodor Mommsen with Paul Krueger. 4 vols. Philadelphia: University of Pennsylvania Press, 1985.

——. (*Institutiones*). *The "Institutes" of Justinian.* Edited by Thomas Collett Sandars. London: Longmans, Green, 1922.

Juvenal. *Saturae.* Edited by J. D. Duff. Cambridge: Cambridge University Press, 1925.

Kempe, Margery. *The Book of Margery Kempe.* Edited by Sanford Brown Meech and Hope Emily Allen. Early English Text Society, 212. London: Oxford University Press, 1940.

Kosmas und Damien. Edited by Ludwig Deubner. Leipzig: B. G. Teubner, 1907.

Labé, Louise. *Oeuvres complètes: Sonnets-élégies, Débat de folie et d'amour.* Edited by François Rigolot. Paris: Flammarion, 1986.

Lactantius. *Opera omnia.* Edited by Samuel Brandt. 2 vols. Corpus scriptorum ecclesiasticorum latinorum, 19, 27. Vienna, 1890-93.

——. *(De ira Dei). Le colère de Dieu.* Edited by Christiane Ingremeau. Sources chretiennes, 289. Paris: Cerf, 1982.

Las Casas, Bartolome de. *Obras completas.* Edited by Angel Losada. 14 vols. Madrid: Aliana, 1988-92.

——. *Apologética historia sumaria*. Edited by Edmundo O'Gorman. Instituto de investigaciones historicas, serie de historiadores y cronistas de Indias, 1. 3d ed. 2 vols. Mexico City: Universidad nacional autónoma de México, 1967.

La Tour-Landry, Geoffroy de. *Le livre du Chevalier de la Tour Landry pour l'enseignement de ses filles*. Edited by A. Montaiglon. Paris, 1854.

Lefèvre d'Étaples, Jacques. *De Maria Magdalena, et triduo Christi disceptatio*. Paris: Henri Estienne, 1517.

——. *De Maria Magdalena, triduo Christi, et ex tribus una Maria, disceptatio. . . secunda emissio*. Paris: Henri Estienne, 1518.

León, Luis de. *La perfecta casada*. Edited by Elizabeth Wallace. University of Chicago Decennial Publications, second series, 6. Chicago: University of Chicago Press, 1903.

Leonardo da Vinci. (*Opera*). *The Literary Works of Leonardo da Vinci*. Edited by Jean Paul Richler. 3d ed. 2 vols. London: Phaidon, 1970.

——. (*Codex urbinas latinus 1270*). *Treatise on Painting*. Edited by A. Philip McMahon. 2 vols. Vol. 2: *Facsimile*. Princeton, N.J.: Princeton University Press, 1956.

Le Picart, François. *Les sermons et instructions chrestiennes, pour tous les iours de caresme, et feries de Pasques*. Paris: Nicolas Chesneau, 1566.

Liébault, Jean. *Trois livres de l'embellissement et ornement du corps humain*. Paris: Jacques du Puys, 1582.

Livy. *Ab urbe condita libri*. Edited by W. Wisenborn and M. Mueller. 10 vols. Berlin, 1873-88.

Lomazzo, Giovanni Paolo. *Trattato dell'arte de la pittura*. Hildesheim: Georg Olms, 1968.

Loyola, Ignatius. *Exercitia spiritualia*. Edited by Joseph Calveras. Monumenta historica societatis Iesu, 100. Rome: Institutum historicum societatis Iesu, 1969.

Lucretius. *De rerum natura*. Edited by Cyril Bailey. 2d ed. Oxford: Clarendon, 1967.

Lucian. *Opera*. Edited by W. D. McLeod. 2 vols. Oxford: Clarendon, 1972-.

Ludolf of Saxony. *Vita Jesu Christi ex Evangelio et approbatis ab Ecclesia Catholica doctoribus sedule collecta*. Edited by L. M. Rigollot. 4 vols. Paris, 1878.

Luigini, Federico. *Il libro della bella donna*. Milan: "L'Aristocratica," 1925.

Luther, *Werke*. 58 vols. Weimar: H. Böhlau. Rpt.: Graz: Akademische, 1964-.

——. *De servo arbitrio*. In *Luthers Werke in Auswahl*, 4:94-293. Edited by Otto Clemen. 6 vols. Berlin: Walter de Gruyter, 1950.

Machiavelli, Niccolò. "Esortazione alla penitenza." In *Tutti gli scritti letterari*, pp. 207-13. Edited by Franco Gaeta. Milan: Feltrinelli, 1965.

Macinghi Strozzi, Alessandra. (*Lettere*). *Tempo di affetti e di mercanti: Lettere ai figli esuli*. Edited by Angela Bianchini. Milan: Garzanti, 1987.

Macrobius. *Opera*. Edited by Francis Eyssenhardt. Leipzig, 1893.

Manetti, Giannozzo. *De dignitate ex excellentia hominis*. Edited by Elizabeth Riley Leonard. Thesaurus mundi, Bibliotheca scriptorum latinorum mediae et recentioris aetatis, 12. Padua: Antenore, 1975.

Manilius. *Astronomicon*. Edited by George P. Goold. Leipzig: Teubner, 1985.

Manuel, Juan. *Libro de los estados*. Edited by R. B. Tate and I. R. Macpherson. Oxford: Clarendon, 1974.

Marguerite de Navarre. *L'Heptameron*. Edited by Michel François. Paris: Garnier, 1964.

Marinella, Lucrezia. *La nobiltà e l'eccellenze delle donne (1600)*. In *Donna e società nel seicento: Lucrezia Marinella e Arcangela Tarabotti*, pp. 114-57. Edited by Ginevra Conti Odorisio. Biblioteca di cultura, 167. Rome: Bulzoni, 1979.

Marinelli, Giovanni. *Gli ornamenti delle donne*. Venice: Francesio de'Franceschi, 1562.

Marino, Giambattista. *Poesie varie*. Edited by Benedetto Croce. Scrittori d'Italia, 51. Bari: Gius. Laterza e Figli, 1913.

Martin Le France. *Le champion des dames.* Edited by Arthur Piaget. Mémoires et documents publiés par la Société d' histoires de la Suisse romande, 3d series, 8. Lausanne: Payot, 1968.

Mary Magdalen. In *The Late Medieval Religious Plays of Bodlein MSS. Digby 133 and E Museo 160*, pp. 24-95. Edited by Donald C. Baker, John L. Murphy, and Louis B. Hall, Jr. Early English Text Society, old series, 283. Oxford: Oxford University Press for Early English Text Society, 1982.

Massa, Niccolò. *Liber introductorius anatomiae.* Venice, 1559 or 1536.

Matthew of Vendôme. *Ars versificatoria.* In *Les arts poétiques du douzième et du treizième siècle: Recherches sur la technique littéraire du Moyen Âge*, pp. 106-93. Edited by Edmond Faral. Paris: Honoré Champion, 1962.

Le ménagier de Paris. Edited by Georgine E. Brereton and Janet M. Ferrier. 2 vols. Oxford: Clarendon, 1981.

Mercati, Michele. "De ceraunica cuneata." In Robert F. Heizer, *Man's Discovery of His Past: A Sourcebook of Original Articles*, pp. 73-77. Palo Alto, Calif.: Peek, 1967.

Mexía, Pedro. *Silva de varia lección.* Edited by Antonio Castro. 2 vols. Madrid: Catedra, 1989.

Mexía, Vicente. *Saludable instrucción del estado del matrimonio.* Córdoba: Juan Baptista Escudero, 1566.

Michel, Jean. (*Le mystère de la passion*). *Le livre du conduite du régisseur et la compte des dépenses pour "Le mystère de la passion" joué à Mons en 1501.* Edited by Gustave Cohen. Bibliothèque du cinquième siècle, 30. Paris: H. Champion, 1925.

Michelangelo. (*Carteggio*). *The "Letters" of Michelangelo.* Edited by E. H. Ramsden. 2 vols. Stanford, Calif.: Stanford University Press, 1963.

——. *Il "carteggio" di Michelangelo.* Edited by Giovanni Poggi, Paola Barocchi, and Renzo Ristori. 5 vols. Florence: Sansoni, 1965-79.

——. (*Rime*). *Michelangelo Buonarroti: "Rime."* Edited by Enzo Noè Girardi. Scrittori d'Italia, 217. Bari: Laterza, 1960.

Minucius Felix. *Octavius.* Edited by G. Quispel. Leiden: E. J. Brill, 1949.

Molanus, Johannes. *De historia ss. imaginum et picturarum pro vero eorum usu contra abusus libri quatuor.* Edited by Johannes Natalis Paquot. Louvain: Typis Academicis, 1771.

Molina, Alonso de. *Vocabulario en lengua castellana y mexicana y mexicana y castellana.* Biblioteca Parrúa, 44. Mexico: Parrúa, 1970.

——. *Vocabulario en lengua castellana y mexicana.* Mexico, 1571. Rpt. Colección de incunables americanos siglo XVI, vol. 4. Madrid: Cultura hispanica, 1944.

Mondeville, Henri de. *"Chirurgia" de maître Henri de Mondeville.* Edited by E. Nicaise. Paris, 1893.

Mondino dei Luzzi. (*Anathomia*). *"Anatomies" de Mondino dei Luzzi et de Guido de Vigevano.* Paris: Droz, 1926. Rpt. Geneva: Slatkine, 1977.

Montaigne. *Les Essais.* Edited by Pierre Villey and V.-L. Saulnier. Paris: Presses universitaires de France, 1965.

Münster, Sebatian. *Cosmographiae universalis libri VI.* Basel: H. Petri, 1559.

Nifo, Agostino. *De pulcro liber.* Leiden: David Lopes de Haro, 1643.

Nogarola, Isotta. *Opera quae supersunt omnia.* Edited by E. Abel. 2 vols. Vienna, 1886.

Odasi, Tifi. "Macaronea." In *Le macaronee padovane: Tradizione e lingua*, pp. 114-33. Edited by Ivano Paccagnella. Medioevo e umanesimo, 35. Padua: Antenore, 1979.

Odo of Cluny. "Sermo de Maria Magdalena." In *Patrologia latina*, 133:713-21.

Oppian. *Halieutica.* In *Oppian, Colluthus, Tryphiodorus*, pp. 200-514. Edited by A. W. Mair. New York: G. P. Putnam's Sons, 1928.

Ordo L. In Michel Andrieu, *Les ordines romani du haut moyen âge*. Vol. 5: *Les textes (Ordo L)*. Spicilegium sacrum lovaniense, études et documents, 11, 23-24, 28-29. 5 vols. Louvain: Spicilegium sacrum lovaniense, administration, 1961.

Origen. *Commentarium in Canticum canticorum*. Translated by Rufinus. Edited by Luc Brésard and Henri Crouzel. 2 vols. Sources chrétiennes, 375-76. Paris: Cerf, 1991-92.

L'Ornement des dames (Ornatus mulierum): Texte Anglo-normand du treizième siècle. Edited by Pierre Ruelle. Brussels: Presses universitaires de Bruxelles, 1967.

Osiander, Andreas. *Gesamtausgabe*. Edited by Gerhard Müller with Gottfried Seebass. 8 vols. Gütersloh: Gerd Mohn, 1975-90.

Ovid. *Amores*. Edited by J. C. McKeown. 2 vols. Liverpool: F. Cairns, 1987.

——. *Amores, Medicamina faciei femineae, Ars amatoria, Remedia amoris*. Edited by E. J. Kenney. Oxford: Clarendon, 1961.

——. *Metamorphoses*. Edited by O. Korn and J. H. Muller. 2 vols. in 1. Berlin: Weidmann, 1915-16.

Paré, Ambroise. *Oeuvres complètes*. Edited by J.-F. Malgaigne. 2 vols. Paris, 1840-41.

——. *De monstres et prodiges*. Edited by Jean Céard. Travaux d'humanisme et Renaissance, 115. Geneva: Droz, 1971.

——. *Dix livres de la chirurgie*. Paris: Jean le Royer, 1564. Rpt. Paris: Cercle du livre précieux, 1964.

Patrologiae cursus completus, series graeca. Edited by J.-P. Migne. 161 vols. Paris: Garnier, 1857-1912.

Patrologiae cursus completus, series latina. Edited by J.-P. Migne. 221 vols. Paris, 1800-75.

Paulinus of Nola. *Epistolae*. In *Patrologia latina*, 61:153-438.

Paulus Aegineta. *Opera*. Paris: V. Richelium, 1542.

Pausanius. *(Descriptio Graeciae). Hellados periegeseos*. 5 vols. Cambridge, Mass.: Harvard University Press, 1918-55.

Pepin, Guillaume. *Conciones quadragesimales ac sacras evangeliorum sensus pro feriis quadragesimae mystice et moraliter explicandos*. Antwerp: Guillelmus Lesteenicus and Engelbertus Gymnicus, 1656.

——. *Rosareum aurem B. Mariae virginis*. Antwerp: Guillelmus Lesteenius and Engelbertus Gymnicus, 1656.

Persius. *Saturae*. In *A. Persius Flacci et D. Iuni Iuvenalis "Saturae,"* pp. 1-34. Edited by W. V. Clausen. Oxford: Clarendon, 1959.

Peter Lombard. *Sententiae in quatuor libris distinctae*. 3d ed. 2 vols. Grottaferata: College of St. Bonaventure at Claras Aquas, 1971-81.

Peter the Chanter. *De penitentia et partibus eius*. In Richard C. Trexler, *The Christian at Prayer: An Illustrated Prayer Manual Attributed to Peter the Chanter (d. 1197)*. Medieval and Renaissance Texts and Studies, 44. Binghamton, N.Y.: Medieval and Renaissance Texts and Studies, 1987.

Petrarch. *Canzoniere*. Edited by Gianfranco Contini. Turin: Einaudi, 1964.

Philo. *Philo*. Edited by F. H. Colson and G. H. Whitaker. 12 vols. Cambridge, Mass.: Harvard University Press, 1962-71.

Piccolomini, Alessandro. *Dialogo de la bella creanza de la donne*. In *Trattati del cinquecento sulla donna*, pp. 3-69. Edited by Giuseppe Zonta. Bari: Gius. Laterza e Figli, 1913.

Pico della Mirandola, Giovanni. *Opera omnia*. Edited by Eugenio Garin. 2 vols. Turin: Bottega d'Erasmo, 1970.

Pietro Martire d'Anghiera. *De orbe novo decades octo*. In *Opera*, pp. 35-268. Graz: Akademische Druk-u.Verlaganstalt, 1966.

Pizzicoli, Ciriaco de'. *Itinerarium*. Florence: Giovanni Paolo Giovannelli, 1742.

Plato. *Opera*. Edited by Ioannes Burnet. 5 vols. Oxford: Clarendon, 1900-7.

Plautus. *Comoediae*. Edited by W. M. Lindsay. 2 vols. Oxford: Clarendon, 1904-5.

Pliny. *Naturalis historia.* Edited by H. Rackham, W. H. S. Jones, and D. E. Eichholz. 10 vols. Cambridge, Mass.: Harvard University Press, 1938-42.

Pliny, the younger. *Epistolae.* Edited by R. A. B. Mynors. Oxford: Clarendon, 1963.

Plotinus. *Opera.* Edited by Paul Henry and Hans-Rudolph Schwyzer. 3 vols. Paris: Desclée de Brouwer, 1951.

Plutarch. *Moralia.* Edited by Harold Fredrik Cherniss. 17 vols. Cambridge, Mass.: Harvard University Press, 1976.

——. *Vitae parallelae.* Edited by Robert Flacelière, Émile Chambry, and Marcel Juneaux. 16 vols. Paris: Belles lettres, 1957-83.

Pollux, Julius. *Onomasticon.* Edited by Eric Bethe. 3 vols. Lexicographi graeci, 9. Leipzig: B. G. Teubner, 1900-66.

Porta, Giambattista della. *De i miracoli et maravigliosi effeti dalla natura.* Venice: Lodovico Avanzi, 1560.

Poullain de la Barre, François. *De l'égalité des deux sexes: Discours physique et morale.* Paris, 1673.

Problemata varia anatomica: The University of Bologna, MS. 1165. Edited by L. R. Lind. University of Kansas Humanistic Studies, 38. Lawrence: University of Kansas Press, 1968.

Prudentius. *Carmina* Edited by Maruice P. Cunningham. Corpus christianorum series latina, 126. Turnhout: Brepols, 1966.

Purchas, Samuel. *Hakluytus posthumus, or Purchas His Pilgrimes.* 20 vols. Glascow: J. MacLehose, 1905-7.

Quintilian. *Institutiones oratoriae.* Edited by Michael Winterbottom. 4 vols. Oxford: Clarendon, 1970.

Rabelais, François. *Gargantua.* Edited by Ruth Calder. Textes littéraires français, 163. Geneva: Droz, 1970.

Ráskai, Lea. *Boldag Margit legendája.* Budapest: Royal Hungarian University Press, 1938.

Richard de Fournival. *"Li bestiaires d'amours" di Maistre Richart de Fourneval e "li response" du bestiaire.* Edited by Cesare Segre. Documenti di filologia, 2. Milan, 1957.

Richard of St. Victor. *De eruditione hominis interioris.* In *Patrologia latina,* 196:1229-1366.

Ripa, Cesare. *Iconologia, overo descrittione di diverse imagini cavate dall'antichità, a di propria inventione.* Edited by Erna Madowsky. Hildesheim: Georg Olms, 1970.

Robert de Blois. *Le chastoiement des dames.* In John Howard Fox, *Robert de Blois, son oeuvre didactique et narrative: Étude linguistique et litteraire,* pp. 133-55. Paris: Nizet, 1950.

Rondelet, Guilluame. *Libri de piscibus marines in quibusverae piscium effigies expressae sunt* Lyon, 1554.

Ronsard, Pierre de. *Oeuvres complètes.* Edited by Gustave Cohen. 2 vols. Bibliothèque de la Pléiade, 45-46. Paris: Gallimard, 1950-66.

Roper, Margaret More. *A Devout Treatise upon the Pater noster, translation of Erasmus, "Precatio dominica inseptem portiones distrubata."* Edited by Richard L. De Molen. In *Erasmus of Rotterdam: A Quincentennial Symposium,* pp. 93-124. New York: Twayne, 1971.

Rudolf of Fulda. *Vita Leobae.* In *Monumentae germaniae historiae scriptores,* 15-1:118-31. Edited by Georg Waite. Hannover, 1887.

(Sacramentarium gregorianum). Le sacramentaire grégorien: Ses principales formes d'après les plus anciens manuscrits. Edited by Jean Deshusses. 3 vols. Spicilegium friburgense, 16, 24, 28. Fribourg: Editions universitaires Fribourg suisse, 1971-82.

Sallust. *Catalina, Iugurtha, fragmenta ampliora.* Edited by Alphonsus Kurfess. Leipzig: B. G. Teubner, 1968.

Salviani, Ippolito. *Aquatilium animalium historiae.* Rome, 1554.

Sánchez, Tomás. *De sancto matrimonii disputationum tomi tres.* 3 vols. in 1. Lyon: Sumptibus Societatis typographorum, 1621.

Sander, Nicholas. *De origine ac progressu schismatis anglicani libri tres.* Ingolstadt: W. Ederi, 1588.

Savonarola, Girolamo. *Prediche e scritti.* Edited by Mario Ferrara. 2 vols. Florence: Olschki, 1952.

Scaliger, Julius Caesar. *Exotericorum exercitationum liber quintus decimus, de subtilitate, ad Hieronymum Cardanum.* Paris: Michel de Vascosan, 1557.

Schurman, Anna Maria van. *Amica dissertatio. . . de capacitate ingenii muliebris ad scientias,* Paris, 1638. Rpt. in eadem, *Opuscula hebrea, graeca, latina, gallica, prosaica et metrica*, pp. 28-95. Leiden, 1648.

Scribonius Largus. *Compositiones.* Edited by Sergio Sconocchia. Leipzig: B. G. Teubner, 1983.

Scritti d'arte del cinquecento. Edited by Paola Barocchi. Letteratura italiana, storia e testi, 32. Milan: Riccardo Ricciardi, 1973.

Select Documents Illustrating the Four Voyages of Columbus. Edited by Lionel Cecil Jane. 2 vols. Hakluyt Society, 2d series, 65, 70. London: Hakluyt Society, 1930-33.

Seneca. *Opera quae supersunt.* Edited by Friedrich Haase. 3 vols. in 2. Leipzig, 1852-53.

Seneca, the Elder. *Controversiae.* Edited by Michael Winterbottom. 2 vols. Cambridge, Mass.: Harvard University Press, 1974.

Sepúlveda, Juan Ginés de. *Democrates segundo, o de las justas causas de la guerra contra los indios.* Edited by Angel Losada. Madrid: Consejo superior de investigaciones científicas, 1951.

Servius. *In Vergilii carmina commentarii.* Edited by George Thilo and Hermann Hagen. Leipzig, 1881-87. Rpt. Hildesheim: Georg Olms, 1961.

Sextus Empiricus. *Opera.* Edited by Hermann Mutschmann. Revised by Jürgen Mau and Karl Janácek. 3 vols. Leipzig: B. G. Teubner, 1958.

Silius Italicus. *Punica.* Edited by Joseph Delz. Stuttgart: B. G. Teubner, 1987.

Sophronius. *Narratio miraculorum sanctorum Cyri et Joannis.* In *Patrologia graeca*, 87-3:3423-3676.

Soranus. *Gynaeciorum libri IV, De signis fracturarum, De fasciis, Vita Hippocratis secundum Soranum.* Edited by Johannes Ilberg. Corpus medicorum graecorum, 4. Leipzig: B. G. Teubner, 1927.

Society of Jesus. *Constitutiones societatis Iesu.* Edited by Arturo Codina. Monumenta historica societatis Iesu, 83. Rome: Borgo S. Spirito 5, 1934.

Les sources du droit du canton de Genève. Edited by Émile Rivoire and Victor van Berchem. Sammlung schweizerischer Rechtsquellen, 22. 4 vols. Arau: H. R. Sauerländer, 1927-35.

Spenser, Edmund. *The Faerie Queene.* Edited by Albert C. Hamilton. London: Longman, 1977.

Sprenger, Jacob and Heinrich Institoris. *Malleus maleficarum.* Translated by Montague Summers. London: John Rodker, 1928.

Stampa, Gaspara. In *"Rime" di Gaspara Stampa e di Veronica Franco*, pp. 1-227. Edited by Abdelkadar Salza. Bari: Gius. Laterza e Figli, 1913.

Steinmann, Ernst and Heinrich Pogatscher. "Dokumente und Forschungen zu Michelangelo," *Repertorium für Kunstwissenschaft* 29 (1906):387-424, 485-517.

Strabo. *Geographica.* Edited by H. L. Jones. Cambridge, Mass.: Harvard University Press, 1982.

Suárez de Peralta, Juan. *Tratado del descubrimento de las Indias (Noticias historicas de Nueva España) compuesto en 1589.* Testimonios mexicanos, historiadores, 3. Mexico: Secretaria de educación pública, 1949.

Suetonius. (*De viris illustribus*). In *Suetonius*. Edited by J. C. Rolfe. 2 vols. Cambridge, Mass.: Harvard University Press, 1913-14.

Synodis dioecesana autisioderensis. In *Concilia galliae A. 511- A. 695*, pp. 264-72. Edited by Caroli de Clercq. Corpus christianorum series latina, 148A. Turnhout: Brepols, 1958.

Studies in Pre-Vesalian Anatomy: Biography, Translations, Documents. Edited by L. R. Lind. Memoirs of the American Philosophical Society, 104. Philadelphia, Pa.: American Philosophical Society, 1975.

Teresa of Avila. *Obras completas*. Edited by Otger Steggink and Efren de la Madre de Dios. 2d ed. rev. Madrid: Biblioteca de autores cristianos, 1967.

Tertullian. (*De cultu feminarum*). *La toilette des femmes*. Edited by Marie Turian. Sources chrétiennes, 173. Paris: Cerf, 1971.

Theocritus. (*Opera*). Edited by A. S. Gow. 2 vols. Cambridge, Mass.: Harvard University Press, 1950-52.

Theophrastus. *De igne: A Post-Aristotelian View of the Nature of Fire*. Edited by Victor Coutant. Assen: Royal Vangorcum, 1971.

Thomas Aquinas. *Summa theologiae*. In *Opera omnia*. 16 vols. Rome: Polyglota s. c. de propaganda fide, 1882-1948.

Thomas of Cantimpré. *Liber de monstruosis hominibus orientis*. Edited by Alfons Hilka. In *Festschrift zum Jahrhundertfeier der Universität Breslau*, pp. 153-65. Breslau, 1911.

——. *Liber de natura rerum*. Edited by Helmut Boese. Berlin: Walter de Gruyter, 1973.

Tommaso da Vio, Cajetan. *Opuscula omnia*. Florence: Philip Tinghi, 1575.

——. *Commentarii in quinque Mosaicos libros*. Paris, 1539.

——. *In quatuor evangelia*. Paris: Iohannes Foucherius, 1542.

Valcoogh, D. Adriaenz. *Regel der Duytsche schoolmeester*. Amsterdam, 1664.

Varro. *De lingua latina*. Edited by Roland G. Kent. 2 vols. Cambridge, Mass.: Harvard University Press, 1951.

Vasari, Giorgio. *La vita di Michelangelo: nelle redazioni del 1550 e del 1568*. Edited by Paola Barocchi. 5 vols. Documenti di filologia, 5. Milan: Riccardo Ricciardi, 1962.

Vecellio, Cesare. *(Corona delle nobili e virtuose donne). Pattern Book of Renaissance Lace: A Reprint of the 1617 Edition of the "Corona delle nobili et virtuose donne."* New York: Dover, 1988.

Vincent of Beauvais. *Speculum quadruplex, sive speculum maius: Naturale, doctrinale, morale, historiale*. 4 vols. Douai, 1624. Rpt. Graz: Akademische Druck, 1964.

Vergil. *Opera*. Edited by R. A. B. Mynors. Rev. ed. Oxford: Clarendon, 1972.

Vesalius, Andreas. *De humani corporis fabrica*. Florence: I. Tornaesium, 1552.

Vita beatae Mariae Magdalenae. In *Patrologia latina*, 112:1431-1508.

Vitruvius. *De architectura*. Edited by Frank Granger. 2 vols. Cambridge, Mass.: Harvard University Press, 1931.

Vocabularium iurisprudentiae romanae. Edited by Otto Gradenwitz, Bernard Kuebler, E. T. Schulze, Rudolf Helm et. al. 5 vols. Berlin: Georgius Reimeri, 1903.

The Voyages of Christopher Columbus. Edited by Lionel Cecil Jane. London: Argonaut, 1930.

Whiterig, John. *The Monk of Farne: The Meditations of a Fourteenth-Century Monk*. Edited by Hugh Farmer. London: Darton, 1961.

Wotton, Edward. *De differentiis animalium libri decim*. Paris, 1552.

Wyatt, George. "The Life of Queen Anne Boleigne." In *The Life of Cardinal Wolsey by George Cavendish*. Edited by S. W. Singer. 2d ed. London, 1827.

Xenophon. *Opera omnia*. Edited by E. C. Marchant. 5 vols. Oxford: Clarendon, 1961-63.

Zayas y Sotomayor, María de. *Novelas amorosas y ejemplares*. Edited by Agustín G. de Amezúa. Madrid: Aldus, 1948.

Zeden-Goede manierlijcke. Edited by Johannis van Vloten. In *De Dietsche Warande* 6 (1864).

INDEX OF NAMES

INDEX OF SUBJECTS

STUDIES IN MEDIEVAL AND REFORMATION THOUGHT

EDITED BY HEIKO A. OBERMAN

1. DOUGLASS, E. J. D. *Justification in Late Medieval Preaching.* 2nd ed. 1989
2. WILLIS, E. D. *Calvin's Catholic Christology.* 1966 *out of print*
3. POST, R. R. *The Modern Devotion.* 1968 *out of print*
4. STEINMETZ, D. C. *Misericordia Dei.* The Theology of Johannes von Staupitz. 1968 *out of print*
5. O'MALLEY, J. W. *Giles of Viterbo on Church and Reform.* 1968 *out of print*
6. OZMENT, S. E. *Homo Spiritualis.* The Anthropology of Tauler, Gerson and Luther. 1969
7. PASCOE, L. B. *Jean Gerson: Principles of Church Reform.* 1973 *out of print*
8. HENDRIX, S. H. *Ecclesia in Via.* Medieval Psalms Exegesis and the *Dictata super Psalterium* (1513-1515) of Martin Luther. 1974
9. TREXLER, R. C. *The Spiritual Power.* Republican Florence under Interdict. 1974
10. TRINKAUS, Ch. with OBERMAN, H. A. (eds.). *The Pursuit of Holiness.* 1974 *out of print*
11. SIDER, R. J. *Andreas Bodenstein von Karlstadt.* 1974
12. HAGEN, K. *A Theology of Testament in the Young Luther.* 1974
13. MOORE, Jr., W. L. *Annotatiunculae D. Iohanne Eckio Praelectore.* 1976
14. OBERMAN, H. A. with BRADY, Jr., Th. A. (eds.). *Itinerarium Italicum.* Dedicated to Paul Oskar Kristeller. 1975
15. KEMPFF, D. *A Bibliography of Calviniana.* 1959-1974. 1975 *out of print*
16. WINDHORST, C. *Täuferisches Taufverständnis.* 1976
17. KITTELSON, J. M. *Wolfgang Capito.* 1975
18. DONNELLY, J. P. *Calvinism and Scholasticism in Vermigli's Doctrine of Man and Grace.* 1976
19. LAMPING, A. J. *Ulrichus Velenus (Oldřich Velenský) and his Treatise against the Papacy.* 1976
20. BAYLOR, M. G. *Action and Person.* Conscience in Late Scholasticism and the Young Luther. 1977
21. COURTENAY, W. J. *Adam Wodeham.* 1978
22. BRADY, Jr., Th. A. *Ruling Class, Regime and Reformation at Strasbourg, 1520-1555.* 1978
23. KLAASSEN, W. *Michael Gaismair.* 1978
24. BERNSTEIN, A. E. *Pierre d'Ailly and the Blanchard Affair.* 1978
25. BUCER, Martin. *Correspondance.* Tome I (Jusqu'en 1524). Publié par J. Rott. 1979
26. POSTHUMUS MEYJES, G. H. M. *Jean Gerson et l'Assemblée de Vincennes (1329).* 1978
27. VIVES, Juan Luis. *In Pseudodialecticos.* Ed. by Ch. Fantazzi. 1979
28. BORNERT, R. *La Réforme Protestante du Culte à Strasbourg au XVIe siècle (1523-1598).* 1981
29. SEBASTIAN CASTELLIO. *De Arte Dubitandi.* Ed. by E. Feist Hirsch. 1981
30. BUCER, Martin. *Opera Latina.* Vol I. Publié par C. Augustijn, P. Fraenkel, M. Lienhard. 1982
31. BÜSSER, F. *Wurzeln der Reformation in Zürich.* 1985 *out of print*
32. FARGE, J. K. *Orthodoxy and Reform in Early Reformation France.* 1985

33, 34. BUCER, Martin. *Etudes sur les relations de Bucer avec les Pays-Bas.* I. Etudes; II. Documents. Par J. V. Pollet. 1985

35: HELLER, H. *The Conquest of Poverty.* The Calvinist Revolt in Sixteenth Century France. 1986

36. MEERHOFF, K. *Rhétorique et poétique au XVIe siècle en France.* 1986
37. GERRITS, G. H. *Inter timorem et spem.* Gerard Zerbolt of Zutphen. 1986
38. ANGELO POLIZIANO. *Lamia.* Ed. by A. Wesseling. 1986
39. BRAW, C. *Bücher im Staube.* Die Theologie Johann Arndts in ihrem Verhältnis zur Mystik. 1986
40. BUCER, Martin. *Opera Latina.* Vol. II. Enarratio in Evangelion Iohannis (1528, 1530, 1536). Publié par I. Backus. 1988
41. BUCER, Martin. *Opera Latina.* Vol. III. Martin Bucer and Matthew Parker: Florilegium Patristicum. Edition critique. Publié par P. Fraenkel. 1988
42. BUCER, Martin. *Opera Latina.* Vol. IV. Consilium Theologicum Privatim Conscriptum. Publié par P. Fraenkel. 1988
43. BUCER, Martin. *Correspondance.* Tome II (1524-1526). Publié par J. Rott. 1989
44. RASMUSSEN, T. *Inimici Ecclesiae.* Das ekklesiologische Feindbild in Luthers "Dictata super Psalterium" (1513-1515) im Horizont der theologischen Tradition. 1989
45. POLLET, J. *Julius Pflug et la crise religieuse dans l'Allemagne du XVIe siècle.* Essai de synthèse biographique et théologique. 1990
46. BUBENHEIMER, U. *Thomas Müntzer.* Herkunft und Bildung. 1989
47. BAUMAN, C. *The Spiritual Legacy of Hans Denck.* Interpretation and Translation of Key Texts. 1991
48. OBERMAN, H. A. and JAMES, F. A., III (eds.). in cooperation with SAAK, E. L. *Via Augustini.* Augustine in the Later Middle Ages, Renaissance and Reformation: Essays in Honor of Damasus Trapp. 1991 *out of print*
49. SEIDEL MENCHI, S. *Erasmus als Ketzer.* Reformation und Inquisition im Italien des 16. Jahrhunderts. 1993
50. SCHILLING, H. *Religion, Political Culture, and the Emergence of Early Modern Society.* Essays in German and Dutch History. 1992
51. DYKEMA, P. A. and OBERMAN, H. A. (eds.). *Anticlericalism in Late Medieval and Early Modern Europe.* 2nd ed. 1994
52, 53. KRIEGER, Chr. and LIENHARD, M. (eds.). *Martin Bucer and Sixteenth Century Europe.* Actes du colloque de Strasbourg (28-31 août 1991). 1993
54. SCREECH, M. A. *Clément Marot: A Renaissance Poet discovers the World.* Lutheranism, Fabrism and Calvinism in the Royal Courts of France and of Navarre and in the Ducal Court of Ferrara. 1994
55. GOW, A. C. *The Red Jews: Antisemitism in an Apocalyptic Age, 1200-1600.* 1995
56. BUCER, Martin. *Correspondance.* Tome III (1527-1529). Publié par Chr. Krieger et J. Rott. 1989
57. SPIJKER, W. VAN 'T. *The Ecclesiastical Offices in the Thought of Martin Bucer.* Translated by J. Vriend (text) and L.D. Bierma (notes). 1996
58. GRAHAM, M.F. *The Uses of Reform.* 'Godly Discipline' and Popular Behavior in Scotland and Beyond, 1560-1610. 1996
59. AUGUSTIJN, C. *Erasmus. Der Humanist als Theologe und Kirchenreformer.* 1996
60. McCOOG SJ, T. M. *The Society of Jesus in Ireland, Scotland, and England 1541-1588.* 'Our Way of Proceeding?' 1996
61. FISCHER, N. und KOBELT-GROCH, M. (Hrsg.). *Außenseiter zwischen Mittelalter und Neuzeit.* Festschrift für Hans-Jürgen Goertz zum 60. Geburtstag. 1997
62. NIEDEN, M. *Organum Deitatis.* Die Christologie des Thomas de Vio Cajetan. 1997
63. BAST, R.J. *Honor Your Fathers.* Catechisms and the Emergence of a Patriarchal Ideology in Germany, 1400-1600. 1997
64. ROBBINS, K.C. *City on the Ocean Sea: La Rochelle, 1530-1650.* Urban Society, Religion, and Politics on the French Atlantic Frontier. 1997
65. BLICKLE, P. *From the Communal Reformation to the Revolution of the Common Man.* 1998
66. FELMBERG, B. A. R. *Die Ablaßtheorie Kardinal Cajetans (1469-1534).* 1998

67. CUNEO, P. F. *Art and Politics in Early Modern Germany.* Jörg Breu the Elder and the Fashioning of Political Identity, ca. 1475-1536. 1998
68. BRADY, Jr., Th. A. *Communities, Politics, and Reformation in Early Modern Europe.* 1998
69. McKEE, E. A. *The Writings of Katharina Schütz Zell.* 1. The Life and Thought of a Sixteenth-Century Reformer. 2. A Critical Edition. 1998
70. BOSTICK, C. V. *The Antichrist and the Lollards.* Apocalyticism in Late Medieval and Reformation England. 1998
71. BOYLE, M. O'ROURKE. *Senses of Touch.* Human Dignity and Deformity from Michelangelo to Calvin. 1998